CONTENTS

PREFACE

The highly successful and comprehensive *Encyclopedic dictionary of psychology* included a dozen psychological specialities. The editors have selected, updated and supplemented material from the original dictionary to provide in this and similar volumes a compact but compendious coverage of the most widely studied of these specialities. In preparing the independent dictionaries we have had in mind the needs of both students and practitioners in many branches of psychology and allied fields. In addition to this volume which concentrates on personality and social psychology, three further volumes cover physiological and clinical psychology, developmental and educational psychology, and ethology and animal learning.

The selected articles have been brought up to date, and the bibliographies have been revised to include the most recent publications. Many new entries have been added to fill the inevitable gaps of the first edition. The number of biographies of great psychologists has been increased to help to bring the research process and its scientific findings to life.

Psychology has developed within several different conceptual frameworks, often treating the same subject matter with very different assumptions and methods. We have tried, we hope without being uncritically eclectic, to reflect a wide range of approaches to human thought and behavior, including those popular in academic, applied and clinical branches of psychology.

Rom Harré and Roger Lamb

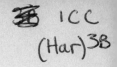

THE DICTIONARY OF

Personality and Social Psychology

THE DICTIONARY OF

Personality and Social Psychology

EDITED BY

Rom Harré and Roger Lamb

BLACKWELL REFERENCE

Based on material from *The encyclopedic dictionary of psychology*, first published 1983.

Copyright © Basil Blackwell Ltd 1986
© Editorial organization Rom Harré and Roger Lamb 1983, 1986

First published 1986

Basil Blackwell Ltd
108 Cowley Road, Oxford OX4 1JF, UK

BRITISH LIBRARY CATALOGUING IN PUBLICATION DATA

The Dictionary of personality and social psychology.
1. Social psychology — Dictionaries
I. Harré, Rom   II. Lamb, Roger
302'.03'21   HM251

ISBN 0-631-14601-6
ISBN 0-631-14602-4 Pbk

Typeset in 9 on 10pt Linotron Ehrhardt
by Oxford Publishing Services, Oxford
Printed in Great Britain by Page Bros (Norwich), Ltd

ACKNOWLEDGMENTS

The Editors and Publisher are grateful to Juliet Field who compiled the index. They are also pleased to acknowledge permission from the publishers to reproduce the following illustrations:

crowd psychology

Addison Wesley. (Redrawn from S. Milgram and H. Toch, "Collective behavior: crowds and social movements". In *Handbook of social psychology*, ed. G. Lindzey and E. Aronson. 2nd edn. (1969), p. 532.)

reticulator activating system

W. H. Freeman and Company. (Redrawn from J. D. French, "The reticular formation". *Scientific American* (May 1957).)

CONTRIBUTORS

Jeffrey W. Adams   JWA
Brunel University

Irving E. Alexander   IEA
Duke University

Irwin Altman   IA
University of Utah

Edgar Anstey   EA
Former Chief Psychologist, Civil Service Department

J. Michael Argyle   JMA
University of Oxford

Solomon E. Asch   SEA
Princeton University

J. Maxwell Atkinson   JMAt
University of Oxford

R. D. Attenborough   RDA
Australian National University

James R. Averill   JRAv
University of Massachusetts

Michael Basseches   MBa
Clinical-Developmental Institute, Belmont, Mass.

Paul Bebbington   PBe
Medical Research Council Social Psychiatry Unit, London

Suzanne Benack   SBe
Union College, Schnectady

Michael Berger   MBe
University of London

Len Berkowitz   LB
University of Winsconsin

Roy Bhaskar   RB
University of London

Frank H. M. Blackler   FHMB
University of Lancaster

Sidney Bloch   SB
Warneford Hospital, Oxford

J. G. Burgoyne   JGB
University of Lancaster

James N. Butcher   JNB
University of Minnesota

George E. Butterworth   GEB
University of Southampton

Hilary Callan   HC
Trent University, Ontario

Anne Campbell   AC
Temple University, Philadelphia

Joseph J. Campos   JJCa
University of Denver

Karen Stojak Caplovitz   KSC
University of Denver

J. K. Chadwick-Jones   JKC
Saint Mary's University, Nova Scotia

A. J. Chapman   AJC
University of Leeds

Neil M. Cheshire   NMC
University College of N. Wales, Bangor

Rebecca M. Cheshire   RMC
University of Hawaii at Manoa

T. Matthew Ciolek   TMC
Australian National University

David D. Clarke   DDC
University of Oxford

Stanley Cohen   SCoh
Hebrew University of Jerusalem

Peter Collett   PC
University of Oxford

Cary L. Cooper   CLC
University of Manchester

John H. Crook   JHC
University of Bristol

Gerald C. Cupchick   GCC
University of Toronto

Christopher Dare   CD
University of London

Nancy Datan   ND
West Virginia University

Richard Dawkins   RD
University of Oxford

Jean-Pierre De Waele   J-PDeW
Vrije Universiteit Brussel

Morton Deutsch   MDe
Columbia University

James E. Dittes   JED
Yale University

Steven W. Duck   SWD
University of Iowa

Muriel Egerton   ME
University of Oxford

J. Richard Eiser   JRE
University of Exeter

Robert Farr   RFa
University of London

Fred E. Fiedler   FEF
University of Washington, Seattle

Esther Flath   EF
*École des Hautes Études en Sciences
Sociales, Paris*

Ronald Fletcher   RF
*University of Reading (Emeritus
Professor)*

Joseph F. Forgas   JFF
University of New South Wales

Fay Fransella   FF
*Centre for Personal Construct
Psychology, London*

Adrian Furnham   AF
University of London

László Garai   LG
Hungarian Academy of Sciences

Marianthi Georgoudi   MG
Temple University, Philadelphia

Kenneth J. Gergen   KJG
Swarthmore College, Pennsylvania

G. P. Ginsburg   GPG
University of Nevada

Jules O. Goddard   JOG
London Business School

Carl F. Graumann   CFG
University of Heidelberg

Horst U. K. Gundlach   HUKG
University of Passau

W. Hacker   WH
*Institut für Ingenieurwissenschaft,
Dresden*

Milton D. Hakel   MDH
Ohio State University

David Hargreaves   DHH
University of Oxford

Rom Harré   RHa
University of Oxford

Stanley G. Harris   SGH
University of Michigan

Daniel P. Harrison   DPH
*State University of New York,
Binghamton*

Paul H. Harvey   PHH
University of Oxford

Paul Heelas   PLFH
University of Lancaster

R. W. Hiorns   RWH
University of Oxford

Robert Hogan   RHo
Johns Hopkins University

Wayne Hudson   WHu
University of Utrecht

Joseph M. F. Jaspars   JMFJ
Formerly of University of Oxford

Robert A. Jensen   RAJ
Southern Illinois University of Carbondale

Thomas C. Kelly   TCK
London

Marcel Kinsbourne   MK
Eunice Kennedy Shriver Center for Mental Retardation

Paul Kline   PK
University of Exeter

Hans Kummer   HK
University of Zurich

Roger Lamb   RL
University of Oxford

Barbara B. Lloyd   BBL
University of Sussex

Edwin A. Locke   EAL
University of Maryland

Robert McHenry   RMcH
University of Oxford

Salvatore R. Maddi   SRM
University of Chicago

Aubrey W. G. Manning   AWGM
University of Edinburgh

Peter E. Marsh   PEM
Oxford Polytechnic

Richard A. Mayou   RAM
University of Oxford

Luciano Mecacci   LM
University of Rome

Roel W. Meertens   RWM
University of Amsterdam

Alexandre Métraux   AM
University of Heidelberg

David L. Miller   DLM
University of Texas at Austin

Jill G. Morawski   JGM
Wesleyan University, Connecticut

S. Moscovici   SMo
École des Hautes Études en Sciences Sociales, Paris

Peter Mühlhäusler   PM
University of Oxford

D. K. B. Nias   DKBN
University of London

William Outhwaite   WO
University of Sussex

W. Ll. Parry-Jones   WLlP-J
University of Oxford

W. Barnett Pearce   WBP
University of Massachusetts, Amherst

David Pears   DP
University of Oxford

Harry F. M. Peeters   HFMP
Tilburg University, The Netherlands

Addie L. Perkins   ALP
University of Michigan

Gerald M. Platt   GMP
University of Massachusetts

Dean G. Pruitt   DGP
State University of New York, Buffalo

V. Reynolds   VR
University of Oxford

P. G. Rivière   PGR
University of Oxford

Daniel N. Robinson   DNR
Georgetown University

John C. Rowan   JCR
London

Joseph F. Rychlak   JFR
Purdue University

John Sabini JS
University of Pennsylvania

E. W. Shepherd EWS
City of London Polytechnic

J. M. Shorter JMS
University of Oxford

John D. Shotter JDS
University of Nottingham

Maury Silver MS
Johns Hopkins University

Dean Keith Simonton DKS
University of California, Davis

Ben R. Slugoski BRS
University of Oxford

Peter K. Smith PKS
University of Sheffield

Siegfried Streufert SSt
Pennsylvania State University

Henri Tajfel HT
University of Bristol

Colin Tatton CT
*International Transactional Analysis
Association, Birmingham*

Insup Taylor IT
University of Toronto

Sybe J. S. Terwee SJST
University of Leiden

Irving G. Thalberg IGT
University of Illinois, Chicago

Alison Thomas AT
University of Reading

Noel M. Tichy NMT
University of Michigan

Richard G. Totman RGT
University of Sussex

Harry C. Triandis HCT
*University of Illinois, Urbana-
Champaign*

Peter Trower PET
University of Leicester

Philip Ullah PU
University of Nottingham

J. O. Urmson JOU
Stanford University (Emeritus Professor)

Ladislav Valach LV
University of Bern

Philippe Van Parijs PVanP
Institut d'Economie, Louvain-la-Neuve

Philip E. Vernon PEV
University of Calgary

Mario von Cranach MvC
University of Bern

Nigel Walker NDW
University of Cambridge

Mary Warnock MW
University of Cambridge

Peter B. Warr PBW
University of Sheffield

H. Weinrich-Haste HW-H
University of Bath

Glayde Whitney GW
Florida State University

Richard S. Williams RSW
London

Glenn D. Wilson GDW
University of London

Gordon Winocur GWi
Trent University, Ontario

Linda A. Wood LAW
University of Guelph, Ontario

Steve W. Woolgar SWW
Brunel University

R. C. Ziller RCZ
University of Florida, Gainseville

EDITORIAL NOTE

Asterisks against titles in the bibliographies indicate items suitable for further reading. The convention 1920 (1986) indicates a work first published in 1920 but widely accessible only in an edition of 1986, to which the publication details given refer.

Cross references to other entries are printed in small capitals in the text. Leads to further additional information can be found from the index.

A

achievement motivation This concept was developed by McClelland (see McClelland et al. 1953) and refers to the motive to achieve some standard of accomplishment or proficiency. People with a strong achievement motive (which McClelland calls need for achievement) prefer moderate to easy or hard goals or risks, want concrete feedback regarding task performance, prefer tasks where skill rather than luck determines the outcome, seek personal responsibility, have a future time perspective, and err somewhat on the side of optimism in estimating their chances for success, especially on new tasks. McClelland (1961) claims that the achievement motive is crucial in entrepreneurship and influences success in entrepreneurial occupations (e.g. selling); he has even claimed that cultural differences in achievement motivation account for differences in economic growth rates. It is argued that the need for achievement is fostered by child rearing practices which encourage independence. It is held by McClelland to be a subconscious motive, and therefore more accurately measured by projective techniques, such as the Thematic Apperception Test, than by self reports. Research on achievement motivation has been criticized on numerous grounds, including: unreliability of the Thematic Apperception Test measures; inconsistency of results; excessive use of post hoc explanations when the results failed to turn out as predicted; and ethnocentrism. Heckhausen (1967) and Atkinson and Raynor (1978) have summarized much of the achievement motivation research. FAL

Bibliography

Atkinson, J.W. and Raynor, J.O. 1978: *Personality, motivation and achievement*. New York: Hemisphere.

Heckhausen, H. 1967: *The anatomy of achievement motivation*. New York: Academic Press.

McClelland, D.C. 1961: *The achieving society*. Princeton: Van Nostrand.

———— et al. 1953: *The achievement motive*. New York: Appleton-Century-Crofts.

act psychology The origins of the concept lie in Brentano's doctrine of intentionality (though he did not use exactly this term). In his *Psychologie vom empirischen Standpunkt* (1874) he suggested the concept "intentional inexistence" to characterize the distinction between mental and physical. Unlike physical phenomena, mental phenomena are "directed upon", "point to", "mean", "refer to", or "contain" objects, which need not actually exist (for we may believe falsehoods, or try to reach for unattainable goals, etc.). In contrast to WUNDT's and Titchener's introspective psychology of contents, Brentano's psychology of acts asserted that mind could not be reduced to a set of elements found in consciousness: the finding of them requires mental activity of one kind or another, and, act psychologists argued, it is the way in which that activity "contains" or is "directed towards" that result which manifests the true nature of mind, not the results alone. This "directedness" of consciousness was investigated empirically by the Würzburg school (begun by Külpe, *c*. 1900), but act psychology and its emphasis on intentionality is only now coming fully into its own, linked with an increased understanding of how people construct socially intelligible accounts of their own actions (see ETHOGENICS; ETHNO-METHODOLOGY). JDS

Bibliography

Brentano, F. 1874 (1973): *Psychology from an empirical standpoint*. London: Routledge and Kegan Paul; New York: Humanities Press.

Humphrey, G. 1951: *Thinking: an introduction to its experimental psychology*. London: Methuen; New York: Wiley.

action theory A theory concerned with the study of human goal-directed behavior and its social basis. Key terms are action, act and actor. A comprehensive definition of action includes the following characteristics: it is consciously goal-directed and planned, it is motivated and deliberate behavior, it is accompanied by emotions and it is socially steered and controlled. An act is defined as a unit of action which occurs in a socially defined situation. An actor is taken to have the capacities of self-reflection and autonomy, and to be capable of experiencing and accepting responsibility.

There are many action theories. We assume, however, that these are to a great extent based on common sense social knowledge about goal oriented action as it has been described by Heider (1958; see ATTRIBUTION THEORY). Naive behavior theory has been further elaborated by Laucken (1973) who argues that assumptions about goal-directed action constitute its nucleus and that concepts such as those of goal, plan, decision, resolution and motive are part of naive action analyses and attributed by the naive psychologist to his own and others' behavior.

Basically, problems in this field can be formulated in three questions. How is action organized, steered and controlled by the individual actor? How is it motivated and what is the role of emotion in the organization of action? How is individual action steered and controlled by society? Let us pursue the problems inherent in these questions to present a few prototypes of action theory.

"Cognitive steering" and systems approach

These theories (also referred to as "action-structure theories" or "action-regulation theories") are based on general systems theory. Their common nucleus consists of the "sequential-hierarchical model", in which action is seen as sequentially ordered on various hierarchical levels, interconnected by feedback loops.

A widely known example is the theory of Miller, Galanter and Pribram (1960). Starting from the analogy between the program-directed computer and the plan-directed behaving organism, the authors assume that behavior is steered and controlled by cognition. Although they do not actually propose a theory of action ("action" and "behavior" are used synonymously, and a goal concept is missing), they have provided some of its most essential concepts: (1) the "image" (following a notion from Boulding) as a general stock of knowledge, serving as the basis for the development of a plan. (2) The plan is a "hierarchy of instruction": instruction as far as these pieces of information direct behavior, and hierarchical since they are ordered on superior and subordinate strategical and tactical levels. (3) The famous TOTE-unit (Test-Operate-Test-Exit) is introduced as the basic unit of the organization of behavior, essentially a feedback-loop. TOTE-units are, in the same plan and at the same time, sequentially as well as hierarchically ordered and thus constitute sequential-hierarchical organization.

In some of the most advanced and fertile action theories these concepts are integrated into the framework of the "Marxist theory of activity" (Rubinstein 1977). In his *Arbeits- und Ingenieur-Psychologie* Hacker (1978) presents an elaborate theory of work activity, essentially an action theory of industrial work.

Work is a basic concept in MARXIST ACTIVITY PSYCHOLOGY. Work is considered the driving force of human development. All mental processes are considered as aspects of activity. Conscious reflection is considered the most important mental process. Two basic problems are the regulation of motive or drive ("Antriebsregulation") and the regulation of execution ("Ausführungsregulation"). Execution-regulation refers to action and is the main concern of the theory. Action is a unit of activity: in action, the activity's motive is dissolved into the (conscious) goal.

Action is a multi-level process; different levels of the hierarchy are linked with different degrees of conscious representation. Hacker distinguishes three "levels of regulation": the level of "intellectual analysis" where plans and strategies are developed (highest level); the level of "perceptive conceptual regulation" where action schemata are worked out; and the "senso-motoric level" of movement orienting representations (lowest). The higher two levels have to be consciously represented, the lowest may be.

Two further concepts should be mentioned. Firstly, a differentiated concept of the "operative representation system" (OAS) is introduced, similar in function to Miller, Galanter and Pribram's "image". This refers to an internal model of all those circumstances of the production process which are relevant for the actor's own regulation of his work activity, namely the influence he thinks he can have, how much freedom he thinks he has, the characteristics of the situation, his knowledge of the work process, his means and materials and a model of the adequate procedures indicated by this information. The OAS culminates in a hierarchy of goals and plans and enables the actor to predict the actions' outcomes. Secondly, Hacker's theory contains the notion of a regulating function unit, similar to Miller, Galanter and Pribram's TOTE-unit. This is the "comparison-change-feedback unit" (VVR) which makes use of information derived from the OAS.

Motivation and emotion in action

Modern western motivation theory constitutes an equally rationalistic but more molar approach. "Motivational psychologists look at the breakpoints in the stream of behavior and try to explain to what end a new action is undertaken" (Heckhausen 1982). Motivation is seen as a product of more or less rational calculation. The basic idea of the "expectancy x value theories" is the assumption that the actor, in his choice between several action-alternatives, prefers the alternative which maximizes the product of the value of the outcome and the probability of success. This basic model is elaborated by the introduction of many other cognitive constructs and processes.

Consequently, the steering function of motivation is stressed and its energizing function neglected. Certainly, the nature of "mental energy" is not yet really understood. Resolve and effort, still indispensible for a realistic action theory, are however energy concepts. The question will eventually arise whether the obsolete concept of will can be dismissed in the long run, or whether it must be reintroduced (e.g. in the form of "conscious mobilization of energy"). Emotion, motivation's sibling, has been more or less neglected in rationalistic action theories.

Social steering and control

Most assumptions about social steering and control are rooted in the ideas of SYMBOLIC INTERACTIONISM. This school has developed into different branches, all of which are relevant to action theory (compare e.g. MEAD 1934, GOFFMAN 1959, and the various exponents of ETHNO-METHODOLOGY). As a common unbroken thread, there are the following ideas: human symbolic interaction leads to the establishment of a personal SELF-CONCEPT. In the course of socialization, society transmits to its members cognitions of objects, situations, actions and the self. These constitute the basis on which to act, especially to interact and to interpret one's own and others' actions. Social steering and control therefore operate to a large degree through implanted social cognitions (indirect control as opposed to direct control, which operates through the direct enforcement of orders and norms). Here we must also mention the theory of social representations (e.g. Farr and Moscovici 1984) which stresses the systemic character and adaptive function of these socially based cognitions and considers them as the basis of social action.

However, we must consider the following questions: How strict is social control? How explicit are social prescriptions? Is there any freedom for the actor and what is the degree and importance of individual variations on these social processes? On the pole of strictness and outer-directedness we find many psychologists who assume that the goal-structure is an attribute of the situation. In his script theory, Abelson (1976) proposes that for given situations actions are more or less completely prescribed by scripts and that the actor's activity consists mainly in the selection and execution of these prefabricated instructions. Harré and Secord (1972) start from Goffman's theater analogy; they assume that action is cognitively regulated, but follows more or less the perceived meaning of the situation and the rules and conventions which are accepted in relation to this meaning. Von Cranach and Harré (1982) grant the actor more freedom. They stress the importance of values, conventions and knowledge which the individual uses in the course of forming attitudes and making decisions about his goals and plans. These latter models can be combined with the viewpoints of systems theory mentioned above. MVC/LV

Bibliography

Abelson, H.P. 1976: Script processing in attitude formation and decision making. In *Cognition and social behavior*, eds. J.S. Carroll and J.W. Payne. New York: L. Erlbaum.

Farr, R.M. and Moscovici, S. eds. 1984: *Social representations*. Cambridge and New York: Cambridge University Press.

Goffman, E. 1959: *The presentation of self in everyday life*. 2nd edn. New York: Doubleday; London: Penguin (1971).

Hacker, W. 1978: *Allgemeine Arbeits- und Ingenieurpsychologie. Psychische Struktur und Regulation von Arbeitstätigkeiten*. Bern, Stuttgart, Wien: Hans Huber Verlag.

Harré, R. and Secord, P.F. 1972: *The explanation of social behavior*. Oxford: Basil Blackwell; Totowa, N.J.: Rowman and Littlefield.

Heckhausen, H. 1982: Models of motivation: progressive unfolding and unremedied deficiencies. In *Cognitive and motivational aspects of action*, eds. W. Hacker, W. Volpert and M. von Cranach. Amsterdam: North Holland.

Heider, F. 1958: *The psychology of interpersonal relations*. New York: Wiley.

Laucken, U. 1973: *Naive Verhaltenstheorie*. Stuttgart: Klett Verlag.

Mead, G.H. 1934: *Mind, self and society*. Chicago: Chicago University Press.

Miller, G.A., Galanter, E. and Pribram, K.H. 1960: *Plans and the structure of behavior*. New York: Holt.

Rubinstein, S.L. 1977: *Grundlagen der All-gemeinen Psychologie*. 9. Auflage, Berlin: Volk und Wissen.

von Cranach, M. 1982: The psychological study of goal-directed action: basic issues. In von Cranach and Harré 1982.

von Cranach, M. and Harré, R. 1982: *The analysis of action: recent theoretical and empirical advances*. Cambridge and New York: Cambridge University Press.

adolescence The period of human development beginning with puberty and culminating in the attainment of adult maturity. It cannot be given any precise limits, but in general it covers the age-span from twelve to eighteen years.

It is a time of rapid physiological and psychological change, of intensive readjustment to family, school, work and social life and of preparation for adult roles. The processes of adolescent socialization and role-change are potentially stressful. Phase-specific maturational tasks can be identified, associated with these changes, particularly the physical, cognitive and emotional development. The sequence of physical changes at puberty involve an increased rate of growth in stature and weight, development of the secondary sexual characteristics and the reproductive system (Tanner 1962). The timing and effects of physical maturation have a number of psychological correlates and, in particular, rapid bodily change can have a powerful effect on SELF-CONCEPT. The variation in the age of onset and rate of the "growth spurt" and the impact of both early and late development have far-reaching effects. In boys, delayed maturation may lead to a feeling of low self-confidence and inferiority. Although the effects in girls are less marked, early menarche may be associated with negative feelings. Following puberty there is an upsurge of sexuality and an increase in heterosexual interests and behavior (Schofield 1965). There may be a passing phase of intense attachment to persons of the same sex but this does not appear to be related to adult homosexuality. The comfortable acceptance of appropriate sex-roles is an important part of identity development. Despite changing social attitudes toward sexual behavior in recent decades, in the direction of greater sexual freedom, and the pressures for early sexual experience, there is no evidence of increasing promiscuity and sexual behavior remains a major source of anxiety and uncertainty for young people. The value of sex education, and the effectiveness of different approaches is difficult to assess. The majority of adolescents, however, favor sex education in a responsible way. Changes in intellectual function have far-reaching implications for behavior and attitudes. Piaget described the transition from the stage of "concrete operations" to "formal operational thinking" following puberty, enabling the adolescent to think in an abstract way, to construct hypotheses and to adopt a deductive approach in solving problems (see Inhelder and Piaget 1958; Elkind 1968). These changes in adolescent reasoning are reflected in scholastic learning, in personality development, in the growth of moral judgment (see Kohlberg 1969) and political thinking. The move toward maturity requires gradual emancipation from the home, the establishment of an independent life-style, a conscious sense of individual uniqueness, commitment to a sexual orientation and a vocational direction and the development of self-control. Self-concept development in adolescence is a complex process (see Coleman 1980). Erikson's contribution to the understanding of identity formation in adolescence has had a major influence (1968; see also Marcia 1980). He described the adolescent tasks of establishing a coherent identity and overcoming identity diffusion, but went further to indicate that some form of crisis was a necessary and expected phase in this process. This concept of a "normative crisis" has, nevertheless, been the most controversial part of Erikson's work and it has not been supported by research.

The course and successful completion of adolescence is influenced by a wide variety of factors. The function of parents is crucial in providing models of adult roles and in facilitating the individuation of adolescents (see Grotevant and Cooper 1985). Despite popular views to the contrary and frequent reference to the "generation gap", conflict between adolescents and parents is rarely substantial or long-standing (see Rutter et al. 1976; White et al. 1983) and parents remain a significant influence throughout adolescence. However, the adolescent's quest for independence and challenge of parental standards, values and attainments can pose a major threat and adolescent behavior can have a disequilibrating effect on marital and family homeostasis. Further, adolescence is often a time of idealism, when society's standards and morals are examined, challenged or rejected. Outside the home, adolescence is shaped by the school, the immediate peer group and contemporary youth culture. Wider social, cultural and political factors also have direct consequences, including increasing social complexity and moral confusion (Kitwood 1980), the ambiguity in the status and role prescription for adolescents, the prolonged dependence of adolescents engaged in further and higher education, the consequences of unemployment and the effects of mixed racial society. Friendships with other young people play an important part in adolescence particularly during the period of detachment from the family. The pattern of these relationships changes during early, middle and late adolescence (Coleman 1974). The peer group has a supportive function and a powerful influence on behavior, particularly in its pressure for conformity and social popularity and, in this way, it plays an important part in adolescent socialization. The relative attractiveness of the peer group is influenced by the quality of relationships within the home, parental attitudes toward it, and the nature of the adolescent problems, since adolescents perceive parents and peers as useful guides in different areas of experience.

Some degree of anxiety and the experience of tension is likely to be related to coping with maturational changes, and the acquisition of new roles, particularly since there are no clear-cut rules about how to progress to adulthood or when the process is complete. Disturbance is most likely to occur at times of transition and the extent of the anxiety is partly a reflection of the adolescent's perception of the balance of stress and support. The idea that adolescence is characterized by "storm and stress" has been a consistent feature of major theories of adolescence. The psychoanalytic view, expressed by Anna Freud (1958) was that 'adolescence is by its nature an interruption of peaceful growth' and this notion was in keeping with Erikson's concept of "identity crisis". There is substantial evidence, however, that although rapid mood swings, feelings of misery, self-doubts and self-consciousness are common in adolescence and may lead to personal suffering, only a small number show emotional distress or do experience a disturbance of identity relating to their sense of self in the present. Psychiatric disorders occurring during adolescence include those present since childhood and those arising initially in this age-period (see Rutter and Hersov 1977). The full range of disorders occurring in later age-periods may be found. The key task in diagnosis is the differentiation of psychiatric disorders from age-appropriate reactions that may settle when stress is reduced or eliminated with further development and the passage of time.   WI.IP-J

Bibliography

Coleman, J.C. 1974: *Relationships in adolescence*. London and Boston: Routledge and Kegan Paul.

—— 1980: *The nature of adolescence*. London and New York: Methuen.

Elkind, D. 1968: Cognitive development in adolescence. In *Understanding adolescent psychology*, ed. J.F. Adams. Boston: Allyn and Bacon.

Erikson, E.H. 1968: *Identity, youth and crisis*. New York: Norton; London: Faber.

Freud, A. 1958: Adolescence. *Psychoanalytic study of the child* 13, 255–78.

Grotevant, H.D. and Cooper, C.R. 1985: Patterns of interaction in family relationships and the development of identity exploration in adolescence. *Child development* 56, 415–28.

Inhelder, B. and Piaget, J. 1958: *The growth of logical thinking*. London: Routledge and Kegan Paul; New York: Basic Books.

Kitwood, T. 1980: *Disclosures to a stranger*. London and Boston: Routledge and Kegan Paul.

Kohlberg, L. 1969: Stage and sequence: the cognitive developmental approach to socialization. In *Handbook of socialization theory and research*, ed. D.A. Goslin. Chicago: Rand McNally.

Marcia, J.E. 1980: Identity in adolescence. In *Handbook of adolescent psychology*, ed. J. Adelson. New York: Wiley.

Rutter, M. et al. 1976: Adolescent turmoil: fact or fiction? *Journal of child psychology and psychiatry* 17, 35–56.

—— and Hersov, L. 1977: *Child psychiatry: modern approaches*. Oxford: Blackwell Scientific; Philadelphia: Lippincott.

Schofield, M.G. 1965: *The sexual behaviour of young people*. London: Longman; Boston: Little, Brown.

Tanner, J.M. 1962: *Growth at adolescence*. 2nd edn. Oxford: Blackwell Scientific; Springfield, Ill.: C.C. Thomas.

White, K.M., Speisman, J.C. and Costes, D. 1983: Young adults and their parents: individuation to mutuality. In *Adolescent development in the family: new directions for child development*, eds. H.D. Grotevant and C.R. Cooper. San Francisco: Jossey-Bass.

Adorno Born Theodor Wiesengrund in Frankfurt am Main, Adorno (1903–1969) was a German Jewish philosopher, an outstanding neo-Marxist intellectual, and a founding father of the Frankfurt School. He made important contributions to aesthetics, musicology and sociology as well as to social psychology.

Adorno's philosophy of non-identity or negative dialectics in some respects anticipated and influenced contemporary French poststructuralism. It involved a method of "immanent criticism" or "metacritique" which sought to expose, in the allegedly autonomous discourses of philosophy, sociology and psychology, antinomies which unintentionally revealed contradictions in the social reality which determined them.

Adorno rejected an autonomous science of psychology concerned with mere inwardness; such a science would have no object. He opposed any hypostatization of "mind" and any permanent division between psychology and sociology. Psyche had to be related to society in an historical framework which recognized the social determination of both psychological states and psychological theories about them, but also to preserve a genuinely psychological moment against sociological reductionism. What was needed was a critical approach which exposed ideological distortions in contemporary psychological and sociological theories and uncovered the psychological impediments to human emancipation. In this context Adorno attempted to use Freudian theory to explain the formation of the individual in capitalist societies. He stressed the importance of the biological and sexual emphases in FREUD ('nothing is true in psycholanalysis except the exaggerations', he once wrote), and defended an ultra-orthodox Freud of the early writings against the sociological revisionism of Karen Horney and Erich Fromm. Adorno denaturalized Freud's basic concepts while preserving his male bias, related his theory to a particular stage of bourgeois society, and proposed amendments appropriate to a later stage in which a new anthropological type was appearing and in which immediate substitute gratification was replacing repression. Adorno's promotion of Freud, from his early "Habilitation" (*The concept of the unconscious in the transcendental theory of the soul*, 1927) onward, had a major influence on the post-war reception of Freudian theory in West Germany and on Jürgen Habermas.

Adorno's association with Max Horkheimer and with the Frankfurt Institute for Social Research, led him to apply his ideas to studies of popular culture, the culture industry, fascism and anti-semitism as well as to high cultural productions. His accounts of the pseudo-individualization and the standardization of human beings in advanced capitalist societies were pessimistic and implied that many people had lost their "psychology" already.

Despite his widely misinterpreted contributions to *The authoritarian personality* (1950), for which he provided qualitative analyses and helped formulate the celebrated scale for testing predispositions to fascism, Adorno opposed all forms of positivism. Far from explaining fascism in psychological terms, he explained its ability to activate unconscious personality structures by reference to the social formation of individuals under monopoly capitalism. In place of the bourgeois family which repressed the individual but also enabled him to become an autonomous ego, individuals increasingly could not regard the father as an authority figure; they ceased to introject their aggression and regressed to narcissistic egoism. Here Adorno provided a critical theory of the family which is an alternative to Fromm's "flight from freedom" model of the psychological bases of fascism.

Adorno was hostile to all affirmativist interpretations of human personality, for example: ego psychology. He rejected attempts to posit a completely autonomous subject; in post-individualistic capitalist societies the individual subject was determined by the lack of a real market and an anonymous mode of domination. At the same time he rejected attempts to eliminate subjectivity entirely and sought to defend what genuine individuality human beings still possessed. Here his views are seen as prophetic of arguments in contemporary postmodernism. He was also fiercely critical of Husserl's notion of constitutive subjectivity and of the existentialist tradition from Kierkegaard to Heidegger. He rejected all ideological uses of humanism. 'Man', he declared, '[was] the ideology of dehumanisation'. In a remarkable convergence of social pessimism and Jewish theological precept, he denied that human beings could achieve psychological maturity as long as "the social whole" remained irrational: the only true image of man was the negative one. Adorno's legacy to psychology is a powerful warning against facile optimism, and an attack on autonomous approaches to the psychological which does not endorse over-simplified ("undialectical") sociological explanations of psychological phenomena. (See AUTHORITARIAN PERSONALITY.)   WHu

Bibliography

Adorno, T.W. 1970: *Gesammelte Werke.* 23 vols, ed. Rolf Tiedemann. Frankfurt am Main: Suhrkamp.

Benjamin, J. 1977: The end of internalization: Adorno's social psychology. *Telos* 32, Summer.

Buck-Morss, S. 1977: *The origin of negative*

dialectics: Theodor W. Adorno, Walter Benjamin and the Frankfurt Institute. Hassocks: The Harvester Press.

Jay, M. 1973: *The dialectical imagination: a history of the Frankfurt School and the Institute of Social Research 1923–50*. London: Heinemann.

—— 1984: *Adorno*. London: Fontana Modern Masters.

Rose, G. 1978: *The melancholy science: an introduction to the thought of Theodor W. Adorno*. London: Macmillan.

aggression The quest for a unitary definition of aggression, acceptable across the many specialist areas within psychology which profess an interest in the subject, has been both prolonged and largely unresolved. Recent text-books on aggression typically open with an extensive introduction to what Bandura (1973) has so aptly described as this "semantic jungle". In some cases the issue is settled by the selection of a definition which accords with a particular theoretical orientation, rather than with a more open appreciation of the variation and complexities of aggressive behavior. Thus, aggression might be viewed as a motivational state, a personality characteristic, a response to frustration, an inherent drive, or the fulfilling of a socially learned role requirement.

Alternatively, some authors viewing the whole issue as essentially irresoluble declare that a unitary concept is not viable. Johnson (1972), for example, maintains that 'it is difficult if not impossible to isolate the necessary and sufficient conditions to produce a satisfactory definition'. He goes on to conclude that 'there is no single kind of behavior which can be called "aggressive" nor any single process which represents "aggression"'. Definition is further complicated by concepts and theoretical stances deriving from related disciplines such as ethology and anthropology. It is not surprising, therefore, to discover more than 250 different definitions of aggression in the psychological literature, discounting pure operationalizations for experimental purposes. An extensive volume of literature reviewing these various definitions and the conceptual stances from which they derive already exists. Rather than providing a review of the reviews it is more appropriate to isolate those components of definitions for which there is broad support and those where lack of consensus is most evident. Further elaboration is to be found in Baron (1977, and Geen and Donnerstein 1983).

Firstly, aggression may be said to occur only between members of the same species. In other words it is distinguishable from predation, anti-predator behavior and encounters arising from competition for the same ecological niche.

Secondly, there is the notion that aggression involves the delivery of a noxious stimulus. In other words, the products of aggression must be perceived negatively by the recipient. Such a definition would allow a wide range of behavior, from nuclear bombing to sarcastic comment, to be classed as aggressive, and this stance is to be preferred to those which limit aggression to the perpetration of physical injury. It is, however, not a *sufficient* condition for aggression since noxious stimuli can clearly be delivered without any aggression present. One would rarely accuse a dentist of being aggressive when he causes pain to a person's mouth. Nor would one suggest that all injurious car accidents are attributable to aggressive drivers.

Clearly the concept of *intention* must be an essential component of any satisfactory definition. It is at this point, however, that the most severe difficulties arise since a very mentalistic concept has been introduced. And while it might be philosophically legitimate to talk of *intentionality* in a discussion of human behavior it would be absurd to use such a concept in relation to aggression in animals. To ask whether one cat *intended* to injure another is to engage in a quite untenable form of anthropomorphism.

There might also be a problem in attempting to define aggression with reference to any limited category of behavior, even though Buss (for example) allows for considerable freedom in this context. This is because behavior may be exhibited only if an appropriate target is available and conditions are such that delivery of a noxious stimulus is possible. Geen (1976) attempts to overcome this limitation by adding a further necessary condition. He insists that there must be "some expectation that the stimulus will reach its target and have its intended effect".

Again, however, we are presented with rather immeasurable criteria and a distinct sense of circularity is evident. Both intention and expectation are to be gleaned only through post hoc rationalization of action. More importantly there is the continuing, restricting assumption that aggression cannot be said to exist unless there are observable, intentional acts directed at specific targets!

So, on the one hand we have an apparent desire to define aggression in terms which accord with the frames of reference of traditional, empirical psychology – i.e. overt behavior. On the other, in order to meet the constraints of simple logic and everyday human experience, mentalistic criteria are introduced (often apologetically). Lacking, however, is any indication of how intention or expectation may be determined in general or specific examples of aggression.

Because of these problems we might be forgiven for adopting Johnson's position. At the same time, however, there exists in everyday language and conceptualization the notion that aggression does indeed have a unitary nature, although the range of psychological states and patterns of behavior might be rather wider than is commonly assumed by psychologists. In everyday talk we use the term "aggression" to refer to acts of hostility, violence etc. in a pejorative manner, but at the same time we speak of an athlete running an aggressive race and of the successful, entrepreneurial businessman conducting an aggressive sales campaign. In the latter examples the sentiment is a positive one.

The two senses in which the term aggression is used have little in common in behavioral terms and in the case of the athlete it is difficult to isolate a "noxious stimulus". What unites them is the presence of competition, establishment of dominance and the subjugation of per-ceived rivals – a broad but meaningful constellation of psychological processes. It is suggested that this might provide the starting point for a more relevant and useful definition of aggression. Such an approach is in keeping with some ethological perspectives, and allows for comparative study. This, however, is not its primary objective. Viewing aggression in this manner allows us to evaluate more clearly the social motives of a wide range of acts which otherwise appear to be quite disparate. Rather than aggression inhering in a limited range of behaviors, it might more reasonably be seen as an internal motivational state. Resultant behavior will be a function not only of the strength of such a state but also of the target and, more importantly, of extant social and cultural frameworks whose primary function is the regularizing and containment of aggressive expression (see below, *ritual aggression*).

From this standpoint acts of violence, with the status of social *events*, may be distinguished clearly from the aggression process itself. Aggression, under certain circumstances, may result in acts of physical injury which can be said to constitute violence. Violence, however, is not a *necessary* consequence of aggression, other means for the expression of dominance and the subjugation of rivals being readily available. Nor need violence necessarily be preceded by a state of aggression, especially when the target of violence is remote or when systematic dehumanization of the target has been achieved. In such cases one might argue that the violent acts are more akin to predation than to expressions of aggression (see Marsh 1978).

The concept of intentionality is, to a large extent, redundant in this formulation because, again, aggression is not determined solely by reference to the particular behavior but may be determined by reference to the relationship between individuals involved in a given encounter and to their respective motives. This can be a distinct advantage in non-laboratory research since these kinds of data are often more readily available than are direct measures of particular behavior.

Major fields of research

Research directly concerned with the antecedents of aggression has occupied the bulk of the literature over the past thirty years. The nature-nurture controversy is as heated in this field as in those of intelligence and personality. The major theoretical approaches within which this research has been conducted can be summarized as follows:

Biological theories: The work of FREUD and his concept of *Thanatos*, which recast Hobbesian notions in a psychoanalytic form was later mirrored by the ethological theory of Lorenz (1966). Subsequent ethological work by Eibl-Eibesfeldt (1971) and Tinbergen (1953) refined some of the more mechanistic assumptions of the earlier approaches, emphasized more strongly the plasticity of inherited characteristics and the important role of social and cultural factors. Within this broad category of perspectives we should also include work on specific genetic abnormalities – e.g. the XYY syndrome.

Drive theories: Work by Dollard et al. (1939) developed from a psychoanalytic position and gave rise to the frustration-aggression model. The unworkable rigidity of this model was, to some extent, tempered in subsequent models proposed by Berkowitz (1962) and the theme has also been explored by Feshbach (1964) and many others. These approaches did much to encourage examination of social factors as antecedents of aggressive behavior. This approach is even more firmly evident in the third category of approaches.

Social learning theories: Work by Bandura (1973) has provided the basis for extensive research, most of which has been laboratory based using children as subjects. Work by Geen (1976) has been particularly influential.

In addition to the numerous general textbooks on aggression (e.g. Baron 1977, Johnson 1972) and those focusing on one of the major approaches (e.g. Eibl-Eibesfeldt 1979), rather extreme polarizations in the nature-nurture debate can be found in Ardrey (1979) and Montagu (1976).

Ritual aggression

Work on ritual aggression has developed in two quite different fields – those of ethology and anthropology. In ethology the term ritualization was coined by Huxley and used to refer to 'the adaptive formalisation or canalisation of emotionally motivated behaviour, under the telenomic pressure of natural selection'. It has been employed in particular in the area of aggressive behavior by writers such as Lorenz (1966), Eibl-Eibesfeldt (1979) and others. Evidence suggests that patterns of fighting behavior are modified to the extent that intra-species agonistic encounters result in relatively little injury to the combatants. Potentially lethal attacks take on the nature of "tournaments" involving threat signals such as color changes, bristling of fur etc.

In anthropology ritual refers to patterned routines of behavior involving a system of signs and conventional relations between the actions in which the ritual is performed and the social act achieved by its successful completion. Many examples of tribal warfare have been described in these terms. The Dani of New Guinea, for example, were described by Gardner and Heider as engaging in highly ceremonial and ritual patterns of inter-group hostility.

More recently, writers such as Fox (1977) have brought these two major approaches together in the explanation of particular patterns of group aggressive activity. Here the assumption is that patterns of ritual aggression in man have essentially the same (largely biological) origins and perform the same adaptive functions. Work by Marsh (1978), however, which has focused on ritual aggression among youth in Britain, suggests that the common origins argument is unnecessary in the explanation of such patterns of behavior.   PEM

Bibliography

Ardrey, R. 1979: *The hunting hypothesis*. London and New York: Methuen.

Bandura, A. 1973: *Aggression: a social learning analysis*. Englewood Cliffs, N.J.: Prentice-Hall.

Baron, R.A. 1977: *Human aggression*. New York: Plenum Press.

Berkowitz, L. 1962: *Aggression: a social psychological analysis*. New York: McGraw-Hill.

Dollard, J. et al. 1939: *Frustration and aggression*. New Haven, Conn.: Yale University Press.

Eibl-Eibesfeldt, I. 1971: *Love and hate*. London: Methuen; New York: Holt, Rinehart and Winston.

—— 1979: *The biology of peace and war*. London: Thames and Hudson.

Feshbach, S. 1964: The function of aggression and the regulation of aggressive drive. *Psychological review* 71, 257–72.

Fox, R. 1977: The inherent rules of violence. In *Social rules and social behavior*, ed. P. Collett. Oxford: Basil Blackwell; Totowa, N.J.: Rowman and Littlefield.

Geen, R.G. 1976: *Personality: the skein of behaviour*. London: Henry Kimpton.

—— and Donnerstein, E.I. eds. 1983: *Aggression: theoretical and empirical reviews*. New York: Academic Press.

Johnson, R.N. 1972: *Aggression in man and animals*. Philadelphia: W.B. Saunders.

Lorenz, K. 1966: *On aggression*. London: Methuen; New York: Harcourt, Brace and World.

Marsh, P. 1978: *Aggro: the illusion of violence*. London: Dent.

Montagu, A. 1976: *The nature of human aggression*. Oxford and New York: Oxford University Press.

Tinbergen, N. 1953: *Social behaviour in animals*. London: Methuen; New York: Wiley.

alienation A state or process in which something is lost by or estranged from the person who originally possessed it. Marx's concept of estranged labor refers primarily to the worker's estrangement, in capitalist relations of production, from his or her product, the act of production, the "species-being" or human nature, and from other workers. This estrangement (*Entfremdung*) is based on the alienation (*Entäusserung*) of the worker's wage-labor to the capitalist. It is therefore a matter of production relations rather than technology, though it may be particularly prominent with machine production.   WO

Bibliography

Lukes, S. 1967: Alienation and anomie. In *Philosophy politics and society*, eds. P. Laslett and W.G. Runciman, series III. Oxford: Basil Blackwell; New York: Barnes and Noble.

Marx, K. 1844 (1975): Economic and philosophical manuscripts. In *Early writings*. Harmondsworth: Penguin.

Allport, Gordon Willard (1897–1967) born in Indiana, was a student at Harvard (AB 1919, majoring in economics and philosophy; PhD 1922 in psychology). He spent one year in Istanbul before doing his PhD, and two years in Berlin, Hamburg and Cambridge before returning to teach at Harvard in 1924. Apart from two years at Dartmouth he remained at Harvard until his death. His main work was on personality, although he also wrote a well-known book on prejudice (1954) in which he outlined many ideas which are still fruitful.

The emphases of Allport's theories about personality were on the individual's uniqueness and on the role of conscious goals in determining the course of people's behavior. He borrowed from Windelband the terms "idiographic" and "nomothetic", although he subsequently (1962) suggested substituting the terms "morphogenic" and "dimensional". He believed that each person has a unique pattern of personality and championed the idiographic (morphogenic) study of individuals, using (e.g.) case histories, rather than the (nomothetic) attempt to establish general laws about human behavior by looking at the co-occurrence of characteristics in large samples of people. This preference was accompanied by a mistrust of methods imported from the natural sciences (1947). Many critics have argued that no science can concern itself with the unique.

Allport also opposed the popularity of assumptions derived from PSYCHOANALYSIS, and the accompanying attempts to bypass conscious beliefs and reach people's "real" unconscious motives by using PROJECTIVE TESTS. He thought that conscious intentions rather than unconscious motives guide behavior. This stress on current contents of consciousness had as its correlate a belief in the comparative unimportance of genetic factors or the person's history as determinants of behavior. This view contrasts sharply with the ideas of psychoanalysts and other theorists who use "instinct" as an explanatory concept, and believe that the first few years of life determine one's whole future adjustment. In Allport's opinion the goals people have are not fixed by biology or any other deterministic mechanism. There is no limit to the range of possible human goals, because of what he called FUNCTIONAL AUTONOMY. This means that any form of behavior may become an end in itself even though it may originally have been adopted as a means to some other end. This concept has come under continuous attack, not least from those who see it as simply another version of secondary reinforcement, and therefore as no less deterministic in its implications than any other behaviorist explanation.

Allport's beliefs in people's uniqueness and the power of their current intentions made him a founding father of HUMANISTIC PSYCHOLOGY. But he was also a TRAIT theorist, whose work can therefore be associated with that of theorists such as CATTEL and EYSENCK. He believed that traits 'initiate . . . equivalent (meaningfully consistent) forms of adaptive and expressive behavior' (1961). In other words, he believed that people have consistent personalities which manifest themselves in many different aspects of their behavior. In 1933 he and Vernon investigated expressive behavior, looking at such things as the length of stride, the speed of counting, the firmness of handshake and handwriting, and claimed that these were related in consistent ways. He suggested that there was some inner core of consistent self, which he called the "proprium", and spoke of the "propriate functions" of the personality. In contrast to most trait theorists, however, he differentiated between "individual" traits and "common" traits (1937). Although he later changed his terminology (1961) and referred to "traits" (=common traits) and "personal dispositions" (=individual traits), the distinction was still the same. As the names suggest the individual traits are "peculiar to the individual" while the common traits are not. So, although on the face of it trait words

describe characteristics which are common to many people, Allport was intent upon the apparently contradictory task of producing a trait theory which preserved the uniqueness of the individual. Furthermore he did not regard attitudes and intentions as significantly less important determinants of behavior than traits.

His theorizing is probably too vague to be of current value in any systematic way, but his books are written in a stimulating style, and contain many incidental riches. In 1951 American clinical psychologists who were asked which personality theorists were of value to their work placed Allport second only to FREUD. Whatever the value of humanistic psychology beyond the therapeutic session, Allport's stands against the shibboleths of natural science and psychoanalysis were salutary. More recent developments of the idiographic approach to personality are still going strong (e.g. Bem 1983).

Allport's major works were: *Personality, a psychological interpretation*. New York: Holt, 1937; *The nature of prejudice*. Reading, Mass. Addison Wesley, 1954; *Becoming: basic considerations for a psychology of personality*. New Haven, Conn. Yale University Press, 1955; *Pattern and growth in personality*. New York: Holt, Rinehart and Winston, 1961.   RI.

Bibliography

Allport, G.W. 1947: Scientific models and human morals. *Psychological review* 54, 182–92.

—— 1962: The general and the unique in psychological science. *Journal of personality* 30, 405–22.

—— and Vernon, P.E. 1933: *Studies in expressive movement*. New York: Macmillan.

Bem, D.J. 1983: Constructing a theory of the triple typology: Some (second) thoughts on nomothetic and idiographic approaches to personality. *Journal of personality* 51, 566–77.

Hall, C.S. and Lindzey, G. 1978: *Theories of personality*. 3rd edn. New York: Wiley.

altruism A term often used synonymously with pro-social (or helping) behavior to indicate some form of unselfish behavior on behalf of others that may involve some self-sacrifice. Types of behavior that have been studied include the donation of blood or money; rendering assistance in an accident; volunteering; challenging shop-lifters; cooperating and competing during games. Many theories exist to explain why people do or do not behave altruistically. They include ideas from SOCIOBIOLOGY, reinforcement theory, PSYCHOANALYSIS, and theories about cognitive development and reciprocity norms.

However, probably the most important and influential research in this area has been the work on *bystander effect* by Latané and Darley (1970). The bystander effect refers to the consistently demonstrated fact that individuals are less likely to help when they are in the presence of others than when they are alone. Apart from the mere presence of a bystander, numerous other variables have been shown to affect altruistic responses: the age, sex and number of bystanders; characteristics of the victim or person in need of help; the help given by others; familiarity or ambiguity of the situation, cultural norms etc. Latané and Darley (1970) cite five critical steps in the process which leads to altruism: notice that something is happening; interpret the situation as one in which help is needed; assume personal responsibility; choose a form of assistance; implement the assistance.

More recently attention has been turned to wider aspects of altruism such as the development and teaching of altruism, individual differences in altruism and the help people offer one another in modern cities (Rushton 1980). See also SOCIO-BIOLOGY.   AF

Bibliography

Latané, Bibb and Darley, John M. 1970: *The unresponsive bystander: why doesn't he help?* New York: Appleton-Century-Crofts.

Rushton, J. 1980: *Altruism, socialization and society*. Englewood Cliffs, N.J.: Prentice-Hall.

androgyny, psychological This recently influential concept, associated particularly with the work of Sandra Bem, denotes the combination of both typically "masculine" and "feminine" traits and behavior in a single individual. Until the 1970s the majority of psychometric research on masculinity-femininity was founded upon the implicit assumption that these constructs represented the opposite poles of a unidimensional continuum. The construction of most M–F scales was such that it was not possible for an individual to show both masculinity and femininity – a high score on one necessarily implied a low score on the other (Constantinople 1973).

Rossi (1964) had already voiced criticisms of traditional sex-typing, proposing instead an "androgynous" conception of the sexes whereby 'each sex will cultivate some of the characteristics usually associated with the other'. It was not until Sandra Bem began to write about psychological androgyny in the early 1970s that the concept received much attention and was recognized as an idea "whose time had come". Bem's formulation of psychological androgyny theory coincided with social changes favoring unisex dress and behavior and a blurring of traditional sex-roles. It consequently found ready acceptance amongst many liberal social psychologists and inspired a new wave of research into aspects of gender and sex-roles.

Although Bem is by no means the sole proponent of the concept of psychological androgyny (for example, see also Spence and Helmreich's studies using the Personal Attributes Questionnaire, or PAQ), she has nevertheless been the most influential, and the Bem Sex-Role Inventory (BSRI) remains the most popular measure of the construct. In its original form this comprises 60 items – 20 masculine, 20 feminine and 20 neutral – each of which is rated on a 7-point scale, from "never or almost never true" (of the self) to "always or almost always true". Scoring was based on the difference between a person's mean masculinity and femininity scores: a high difference score represented a correspondingly high degree of sextyping, while a low score indicated an M–F balance and thus "psychological androgyny". This reflects Bem's initial exposition of the theory (1974) in which she proposed that those who were psychologically androgynous showed a more or less equal balance of masculine and feminine characteristics (e.g. they were both assertive and compassionate). This was in contrast to traditionally sex-typed people who displayed either masculine or feminine traits, but not both. Following criticisms of this balance model of androgyny and the scoring methods associated with it Bem later revised her initial criteria (1977) such that only those whose masculinity and femininity scores both fall above the median (i.e. showing high M and high F) are classified as androgynous. In spite of some continuing criticisms, especially with regard to item selection, and further suggestions for more sophisticated scoring methods, the sole modification to the BSRI has been the provision of an alternative shorter form of the inventory consisting of 30 items. But this has not proved comparable to the original BSRI, so Bem herself no longer recommends it (Frable and Bem 1985).

Bem's early studies (1974) using the BSRI demonstrated both that androgynous subjects were able to show suitably masculine behavior in an Asch-type conformity experiment (see ASCH), in which they made independent judgments; and that they could similarly behave in an appropriately feminine manner when, for example, they showed nurturant behavior with a small baby. Other studies indicated that androgynous subjects were also more willing to engage in cross-sex activities than sex-typed individuals (Bem 1975). This element of behavioral flexibility lies at the heart of Bem's conception of psychological androgyny, and she emphasizes the personal and social benefits of being able to behave in both masculine and feminine ways rather than being tied to a rigid repertoire of sex-appropriate behavior.

Androgyny theory holds that every person has the potential to develop both the masculine and feminine aspects of their nature instead of suppressing those traits that society labels as appropriate only for the opposite sex, and thus becoming sex-typed. In fact Spence (1984) has objected to Bem's approach on the grounds that it is presented as a claim that masculinity and femininity are unrelated, but actually substitutes one crude, bipolar,

unidimensional scheme for another. Traditionally masculinity and femininity were treated as opposites. In Bem's scheme they lie at the same extreme, with those who are highly masculine or highly feminine (but not both) lumped together as 'sex-typed'. Whether or not individuals do actually become "androgynous" rather than sex-typed depends, according to Bem, on 'the extent to which one's particular socialization history has stressed the functional importance of the gender dichotomy.'

In the last ten years psychological androgyny has been studied in relation to self-esteem, anxiety, interpersonal relations, sexual behavior, sex-role attitudes and political ideology, to name only a few examples. The majority of such studies conclude in support of Bem's view that psychological androgyny is both adaptive and desirable, and leave one in little doubt that this concept, with its liberationist ideology, has become the new orthodoxy. In so far as it views masculinity and femininity as independent rather than as bipolar opposites it does certainly represent progress. However it has not gone sufficiently far in recognizing the multidimensionality of both masculinity and femininity.

Spence herself (1984) now argues that her own questionnaire (the PAQ) and the BSRI both tap 'desirable self-assertive, self-oriented personality traits' and 'desirable nurturant, interpersonally oriented traits'. These two sets of traits are gender-related, and in work which uses these questionnaires they are labeled "masculinity" and "feminity". But Spence suggests that the questionnaires are only successful in predicting behavior 'that might reasonably be expected to be influenced by self-assertive and interpersonally oriented characteristics per se', and that there are often only insignificant relationships between the questionnaires and sex-role behavior which is not of these two kinds. She therefore concludes that 'all that could legitimately be claimed from the . . . data obtained from that BSRI and PAQ is that self-reports of two specific constellations of gender-related traits are uncorrelated.'

Bem's (1984) response to these criticisms is that it is 'wrong to assume that just because the BSRI cannot predict everything about an individual's gender psychology it cannot predict anything about it.' In support of her contention she cites studies which suggest that androgyny (as defined by the BSRI) may not only be related to nurturance and assertiveness. For instance she and Lenney (1976) found that in an experimental setting sex-typed individuals were more likely than androgynous individuals to choose activities which were stereotypically consistent with their own gender (e.g. oiling squeaky hinges vs ironing). Sex-typed individuals also felt worse than androgynous individuals after performing gender-inconsistent activities. Bem also cites work on non-verbal communication, such as that of LaFrance and Carmen (1980), who found that in a conversation BSRI sex-typed people were more inclined than androgynous people to display paralinguistic behavior typical of their own sex. However, the four kinds of behaviour investigated – filled pauses and interruptions (masculine), and gaze and smiling (feminine) – might well be regarded as assertiveness and nurturance.

Studies continue to support the idea that the sex-typed vs androgynous dimension has important correlates. Coleman and Ganong (1985), for instance, found (on self-report) that androgynous students were more tolerant of their romantic partners' faults, more aware of their own feelings and more willing to express them than either masculine or feminine sex-typed students. Nevertheless some of the more striking claims for androgyny, such as its supposed relationship with self-esteem and mental health, now seem very questionable. Reviews suggest that for both sexes high masculinity is associated with self-esteem and mental health. So it seems that when androgynous individuals are distinguished from "undifferentiated" individuals (by the criterion that they are highly masculine *and* highly feminine rather than low on both), it is their high masculinity which is good for them (Taylor and Hall 1982; Whitley 1983). It is therefore as profitable to be masculine sex-typed (regardless of sex) as to be androgynous. This means that it is misleading to lump together both the masculine and the feminine sex-typed, and that Spence's arguments against the value of the sex-typed vs androgynous distinction are probably valid.   AMT/RL

Bibliography

Bem, S.L. 1974: The measurement of psychological androgyny. *Journal of consulting and clinical psychology* 42, 155–62.

────── 1975: Sex-role adaptability: one consequence of psychological androgyny. *Journal of personality and social psychology* 31, 634–43.

────── 1977: On the utility of alternative procedures for assessing psychological androgyny. *Journal of consulting and clinical psychology* 45, 196–205.

────── 1984: Androgyny and gender schema theory: a conceptual and empirical integration. *Nebraska symposium on motivation* 32, 179–226.

────── and Lenney, E. 1976: Sex-typing and avoidance of cross-sex behavior. *Journal of personality and social psychology* 33, 48–54.

Coleman, M. and Gangong, L.H. 1985: Love and sex role stereotypes: do macho men and feminine women make better lovers? *Journal of personality and social psychology* 49, 170–6.

Constantinople, A. 1973: Masculinity-feminity: an exception to a famous dictum? *Psychological bulletin* 80, 389–407.

Frable, D.E.S. and Bem, S.L. 1985: If you are gender-schematic, all members of the opposite sex look alike. *Journal of personality and social psychology* 38, 459–68.

LaFrance, M. and Carmen, B. 1980: The non-verbal display of psychological androgyny. *Journal of personality and social psychology* 38, 36–49.

Rossi, A.S. 1964: Equality between the sexes: an immodest proposal. *Daedalus* 93, 607–52.

Spence, J.T. 1984: Gender identity and its implications for the concepts of masculinity and feminity. *Nebraska symposium on motivation* 32, 59–95.

────── , Helmreich, R. and Stapp, J. 1975: Ratings of self and peers on sex-role attributes and their relation to self-esteem and conceptions of masculinity and feminity. *Journal of personality and social psychology* 32, 29–39.

Taylor, M.C. and Hall, J.A. 1982: Psychological androgyny: A review and reformulation of theories, methods, and conclusions. *Psychological bulletin* 92, 347–66.

Whitley, B.E. 1983: Sex role orientation and self-esteem: A critical meta-analytic review. *Journal of personality and social psychology* 44, 765–78.

anomie A state of normlessness or lack of regulation (Greek: *nomos*=law). Emile DURKHEIM (1858–1917) coined the term to describe a lack of the social control which he saw as essential to any human society. Human nature needed to be formed and regulated by society. Durkheim's early concept of the *conscience collective* neatly expresses the dual (cognitive and moral) aspect of this regulation. (See SOCIAL REPRESENTATION.)

The social division of labor may become anomic under capitalism; it needs to be regulated and given a moral character by occupational corporations similar to medieval guilds. The anomic form of suicide results from the frustration of desires which, in the absence of the necessary social regulation, have grown beyond all possibility of their satisfaction.

Durkheim's "anomie" is structurally similar to Marx's "estrangement"/ "ALIENATION", in that they describe an objective process with subjective consequences. They seem however to rest on divergent views of human nature, Durkheim stressing the need for social regulation in *any* society.   WO

Bibliography

Lukes, S. 1967: Alienation and anomie. In *Philosophy, politics and society*, series III, eds. P. Laslett and W.G. Runciman. Oxford: Basil Blackwell; New York: Barnes and Noble.

anxiety: in personality theory This is a crucial concept, especially in psychoanalytic theories, where it is seen to be of primary importance in the dynamics of behavior (see PERSONALITY THEORY, PSYCHOANALYTICAL). It is often said that the state or feeling of anxiety is more closely associated with uncertainty than is the feeling of fear. The agitation produced in animals which cannot distinguish signals for shock from signals for food may be regarded as an analogue of human anxiety. The feeling is accompanied by fairly well-defined bodily changes which are manifested in raised heart-rate and GALVANIC SKIN RESPONSE (GSR). The primacy of uncertainty in the causes of anxiety was shown by Epstein (1972), who found that people who were told that they had a 5% chance of receiving an electric shock had higher heart-rate and GSR than people who were told they had a 95% chance.

In FREUD's earlier writings (1917), anxiety is said to result from the undischarged energy of the ID, which expresses itself in this form when there is a lack of libidinal gratification. In his later theory (1926) the EGO 'inoculates' itself with anxiety when the gratification of a desire will cause more pain than pleasure. To avoid this experience of anxiety the ego makes use of DEFENSE MECHANISMS, both to prevent the unacceptable gratification and to resolve the conflict by allowing the urge to be expressed in a socially acceptable form. Both these explanations can be seen to involve the elements of uncertainty or inability to act effectively to fulfil a desire.

In the writings of the neo-Freudians Horney and Sullivan, anxiety is said to result from feelings of insecurity, which begin in infancy and may be due to actual helplessness or to the experience of parental disapproval. Both Horney and Sullivan stress the importance of interpersonal relationships in causing and reducing such feelings of insecurity (see NEO-FREUDIAN THEORY).

Existential personality theorists also believe that anxiety is a fundamental part of human experience. In their view, however, it results from the uncertainty and changeability of the future. They stress the value of willingness to change and therefore, since change involves anxiety, they also stress the necessity of confronting anxiety rather than running away from it if one is to grow and develop one's personal potential. KELLY similarly believed that uncertainty causes anxiety, but in his view the uncertainty arises when we can only partially understand events or people we encounter (see PERSONAL CONSTRUCT THEORY).

Spielberger (1971) distinguished the

transitory emotion or mood of anxiety from the characteristic of being an anxious person. This distinction between state and trait anxiety has informed a good deal of recent research. Individuals who have more than usual trait anxiety also have unusually intense state anxiety in response to stressors, particularly to psychological rather than physical threat (Lamb 1978). In CATTELL's work trait anxiety is one of the two best replicated second-order factors produced by factor analysing the intercorrelations among his 16 'source traits'. As such it is probably to be identified with WUNDT's dimension of emotionality and EYSENCK's dimension of neuroticism (see TRAITS, TYPE).   RL

Bibliography

Epstein, S. 1972: In Spielberger 1972.

Freud, S. (1917) 1963: *Introductory lectures on psychoanalysis*. Trans. J. Strachey. London: Hogarth.

——— (1926) 1963: *Inhibitions, symptoms and anxiety*. Trans. J. Strachey. London: Hogarth.

Kobasa, S.C. and Maddi, S.R. 1977: Existential personality theory. In *Current personality theories*, ed. R.J. Corsini. Ithaca, Ill.: F.E. Peacock.

Lamb, D. 1978: Anxiety. In *Dimensions of personality*, eds. H. London and J.E. Exner. New York: Wiley.

Spielberger, C.D. ed. 1971, 1972: *Anxiety: current trends in theory and research*. 2 vols. New York: Academic Press.

anxiety: in social psychology The study of anxiety, as a specific subjective experience, a physiological state or a personality trait, has received attention in social psychology mainly as a determinant of affiliative behavior. Research by Schachter (1959) showed that the induction of anxiety leads to a preference for being in the company of others who are in the same emotional state. The social comparison which such company affords plays an important role in Schachter's theory of emotions, which suggests that the interpretation of emotions depends crucially upon such social comparison procedures where people are ignorant about the source of arousal which they experience. The affiliation effect of induced anxiety appears to be stronger in first-born and only children.

Social anxiety and shyness have also been intensively studied, and have been cited as major causes of loneliness and mental disorders (Buss 1980). More recently there has been interest in the relation between social anxiety and *self-presentation*. Snyder et al. (1985) have produced evidence which suggests that in socially anxious men shyness may (partly) be maintained because it is a ready-made excuse for failure.   JMFJ

Bibliography

Buss, A.H. 1980: *Self-consciousness and social anxiety*. San Francisco: Freeman.

Schachter, S. 1959: *The psychology of affiliation*. Stanford, Calif.: Stanford University Press.

Snyder, C.R., Smith, T.W., Angelli, R.W. and Ingram, R.E. 1985: On the self-serving function of social anxiety: Shyness as a self-handicapping strategy. *Journal of personality and social psychology* 48, 950–80.

approach/avoidance conflict: social psychology One of the three possible types of CONFLICT, distinguished by LEWIN (1935), in which the tendency to approach and avoid a goal are of equal strength. Approach leads to an increase of negative valence and hence to compensatory withdrawal from the goal; avoidance to a relative increase of positive valence and therefore to compensatory approach movements. The approach/avoidance conflict is relatively stable and leads to a great deal of vacillating and "Übersprung" behavior, as observed by ethologists in animals. In children it may lead to minimal task performance, rejecting the goal or attempting to reach the goal in other ways.

The most influential research on approach/avoidance conflicts has been conducted by Miller (1944). Most of his work was concerned with learning in animals.   JMFJ

Bibliography

Lewin, K. 1935: *A dynamic theory of personality*. New York: McGraw-Hill.

Miller, N.E. 1944: Experimental studies of conflict. In *Personality and behavior disorders: a handbook based on experimental and clinical research*, vol. 1, ed. J. McV. Hunt. New York: Ronald.

Weiner, B. 1980: *Human motivation*. New York: Holt, Rinehart and Winston.

archival method

archival method A method of research involving the systematic analysis of previously recorded or preserved information. Archives are typically documents and public records, although research is not restricted to printed materials and may deal with artifacts such as tools, toys, architecture or clothing. The outstanding feature of archival methods is that they help with the study of psychological phenomena cross-time, and cross-culturally. The method is generally economical, permits re-analysis of materials, and involves a procedure of nonreactive or unobtrusive assessment of phenomena. On the other hand archival studies are susceptible to biases in the recording, survival and retrieval of information.

Archival materials may be subjected to quantitative analysis. The findings then often resemble social statistics as exemplified in DURKHEIM's classic study of suicide. Research problems requiring qualitative or higher-order analysis may use various techniques of content analysis. Archival research in psychology has conventionally been distinguished from historical research by its use of quantitative measures, but the distinction is superficial as some historians employ quantitative measures and some psychologists use qualitative ones. Owing to these mutual interests in methodology and in psychological explanations, a comprehensive account of archival methods must include studies in psychology and history.   JGM

Bibliography

Durkheim, E. (1897) 1951: *Suicide: a study in sociology*. Trans. J.A. Spalding and G. Simpson. Glencoe: Free Press; London: Routledge (1952).

Gergen, K. and Gergen, M. eds 1983: *Historical social psychology*. New York: Erlbaum.

Simonton, D.K. 1981: The library laboratory: archival data in personality and social psychology. In *Review of personality and social psychology*, vol. 2, ed. L. Wheeler. Beverly Hills and London: Sage.

arousal A psychophysiological concept that is used in all branches of psychology, particularly personality theory. The idea of arousal can be traced back to Pavlovian ideas of the excitatory strength of the nervous system, but is perhaps more widely known in the work of EYSENCK (1967) and Gray (1971). Both see arousal level as an inherited biological phenomenon on which individuals may differ along a dimension. Furthermore both have the notion of an optimal level of arousal.

Russian and Polish researchers have looked at arousal in terms of the concept of reactivity of the nervous system – that is the relationship between the intensity of the stimulus and the amplitude of response. Stimuli of equal physical activity are demonstrated to evoke a lower level of arousal in low-reactive than in high-reactive subjects. The low-reactive individual augments stimulation, and the high-reactive individual reduces stimulation, both aiming at maintaining or restoring a genetically fixed optimal level of activation.

Eysenck (1967) has argued that extraversion and introversion are closely related with habitual levels of arousal in the cortex (particularly the reticular activating system). Introverts have a higher level of arousal and hence are more inhibited, seek less stimulation and are better at learning, remembering and conditioning. Extraverts have a lower level of arousal and hence are more excitable, seek more stimulation and are less easily conditioned. They are therefore not so good at learning.

Numerous studies have looked at the relationship between various self-report and physiological measures of arousal (see Paisey and Mangan 1980). A lot of work in human experimental psychology has also been concerned with the effects of induced rather than inherited levels of arousal on performance. An inverted U curve has been found for the relationship between arousal level and performance at a wide variety of different tasks. At very low levels of arousal the nervous system may not function properly, whereas at very high levels it may lead to intense emotions that disrupt performance. A moderate optimal level of arousal tends to produce alertness and interest in the task at hand.　　　AF

Bibliography

Eysenck, H.J. 1967: *The biological basis of personality*. Springfield, Ill.: C.C. Thomas.

Gray, J.A. 1971: *The psychology of fear and stress*. London: Weidenfeld and Nicolson; New York: McGraw Hill.

Paisey, T. and Mangan, G. 1980: The relationship of extroversion, neuroticism, and sensation-seeking to questionnaire derived measures of the nervous system. *Pavlovian journal of biological science* 15, 123–30.

Asch, Solomon Eliot Born 1907, in Warsaw. At thirteen Asch moved to the USA where he was educated in New York (BS, College of the City of New York 1928; PhD, Columbia, 1932). While he was an assistant professor at Brooklyn College (1932–1943), he met and was profoundly influenced by the gestalt psychologist, Wertheimer. When the latter died in 1944 Asch took over his position at the New School for Social Research in New York. From 1947 to 1966 he was professor at Swarthmore College, and after that he was at Rutgers (1967–72), Pennsylvania and then Princeton.

Asch's work has been seminal in the study of both CONFORMITY and impression formation. In both areas he has been concerned with how people make sense of information they receive. He was guided by the gestalt psychologists' belief that the elements of incoming information are transformed by their relationships with each other, so that any element may appear different when it occurs in a different structure. In other words the meaning of a unit to which the elements belong affects the meaning of the individual elements, and is not itself determined by the meaning which the elements have in isolation from each other. He has also been guided by the idea that the recognition of consciousness and judgment in others makes our responses to them quite different in kind from our responses to other entities. For

this reason social psychology cannot be reduced to individual psychology (Asch 1952, 1958).

In 1938 Asch, Block and Hertzman described several studies on judgments of persons shown in photographs, of politicians, of professional groups and of political slogans! Apart from *halo effects* (a tendency for individuals' judgments to be all in a favorable or all in an unfavorable direction), they also found that people were influenced by reports of the opinions of "a large number of people" or "the country's leading psychologists". They concluded, however, that "when the subject has some objective knowledge of a situation . . . [this] . . . produces a more stable attitude and one more resistant to change".

Later, however, Asch found that people are prepared to follow the lead of a group of strangers even when the others say something which they can clearly perceive to be false (Asch 1951, 1956). Groups were composed of just a single subject and a set of stooges (usually five or seven). The task was simple and unambiguous. Each member in turn stated which of three clearly different comparison lines was the same length as a stimulus line. On selected trials the stooges all gave the wrong answer. on thirty-two percent of these occasions the subject followed the group and also gave the wrong answer. About seventy-five percent of the subjects gave an incorrect answer at least once, and a third of them did so on half or more of the twelve trials. Controls, who were not subjected to influence, made virtually no mistakes.

When questioned afterwards, some who had conformed said they had simply lied so as not to appear different or inferior, although others said they had lacked confidence and felt that their perception must have been wrong. A few said that they were unaware that their judgment had been distorted by the majority. In subsequent studies of the same kind Asch showed that one dissenter from the opinion of the majority would reduce conformity, even if the dissenter selected the other wrong line rather than the correct line. If there were two naive subjects the total number of promajority errors dropped to just over ten percent, and if there was a stooge who preceded the subject and always responded correctly the number dropped to just over five percent. Asch used a variety of different sized groups, and found that a group of four, with three stooges, was sufficient to produce the full effect. The elegance and simplicity of these experiments dominated work on conformity for two decades, but their fame is somewhat ironic. Because people conformed to the majority without any coercion or threat, the results were taken to prove how readily people comply. But Asch himself was interested in independence as well as conformity. He questioned the subjects because he wanted to know how someone thought when he "faced, possibly for the first time in his life, a situation in which a group unanimously contradicted the evidence of his senses". He wanted "to establish the grounds of the subject's independence or yielding" and he stressed the characteristics and comments of different types of resistance (the cool vs the perturbed) just as much as different types of compliance. He was also interested in how much conformity was a matter of conscious awareness and choice.

A more abiding interest of Asch's has been in the integration of information in IMPRESSION FORMATION. In 1946 he reported ten experiments on this. The best known results were the demonstration of the impact of primacy on judgments of personality, and the warm/cold effect. In one experiment (no. 6) he asked subjects to imagine someone who was "intelligent, industrious, impulsive, critical, stubborn, envious". He asked others to imagine someone with the same traits, but listed them in the opposite order. The first group received the better impression. Since intelligent is more complimentary than envious, and the first list seems to show a descending order of desirability, Asch considered this a "primacy effect" in which the information acquired first sets up 'a direction which then exerts a continuous effect on the latter terms'. Such primacy effects have also been shown in studies which used vignettes (Luchins 1957) and even when the subjects were given no

information but merely observed others' behavior (Jones et al. 1968).

In another experiment (no. 1) Asch asked subjects to imagine a person who was 'intelligent, skilful, industrious, warm, determined, practical, cautious'. Other subjects received the same adjectives, with the exception that cold replaced warm. Again the two groups' impressions differed. Asch argued that warm and cold are central qualities in this array. He felt this view was supported by the fact that forty-nine percent who received warm and forty-eight percent who received cold ranked these traits in first or second place for their importance in determining their impressions.

Asch believed that the changes produced in the impressions by order effects and by the substitution of only one word in a list could only be interpreted in gestalt terms, since it was clear that the traits were not summed additively but "integrated" in 'the perception of a particular form of relation between' them. These studies of impression formation, like those of conformity, are regarded as classics, and have inspired numerous imitators and much debate (see SOCIAL INFLUENCE; IMPRESSION FORMATION; SOCIAL COGNITION). In particular the processes involved in impression formation have constantly been disputed but even those who have attempted to demonstrate that Asch's gestalt interpretation of his own results is mistaken have acknowledged the importance of the example he set (e.g. Anderson 1962).

Asch subsequently became interested in the fact that we describe personal characteristics in metaphors. Descriptions 'of emotions, ideas or trends of character . . . employ terms that also denote properties and processes observable in the world of nature' (1958). He found this to be true of other languages such as Homeric Greek, Chinese and Hausa. He suggested that physical object and personal characteristic are described in the same words because each involves a similar "mode of interaction". For example "hardness is resistance to change imposed by external forces" whether it is hardness of an object or of a character. In the 1960s he applied his gestalt principles to a series of experiments on the role of organization and recognition in the recall of shapes and nonsense syllables (1969).

Most recently, taking up from where he left off in 1946, he and Zukier (1984) have looked at how people reconcile conflicting trait information. They found that people can construct a coherent personality profile even from a pair of adjectives in which one appears to contradict the other (e.g. brilliant-foolish, sociable-lonely). They inferred various rules which determined how incongruences were eliminated, such as that 'phenomenally inner attributes dominated over outer attributes'. In the case of sociable-lonely, for example, people typically suggested that someone might appear sociable but be "inwardly . . . lonely". Brillant-foolish, were reconciled by "segregation" of domain, as in "brilliant intellectually but foolish in practical . . . matters". As before, the conclusion was that 'relations discerned between two dispositions . . . produced marked changes in the content, scope, and significance of one or both terms', and that people were motivated to work out such different meanings, because 'unity of the person was one assumption that was not questioned'.

RI.

Bibliography

Anderson, N.H. 1962: Application of an additive model to impression formation. *Science* 138, 817–18.

Asch, S.E. 1946: Forming impressions of personality, *Journal of abnormal and social psychology* 41, 258–90.

——— 1951: Effects of group pressure upon the modification and distortion of judgments. In *Groups, leadership and men*, ed. H. Guetzkow. Pittsburgh: Carnegie Press. (Reprinted in *Group dynamics: research and theory*, eds. D. Cartwright and A. Zander. Evanston, Ill.: Row, Peterson 1953).

——— 1952: *Social psychology*. Englewood Cliffs, N.J.: Prentice-Hall.

——— 1956: Studies of independence and conformity: I. A minority of one against a unanimous majority. *Psychological monographs* 70 (9, Whole No. 416).

——— 1958: The metaphor: a psychological inquiry. In *Person perception and interpersonal behavior*, eds. R. Tagiuri and L. Petrullo. Stanford: Stanford University Press.

——— 1969: A reformulation of the problem of association. *American psychologist* 24, 92–102.

——— Block, H. and Hertzman, M. 1938: Studies in the principles of judgments and attitudes: I. Two basic principles of judgment. *Journal of psychology* 5, 219–51.

——— and Zukier, H. 1984: Thinking about persons. *Journal of personality and social psychology* 46, 1230–40.

Jones, E.E., Rock, L., Shaver, K.G., Goethals, G.R. and Ward, L.M. 1968: Pattern of performance and ability attribution: an unexpected primacy effect. *Journal of personality and social psychology* 9, 133–41.

Luchins, A.S. 1957: Primacy-recency in impression formation. In *The order of presentation in persuasion*, ed. C.I. Hovland. New Haven: Yale University Press.

aspiration level In a brilliant series of studies inspired by LEWIN, Dembo and Hoppe conducted some of the first experimental studies in human motivation. This early research indicated that the experience of success and failure depends more upon the person's aspirations than on some objective standard of performance. These studies also showed that the motivation for success does not lead to levels of aspiration which guarantee easy success. When translated into English (in Frank 1935 a,b), this research led to a flood of studies by American investigators, giving rise to important work on SOCIAL COMPARISON processes, self-evaluation, IDEAL SELF/actual self and ACHIEVEMENT MOTIVATION, and also to the use of self-anchoring scales to study patterns of human concern around the world.   JMFJ

Bibliography

Frank, J.D. 1935a: Individual differences in certain aspects of the level of aspiration. *American journal of psychology* 47, 119–28.

——— 1935b: The influence of level of performance in one task on the level of aspiration in another. *Journal of experimental psychology* 18, 159–71.

attachment An affective tie between an infant and caregiver construed either as an indicator of dependence motivation or as an organizational construct within a systems-theoretic view of development. Initially concerned with the psychiatric sequellae of disturbed early development Bowlby (1969) used an evolutionary perspective in recasting explanations of early infant-caregiver interaction. He proposed that smiling, clinging and vocal signaling be viewed as functionally-related proximity maintaining devices which ensured the safety of the infant and the reproductive success of the parents. Concern with safety from predation was broadened to include a view of the primary caregiver as a secure base which allowed exploration and which provided comfort in distress. The strength of an organizational approach lies in its ability to integrate a diverse set of behavior and provide a theoretical account of individual differences and developmental changes (Sroufe and Waters 1977). Bowlby's theory provoked much empirical research, particularly into the presumed privileged status of the mother. Evidence has since shown that the mother need not be the primary attachment figure and that an infant can form bonds with a number of responsive caregivers, including other children. (See also SEPARATION.)   BBL

Bibliography

Bowlby, J. 1969: *Attachment and loss*. vol. 1. *Attachment*. London: Hogarth Press; New York: Basic Books.

Sroufe, L.A. and Waters, E. 1977: Attachment as an organizational construct. *Child development* 48, 1184–99.

attitudes Generally regarded as acquired behavioral dispositions, which are introduced in the analysis of SOCIAL BE-HAVIOR as hypothetical constructs to account for variations in behavior under seemingly similar circumstances. As latent states of readiness to respond in particular ways they represent residues of past experience which guide, bias or otherwise influence behavior. By definition, attitudes cannot be measured directly but have to be inferred from overt behavior.

The concept of attitude is often treated in a global and undifferentiated way; but the etymology of the word itself and a conceptual analysis of definitions suggest that an attitude is regarded either as an implicit response, by learning theorists, or as a perceptual template, by cognitive social psychologists. These two views are combined in modern expectancy-value theories of attitudes (Ajzen and Fishbein 1980). The expectancy component of an attitude refers to the perceived instrumentality of the attitude object to the person's goals or the perception that the attitude object has certain attributes. The value component refers to the evaluation of the goals or attributes related to the attitude object. An attitude is thus defined as the sum of evaluative weighted expectancies or beliefs. As such, an attitude is not a very discriminating concept. It reflects the general and prevalent notion of behavioral decision theory that human action is guided by considerations of subjectively expected utility.

Ideally attitudes should be inferred by observing behavioral responses in a wide variety of situations. In practice it is of course not feasible to follow persons around in their natural surroundings and observe all their reactions to a variety of stimuli and hence it has become more or less standard procedure in attitude measurements to consider mainly verbal (evaluative) reactions to symbolic representations of the attitude object. Other reactions, such as cognitive and perceptual distortions and physiological measures, are sometimes used but their validity appears to be relatively low due to measurement problems. Standard procedures for measuring attitudes consist of constructing scales following traditionally either a subject, stimulus or response approach.

The most common type of attitude scale is the subject-centered type which was introduced by Likert (see Jaspars 1978). This approach represents a direct application of test theory as developed from the measurement of general cognitive activities. The construction of a Likert scale starts with the collection of a large number of prima facie relevant statements which are administered to a sample of subjects who are asked to indicate their agreement or disagreement with each statement. Item analysis or factor analysis is then used to remove from the initial collection those statements that do not show sufficiently high correlations with either the initial total score or other items, in order to ensure a scale with high internal consistency and reliability.

A stimulus approach, which stems from the psychophysical tradition in psychology, aims first at assigning scale values to attitude statements (Jaspars 1978) and arrives at a score for a respondent by calculating the median scale value for those statements with which a subject agrees.

The response-centered approach introduced by Guttman (see Jaspars 1978) is based on the analysis of the response patterns produced by respondents. Scale values for statements and subjects are simultaneously obtained. In recent years non-metric multidimensional scaling techniques have been developed which make use of computerized iterative procedures to obtain scale values for respondents and stimuli on as many scales as are required to account for the observed response patterns (Carroll and Arabie 1980).

The main purpose of measuring attitudes is to predict behavior. Initially the predictive validity of attitudes in this sense was tested by correlating scores obtained on general attitude scales with specific overt behavior in situ. Results were quite disappointing (Wicker 1969) but Fishbein and Ajzen have recently shown that attitudes do predict behavior quite well if the attitude measured is congruent with the behavior to be predicted and is specific rather than general (see Pagel and Davidson 1984). The attitude to the action itself is often more predictive than the attitude to the object. It has been realized moreover that the search for positive correlations between attitudes and behavior is a misguided effort (Jaspars 1978) because one cannot test whether a latent disposition is a determinant of overt behavior by correlating what people say and do. Path analytical models using latent variables show that attitudes do have an important effect on overt behavior. The correlation between

verbal attitude measures and overt behavior is also an incorrect measure of the association between attitudes and behavior because it assumes that attitudes might be sufficient causes for behavior, but it is abundantly clear from a large number of studies that social behavior in particular situations is determined by many other factors. This leads to the typical finding of a discrepancy or asymmetric relation between what people say and do. In many situations normative influences make it more difficult or costly for a person to practice what he or she preaches and hence we find that expressing a counter-normative attitude is not very predictive of actual behavior whereas showing the behavior predicts the attitude of the person very well. Conversely the absence of counter-normative attitudes is strongly predictive of normative behavior. The verbal expression of a latent attitude appears to have a lower threshold than overt behavior, as Campbell has suggested (see Jaspars 1978). Verbal attitudes based on direct, previous experience with the attitude object should raise the threshold of verbal attitude expressions and lead to a better prediction of behavior. This is exactly what recent research has shown to be the case.

The study of attitude change has been a major area of research in social psychology during the past 40 years. The traditional approach has been to regard attitude change as a problem of information processing based on persuasive communication. Under the influence of persuasive communication studies conducted during the second world war in the American Armed Forces and the Yale School (see McGuire 1969), numerous studies have been made to discover the determinants of successful persuasion. The model underlying these studies assumes that attitude change depends upon the discrepancy between the attitude originally held by the receiver and the position advocated by the source of the message. The amount of change produced in the receiver is thought to be a function of the relative weights of the source and the receiver. This proportional change model can be expressed as:

$$\triangle A_r = \frac{W_s}{W_s + W_r} (A_s - A_r)$$

where

$\triangle A_r$ = change in attitude of the receiver

W_s and W_r = weights assigned to the values of the attitudes expressed or held by the source and receiver

A_s and A_r = the initial attitudes expressed by source and receiver.

Many studies have shown that the weight of the source depends to a large extent upon the attitude of the receiver to the source of communication. In general, the greater the expertness, attraction, reward or coercive power of the source over the receiver, the greater the attitude change.

The second major category of determinants studied is related to the discrepancy between the attitudes of source and receiver as perceived by the receiver. Numerous studies have investigated the effect of the message structure on attitude change, but very few robust findings have been reported. It appears that such factors as emotional appeal, fear, arousal, style of delivery, explicit drawing of conclusions, refuting of counter-arguments, repetition and order of presentation have different effects depending upon the content of the message and the nature of the receiver.

Findings are similarly inconclusive with respect to the influence of characteristics of the receiver on attitude change. There is only weak evidence of a general factor of susceptibility. McGuire (1985) has suggested that contradictory findings about the effect of message and receiver factors can be reconciled if one assumes that many of these factors have opposite effects upon comprehension of a message and yielding once the message is understood. Experimental evidence and results from field studies largely support McGuire's explanation.

A completely different tradition of research on attitude change was instigated by Festinger's theory of COGNITIVE DISSO-NANCE. This theory suggests that people in general will show a tendency to reduce dissonant cognitions. One would therefore expect that when individuals are forced to comply at a behavioral level, they will tend to change their attitudes in accordance with their behavior. Experimental evidence supports this prediction although it is not clear whether dissonance reduction is the cause of the observed attitude change. Moreover it is obvious from later research that the process only appears to operate under certain conditions, one of which is that the person must perceive his or her own commitment to the action as voluntary. A third strategy of attitude change is to expose the receiver directly to the attitude object. Research has shown that mere exposure to a stimulus may be sufficient to induce a positive evaluation of the stimulus (see MERE EXPOSURE EFFECT). Recently it has been shown that such preferences can even develop without being able to discriminate between stimuli (Zajonc 1980).

It has been argued that the effectiveness of these three strategies depends upon the extent to which the content of a message is related more to the source or to the receiver of the communication. In general it is assumed that a matching of strategy and context will result in more attitude change. Thus an external source may be very persuasive when the content of the message is related to his own expertise, but less so when the communication refers to values held by the receiver. Changing the views a person holds of himself or herself should be more influenced by getting the person to focus on his or her own behavior.

JMFJ

Bibliography

Ajzen, I. and Fishbein, H. 1980: *Understanding attitudes and predicting social behavior.* Englewood Cliffs, N.J.: Prentice-Hall.

Caroll, J.D. and Arabie, P. 1980: Multidimensional scaling. *Annual review of psychology* 31, 607–50.

Cooper, J. and Croyle, R.T. 1984: Attitude and attitude change. *Annual review of psychology* 35, 395–426.

Jaspars, J. 1978: The nature and measurement

of attitudes: determinants of attitudes and attitude change. In *Introducing social psychology*, eds. H. Tajfel and C. Fraser. Harmondsworth: Penguin.

McGuire, W.J. 1985: Attitudes and attitude change. In *Handbook of social psychology*, 3rd edn., vol. 2, eds. G. Lindzey and E. Aronson. Reading, Mass.: Addison-Wesley.

Pagel, M.D. and Davidson, A.R. 1984: A comparison of three social-psychological models of attitude and behavioral plan. *Journal of personality and social psychology* 47, 517–33.

Wicker, A.W. 1969: Attitudes vs actions: the relationship between verbal and overt behavioral responses to attitude objects. *Journal of social issues* 25, 41–78.

Zajonc, R. 1980: Feeling and thinking: preferences need no inferences. *American psychologist* 35, 151–75.

attraction to strangers encountered in the laboratory received a good deal of attention in the years 1960–1975 or so, but has declined in recent years as researchers have moved on to study real-life RELATIONSHIPS. In part the decline is due to growing dissatisfaction with the reductionism necessary to study liking in a laboratory, but in part it is due to the development of more complex methods for studying real-life encounters, to a greater understanding of the rules of friendship in everyday life, and to a greater willingness to explore COMMUNICATION in extended interactions.

Attraction has been defined and used in so many ways that it is impossible to give an encapsulated definition of the term. This itself has proved to be a great obstacle to research since one major issure has been the extent to which different workers are talking about the same phenomenon. In its most general usage (e.g. Berscheid and Walster 1978) attraction refers to a positive inner ATTITUDE felt by one person toward another. However, in the best known of the attraction paradigms (i.e. that of Byrne 1971), attraction refers specifically to the liking expressed by a subject for a *stranger*, and Byrne does not concern himself with the question of whether expressed liking reflects an inner state. A third, and confusing, use of the word "attraction"

indicates *growth* of liking during acquaintance, and Levinger's (1974) schematic approach to attraction has muddied the water by thus failing to distinguish initial attraction and more complex forms of liking and commitment that develop as relationships grow. Fourth, the "word" attraction is used (Berscheid and Walster 1978) to refer to the whole area of research into personal liking, and hence to a variety of different forms of relationship (e.g. friendship, courtship, marriage) without concern for their possible differences in form, intensity and expressive nature of liking.

The most consistent use of the term takes attraction to be one individual's attitude towards another, with consequent structural division into affective (feelings), behavioral (action) and cognitive (intentional) components. Alternatively and more usefully, research into relationships has stressed the diversity of behavior and of joint social action that characterize relationships and has placed much less emphasis on the internal psychological processes occurring in only one of the individuals involved.

The bulk of work into attraction has tested explanations of the antecedents of liking (particularly features that make persons attractive to others), although a lesser amount of work has explored the consequences of attraction on other social behavior, such as obtaining a bank loan (Golightly, Huffman and Byrne 1972). Numerous items have been studied; examples can be found under COOPERATION, EQUITY THEORY, SOCIAL EXCHANGE, NONVERBAL COMMUNICATION, SOCIAL SKILLS and MERE EXPOSURE EFFECTS. A major limitation of all such work was that it did not explore the ways and means by which feelings of liking or attraction were translated into everyday relationships nor the reasons why this did not always happen (Duck and Sants 1983).

For instance, work on physical attractiveness, despite an increasing sophistication, clung to the idea that individuals had properties that made them *invariably* attractive to other people (e.g. beauty, height, generosity). Such work ignored the processes by which such features exerted their influence through actual behavior (Duck and Sants 1983). Researchers have only recently asked themselves how physical attractiveness influenced actual experience of social encounters and have attempted, in parallel, to identify the personality features that were most generally attractive, on the assumption that interrelationship of the personalities of the two partners (e.g. their similarity or their oppositeness) was at least as important as the personal qualities of either individual alone (a finding explained variously by COGNITIVE CONSISTENCY and COGNITIVE BALANCE). The main effort of such research went into the issue of whether similarity or complementarity was more attractive. Complementarity of personality needs was proposed by Winch (1958) to explain selection of marital partners and he argued that certain types of persons (e.g. dominant ones) would seek partners who had complementary styles (i.e. submissive, in the above example). However, much research challenged this. Tharp (1963) showed the methodological and conceptual weaknesses in the complementary needs hypothesis. A possible resolution of the debate was provided by Kerckhoff and Davis (1962). They suggested that courtship partners first assessed their partners on similarity of backgrounds and interests; subsequently similarity of attitudes would become salient; and then partners would use "need fit" as the criterion – a sequence of events that they referred to as "filtering". This useful idea has never been well supported in relation to courtship, for which it was proposed, although (importantly) it is based on a fundamental reorientation to the nature of attraction: namely, one which sees the research task as explaining the *growth* of liking rather than its initial inducement (see Huston et al. 1981).

Although the work on personality was undoubtedly important in the history of attraction research, it is perhaps little more than an historical curiosity. One striking and careful set of studies was carried out by Byrne (1971) into the effects of attitude similarity on attraction to strangers. Arguing that individuals had an innate

need for "effectance" (i.e. to validate themselves and demonstrate their competence at dealing with the world), Byrne (1971) suggested that attitudes, being uncertain propositions, would need to be *socially* validated (see SOCIAL COMPARISON) and that people would thus find similarity of attitudes validating, rewarding and attractive. Byrne (1971) argued that attraction would result in direct proportion to the amount of reinforcing similarity and the importance of the attitude to the person. In a cleverly-designed, but much criticized, paradigm known as the Bogus Stranger Paradigm, Byrne was able to present subjects with a precisely measured amount of similarity to another person (the stranger) as follows: the subject completed an attitude format; Byrne collected it and gave the subject some other task to do; Byrne rigged another attitude format to reflect the subject's to a precise extent (10, 20 .... 80 percent similar) and handed it back to the subject as though it had been completed by an independent stranger. The subject's ratings of the person who was thought to have completed the attitude format were then taken as the measure of liking created by the known degree of attitudinal similarity. Byrne (1971) presented a mountain of evidence to show that attraction was directly related to attitudinal similarity.

Critics of Byrne (e.g. Murstein 1971) claimed artificiality in the paradigm because the subject does not meet the stranger (obviously he or she cannot), and because attitudes expressed on an attitude scale may not find adequate expression in social behavior, or may not exert the power of effect in real life that they do in Byrne's paradigm. It is now clearly recognized that, despite the strengths of the paradigm, similarity of attitudes creates attraction through processes of communication in acquaintance (Duck 1977, 1985) and that it does so most effectively only at certain points of interaction or acquainting.

The filtering theory of Kerckhoff and Davis (1962) provides the best basis for a resolution of the relative roles of attitudes, personality and communication in attraction, if one extends the idea of filtering from courtship to all friendships, and from attitudes or needs to a more complex view of the processes involved (Duck 1977, 1985). Thus individuals are conceptualized as communicating, by a variety of means, those aspects of their cognitive make-up that will assist them and their partners to create models of each other through which to assess their SOCIAL COMPARISON value and their provision of validational support for each other. As the relationship grows, so the relevant filters change, although in this new approach the ultimate purpose of their use is the same: seeking self-validation.

The history of research into attraction has a number of embarrassing mistakes that mark its track: a limited experimental base; a restricted range of concerns; a prolonged obsession with initial attraction rather than growth relationship; over-hasty dismissal of the study of real-life relationships; and too little concern for the validity of its laboratory findings when extended to explain naturally occurring relationships. Its value can be seen to lie in the fact that it provided a number of small but critical building blocks for the more promising area of relationship research.

SWD

Bibliography

Argyle, M. and Henderson, M. 1984: The rules of friendship. *Journal of social and personal relationships* 1, 211–37.

*Berscheid, E. and Walster, E.H. 1978: *Interpersonal attraction*. 2nd edn. Reading, Mass.: Addison-Wesley.

*Byrne, D. 1971: *The attraction paradigm*. New York and London: Academic Press.

Duck, S.W. 1977: *The study of acquaintance*. Farnborough, London: Saxon House/Teakfields/Gower Press.

—— 1985: Social and personal relationships. In *Explorations in interpersonal communication*, eds. G.R. Middler and M.L. Knapp. Beverly Hills: Sage.

—— and Sants, H.K.A. 1983: On the origin of the specious: are personal relationships really interpersonal states? *Journal of clinical and social psychology* 1, 27–41.

Golightly, C., Huffman, D.M. and Byrne, D. 1972: Liking and loaning. *Journal of applied psychology* 56, 521–3.

Huston, T.L., Surra, C., Fitzgerald, N. and Cate, R. 1981: From courtship to marriage: mate selection as an interpersonal process. In *Personal relationships 2: Developing personal relationships*, eds. S.W. Duck and R. Gilmour. London: Academic Press.

Kerckhoff, A.C. and Davis, K.E. 1962: Value consensus and need complementarity in mate selection. *American sociological review* 27, 295–303.

Levinger, G. 1974: A three level approach to attraction: toward an understanding of pair relatedness. In *Foundations of interpersonal attraction*. New York: Academic Press.

Murstein, B.I. 1971: Critique of models of dyadic attraction. In *Theories of attraction and love*, ed. B.I. Murstein. New York: Springer Publishing Company.

Tharp, R.G. 1963: Psychological patterning in marriage. *Psychological bulletin* 60, 97–117.

Winch, R.F. 1958: *Mate selection: a study in complementary needs*. New York: Harper and Row.

attribution theory A theory concerned with the study of common-sense explanations of human behavior and of its direct or indirect effects. People are said to be making attributions when they explain events by attributing them to causes. The idea that common-sense psychology is a fruitful area of study for social psychology was first suggested by HEIDER, whose discussion of the everyday analysis of action (1958) has greatly influenced more recent work on attribution theory. The notion of common-sense psychology developed by Heider is akin to ideas put forward in ETHNOMETHODOLOGY and ETHNOGENICS. However, in social psychology Heider's work has given rise mainly to experimental studies, especially in the formulations of causal attribution theory suggested by Kelley (see Kelley and Michela 1980) and Jones (1979).

Heider suggested that our everyday analysis of action is in a way analogous to experimental methods. We infer from observation whether the behavior of ourselves and of others is caused by environmental or personal forces. Among the latter Heider distinguishes power and ability (i.e. whether a person can do something) from motivation (i.e. what he is trying to do and how hard he is trying). Environmental forces are seen as divided into non-social factors (e.g. the difficulty of the task), and either interpersonal social forces such as requests or commands or objective social forces such as values. Heider argues that these factors are not seen as completely independent of each other. He points out that what a person "can" do encompasses both personal ability and situational difficulty. He also stresses the fact that in common sense, the less power or ability someone has, the more he will have to exert himself, and that in general how he performs will be determined both by what he can do and by what he is motivated to do.

Which forces are seen as causal in a particular instance depends on such factors as proximity, contiguity and the perceived strength and simplicity of connections, which determine whether actor and act or act and outcome are perceived as forming cause and effect units. Heider points out that in general a personal attribution is much more likely to occur than a situational attribution because actor and act are perceived as a much stronger unit than are situation and behavior, but he also considers that personal attribution is more common because a person is seen as a first or "local" cause beyond which we do not trace the causal chain. Our tendency in everyday thought to attribute behavior too often to personal factors has more recently been confirmed experimentally and labeled the "fundamental attribution error".

In contrast to Heider, Kelley (1967, 1973) suggested that an observer arrives at a causal understanding of perceived behavior either on the basis of observed covariation of the behavior and its possible causes or, in the case of a single observation, the configuration of the plausible causes. In the first case Kelley suggests that the process of causal attribution is a common-sense replica of the method of analysis of variance as utilized in scientific psychology where persons, entities and times/occasions are the independent variables. When an effect (action or behavior) occurs in one person only, but it occurs in him or her at various times and for various

entities, the covariance suggests, according to Kelley's theory, that the effect is "caused" by some property, characteristic or predisposition of the person. However, when the behavior occurs all the time in almost everyone in respect to only one entity, the entity is seen as the cause of the behavior. Experiments conducted by McArthur and others (see Kelley and Michela 1980) confirm that consistency (same reaction occurring in different situations), consensus (same reaction occurring in different persons) and distinctiveness (reaction occurring only with respect to a particular entity) do indeed affect the attribution of causality in the way predicted by Kelley, although not all factors are of equal importance.

It appears, however, that in general people are not very good at assessing covariation. Perception of covariation in the social domain is largely a function of the pre-existing theories people have, as Nisbett and Ross (1980) have recently shown. The use of information in making causal inferences depends, as Tversky and Kahneman (1974) have argued, on its representativeness and availability. The reason why consensus information is apparently less important for ordinary people in making causal inferences is probably because such information is less available, since it is less vivid and less direct than the entity and the actor. Only in the case of the attribution of performance to personal abilities does it appear that consensus information is used appropriately.

Kelley has also argued that the analysis of variance conception of the attribution process can be used to understand the phenomenon of attributional validity. A person can, according to Kelley, know that his perceptions, judgments and evaluation of the world are true to the extent that he can confidently make an entity attribution for a perception, judgment or evaluation. Kelley suggests, moreover, that the ratio of between-entity distinctions to within-entity variance between persons can be used as a measure of an individual's level of information.

In the case of a single observation Kelley has suggested several principles or causal schemata which observers may use to arrive at causal attributions. The first principle is known as the discounting principle, and states that the role of a given cause in producing a given effect is discounted if other plausible causes are present. The second principle is called the augmentation principle and refers to the familiar idea that when there are known to be constraints, costs, sacrifices or risks involved in taking an action, the action is attributed more to the actor than it would be otherwise. The discounting principle and the augmentation principle are examples of what Kelley calls a multiple sufficient cause schema and a compensatory cause schema. In addition to these two schemata Kelley distinguishes a multiple necessary cause schema, a person attribution schema, (one-to-one) pairing, and grouping schemata. Kelley holds that the layman has a repertoire of such schemata available in trying to interpret social reality.

The third major approach to the study of common-sense explanations of human behavior is the theory of correspondent inferences of Jones and Davis (1965), who have suggested that the fewer distinctive reasons an actor has for an action and the less these reasons are widely shared in the culture, the more informative is that action about the intentions or dispositions of the actor. More specifically, Jones and Davis argue that the disposition or the intention governing an action is indicated by those of its consequences not common to the alternative actions and the fewer such non-common effects, the less ambiguous is the attribution of the intention or the disposition (the principle of non-common effect). The second factor which affects causal attribution, according to Jones and Davis, is the belief of the observer about what other actors would do in the same situations (the principle of social desirability). If few persons would have acted as the actor does, the action is seen as revealing the person's intentions and dispositions.

In the third place Jones and Davis suggest that the observer makes a personal attribution if the action affects the person's personal welfare in a positive sense (the principle of hedonic relevance). Research based on correspondent inference theory has by and large confirmed that these factors do indeed affect causal attribution to persons.

The three approaches to attribution theory have given rise to a great deal of research during the last fifteen years. Apart from the research already mentioned, motivational aspects of attribution processes, especially the defensive nature of certain attributions, have been investigated. The most popular area of research has been the study of differences in attributions made by actors and observers of the same behavior. The general finding here is that we are inclined to explain our own behavior in terms of situational factors, whereas the behavior of other people is more often explained in terms of their intentions and dispositions.

The consequences of differences in causal attributions have not been studied as often as the conditions which lead to these differences (Fincham and Jaspars 1981). Moreover, common-sense explanations have hardly been studied in social psychology as part of the natural social context in which they are called for. Interest in both problems appears to be growing. It is hoped that this will lead to a theory of common-sense explanation which takes social factors into account.   JMFJ

Bibliography

Fincham, F. and Jaspars, J. 1981: Attributions of responsibility. In *Advances in experimental social psychology*, vol. 13, ed. L. Berkowitz. New York and London: Academic Press.

Harvey, J.H. and Weary, G. 1985: *Attribution: basic issues and applications*. Orlando, Fla. and London: Academic Press.

—— 1958: *The psychology of interpersonal relations*. New York: John Wiley; London: Chapman and Hall.

Jones, E.E. 1979: The rocky road from acts to dispositions. *American psychologist* 34, 107–17.

—— and Davis, K.E. 1965: From acts to dispositions: the attribution process in future perception. In *Advances in experimental social psychology*, vol. 2, ed. L. Berkowitz. New York and London: Academic Press.

Kelley, H.H. 1967: Attribution theory in social

psychology. In *Nebraska symposium on motivation*, ed. D. Levine. Lincoln: University of Nebraska Press.

—— 1973: The process of causal attribution. *American psychologist* 28, 107–28.

—— and Michela, J.L. 1980: Attribution theory and research. *Annual review of psychology* 81.

Nisbet, R. and Ross, L. 1980: *Human inference: strategies and shortcomings of social judgement.* Englewood Cliffs, N.J. and London: Prentice-Hall.

Tversky, A. and Kahneman, D. 1974. Judgement under uncertainty: heuristics and biases. *Science*, 185, 1124–31.

authoritarian personality A term introduced in social psychology as the title of a famous study of the psychological origins of anti-semitism. Heavily influenced by psychoanalytic theory, the authors of *The authoritarian personality* suggest that anti-semitism is a specific instance of a more general ethnocentric ATTITUDE which is held by individuals who, as a result of an authoritarian upbringing, have failed to internalize their SUPEREGO and who exhibit a strong ID and weak EGO. According to the theory the ambivalent attitude towards authority leads such individuals to express their hostile feelings towards members of outgroups. The authoritarian personality is supposed to be characterized by respect for convention, submission to authority, lack of introspection, superstition, stereotypical beliefs, admiration for power and toughness, destructive and cynical tendencies, projection and an exaggerated concern with sexual mores. The F (fascism) scale, which was constructed to measure the authoritarian personality and which contains questions about all of these aspects, appears to be multi-dimensional, indicating that not all aspects are related in the way the theory suggests. However the F scale has in general, a high predictive validity which suggests that it taps some important aspects of human personality (see Cherry and Byrne 1977). (See ADORNO.) JMFJ

Bibliography

Adorno, T.W., Frehkel-Brunswik, E., Levinson, D.J. and Sanford, R.N. 1950: *The authoritarian personality*. New York: Harper.

Billig, M. 1982: *Ideology and social psychology*. Oxford: Basil Blackwell.

Cherry, F. and Byrne, D. 1977: Authoritarianism. In *Personality variables in social behavior*, ed. T. Blass. Hillside, NJ: Lawrence Erlbaum.

autonomy Independence: ability to act according to one's own priorities or principles without being overwhelmed by external constraints or internal pressures such as unwanted but uncontrolable desires. Kant's classic definition of enlightenment also defines intellectual autonomy. Enlightenment is 'man's emergence from his self-incurred immaturity. Immaturity is the inability to use one's understanding without the guidance of another person.' Some modern critical theorists, however, have argued that the enlightenment principles of freedom and reason have come to be realized in a limited form which actually *restricts* human freedom and the possibility of a rational society. In modern society reason is confined to the cataloguing of empirical facts, autonomy takes the form of individuals repressing their own reasonable aspirations for a better life, and, as Marcuse put it (1964, p.23), "Free election of masters and slaves does not abolish the masters or the slaves". WO

Bibliography

Marcuse, H. 1936 (1972): A study in authority. In *Studies in critical philosophy*. London: New Left Books.

—— 1964: *One dimensional man*. Boston: Beacon; London: Routledge and Kegan Paul.

B

Bandura, Albert Born in 1925 in
Alberta, Canada Bandura attended the
University of British Columbia. After
graduating (1949) he studied clinical psychology at the University of Iowa (PhD
1952) where he was influenced by Spence
and the writings of Miller and Dollard.
After Iowa Bandura went to Wichita for an
internship, and then to Stanford. His
importance as a theorist and experimenter
on SOCIAL LEARNING THEORY lies in his
development of ideas far beyond the
reinforcement-contingency models with
which it began. Bandura was particularly
interested in the causes of AGGRESSION in
children. He argued against the view that
aggression is necessarily 'an impulsive,
emotional pathological manifestation'
rather than 'a method for getting what (the
aggressor) wants when other options have
failed' (1973a). He also argued against
earlier social learning theorists' ideas about
the necessary connection between frustration and aggression.

Bandura's work with Richard Walters
(1918–67) and others emphasized the
central role of observational learning. They
found that children could learn from
watching an adult act aggressively
(Bandura, Ross and Ross 1963). Children
who had seen an adult punished for
aggression were less likely than other
children to imitate when given a chance;
but if the children were then offered a
reward for imitating the model, those who
had watched the punished adult behaved
no differently from the others. This
showed that the children could learn to do
things by watching someone who was not
rewarded. Neither reward nor the observation of reward were therefore necessary for
the acquisition of the learning, although
reward or its observation would influence
whether the child actually imitated what
had been seen. Bandura therefore dis-

tinguished *acquisition* from *performance*. He
also distinguished the process illustrated in
this experiment from IMITATION on the one
hand, and IDENTIFICATION on the other.
Imitation implies literal mimicry of
another's behavior, while identification
implies an attempt to be as completely like
another person as one can. Bandura called
the observational learning seen in his
experiments "modeling". This process has
proved effective in the treatment of various
phobias (Bandura 1969a).

Bandura suggested that observational
learning is indispensable in 'situations
where errors are likely to produce costly or
fatal consequences', and that reinforcement could hardly suffice to explain the
acquisition of 'language ... customs, ...
and educational, social and political practice' (1969b). BEHAVIORAL THEORIES OF
PERSONALITY, in fact, cannot easily account
for the appearance of entire organized
patterns of behavior, for the acquisition of
learning in the absence of reward, or for the
fact that actions may be performed for the
first time long after the observation of the
model on which they are based. Cognitive
social learning, on the other hand, recognizes processes which explain the
demonstrable fact that observers 'abstract
common features from seemingly diverse
responses and formulate generative rules
of behavior that enable them to go beyond
what they have seen or heard' (1974).

Bandura subsequently continued to
develop his ideas about the cognitive
processes involved in social learning. In
particular he has placed great emphasis on
the important role of the *expectancy* one has
about the consequences of one's actions.
His ideas about therapy and well-being
resemble those of Rotter (see LOCUS OF
CONTROL) and Seligman's conceptions of
learned helplessness. He uses the terms
"self-efficacy" and "self-inefficacy" to

denote the states in which one perceives oneself as able or unable to cope. Self-efficacy involves expectations that one will bring about desirable and desired results, while self-inefficacy, involving opposite expectations, leads to anxiety and avoidance of difficult or threatening situations. Bandura believes that perceptions of self-efficacy determine whether people who know what to do act on the basis of that knowledge. Perceptions of self-inefficacy therefore help to explain why 'people often do not behave optimally, even though they know full well what to do' (1982).

The work of Bandura and others on the relationship between perceived self-efficacy and achievement, career interests, or favorable response to therapy confirms that the belief that one *can* do something is a predictor of one's choice to do it, and of the effort one makes in trying to achieve one's goals. This work therefore has a great deal in common with other cognitive theories of motivation which have developed in ATTRIBUTION THEORY (see Weiner 1980), and leads to similar conclusions about the causal role of belief and expectancy in determining what people (try to) do.

Bandura's concern with cognitive processes, however, has been pursued as part of a larger effort to establish a model of man as a self-determining agent who plans for long-term goals, and is capable of exercising self-control in an effort to reach them. This model is quite conventional in our culture. Bandura is unusual because he has tried to demonstrate that the model is correct by drawing on the theories and laboratory methods which have often been taken to show that it is useless or downright wrong. In the process he has broadened the scope of learning theory and made its application to humans appear less perverse. He has also been in the forefront of those who have tried to extract practical benefits from the tradition of laboratory study. These aims and achievements were recognized by the American Psychological Association's award (1980) to Bandura for his distinguished scientific contributions; the citation referred to his and his followers'

work on 'moral development, observational learning, fear acquisition, treatment strategies, self-control, standard setting, self-referent processes, and the cogntive regulation of behavior'. RL

Bibliography

Bandura, A. 1969a: *Principles of behavior modification*. New York: Holt, Rinehart and Winston.

—— 1969b: Social-learning theory of identificatory processes. In *Handbook of socialization theory and research*, ed. D.A. Goslin. Chicago: Rand McNally.

—— 1973a: Social learning theory of aggression. In *The control of aggression*, ed. J.F. Knutson. Chicago: Aldine.

—— 1973b: *Aggression: a social learning analysis*. Englewood Cliffs, N.J.: Prentice-Hall.

—— 1974: Behavior theory and the models of man. *American psychologist* 29, 859–69.

—— 1977: *Social learning theory*. Englewood Cliffs, N.J.: Prentice-Hall.

—— 1982: Self-efficacy mechanism in human agency. *American psychologist* 37, 122–47.

—— Ross, D. and Ross, S. 1963: Vicarious reinforcement and imitative learning. *Journal of abnormal and social psychology* 67, 601–7.

Weiner, B. 1980: *Human motivation*. New York: Holt, Rinehart and Winston.

Bateson, Gregory (1904–1980) Bateson studied in Geneva and got his doctorate at Cambridge University (1930). He went to New Guinea (1927–30) and Bali (1936–38) where he collected data for a book he subsequently wrote with the anthropologist Margaret Mead (1942). He held many research and teaching posts: ethnologist at the Veterans Hospital of Palo Alto in California (1950–62), director of the Institute of Communication Research at St Thomas, in the Virgin Islands, director of Research at the Oceanic Institute of Hawaii (1964–72), and lecturer at Kresge College at the University of California in Santa Cruz. Bateson was the main representative of the Palo Alto Group, and applied his anthropological expertise to psychiatry. His studies on the processes of communication in mental disorders are fundamental (see COMMUNICATION, HUMAN GENERAL). LM

Bibliography

Bateson, G. 1936: *Naven*. Cambridge: Cambridge University Press; New York: Macmillan, 1937.

────── 1942: *Balinese character*. New York: New York Academy of Sciences. (2nd. edn. 1958: Stanford: Stanford University Press; Oxford: Oxford University Press.)

────── 1972 (1973): *Steps to an ecology of mind: collected essays in anthropology, psychiatry, evolution and epistemology*. St. Albans: Granada.

behavior genetics Is concerned with the effects of genes on the expression of behavior. Any form of genetic analysis requires the identification of differences. This may take the form of a clear distinction between the behavior of two individuals, or there may be continuous variation in the expression of some type of behavior within a population. Breeding tests or examination of relatives can then be made to establish how far such differences are genetic. Behavior genetics is not a unified field of investigation and within this broad outline are to be found a diverse set of aims and approaches which may have little contact with each other. Fuller and Thompson (1978) provide much the best survey of the whole field.

On the one hand, much research is directed toward the nature of gene action upon behavior. Single gene mutations are studied in convenient organisms such as *Drosophila* or mice, and attempts are made to relate behavioral differences between mutant and normal individuals to gene action on physiology, neural structure or neurochemistry. At the other end of the range the techniques of quantitative genetics are used to analyse the variation within a population for a complex trait like learning ability. This will certainly involve many genes and there is no possibility of identifying the action of any one, the aim may be to use genetic analysis to help partition the trait and distinguish between variation of genetic and environmental origin (see TRAITS).

There is an inevitable diversity imposed on the field by the nature of the character being studied. Some branches of genetics are concerned with systems whose control is quite well known and where it is possible to relate the known action of genes (i.e. controlling the synthesis of proteins) to the end product. It is no coincidence that the most spectacular recent advances in genetics have come at its interface with molecular biology. Behavior presents many more problems for genetic analysis. Firstly, the phenotype itself is extremely diverse and indeed demands many completely different levels of analysis. We may be interested in the phototactic behavior of fruit flies, the control of balance and locomotion in mice, the maze-learning of rats, levels of aggression in different breeds of dog, courtship displays in chickens or spatial components of intelligence tests in human beings (all of which have been the subject of behavior-genetic analysis). Secondly, for many such phenomena the gap between gene action at the cellular level and the end-product we are studying is maximal. Nor can we expect to be able to generalize about the pathways along which genes operate to exercise their effects on such diverse behavioral phenotypes. Not all the pathways are of much interest in any case—a mutant mouse may show inferior avoidance learning, but turn out to have an elevated pain threshold to the electric shock which serves as reinforcer in the learning situation. It will always be necessary to screen out trivial effects of this type.

It has been argued that since behavior is usually manifested only intermittently as a sequence of events through time, its genetic basis exists only in so far as we can identify some underlying structure upon which it is based. Certainly some people feel that only by working with identified single genes of known effect can we hope to make any progress (see Quinn and Gould 1979 for an extreme statement of this reductionist position). However this type of approach is scarcely possible, except in one or two favored invertebrates whose genetics are well known, and much more that is of interest to psychologists has been achieved by behavior genetic analysis at other levels. We can consider some examples of each type.

Single-gene studies

There has been extensive work on *Drosophila melanogaster* where hundreds of mutant stocks are easily available, but these may have diverged genetically in other ways over generations of culturing, so it is often more useful to treat normal flies with a mutagen and screen the progeny for behavioral changes. Using this technique mutants have been isolated which affect a wide variety of behavioral phenotypes–phototaxis, locomotor activity, circadian rhythms, courtship behavior and learning ability (see Benzer 1983). Screening for behavior mutants requires some ingenuity and many trivial effects will have to be discarded along the way, e.g. flies which fail to respond because they cannot walk properly. The mutants affecting learning were mostly derived from a screening test in which flies learnt to avoid an odor which had been associated with electric shock. As their names, *dunce*, *amnesiac* and *turnip*, suggest their effect is to reduce learning and retention. It is obviously important to discover whether such mutants affect only olfactory conditioning, or whether they act more generally. It is not easy to get a range of learning situations for *Drosophila* but some visual, and simple operant conditioning has proved possible; *dunce* and *amnesiac* flies show some learning ability in these situations but certainly reduced from normal (see Folkers 1982). The genes appear to have both general and specific effects and attempts are being made to link them with changes to brain biochemistry. Using special stocks of *Drosophila* it is possible to generate flies some of whose cells express the effects of a mutant gene while others are normal. Study of such mosaic individuals helps to reveal in which parts of the body the gene acts to produce its effect–its "primary focus" (see Hotta and Benzer 1972).

Behavioral analysis involving many genes

The great majority of behavioral characters will be affected by many genes and we may not be able to identify the effects of any particular locus. Nevertheless the study of different strains of breeds or inbred lines of animals has often yielded interesting results. Nearly always they show differences on a wide variety of behavioral measures which can be shown to be of genetic origin, but the scale and sometimes direction of such genetic effects can be markedly affected by the environment. For example Henderson (1970) compared mouse strains reared in complex or standard cage environments in a feeding situation which involved exploratory behavior and agility. The genetic contribution to variance between the strains was four times greater in mice from complex cages, indicating extreme gene/environment interaction. We must expect such interactions to be the rule in behavioral development.

Artificial selection for behavioral characters has often been successful and reveals that natural populations are variable for genes affecting behavioral traits. Aggression in mice, mating speed in *Drosophila*, maze learning in rats–all have responded strongly to selection. Tryon's experiment with maze learning was one of the first of its type. He produced "maze-dull" and "maze-bright" rats with virtually no overlap in performance. However, when tested in other types of learning situation, the brights performed no better or even less well than the dulls. Analysis showed that Tryon's selection had isolated factors relating to the main cues the rats responded to when learning the maze. The brights were genetically predisposed to concentrate on kinesthetic cues in which Tryon's original maze was rich; the dulls' behavior was more visually controlled. Such a result contributed to our understanding of learning and illustrates the use of genetics as a tool for the study of behavior itself over and above its intrinsic genetic interest (see Manning 1976). By separating and exaggerating the effects of components which are normally associated together behavioral analysis is facilitated.

Human behavior genetics

Human behavior genetics mainly operates in two highly contrasted areas. First there is the study of gross genetic abnormalities, both those associated with single genes such as phenylketonuria or microcephaly, and also the chromosome abnormalities responsible for Down's syndrome, Turner's syndrome and others. With the single genes the nature of the primary action is often a clear enzyme deficiency which can be related to the effects on the functioning of the nervous system and it can sometimes be counteracted using a controlled diet. Study of the genetics of brain metabolites backed up with experimental animal studies may help us to understand certain types of mental illness where neurochemistry is implicated (see Petersen, Collins and Miles 1982; Kety 1982).

The other type of human behavior genetics uses quantitative genetic approaches to study continuously varying traits such as intellectual ability and personality. The genetic analyses can be of impressive sophistication with data from extended families, mono- and dizygotic twins reared together and apart etc. The unresolved problem concerns the realistic separation of genetic and environmental influences upon such complex and controversial traits. (See also GENETICS, EVOLUTION AND BEHAVIOR). AWGM

Bibliography

Benser, S. 1983: The Croonian Lecture. Genes, neurons and behavior in *Drosophila. Proceedings of the Royal Society B.*

Folkers, E. 1982: Visual learning and memory of *Drosophila melanogastor* wild type C-S and the mutants *dunce, amnesiac, turnip* and *rutabaga. Journal of insect physiology* 28, 535–9.

Fuller, John L. and Thompson, William R. 1978: *Foundations of behavior genetics.* St. Louis: C.V. Mosby. No UK edn. but distributed in UK by: London: Y.B. Medical Publishers.

Henderson, N.D. 1970: Genetic influences on the behavior of mice can be obscured by laboratory rearing. *Journal of comparative physiological psychology* 72, 505–11.

Hotta, Y. and Benser, S. 1972: The mapping of behavior in *Drosophila* mosaics. *Nature* 240, 527–35.

Kety, S. 1982: Neurochemical and genetic bases of psychopathology: current status. *Behavior genetics* 12, 93–100.

Manning, A. 1976: The place of genetics in the study of behavior. pp. 327–43. In *Growing points in ethology*, eds. P.P.G Bateson and R.A. Hinde.

Cambridge and New York: Cambridge University Press.

Petersen, D.R., Collins, A.C. and Miles, R.G., 1982: An overview of the genetics of psychopathology. *Behavior genetics* 12, 3–10.

Quinn, W.G. and Gould, J.L. 1979: Nerves and genes. *Nature* 278, 19–23.

behavioral theories of personality

Attempts to apply the precepts of learning theory, and the laboratory findings it has inspired, to explain individual differences. The approach therefore stresses the behaviorist pantheon of accurate objective measurement in controlled conditions and the avoidance of reference to unobservable processes within the organism. Much reliance is placed on inferences drawn from discoveries about the laboratory behavior of non-human species such as rats and pigeons; as in all traditional behaviorism, there are assumptions about the plasticity of the behavioral repertoire and the universality of the principles underlying learning. In its pure forms the behavioral approach to personality plays down genetic factors and suggests that personality development can be explained by the reinforcements (rewards and punishments) which the individual has received from the environment in the course of his or her development.

The mechanisms of association involved in the processes of conditioning (classical and operant or instrumental) are taken to be sufficient to explain differences in motivation, competence, and emotional adjustment. The theorizing leads to a faintly paradoxical set of ideas which are at once egalitarian (and libertarian) since anyone can become anything (Watson 1930), yet at the same time highly deterministic, implying that people are entirely the product (and toys) of environmental forces over which they have no control. The vocabulary is one in which the individual is "shaped" and "conditioned" in a passive way.

Such approaches may lead to a belief in social engineering (Skinner 1971) in which the benign psychologist takes control of the contingencies which determine others' development. This vision has not proved universally attractive, and has led, somewhat prematurely, to fears of a state which "brain-washes" its citizens into calm or murderous compliance. Not surprisingly the most interesting application of such behavioral approaches has been in the concoction of training programs, and particularly in the clinical field. There have now been innumerable attempts to "shape" the behavior of the unruly (O'Leary and O'Leary 1977), or the lethargic and institutionalized (Ayllon and Azrin 1968), and to eliminate phobias and anxieties by procedures drawn from animal research (e.g. Masserman 1943) and explained by "basic" mechanisms of learning (e.g. Wolpe's dubious "reciprocal inhibition" – or counterconditioning – in the removal of anxiety). Many of these attempts have reputedly been successful (see Rachman and Wilson 1980).

The most concerted efforts to apply the experimental approach and ideas derived from learning theory to a wide range of personality and developmental issues has been that of the various proponents of SOCIAL LEARNING THEORY. Mischel (1973, 1983), for instance, has attempted to undermine many of the assumptions of personality theory, and to substitute a social learning model in their place (see PERSON/SITUATION CONTROVERSY). As social learning theory has become more comprehensive, however, it has abandoned the simple reinforcement models of its pioneers, and has taken up with cognitive processes such as planning and expectation, and has thereby arrived at a picture of the person as an active shaper of the environment rather than its product. It is therefore hardly to be reckoned a behavioral theory of personality.

Of course learning theories have themselves changed. The serious welcome given to Seligman's ideas about "preparedness" (1971) shows that the infinite plasticity of behavior and the supposed possibility of conditioning and response to just any conditional stimulus are no longer taken for granted as they appear to have been by Watson (1925; Watson and Rayner 1921). Furthermore, where the behaviorist's assumptions have been imported into

personality research they have often been watered down (or totally submerged) by assumptions which contradict the shibboleths of behaviorism. EYSENCK, for example, has embraced learning theory both in his approach to therapy and to personality, but has argued for the importance of genetic factors in determining behavior and personality, through their influence on the individual's susceptibility to conditioning or different kinds of conditioning. Eysenck therefore builds learning theory into his conception of personality development, but in such a way that the final product seems the antithesis of a behavioral or even social learning model.   RL

Bibliography

Ayllon, T. and Azrin, N.H. 1968: *The token economy*. New York: Appleton-Century Crofts.

Eysenck, H.J and Eysenck, M.W. 1985: *Personality and individual differences*. New York: Plenum.

Masserman, J.H. 1943: *Behavior and neurosis*. Chicago: University of Chicago Press.

Mischel, W. 1973: Toward a cognitive social learning reconceptualization of personality. *Psychological review* 80, 252–83.

——— 1983: Alternatives in the pursuit of predictability and consistency of persons: stable data that yield unstable interpretations. *Journal of personality* 51, 578–604.

O'Leary, D.K. and O'Leary, S.G. 1977: *Classroom management*. Oxford and New York: Pergamon.

Rachman, S.J. and Wilson, G.T. 1980: *The effects of psychological therapy*. Oxford and New York: Pergamon.

Seligman, M.E.P. 1970: On the generality of the laws of learning. *Psychological review* 77, 406–18.

Skinner, B.F. 1971: *Beyond freedom and dignity*. New York: Knopf.

Watson, J.B. 1925, 1930: *Behaviorism*. New York: 1st edn. People's Institute Publishing Co. (1925); rev. edn. Norton (1930).

——— and Rayner, R. 1920: Conditioned emotional reactions. *Journal of experimental psychology* 3, 1–14.

Wolpe, J. 1958: *Psychotherapy by reciprocal inhibitions*. Stanford: Stanford University Press.

bond A relationship in which an individual maintains and restores proximity to an inanimate object (such as a nest) or to an animate object (such as a parent or mate) towards which certain behavior is exclusively or preferentially directed (Lorenz 1966; Wickler 1976). Ethology has been concerned mainly with bonding among conspecifics, which generally is mutual though not necessarily symmetric. Bonding partners recognize each other as individuals. Bond formation occurs rapidly between parent and young. Among adults, it requires extended interactions and may then be regarded as an investment (Kummer 1978). Bonded partners tend to defend one another. Attachment theory holds that evolved behavioral and motivational systems underlie the differential preferences of individuals for forming particular bonds (e.g. Bowlby 1969; Reynolds 1976). HK

Bibliography

Bowlby, John 1969–80: *Attachment and loss*. vol. 1. *Attachment*. 1969. New York: Basic Books; London: Hogarth Press; Institute of Psychoanalysis.

Kummer, H. 1978: On the value of social relationships to nonhuman primates: a heuristic scheme. *Social science information* 17, 687–705.

Lorenz, Konrad Z. 1966: *On aggression*. New York: Harcourt, Brace and World; London: Methuen.

Reynolds, P.C. 1976: The emergence of early hominid social organisation: I. The attachment systems. *Yearbook of physical anthropology* 20, 73–95.

Wickler, W. 1976: The ethological analysis of attachment. *Zeitschrift für Tierpsychologie* 42, 12–28.

C

Cattell, Raymond B. Born in 1905 in Staffordshire, England, Cattell studied chemistry at London University, but subsequently turned to psychology in which he worked under Spearman. He was a lecturer at Exeter University (1927–32), and then worked at the City of Leicester Child Guidance Clinic (1932–37). He moved to New York as a research associate of Thorndike. He held positions at Harvard, Clark and Duke Universities. In 1945 he became research professor at the University of Illinois. He currently lives in Hawaii.

Along with ALLPORT and EYSENCK Cattell has been the most famous contributor to trait theories of personality (see TRAITS). In their 1936 monograph Allport and Odbert had found over 4500 adjectives applicable to humans. Cattell reduced this list to 171 by the removal of synonyms. He asked students to describe friends using these 171 words (which he referred to as "trait elements"). He then factor analysed the resulting ratings, and found thirty-six factors. He referred to these as "surface traits". He added ten more terms from psychological and psychiatric texts. He called these forty-six characteristics the 'standard reduced personality sphere'. Subsequently the forty-six were again reduced to sixteen dimensions, which he referred to as "source traits". These sixteen traits formed the basis of his later work, which included the design of a questionnaire (the 16 Personality Factor or 16PF) to tap them. Cattell named them: sizia/affectia (a reserved person vs an outgoing person), intelligence, ego strength (emotionally stable vs unstable), submissiveness/dominance, desurgency/ surgency (sober vs happy-go-lucky), superego strength (conscientious vs not), threctia/parmia (shy vs uninhibited), harria/premsia (tough-minded vs tender-

minded), alaxia/protension (trusting vs suspicious), praxernia/autia (practical vs imaginative), artlessness/shrewdness, untroubled adequacy/guilt proneness, conservatism/radicalism, group adherence/ self-sufficiency, self-sentiment integration (undisciplined vs controlled), and ergic tension (tranquil vs tense). These sixteen dimensions are correlated with each other so they may in turn be reduced by factor analysis. Doing this produces four- to eight-second order factors, of which intoversion-extraversion (which he calls invia and exvia) and anxiety are the best replicated in different studies (see TYPE).

Cattell went beyond the questionnaire (Q) data to collect what he called L data, i.e. ratings by peers or observers. He has found that the last four of the sixteen factors mentioned above do not appear in the analyses of L data, but the others do (see Cattell 1973). He has also found four further factors in L data. He feels that this degree of match shows that these two kinds of data are mutually supportive. He is nevertheless aware of the difficulties with both sorts of data. There are practical problems with QUESTIONNAIRES: people may lie or have response biases, such as saying yes to every question (Cronbach 1946). However Krug (1970) gave the 16PF questionnaire to subjects in a variety of (role-play) situations and found that the role factor did not outweigh the consistency among the responses in the different settings. Nevertheless, as Anastasi (1982) reports in reviewing Cattell's work, the reliability of the 16PF is not high. Correlations between scores on parallel forms of the questionnaire are in the region of 0.5, while retests after a week or less often correlate with the original score at less than 0.8 (see Baird 1981). Lanyon (1984) concludes that it is necessary to accept the verdict of previous reviewers that the 16PF cannot be recommended unreservedly for any use.

In the case of L data there are always problems with raters, who may use a scale differently from each other. Frequently raters simply disagree. There are other more subtle problems such as the *halo effect*, which is the tendency of a rater to perceive that a person has one characteristic and to attribute another to him because of an implicit assumption that certain characteristics are found together in the same person. Cattell has therefore suggested that for L data it is necessary for the rater to have known the subject for at least two to three months before making the assessments, and for there to be more than one rater. To reduce the halo effect only one trait should be rated at a time, and the behavior to be rated should be highly defined on a checklist. Even with all these precautions, however, there is evidence that the high degree of correlation between Q and L data may result from the fact that they are both tapping STEREOTYPES or culturally transmitted IMPLICIT PERSONALITY THEORIES which are shared by the raters and the people they are rating (D'Andrade, 1965; see also PERSON/SITUATION DEBATE).

This objection would obviously be overcome by Cattell's third kind of data, which he collects from objective tests that are not clearly connected with personality, and are in most cases very difficult for the subject to fake. Cattell has used over 400 of these tests to produce what he calls T data. They include standard projective tests like the thematic apperception test and also some less common tests like blowing up a balloon and drawing a line very slowly. Unfortunately for Cattell's ingenuity, analyses of these tests have produced twenty factors which are very different from those which result from analyses of the Q and L data (with anxiety and introversion/extroversion ninth and seventeenth among the factors rather than first and second). Had Cattell been able to find a similar factor structure among the scores on the objective tests, his theorizing about personality would have seemed far more soundly based than it now does. Nevertheless, if he had only shown us our way round the stereotypical notions of personality which people in our society hold, this would be an important achievement. On the other hand, even if his discoveries are about the way in which people really do differ from each other, his approach to both his original list of adjectives and to his objective tests has been resolutely empirical and atheoretical. It therefore invites the criticism of personality theorists such as Eysenck, who have attempted to make sense of their (quite similar) questionnaire and factor analytic results by grounding them in physiology (e.g. Eysenck 1972).   RL

Bibliography

Allport, G.W. and Odbert, H.S. 1936: Trait names: a psycholexical survey. *Psychological monographs* 47, no. 211, 1–171, 63.

Anastasi, A. 1982: *Psychological testing*. 5th. edn. New York: Macmillan.

Baird, Jr J.S. 1981: Reliability of the 16PF questionnaire for security guard applicants. *Journal of personality assessment* 45, 545–6.

Cattell, R.B. 1965: *The scientific analysis of personality*. Baltimore and London: Penguin.

—— 1973: *Personality and mood by questionnaire*. New York: Jossey Bass.

—— and Kline, P. 1977: *The scientific analysis of personality and motivation*. New York and London: Academic Press.

Cronbach, L.J. 1946: Response sets and test validity. *Educational and psychological measurement* 6, 475–94.

D'Andrade, R.G. 1965: Trait psychology and componential analysis. *American anthropologist* 67, 215–28.

Eysenck, H.J. 1972: Human typology, higher nervous activity, and factor analysis. In *Biological bases of individual behavior*, eds. V.D. Nebylitsyn and J.A. Gray. New York and London: Academic Press.

Krug, S. 1970: see Cattell 1973.

Lanyon, R.I. 1984: Personality assessment. *Annual review of psychology* 35, 667–701.

cognitive balance A term introduced by HEIDER (1958) to describe the cognitive tendency towards a balanced state in which perceived relationships between persons and/or objects coexist without stress. Perceived relational triads are said to be balanced when all relations are positive or when one relation is positive and two are negative. Jaspars (see Eiser 1980) has shown, however, that the balanced or imbalanced state of a cognitive system depends upon the nature of the underlying cognitive representation. Cognitive balance affects the learning and completion of cognitive structures relating to social relationships. It also has an effect on the evaluation of social relationships, although other factors (agreement, positivity) have in general a stronger impact. Later research (Wyer 1974; Schank and Abelson 1977) shows that the effect is not as general as Heider originally suggested but depends on the nature of the relationships involved (see also COGNITIVE CONSISTENCY).   JMFJ

Bibliography

Eiser, J.R. 1980: *Cognitive social psychology*. London: McGraw-Hill.

Heider, F. 1958: *The psychology of interpersonal relations*. New York: Wiley.

Schank, R.C. and Abelson, R.P. 1977: *Scripts, plans, goals and understanding*. Hillsdale, N.J.: Erlbaum.

Wyer, R.S. 1974: *Cognitive organization and chance: an information processing approach*. New York: Wiley.

cognitive complexity Reflects a style of thinking (cognition) and describes the number of dimensions and the relationship among dimensions on which a person places stimulus information in the process of translating a stimulus into a response. The use of several more or less independent dimensions of perception, judgment or behavior is called differentiation (e.g. Bieri 1961). Use of differentiated dimensions provides the person with the option of responding to the same stimulus (the same environmental situation) in a number of different ways. The outcome of differentiation could be the choice of (any) one response from those available, or it could be the use of some superordinate judgmental dimension(s) to select (in a strategic purposeful fashion) one of a number of behavioral options. The latter process is called integration (Streufert and Streufert 1978). The degree of cognitive complexity identified for any individual reflects the

degree of differentiation and/or integration which he or she displays.

While some have argued that complexity might reflect an ability or a cognitive preference, the general opinion appears to be that the degree to which persons differentiate and integrate is a learned style. Recent evidence of physiological (cardiovascular and electroencephalographic) differences between more and less complex persons suggests the possibility of potential physiological determinants. Complexity appears unrelated to other measures of ability (including intelligence) or cognitive style.

Considerable research has shown that cognitive complexity predicts a wide range of phenomena, including attitude change, decision making and perceptual responses. Scott has provided evidence that predictions of behavior may, however, hold only for those specific cognitive domains for which a level of cognitive complexity (degree of differentiation and integration) has been established.   SSt

Bibliography

Bieri, J. 1961: Complexity-simplicity as a personality variable in cognitive and preferential behavior. In *Functions of varied experience*, eds. D.W. Fiske and S.R. Maddi. Homewood, Ill.: Dorsey.

Streufert, S. and Streufert, S.C. 1978: *Behavior in the complex environment*. Washington, D.C.: Victor H. Winston and Sons.

cognitive consistency The tendency to avoid contradictory cognitions about social reality. During the 1950s Newcomb (1953), Festinger (1957), HEIDER (1958) and Osgood et al. (1957) published, to some extent independently of each other, a number of similar theories in which the tension arising from imbalanced, dissonant or incongruent beliefs, knowledge or attitudes is seen as a motivating force in human behavior. In a general sense these theories were neither new nor remarkable. They followed in the tradition of rationalistic philosophers such as Spinoza and Herbart and can be regarded to some extent as the application of gestalt principles in the domain of SOCIAL COGNITION. For two decades, however, these theories had a great influence in social psychology and stimulated an enormous amount of research. In quantitative terms Festinger's theory of COGNITIVE DISSONANCE has perhaps been the most productive, whereas Heider's theory of Balanced States has been more influential in the long run because it is part of his general theory about common-sense knowledge.

The basic postulates of Festinger's theory are simple and somewhat vague. The theory states that relations between cognitive elements can be irrelevant, consonant or dissonant. Cognitive elements are only defined in a very general way as "the things a person knows". Dissonance exists between two elements when, considering these two alone, the opposite of one element follows from the other. Again it is not clear whether we are concerned here with logical or psychological inconsistency. Whatever the case may be, dissonance is, according to Festinger's theory, experienced as an unpleasant state which the individual will try to reduce by changing cognitions or by introducing new elements in his or her cognitive system. The tendency to reduce dissonance will be stronger, the higher is the ratio of dissonant to consonant elements in a cognitive system (see COGNITIVE DISSONANCE).

Heider's theory of balanced states is part of his general attempt to unveil the principles of common-sense psychology. In this theory the concepts of sentiment, unit formation and balanced state play an important role. Sentiments refer to the positive or negative feelings a person can have about other persons or non-personal entities. A (cognitive) unit arises when several entities are perceived as belonging together due to proximity, similarity, common fate or other gestalt factors. According to the theory, unit and sentiment relations tend towards a balanced state; that is, a situation in which both types of relations can coexist without stress and do not show a tendency towards change. When balance is disturbed there will be a tendency towards restoring the balanced state. Heider distinguishes three types of balanced states. The first applies to

the homogeneity of sentiment or unit relations with respect to other people, better known as the *halo effect*. The second group of balanced states applies to the relationship between sentiment and unit relations with respect to one other person. In this case there is a balanced state when all relations are either positive or negative. The third and most interesting group of balanced states is concerned with the relationships between a person and two other people and/or non-personal entities. Such a triadic set of relations is balanced, according to Heider's theory, when all relations are positive or when one relation is positive and the others are negative.

The theory has later been formalized and extended using graph theory, and numerous experiments have tested various predictions which follow from Heider's basic postulates. In general it appears that the strongest confirmation of the tendency towards balanced states can be found in learning and perception experiments, whereas the effect of imbalance on evaluative ratings of the social situation is much less pronounced. This is due to the fact that the pleasant or unpleasant nature of a situation is determined also by the attitude towards the other person in the situation and the extent to which persons in the situation agree with each other. In fact it is much easier to understand Heider's theory of balanced states when one realizes that the relations he is concerned with can be reformulated as linguistic relations between subject, object and verb in a sentence. This reformulation also makes clear that the balanced effects suggested are far less general than was originally thought because they depend very much upon the specific nature of the relationships.

Osgood's congruity principle and Newcomb's analysis of communicative acts do not differ essentially from the theories of Festinger and Heider and will therefore not be discussed here.

Research on cognitive consistency has decreased in recent years (Abelson 1983), but the ideas of the originators are still very much alive in a disguised form in various other areas of research. Most theories about attitude change regard a discrepancy between a person's original attitude and the attitude advocated in a persuasive communication as the core of the attitude change process. One of the major strategies of attitude change derives in fact from Festinger's idea that attitude change can be brought about indirectly by first changing a person's behavior, as in a forced compliance situation, and relying on dissonance for a change of the person's attitude. (See ATTITUDES.)

There is also a good deal of interest within cognitive social psychology in people's attention to and memory for information which is inconsistent with their attitudes and expectations. (For a review see Fiske and Taylor 1984, chapter 12).

JMFJ

Bibliography

Abelson, R.P. 1983: Whatever became of consistency theory? *Personality and social psychology bulletin* 9, 37–54.

Festinger, L. 1957: *A theory of cognitive dissonance*. Stanford, Calif.: Stanford University Press.

Fiske, S.T. and Taylor, S.E. 1984: *Social cognition*. Reading, Mass.: Addison-Wesley.

Heider, F. 1958: *The psychology of interpersonal relations*. New York: Wiley.

Newcomb, T.M. 1953: An approach to the study of communicative acts. *Psychological review* 60, 393–404.

Osgood, O.E., Suci, G.J. and Tannenbaum, P.H. 1957: *The measurement of meaning*. Urbana: University of Illinois Press.

Zajonc, R.B. 1969: Cognitive theories in social psychology. In *Handbook of social psychology*. 2nd edn, eds. G. Lindzey and E. Aronson. Reading, Mass.: Addison-Wesley.

cognitive dissonance One of the consistency theories of attitude change that assumes that a person behaves in a way which will maximize the internal consistency of his or her cognitive system and that groups also strive to maximize the internal consistency of their interpersonal relations. Apart from cognitive dissonance theory (Festinger 1957) there are Heider's balance theory (1946) (see COGNITIVE BALANCE; COGNITIVE CONSISTENCY), and Osgood and Tannenbaum's congruity theory (1955). Cognitive dissonance theory was, however, by far the most influential and dominated attitude research for over a decade.

The core of the theory is deceptively simple: two cognitive elements (thoughts, attitudes, beliefs) are said to be in a dissonant relation, if the obverse of the one would follow from the other. Because dissonance is psychologically uncomfortable, its existence will motivate a person to reduce it and achieve consonance. Further, when dissonance is present, a person will actively avoid situations and information which would be likely to increase it.

The strength of the theory is not its clarity but the fact that it has generated a large number of hypotheses which have been tested in a wide variety of situations. In this sense the theory has been extraordinarily fertile although not all its hypotheses have been confirmed, and for some of the phenomena alternative explanations have been offered. Originally Festinger suggested various hypotheses with respect to decision making, exposure to information, seeking of social support and acting under forced compliance. It is especially the latter application in the area of attitude change which has probably had the greatest impact. In one of the most influential experimental studies Festinger and Carlsmith (see Wicklund and Brehm 1976) showed that smaller bribes are more effective in making a person change his mind than larger payments. This counter-intuitive finding, which also seemed to contradict reinforcement theory, was derived from dissonance theory, but later research has shown that this finding only holds under particular circumstances. Two conditions are apparently very important. Although we are concerned with a situation of forced compliance, the person involved should have the impression that he or she has freely chosen to act in this particular way; and secondly it must then be impossible for the person to undo what he or she has done. Similar restrictions hold with respect to some of the other areas of research to which dissonance theory has been applied and certainly with respect to applications in the fields of marketing, politics, mass media, religion, clinical psychology, marriage counseling, gambling and treatment of smoking. A complete review can be found in Wicklund and Brehm (1976).

The theory and research are not without their critics. It has been attacked for being vague and simplistic and not clearly defining its terms "cognitive element", "follow from" etc. The very parsimoniousness of the theory is seen as a problem rather than an asset. The methodology of experiments to "prove" the theory has also been attacked because of artifacts, confounding variables and problems of external validity. Others have maintained that cognitive dissonance is a new name for an old theory, or that individual differences have been ignored. The most widely quoted as well as hotly disputed criticism of the theory is that of Chapanis and Chapanis (1964).   AF/JMFJ

Bibliography

Chapanis, N. and A. 1964: Cognitive dissonance: Five years later. *Psychological bulletin* 61, 1–22.

Festinger, L. 1957: *A theory of cognitive dissonance*. Stanford: Stanford University Press.

——— and Carlsmith. J. 1959: Cognitive consequences of forced compliance. *Journal of abnormal and social psychology* 58, 203–10.

Heider, F. 1946: Attitudes and cognitive organization. *Journal of psychology* 21, 107–12.

Osgood, C. and Tannenbaum, P. 1955: The principle of congruity in the prediction of attitude change. *Psychological review* 62, 42–55.

Wicklund, R.A. and Brehm, J.W. 1976: *Perspectives on cognitive dissonance*. Hillsdale, N.J.: Erlbaum.

cognitive personality theory Is concerned with the development of individual differences in the processes of thinking as they affect the perceptions and behavior of individuals. While the early personality theorists (FREUD, JUNG, Adler) were more concerned with biological and (later) social needs, some evidence of cognitive components of personality was nonetheless present. An example is found in Freud's concept of the EGO as a (potentially) cognitive mediator between the id and the SUPEREGO. It was, however, not until the advent of NEO-FREUDIAN THEORY that writers such as Sullivan utilized developmental formulations (helped in part by the work of G.H. MEAD) to point towards emerging individual differences as cognitive in character. Sullivan, for example, distinguished between prototaxic thought (a direct series of momentary states in the sensitive organism, not unlike what James called the "stream of consciousness"), parataxic thought (identifying events that occur at the same time or in the same space as causally related), and syntaxic thought (use of consensually validated, primarily verbal thought resulting in the potential of communication among persons). Sullivan argued that cognitive development progresses from prototaxic to syntaxic cognition. Obviously, individual differences may emerge in both the degree and the rapidity of advancement toward higher syntaxic cognitive levels.

The work of Piaget, based on experiments with children and adolescents (rather than on psychiatric observation, as was the case with most Freudian and neo-Freudian efforts) differs greatly from Freudian and even neo-Freudian viewpoints in its emphasis on the development of thought as opposed to need-states or other affective components as driving forces of the personality. Inhelder and Piaget (1958) describe the growth of formal thinking (cognition) and explore the implications of cognitive maturation as they influence personality development, resulting in specific rates of progress towards identity formation, growth of autonomy, future orientation and other cognitively more mature processes. Although it has recently been argued that the developmental sequences observed by Piaget, Kohlberg, and others are in part misplaced on the developmental time dimension and are ethnocentric (see Gardner 1984), they have been and continue to be aids for the understanding of how individual differences in cognitive characteristics of people emerge during childhood and adolescence.

It has generally been recognized that regularities and universals (i.e. the absence of differences among individuals) are greater in younger than in older children. In other words variability, including the degree of individual differences in cognitive characteristics, tends to increase with increasing age into adulthood. The lesser differences among young children are, however, often credited with being the origin of the much greater cognitive discrepancies which we see in the adult personality. As a result a number of theorists have explored the cognitive development of children to find causes for later personality characteristics. Most frequently it has been assumed that the child or adolescent can become arrested at some stage of development, producing some degree of immature adult cognition and with it inappropriate and immature behavior. Unfortunately most attempts to identify stages of development reflecting specific individual differences (for example Harvey, Hunt and Schroder's "System Theory") have suffered from the confounding of personality structure with the content of persons' attitudes or belief systems.

A somewhat different approach to cognitive personality theory grew out of the concept that individuals have mental models of reality. From this point of view a person is conceived as a complex information processing system. Cognition represents the process of translating a stimulus input into a perception and, subsequently, into a potential behavioral output. Mental models would be likely to differ among people who have experienced different environments, have lived in different cultures, and have had different learning experiences. On the other hand common experiences can lead to shared mental models. People with shared models (i.e. people who would respond to specific inputs from the environment in the same or similar fashion) are often seen as having the same personality type.

An individual's well-established mental model is likely to identify input stimuli as belonging to specific groups. Identifications of this kind are made in the attempt to organize experience into meaningful patterns. Input information may well be misinterpreted in the process. If, for example, a person's mental model would suggest that persons from country X typically behave in a certain way, then the behavior of any representative of that country would be seen in exactly that fashion, even if the actual behavior was somewhat different. (See STEREOTYPES.)

Early assumptions of commonalities in behavior among certain groups resulted in theories exemplified by the identification of the Authoritarian Personality (Adorno et al. 1950 and see ADORNO). It was assumed that the authoritarian (pre-Nazi) personality had certain characteristics that would be common across cultures, but would occur with particular frequency in Germany and other one-time fascist countries. While authoritarianism was, for a time, the most popular concept in personality theory, it did not fulfill much of its promise. Authoritarians were found in all cultures. The behavior of the authoritarian was not necessarily violent as had been expected by many. Most of all, an authoritarian, as measured by the Adorno et al. F scale, turned out to be a person with two separate characteristics: someone with conservative attitudes or beliefs, and an acquiescent responder who is likely to agree with any strongly worded statement regardless of the content of the statement. While the first characteristic of the authoritarian represents the content (attitude, belief) of thought, the second (acquiescing in strongly worded statements) represents a cognitive characteristic. To the degree to which a person with strong liberal or politically leftwing attitudes is likely to be acquiescent, that person would be equally as authoritarian as the potential fascist.

In an attempt to develop a more purely cognitive measure of personality Rokeach (1960) focused on rigidity and on dogmatism. His dogmatism scale is designed primarily to measure fixed and strongly held (inflexible) cognitions across a number of domains. Scoring is based on agreement with dogmatic statements, even in the face of inherent inconsistencies worked into the statements. Dogmatic cognition has been shown to relate to prejudice, to attitude change characteristics, and to abnormal behavior. The work of Rokeach moved in the direction of a stylistic approach to cognition: persons are assumed to learn specific cognitive patterns i.e. styles in dealing with environmental stimulation. All cognitive style theories have at least one major factor in common: they tend to emphasize structure of thought rather than content of thought. Structure reflects how cognition is organized, in other words, how people think (how they relate perceptions, ideas, etc. to each other). Content refers to what knowledge is available, what a person's attitudes and beliefs are, and so on.

The cognitive styles on which persons differ have been described by a number of theorists as influencing specific cognitive perceptions or behavior. Among those styles are:
(1) tolerance for unrealistic experiences, the readiness to accept experiences that are at variance with conventional reality;
(2) conceptual differentiation, the tendency to use many or few categories;
(3) constricted-flexible control, the degree to which persons are free of influence by single powerful cues;
(4) leveling-sharpening, the degree to which previous information stored in memory is integrated into present perceptions;
(5) focusing-scanning, the breadth with which an individual verifies the judgments he or she makes;
(6) field dependence-independence, the degree to which individuals structure their perceptual field or require externally imposed structure (see COGNITIVE STYLE);
(7) category width, the range of events which individuals consider likely to occur;
(8) cognitive complexity, the number and interaction of cognitive judgment dimensions brought to bear on a stimulus configuration (see COGNITIVE COMPLEXITY);
(9) reflection-impulsivity, the speed with which a person makes decisions under conditions of uncertainty.

A number of attempts have been made to integrate the various cognitive styles into an overall conceptualization of cognitive personality structure. A generally satisfactory integration has yet to be found. Nonetheless a number of cognitive styles (parti-cularly cognitive complexity and field dependence-independence) have been quite useful for the prediction of a wide range of behavior.

Among the most widely discussed and widely used cognitive personality theories are those of KELLY and Rotter. (See PERSONAL CONSTRUCT THEORY and LOCUS OF CONTROL). Another impetus toward the emphasis on cognitive personality theory has come from artificial intelligence (Loehlin, 1968). More recently there has been an enormous amount of work on information-processing approaches to personality (see Cantor and Kihlstrom 1981; Pervin 1985). Much of this has been preoccupied with how people perceive others rather than with individual differences in cognition and their impact on behavior (e.g. Cantor and Mischel 1979), but a more co-ordinated control-systems approach has been suggested by Carver and Scheier (1982). In ATTRIBUTION THEORY and particularly in its application in the clinical domain (Peterson and Seligman, 1984) emphasis has been placed on how individual differences in cognition affect emotion and behavior.   SS/RL

Bibliography

Adorno, T.W. et al. 1950: *The authoritarian personality*. New York: Harper.

Cantor, N. and Kihlstrom, J.F. eds. 1981: *Personality, cognition and social interaction*. Hillsdale, N.J.: Erlbaum.

───── and Mischel, W. 1979: Prototypes in person perception. *Advances in experimental social psychology* 12, 3–52.

Carver, C.S. and Scheier, M.F. 1982: Control theory: a useful conceptual frame-work in personality – social, clinical and health psychology. *Psychological bulletin* 92, 111–35.

Gardner, H. 1983: *Frames of mind*. New York: Basic Books; London: Heinemann (1984).

Inhelder, B. and Piaget, J. 1958: *The growth of logical thinking from childhood to adolescence*. New York: Basic Books.

Loehlin, J.C. 1968: *Computer models of personality*. New York: Random House.

Pervin, L.A. 1985: Personality: current controversies, issues and directions. *Annual review of psychology* 36, 83–114.

Peterson, C. and Seligman, M.E.P. 1984: Causal explanations as a risk factor for depression: theory and evidence. *Psychological review* 91, 347–79.

Rokeach, M. 1960: *The open and closed mind.* New York: Basic Books.

cognitive style Cognitive style is defined as an individual's characteristic and consistent manner of processing and organizing what he sees and thinks about (Messick 1976; Witkin et al. 1971). Nineteen major cognitive styles have been distinguished (Messick 1976) which can be classified as one of three types.

First, there are cognitive styles which are related to abilities to perform a specific task and which are assessed in terms of the accuracy or correctness of performance (Messick 1976). An example of this cognitive style is field-independence versus FIELD-DEPENDENCE which refers to the tendency to approach situations and tasks in an analytical as opposed to a global way. It is assessed in tasks which test the ability to discriminate a figure from its background.

Second, there are cognitive styles which differ in the value which can be attributed to them. An instance of this type of cognitive style is COGNITIVE COMPLEXITY versus cognitive simplicity which refers to the extent to which people organize events, and especially social behavior, in a complex, multidimensional, and discriminating manner. In processing certain types of information a cognitively complex style is valued more highly than a cognitively simple style (Goldstein and Blackman 1977).

Third, some cognitive styles do not relate to abilities, and values are not attributed to them. An example is the cognitive style "breadth of categorization", which describes a tendency to think of specified categories as broad and inclusive or as narrow and exclusive.

A number of questions remain unresolved in cognitive style research. These include how cognitive styles are produced, e.g. consciously or unconsciously; the extent to which they are open to self-control and modification; and whether they indicate an actual capacity to process information in a certain manner or merely a preference for doing so. The conceptual adequacy of cognitive style and its related concepts has also been questioned (Kurtz 1969).   DPH

Bibliography

Goldstein, K.M. and Blackman S. 1977: Assessment of cognitive style. In *Advances in psychological measurement*, vol. 4, ed. P. McReynolds. London and San Francisco: Jossey-Bass.

Kurtz, R.M. 1969: A conceptual investigation of Witkin's notion or perceptual style. *Mind* 78, 522–33.

Messick, S. 1976: Personality differences in cognition and creativity. In *Individuality in learning*, eds. S. Messick et al. London and San Francisco: Jossey-Bass.

Witkin, H.A. et al. 1971: *A manual for the embedded figures tests.* Palo Alto, Calif.: Consulting Psychologists Press.

cohesiveness Refers to the forces that hold a group together. Cohesiveness is based upon the attraction that the members of the group feel for each other and/or the sharing of the common group goal. Cohesive groups are not necessarily more productive than non-cohesive groups. As Shaw (1976) noted, group members who are attracted to the group work harder to achieve its goals. If the norms of the group favor productivity, cohesiveness has a positive influence. If the norm is to avoid work, cohesive groups are less productive than non-cohesive groups.

Janis (1972) argues that cohesiveness constitutes in particular a danger for decision making in groups, since it will induce pressures towards uniformity and conformity, leading to "group think".   JMFJ

Bibliography

Janis, I.L. 1972: *Victims of group think.* Boston: Houghton Mifflin.

Shaw, M.E. 1976: *Group dynamics: the dynamics of small group behavior.* New York: McGraw-Hill.

communication: human general Although the term "communication" is of fundamental importance in social and behavioral science there is no consensus as to its definition. There are three distinct approaches to communication: informational, interactional and relational. Despite apparent similarities of concepts, terminology and research techniques, each approach is grounded in different philosophical traditions and offers complementary yet different accounts of the phenomenon in question.

Informational approaches evolved mainly during the 1930s and 40s and have become widely accepted since then. They deal with transmission of messages, mainly factual ones, between interacting "parties" (e.g. societies, organizations, individuals, telecommunication devices etc.) that are capable of sending or receiving information through some common system of signals or symbols. The theoretical roots of informational approaches are three-fold: (a) an assumption that meaning or information is encapsulated in words, gestures, appearances or objects and that these have to be untangled or decoded to have their content revealed; (b) an assumption that people's bodies, especially their faces, eyes and hands, constitute a screen on which various thoughts, emotions and attitudes are displayed; (c) an Aristotelian and Newtonian view of the world as a neutral space in which discrete entities (organisms, objects etc.) occasionally act (exert some influence) on one another. Such mutual influences are often conceptualized in terms of a linear sequence of events occurring within a dyadic framework (e.g. A acts; B reacts; A reacts to B's reaction and so forth).

There are two major groups of informational studies. The first deals with the theory and practice of conversion of messages and meanings into various icons, signs, signals, symbols, languages or codes and their subsequent decoding. The most important model was developed by Shannon and Weaver (1949) in their work on the mathematical theory of transmission of electronic signals. Their model originally consisted of five elements: (1) an information source; (2) a transmitter (encoder); (3) a channel for transmission of signals; (4) a receiver (decoder) and (5) a destination – all arranged in a linear order. Later studies improved on this simple scheme by drawing a distinction between a "message" and its "source" and by introducing such

important notions as "feedback" (destination's response which enables the source to modify its subsequent transmissions), "noise" (interference with the message travelling along a channel); "redundancy" (repetitions in coding of the message so that it is correctly decoded) and "filters" (modifiers of the message when it is arriving at the encoder or leaving the decoder). This model exhibited several virtues – simplicity, ready quantifiability and generality – making it attractive to a number of disciplines (Cherry 1957), with the result that the potential utility of other views of communication, or even their existence, tended to be overlooked.

The second group of studies in this tradition was developed mainly during the 1960s and focused on the socially organized conditions for the circulation of information between members of a given commununity or face-to-face gathering. The main work in this area is by GOFFMAN, whose model of communicational exchange has four elements: (a) communicational arrangements established among a given set of individuals (e.g. direct vs. indirect; symmetrical vs. asymmetrical transmissions of messages); (b) communicational conduct (strategies) that interacting parties adopt while dealing with each other; (c) communicational constraints, that is ecological, technical, intellectual and emotional factors limiting people's choice of strategy; and finally (d) interpretational frames governing the way people perceive and account for their conduct with regard to one another. It is this model that bridges most fully the gap separating informational and interactional studies.

Interactional approaches evolved mainly in the 1960s and 70s. They define communication not as a transaction but as an occasion that individuals (mainly humans, but also animals) cooperatively establish and maintain through the skillful deployment of behavior, appearances and artifacts. This behavioral management of co-presence takes place irrespective of the wishes or intentions of the individuals engaged in it. Although they do have control over their entering into and departure from situations of co-presence, as long as the parties perceive each other's monitoring they cannot avoid continuous co-ordination of behavior in relation to one another. The interactional approach recognizes that every interaction involves an exchange of messages but the key research interest is in the organization of behavior rather than in "what does it mean?" The theoretical roots of this approach are three-fold: (a) the interest of behavioral sciences in fine-grained analyses of behavior under a variety of circumstances, including interactions with conspecifics and the immediate environment; (b) an assumption that behavior is not so much a function of the individual's internal drives, motivations or personality as of the situation and of the social relationships established with others; (c) General Systems Theory which leads to the introduction of such fundamental notions as "systems", "dynamic equilibrium", "self-regulation", "feedback" and "program".

A number of theoretical models attempt to describe and explain the way social occasions are structured and managed by behavioral means. Five of the most important constructs are: (i) the "linguistic" model, proposed in the early 1960s by Birdwhistell (1970) which argues that despite the variety of interactions they are all constructed from the same limited repertoire of fifty to sixty elementary bodily movements and positions. It hypothesizes that behavioral sequences formed from those elementary units are organized in the way in which sequences of sound patterns are organized into words, sentences and passages of speech; (ii) the "social skill" model (Argyle and Kendon 1967) which postulates that interpersonal transactions, like other learnable skills (e.g. driving, dancing, playing card games) are hierarchically organized and formed by a series of small, goal-oriented yet often tentative and ambiguous "steps"; (iii) the "equilibrium" model (Argyle and Dean 1965) which assumes that the interacting parties always strive to maintain a certain overall "balance" in the way they deploy their behavior in relation to each other's presence and activity. Any change in the

use of behavior type X is usually compensated for by appropriate changes in the use of behavior type Y and vice versa; (iv) Scheflen's "programs" model (1968) of social interaction which postulates that the overall synchronic and diachronic structure of the face-to-face encounter is generated by the operation of at least three sets of programs. The first deals with simple coordination of activities. The second controls modifications to the individuals' activities whenever some contingencies or ambiguities arise. The third program modifies the modification procedures, that is, handles the complex task of meta-communication. These programs are internalized as individuals learn to function as fully-fledged members of a given group, community and culture and permit organization of diverse behavioral material into meaningful and appropriate interchanges. They are culture and context specific; that is, a given situation, a given task and a given social organization evoke performance of a given program; (v) the "systems" model (Kendon 1977) which envisages interaction as a configuration of systems of behavior each managing a separate aspect of an interpersonal transaction. So far two such systems have been identified and analysed. The first one is a system of behavior managing an "exchange of utterances" while the other one is a system of behavior managing orderly use of interactional spaces and territories.

Of these five models it is the "programs" model which displays the greatest affinity to the relational theory of communication.

The *relational* approach has been gradually developing since the mid-1950s (Birdwhistell 1968). It postulates that people's environmental and social contexts constitute not so much the circumstances under which transfer of information and occasions of face-to-face interaction occur as the very phenomenon of communication itself. In other words, "communication" is a name for the overall system of relationships people develop between each other and with the community and habitat in which they live. Any difference (i.e. change or transformation) which makes the difference to any part of this system is called "information" (Bateson 1973). People (or animals and other organisms) cannot be said to engage in communication (informational approach) or participate in it (interactional approach) for they are already an indispensable part of it in the same way as they are, whether they want it or not, a part of the local as well as global ecosystem. They became immersed in it at the moment of their birth and do not leave it until the moment of their death. Three sets of theoretical developments have been instrumental in bringing the relational theory of communication about: (a) cybernetics and General Systems Theory; (b) the Theory of Logical Types which identifies discontinuities between different levels of abstraction (e.g. between a statement and meta-statement) and enables comparisons between logical structures of such diverse phenomena as play, non-play, metaphor, humor, confidence-tricks or schizophrenia; (c) the biological research on ecology and ecosystems in general and on constancy and change in the relationships between organisms and their contexts in particular.

The most important research carried out within the framework of the relational approach has been generated by the "double bind" model of psychopathology (Bateson et al. 1956). This model has, for example, challenged the traditional view of schizophrenia as a distortion in the behavior of an individual by advancing a view of schizophrenia as a permanent disturbance or distortion in the pattern of relations between an individual and other persons (Laing 1959). This distortion is thought to arise whenever people conduct themselves in such a way that (i) one or more of them is subjected to mutually exclusive demands such that to obey one is to disobey the other; (ii) this disobedience is punished; (iii) the paradoxical nature of these demands cannot be acknowledged or discussed, and (iv) people cannot escape from dealing with each other. There has, however, been no satisfactory empirical support for the idea that double binds distinguish the families of schizophrenics from other families, partly because proponents of the double bind hypothesis are unable to agree about when a double bind is occurring.

The relational theory of communication is in an almost embryonic stage of development. It may take several years before it will be employed as widely as is currently the case with the informational and interactional approaches. However, even at this early stage, it clearly represents one of the most seminal and revolutionary approaches to the phenomena of society, of communication, of interaction and of behavior that the social and behavioral sciences have ever known. Its strength and potential rests in the fact that it replaces the handy but restrictive framework of Aristotelian epistemology with the "systems approach". Unlike the former, which has proved valuable for analysing simple systems, the latter has proved to be uniquely suited to dealing with moderately to highly complex phenomena. (See also COMMUNICATION: NON-VERBAL.)   TMC

Bibliography

Argyle, M. and Dean, J. 1965: Eye-contact, distance and affiliation. *Sociometry* 28, 289–304.

—— and Kendon, A. 1967: The experimental analysis of social performance. In *Advances in experimental social psychology*, ed. L. Berkowitz. London: Academic Press.

Bateson, G. 1973: *Steps to an ecology of mind: collected essays in anthropology, psychiatry, evolution and epistemology*. Frogmore: Paladin Granada Publishing Ltd.

—— et al. 1956: Towards a theory of schizophrenia. *Behavioral science* 1, 251–64.

*Birdwhistell, R.L. 1968: Communication. In *International encyclopedia of the social sciences*, vol. 3, ed. D.J. Shils. New York: McMillan and Co. and The Free Press.

—— 1970: *Kinesics and context: essays on body-motion communication*. Philadelphia: University of Pennsylvania Press; London: Allen Lane (1971).

Cherry, C. 1957. *On human communication: a review, a survey, and a criticism*. Cambridge, Mass.: MIT Press.

Goffman, E. 1963: *Behavior in public places: notes on the social organization of gatherings*. New York: Free Press.

—— 1969: *Strategic interaction*. Pennsylvania: The Trustees of the University of Pennsylvania; Oxford: Blackwell Scientific (1970).

———— 1975: *Frame analysis: an essay on the organization of experience*. New York: Harper and Row.

Hinde, R.A. ed. 1972. *Non-verbal communication*. Cambridge and New York: Cambridge University Press.

Kendon, A. 1977: *Studies in the behavior of social interaction*. Bloomington: Indiana University; Lisse: Peter de Ridder.

Laing, R.D. 1959: *The divided self: an extended study in sanity and madness*. London: Tavistock.

Scheflen, A. 1968. Human communications: behavioral programs and their integration. *Behavioral science* 13, 44–55.

Shannon, C.E. and Weaver, W. 1949: *A mathematical theory of communication*. Urbana: University of Illinois Press.

communication: non-verbal Transmission of information by means of interactional instrumentalities (i.e. behavior, appearance and artifacts) other than language in its spoken, written, or otherwise coded form. The information exchanged by these means is diverse and can be divided into three broad categories–factual, indexical and regulatory. "Factual" messages are those dealing with requests for, and provision of, goods, services and information. They also include performance of socially significant, often ritualized behavior (e.g. decorating a person with a medal). Indexical signals convey information about the people themselves. These signals are about the sender's biological and psychological characteristics; his social and cultural affiliations; his relations with and attitudes toward those co-present; his relation to the present interaction as well as his relation to the immediate physical environment. The third category of information concerns the adequate and orderly joint management of interpersonal transactions. This consists of information about the spatial and temporal boundaries of the interaction at hand; its nature (e.g. whether a chat or an interrogation); the spatial and temporal coordination of behavior and action (e.g. the taking of turns in a conversation); definition of roles for each participant and of the required level of participants' involvement in the transaction.

For such a transmission of information to occur some communicational relationship between two or more individuals must be established. Communicating parties form such a relationship by attending to each other's deployment and usage of various interactional instrumentalities and by coordinating performances with each other. This means that people's appearance, behavior and use of objects constitute not only the source of information individuals acquire from each other but also the essential context for the acquisition of such information.

In a series of classic analyses of people's communicational conduct GOFFMAN (1959, 1969) suggested that there are four basic types of communicational relations and that every community and every social occasion has a particular repertoire of such relations. Thus information that individuals provide (irrespective of whether it is done consciously and voluntarily) can be transmitted either directly or indirectly and, simultaneously, in either a symmetrical or an asymmetrical fashion. A direct communication (such as an exchange of smoke signals) occurs when the information is transmitted by the sender's current (usually bodily) activity, which is taking place within the operational range of the receiver's senses. Indirect communication, on the other hand, utilizes people's ability to decode messages in the form of behavioral traces or in the form of positioning and appearances of artifacts. Good examples of such disembodied messages are a burglar's footprints on a window sill, or a bouquet of red roses brought by a messenger.

Communicational arrangements differ also in the symmetry of roles adopted by the communicating parties. A symmetrical transaction is one in which people are simultaneously receiving and feeding back information. In an asymmetrical transaction (e.g. when somebody is spying or eavesdropping on someone else) the roles of senders and receivers of signals are kept separate, providing no feedback and *they* are not reversible in a given transaction.

In the course of the behavioral process appropriate conditions for transfer of information become created, defined and skillfully managed moment by moment (this process is known as "coenesis" see Ciolek, Elzinga and McHoul 1979); arrays of variously combined instrumentalities can be seen to be deployed in ever-changing spatio-temporal configurations. Along acoustic channels of communication, for example, there is a widespread use of (a) speech, (b) paralanguage, (c) strepitus (non-vocal body noise), and (d) mechanically created noises and sounds. Visual communication uses (e) spacing and orientation in relation to the physical and human context, (f) body movements such as gestures, gesticulation, nods and shifts of posture, as well as facial expressions and gaze behavior; (g) physical appearance; and (h) artifacts such as dress, make-up, jewelery, etc. Transfer of information by touch and smell is usually conducted at close and very close range, and involves (j) tactile behavior such as caressing, holding, manipulation; (k) tactile and thermal appearances of the skin surface; and (l) natural bodily smells and odors, as well as their modifications by cosmetics, food, tobacco or medicaments.

Deployed behavior, appearances and artifacts are never neutral or non-significant. It has been pointed out that a given behavior can be received and reacted to at a number of levels: as a physical stimulus requiring appropriate bodily response on the part of the receiver; as a simple symptom or indicator of something else; or as a symbol or even as an element of a code or language of some kind. This means that in man-made environments or in the presence of other people a person cannot avoid reacting to one, at least, of these levels of behavior of other people. Similarly, no one can totally stop transmitting information of some sort, and therefore no one can stop influencing the behavior of others. Some balance, however, between the degree of sensory exposure and access can be and usually is established. This balance, often referred to as privacy of a certain degree, is, according to Altman (1975), achieved by a combined application of various control measures. These may include avoidance or modifi-cation of certain types of behavior (e.g. of the amount of mutual gaze), manipulation of spatial relationships between people, division of the environment into variously marked, controlled and defended spaces, and finally extensive reliance on furniture, barriers and concealments of various kinds. In this context it was observed that whenever the overwhelming and/or prolonged presence of others leads to a person's loss of control over the amount of information he or she receives or emits, such an individual is likely to experience a more or less acute sense of crowding.

Ways of communicating vary from community to community, from place to place and from one person to another. Cultural factors play an important role in shaping people's communicational conduct and so do numerous situational and individual variables (Argyle 1975). Another important source of variability in people's behavior is to be found in communicational transactions themselves, for these can frequently be accomplished according to more than one format or program (Scheflen 1968). There is thus a wide choice of possible strategies: sometimes people will organize their mutual conduct in terms of only one or two aspects of a single instrumentality and sometimes they will do it at the level of all the types of behavior they have at their disposal. This means that human communication can occasionally become exceedingly intricate. Further, it means that there are circumstances under which both verbal and non-verbal components of a communicational exchange form a joint system of closely interrelated instrumentalities which cannot occur separately. For this reason many researchers argue that, while the distinction between verbal and non-verbal behavior is valid, that between verbal and non-verbal communication is not always meaningful and is in fact artificial, rather like the distinction between cardiac and non-cardiac physiology (Birdwhistell 1970).

There are a number of stages in the history of communication studies, each reflecting the theoretical and methodological stance of a discipline current at the time of the research. Until the mid-1950s there was a tendency to study asymmetrical and disembodied modes of communication (Ruesch and Kees 1972). Contemporary research, however, deals primarily with those communicational arrangements which are either direct or symmetrical, or both (Kendon 1977). At the same time a significant shift in emphasis can be observed from studies of "*what* behavior means" towards research into "*how* behavior means" (Scheflen 1974). During the past twenty years these developments have led to a surge of interest in the behavioral structuring and moment-to-moment regulation of face-to-face encounters. According to the three pioneers of modern communication studies – Bateson (1973), Scheflen (1975) and Birdwhistell (1970) – all these transformations mark the steadily growing influence of the "systems approach", which has been found to constitute the most suitable tool for dealing with complex issues of human behavior. (See also COMMUNICATION: HUMAN GENERAL; PROXEMICS; and for particular topics and alternative approaches: ETHOLOGY; FACIAL EXPRESSION AND EMOTION; GESTURE; GAZE; SOCIAL INTERACTION; TOUCH.)   TMC

Bibliography

Altman, I. 1975: *The environment and social behavior: privacy, personal space, territory, crowding.* Monterey, Calif.: Brooks/Cole.

Argyle, M. 1975: *Bodily communication.* London: Methuen; New York: Barnes and Noble.

Bateson, G. 1973: *Steps to an ecology of mind: collected essays in anthropology, psychiatry, evolution and epistemology.* Frogmore: Paladin Granada.

Birdwhistell, R.L. 1970: *Kinesics and context: essays on body-motion communication.* Philadelphia: University of Pennsylvania Press; London: Penguin (1971).

—— 1976: Background considerations to the study of the body as a medium of "expression". In *The body as a medium of expression*, eds. J. Benthall and T. Polhemus. New York: E.P. Dutton.

Ciolek, T.M., Ezinga, R.H. and McHoul, A.W. 1979: Selected references to coenetics – the study of behavioral organization of face-to-face interactions. *Sign language studies* 22, 1–74.

Goffman, E. 1959: *The presentation of self in everyday life.* New York: Doubleday; London: Penguin (1969).

—— 1969: *Strategic interaction.* Pennsylvania: Trustees of the University of Pennsylvania; Oxford: Blackwell Scientific (1970).

*Kendon, A. 1977: *Studies in the behavior of social interaction.* Bloomington: Indiana University; Lisse: Peter de Ridder.

Ruesch, J. and Kees, W. 1972: *Non-verbal communication: notes on the visual perception of human relations.* 2nd edn. Berkeley: University of California Press.

Scheflen, A. 1968: Human communication: behavioral programs and their integration. *Behavioral science* 13, 44–55.

—— 1974: *How behavior means.* New York: Anchor Press and Doubleday.

—— 1975: Models and epistemologies in the study of interaction. In *The organization of behavior in face-to-face interaction*, eds. A. Kendon, R.M. Harris and M.R. Key. The Hague: Mouton.

communication network Communication between group members is often restricted by available communication channels. Communication networks are defined by the nature and number of communication channels available in a group. Communication networks can be distinguished according to their degree of centrality, peripherality and independence. A wheel structure, in which all communication is channeled through one person, has a high degree of centrality whereas a circle structure, in which members can communicate only with "adjacent" members, has a low degree of centrality. Experimental studies have shown that centralized structures are usually more efficient than more haphazard structures for simple tasks, but the reverse is true for more complex tasks. Satisfaction is generally higher in less centralized structures. Mulder (see Shaw 1976) has shown, however, that both effects do not depend wholly on the communication network available, since people can, for example, centralize a structure by deciding not to use certain channels. Cohen (see Shaw 1976) has proposed a general theory which suggests that a matching of task and communication structure leads to higher productivity.   JMFJ

Bibliography

Shaw, M.E. 1976: *Group dynamics.* New York: McGraw-Hill.

competition Striving to excel in order to obtain an exclusive goal; in psychology, often studied as maximizing one's own outcomes at the expense of others in game theory experiments (see GAMES). Factors which have been shown to affect cooperative and competitive behavior in these situations are: (1) the structure of the pay-off matrix; (2) the cooperative or competitive behavior shown by others; (3) attributions concerning the motives of others; (4) the possibility of communicating with adversaries. Recent evidence suggests that in humans and animals alike, competition serves to establish a social structure and to provide information about one's activities through social comparison. (See also COOPERATION.)   JMFJ

Bibliography

Passingham, R. 1981: *The human primate.* New York: Academic Press.

conflict A psychological state of indecision which occurs when a person is influenced simultaneously by two opposing forces of approximately equal strength. According to LEWIN (1935), there are three fundamental types of conflict situation:

(1) An individual may be caught at a midway point between two positive valences of nearly equal strength (i.e. the choices are equally attractive). FIELD THEORY predicts that the strength of the force toward the goal region increases as the individual approaches it; thus, chance factors alone make it likely that the individual will accidentally move toward one goal and away from the other, destroying the point of equilibrium. What results is a natural acceleration of the force toward that particular region as a consequence of an increase in proximity to the goal.

(2) An individual may be caught between two negative valences of approximately equal strength (i.e. the choices are both undesirable). Punishment is an example of this type of conflict. There are three subtypes of situations in which conflict occurs between equal negative valences: the individual is confronted by two negative valences, but it is possible to escape the situation entirely; the individual is placed between two negative valences, yet cannot leave the field; and the individual can leave an area of negative valence only by going through another region of negative valence.

(3) An individual may be exposed to opposing forces deriving from a positive and a negative valence. Conflict involving both attractive and unattractive components can also be divided into three subtypes: one situation is simply that the region, or psychological activity involved, has both negative and positive aspects. This can be recognized as the familiar Freudian concept of ambivalence. A second subtype involves an individual who is encircled by a negative region but attracted by a goal outside the negative region. In a third situation a region of positive valence is encircled by a region of negative valence. This is different from the example just cited in that the region of positive valence, rather than the region in which the person is to be found, is encircled by the negative valence.

Much research has been generated by Lewin's theoretical exploration of conflict. The most widely-known work has probably been that of Festinger's COGNITIVE DISSONANCE (1957) which elaborates Lewin's view that the situation prior to decision differs from that after the decision. More recent work of Deutsch's in this area was also influenced by Lewin (Deutsch 1973).
                    MDe

Bibliography

Deutsch, M. 1973: *The resolution of conflict.* New Haven: Yale University Press.

Festinger, L. 1957: *A theory of cognitive dissonance.* Stanford, Calif.: Stanford University Press.

Lewin, K. 1935: *A dynamic theory of personality.* New York: McGraw-Hill.

conformity *See* social influence; Asch.

congruity principle A quantitative extension of Heider's theory of balanced states (see COGNITIVE CONSISTENCY) suggested by Osgood and Tannenbaum (1955), in particular applicable to persuasive communication processes. According to Osgood's congruity principle, attitude change depends upon the discrepancy between the initial attitudes of the receiver towards the source and the content of the message, taking into account the positive or negative nature of the communication. Predictions of actual attitude change are only moderately successful and require various additional assumptions, which suggests that a weighted averaging model (in which the relative weight of the source depends on the attitude of the receiver to the source) describes attitude change better than the congruity principle.   JMFJ

Bibliography

Jaspars, J. 1978: Determinants of attitudes and attitude change. In *Introducing social psychology*, eds. H. Tajfel and C. Fraser. Harmondsworth: Penguin.

Osgood, C.E. and Tannenbaum, P.H. 1955: The principle of congruity in the prediction of attitude change. *Psychological review* 62, 42–55.

conscience A set of personal rules and values that usually parallel the norms of society and guide individual social conduct. These rules are generally thought to be learned and are therefore initially implanted by external influences (e.g. through the rewards and punishment of authority figures). Once the rules are internalized, however, social conduct becomes privately regulated (e.g. guilt is experienced when these internalized rules are violated). See SUPEREGO for Freud's views on the development and operation of the conscience.
                                                RHo

constitutional psychology Theory that specific psychological characteristics, especially personality TRAITS, are associated with aspects of physical constitution. In the 1920s Kretschmer applied this ancient idea to his psychotic patients and observed that schizophrenics tended to have a tall,

linear build (asthenic or asthenic-athletic) while manic-depressives tended to be shorter and rounded (pyknic; but he did not control for the different age of onset of these disorders. He regarded these as extreme or disordered cases of a general trend linking the temperament of schizothymia with the one build and that of cyclothymia with the other.

In the 1940s Sheldon analysed body-build into three contributory components which could each be measured objectively and used to yield standardized scores on a 7-point scale: ectomorphy (linearity), mesomorphy (bone and muscle) and endomorphy (roundness and fat). The mixture of these components in an individual's body is its somatotype, which can be expressed in a three-digit code. These somatic components were correlated with three parameters of temperament respectively: cerebrotonia (emotional reserve and cognitive control), somatotonia (aggressive activity) and viscerotonia (sociability, physical relaxation). Subsequent researchers have not found such high correlations, and endomorphy seems a doubtful component. Rees and Eysenck argue that two factors, one of linearity and one of size, are enough to cover the variety observed; but Parnell confirms the link between ectomorphy and schizoid intellectual temperament (see Hall and Lindzey 1978, ch. 13). Eysenck's theory of personality (1967) links two dimensions of introversion–extraversion and neuroticism–stability to the constitution of the nervous system (see EYSENCK).   NMC

Bibliography

Eysenck, H.J. 1967: *The biological basis of personality*. Springfield, Ill.: Thomas.

Hall, C.S. and Lindzey, G. eds. 1978: *Theories of personality*. 3rd edn. New York: Wiley.

contagion In contagion theories collective behavior is a process in which emotions and behavioral patterns spread rapidly and are accepted uncritically by the members of a collective. Social contagion is a form of collective excitement. It is a relatively rapid and non-rational dissemination of a mood, impulse or form of conduct. It can bring in what were initially detached observers and lead them to behave like the others involved.

Social contagion may often be seen in crowd or mass behavior. Research is mainly concerned with explaining how the absence of regulative interaction between individuals in crowds produces illusions of power and feelings of "universality" which involve a transition of responsibility to the crowd, increased similarity of the individuals' behavior and processes of emotional fusion and identification with a leader. (See CROWD PSYCHOLOGY.)   AF

Bibliography
Kerckhoff, A.C. and Back, K.W. 1968: *The June bug: a study of hysterical contagion.* New York: Appleton-Century-Crofts.

contextualism   Emphasizes   the importance of contextual factors in the explanation of social, psychological and historical events. From the 1960s onwards several authors have considered contextual theory (or "contextualism") as an alternative to the traditional view that human action can be explained by reference to laws and initial conditions (the covering-law model). The search for laws – in psychology mainly correlations between dependent and independent variables – is argued to detract from a careful investigation of the situation in which the action was performed.

Influenced by the work of Wittgenstein, theorists working from this point of view maintain that "meaning" is not a private, subjective entity, but is created by the use of expressions in social interaction (cf. Wittgenstein's attack on private languages). So only an analysis of the context of human action can give insight into both its determinants and its meaning.   SJST

Bibliography
*Sarbin, T.R. 1977: Contextualism: a world view for modern psychology. In *Nebraska symposium on motivation*, ed. A.W. Landfield. Lincoln: University of Nebraska Press.
Wittgenstein, L. 1980: *Understanding and meaning*, eds. G.S. Baker and P.M.S. Hacker. Oxford: Basil Blackwell; Chicago: University of Chicago Press.

contingency theories of leadership
An approach to understanding LEADERSHIP in small groups which asserts that the effectiveness of a leader depends upon the particular circumstances in which he or she is operating. In exploring the relevance of contextual features contingency approaches stand in marked contrast to earlier approaches that sought to identify the personality traits that might be associated with effective leadership or to identify a universally preferred style of leadership (see INITIATING STRUCTURE; MANAGEMENT).

One leading contingency theorist is Fiedler, who suggests that certain situations are more favorable to leaders than others. Factors which he identifies as determining "situational favorableness" are the leader's popularity with his group, the extent to which a group task is straightforward and unambiguous, and the leader's ability to administer rewards and sanctions. He predicts that task oriented leaders are more effective when easy and difficult decisions have to be made, while relation oriented leaders are more effective in situations of intermediate difficulty. An important implication of this theory is that, rather than attempting to train people to adopt new and unfamiliar leadership styles, it would be more effective to fit people into the leadership situations most suited to their characteristics. Other contingency models however have adopted a different objective, having been devised to help leaders develop more flexible approaches to their roles. Notable here is the approach of Vroom and Yetton. These writers have developed a decision-process flow chart which, according to factors such as the importance of the decision that a group has to make, its difficulty, the leader's expertise in the matter, and the degree of commitment required of the group's membership, sets out to indicate whether directive, consultative or participative styles would be the most appropriate for the leader to adopt.   FHMB

Bibliography

Fiedler, F.E. 1967: *A theory of leadership effectiveness*. New York: McGraw-Hill.

—— 1978: A contingency model of leadership effectiveness. In *Group processes*, ed. L. Berkowitz. New York: Academic Press.

Peters, L.H., Hartke, D.D. and Pohlmann, J.T. 1985: Fiedler's contingency theory of leadership: an application of the meta-analysis of Schmidt and Hunter. *Psychological bulletin* 97, 274–85.

*Porter, L.W. et al. 1977: A symposium on leadership. In *Perspectives on behaviour in organisations*, ed. R.J. Hackman. New York: McGraw-Hill.

Vroom, V.H. and Yetton, P.W. 1973: *Leadership and decision making*. Pittsburg: University of Pittsburg Press.

cooperation: social psychology

Working together towards the same end, purpose or effect; in psychology, especially working together for mutual benefit by maximizing joint profits or rewards and minimizing joint costs or losses. Innumerable studies have been conducted making use of matrices representing (often imaginary) pay-offs to both persons, an idea initially suggested by von Neuman and Morgenstern (1944) and introduced in psychology by Luce and Raiffa (1957). The best known game theory paradigm of cooperation experiments is the so-called prisoner's dilemma game (see GAMES) in which both players have to make a choice between maximizing personal or joint pay-offs, a conflict which in many conditions leads to the least preferred outcome for both parties.

Cooperation is often the response to helpful and cooperative behavior from others, although Shure et al. (1965) found that 90% of their subjects exploited an opponent who was totally cooperative.

Cooperation between groups has been suggested as a possible antidote to PREJUDICE. Sherif (1966) found that boys at summer camp developed strong feelings of identification with the group to which they had been assigned. COMPETITION then produced hostility towards opponents. This hostility could be overcome only if groups worked together cooperatively.

Deschamps and Brown (1983) however, found that in some circumstances cooperation between groups may increase rather than decrease intergroup discrimination which favors the ingroup.   JMFJ

Bibliography

Deschamps, J.C. and Brown, R.J. 1983: Superordinate goals and intergroup conflict. *British journal of social psychology* 22, 189–95.

Luce, R.D. and Raiffa, H. 1957: *Games and decisions: introduction and critical survey*. New York: Wiley.

Pruitt, D.G. and Kimmel, M.J. 1977: Twenty years of experimental gaming: critique, synthesis and suggestions for the future. *Annual review of psychology* 28, 363–92.

Sherif, M. 1966: *In common predicament: social psychology of intergroup conflict and cooperation*. Boston: Houghton Mifflin.

Shure, G.H., Meeker, R.J. and Hansford, E.A. 1965: The effectiveness of pacifist strategies in bargaining games. *Journal of conflict resolution* 9, 106–17.

von Neuman, J. and Morgenstern, D. 1944: *Theory of games and economic behavior*. Princeton, N.J.: Princeton University Press.

coronary-prone behavior

Usually refers to the Type A coronary-prone personality pattern described by Friedman and Rosenman (see TYPE-A PERSONALITY). Other psychometric work has been done, however, linking personality factors to coronary heart disease.

The conclusion from six studies using the Minnesota Multiphasic Personality Inventory (MMPI) seems to be that before their illness, patients with coronary disease differ from persons who remain healthy on several scales of the inventory, particularly those in the "neurotic" triad of hypochondriasis (Hs), depression (D), and hysteria (Hy). The occurrence of manifest coronary heart disease (CHD) increases the deviation of patients' MMPI scores further and, in addition, there is ego defense breakdown. As Jenkins (1971) summarizes: 'patients with fatal disease tend to show greater neuroticism (particularly depression) in prospective MMPIs than those who incur and survive coronary disease'.

Three major studies have utilized the sixteen Personality Factor inventory. All three investigations portray patients with CHD or related illness as emotionally unstable and introverted, which is consistent with the six MMPI studies. The limitation of these investigations is that they are, on balance, retrospective. That is, anxiety and neuroticism may well be reactions with CHD and other stress-related illnesses rather than precursors of it. Paffenberger, Wolf and Notkin (1966) report an interesting prospective study in which they linked university psychometric data on students with death certificates filed years later. They found a number of significant precursors to fatal CHD, one of which was a high anxiety or neuroticism score for the fatal cases.   CLC

Bibliography

Jenkins, C.D. 1971: Psychological and social precursors of coronary disease. *New England journal of medicine* 283, 244–55.

Paffenberger, R.S., Wolf, P.A. and Notkin, J. 1966: Chronic disease in former college students. *American journal of epidemiology* 83, 314–28.

creativity Many diverse definitions have been proposed, but the following is probably representative: man's capacity to produce new ideas, insights, inventions or artistic objects, which are accepted as being of social, spiritual, aesthetic, scientific or technological value. This emphasizes novelty and originality in the production of new combinations of familiar patterns, as in poetry or music, or reorganization of concepts and theories in the sciences. But unconventionality is not sufficient: a lunatic's ravings are not creative. The product must be recognized by capable people, even if initially rejected and not appreciated until later.

Traditionally, creativity was considered a rare and mysterious phenomenon, occurring mainly in a few outstanding geniuses such as Da Vinci, Mozart or Einstein, although it was realized that many other generally more mediocre artists or scientists produced occasional or minor creative works. The present trend, however, particularly in the USA is to see creativity as spread through almost the entire population, though varying in degree. The dramatic play of the young child often appears as imaginative and creative. Indeed creativity can even be observed in young animals at play or among chimpanzees who, according to Köhler (1925), display inventive thinking or "insight".

The older view often linked creativity with insanity (e.g. Lombroso and Kretschmer), though Havelock Ellis's early survey of British geniuses in 1904 found only a very small proportion who could be called psychotic. Minor emotional difficulties, ill health and neuroses were more common. Even more extensive was Terman's study (Cox 1926) of 300 eminent historical figures including many artists and scientists. Terman expected them to have possessed outstanding intelligence, but on assessing their mental capacities from their recorded achievements he found only a few with very high IQs of 170 to 200. The average was 135, and some were as low as 100–110. The geniuses were distinguished more by the character traits of perseverance and drive and the encouraging environment in which most of them were reared. Neurotic tendencies were apparent only in a minority.

Anne Roe's intensive analysis (1952) of the personalities of sixty-four highly creative living scientists, and MacKinnon's and Barron's investigations (1962 and 1969) of architects and other groups of professionals, have thrown much light on the psychology of creative individuals. Scientists, especially physical scientists, were characterized by intense absorption in their work and relative lack of interest in social or recreational activities. Though there were wide individual differences, they were the most emotionally stable group. Social scientists and Barron's writers showed more emotional disturbances, but Barron also found the writers high in ego strength, that is self-control and personal effectiveness. Many of these individuals were notably gifted as children, though not necessarily in the same special field; while others did not discover their talent and interest until early adulthood. On the other hand gifted children may be highly intelligent yet not specially talented or creative since they lack the mature technique and the strong inner drive characteristic of creative adults. Nevertheless those adolescents who do show artistic or scientific gifts, e.g. in science projects, are more likely to become involved in creative research and activities at university or in their subsequent jobs. The much lower frequency of creative accomplishments among women than among men is generally attributed to cultural expectations of sex roles, but women have also traditionally had to balance marriage and children against the ambition to follow a creative career.

A different approach is based on studying the creative process. Psychologists have reported many experiments on problem-solving, a process which is certainly useful though not highly creative or original. Several writers, musicians, scientists and mathematicians have described their methods of work and the nature of their inspiration (see Ghiselin 1952). Graham Wallas (1926) recognized four main stages; first that of preparation, including the acquisition of artistic skills or scientific information relevant to the particular problem. Although creative people may rebel against accepted conventions, they must be conversant with the methods and knowledge of their field in order to have something to be creative with. Secondly there is so called unconscious cerebration, where a strong emotional drive to create interacts, largely subconsciously, with the skills or information. Next there is inspiration regarding the solution or the artistic product; this sometimes arises quite suddenly. Finally a long period of working out and elaboration occurs and, in science, of verification of the solution. This of course is an over-rigid formulation. There is often an interplay of all four stages spread over a considerable period, as in writing a symphony or novel, or developing a scientific discovery.

Much has been written on creativity by Freud and his followers. In 1908 Freud pointed out the resemblance between children's play, fantasy or daydreaming and the work of the poet. In his view all these activities are expressive of people's inner needs and their imagined solutions. But the poet's feelings and conflicts are more repressed or inhibited, and they emerge in a disguised and socially acceptable form in his finished poems. Freud further distinguished "primary process" thinking, arising from the unconscious, from "secondary process", which is thinking under the control of the ego. He saw both as involved in creative production.

Other writers criticized Freud's implication that artistic and scientific creation derive from the sublimation of repressed and aggressive tendencies, and that creativity is essentially a neurotic defense mechanism, for there are innumerable neurotics who are not at all creative. Kris (1952) and Koestler (1964) modified the original theory paying more attention to the critical processes of the ego. They considered the creative artist to be a person who is more than usually in touch with his primary process fantasies and thus, like young children, more spontaneously imaginative. This underlies the original inspiration which is then taken over by the ego and fashioned through secondary process into the complete product. Moreover we gain aesthetic pleasure from a work of art because we are all prone to unconscious conflicts similar to the artist's. Kris refers to this as "regression in the service of the ego". It fits in with Barron's discussion of neuroticism and ego control among creative individuals and it helps to explain the greater part played by emotion in artistic as opposed to scientific production. Scientists do sometimes experience inspirations, but clearly most of their work is at the secondary level.

From about 1950 many industrial firms made use of schemes for stimulating creative thinking, such as Osborn's "Applied Imagination" and W. J. Gordon's "Synectics". These provide a fresh approach to such problems as designing and marketing a new product. Several staff members cooperate, and they are encouraged to put forward any suggestions that come to mind, however wild, not stopping to criticize or follow through. This is called "free wheeling", or the principle of deferred judgment. At a later session all ideas are considered critically by the group. This owes something to Freudian theory since the participants are told to relax all inhibitions and give free rein to creative imagination. Several other related techniques may be used. There is little or no scientific evidence that it works; but it has also spread from business into college courses where, it is claimed, training can be given in creative problem-solving with beneficial effects on academic work generally.

In 1950 Guilford drew attention to psychologists' neglect of creative abilities. Aptitude or achievement tests are "convergent" in the sense that the student's answers must converge to the one right solution. But some tests are available in which people are encouraged to put forward a variety of their own answers, i.e. to think "divergently". For example they may be asked to write down as many uses as they can think of for an empty tin can, and their responses are scored both for the quantity or fluency of ideas, and for quality as shown by the usefulness of the ideas. Many other similar divergent tests have been devised in the United States in the belief that American education has become too conventional and convergent, and that those children who will become the creative leaders of the next generation need to be discovered and encouraged. The tests, however, are rather trivial in content and they correlate very little with assessments or other criteria of creative behavior. As with most verbal tests girls tend to score more highly, whereas boys are more attracted to science, which chiefly involves convergent thinking. The tests are also very troublesome to score and they appear to have declined in popularity since the 1960s.   PEV

Bibliography

*Albert, R.S. ed. 1983: *Genuis and eminence*. Oxford: Pergamon.

Barron, F. 1969: *Creative person and creative process*. New York: Holt, Rinehart and Winston.

Cox, C.M. 1926: *The early mental traits of three hundred geniuses*. Stanford, Calif.: California University Press.

Freud, S. 1908: Creative writers and daydreaming. In *Standard edition of the complete psychological works of Sigmund Freud*, vol. 9, 1959. London: Hogarth; New York: Norton..

*Ghiselin, B., ed. 1952: *The creative process: a symposium*. Berkeley, Calif.: University of California Press.

Gordon, W.J.J. 1961: *Synectics: the development of creative capacity*. New York: Harper and Row.

Guilford, J.P. 1950: Creativity. *American psychologist* 5, 444–54.

Köhler, W. 1925: *The mentality of apes*. London: Kegan Paul; New York: Harcourt Brace; New York: Macmillan.

Koestler, A. 1964: *The act of creation*. London: Hutchinson.

Kris, E. 1952: *Psychoanalytic explorations in art*. New York: International Universities Press.

MacKinnon, D.W. 1962: The personality correlates of creativity: a study of American architects. *Proceedings of XIV Congress of Applied Psychology* 2, 11–39.

Osborn, A.F. 1953: *Applied imagination*. New York: Scribner.

Roe, A. 1952: *The making of a scientist*. New York: Dodd Mead.

Wallas, G. 1926: *The art of thought*. London: Jonathan Cape; New York: Harcourt Brace.

criminal psychology The study of the motives, personalities and decisions which lead to crime. The motives for most offenses – whether acquisitive, violent, sexual or connected with traffic – are normal in the sense that they are of kinds experienced by ordinary adults from time to time: greed, rage, lust, impatience, the desire for excitement. What has interested clinical psychologists, psychiatrists and psychoanalysts is the motive which is abnormal either in its strength, so that the offender finds it difficult to resist even when it is clearly dangerous to yield to it, or in its nature, sadism or pedophilia being examples.

Explanations of such motives belong to abnormal psychology. A few forms of mental disorder seem to be associated with certain kinds of objectionable behavior, although there is no good evidence that mental disorder in general increases the likelihood of being in trouble with the law. People who have committed serious personal violence are not infrequently found to be depressed, schizophrenic or "aggressive psychopaths". Some chronic confidence tricksters are said to have hysterical personalities. Some sexual offenders, especially against children, are found to be mentally handicapped. Arson, when committed for excitement rather than for gain or revenge, often seems to be compulsive.

The extent to which a predisposition to anti-social forms of behavior can be congenital has long been the subject of research and controversy. What cannot be disputed is the genetic transmission of a few diagnosable disorders (such as Huntington's Chorea) which sometimes involve sufferers in social trouble. There are also indisputable chromosomal abnormalities (not necessarily inherited) such as the XYY condition, which is associated with above average height, below average intelligence and a slightly increased likelihood of being involved in violence, including sexual violence.

The overwhelming majority of offenders are not suffering from such abnormalities. Their offences are often simply the result of circumstances: a speeding driver may have been late for an appointment; an assaulter may have been provoked by taunts; a sexual offender's self-control may have been reduced by alcohol or the behavior of his companion. (Indeed it is sometimes the victim's conduct that calls for explanation.) When the offense is premeditated or repeated, however, we feel the need for a fuller explanation. This may be the offender's imprudence or deliberate risk-taking; it may be lack of conscience or shame; or it may be a preference for the criminal's way of life. In other contexts what seems to call for explanation is not the frequency with which an individual offends but the frequency of offences of certain kinds among certain groups, such as vandalism among schoolboys. Current explanations may emphasize child-training methods, the values of a culture or subculture, low intelligence or impaired capacity for social learning.

Child-training methods are important because they may fail to result in the child internalizing the rules of conduct of the culture or SUBCULTURE to which he belongs. In this case he will be readier to breach them when it seems in his interest to do so. Internalization seems most likely to take place when parents explain the reasons for a rule and withdraw affection when the child breaks it. Physical punishment, especially if harsh or erratic, seems less effective (and may teach the child violent behavior). The effect is also weaker if parents' reactions are inconsistent, or if the child's dependence on their affection is weakened (e.g. by frequent absences). There are also types of anti-social conduct which become likely only in the teens or later, when children are less influenced by their parents and more by their peers (e.g. the abuse of drugs). It may be significant that the rate of DELINQUENCY rises with every year of compulsory schooling, and begins to decline at about the age when most young people leave school and mix with older people.

In any case, the child, the teenager or the adult may belong to a subculture whose values do not condemn everything that the law forbids. It may for example view dishonest acquisition no more seriously than many motorists regard speeding. It may respect rather than censure a man who uses violence to settle a quarrel. In some white-collared subcultures tax evasion and the acceptance of corrupt favors are "smart". Again, an individual may belong to, or join, a subculture which condones what he or she likes doing. Even in societies which condemn pedophilia (as not all do) pedophiles can sometimes join or form like-minded groups. Such groups often adopt "neutralizing" arguments to counterbalance the condemnation of others (or in some cases their own consciences). Pedophilia is said to benefit children by introducing them to a more mature kind of affection than they get from their contemporaries. Burglars assure themselves that householders' insurance policies indemnify them. Football fans excuse their violence to rivals by claiming that the latter "began it", or "asked for it" by entering their territory. Like other groups, such as street gangs or terrorists, they may invoke loyalty to a group or a cause, which can be used to justify revenge for an injury to a group member, or an unprovoked assassination. Another technique is the denial of legitimacy: "Property is theft". The concept of "neutralization" is more often used by sociologists than psychologists, perhaps because of the latter's preoccupation with measurable characteristics.

A controversial figure is "the psychopath". Many psychologists and psychiatrists believe that even when allowances are made for the influence of subcultures which are tolerant of dishonesty, violence, sexual promiscuity, drug abuse and other hedonistic conduct, there are some men and women whose proneness to one or more of these kinds of behavior is so impulsive or unheeding of other people's disapproval that it is in some way pathological: attributable, that is, to some sort of defect. Descriptions and explanations of the defect vary, from congenital abnormalities or perinatal brain damage to grossly affectionless upbringing. Some investigators find that samples of "psychopaths" contain individuals who do not show the normal responses to stimuli which should arouse anxiety, although the samples also seem to include others whose responses are more or less normal. Psychiatrists have succeeded in having the concept of psychopathic disorder written into legislation. For example, Section 4 of the English Mental Health Act 1959 (as amended) defines it as 'a persistent disorder or disability of mind ... which results in abnormally aggressive or seriously irresponsible conduct ...' In the USA statutory definitions (e.g. of "sexual psychopaths") vary from state to state. The more precise term now approved by the American Psychiatric Association (in its *Diagnostic and Statistical Manual*) is "anti-social personality disorder" in which there is 'a history of continuous and chronic anti-social behavior in which the rights of others are violated, persistence into adult life of a pattern ... that begins before the age of fifteen not due to ... severe mental retardation, schizophrenia or manic epi-

sodes'. These definitions, however, are descriptive and generic, leaving room for a variety of more specific diagnoses, such as those of the International Classification of Disorders (published by the World Health Organization). It is possible that this generic group will eventually prove divisible into sub-groups with more or less specific etiology; but this is unlikely to happen until research workers develop more exact diagnostic criteria and explanatory hypotheses.

An aspect of law-breaking which is only beginning to receive attention is what can be loosely called the decision-making stage, although many offences are the result of processes which can hardly be called "decisions", being impulsive, compulsive, negligent or habitual. These apart, however, even very strong motivation does not mean that every opportunity for the offence will be taken. The situation may be perceived as too risky, the penalty as too great, accomplishment as too difficult (as when a car thief is attracted by a car but desists because he would be too conspicuous, because he knows that his next prison sentence would be a long one, or because he knows that its lock is hard to force). NDW

Bibliography

Feldman, M.P. 1977: *Criminal behaviour: a psychological analysis*. New York and London: John Wiley.

Walker, N. 1977: *Behaviour and misbehaviour: explanations and non-explanations*. Oxford: Basil Blackwell; New York: Basic Books.

West, D.J. 1982: *Delinquency: its roots, careers and prospects*. London: Heinemann; Cambridge, Mass.: Harvard University Press.

critical theory A body of neo-Marxist social theory originating in the Frankfurt Institute for Social Research (hence the later term "Frankfurt School"). The Institute was founded in 1923 as a center for interdisciplinary Marxist research and began to take on a distinctive character after Max Horkheimer (1895–1973) became Director in 1930. Horkheimer and Theodor ADORNO (1903–69) formed the nucleus of the Institute, but many of the leading figures of German intellectual life were associated with it at one time or another. Probably the best known are the literary theorist Walter Benjamin, the philosopher Herbert Marcuse and the psychologist Erich Fromm; others include Otto Kirchheimer and Franz Neumann (politics and law), Friedrich Pollock, Henryk Grossman and Arkady Gurland (political economy), Leo Löwenthal (literature) and Bruno Bettelheim, Nathan Ackerman and Marie Jahoda (psychology).

The Institute was forced to leave Frankfurt in 1923, settling in the USA in 1935. In 1950 it was re-established in Frankfurt, under the direction of Horkheimer and Adorno. It was the center of a distinctive conception of society and culture, represented to a greater or lesser degree in the work of individual members and associates.

Critical theory may first be viewed as part of a more general trend in western Marxism, since around 1930 characterized by a move towards a closer relationship with non-Marxist thought, a growing preoccupation with cultural and ideological issues at the expense of political economy, and a scholarly rather than a proletarian audience (Anderson 1976). In addition, critical theory must be seen in terms of the intellectual situation of western European Marxists, confronted in the 1930s by the unholy trio of liberal capitalism, Stalinism and fascism. The writers connected with the Institute were not content, like more orthodox Marxists, to analyse fascism as simply a mutant form of monopoly capitalism, nor, like the post-war theorists of totalitarianism, to equate Stalinism with fascism and to contrast both with an idealized image of liberal democracy. They were struck by the similarities in terms of organization, technology, culture and personality structure in all forms of society, and hence gave these phenomena a more prominent place in their analyses than had the majority of Marxist writers.

Critical theory was understood from the outset as a totalizing theory which viewed society from the standpoint of the need to change it. The theory was to be reflexive about its own status and that of its interpretive categories: 'the critical acceptance of the categories which rule social life contains simultaneously their condemnation'. Fascism, for example, could not really be understood in the categories of western liberalism, since this was the ideology of a social order which had produced fascism. 'He who does not wish to speak of capitalism should also be silent about fascism' (cited in Jay 1973, p.156). Critical theory was also hostile to traditional disciplinary boundaries: the early *Studies in authority and the family* (1936) contained lengthy discussions of social and political thought as well as social psychological material, and *The authoritarian personality* (1950) was intended to be understood in terms of the more sociocultural analysis of *Dialectic of enlightenment* (1947), where anti-semitism is seen in the context of the rational domination inaugurated by the Enlightenment. Fascism 'seeks to make the rebellion of suppressed nature against domination directly useful to domination' (1947, p.185).

The concepts of domination and authority pervade the Institute's work. Domination, although exemplified par excellence in fascism, was also the central principle of liberal societies, possibly more important than the categories of Marxian political economy. As Adorno put it in a late article, 'Behind the reduction of men to agents and bearers of exchange value lies the domination of men over men'. Marcuse's concept of surplus-repression, developed in his critique (1954) of Freud's *Civilisation and its discontents* (1930) is defined as 'the restrictions necessitated by social domination', over and above those which, as FREUD had argued, were necessary for *any* ordered society and which Marcuse calls the 'rational exercise of authority' (1954, p.45).

This distinction is crucial to the critical theorists' account of the relation between reason and domination. They criticized existing social arrangements in the name of reason and of a more rational alternative society, with the conviction that 'social freedom is inseparable from enlightened thought' (1947, p.xiii). At the same time, however, they increasingly saw instrumental or technological rationality as the basis of the 'comfortable, smooth, reasonable, democratic unfreedom (which) prevails in advanced industrial civilisation' (Marcuse 1964, p.19). And though Marcuse's critique drew heavily on his American experience, it applied increasingly, he thought, to state socialist societies: 'it is not the West but the East which, in the name of socialism, has developed modern occidental rationality in its extreme form' (1968, pp. 201f.).

Marcuse's critique of industrial society in *Eros and civilisation* and *One dimensional man*, and some of his later writings, was prefigured in a more speculative form in Adorno and Horkheimer's *Dialectic of enlightenment*. Here the domination of nature by means of reason leads inevitably to the domination of man. In the lapidary formula on p.6, 'enlightenment is totalitarian'.

Dialectic of enlightenment also contains a critique of mass culture, or as Horkheimer and Adorno preferred to call it, the "culture industry"; they saw this as a homogeneous system of entertainment, devoid of the critical potential which high culture had once possessed and serving only to stabilize a system of domination. Here again one sees the emphasis on the interplay between sociology and psychology: 'the might of industrial society is lodged in men's minds' (p.127). Cultural theory is perhaps the area for which these writers will mostly be remembered; Adorno in particular produced a substantial body of work on aesthetic questions, especially on music. In philosophy, their contribution was mainly confined to expositions and critiques: Horkheimer's work on philosophies of history, Adorno's critiques of Husserl and Heidegger and Marcuse's book on Hegel, *Reason and revolution* (1941). Adorno's major work, *Negative dialectics* (1966), will surely remain as one of the classic texts of twentieth-century philosophy.

Once the Institute was re-established in Frankfurt, the "Frankfurt School", as it then came to be known, had a powerful influence in an otherwise rather conservative West Germany. The major intellectual event was the School's attack on positivism and empiricism in the social sciences, the *Positivismusstreit*; the main political event was of course the challenge of the student movement and the extra-parliamentary opposition, with which the Frankfurt School had an uneasy and ultimately hostile relationship.

After the death of Adorno in 1969 critical theory developed in a more diffuse form, in the work of Jürgen Habermas, Karl-Otto Apel, Claus Offe, Alfred Schmidt, Albrecht Wellmer, and others. Habermas was a leading participant in the *Positivismusstreit* in which he linked, in a classically Frankfurt way, questions of philosophy of science with a political critique of technocracy or the "scientisation of politics". His most recent work has been concerned with "reconstructing" historical materialism as a cognitively oriented evolutionary theory of society, and to develop from this a new theory of crisis tendencies in advanced societies. In doing so he has made imaginative use of the work of Chomsky, Searle and others in linguistics, and Piaget and Kohlberg in psychology. He seems less interested than the earlier generation in psychology *per se*, though he remains fascinated by the meta-theory of psychoanalysis: the idea of a theory whose validation consists in its rationally grounded acceptance by its addressee. For Habermas, this is also the case for Marxism, understood as the critique of ideology. Habermas's work, *Theorie des kommunikativen Handelns* (1981) sets his earlier reflections on science and communication within a more general context of the rationalization (in Max Weber's sense) of the Lebenswelt or lifeworld (see PHENOMENOLOGY).   WO

Bibliography

Adorno, T.W. et al. 1950: *The authoritarian personality*. New York: Harper.

—— 1966 (1973): *Negative dialectics*. New York: Seabury Press.

—— 1976: *The positivism dispute in German sociology*. London: Heinemann.

Anderson, Perry 1976: *Considerations of Western Marxism*. London: New Left Books.

Freud, Sigmund 1930 (1969): *Civilisation and its discontents*. London: Hogarth Press; New York: Norton.

Habermas, Jürgen. 1981: *Theorie des kommunikativen Handelns*. 2 vols. Frankfurt: Suhrkamp.

Horkheimer, Max and Adorno, Theodor W. 1947 (1972): *Dialectic of enlightenment*. New York: Herder and Herder; London: Allen Lane (1973). Institut für Sozialforschung 1936: *Studien über Autorität und Familie*. Paris: F. Alcan.

Jay, Martin 1973: *The dialectical imagination*. London: Heinemann.

Marcuse, Herbert 1941 (1955): *Reason and revolution*. 2nd edn. London: Routledge and Kegan Paul.

——— 1964: *Eros and civilisation*. Boston: Beacon Press.

cross-lagged correlation A statistical procedure to shed light on causal relationships between variables in research settings where no experimental manipulation is possible. It has been widely used in occupational psychological research within organizations (Clegg, Jackson and Wall 1977). The correlation between two variables, x and y, is calculated on two occasions (x_1y_1 and x_2y_2), also permitting the calculation of correlations between x on both occasions (x_1x_2), between y on both occasions (y_1y_2), and the cross-correlations which are lagged in time (x_1y_2 and y_1x_2). In situations where x_1y_2 is found to be substantially larger than y_1x_2, it is often appropriate to infer causal priority from x to y rather than in the opposite direction.

PBW

Bibliography

Clegg, C.W., Jackson, P.R. and Wall, T.D. 1977: The potential of cross-lagged correlation analysis in field research. *Journal of occupational psychology* 50, 177–96.

cross-sectional research A research design in which a range of variation in a given variable is examined by sampling several different cases at the same time: in contrast to longitudinal research in which a range of variation in a given variable is sampled by observing the same cases at different points in time. For example, a cross-sectional study of the relationship between a person's age and height would compare the heights of individuals who are at different ages, while a longitudinal study would compare the height attained by a given individual at different points in the lifespan. (See also LONGITUDINAL RESEARCH.)

SBe

Bibliography

Wolman, B.B. ed. 1982: *Handbook of developmental psychology*. Englewood Cliffs, N.J.: Prentice-Hall.

crowd psychology The psychology of crowd and mass behavior is a psychology of history both in its subject matter and its models and in its initial aim of reforming the theory and practice of politics.

The theory of crowd psychology took shape in Europe, and more particularly in France, at the beginning of this century, after an era of traumatic events stretching from the French Revolution to the Commune of 1871, an era that saw in Napoleon the dazzling appearance of one of the greatest leaders of all times.

Gustave Le Bon, a true pioneer in the field addressed himself to those members of the politically conscious classes whose failure to understand the irresistible rise of crowd phenomena seemed to him a major threat to civilization (1903, 1910). It was Le Bon who made people recognize crowd phenomena as an essential element of social behavior. His description, which still prevails over common sense, stresses the radical difference between the psyche of the individual which is conscious, reasonable and peaceful, and that of the spontaneous crowd, which is subconscious, passionate and even violent; in the heat generated by the crowd, the fusion of individuals into a common sentiment or spirit blurs differences of personality and social status, blunts the intellectual faculties and propels the enthusiastic and credulous mass into patterns of behavior that are sometimes heroic but, rather more often, destructive and anarchic.

An explanation for the opposition between the conscious, which is individual, and the subconscious, whose collective nature is manifested in the crowd, is to be found in the theory which fascinated Le Bon and his contemporaries, namely that of hypnosis. Hypnosis helps to explain two things: firstly, the state of suggestibility or receptivity of individuals in a crowd, and, secondly, the way in which a leader can gain control of a crowd. As Le Bon says (1903) 'The leader has most often started as one of the led. He has himself been hypnotized by the idea, whose apostle he has since become' and one can add that he must be hypnotized also by the echo of his own ideas which the crowd sends back to him as it acclaims him.

Le Bon's discoveries in the psychology of natural crowds were taken up and considerably amplified by Gabriel Tarde (1903, 1910). His descriptive theory is a very general one and can be applied to all forms of social behavior. Artificial or organized crowds, henceforth called masses, become the center of his interest. Their prototypes are the army and the church, but political parties, trades unions and all the administrative structures of the state are obviously part and parcel of the same phenomenon.

Masses, that is institutionalized crowds, become the guiding principle that explains the whole evolution of society, and implicit in all this is the resolution of a paradox. For, in the model proposed by Tarde, crowds must be capable of creativity, a quality which they lack in Le Bon's system.

The solution adopted by Tarde ascribes the advance of humanity to the progress and discoveries accomplished by the leader, who becomes the driving force behind the system. This is possible thanks to an analogue of suggestibility, namely imitation, which ensures the cognitive and affective uniformity of the mass at the same time as its submission to the leader.

And finally one must not forget Tarde's most original contribution which makes him a precursor of the theories of mass culture. Taking as his starting point the example of the press, he describes a type of long range, indirect, imitative suggestibility. The journalist, who is compared with the hypnotist, prefigures what today we should call a leader of opinion. Tarde foresees, therefore, from its earliest days, the era which will witness the triumph of mass communications, of crowds transformed into publics, of the masses at home.

The originality and the prophetic nature of the works of Le Bon and Tarde are undeniable but it is only with FREUD that their hypotheses become deductions in an all-embracing theoretical system. Freud's theory of mass psychology is a generalized psychoanalytical system concerned with the history of the origins of those fundamental social institutions, the family and religion (which Freud, like his predecessors, considers as the prototype of all collective beliefs).

However, though Freud expresses admiration for Le Bon's descriptions he cannot accept his idea of a collective unconscious which might explain the changes that take place in individuals when they become part of a crowd. For Freud the unconscious springs from repression, the characteristics that an individual exhibits in a crowd are his own, and it is the individual's regression towards the mass, towards the primitive state, which provokes or permits the relaxation of this repression. 'The apparently new characteristics which he then displays are in fact the manifestations of this unconscious, in which all that is evil in the human mind is contained as a predisposition. We can find no difficulty in understanding the disappearance of conscience or of a sense of responsibility in these circumstances' (1921).

Once the unconscious has been put back in its rightful place there remains the question of elucidating the nature of the mechanisms which explain the formation of the mass and the fundamental role played by the leader.

The intuitive suggestion by Le Bon and Tarde, that there is a kind of love that binds together the mass on the one hand and the mass and the leader on the other, is taken up and clarified in Freud's concept of libido, which describes a two-fold reality: firstly, the narcissistic libido, that love of self into which the leader can and must retreat by himself if he wants to be and to remain leader, and, secondly, the erotic libido, which makes possible the social bond in general and also, in particular, what one observes in the crowd.

The second concept which is indispensable for the study of crowd psychology, identification, is a development of Tarde's theory of imitation. It expresses the differentiation of the psychic apparatus through the interiorizing of exterior authorities, of social ideals and models: 'We are aware that what we have been able to contribute towards the explanation of the libidinal structure of a mass leads back to the distinction between the ego and the ego ideal and to the double kind of tie which this makes possible – identification, and putting the object in the place of the ego ideal' (Freud 1921).

If one considers the two factors, Eros and Mimesis, as autonomous and irreducible, responsible both of them for the multiple conflicts that arise in their own spheres, but also for an almost permanent conflict which is due to their co-presence, one can arrive at a new and theoretically coherent explanation of the crowd/individual opposition: whereas in the individual the erotic factor dominates the mimetic factor, in the mass this relationship is reversed.

The whole system hangs together for the leader and through the leader. For the leader, thanks to the mechanisms already described; through the leader because for Freud the passage from the natural crowd to the artificial crowd is marked by that fundamental event of the psychoanalytical theory of the mass: the murder of the leader. From Moses to Mao, all the leaders in history would be, from this point of view, resurrections of this image.

The foregoing paragraphs constitute a reconstruction and an integration of the classical theories concerning the psychology of the masses. These theories were visionary in nature. The phenomenon they analyze is still unrolling today before our very eyes 'on a scale hitherto unknown, hence its absolute historical novelty' (Moscovici 1981).

Moreover, these theories have had a considerable influence on recent and contemporary history. Mussolini and Hitler knew and put into practice the ideas of Le Bon. Psychoanalysis has inspired an opposing school of thought which incorporates various theoretical elements drawn from Marxism. Among the most influential tendencies we find Reich, with *The mass psychology of fascism* (1933, 1946), and above all the Frankfurt School, which saw a powerful reverberation in the social movements of the 1960s.

Another scientific tradition, based on an empirical and experimental social psychology, has, since the last world war, made an important contribution to our understanding of particular aspects of crowd phenomena.

We speak here of crowds and not of masses because by definition mass institutions and organizations, organized crowds, are excluded by epistemological distinction: 'The conceptual requirements of spontaneity, planlessness, and relative lack of organization distinguish collective behavior from established groups such as the Methodist Church, Harvard University, and the Republican Party' (Milgram and Toch 1969).

The definition of the phenomenon is both simple and all-embracing. It includes all human assemblies in which nearness is in itself sufficient to provoke a significant change in behavior.

Urbanization provides the sociological and ecological framework for a detailed description of the characteristics of crowds. The shape, often circular, the size, the movement, the circulation of information in the shape of a rumor and even the facilitating role of the ambient temperature, are photographed, measured and evaluated.

Experimental studies are carried out to verify partial hypotheses. Thus, the "crowd crystals" invoked by Canetti (1962) to describe the initial formation of a crowd become, in Milgram's ingenious field experiment (1969), "precipitating groups", the efficacy of the theory being tested and measured in a busy street in New York.

This experiment is illustrative of a theoretical orientation according to which crowds are among the elementary phenomena of social life. By way of contrast one finds theories which situate crowds in

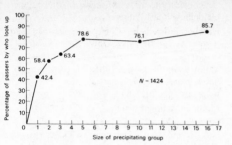

the domain of deviance or even of pathology. To describe the homogeneity of behavior in these violent and destructive crowds, one uses terms such as "CONTAGION" and "infection" and mathematical models derived from research into "epidemics".

Closer to the psychosocial perspective of group dynamics, the Emergent Norm Theory (Turner and Killian 1957) proposes a model which dismisses the homogeneity of crowd behavior, as merely an illusion of the observer. According to this theory a small number of active participants impose on the mass of the crowd which then conforms with them, a mode of action which is perceived as a dominant norm.

In conclusion we should note that there are two distinct avenues of research in the domain of crowd psychology: the classical explicative theory whose scientific status is still rather fragile, and a corpus of research based on methods which are reputedly more rigorous but whose field of investigation is restricted by theoretical and ideological presuppositions. One can only hope that the two currents will gather strength and come closer together, perhaps in the street as in Milgram's experiment, but in any case somewhere where there is a crowd to surround us.   MG/SM

Bibliography

Canetti, E. 1962: *Crowds and power*. London: Gollancz.

Cantril, H. 1941: *The psychology of social movement*. New York: Wiley.

*Freud, S. 1921: Group psychology and the analysis of the Ego. *Standard edition of the complete psychological works of Sigmund Freud*, vol. 18. London: Hogarth Press; New York: Norton.

*——— 1939: Moses and monotheism. *Standard edition*, vol. 23.

Graumann, C.F. and Moscovici, S. 1985: *Changing conceptions of crowd mind and behavior*. New York: Springer Verlag.

Le Bon, G. 1903: *The crowd*. London: Unwin.

——— 1910: *La psychologie politique*. Paris: Flammarion.

*Milgram, S. and Toch, H. 1969: Collective behavior: crowds and social movements. In *The handbook of social psychology*. 2nd edn., eds. G. Lindzey and E. Aronson. Reading, Mass.: Addison-Wesley.

*Moscovici, S. 1985: *The age of the crowd*. Cambridge: Cambridge University Press.

Reich, W. 1946: *The mass psychology of fascism*. New York: Orgon Institute Press.

Rudé, G. 1959: *The crowd in the French Revolution*. Oxford: Oxford University Press.

Sighele, S. 1901: *La foule criminelle*. Paris: Alcan.

Tarde, G. 1903: *The laws of imitation*. New York: Holt, Rinehart & Winston.

——— 1910: *L'opinion et la foule*. Paris: Alcan.

Turner, R.H. and Killian, L.M. 1957: *Collective behavior*. Englewood Cliffs, N.J.: Prentice-Hall.

cultural determinism The view that patterns of behavior are determined by cultural rather than biological or other factors. Some patterns of behavior persist across time within a culture although the persons who behave in a particular way are entirely different. Some customs, attitudes, values or role perceptions remain unchanged over several generations. This observation does not imply that individuals do not influence culture or that biology, situations or other determinants are unimportant in shaping human behavior. However, cultural determinism emphasizes the role of culture in the continuation of pattern across time. While humans can plan and plot they are to some extent swept along by the historic stream of their cultures. For example Kroeber and Richardson (see Kroeber 1952) examined the dimensions of women's dresses from 1605 to 1936 and found strong evidence of cultural determinism, despite attempts of dress designers to innovate and create new fashions. Learned behavior is handed down from one generation to another, creating stability which can be studied as a phenomenon. The observed continuity in such data suggests cultural determinism. This does not, of course, preclude individual innovations or variations of behavior within each culture. (See also DURKHEIM, SOCIAL REPRESENTATION.)   HCT

Bibliography

Kroeber, A.L. 1952: *The nature of culture*. Chicago: University of Chicago Press.

cultural diffusion The spread of cultural traits through contact across societies. Some objects (customs, beliefs, attitudes, values or role perceptions) are found in one society in a particular historical period and also in neighboring societies at a later historical period. Culture change occurs through both innovation and diffusion. Among anthropologists, theoretical battles about diffusion included the question of how much cultural change is due to one or the other of these factors. A second battle was concerned with whether anthropologists should study diffusion at all, or confine themselves to examining the way institutions, operating on a single time-plane, reinforce each other. The latter, anti-diffusionist, position was championed by B. Malinowski, and is known as functionalism. Functionalism contrasts with several diffusionist schools. Three major schools can be identified: the English (Elliot Smith and W.J. Perry), German-Austrian (Father Schmidt and F. Graebner) and American (F. Boas and his students). Elliot Smith considered borrowing to be virtually the sole means by which cultures change, a view which denied the inventiveness of humans. Graebner established diffusion by noting the number of similarities and the complexity of similar cultural elements. The American school examined not only similarities but also the inner relations among the elements that were diffused, and emphasized the known historic links between the cultures where diffusion has taken place.   HCT

Bibliography

Boas, Franz 1938: *General anthropology*. New York: D.C. Heath.

Graebner, Fritz 1911: *Methode der Ethnologie*. Heidelberg: Carl Winter.

Kroeber, Alfred L. 1944: *Configurations of cultural growth*. Berkeley: University of California Press.

Malinowski, Bronislaw 1961: *The dynamics of culture change*. New Haven: Yale Press.

Perry, William J. 1927: *Children of the sun*. London: Methuen.

Schaefer, J.M. 1974: *Studies of cultural diffusion*. New Haven: Human Relations Area Files Press.

Schmidt, Wilhelm 1939: *The cultural historical method of ethnology*. New York: Fortuny's.

Smith, Grafton Elliot 1927: *Culture: the diffusion controversy*. New York: Norton.

cultural relativism The view that patterns of understanding found in different cultures are as good as each other. This viewpoint has implications for method, philosophic position, the evaluation of values and for attitudes toward culture change. Methodologically, it implies that phenomena must be described from the perspective of adherents of a given culture. Philosophically it implies that there is no reality other than the symbolic forms which constitute culture and hence all reality is cultural (see CULTURAL DETERMINISM). Cultural relativism also guides the evaluation of values, which are seen as dependent on social organization and as varying with the modes and interests of each society. It follows that there is no way to judge the superiority of values outside the particular cultural contexts in which they were developed. Finally, this viewpoint implies that since the values of each cultural group are equally acceptable, reform should not attempt to change another group's values. Ethnocentrism is the opposite of cultural relativism. A person making ethnocentric judgments uses his or her own culture as the standard against which to measure other cultures. By contrast, in cultural relativism judgments are said to be based on experience and experience is interpreted by each individual in terms of his or her own enculturation. Judgments of right and wrong, normal and abnormal, beautiful and ugly depend on the judge's experience and are shaped by events that occur in particular ecologies and cultures. What is desirable in one ecology may be undesirable in another. Even the facts of the physical world are discerned through the acculturation screen. So the perception of time, distance, weight, size and other realities is mediated by the conventions of cultural groups.   HCT

Bibliography
Herskovits, M.J. 1972: *Cultural relativism.* New York: Random House.

cyclical change in history Model of the pattern of human change as a recurrent and cyclic process of growth and decay. The cyclical model of history is generally placed against two alternatives: the linear or evolutionary pattern and the discontinuous or revolutionary pattern. A cyclical model of historical change does not necessarily imply continued repetition for it may be claimed that the periods of growth are progressive ones. The works of the Italian historian, Giambattista Vico, are often cited as exemplifying a cyclical model. Sociologists interested in the processes of social change have also contemplated a cyclical model; most notable of these are Pitrim Sorokin and Vilfredo Pareto. The idea of recurrent yet developing cycles of change in phenomena has recently gained attention in psychology (Rosnow 1978).   JGM

Bibliography
Rosnow, R.L. 1978: The prophetic vision of Giambattista Vico: Implications for the state of social psychological theory. *Journal of personality and social psychology* 36, 1322–31.

D

Darwinism, social Conventionally refers to the set of (psychological, sociological, ethnological, etc.) theories which arose from the application of Charles Darwin's views on evolution to the understanding both of social phenomena and of the processes determining the changes of sociosystems. In some instances, the term also denotes social doctrines of whatever scientific status supposedly supported by Darwinian evolutionism. This definition masks the complexity of the origins and the ramifications of this movement of thought.

The emergence of the movement of thought referred to as "Social Darwinism" took place roughly between 1850 and 1880. It reached its peak of scientific, political, social and ideological fascination and visibility in Europe and in North America between 1880 and the end of the first world war. Yet its origins can be traced back to *two* separate traditions beginning at the turn of the nineteenth century. Indeed, Malthus's *Essay on the principle of population*, first published in 1798, marks a first and decisive step in the early phase of the history of Social Darwinism, for it was instrumental in shaping both the Darwinian theory of natural selection and the theory of social evolution which eventually led to Social Darwinism proper.

Ironically, the progressive theory of natural selection drew from a work which was pessimistic in its whole outlook and politically reactionary. In his *Essay*, Malthus endeavored to rebut the theories of progress of the French *philosophes* (such as Turgot, Diderot, Condorcet) which consisted merely of 'speculations on the perfectibility of man and society'. According to Malthus the possibility of progress through education and political or social revolution met an insurmountable obstacle in the imbalance between the geometric increase of population and the arithmetic growth of food supply.

It was to his reading of Malthus's book that Darwin attributed his discovery of the principle of natural selection and traces of Malthus's influence on Darwin are prominent in *The origin of species* (1859) as well as in *The descent of man* (1871). But unlike Malthus, Darwin optimistically put the emphasis on the goodness of the struggle for life which results from the imbalance set forth by Malthus and pointed to the inevitability of progress through selection conceived as a law of nature (*Origin of species* pp. 86 and 449). Thus the frame of a sociocultural theory worked as a conceptual matrix within which Darwin discussed the main topics of natural evolution.

The second tradition of social evolutionism was prominently represented in the early nineteenth century by such authors as Hegel, Saint-Simon, and Comte. Herbert Spencer elaborated a general theory of evolution of sociosystems which directly addressed the issues raised by Malthus. His early contribution on *The proper sphere of government* (1842) and his first book on *Social statics* (1850) not only contain an attempt to find an exit from the Malthusian dilemma by means of a physiologically oriented theory of the inverse relationship between intelligence and fertility, but also include most of the ideas Spencer is said to have taken from Darwin. And though he often refers to the Lamarckian notion of individual adaptation by the constant use of the sensory, motor, secretory etc. parts of the organism as one element of sociocultural progress, his conception resorts to the ideas of struggle for existence, survival of the fittest and other ideas of social-Darwinistic type. When the *Origin of species* was published, Spencer and his disciples welcomed its overall message as a confirmation of their own social evolutionism which would now definitely rest on a firm scientific, i.e. biological, ground (for further developments see Wiltshire 1978).

It should also be noted that Spencer had popularized the term "evolution" by 1857 and in his *Principles of biology*, the phrase "survival of the fittest". Darwin duly acknowledged this fact in the fifth edition of the *Origin* by pointing out that 'I have called this principle, by which each slight variation, if useful, is preserved by the term Natural Selection, in order to mark its relation to man's power of selection. But the expression often used by Mr. Herbert Spencer of the Survival of the Fittest is more accurate, and is sometimes equally convenient' (p.74).

This summary makes it clear that the biological and social sciences in England developed in a parallel manner up to approximately 1860 and then converged upon a general theory of evolution in which the concepts of struggle for existence, competition, adaptation and the survival of the fittest were given great explanatory power. The summary also shows that Darwin's doctrines made possible the synthesis of the traditions mentioned above, thereby supposedly confirming in terms of biology what had already been assumed in the doctrines of sociocultural progress, so that, as Bayertz (1982, p.113) put it, one could have construed the main principles of Social Darwinism without Darwin (see also Young 1973).

When the *Origin* was published English scientists interested in the topic of evolution (whether of the cosmos, the earth, nature or society) were rapidly converted to Darwin's doctrines. Darwinism was seen as a new and valid standard within the scientific community by 1870, when the Darwinians had succeeded in taking control of the scientific institutions. And, due to the publicizing of Darwinism by such figures as Huxley, Hooker and Lyell in England, Asa Gray in the United States, and Ernst Haeckel in Germany, the new evolutionism attracted more and more intellectuals fascinated by the possibility of giving their social doctrines a scientific outlook (see Ruse 1979, pp. 257–68).

Paradoxically, from 1870 on, whereas the number of severe controversies over *specific* problems of Darwinian biology grew in number, evolutionism in its trivial version of Social Darwinism – or, as Harris (1969, p.129) prefers to call it, Biological Spencerism – became a rather fashionable ideological vehicle for the justification of social, economic and political practices.

Indeed, from the early 1870s to the mid-1890s, the economy of the industrialized nations suffered from a severe deflation. This explains why politicians and economists in Europe and in the United States sought a remedy against the economic crises in the strengthening of the policies of protective tariffs, conquest of new markets, increase of industrial production by means of reducing the impact of governmental control and stronger exploitation of colonial resources and manpower. These policies of economic *laissez-faire* and of political imperialism were argued for precisely in terms of those ideas which Social Darwinism were offering as a scientifically supported ideology (Koch 1973, passim).

In historical accounts of Social Darwinism as ideology, however, it has often been overlooked that a rigorous adherence to the principles of struggle through *laissez-faire* economics and imperialism leads to a paradoxical situation. The paradox is that since individuals, groups, classes, states or nations are all conceived as entities or units corresponding to the organisms as units subjected to the law of natural selection, too strong a competition between individuals and groups *within* a State or nation would weaken the latter in its struggle with other States or nations. One ought therefore to distinguish analytically between the two trends of "external Social Darwinism", and "internal Social Darwinism" (Koch 1973, p.131).

The first trend postulated progress through elimination of weak, i.e. unfit, States or nations and the expansion of fit States through war on the one hand, and on the other, the elimination of unfit races through the deployment of eugenic techniques or, as in *National life from the standpoint of science* (1901) by the noted statistician Charles Pearson, by means of war, trade and industry.

The second trend, in contradistinction, postulated a restriction of domestic *laissez-faire* through social reform, so that the chances of survival in external struggle and competition would increase. Instead of maintaining the principle of selection modeled after that of natural selection proper, the proponents of social reform based their arguments on the possibility of man-made selection and therefore included the manipulation of social (or societal) conditions in their doctrines. A typical representative of this trend is Benjamin Kidd, whose monograph on *Social evolution* of 1894 contained a theoretical frame for social reformism, according to which the State must guarantee equal conditions of fair competition for all its members through just distribution of income and taxes, general education and change of the social and physical conditions of industrial production.

Social Darwinism as ideology had in turn some influence on the rise of the early modern social and behavioral sciences in England, the United States and in several European countries such as Germany, Austria and France. In Germany, for example, the monism of Ernst Haeckel easily amalgamated with Social Darwinism in its moderate, internally oriented version and helped to orient the hesitant steps of early German sociology and social psychology. In France, the crowd psychologists led by Le Bon and Tarde not only propagated racism, but also used social Darwinistic ideas in their theory of regression to a prior stage of evolution through suggestion by a (usually anarchistic, socialist, trade-unionist) leader. Finally, the first generation of social psychologists of the Chicago School such as Dewey and MEAD had a more rigorous theory of the continuity of evolution from animal to man than their overtly ideological contemporaries blinded by Social Darwinism, and elaborated their conceptions in view of making the various techniques of social reform scientific.

Other behavioral and social scientists with a penchant for Social Darwinism or working within a frame derived from it were Lester Ward, Franklin H. Giddings, Edward B. Tylor, William G. Sumner, Edward A. Westermarck, Ludwig Gumplowicz, Alfred Fouillée (for further details see Hofstadter 1955 and Mitchell 1968).

AM

Bibliography

Bayertz, K. 1982: Darwinismus als Ideologie. *Darwin und die Evolutionstheorie* (= Dialektik, vol. 5). Köln: Pahl Rugenstein, 101–116.

Darwin, Charles 1859 (1958): *On the origin of species*. New York: New American Library.

Harris, M. 1969: *The rise of anthropological theory*. London: Routledge and Kegan Paul.

Hofstadter, R. 1944 (1955): *Social Darwinism and American thought*. Boston: Beacon Press.

Koch, H.W. 1973: *Der Sozialdarwinismus. Seine Genese und sein Einfluss auf das imperialistische Denken*. Munich: Verlag C.H. Beck.

Mitchell, G.D. 1968: *A hundred years of sociology*. Chicago: Aldine.

Ruse, M. 1979: *The Darwinian revolution: science red in tooth and claw*. Chicago: Chicago University Press.

Wiltshire, D. 1978: *The social and political thought of Herbert Spencer*. Oxford and New York: Oxford University Press.

Young, R. 1973: The historiographic and ideological contexts of the nineteenth-century debate on man's place in nature. In *Changing perspectives in the history of science*, eds. M. Teich and R. Young. London: Heinemann.

defense mechanism: in psychoanalytic theory One of a number of techniques used by the EGO to defend itself from ANXIETY, which may arise from three sources: when an instinctual impulse in the id is pressing for gratification; when the superego exerts moral pressure against a wish, intention or idea; or when there is a realistic danger of pain or injury (ego-anxiety). The aim of defense mechanisms is to divert anxiety away from the ego's consciousness. This can be done in about a dozen different ways, according to psychoanalytic literature, which vary in the extent to which they are consistent with reason and perceived reality; one that is consistent is "ego-syntonic", and one that is not is "ego-dystonic". The severity of a psychological disturbance is often assessed by the quality (in terms of ego-syntonicity) of the prevailing defenses, which PROJECTIVE TESTS especially are designed to elicit. The ego-defenses have been extensively discussed by Anna Freud (1937) and by Laughlin (1970).

The principal defense is REPRESSION, which covers both preventing a mental element (idea, wish, anxiety, impulse, image) from becoming conscious, and rejecting from consciousness to the UNCONSCIOUS MIND one which had been. The commonest of the others are: "projection", by which one attributes to others a property of oneself and can therefore blame them instead of feeling guilt (a form of anxiety) oneself; "reaction-formation", by which one's anxiety about (say) aggressive feelings towards someone is kept at bay by overtly adopting the opposite attitude of solicitude and compliance; "identification", by which either depressive anxiety over "object-loss" is mitigated by perpetuating in one's own behavior some psychological property of (say) a parent or spouse who has been emotionally lost (cf. Freud on depression: 1917a, p.239), or the threat of an aggressor is annulled by one's adopting his/her characteristics (see SUPEREGO); denial, a relatively ego-dystonic defense because if some unpleasant feature of the perceptual world is simply denied, then this defies the "reality principle" and may lead to delusion or hallucination, whereas, if one denies some painful aspect of one's emotional make-up (say depression), one is tending towards mania; SUBLIMATION and rationalization, both much more ego-syntonic, and the latter meaning to give an intellectual rationale for what was in fact an emotionally determined action or response; "isolation" by which the mental image of a disturbing experience or action is disconnected in one's thinking from its temporal and associative context, drained of its feeling-tone, and left cognitively and emotionally isolated; "splitting", by which a single "object" is treated as two separate ones so that a separate set of feelings can be directed to either part-object, and the anxious dissonance between (say) wanting and rejecting the same thing be conse-

quently resolved (see PERSONALITY THEORY, PSYCHOANALYTICAL for Kleinian usage); "regression", by which one reverts to the gratification techniques of an earlier psychosexual stage to compensate for a current anxiety (see PERSONALITY THEORY, PSYCHOANALYTICAL for the account of "stages").

The theoretical relation between repression and the other defenses is problematic, with the exception of regression, for the latter is the only one which depends upon the chronology of personality development (Freud 1917b, ch. 22). Freud recognized (1926, ch. 11A) that he had been using the word repression to cover different forms of defense against anxiety (on the assumption that all defenses except regression would involve repression). He proposed to revert to the concept of a class of defense-mechanisms of which repression would be a particular case. Madison (1961) has argued that Freud does not maintain this program in subsequent writings. Freud also considers (1926) the possibility that the neuroses should be understood in terms of which defense mechanisms dominate their respective psychopathologies, and Fairbairn (1941) proposed a realization of this idea in the context of "object-relations theory".

Kline has reviewed a great many ingenious empirical investigations into defense-mechanisms (1981, ch. 8), and concludes that, although a number of them are poorly designed or irrelevant, there is undoubted support for repression, and a certain amount for isolation, projection, reaction-formation and denial.   NMC

Bibliography

Fairbairn, W.R.D. 1941 (1952): A revised psychopathology. Reprinted in *Psychoanalytic studies of the personality*. London: Tavistock.

Freud, A. 1937: *The ego and the mechanisms of defence*. London: Hogarth; New York: International Universities Press (1946).

Freud, S. 1917a: 1917b: 1926: Mourning and melancholia, vol. 14; Introductory lectures, vol. 16; Inhibitions, symptoms and anxiety, vol. 20. In *Standard edition of the complete psychological works of Sigmund Freud*, vols. as indicated. London: Hogarth Press; New York: Norton.

Kline, P. 1981: *Fact and fantasy in Freudian theory*. London and New York: Methuen.

Laughlin, H.P. 1970: *The ego and its defenses*. New York: Appleton-Century-Croft.

Madison, P. 1961: *Freud's concept of repression and defense*. Minneapolis: Minnesota University Press.

deindividuation

deindividuation A state of relative anonymity in which a person cannot be identified as a particular individual but only as a group member. Experiments by Zimbardo (1970) have found that people show an increased tendency towards aggressive behavior in conditions of relative anonymity. The threshold for non-normative acts is lowered because sanctions cannot be easily implemented in such conditions. This in turn may lead to the weakening of such internalized controls as shame, guilt or fear. Milgram (1974) has shown that deindividuating the victim also leads to an increase in aggression.

Gergen et al. (1973) found that deindividuation could increase intimacy. People who entered and left a lightless room individually, and had no opportunity to meet outside it, gave up conversation after about forty minutes and began touching and feeling each other. The mechanism involved in producing this friendly behavior is again assumed to be the breakdown of internalized controls.

All these experiments may be criticized for their extreme artificiality and doubtful generalizability. This criticism is less easily leveled at a study by Diener et al. (1976) in which deindividuation was found to increase the mischievousness of trick-or-treat children on Hallowe'en.   JMFJ/RL

Bibliography

Diener, E., Fraser, S.C., Beaman, A.L. and Kelem, R.T. 1976: Effects of deindividuation variables on stealing among Halloween trick-or-treaters. *Journal of personality and social psychology* 33, 178–83.

Gergen, K.J., Gergen, M.M. and Barton, W. 1973: Deviance in the dark. *Psychology today* 7, 129–30.

Milgram, S. 1974: *Obedience to authority: an experimental view*. New York: Harper.

Zimbardo, P.G. 1970: The human choice: individuation, reason and order versus deindividuation, impulse and chaos. In *Nebraska symposium on motivation*, eds. W.J. Arnold and D. Levine. Lincoln: University of Nebraska Press.

delinquency Conduct disorder in young persons involving offenses against the law. In Britain, juvenile delinquents could be considered legally as persons under the age of seventeen with criminal convictions. However, no widely accepted definition exists, the term often including any antisocial, deviant or immoral behavior whether or not it forms part of a criminal offence. Delinquency is a serious cause for concern worldwide, but rates are difficult to estimate reliably. West and Farrington (1973) showed that 30.8 per cent of working-class boys in London had at least one conviction at twenty-one years. Boys have outnumbered girls in a ratio of up to ten to one. The most common offenses involve theft. A popular distinction is drawn between socialized and unsocialized delinquents (Hewitt and Jenkins 1946).

Causation is multifactorial, including genetic, psychological, social and cultural factors. Over-simplified causal explanations are misleading. Prevalence is high in depressed urban environments and one view relates delinquency particularly to disadvantaged subcultures. There is a well-established connection between delinquency and disturbed home background and family conflict. Schools may have differing rates of delinquency and may play a part in fostering delinquent behavior (Reynolds 1976). Longitudinal studies suggest that future delinquents may be differentiated from others during late childhood on the basis of their attitudes and behavior (West and Farrington 1973). The "labeling" of children as failures and troublemakers, especially by teachers, contributes to the acquisition of deviant status (Hargreaves 1975).   WLIP-J

Bibliography

Hargreaves, D. H., Hester. F. and Mellor, S. 1975: *Deviance in classrooms*. London and Boston: Routledge and Kegan Paul.

Hewitt, L.E. and Jenkins, R.L. 1946: *Fundamen-*

tal patterns of maladjustment: the dynamics of their origin. Springfield, Ill.: State of Illinois.

Loeber, R. and Dishion, T. 1983: Early predictors of male delinquency: a review. *Psychological bulletin* 94, 68–99.

Reynolds, D. 1976: The delinquent school. In *The process of schooling*, eds. M. Hammersley and P. Woods. London and Boston: Routledge and Kegan Paul.

West, D.J. and Farrington, D.P. 1973: *Who becomes delinquent?* London: Heinemann Educational.

*——— 1977: *The delinquent way of life.* London: Heinemann Educational.

——— 1982: *Delinquency: its roots, careers and prospects.* London: Heinemann; Cambridge, Mass.: Harvard University Press.

demand characteristics

A phrase referring to the fact that certain features of the experimental setting may impose certain perceived demands upon the experimental subject. Subjects tend to act in the way that they think the experimenter would wish. Orne (1962) was one of the first to point to the demand characteristics of psychological research which he defined as 'the totality of cues which convey an experimental hypothesis to the subject' (p.779). Many famous experiments such as the obedience study of Milgram (1965) have been interpreted in terms of demand characteristics (Mixon 1972). It is, of course, possible that while some subjects in an experiment will feel the need to confirm the experimental hypothesis others will not.

A related experimental artifact is evaluation apprehension, which refers to the anxiety and self-consciousness that a subject has about being observed and judged while in a laboratory or similar setting. Because subjects realize that some aspects of their behavior are being measured or observed, they may try to present themselves in a favorable light. Evaluation apprehension has been studied by Sigall, Aronson and Van Hoose (1970) who found that if subjects were faced with the choice between giving negative information about themselves while cooperating with the experimenter, and presenting positive information but negating the experi-menters' demands they chose the latter. This suggests the limited effects of demand characteristics when the demand is for a display of negative aspects of the person.   AF

Bibliography

Milgram, S. 1965: Some conditions of obedience and disobedience to authority. *Human relations* 18, 57–76.

Mixon, D. 1972: Instead of deception. *Journal for the theory of social behavior* 2, 145–77.

Orne, M. 1962: On the social psychology of the psychological experiment: with particular reference to demand characteristics and their implication. *American psychologist* 17, 776–83.

Sigall, H., Aronson, E. and Van Hoose, T. 1970: The cooperative subject: myth or reality. *Journal of experimental social psychology* 28, 218–24.

dialectic theory

In its most general sense, dialectic has come to signify any more or less intricate process of conceptual or social conflict, interconnection and change, in which the generation, interpenetration and clash of oppositions, leading to their transcendence in a fuller or more adequate mode of thought or form of life, plays a key role. But dialectic is itself one of the most complex – and contested – concepts in the story of philosophical and social thought. The most important historical figures for the contemporary human sciences in this conceptual area are undoubtedly Karl Marx (1818–83) and G.W.F. Hegel (1770–1831), but Marx's dialectic cannot be understood in abstraction from its relation to Hegel's, and to understand Hegel's one must go back to the roots of western culture in ancient Greek thought.

Derived from the Greek verb meaning "to converse (or discourse)" Aristotle (384–322 BC) credited Zeno of Elea (464 BC) with the invention of the term dialectic, in his famous paradoxes (e.g. of motion) which were designed to refute his antagonists' hypotheses by drawing intuitively unacceptable conclusions from them. But the term was first generally applied to Socrates' mode of argument, or *elenchus*, which was differentiated from the Sophistic *eristic*, or art of disputation for the sake of rhetorical success, by the orientation of the Socratic dialogue towards the disinterested pursuit of truth. Plato (429–348 BC) himself regarded dialectic as the supreme philosophic method – the 'coping-stone of the sciences' – using it to designate both the definition of ideas by genus and species (founding logic) and their interconnection in the light of a single principle, the Form of the Good (founding metaphysics). Aristotle's opinion of dialectic was considerably less exalted. For him dialectic was at best a propaedeutic to the syllogistic reasoning expounded in his *Analytics*, in as much as, unlike the latter, it was based on premises which were merely probable, depending upon the agreement of the interlocutors. The sense of conversational interplay, involving the assertion and contradiction of theses, was retained in the practice of medieval disputation; and it was this sense that was probably most familiar to Kant (1724–1804) who also took over the Aristotelian conception of dialectic as relying upon inadequate premises and his dialectical/analytical contrast. For Kant, dialectic was that part of transcendental logic which showed the mutually contradictory or antinomic state in which the intellect fell when not harnessed to the data of experience. This spread of connotations of dialectic includes, then, argument and conflict, disputation, dialogue and exchange, but also enlightenment, demystification and the critique of illusion.

Hegel synthesized this Eleatic idea of dialectic as *reason* with another ancient strand, the Ionian idea of dialectic as *process* in his idea of dialectic as a self-generating, self-differentiating and self-particularizing *process of reason*. The second idea typically assumed a dual form, in an *ascending* dialectic the existence of a high reality (e.g. the Forms or God) was demonstrated; and in a *descending* dialectic its manifestation in the phenomenal world was explained.

Combination of the ascending and descending phases results in a quasi-temporal pattern of original unity, loss or division and return or reunification (graphically portrayed in Schiller's influential *Letters on the aesthetic education of mankind* (1794–5)) or a quasi-logical pattern of hypostasis and actualization. Combination of the Eleatic and Ionian strands yields the Hegelian Absolute – a logical process or *dialectic* which actualizes itself by alienating itself and which restores its self-unity by recognizing this alienation as nothing other than its own free expression or manifestation; and which is recapitulated and completed as the Hegelian System itself.

However, in addition to dialectic as a logical process, there is another inflection of the dialectic in Hegel, in which it is conceived, more narrowly, as the dynamo of this process, the second, essentially negative, moment of "actual thought". Hegel styles this moment as the 'grasping of opposites in their unity or of the positive in the negative' (1969 edn., p.56). Dialectic in this narrower sense is the method which enables the dialectical commentator to observe the process by which categories, notions or forms of consciousness arise out of each other to form ever more inclusive totalities, until the system of categories, notions or forms as a whole is completed. For Hegel truth is the whole and error lies in one-sidedness, incompleteness and abstraction: its symptom is the contradictions it generates and its cure their incorporation into fuller, richer, more concrete and highly mediated conceptual forms. In the course of this process the famous principle of *sublation* is observed: as the dialectic infolds no partial insight is ever lost. In fact the Hegelian dialectic progresses in two basic modes: by bringing out what is implicit, but not explicitly articulated, in some notion; or by repairing some want, lack or inadequacy in it. "Dialectical", in contrast to "reflective" (or analytical), thought grasps conceptual forms in their systematic interconnections, not just their determinate differences and conceives each development as the product of a previous, less developed phase, whose necessary truth or fulfillment it is; so that there is always a tension, latent irony or incipient surprise between any form and what it is in the process of becoming.

Four main issues have dominated intellectual controversy about dialectic in the Marxist idiom: the difference between the

Marxian ("materialist") and Hegelian dialectics; the role of the dialectic within Marx's work, and more broadly in any Marxian social science; the compatibility of dialectics with formal logic, materialism, scientific practice and rationality generally; and the status of Engels's attempt to extend Marx's dialectic from the historical realm to encompass nature and the whole of being generally.

After his brilliant early analyses of its mystified logic and idealist concept of labor in 1843–44, Marx's critique of the Hegelian dialectic became subsumed in the works of 1844–47 under a ferocious polemical assault on speculative philosophy. But from the time of the *Grundrisse* (1857–8) on, a definite positive re-evaluation of the Hegelian dialectic occurs. The extent of this remains a matter of live controversy. But two points seem indisputable: that Marx continued to be critical of the Hegelian dialectic as such and yet believed himself to be working with a dialectic related to the Hegelian one. Thus he writes in the 1873 Afterword to *Capital* vol. I that 'the mystification which the dialectic suffers in Hegel's hands by no means prevents him from being the first to present its general forms of motion in a comprehensive and conscious manner. With him it is standing on its head. It must be inverted to discover the rational kernel within the mystical shell' (Marx 1976, p.103). These two metaphors – of the inversion and the kernel – do seem to indicate that Marx thought it possible to extract part of the Hegelian dialectic without being compromised by Hegel's idealism.

For Marx, following Feuerbach here, infinite mind is nothing but the illusory projection of (alienated) finite beings and nature is transcendentally real. Thus Marx replaces Hegel's immanent spiritual ideology or *Geistodyssey* of infinite, petrified and finite mind (represented by logic, nature and spirit) with a methodological commitment to the empirically controlled investigation of the causal relations within and between historically emergent, developing humanity and irreducibly real, but modifiable nature.

In his later work Marx often uses "dialectical" in close association with, or even just as a synonym for, "scientific". He understood his dialectic as *scientific*, because it set out to explain the contradictions in thought and the crises of socio-economic life in terms of the particular contradictory essential relations generating them; as *historical*, because it was both rooted in, and (conditionally) an agent of, the changes in the very relations and circumstances it described; as *critical*, because it demonstrated the historical conditions of validity and limits of adequacy of the categories, doctrines, practices and forms of life it explained; and as *systematic*, because it sought to trace the various historical tendencies and contradictions of capitalism back to certain structurally constitutive contradictions of its mode of production.

In the relationship between a feature of social life and its systematic misrepresentation (most generally, in IDEOLOGIES), there seems to be a species of contradiction analogous to that between a notion and its dialectical comment in Hegel. And it can be plausibly maintained that such an essence/appearance contradiction is susceptible of a purely analytical description, a possibility that is a condition of *any* human science.

The three most common positions on dialectics are that it is unintelligible nonsense, that it is universally applicable, and that it is applicable to the conceptual and/or social, but not the natural, domains. The second, universalist position must be problematic for a realist committed to the notion of the existence of nature independently of thought and for a materialist committed to the notion of its causal primacy. Yet Engels, underwriting both commitments, nevertheless took dialectic in its essentially Hegelian sense and sought to apply it to being as a whole. According to him, dialectics is 'the science of the general laws of motion and development of nature, human society and thought' (1969 edn., p.169), laws which he identified as (1) the transformation of quantity into quality and vice-versa; (2) the interpenetration of opposites and (3) the negation of the negation. While Marx did not repudiate Engels's cosmology, his critique of political economy neither presupposes nor entails a dialectics of nature, and his critique of a priorism implies the a posteriori and subject-specific character of claims about the existence of dialectical, as other types of processes of reality.

The very supposition of a dialectics of nature has appeared to a line of critics from Lukács to Sartre as categorically mistaken, in as much as it involves anthropomorphically (and hence idealistically) retrojecting onto nature, categories, such as contradiction and negation, which only make sense in the human realm. Such critics do not deny that *natural science*, as part of the socio-historical world, may be dialectical; what is at stake is whether there can be a dialectics of *nature per se*. Obviously there are differences between the natural and social spheres. But are these specific differences more or less important than their generic similarities? In effect the problem of the dialectics of nature reduces to a variant of the general problem of naturalism, with the way it is resolved depending upon whether dialectics is conceived sufficiently broadly and the human world sufficiently naturalistically to make its extension to nature plausible.

Throughout its long and complex history, five basic strands of meaning in dialectic stand out:
(1) *dialectical contradictions*, involving inclusive oppositions or forces of non-independent origins;
(2) *dialectical* or discursive *argumentation*, oriented to the pursuit of groundable ideals;
(3) *dialectical reason* which encompasses a spread of connotations ranging from that imaginative and conceptually flexible thinking which, under the discipline of empirical, logical and contextual constraints, plays such a crucial role in scientific development through enlightenment and demystification to the depth rationality of emancipatory praxes;
(4) *dialectical process*, involving a schema of original unity, historical diremption and eventual return, which is a recurrent and deep-rooted motif in western thought;

(5) *dialectical intelligibility*, comprehending both the teleologically (in Hegel) or causally (in Marx) generated presentation of social and cultural forms (including beliefs) and their explanatory critique. In recent years there has been a tendency to return to the great classics of modern "dialectical theory", Hegel's *Phenomenology of spirit* (1807) and *Science of logic* (1812–16) and Marx's *Grundrisse* (1857–8) and *Capital* vol. I (1867). These will remain permanent resources for psychologists and other social scientists. But their critical assimilation, empirical exploitation and theoretical development have in the past been hindered by the conceptual confusions surrounding dialectics, and the political interest to which these confusions have, regrettably, become attached.   RB

Bibliography

*Bhaskar, R. 1983: *Dialectic, materialism and human emancipation*. London: New Left Books.

Engels, F. 1878 (1969): *Anti-Duhring*. Moscow: Progress Publishers.

Hegel, G.W.F. 1812–16 (1969): *Science of logic*. Trans. A. Miller. London: George Allen and Unwin.

Marx, K. 1867 (1976): *Capital*, vol. I. Trans. B. Fowkes. London: New Left Review/Pelican.

—— and Engels, F. (1975): *Selected correspondence*. Moscow: Progress Publishers.

discrimination: social psychology

Any behavior which implies the acceptance or rejection of another person solely on the basis of that person's membership of a particular group. In general, discrimination is seen as related to (racial, ethnic or other group) prejudice, which consists of unjustified evaluative judgments based solely on another person's group membership. Discrimination and prejudice can to some extent be explained by historically developed socio-economic conditions which may lead to competitive relations between social groups, and by psychodynamic processes which are perhaps characteristic of certain types of people (AUTHORITARIAN PERSONALITY). Recent research by Tajfel (1982) and his colleagues (see PREJUDICE) has shown that the cognitive process of categorization *per se* may already play an important role in discriminating against members of other social groups.   JMFJ

Bibliography

Tajfel, H. 1982: Social psychology of intergroup relations. *Annual review of psychology* 33, 1–39.

disposition: philosophical usage

The word "disposition" is often used in philosophical writings to cover not only such items as character traits, attitudes and inclinations but also much more broadly to include any sort of tendency, as well as such things as abilities and capacities. The principal difference between the concept of a tendency and that of an ability is that the latter is intimately connected with the idea of an aim. I may have the ability to run a marathon in that if I made the attempt I would last the course, but if nothing would induce me to try I could not be said to have any tendency or inclination to do so.

Statements ascribing dispositions have been analysed, broadly speaking, in two ways. According to Ryle (1949, ch. 5) they are purely hypothetical and say merely how something does, or would, behave in certain circumstances, or what somebody would succeed in doing if he made the right sort of attempt in the right sort of circumstances. On this view a disposition is to be contrasted with what may be called an "occurrent state" like being of a certain shape or molecular structure. Alternatively it may be claimed that a dispositional statement does ascribe an occurrent state but only in an hypothetical manner – to be brittle is to be in some (unspecified) occurrent state which makes the object in question likely to fly into fragments if struck.   JMS

Bibliography

Ryle, G. 1949: *The concept of mind*. London: Hutchinson; Totowa, N. J.: Barnes and Noble (1975).

disposition: psychological usage

Disposition, like temperament, character and constitution, refers to well ingrained personality characteristics or tendencies for the individual to behave in particular ways. Stable and consistent over time and across situations, the dispositional characteristics are viewed as more or less permanent or "given" personality characteristics. These characteristics, if not purely genetically endowed, are considered to be the result of genetic pre-conditions and early learning experiences which combine and interact to provide persistent reaction tendencies. For example, the individual who has an extraverted disposition may behave in a socially outgoing manner in a wide variety of situations and over a long period of time. The personality characteristics comprising extraversion (social facility, talkativeness, interest in social relationships, enthusiasm, etc.) appear to be more or less permanent aspects of the individual's personality makeup. Research has suggested that extraversion may have high genetic heritability. Recently, in the critical discussion of "trait" theories, it has been suggested that apparently stable dispositions are ephemeral effects of placing a person in one kind of situation, rather than another. In the latter different dispositions would be manifested (see TRAITS; PERSON/SITUATION CONTROVERSY). The word disposition is also used especially in ATTRIBUTION THEORY, to mean any characteristic or inclination of a person however fleeting. In this usage "dispositions" are seen as possible causes of behavior and are contrasted with other possible causes which lie outside the person ("situational" factors).   JNB/RL

dogmatism

dogmatism A somewhat unfashionable term, related to the idea of closed-mindedness or the inability to form new cognitive systems of various kinds (perceptual, conceptual etc.). (See COGNITIVE PERSONALITY THEORY.)

Closed-mindedness or dogmatism is characterized by total rejection of opposing beliefs, a relatively poorly interconnected belief system and greater complexity of cognition about objects, people and groups which are positively evaluated compared to those which are negatively evaluated. The more dogmatic a person is, the more his or her cognitions are also said to depend on irrelevant desires and external authority.

Authoritarians are said to exhibit high amounts of dogmatism. They appear to have rigid and inflexible styles of thought and problem-solving abilities; to have low tolerance for ambiguity; to be highly susceptible to social influence, and to be highly conventional. To quote Eckhardt and Newcombe (1969):

> Both authoritarianism and dogmatism were negatively correlated with intellectual conviction and with education, so that the authoritarian, dogmatic, militarist is anti-intellectual. He already "knows" all that he wants to know. Knowledge is a threat to his ego-defensive orientation, and is, therefore, rejected. What he claims to be "knowledge" is actually a faith, so that the essence of dogmatism is a basic confusion between "faith and knowledge".

(See also PREJUDICE).   AF

Bibliography

Eckhardt, W. and Newcombe, A. 1969: Militarism, personality and other social attitudes. *Journal of conflict resolution* 13, 210–19.

Rokeach, M. 1960: *The open and closed mind*. New York: Basic Books.

Durkheim, Émile (1858–1917) A French sociologist who was, with WEBER, the dominant influence on modern sociological thought. Durkheim was born in Épinal, near Strasbourg. His father was a rabbi, and although Durkheim was an agnostic in adult life, he remained fascinated by religion. He was educated at École Normale Supérieure, after which he taught in lycées while working on his theses. One of these was about Montesquieu; the other became his first major book, on the division of labor (1893, 1933). In 1885–6 Durkheim spent a year in Germany. He was attracted by the ideas of WUNDT, and was probably influenced by the latter's interest in moral behavior and the possibility of studying morality in a scientific manner. In 1887 he moved to Bordeaux University, where he became a full professor in 1896. In 1898 he founded *L'Année Sociologique*, which became a major

medium for the transmission of his ideas. In 1902 he joined the University of Paris, becoming full professor (in education) in 1906.

From the time Durkheim conceived the theme of *The division of labor in society*, he was preoccupied with 'the relation of the individual to social solidarity'. In Durkheim's view however, the relationship is very one-sided. He claimed that, 'society is not a mere sum of individuals; rather the system formed by their association represents a specific reality which has its own characteristics' (1895, 1938). Furthermore this reality exists 'prior to the individual', and not only influences the individual but, as Lukes (1973) puts it, 'largely constitutes' what the individual is. The primacy of society over its members and the ways in which it guides and controls their actions and their thoughts, even while they may remain unaware of this remained his theme throughout his career. Because society determines what the individual does and is, we must look at society for an understanding of much individual behavior rather than looking at individual behavior for an understanding of society. This point is summed up in a much-quoted passage from a review he wrote of Labriola (1897): 'I consider extremely fruitful this idea that the social life should be explained, not by the notions of those who participate in it, but by more profound causes which are unperceived by consciousness, and I think also that these causes are to be sought mainly in the manner according to which the associated individuals are grouped'.

This stress on society at the expense of the individual was partly a reaction against the methodological individualism of Utilitarian theories of social and economic activity which derived from the ideas of Mill. They explained social developments by reference to individual behavior which was motivated by the self-interested search for satisfaction. Durkheim in contrast argued that individualistic ideas are based on moral assumptions which arise when society is in a particular state of development. Part of Durkheim's motive in insisting on the clear primacy of society may also have been his desire to establish an academic discipline of sociology, which would be distinct from individual psychology and have its own subject matter.

Durkheim was initially influenced by Spencer, who was the most prominent social theorist in the late nineteenth century. This is clear in *The division of labor*. Spencer used functional analogies between processes of organisms and societies, and put forward an evolutionary typology of societies in which more advanced societies display greater complexity of structure which involves greater differentiation among their parts. This leads to greater integration and interdependence among the parts. Spencer held that sociology should analyze the structure of societies to show how the different parts contribute to the whole. Durkheim (1893) presented a similar model of social evolution. At this stage Durkheim saw the primary sources of change in social structure as material. The increase of population leads to greater rivalry for resources and this leads to the breakdown of constraints present in a simple society; Durkheim called this "mechanical solidarity". Increased competition is reduced by specialization of labor which makes people dependent on each other. This leads to a morality of mutual obligation in which individual differences are recognized (because of different social functions). This transition produces a society which has "organic solidarity", on the Spencerian analogy of a complex organism with highly differentiated and interdependent parts. (Durkheim's use of "mechanical" and "organic" provides an amusing contrast with the more common use of these metaphors in which simple societies are "organic" and "natural", while complex societies are "mechanical" cf. Tönnies, *Gemeinschaft und Gesellschaft.*) The important point of Durkheim's analysis here is that ideas are the result of changes in social organizations which are themselves not the result of material ("morphological") changes. Such an analysis is not, of course, very different from Marxist conceptions of the economic forces at work in society which produce both the material conditions of life and the ideologies which govern men's thinking.

Durkheim, however, was concerned with the "social solidarity" and the beliefs and institutions which maintain it in different types of society. He made use of the concept of *conscience collective*, which he defined as 'the set of beliefs and sentiments common to the average members of a given society (which) forms a determinate system that has its own life.' The word "*conscience*" in French means both "conscience" and "consciousness", and this allows its contents to be both moral and non-moral beliefs. The *conscience collective*, is said to be independent of individuals since 'they pass on and it remains', but, on the other hand 'it can only be realized through individuals'. He was accused of suggesting that society has its own group mind (see, for example, Catlin's introduction to the English translation of *The rules of sociological method*, 1938). He always denied this, but in later work he made much less use of the concept of *conscience collective*, using instead the phrase *représentations collectives*, which may be understood as various kinds of mental contents of the hypothetical *conscience collective*. Such contents may be modes of thinking as well as what is thought. They may clearly have an existence which is not dependent on any living individual, or indeed all living individuals, since they existed before the individuals and may still exist when all contemporary individuals are dead.

For Durkheim the moral conscience aspect of *conscience collective* is very important, and it comes close at times to meaning a shared moral and religious consensus. This is why he could apparently suppose (1893) that its role in maintaining social solidarity might be replaced by the contractual commitments of a heterogeneous society. He later abandoned this idea.

In *The rules of sociological method* (1895, 1938), Durkheim attempted to clarify the subject matter of sociology, and the nature of society's independence from and influence upon its members. He suggested that "social facts" (*faits sociaux*) are sociology's subject. They exist outside individuals and should be considered as objective "things" (*choses*). Furthermore 'the determining cause of a social fact should be sought among the social facts preceding it and not among the states of the individual consciousness'. They include structural or "morphological" facts, such as the distribution and density of population, the forms of dwellings and the number and nature of channels of communication. This is the material substrate of society which was given a primary role in social evolution in *The division of labor*. Social facts also include INSTITUTIONS such as legal or moral rules, religious dogmas, and financial systems. Finally there are social facts which are not institutionalized, but which 'have both the same objectivity and same ascendancy over the individual'. Among these are "social currents" and "transitory outbreaks" of indignation or of pity in a crowd (see CROWD PSYCHOLOGY). Such facts are 'general throughout the extent of a given society', 'outside individual *consciences*', and 'capable of exercising over the individual exterior constraint'.

The types of constraint Durkheim envisaged are multifarious, and some of them would hardly be considered coercive (see Lukes 1973, p.12). Durkheim includes the "determinate sanction" which attaches to breaking laws, but also the constraints imposed by language which must be followed if one is to be understood, the compulsion of SOCIAL INFLUENCE, the restrictions imposed by the material or technological development of society, and the general beliefs, values and rules of conduct which the individual learns in the course of socialization. All these are aspects of society which make the individual's behavior and thoughts different from what they might have been if he or she had belonged to a different society. In that sense the individual is determined by the society (and not vice versa).

In *Suicide* (1897) Durkheim declared, 'The basic proposition that social facts are objective ... finds a new and especially conclusive proof ... in the statistics of suicide'. This was because rates of suicide and different types of suicide could, according to Durkheim, be explained by reference to social facts which exist apart from the persons who commit suicide or

their feelings and ideas. He defined "suicide" with the minimum references to mental elements commensurate with distinguishing it from accidental death. Suicides were 'all cases of death resulting directly or indirectly from an ... act of the victim himself, which he knows will produce this result'. Given this definition, death in battle may be an example of suicide. Critics have pilloried Durkheim's refusal to distinguish *intending* an effect and *knowing* an effect will follow from a chosen action.

He divided suicide into different types, the causes of which were located in the relationship between the individual and society. Suicide could be occasioned by over-integration, as in *altruistic* suicide or self-sacrifice which occurs when one has an underdeveloped sense of one's individuality. This happens in primitive societies or the army. Under-integration could also be a cause, when there is no meaning in group life and the individual is isolated. Durkheim believed this was responsible for higher suicide rates among Protestants than among Catholics and perhaps for the higher rate among the unmarried. Durkheim called suicide due to under-integration *egoistic*. Suicide could also result from too much or too little *regulation*. When there is too much, one's freedom is curtailed. Suicide in these circumstances (about which Durkheim actually says next to nothing) is *fatalistic*. When there is too little regulation one is in a state of *anomie*.

Anomie is caused by the weakening of accepted norms. There can be economic anomie or domestic, conjugal anomie. Both take acute and chronic forms. In economic disasters people lose their wealth and 'are not adjusted to the condition imposed on them'. Equally, however, in sudden prosperity one also lacks adjustment. One's appetites and desires are heightened. One becomes disoriented and dissatisfied. In contemporary societies, according to Durkheim, there is chronic economic anomie, because "greed" and "thirst for novelty" are endemic. Domestic anomie is caused in men particularly by divorce, although it also has a chronic form in societies where divorce is common due to "weakening of matrimonial regulation" and the consequent fact that a man may not be "content with what he has". Durkheim believed that a certain rate of suicide was normal, but that the rate was (pathologically) high in nineteenth-century Europe, although he did not have adequate evidence of any increase. The cause was the spread of egoism and anomie fostered by the breakdown of mechanical solidarity and the lack of a satisfactory organic solidarity to replace it.

Durkheim's arguments appear very weak. As Lukes (1973) says, Durkheim was 'by implication proposing a social-psychological theory' that 'only in certain social conditions ... can the individual achieve psychological ... health and equilibrium'. Durkheim wanted to distinguish normal from pathological states of society, and in *The rules* defined "normal" as what is average for a given type of society at a particular stage of development. On this definition the widespread anomie, egoism (and, supposedly, suicide) of nineteenth-century Europe are normal, and therefore, presumably, healthy. Indeed Durkheim actually says that the anomic 'passion for the infinite is daily presented as a mark of moral distinction', which implies that it is valued in the *représentations collectives*. Anomie and egoism might be regarded as pathological because they cause suicide. But it is simply an assertion that any particular rate of suicide is pathological. Or they might be pathological because they do not produce (a particular form of) social solidarity. Again it seems simply an assertion that (one form of) solidarity is normal and other social arrangements are pathological. There are other problems, such as the doubt cast upon the whole enterprise by the possibility that different cultural values may make a verdict of suicide more likely in one society than another (see Douglas 1967; and ETHNOMETHODOLOGY). Nevertheless the book is regarded as a classic, both on suicide and as an example of sociological analysis.

In his later works *Primitive classification* (1903, 1963; with Mauss) and *The elementary forms of the religious life* (1912,

1915) Durkheim turned his attention to "primitive" societies to show that social, and particularly religious organization give rise to the basic categories of thought, viz. 'ideas of time, space, class, number, cause, substance, personality etc.' These categories are 'at the roots of all judgements' and 'dominate all our intellectual life'. Kant proposed that we cannot help but comprehend the world in terms of such basic categories. Now Durkheim proposed that such categories derive from our culture. Because they are the basis of all comprehension, this is clearly the ultimate social constraint. There is however a change in this from the materialist arguments of *The division of labor* where material conditions gave rise to collective representations. In *The elementary forms* Durkheim says that 'the world of representations in which social life passes is superimposed upon its material substratum, far from arising from it'. Durkheim used evidence from accounts of totemism in Australia and North America. He assumed that the totem system always mirrors a clan system and explained the function of religious beliefs and rights as bolstering the social order. He has been extensively criticized by anthropologists because the facts of totemism do not bear out his thesis, because the distinction he made between the "sacred" and the "profane" 'as two worlds between which there is nothing in common' does not appear in all societies (Evans-Pritchard 1965), or again on the grounds that religious belief is frequently socially divisive. On the other hand this book was praised by Gellner (1970) for its attempt, in anticipating Wittgenstein, to demonstrate that 'concepts, as opposed to sensations, are only possible in a social context'.

Altogether Durkheim has been the frequent butt of attacks, for instance as the founder of FUNCTIONALISM, or because of his deification of society or his commitment to social order (which brands him as highly conservative), because of the weakness or circularity of his reasoning (see Lukes 1973, *passim*), or his high-handed way with evidence (see Evans-Pritchard op. cit.). Some of these attacks are clearly groundless, although the methodological ones are not. He was not, for example, conservative. He believed that society must change and the changes he would have liked were those advocated by socialists, such as equality of opportunity and abolition of inheritance (1893, 1933). The functionalism generally attacked is the brainchild of Radcliffe-Brown and Parsons. Durkheim believed, 'When . . . the explanation of a social phenomenon is undertaken, we must seek separately the efficient cause which produces it and the function it fulfils' (1895, 1938). He and the writers on the *Année sociologique* were constantly concerned to explain social facts initially in historical, causal terms, whereas "structural-functionalist" explanations have been largely ahistorical (and circular).

The acrimony aimed at Durkheim testifies to his influence, which has been greater than that of any other twentieth-century social thinker (with the possible exception of FREUD). The most obvious early influence was on anthropology through Radcliffe-Brown, who in turn influenced American sociology. This influence has continued in work quite unlike Durkheim's. For instance Parson's (1949) ideas about the functions of professional etiquette can be seen as a direct precursor of GOFFMAN's work. Goffman acknowledges Durkheim's influence on his conception of *interaction ritual* and its role in expressing and defining society's moral order. Durkheim's concept of anomie was taken up by Merton who used it in a somewhat different sense to explain deviance in obtaining goods when no legitimate means are available. Durkheim's idea that 'We do not reprove (an act) because it is a crime, but it is a crime because we reprove it' (1893, 1933) is an ancestor of LABELING THEORY. His claim that culture provides one's basic cognitive tools clearly influenced Malinowski's ideas which have fuelled innumerable debates on the possibility of cross-cultural comparison and comprehension (see EMIC VS. ETIC). It is also kept alive in the continuing debate about the restrictions imposed on one by the categories embodied in one's language (see Kay and Kempton 1984).

It is, however, in French thought that his most striking influence has been felt. The historians Bloch and Febvre who founded the journal *Annales* in 1929 were profoundly influenced by Durkheim and *L'Année sociologique*. The work of the "Annales school" of historians such as Braudel and LeRoy Ladurie is now renowned for its treatment of social facts and its attempt to demonstrate the interconnections between the material substructure of societies and the beliefs and activities of their members. This, of course, is Durkheimian history. Finally Durkheim stands squarely behind modern STRUCTURALISM. Lévi-Strauss explicitly acknowledges Durkheim's suggestion (in the preface to *The rules*. 2nd edn., 1901) that 'Myths, popular legends, religious conceptions of all sorts, moral beliefs, etc. reflect a reality different from the individual's reality. We need to investigate . . . the manner in which (these) social representations adhere to and repel one another . . .' This is like a manifesto for much of Lévi-Strauss's own work, in which he also employs binary oppositions (as between the "raw" and the "cooked") like Durkheim's between the sacred and the profane. Furthermore Durkheim's belief that language 'functions independently of my use of it' and his entire conception of social facts constraining and determining the individual's behavior lie behind the structuralist ideas of Derrida and Barthes about language and literary texts.

Durkheim's main works were: *The division of labor in society*. Trans. G. Simpson. New York: Macmillan, 1933. (*De la division du travail social: étude sur l'organisation des sociétés supérieures*. Paris: Alcan, 1893); *The rules of sociological method*. Trans. S.A. Solovay and J.H. Mueller. Chicago: University of Chicago Press, 1938. (*Les règles de la méthode sociologique*. Paris: Alcan, 1895); *Suicide: a study in sociology*. Trans. J.A. Spaulding and G. Simpson. Glencoe, Ill.: Free Press, 1951; London: Routledge and Paul, 1952. (*Le suicide: étude de sociologie*. Paris: Alcan, 1897); *The elementary forms of the religious life: a study in religious sociology*. Trans. J.W. Swain. London: Allen and Unwin; New York: Macmillan, 1915. (*Les formes élémentaires de la via religieuse: le système totémique en Australie.* Paris: Alcan, 1912); Durkheim, E. and Mauss, M. 1903: De quelques formes primitives de classification: contribution a l'étude des représentations collectives. *L'Année sociologique* 6, 1–72. (*Primitive classification.* Trans. R. Needham. London: Cohen and West; Chicago: University of Chicago Press, 1963).

A selection appears in:
*Giddens, A. 1972: *Emile Durkheim: selected writings.* Cambridge: Cambridge University Press.

Good secondary sources in English are: Giddens, A. 1978: *Durkheim.* London: Fontana; *Lukes, S. 1973: *Emile Durk-*heim: his life and work.* London: Allen Lane; Nisbet, R. 1975: *The sociology of Emile Durkheim.* London: Heinemann.   RL

Bibliography

Douglas, J.D. 1967: *The social meanings of suicide.* Princeton: Princeton University Press.

Evans-Pritchard, E.E. 1965: *Theories of primitive religion.* Oxford: Oxford University Press.

Gellner, E. 1970: Concepts and society. In *Rationality*, ed. B.R. Wilson. Oxford: Blackwell.

Kay, P. and Kempton, W. 1984: What is the Sapir-Whorf hypothesis? *American anthropologist* 86, 65–79.

Parsons, T. 1949: *Essays in sociological theory.* Glencoe, Ill.: Free Press.

E

ego ideal Term in PSYCHOANALYTICAL PER-
SONALITY THEORY for the ideal standard
against which the ego evaluates its activity
and qualities. Hence FREUD at one time gave
it a role in dream-censorship, but for the
most part he drops the term once he has
attributed its function to the positive aspect
of the SUPEREGO (Freud 1923, esp. pp.
9–11). The young child sets up this psychic
standard as part of that internalization of
(or IDENTIFICATION with) parental values and
controls which allows it to resolve the
OEDIPUS AND ELEKTRA COMPLEXES. As such, it
is "the expression of the admiration for the
perfection" which the child then attributes
to its parents, as opposed to representing
their forbidding and punitive aspect which
the superego also embodies. Elsewhere the
term is used, even by Freud, synonymously
with "superego".   NMC

Bibliography

Freud, Sigmund 1923: The ego and the id.
*Standard edition of the complete psychological works
of Sigmund Freud*, vol. 19. London: Hogarth
Press; New York: Norton.

ego: philosophical usage The word
"ego" is the Latin equivalent of the English
"I", but is used technically as a common
noun rather than as a pronoun. The most
common use is as the name of a putative
substantial self distinct from the body. The
most famous development of such a use is
to be found in Kant's doctrine of the
transcendental ego; in this theory there is
no phenomenal entity, the ego or self, open
to observation or introspection, but the
existence of such an ego must be allowed if
we are to explain mental phenomena and in
particular the unity of the self. It is the
transcendental ego which imposes the
categories on phenomena.   JOU

Bibliography

Kant, I. 1781, 1787 (1929): *Critique of pure
reason*. Trans. N. Kemp Smith. London:
Macmillan.

ego: psychological usage Although
the word has a philosophical history in
English as denoting the essential "self" or
seat of identity (see EGO: PHILOSOPHICAL
USAGE), in psychology, it has come to mean
the system of rational and realistic functions of the personality. This usage is
largely influenced by PSYCHOANALYTICAL
PERSONALITY THEORY, in which the word ego
is a translation of Freud's *Ich* (1923), where
it is contrasted with the instinctually impulsive ID, and with the evaluative SUPEREGO;
but it is not equated with consciousness,
since Freud argued that much of it would
have to be unconscious or "preconscious".
Its function in that theory leads to opera-
tionally definable concepts such as "ego-
strength" and "ego-control", whose
development in childhood and efficacy in
maturity can be assessed by means
independent of psychoanalysis (Cattell
1965, ch. 3). Those theorists who give
greater weight to ego-processes (such as
reality-perception, conscious learning and
voluntary control) in their accounts of
personality development and in techniques
of psychotherapy are known as ego-
psychologists (Hartmann 1964). (See also
DEFENSE MECHANISM.)   RMC

Bibliography

Cattell, R.B. 1965: *The scientific analysis of
personality*. Harmondsworth: Penguin.

Freud, S. 1923: The ego and the id. *Standard
edition of the complete psychological works of
Sigmund Freud*, vol. 19. London: Hogarth Press:
New York: Norton.

Hartmann, H. 1964: *Essays in ego-psychology*. London: Hogarth Press.

egocentrism A term first proposed in 1923 by the psychologist Jean Piaget to designate a cognitive state in which the individual comprehends the world only from his own point of view, without awareness of the existence of other possible points of view. Although typical of childish thought, egocentrism can be observed throughout the lifespan. It is a state of mind characterized by failure to differentiate between subjective and objective components of experience, with a consequent unwitting imposition of a personal point of view (see Cox 1980).

A classic example of spatial egocentrism in childhood is Piaget's "three mountains" task. The child of about five years is seated in front of a papier mâché model of three mountains and asked to imagine how the scene would appear to a doll at another position. The child consistently describes his own viewpoint as though it were characteristic of the doll's.

An example of social egocentrism from adulthood might be the case of the teacher with specialized knowledge who fails to take sufficient account of the lesser knowledge of his pupils, with the consequence that they fail to comprehend. This could be considered an example of "egocentric speech", since the teacher intends but fails to communicate.

A similar phenomenon is the "false consensus" or "egocentric attribution" bias (Ross 1977). In various experiments by Ross and his colleagues people were faced with decisions. They were also asked how many other (comparable) people would make the decision they had made. People generally tended to overestimate the number of those who would make the same decision as themselves. Ross suggests this may be explained both by the salience of one's own viewpoint, which obscures alternatives (as with the child's literal viewpoint), and by the fact that a majority of one's acquaintances *are* likely to share one's opinions and make decisions like one's own.   GEB/RL

Bibliography

Cox, Maureen V. 1980: *Are young children egocentric?* London: Batsford; New York: St Martin's Press.

Piaget, Jean 1923: *The language and thought of the child*. 3rd edn., 1959. London: Routledge and Kegan Paul; New York: Humanities Press.

Ross, L. 1977: The intuitive psychologist and his shortcomings: distortions in the attribution process. In *Advances in experimental social psychology*, vol. 10, ed. L. Berkowitz. New York: Academic Press.

emic vs. etic Conceptions derived from the internal logic of a culture are emic; universal conceptions, cutting across cultures, are etic. This distinction was made by Pike (1954) in discussing phon*emics* vs. phon*etics*. To illustrate this emic polarity the Greek concept of *philotimia* is central to the functioning of Greek culture (Triandis 1972). It refers to a person behaving according to the norms of the ingroup – usually family and close friends. A person who is *philotimos* is highly valued; one who is *aphilotimos* is despised. People in traditional Greek culture use the word *philotimos* more often than any other to describe themselves. It is a concept that is very useful in explaining Greek culture and cannot be fully translated because of the many spontaneous associations that Greeks have with this concept.

An example of an etic concept is *social structure*. All groups have structure. That is, people communicate with others, value others, like others, respect others, avoid others, and so on in a patterned way. Sociometric studies show that some persons are over-chosen and others are under-chosen. This occurs in all cultures. Thus social structure is a concept that does not depend on a particular culture but is a universal. In cross-cultural studies researchers attempt to use emic concepts but relate them to etic constructs. By using emic concepts it is believed that one can capture some of the essence or idiosyncratic reality of a culture; by using etic constructs one attempts to communicate this information to persons outside the culture.   HCT

Bibliography

Brislin, R.W. 1983: Cross-cultural research in psychology. *Annual review of psychology* 34, 363–400.

Pike, K.L. 1954: *Language in relation to a unified theory of the structure of human behavior.* Glendale, Calif.: Summer Institute of Linguistics.

Triandis, H.C. 1972: *The analysis of subjective culture.* New York: Wiley.

emotion and self These are intimately linked, although the nature of the self that influences emotionality changes dramatically with development. Young infants' selves are *biological, reactive,* and inaccessible to babies' awareness. Adults' selves are highly complex; they have been evaluated and modified by the individuals and others throughout individuals' lives.

The self influences both the *elicitation* and the *expression* of emotion. Emotions are initiated by an "appraisal" process, wherein events are related to the self. Appraisal may occur at an extremely low, reflexive level (e.g. a neonate, because of biological endowment, reacts with disgust when a foul-tasting liquid is placed in its mouth), or at a highly sophisticated level (e.g. an adult is ashamed at having made a naive remark, since this is contrary to his or her self-concept). Emotions such as shame and guilt may depend on the existence of a self-concept and appear later in development than disgust or fear.

Older children or adults' selves influence their *expression* of emotion as well; expression of certain emotions may be either congruent or incongruent with a person's self-concepts (e.g. a man who is afraid may hide his fear if fearfulness is contrary to his self-image). For a discussion of this see Baumeister 1982.   JJCa/KSA

Bibliography

Arnold, M., ed. 1970: *Feelings and emotions: The Loyola symposium.* New York: Academic Press.

Baumeister, R.F. 1982: The self-presentational view of social phenomena. *Psychological bulletin* 91, 3–26.

Campos, J. et al. 1983: Socioemotional development. In *Carmichael's manual of child psychology: Infancy and developmental psychobiology,* eds. M. Haith and J. Campos. New York: Wiley.

Harter, S. 1982: Developmental perspectives on the self-system. In *Carmichael's manual of child psychology: Social and personality development,* ed. M. Hetherington. New York: Wiley.

emotion and social behavior Confronted by an armed robber one is understandably afraid. It is not so much the gun as the presumed intentions of the robber that provoke the emotion. It is an emotion at least partly caused by another person and to that extent social. But fear can be provoked by circumstances not at all social. A mountain climber can fear a rock slide. Other emotions, such as anger, greed, shame, guilt, envy, are social in that they involve social norms, i.e. shared expectations about appropriate conduct (Averill 1980). For instance: what makes pangs of acquisitiveness greed is not their intensity, nor the number of things the pangs stimulate one to acquire. Greed has to do with wanting more than one's due; "coveting" one's own goods is not greed. Any emotion might involve social standards – one might fear being ostracized because one hasn't lived up to them, or sorrow over their decline – but sorrow and fear can be felt over objects unconnected to standards. Some emotions are social in a strong sense: they require standards and their appraisal to be intelligible.

The idea that some emotions require an understanding of standards is new to the discipline of psychology, though Aristotle had a normative account of anger: anger is a perception of transgression wedded to an impulse toward revenge; transgression and revenge entail moral standards. Let us trace psychology's path away from standards and back again, beginning with Descartes.

In psychology's (and the British empiricists') version of Descartes's scheme, emotions are events (mental or behavioral) having causes and effects. William James, for example, analyzed emotions as effects stirred up by perceptions, not as patterns of behaving and thinking intrinsically involving appraisal.

Our natural way of thinking about these standard emotions is that the mental perception of some fact excites the mental affection called the emotion, and that this latter state of mind gives rise to the bodily expression. My thesis on the contrary is that *the bodily changes follow directly the perception of the exciting fact, and that our feeling of the same changes as they occur is the emotion* . . . We feel sorry because we cry, angry because we strike, afraid because we tremble . . . (1884 (*1968*), p.18).

James illustrates his thesis: 'If we abruptly see a dark moving form in the woods, our heart stops beating, and we catch our breath instantly and before any articulate idea of danger can arise' (ibid. p.26). But why should this perception provoke trembling unless we appraise the form as dangerous? James invokes instincts: 'In advance of all experience of elephants no child can but be frightened if he suddenly finds one trumpeting and charging upon him. No woman can see a handsome little naked baby without delight . . .' (ibid. p.20).

James realized that a nativist account makes more sense for fear of elephants than fear of a stock-market crash, so he added that once the neural pathways for fear of trumpeting elephants have been exercised, they can be pressed in to the service of stock-market dread: 'A nervous tendency to discharge being once there, all sorts of unforseen things may pull the trigger and let loose the effect' (ibid. p.24). On James's account, then, the various emotions are the experience of the effects of innate patterns of neural discharge. The provocative conditions just set them off. But not all psychologists were so beguiled.

Consider Titchener's discussion of anger (1897): 'It contains, for example, the idea of the person with whom one is angry; the idea of the act of his, at which one is displeased; the idea of retaliatory action on one's own part; a mass of bodily sensations, attending the flushing of one's face, the tendency to clench the fist . . .' (p.13). Maranon (1924) (see Mandler 1979) tried to decide between James and Titchener. According to James if a person experiences the physical state characteristic of an

emotion he or she will experience that emotion. The experimental trick is to put people in the bodily state without the context appropriate to the emotion. But to do this one has to specify the bodily state characteristic of a particular emotion. James did not consistently commit himself to any particular state for any particular emotion, but the tradition fastened on physiological arousal. Arousal of the sympathetic nervous system (producing trembling, blanching, sweating, etc.) was the plausible candidate for anger or fear. So Maranon injected subjects with epinephrine (adrenaline) which mimics arousal of the sympathetic nervous system, and asked them to report their experiences. The results supported Titchener. About two-thirds of the subjects reported no emotion – merely physiological symptoms. Most of the rest reported "as if" emotions, e.g. they said they felt as if they were afraid, but they weren't afraid. Sympathetic activity was not sufficient to produce emotion. Schachter and Singer (1962), in a famous, controversial experiment, sought to extend this account by showing that what sympathetic arousal lacked was the person's appraisal of the situation.

Schachter and Singer's results supported, although not strongly, the Titchnerian position. Although the replicability of the Schachter and Singer study is controversial, Zillman, in a series of studies, provided further indirect support of their position (Zillman 1979). The experimental evidence, then, is not compelling, but generally points toward a contextual account. But the view that appraisals are part of emotion has also been affected by current philosophy in the spirit of the later Wittgenstein, Ryle or Austin.

Kenny (1963), for example, argued that appraisals are part of our concept of, say, anger. While a person could be angry without perceiving a transgression, transgression is nonetheless implicated in anger. Consider this example: though we can imagine a car without an engine, the concept "car" nonetheless involves the notion of being self-propelled. In parallel, although we can understand a particular case of being angry without perceiving (or fancying) a transgression, still what defines anger is (at least in some cases) the perception of transgression. Still, all of this only shows that appraisals are central, not that social norms are essential. We must show that accounts of particular emotions divorced from social norms do not do their job. Psychology has provided a nice example of this failure.

Behaviorists analyzed anger (which they called aggression, see Sabini and Silver 1982) as a response always and only produced by frustration (frustration, they allowed, was being blocked on the way to a goal). But Pastore (1952) pointed out that whether a frustration was justified or not determined whether it produced anger. For example, after you have waited for hours on a wintry street corner a friend finally arrives with his apology: contrast (A) "Sorry I'm late, I couldn't tear myself away from the television" with (B) "I'm sorry, my brother just died and I have been wandering the streets". A and B are equally "frustrating" but it would be surprising if A did not cause anger or if B did. The appraisal in anger is not "being frustrated", but, as Aristotle argued, being transgressed against. To understand what is and is not a transgression, what will or will not provoke anger one has to understand the "form of life" using accusations, justifications, excuses, mitigations, exacerbations (see Averill 1978, 1980).

Envy also involves shared standards. Silver and Sabini argued that envy involves a transgression: perceiving oneself as demeaned by another's accomplishment (or worth), and, because of that, attempting (or wanting) to undercut the other person or his or her accomplishment. Of course attacking someone or his or her "accomplishments" is not necessarily a transgression. If there is truth in the attack then saying it (or wanting to say it) isn't envy but righteous indignation (see Sabini and Silver 1982). Anger and envy are social emotions in the strong sense of entailing shared social standards. Embarrassment too is a social emotion, a curious one.

The curious aspect of embarrassment is the sort of appraisal it involves. For example: you are giving a lecture; as the students begin to nod off you recognize what a miserable job you are doing. The job is so bad that you are embarrassed on seeing your students the next day. What is the appraisal here? Modigliani (1968) argues that we are embarrassed when we perceive others as perceiving us as inadequate. This also seems to explain why embarrassment is so unpleasant: it is connected to a diminution of our sense of self-worth. But suppose the lecturer knows that he or she is a good lecturer, and that the poor performance was a consequence of loss of the lecture notes and has little to do with lecturing abilities. There is no reason then to feel demeaned. But Modigliani's data (and everyday reflection) suggest that people do become embarrassed though they know that they are not at fault.

GOFFMAN has a different approach which avoids this problem. Goffman (1967) argues that what produces embarrassment is the recognition that the self a person is sustaining in a social interaction has been upset by something he or she has done or some personal fact that has slipped out. This account avoids the difficulty but at a cost. The difficulty is avoided because what the lecturer knows about himself or herself is irrelevant to the embarrassment. The issue is whether the poor lecture upsets the consensus between lecturer and students that he or she is an adequate lecturer. This account has several virtues. For one, the appraisal involved need not be distorted. For another it can handle "positive embarrassment", e.g. the embarrassment felt on being congratulated; the pauper discovered to be a prince is embarrassed but so is the prince discovered to be a pauper. It just happens that paupers are more motivated to pretend to be princes than vice-versa. But this account cannot explain why finding one's projected self contradicted is so painful. Goffman would answer that conflicts in SELF-PRESENTATION upset interactions. Interacting with other people is predicated on knowing how to treat them, and this requires a consensus on who they are. The power of embarrassment derives from the importance of social interactions. But, while some interactions are important, and surely the ability to have interactions is important, this does not quite explain why every social interaction should be loaded with the potential to produce embarrassment. This issue is unsettled.

This article has summarized ways in which several emotions involve social norms. Not all emotions do. Further work will, no doubt, expand the list of social emotions and the ways assessments enter them.   MS/JS

Bibliography

Averill, J. 1978: Anger. *Nebraska symposium on motivation*. Lincoln: University of Nebraska Press.

—— 1980: A constructivist view of emotion. In *Emotion: theory, research, and experience*, eds. R. Plutchik and H. Kellerman. New York: Academic Press.

Goffman, E. 1967: *Interaction ritual*. New York: Anchor.

James, W. 1884 (1968): What is an emotion? Reprinted in *The nature of emotion*, ed. M. Arnold. London: Penguin.

Kenny, A. 1963: *Action, emotion and will*. New York: Humanities Press.

Mandler, G. 1979: Emotion. In *The first century of experimental psychology*, ed. E. Herst. Hillsdale, N.J.: LEA.

Modigliani, A. 1968: Embarrassment and embarrassability. *Sociometry* 31 (3), 313–26.

Pastore, N. 1952: The role of arbitrariness in the frustration aggression hypothesis. *Journal of abnormal and social psychology*. 47, 728–31.

Sabini, J. and Silver, M. 1982: *Moralities of everyday life*. New York: Oxford University Press.

Schachter, S. and Singer, J. 1962: Cognitive, social and physiological determinants of emotional state. *Psychological review* 69, 379–99.

Titchener, E. 1897: *An outline of psychology*. New York: Macmillan.

Zillmann, D. 1979: *Hostility and aggression*. Hillsdale, N.J.: LEA.

emotional roles in groups

The idea that two behavioral patterns or roles will become differentiated in every group. The instrumental or task role is directed towards the accomplishment of specific tasks or goals; to that extent, attention will be given to emotion only in an effort to minimize emotional involvement and expression. In contrast, the expressive or socioemotional role is focused upon emotion. The concern is to ensure positive emotional experiences and to enhance the relationships between group members.

The differentiation of these roles is presumed to derive from the necessity for all groups to manage two basic problems: coping with externally imposed demands upon the group; and maintaining the internal integrity of the group by fulfilling the social-psychological requirements of its members. It was initially proposed that because the requirements of the two roles may be incompatible, the same person could not enact both roles in a particular group. Further, it was suggested that the Instrumental role is more likely to be taken by males and the expressive role by females, particularly within family groups. But these assumptions may not be warranted, depending upon such factors as the size and composition of the group, the kind of tasks involved and the group's orientation towards the task.   LAW

Bibliography

Bales, R.F. and Slater, P.E. 1955: Role differentiation in small groups. In *The family: socialization and interaction process*, eds. T. Parsons and R.F. Bales. Glencoe: Ill.: Free Press.

empathy

The understanding and sharing of another person's emotional experience in a particular situation. In the early nineteenth century Lipps described empathy (an English rendering of the German *Einfühlung*) as a process of "feeling into" the emotions expressed in the movements or dynamic postures of people, aesthetic objects or natural scenes. The spontaneous imitation of these cues produces kinesthetic sensations associated with corresponding emotions. The alternative theory of representation emphasized the need to understand the person's situation intellectually thereby evoking emotional memories previously associated with similar situations. Most disagreement about the definition is centered on whether empathy necessarily involves vicarious experience of an emotional state (see Davies et al. 1983). However it is defined, the distinction between it and sympathy (which may also mean "affected with the same feelings as another") lies in the central, and unclear, criterion of some sort of (temporary) identification with the other (see Hogan 1969).

Empathy requires a receptive set ('taking the role of the other', Mead 1934), an appreciation of the meaning of the emotion-eliciting situation for the person and an accurate interpretation of the person's verbal and nonverbal behavior. Dymond (1949) created a measure of this kind of empathy; her test required people to make predictions about the feelings, thoughts or behavior of a person they had met briefly. Although she produced some support for the validity of her scale, Lindgren and Robinson (1953) found evidence that it merely picked up the respondents' recognition of cultural STEREOTYPES.

Two other scales for capturing individual differences in empathy are Hogan's (1969) EM scale and Mehrabian and Epstein's (1972) Questionnaire Measure of Emotional Empathy (QMEE). The Hogan scale is designed to pick out those who have 'the knack of "sizing up" social situations and of making sound and dependable evaluations of people'. The QMEE, on the other hand, questions people about their "susceptibility to emotional contagion", "tendency to be moved by others' . . . emotional experiences" and other aspects of "emotional responsiveness".

Chlopan et al. (1985) review evidence which suggests that both scales have adequate validity in distinguishing the helpful from the less generous, and the aggressive or deviant from the less aggressive. Letourneau (1981) found that both scales distinguished child-abusing mothers from others (the EM being better at this). On the other hand, a predictable difference is found between personality characteristics of high scorers on the two scales. Those on the EM are low in anxiety, and well adjusted. Those on the QMEE have high neuroticism scores on various EYSENCK personality questionnaires (e.g.

Rim 1974). The high emotionality of those with QMEE empathy, and the corresponding low emotionality of those with high EM empathy fit the original constructs of the two scales' inventors. They also show that although they have similar predictive validity, the two scales are not capturing the same thing. They may, of course, be thought to be revealing the different facets of empathy outlined and argued over by earlier theorists.

Hoffmann (1976) has studied the development of forms of empathy through childhood, and ROGERS stresses the vital importance of empathy in the therapeutic relationship. Several psychoanalytical writers also discuss the importance of empathy in therapy; Schafer (1959) presents a model of "generative empathy" which represents the ideal, mature forms of empathy the analyst should direct toward his patient. (See Luborsky et al. 1975 for the psychotherapy literature.)   SB/GCC/RL

Bibliography

Chlopan, B.E., McCain, M.L., Carbonell, J.L. and Hagen, R.L. 1985: Empathy: a review of available measures. *Journal of personality and social psychology* 48, 635–53.

Hoffmann, M.L. 1976: Empathy, role-taking, guilt and the development of altruistic motives. In *Moral development and behavior*, ed. T. Lickona. New York: Holt, Rinehart and Winston.

Katz, R.L. 1963: *Empathy*. London: Collier-Macmillan.

Lipps, T. 1965: Empathy and aesthetic pleasure. In *Aesthetic theories: studies in the philosophy of art*, eds. K. Aschenbrenner and A. Isenberg. Englewood Cliffs, N.J.: Prentice-Hall.

Luborsky, L., Singer, B. and Luborsky, L. 1975: Comparative studies of psychotherapies. *Archives of general psychiatry* 32, 995–1008.

Mead, G.H. 1934: *Mind, self and society*. Chicago: University of Chicago Press.

Schafer, Roy 1959: Generative empathy in the treatment situation *Psychoanalytic quarterly* 28, 342–73.

Stotland, E. 1969: Exploratory investigations of empathy. In *Advances in experimental social psychology*, vol. 4, ed. L. Berkowitz. New York: Academic Press.

Other references may be found in Chlopan et al. 1985.

empirical methods in social inquiry Special techniques for the collection and treatment of observational data. Their importance lies in their relation to psychology in its modern phase as a behavioral science. This is because those psychologists who currently think of themselves as research scientists (and it must be remembered that not all professional psychologists would by any means place themselves in that category), claim that it is their use of such methods which makes their form of psychology scientific, and marks it off from other, supposedly non-scientific forms (psychoanalysis being the case typically cited in this respect). Although there is still no widespread agreement as to quite what it is which makes science *science*, whether there are in fact any basic methods at all (see Feyerabend 1975), empirical psychologists nonetheless see what they do as science because they proceed (a) by proposing causal theories from which (b) they derive particular hypotheses, which (c) they then test, not actually against experience, but by reference to publicly observable events – in short, because they use a version of the *hypothetico-deductive method*. It is, however, a specialized version of that method. For while empiricism as a philosophy only demands of our general theories that all their verifiable consequences are such as experience will confirm, psychologists feel that only data available to third person external observers are adequate for their purposes as behavioral scientists.

This methodological shift – a shift from a concern with experience in general (both "inner" and "outer") to its specialization solely in external observation – occurred after the débâcle of introspectionism. Under Watson's (1930) influence, psychology changed from being "the Science of Mental Life" to being the science of behavior. So, while it is currently entering a cognitive phase and is now concerned with the function and structure of mental states, it still remains behaviorist in the sense of drawing all its relevant data from external observation, by use of one kind of empirical method or another.

Broadly speaking such methods may be divided into two main types: experimental and observational. In an experiment, psychologists attempt to isolate and identify the separate causal processes or mechanisms thought to underlie observed behavior. They do so by establishing the appropriate initial (controlled or closed) conditions for the alleged mechanisms to make themselves manifest. Typically, experimenters vary these initial conditions (the *independent variables*) and observe regularities in the resulting behavior (the *dependent variables*). As the aim in such a procedure is to study the causes of behavior in themselves, objectively, in isolation from one another, the results ought not to be solely or predominately a function of the investigatory process itself (i.e. artifacts). As Bhaskar (1979, p.12) says, 'What distinguishes the phenomena the scientist *actually* produces out of the totality of the phenomena he *could* produce is that, when his experiment is successful, it is an index of what he does *not* produce.' But, as he goes on to argue, such is the case only under the *closed* conditions of the experiment. In other words, observable regularities occur because scientists have pre-arranged experimental conditions so that, as Bhaskar puts it, the constant conjunction of events obtains. Psychologists may (but only with the tacit agreement or compliance of their subjects) approximate such conditions. But normally the conditions under which psychological and social phenomena actually occur and have their being do not seem to be closed in this sense – far from it. As far as we can tell all such circumstances must be characterized as *open*, in which a large number of causal agents may or may not be active at the same time, and therefore in which no constant conjunctions of events certainly obtain.

Observational methods work within such open systems as given. There is no overt attempt to establish the closed conditions appropriate to experiments. Scientists merely attempt, by a combination of deductive and inductive techniques, to extract regularities from the data they collect in what they would claim to be naturalistic circumstances. Observational studies may be further subdivided into *survey* and *field* studies: in field studies, observers attempt to describe an aspect of behavior in all its different manifestations within a circumscribed sphere of life, e.g. as in a *sociometric* account of friendships among a group of people. In survey studies, a system is studied by observing its response to an input; usually but not always by studying the answers given by a sample group of people to a specially designed QUESTIONNAIRE. By arranging for such answers to be given either in one of a fixed number of categories, or on a five-point (Likert) scale, the objective data collected may be subjected to various statistical procedures, especially those of correlation and factor analysis, to reveal previously unknown relationships. In open systems, however, correlations cannot be taken as directly indicating causal relations. Hence caution is required in interpreting such results.

Questionnaire methods may also be used as tests of one kind or another in the exploration of both individual differences in people's abilities and in their personality characteristics, as well as the attitudes and beliefs of individuals (including their implicit theories of psychology – see ATTRIBUTION THEORY). Such tests have also been employed by cross-cultural psychologists in their field work, in an attempt to place the psychology of those they study in an intelligible relation to the psychology already familiar to them. As such they may be used as an adjunct to ETHNOGRAPHY, which cannot itself, be counted as an empirical method *per se*, for it also makes use of experiences gained from first- and second-person standpoints, as well as prior first-person intuitions. In fact, in this respect, even when it is claimed that "verbal reports" are being observed and studied, all data gathered from interviews and in clinical studies become suspect. It is crucial, if a method is to be truly empirical, that the third-person, external observer point of view is maintained.

Such methods are not without their critics (Orne 1962; Rosenthal 1966; Harré and Secord 1972; McGuire 1973; Gergen 1973; to name but a few). Such methods, critics maintain, distort and limit the normal and open conditions of actual everyday life – the conditions necessary for our very being – and institute in its place another kind of social life. For instance, (a) surveys and questionnaires proscribe the dialogue, the continued exchanges, by which people normally avoid misunderstanding and express subtleties of opinion, attitude and belief to one another; (b) experimental situations meant to be objective contain hidden social factors; or (c) they are all structured by the overriding fact that they are exchanges between anonymous strangers observing one another – and acting under such surveillance produces a certain state of (objective) self-awareness (Duval and Wicklund 1972) inimical to normal, spontaneous behavior. Objections of this kind may be multiplied. All essentially stem from the requirement that psychological data employing empirical methods is acquired, not from experience, but only by external observation.

Another, even more crucial objection is beginning to emerge, one of a seemingly paradoxical kind: in psychology empirical methods do not seem to yield objective facts, i.e. facts not produced by the investigatory process itself. As McGuire (1973, p.449) points out, 'If (an) experiment does not come out "right", then the researcher does not say that the hypothesis is wrong, but rather that something was wrong with the experiment. . . .' And the fact seems to be, owing to the intentional nature of human action, one can always make such a claim. One can always say that what happened was not what was meant or intended to happen. What experiments test, suggests McGuire, is not whether hypotheses are true, but rather whether experimenters are 'sufficiently ingenious stage managers' to demonstrate in the laboratory the effective use of a principle they already know to be true. And there is no escape from this conclusion, for example into *field-experiments*, for there we merely test our abilities as "finders" of natural settings which illustrate principles we also already know to be true.

Clearly, as heirs to the modern philosophy of science (Hanson 1958; Kuhn

1962; Bhaskar 1978), we now realize that what the empirical and behavioral sciences call *data* are not simply given us in the phenomena we study, but are theory-laden, i.e., they only appear to us as the facts they are in terms of a theory constructed by us. Instead of being called data they could more correctly be called *capta* (Laing 1967, pp.52–3). for, rather than their being simply given us by Nature, we in fact *take* them out of a constantly changing flux of events. Hence, we can no longer accept that experiments provide inescapable "findings", for the results obtained depend to an extent upon our own "makings". There is a degree of arbitrary choice open to us in the determination of empirical facts. Is there anywhere else we might turn to for *data* in the sense of indubitable givens? Before embarking upon any psychological research, what we must already know, if we are to be competent members of our society, is not an arbitrary matter of our choice. The general nature of our social being is already determined (Smedslund 1980). On this view, the real *data* of experience, the givens, are what we can render explicit of what intuitively we must already know in our experience as social beings. Only these data, the facts of our mental life as persons in a society, which appear at first sight to be arbitrarily chosen, subjective, and idiosyncratic, seem in the final analysis to be inescapable, and to be the proper "givens" from which to begin.

JDS

Bibliography

Bhaskar, R. 1978: *A realist theory of science*. 2nd edn. Brighton: Harvester Press; Atlantic Highlands, N.J.; Humanities Press.

——— 1979: *The possibility of naturalism*. Brighton: Harvester Press.

Duval, S. and Wicklund. R.V. 1972: *A theory of objective self-awareness*. New York: Academic Press.

Feyerabend, P. 1975: *Against method: outline of an anarchist theory of knowledge*. London: New Left; Atlantic Highlands, N.J.: Humanities Press.

Gergen, K.J. 1973: Social psychology as history. *Journal of personality and social psychology* 26, 309–20.

Hanson, N.R. 1958: *Patterns of discovery*. Cambridge: Cambridge University Press.

Harré, R. and Secord, P.F. 1972: *The explanation of social behaviour*. Oxford: Basil Blackwell.

Kuhn, T.S. 1962: *The structure of scientific revolutions*. Chicago: University of Chicago Press.

Laing, R.D. 1967: *The politics of experience*. London: Penguin: New York: Pantheon.

McGuire, W.J. 1973: The yin and yang of progress in social psychology. *Journal of personality and social psychology* 26, 446–56.

Orne, M.T. 1962: On the social psychology of the psychological experiment: with particular reference to demand characteristics and their implications. *American psychologist* 17, 776–83.

Rosenthal, R. 1966: *Experimenter effects in behavioral research*. New York: Appleton-Century-Crofts.

Smedslund, J. 1980: Analysing the primary code: from empiricism to apriorism. In *The social foundations of language and thought: essays in honor of Jerome S. Bruner*, ed. D.R. Olsen. New York: Norton.

Watson, J.B. 1930: *Behaviorism*. New York: Norton.

enlightenment effects The effects of a given psychological theory on those who come to understand its premises and predictions. The most celebrated form of enlightenment effect is the self-fulfilling prophecy, initially described by Merton, in which a theory's predictions come true because of people's knowledge of the theory. Such effects may be contrasted with suicidal prophecies in which the dissemination of the theory negates its predictions. The potential for such effects has been used by both psychologists and economists to question the cumulativeness of behavioral research. If theories enter into the life of the culture, then it may be more important to ask about the potential effects of the theory than about the validity of its predictions.

KJG

Bibliography

Gergen, K.J. 1982: *Toward transformation in social knowledge*. New York: Springer.

Merton, R.K. 1949: Social theory and social structure. Glencoe, Ill.: Free Press.

environmental psychology The mutual relationship between people and the physical environment. Environmental psychology emerged as a field in the early 1960s, stimulated in part by environmental problems of the period and in part by changing values in traditional psychology which had previously adhered to an analytic, laboratory tradition of research and which had not studied human behavior in relationship to the large-scale physical environment (Craik 1973).

Over the years environmental psychology has since developed in the following ways: (1) *a holistic molar perspective*, in which research examines behavior in context, and attempts to study complex networks of psychological processes and environmental factors; (2) *an applied, problem solving perspective* in which research is simultaneously designed to uncover basic principles of behavior and to contribute to the solution of social problems involving the physical environment in the action research tradition; (3) *a broad and eclectic methodology* that accepts the use of laboratory experiments, field experiments, surveys and naturalistic observational studies, because the problems of the field are diverse and not amenable to study by a single procedure; (4) *a range of levels of analysis*: from micro-levels of study such as the impact of noise on task performance, to the study of social processes such as seating positions at tables in relation to social interaction and personal spacing, to moderate scale analyses of home design and use, to large-scale units of study such as community and city design, and the perception of the large-scale environment of cities and countries; (5) *a range of approaches to concepts and theory*: as a young and interdisciplinary field, environmental psychology has not yet developed its own theoretical perspectives. Although the work of Barker and his associates (Barker 1968) emphasizes an approach to research that focuses on the analysis of behavior-settings that is the confluence of people, physical settings and functions or goals, the field of environmental psychology has, to date, tended to adopt substantive theoretical ideas from other areas in psychology and from other social sciences.

Environmental psychologists collaborate with researchers from other disciplines and with environmental design professionals in architecture, interior design and related fields. Collaborative work with environmental designers takes many forms, including the application of psychological principles, theories and findings to design, and evaluations and assessments of the actual and predicted impact on human functioning of environmental designs and changes. The result of cross-disciplinary projects appear in many places, most notably in the annual *Proceedings of the Environmental Design Research Association*. (For descriptions of organizations, publication outlets and educational programmes see White 1979).

Research in environmental psychology encompasses a broad spectrum of topics, including perceptual and cognitive processes, orientations to places and settings, social and behavioral processes, and environmental design and environmental problems. These topics have been studied in relationship to the built or designed environments of homes, buildings, neighborhoods, cities and regions, and in relationship to "natural" environments of wilderness, parks, seashores and the like. Moreover, various psychological processes have been investigated in relation to a variety of individuals and groups, including children, families, the elderly, various cultural and ethnic groups, and special populations such as the handicapped, prisoners, institutionalized people, children, etc. (general reviews of work in the field appear in Craik 1973; Russell and Ward 1982; Altman and Wohlwill 1976–82; Baum and Singer 1978–81; Bell, Fisher and Loomis 1978; Holohan 1986).

A considerable body of research in environmental psychology has focused on places ranging from regions and cities, to places as small as rooms or areas in rooms. Research has investigated attitudes, cognitions and perceptions of urban environments, behavior such as way-finding, helping, transportation, etc. There has also been study of the design and use of neighborhoods, institutional environments such as schools, prisons and hospitals, and housing developments for the poor, aged and other special groups. On a smaller scale, environmental psychologists have conducted research on home environments, including use of interior spaces, living and social behavior, privacy and the ways in which people define, mark and recognize territories.

An increasing body of knowledge and theory has focused on cognitions, perceptions, meanings, attachments and attitudes to places at all levels of scale (Downs and Stea 1973). Such research includes studies of environmental meaning, the feelings people have about places, the effect of various dimensions of places on behavior, ways in which children learn about locations and the distances between places, and the preferences people have with respect to a variety of settings. This research has examined these topics in "natural" environments both because they are interesting phenomena in their own right, and to assist in the development of policies for the use and for the modification of such environments.

Another aspect of environmental psychology concerns social processes, such as the regulation of privacy, personal spacing and territoriality (Altman 1975). The ways in which people make themselves more or less accessible to others, through use and design of the physical environment, is a topic of emerging interest. The process of personal spacing or distancing of people from one another is one of the most well-researched topics in environmental psychology. Physical distancing and separation has been studied in relation to individual factors such as personality and biography, in relation to interpersonal factors involving group composition and personal attraction, and in relation to situational factors. Territoriality, or the occupancy and control of places, has been studied in terms of different types of territories (primary, secondary and public), intrusion and reactions to territorial intrusion, and in terms of the various mechanisms for protecting and marking territories. Other research on spatial behavior involves studies of seating and physical locations in relation to social interaction, status, etc,

Another topic of concern to environmental psychology is environmental problems, such as crowding, noise, transportation, and their various associated stresses. For example, studies of crowding (Baum and Epstein 1978) have investigated the effect on behavior of the amount of space per person (spatial density), number of people in a given space (social density), and the interaction of crowding with personal and social factors. The analysis of density and crowding in relation to stress, performance, social interaction and other behavior has resulted in a large number of studies and theoretical perspectives. Studies of noise have investigated the impact of duration, predictability, controllability and other aspects of noise on physiological functioning, short- and long-term performance on intellectual and other tasks, and on social behavior. Research on other environmental problems include studies of lighting, weather, temperature, air pollution, transportation, etc.

Research in environmental psychology has been designed to develop a body of scientific knowledge regarding various aspects of human functioning in relation to various aspects of the physical environment. In addition, a considerable amount of knowledge has been accumulated about the application of environmental psychology principles and findings to the design and evaluation of different environments. This research, often involving cooperation between behavioral scientists and environmental designers, has spanned all aspects of the design process, including help in the early stages of environmental design through to the evaluation of designed or used environments when they have been occupied. In the coming decades environmental psychologists will probably work on newly emerging social problems that relate to the environment, they will continue to cooperate with other fields both inside and outside psychology in relation to methodology and theory, and they will gradually develop methods and theory unique to the study of the relationship between people and the physical environment. IA

Bibliography

Altman, I. 1975: *Environment and social behavior: privacy space, crowding and territory*. Monterey, Calif.: Brooks/Cole.

—— and Wohlwill, J.F. eds. 1976–82: *Human behavior and environment: advances in theory and research*. 4 vols. New York: Plenum.

Barker, R.G. 1968: *Ecological psychology*. Stanford. Calif.: Stanford University Press.

Baum, A. and Epstein, Y.M. eds. 1978: *Human response to crowding*. Hillsdale, N.J.: Erlbaum.

—— and Singer, J. eds. 1978–81: *Advances in environmental psychology*. Series in progress. Hillsdale, N.J.: Erlbaum.

Bell, P.A., Fisher, J.D. and Loomis, R.J. 1978: *Environmental psychology*. Philadelphia and London: W.B. Saunders.

Craik, K. 1973: Environmental psychology. *Annual review of psychology*. 24, pp. 403–22.

Downs, R.N. and Stea, D. eds. 1973: *Image and environment: cognitive mapping and spatial behavior*. Chicago: Aldine.

Holohan, C.J. 1986: Environmental psychology. *Annual review of psychology* 37, 381–407.

Russell, J.A. and Ward, L.M. 1982: Environmental psychology. *Annual review of psychology* 33, 651–88.

White, W.P. ed. 1979: *Resources in environment and behavior*. Washington, D.C.: American Psychological Association.

epigenetic sequence The biological or psychological development of the individual within his lifespan, conceived as a series of stages, each of which results from the interactions between the person and the environment and among the parts of the organism or psyche, and each of which contains new phenomena or properties not present in earlier stages. Distinguished from *phylogenetic sequence*, the development of properties in the species through biological evolution, and from *preformism*, the doctrine that all properties which arise in development are present in miniature form in the original organism. Major examples of views of psychological epigenesis are FREUD's description of personality development and Piaget's description of cognitive development.   SBe

equity theory A theory of social behavior which suggests that individuals attempt to establish perceived equality of the outcome/input ratios in relationships. The most intriguing implication of the theory is that becoming better off may make one less satisfied. This in turn will lead one to try to "restore equity". Certainly Adams and Rosenbaum (1962) found that people who were told they were going to be paid more than their qualifications warranted did work harder than others. But later research has suggested that they may have wanted to prove themselves (because their self-esteem had been slighted), rather than "restore equity". In such experiments overwork is not kept up long.

The theory has been applied to various forms of social exchange and relationships. Walster et al. (1978) have studied in particular the extent to which intimate and long-term relationships are governed by the principle of equity. As yet the results of these studies are equivocal. One study by Lujansky and Mikula (1983) showed that different methods of assessing equity in a romantic relationship did not correlate with each other. It also showed that equity and its absence (however assessed) did not predict the survival or demise of the relationship five months later. The latter result, however, was not conclusive, as only the male partners might have disagreed about the relationship's equity. Newcomb (Newcomb and Bentler 1981) found that in divorced couples one spouse always felt significantly less *satisfied* with the relationship than the other. If there is any relation between equity and satisfaction, they would presumably have disagreed about equity as well.

Judgments of fairness are also based upon other rules and standards, such as equality and relative need. Each of these may be relevant in different circumstances. If an exchange or relationship is perceived to be inequitable, equity can be re-established by altering inputs, withdrawing from the relationship and/or changing one's perception of the relationship. The possibility that one can come to see circumstances as equitable rather than inequitable, even though no actual change has taken place, also tends to reduce the predictive power of the theory.   JMFJ/RL

Bibliography

Adams, J.S. and Rosenbaum, W.B. 1962: The relationship of worker productivity to cognitive dissonance about wage inequities. *Journal of applied psychology* 46, 161–4.

Lujansky, H. and Mikula, G. 1983: Can equity theory explain the quality and stability of romantic relationships? *British journal of social psychology* 22, 101–12.

Messick, R.M. and Cook, K.S. eds. 1983: *Equity theory: psychological and sociological perspectives.* New York: Praeger.

Newcomb, M.D. and Bentler, P.M. 1981: Marital breakdown. In *Personal relationships*, vol. 3. *Personal relationships in disorder*, eds. S. Duck and R. Gilmour. London and New York: Academic Press.

Walster, E., Walster, G.W. and Berscheid, E. 1978: *Equity: theory and research.* Boston: Allyn and Bacon.

ethnography A method of unstructured observational research developed by social anthropologists for studying the workings of human cultures "from within". It involves the researcher's participation in the everyday lives of the group under study, and its analytic potential was first demonstrated in a series of classic field studies in the Trobriand Islands by Bronislaw Malinowski who, as a German citizen, had been interned there by the British during the first world war.

Sometimes referred to as "participant observation", the method has also been widely used by sociologists for studying the behavior of particular groups and organizations in advanced industrial societies. It has been especially important in the development of approaches to sociology and social psychology which are concerned with studying human conduct in natural, rather than experimentally contrived, settings, and with obtaining observational access to the ways in which people orient to, produce and interpret their everyday activities. As such, it has featured prominently in the emergence of SYMBOLIC INTERACTION and ETHNOMETHODOLOGY. JMAt

Bibliography

Malinowski, B. 1922: *Argonauts of the Western Pacific.* London: Routledge and Kegan Paul.

Sudnow, D. 1967: *Passing on: the social organization of dying.* Englewood Cliffs, N.J.: Prentice-Hall.

Whyte, W.F. 1955: *Street corner society.* Chicago: Chicago University Press.

ethnomethodology The study of the everyday methods of practical reasoning used in the production and interpretation of social action. Although the term now tends to be used to refer to a number of related analytic approaches it was not originally intended to denote a social scientific methodology in the sense that surveys, experiments or ethnography are methodologies. In coining the word its originator, Harold Garfinkel, was looking for a shorthand way of describing what he had come to regard as a previously neglected, but nonetheless important, *topic* for analysis (on the origins of the word ethnomethodology, see Garfinkel 1974). In combining the words "ethno" and "methodology" to refer to the proposed new domain Garfinkel was influenced by the use of such terms as ethnobotany and ethnomedicine for referring to folk systems of botanical and medical analysis and classification. What he was recommending as a focus for study was a folk methodology, comprising a range of "seen but unnoticed" procedures or practices that make it possible for persons to analyze, make sense of and produce recognizable social activities.

Central to Garfinkel's argument and to the development of research in ethnomethodology is the idea that social scientists have paid too little attention to the implications of their own membership of, and familiarity with, the subject matter of their inquiries. Thus the claim is that any competent member of society, including the professional social scientist, is equipped with a methodology for analyzing social phenomena, and that these interpretive procedures are what enable people to make sense of and to produce contextually relevant activities within the potentially infinite range of different settings they encounter in living their lives. Social scientists, however, have tended not to treat these methodic practices as matters worthy of serious investigation in their own right, but have used and relied on them as a taken-for-granted and largely unexplicated resource in carrying out their research. According to the ethnomethodologists many of the more important theoretical and methodological difficulties associated with social science result from this long-standing willingness of researchers to regard their own native competences as a resource, rather than as a topic for investigation.

In studying phenomena such as delinquency and suicide, for example, social scientists have tended to direct their efforts towards finding explanations of these forms of behavior, and a commonly used data base has been official records and statistics on the incidence of such forms of behavior. However, questions such as "why delinquency?" and "why suicide?" are also ones which are asked by laymen and in response to which there are a variety of common sense explanations. Some of the early studies in ethnomethodology focused on the methods of reasoning used by officials to categorize behavior as "delinquent" or "suicidal", and hence to produce "the facts" that social scientists then sought to explain (e.g. Garfinkel 1967; Cicourel 1968; Atkinson 1978). A common finding from this work was that the process of arriving at official categorizations involved the deployment and testing of common-sense hypotheses about causation that closely resemble those which professional researchers have proposed as "scientific" explanations. For example, evidence that a child came from a broken home would make it more likely that he would be taken to court than a child from a more stable background. Similarly, if coroners and others responsible for processing sudden deaths cannot find evidence that a deceased person had been depressed or isolated, they are unlikely to record the death as a suicide. In other words, the presence or absence of a plausible explanation of *why* a particular individual became delinquent or suicidal has been shown to be a crucially important part of deciding that a case *is* one of delinquency

or suicide. Viewed in these terms, it is not very surprising that social scientists who also ask the question *why*, and who hope to find the answer by studying samples of officially categorized delinquents or suicides, tend to rediscover the common sense explanations that were used to produce the official decisions in the first place. Nor is it particularly surprising that researchers may find it difficult to convince lay persons that a causal relationship between broken homes and delinquency, or isolation and/or depression and suicide is properly to be regarded as a victory of science.

Ethnomethodological studies of official categorization procedures are sometimes regarded as being merely negative critiques of the way in which social scientists have traditionally used data from official sources for research purposes. They are also sometimes read as recommendations to the effect that previous methodological procedures should be reformed or improved, so that "more careful" or "more accurate" studies could be done in the future. These are not, however, the lessons that the ethnomethodologists themselves take from their work on official categorizations. Rather they see them as confirming the promise of treating methods of reasoning, hitherto taken for granted, as the topic for inquiry, and of the uninteresting and un-newsworthy character of research that relies on them as an unexplicated resource. Accordingly traditional approaches to the social and behavioral sciences are viewed as interesting only in so far as they, like the analyses by social workers, coroners and others, testify to the methodic ways in which people are well equipped and readily able to construct plausible descriptions and explanations of social behavior. A major challenge posed by the earlier writings of Garfinkel (1967) and other ethno-methodologists, then, was to find ways of identifying these methodic practices, and to show how they work. As such, the approach involves a marked shift away from deterministic traditions which seek to construct causal theories of behavior. Instead of trying to explain *why* some particular type of conduct occurs, ethno-methodological research sets out to describe *how* it works.

Since its emergence in the 1960s, ethnomethodology has diversified to a point where it is now somewhat misleading to refer to it as though it were a unified or homogeneous style of research. Of the various developments which have taken place, however, there can be little doubt that the approach which has had the widest interdisciplinary impact outside sociology is that which has become known as *conversation analysis*. As the name suggests, this work has concentrated on the study of the methodic practices used in the production of mundane conversational interaction, and its approach and findings are having a growing impact in various areas of psychology, linguistics, anthropology and sociology. Research done so far has concentrated on a range of topics, including how interactants categorize persons, actions, places, events etc., the organization of turn-taking in conversation, how stories and jokes are constructed and responded to, the ways in which laughter can be invited and coordinated with talk, and on the production and treatment of actions such as assessments, invitations, complaints, accusations, etc.

While much of the pioneering work in this area concentrated on the analysis of everyday conversational interaction, subsequent developments have already made the term "conversation analysis" appear too narrow a description for research that is conducted within this methodological framework. Thus the approach and findings of conversation analysis are now being applied in studies of various institutional or specialized forms of interaction, including news interviews, doctor-patient consultations, courtroom interaction, plea-bargaining, classroom interaction, child language, and public speaking. A related research program being developed by Garfinkel and his colleagues involves what are becoming known as ethnomethodological studies of work. These are concerned with identifying task-specific properties ("essential quiddities") of particular activities, such as the work of lecturing, electron microscopy, mathematics, and law.

Although research in ethnomethodology and conversation analysis has diversified over the years, there is a wide consensus among those working within the field on at least three central methodological points. The first is that the main focus of any analysis should be on how participants themselves produce and interpret their respective activities. The second is that access to the methodic practices involved depends upon the analyst adopting an orientation to interactional data which seeks to regard such materials as "anthropologically strange". In other words, analysts must be willing to treat even the most mundane and apparently ordinary events as sufficiently puzzling to be worthy of serious analytic attention. Otherwise, he too is likely to overlook, or take for granted the very taken-for-granted practices that he is trying to identify and describe. Third, there is a strong preference for working with naturally occurring interactions, rather than ones arising from experimental situations, survey interviews, or other methods involving observer intervention or manipulation.

This naturalistic approach to data collection and analysis has been greatly facilitated by the development of audio and video-recording technology, which enable real-world interactions to be preserved and subjected to repeated and detailed study. The extensive use of tape-recordings also means that the data about which analytic claims are being made are openly available for critical inspection by readers or hearers of research reports.　　　　JMAt

Bibliography

Atkinson, J.M. 1978: *Discovering suicide: studies in the social organisation of sudden death*. London: Macmillan; Pittsburgh: University Press.

—— and Drew, P. 1979: *Order in court: the organisation of verbal interaction in judicial settings*. London: Macmillan; Atlantic Highlands, N.J.: Humanities Press.

—— and Heritage, J.C. eds. 1983: *Structures of social action: studies in conversation analysis*. Cambridge and New York: Cambridge University Press.

Cicourel, A.V. 1968: *The social organization of juvenile justice*. New York: John Wiley.

Garfinkel, H. 1967: *Studies in ethnomethodology*. Englewood Cliffs, N.J.: Prentice-Hall.

—— 1974: The origin of the term ethnomethodology. In Turner (ed.) op. cit.

Heritage, J.C. 1983: *Harold Garfinkel and ethnomethodology*. London and New York: Macmillan.

Psathas, G. ed. 1979: *Everyday language: studies in ethnomethodology*. New York: Irvington.

Sacks, H., Schegloff, E.A. and Jefferson, G. 1974: A simplest systematics for the organization of turn-taking for conversation. *Language* 50, 696–735.

Schenkein, J.N. ed. 1978: *Studies in the organization of conversational interaction*. New York: Academic Press.

Sudnow, D. ed. 1972: *Studies in social interaction*. New York: Free Press.

Turner, R. ed. 1974: *Ethnomethodology*. London: Penguin.

ethogenics A theory and associated methodology for the analysis and explanation of social interaction. Ethogenics grew out of the attempt to devise an approach to the study of social behavior that was in accordance with the most advanced understanding of the method of the physical sciences. It involved a sharp break with the positivist philosophy upon which experimental social psychology had hitherto been based. In the advanced sciences conceptual systems are used both to create "facts" and to invent hypotheses about processes by which such facts are generated. In the ethogenic approach explicit attention is given to the formulation of an analytical conceptual scheme by means of which observations and identifications of social actions, structures etc. are made, and a coordinated explanatory scheme appropriate to the subject matter. In respect of the former feature it has much in common with aspects of ETHNOMETHODO-LOGY, and in respect of the latter with the cognitive psychology of action.

Three kinds of coordinated social interaction are identified. In automatic interaction actors are not aware of either the fact or the process of coordination. Matching of postures in a conversational setting occurs without the participants being aware of it. Interaction of this sort could be set within a natural order and treated us the effect of the operation of causal mechanisms (or quasi-causal mechanisms such as habits). But in autonomous action actors are aware both of the actions they are performing and of the rules and conventions that require them. Ceremonial action is typically controlled by reference to explicit and known rules. Such interaction is set within a moral order, that is people can be called to account for failures and infelicities in carrying out what was required of them. But much social interaction is not readily classified in either of these categories. The ethogenic methodology is directed to the understanding of social interaction that is neither automatic nor autonomous. It is based on the application of a conceptual system that is a generalization of that required to understand autonomous action. The actions people perform together in, say, managing a discussion, or developing a friendship, or following out the instructions of a superior, are assumed to be effective by virtue of their meanings to the actors. The genesis of meaningful action is thought to be by means similar to those by which people knowingly follow the prescriptions of a system of rules or conventions. Meanings, rules and conventions form systems of belief related to the demands of specific social situations, episodes and encounters. Included among those beliefs must be both representations of the goals appropriate for each role-player in the defined situation, and the locally accepted ways of achieving them. Like a theory in the advanced sciences the ethogenic approach exploits a system of metaphors.

A distinction needs to be drawn between the means by which a social episode is analyzed so that its structure and components are revealed, and the way the production of that episode by those involved is to be explained. The ethogenic analysis of episodes depends on the threefold distinction between behavior, actions and acts. An act is an action or several actions described or defined in a way which makes clear their social meaning, as for instance the signing of a document can be an act of surrender. Acts are realized by human actions, that is behavior carried out intentionally. The concept of "behavior" is reserved for any kind of physically realized response. The act-action-behavior distinction has also been used in ethology (Reynolds 1980). A special case of the distinction is the partition of the efficacy of SPEECH ACTS into locutionary, illocutionary and perlocutionary forces. It follows from this that the socially potent elements in an episode are defined only by the co-ordination of actors' intentions (the acts attempted) and interactors' interpretations (the acts as understood). It further follows that the structure of an episode is determined by semantic not by causal relations between its components. Finally it is most important to notice that acts and actions are not in 1–1 correspondence. The same act (say "farewelling") can be performed in a variety of ways (one is saying "goodbye", another is merely waving), while the same action (turning one's back) can be the expression of many different acts. This fact has profound consequences for methodology.

In studying the sequential structure of human performances in social episodes the act sequence can be related to the general typology according to which each episode is classified with respect to the social structure of the situations and encounters it includes. In courtroom encounters (such as trials) characteristic act sequences occur. But the action sequences by which act sequences are realized may be very different in different communities and cultures. To discover just what acts are being performed actors' meanings must be investigated. Since actors are not always aware of the moment by moment significance of their actions as acts, in non-ceremonial episodes, a joint method of ethnographic analysis and the collection and analysis of accounts is required to formulate hypotheses about the belief system which is being used by actors in generating typical episodes. GOFFMAN's microsociological analyses (Goffman 1959, 1963 and 1972) have proved very helpful in suggesting ethnographic hypotheses, exploiting as they do the dramaturgical and liturgical models of social action. But it is in the accounts that actors produce to comment on, correct and reinterpret the action that rules, conventions and other social beliefs are explicitly formulated. It is in the match between the content of accounts and the ethnographic analysis that a growing grasp of the belief system underlying the action can be achieved (Marsh, Rosser and Harré 1978).

Considered methodologically the joint method of ethnographic description and account analysis leads to competence theories, that is to theories about the knowledge and beliefs which form the resource on which competent actors draw in acting. It must be emphasized that ethogenic analysis does not lead to a set of hypotheses about what is known by individual actors. Rather it is the socially distributed knowledge located in the collectives to which they belong. Much social action is created by cognitive processes that occur in the discourse of the collective and not in the minds of individuals. For instance, one person may know what act should be performed, while another may know how that act, say "protesting", is to be performed in the existing circumstances. The cognitive processing of those components may itself be a social process, involving hierarchical relations between the actors.

The ubiquitous use of the act-action distinction (Kreckel 1981) in ethogenic analyses suggests that performance theories, about the processes by which social knowledge and belief are utilized by actors, should take a means-end form. In most cases the immediate or remote end of social action is some social effect mediated by an act, while the proper performance of that act requires knowledge of means, that is of the right action in that milieu. Ethogenic performance theories take the form of cognitive ACTION THEORY (von Cranach and Harré 1982). Essentially this approach involves the supposition of hierarchies of means-end pairs, involving several distinctive cognitive processes, such as goal setting, goal realization, feedback and other processes etc. Since in most cases of interest actors are not paying attention to the cognitive processes by which they are controlling their actions, account analysis has little to contribute to performance theory. However, von Cranach and others have found that when the smooth unfolding of an episode is interrupted people do become aware both of what they were trying to do (act) and how they were trying to do it (action); consciously accessing that part of the hypothetical means-end hierarchy that should have been operative at that moment in the development of the episode. By clever exploitation of this fact action psychologists have been able to make considerable progress in studying the way means-end hierarchies are developed and used (von Cranach and Harré 1982).

In this approach great emphasis has been laid on discourse (and other forms of symbolic interchange) as the main medium of social interaction. This suggests paying attention to the rhetorics of characteristic forms of discourse, including that of social psychology itself. In traditional experimental social psychology a characteristic scientistic rhetoric appears, using metaphors drawn from the superficial features of the language of the physical sciences. Typical instances are the rhetorical use of words such as "measure", "variable", "experiment" and so on, words which have a literal application in the physical sciences. In studying the use of a rhetoric one must ask for what self-presentational purposes that way of writing or speaking is chosen. This is to set it in the expressive order of action, rather than the practical order. The distinction between expressive and practical orders (or alternatively of expressive and practical motivations) is of central importance for ethogenics, since it is by reference to these orders or systems of motivation that the role of particular rhetorics is to be understood. In traditional social psychology the expressive project realized by the scientistic rhetoric is presentation of oneself as "scientist".

However, choice of one rhetoric rather than another has further consequences. The combination of positivistic philosophy with the effect of the use of superficial scientistic rhetoric had the effect of obscuring both the structural properties of social episodes and encounters and the importance of the meanings of the component acts which formed structural episodes and encounters. Adherents of the old "experimental" methodology seemed literally unable to see structures of meanings. In contrast the ethogenic approach emphasizes the importance of structure not only us a desideratum in analysis of social interaction, but also in explanation. The principle of structural explanation – "Structured products derive from structured templates" – can be used to control the detailed study of performance processes. According to that principle the best hypothesis is that there is likely to be some preformed "template" in which the structure to be realized pre-exists.

A similar explanation of the orderliness of social interactions has been proposed by Abelson. People control their actions by reference to "scripts", belief-systems seemingly identical with the "collective social knowledge" of ethogenics. "Scripts" or "belief-systems" form the cognitive "templates" which are the basis of structural explanations. RHa

Bibliography

Collett, P. ed. 1977: *Social rules and social behavior*. Oxford: Basil Blackwell; Totowa, N.J.: Rowman and Littlefield.

Ginsburg, G.P. 1978: *Emerging strategies of social psychological research*. New York: Wiley.

Goffman, F. 1959: *The presentation of self in everyday life*. New York: Doubleday-Anchor.

—— 1963: *Stigma*. Englewood Cliffs, N.J.: Prentice-Hall.

—— 1972: *Interaction ritual*. London: Allen Lane.

Harré, R. 1979: *Social being*. Oxford: Basil Blackwell; Totowa, N.J.: Rowman Littlefield (1980).

—— and Secord, P.F. 1961: *The explanation of social behavior*. Oxford: Basil Blackwell; Totowa, N.J.: Rowman Littlefield Adams (1964).

Kreckel, M. 1981: *Communicative acts and shared knowledge in natural discourse*. London and New York: Academic Press.

Marsh, P., Rosser, F. and Harré, R. 1978: *The rules of disorder*. London: Routledge and Kegan Paul.

Reynolds, V. 1980: *The biology of human action*. Oxford: Freeman.

von Cranach, M. and Harré, R. 1982: *The analysis of action: empirical and theoretical advances.* Cambridge and New York: Cambridge University Press.

ethologism The appeal to concepts and findings derived from ethological studies of the behavior of non-human animals as a source of immediate diagnosis of the dilemmas of the human condition and of prescriptions for change. The term "ethologism" was introduced by Callan (1970) in an attempt to account for the mass appeal of works of popular ethology such as those of Ardrey (e.g. 1966), Lorenz (e.g. 1966) and Morris (e.g. 1967), and their influence on both popular and scientific conceptions of human nature. It was suggested that the roots of ethologism lay in (a) loss of confidence in the solubility of human problems, such as overpopulation and warfare, by human means; (b) a romantic yearning for the apparent simplicity and innocence of animal life; and (c) the scientific success of ethology. A linguistic feature of ethologism is the adoption of terms such as "ritualization", "pair-bond" and "dominance" which have acquired a technical meaning in ethology but are nevertheless derived from human experience. These are then re-applied to social action in man under the guise of new discoveries *about* social action. Ethologism has a place in the sociology and history of ideas as a manifestation local to the scientific and popular culture of the western world of a more general – perhaps universal – human inclination to speculate about the relation of nature to that of man, and to use animal images as tools for thought about problematic or painful aspects of being human. (See also ETHOLOGY.)   HC

Bibliography

Ardrey, R. 1966: *The territorial imperative.* New York: Atheneum; London: Collins (1967).

Callan, H. 1970: *Ethology and society: towards an anthropological view.* Oxford: Clarendon Press; New York: OUP.

Lorenz, Konrad Z. 1966: *On aggression.* London: Methuen; New York: Harcourt, Brace and World Inc.

Morris, D. 1967: *The naked ape.* London: Cape; New York: McGraw-Hill.

ethology This refers to the application of ideas from ethology and SOCIOBIOLOGY to the study of human behavior. The models and concepts of both classical and modern ethology began to be applied systematically in the 1960s; after a series of meetings, the International Society for Human Ethology was formally founded in 1978. Through the 1970s, human ethology was increasingly influenced by sociobiology, and a specialist journal devoted to human applications, *Ethology and sociobiology*, commenced publication in 1979.

Despite their simplicity, some ideas of classical ethology have found human application. Theorists such as Lorenz, Tinbergen and Eibl-Eibesfeldt have looked for the presence of "sign stimuli" in humans; for example, elevated shoulders or posture-releasing submissive behavior, or babylike expressions releasing parental care. The concepts of DISPLACEMENT ACTIVITY and VACUUM ACTIVITY have been used, for example in Lorenz's controversial book *Human aggression* (1966). Eibl-Eibesfeldt has filmed and documented many "fixed action patterns" (for example facial expressions and gestures) found cross-culturally; an extensive article of his with open peer commentary (Eibl-Eibesfeldt 1979) exemplifies this fairly traditional approach to the ethological study of human behavior.

In the UK and USA, human ethologists concentrated on the observation of behavior in natural settings, without such a tight theoretical framework. Blurton Jones (1967) described the differences between rough-and-tumble play, and real aggression, in a study of nursery school children. This proved to be the precursor to a large number of observational studies on children, and renewed interest in sampling techniques, problems of category definitions and the effects of the observer on behavior. These were approaches and issues which had been undeveloped since the observational studies of child development in the USA in the 1930s. Blurton Jones's edited volume, *Ethological studies of child behaviour*, proved a landmark in these respects. Because of the ease of observation, preschool children have been a rich source for human ethological studies; other examples are aggression and dominance, attention structure, and altruism. For similar reasons, several ethological studies were carried out in medical or mental institutions. Several ethological studies have been made on autistic children.

Besides utilizing ethological concepts such as dominance hierarchy or attention structure, such studies were characterized by attempts at child or human ethograms. An ethogram is a comprehensive list of units of behavior and the contexts and sequences in which they occur. An ambitious example of an attempt at an ethogram for preschool children is that of McGrew (1972). Ekman and Friesen (1976) attempted to analyze human facial expression. Both these approaches, and the cross-cultural work of Eibl-Eibesfeldt, have been important influences in the study of non-verbal communication.

Studies of animals have shown interest in the influence of the environment on social structure and behavior. Following this concern, some human ethologists have investigated areas such as the effects of crowding on behavior (McGrew 1972). Smith and Connolly (1980) combined observational methods and a child ethogram based on those of McGrew and others, together with experimental methodology, to assess the impact of different environments on the behavior of children in different preschool settings.

Some investigations were more explicitly concerned with the functional significance of certain human behaviors. The work of Bowlby (1969) on the parent-infant attachment system is a most notable example. These and other studies have considered the adaptiveness of behavior in the natural environment, often assuming that the "natural environment" of the human species – what Bowlby calls "the environment of evolutionary adaptedness" – is similar to the environment of present-day peoples living in a hunter-gatherer subsistence economy.   PKS

Bibliography

Blurton Jones, N.G. 1967. An ethological study of some aspects of social behaviour of children in nursery school. In *Primate ethology*, ed. D. Morris. London: Weidenfeld and Nicholson. pp. 347–68.

*———— ed. 1972: *Ethological studies of child behaviour*. Cambridge and New York: Cambridge University Press.

Bowlby, J. 1969: *Attachment and loss*. vol 1. *Attachment*. London: Hogarth Press; New York: Basic Books.

*Eibl-Eibesfeldt, I. 1979: Human ethology: concepts and implications for the sciences of man. *Behavioral and brain sciences* 2, 1–57.

Ekman, P. and Friesen, W.V. 1976. Measuring facial movement. *Environmental psychology and nonverbal behavior* 1, 56–75.

Lorenz, K. 1966: *On aggression*. London: Methuen; New York: Harcourt, Brace and World.

McGrew, W.C. 1972: *An ethological study of children's behaviour*. London and New York: Academic Press.

Smith, P.K. and Connolly, K.K. 1980: *The ethology of preschool behaviour*. Cambridge and New York: Cambridge University Press.

expectancy theory In the field of work motivation this theory was first developed by Vroom (1964) based on earlier theories of LEWIN and Tolman. Conceived primarily as a theory of choice, it asserts that the force to perform a certain act is the sum of the products of the "valences" of the outcomes of the act and the degree of expectancy that a given act will be followed by those outcomes. Valence is defined as anticipated satisfaction; thus expectancy theory is a type of calculative hedonism in that it is assumed that people will attempt to maximize satisfaction. Subsequent developments have led both to elaborations of the theory and to the questioning of some of its basic assumptions (Campbell and Pritchard 1976). The elaborations have involved positing two types of expectancies: that the subject will be able to perform the act (often a surrogate ability measure), and that if it is performed the outcome will follow (instrumentality). It has also been argued that expectancy theory predicts goal choice or goal acceptance better than it does behavior. The theory seems to predict action best when only positive valences are used, when the task situation is highly structured, and when small or moderate numbers of outcomes are considered. Theoretically, the assumption of hedonism has been criticized as has the premise that people are aware of all their VALUES or valences (Locke 1975). (See also ATTITUDES.)

EAL

Bibliography

Campbell, J.P. and Pritchard. R.D. 1976: Motivation theory in industrial and organizational psychology. In *Handbook of industrial and organizational psychology*, ed. M.D. Dunnette. Chicago: Rand McNally.

Locke, E.A. 1975: Personnel attitudes and motivation. *Annual review of psychology*, 26, 457–80.

Vroom, V.H. 1964: *Work and motivation*. New York: Wiley.

extraversion *See* Eysenck; Jung; type.

eye contact *See* gaze.

Eysenck, Hans Jürgen is a major personality theorist. Along with ALLPORT and CATTELL, Eysenck is the most famous proponent of the TRAIT approach to personality. He was born in Germany in 1916. After education in Germany, France and England he obtained his PhD from London University, and has spent the majority of his working life in London at the Institute of Psychiatry at the Maudsley Hospital. Eysenck believes that there are three factors underlying the observable variations in personality. He labels these: extraversion/introversion, neuroticism, and psychoticism (see TYPE). As he was a clinical psychologist, his work began with neurotics. This has sometimes been claimed to have affected his theories and his results (e.g. by Cattell and Kline 1977). He outlined the concepts of introversion/extraversion (E) and neuroticism (N) in a 1944 paper. He arrived at these dimensions by factor analyzing the responses on a thirty-nine item questionnaire filled in by psychiatrists to describe 700 neurotic patients. Those who were high on neuroticism were characterized by "badly organized personality, abnormal before illness, little energy, narrow interests". Those who were at the extravert end of the E factor showed symptoms of hysteria and sex anomalies. Those at the introvert end showed depression, obsession and apathy.

In *Dimensions of personality* (1947) he proposed that these dimensions were sufficient to define all personality variations. He claims that Cattell's second-order factors from the 16PF, invia/exvia and anxiety, are the same as E and N, a view which Cattell (somewhat grudgingly) seems to accept. Eysenck and Eysenck (1969) factored together items from scales devised by Cattell, Guilford and Eysenck himself (the EPI; see below). 600 males' and 600 females' scores were factor analyzed separately. As expected, two large, third-order factors (E and N) accounted for most of the variance in both groups. This suggested that the other personality scales do show the same interrelation among items as the EPI. The analysis, however, was loaded somewhat in Eysenck's favor. Although fewer items were included from the EPI than from either Cattell or Guilford, all items on the EPI are designed to cover only the E and N dimensions, whereas Cattell's items had originally been designed to tap fifteen dimensions and Guilford's thirteen. Hence far more intercorrelated items loaded on Eysenck's E and N than on any other dimensions which the conglomerate questionnaire might have tapped. This clearly improved their chances of emerging from the data. In a later paper, however, Eysenck (1972) showed that in Cattell's own data the second-order factors, exvia-invia and anxiety account for almost all the variance, implying that Cattell's sixteen primary dimensions are really only measuring E and N.

Eysenck explicitly compared his theory to the doctrine of the four humors and their associated temperaments (see TYPE), and was anxious to set his empirical discoveries on a theoretical basis which took into account inherited physiological differences. As he himself said (1972),

'Critics of factor analysis have often pointed out the essential element of subjectivity in its purely descriptive methodology; this criticism . . . can only be escaped by linking the resulting concepts with causal theories derived from modern learning theory, behavioral genetics, and experimental laboratory work.' His attempt has therefore been to build a theory which would link anatomy, particularly the RETICULAR ACTIVATING SYSTEM and the visceral brain or limbic system with the factors discovered from responses to questionnaires, and to phenomena such as neurosis, crime and accident-proneness.

The limbic system is associated with emotion. For Eysenck neuroticism is a matter of emotional (in)stability. The reticular system is associated with wakefulness and levels of cortical arousal. Eysenck (1957) held that extraverts had less excitation and more reactive inhibition than introverts. As he himself said, however, 'As long as we . . . can . . . only assess their influence in terms of some other observable variable, it seems impossible to separate out the particular influences of excitation and inhibition . . .' (1967). Inhibition has therefore dropped out of Eysenck's thinking. He now holds that extraverts are less aroused than introverts. Both the inhibition and the arousal theories predict that extraverts seek sensations and have greater difficulty than introverts in concentrating. Eysenck, however, does not regard the two theories as identical, as they lead to some different predictions (see Eysenck and Eysenck 1985). In these theories the links between the physiological levels and the personality and behavioral levels allow measurable differences between people in cortical arousal (measured by electroencephalogram (EEG)) and emotional arousal (measured in terms of heart rate, blood pressure, breathing and GALVANIC SKIN RESPONSE (GSR)). Differences are also predicted in conditioning, motivation and sensory thresholds. Eysenck (1967, 1976) cites a large amount of data which supports his predictions.

The evidence about the differences between neurotics and normals leaves 'a definite impression that neurotic and anxious subjects . . . respond more strongly to stimuli . . . and in particular take much longer to return to their prestimulation base lines.' (1967). Malmo and Shagass (1952), for example, found that neurotics had a higher systolic blood pressure, particularly when they were under stress. S. Eysenck (1956), using GSR measures, and Rubin (1964), measuring the time that pupils remained dilated after noxious stimulation, both found that neurotics calmed down more slowly than normals.

Evidence about extraversion and introversion has again tended to show the expected differences which imply greater arousal in introverts. When depressant drugs such as sodium amytal are administered to introverts and extraverts, the extraverts are more readily sedated (Shagass 1954; Claridge and Herrington 1960). Extraverts are less vigilant than introverts (Thackray et al. 1974), but this difference is eliminated if both groups are given the stimulant caffeine (Keister and McLaughlin 1972). These results suggest that introverts have greater cortical arousal (wakefulness), but that the drug stimulates the extraverts sufficiently for them to reach the same level. Similarly, Corcoran (1965) found that extraverts performed worse than introverts, and that low arousal caused by loss of sleep produced more deterioration in the extraverts' performance when there was no arousing incentive. Introverts' performance may be less hindered by lowered arousal because they are normally more aroused than extraverts.

More direct evidence in favor of the arousal hypothesis is provided by studies which use physiological measures. For instance Corcoran (1964), and Eysenck and Eysenck (1967) found that introverts salivated more than extraverts when four drops of lemon juice were placed on the tongue, while Gale et al. (1969) found differences in the EEG-measured brainwave patterns of introverts and extraverts, although they accepted that the differences were not easy to interpret. More recent evidence is reviewed in Eysenck (1981) and Eysenck and Eysenck (1985).

If personality differences rest on differences in physiology, a large part of the variance among people must be due to inheritance. Eysenck has taken on the mantle of GALTON in championing nature in the nature/nurture debate. He has, of course, been able to find somewhat more adequate evidence than Galton had, by drawing on the many available studies of intrafamilial similarities and especially concordance rates between identical and fraternal twins. He believes that these show the role of genetic inheritance in causing mental disorders and also in causing deviance and criminality (1964, 1973). Not unnaturally, the consensus of informed opinion is much happier with the claims about mental disorders, or at least extreme disorders like schizophrenia.

Eysenck has developed a series of questionnaires starting with the Maudsley Medical Questionnaire (MMQ), which covered the presenting symptoms of patients, and was therefore not suitable for use with a normal population. Since then he has produced the Maudsley Personality Inventory (MPI), which was derived from the MMQ and items from Guilford, and the Eysenck Personality Inventory (EPI), which has been tested with over 30,000 people and proved more reliable than the MPI. These questionnaires tap the dimensions of introversion and extraversion, and may be assumed to be worse when they are used for selection than for clinical or guidance purposes. Eysenck relies on the external validity of his questionnaires, arguing that the truth or falsity of the individual answers is not an issue, since it is only important that responding (truly or falsely) in a particular way should be associated with having one sort of personality rather than another. This argument obviously requires that most people should tell the same lies if the questionnaire is to categorize similar people together. Since developing the EPI, Eysenck has also paid attention to the dimension of psychoticism (see TYPE). He has added new psychoticism items to the EPI to produce the EPQ (Eysenck and Eysenck 1968, 1975). In 1968 the new items were found to load on a third factor, which did however correlate (r=0.3) with neuroticism.

Apart from his work on personality,

Eysenck has also been a major figure in the development of clinical psychology in the United Kingdom since the second world war. He has consistently championed, and contributed to the rise of behavioral treatments for neurosis (Eysenck and Rachman 1965). This has led him to attack PSYCHOANALYSIS in a way which sometimes seems unnecessarily vitriolic, even though many of his criticisms are clearly justified (Eysenck and Wilson 1973; Eysenck 1985). The vitriol may presumably be explained by Eysenck's commitment to a scientifically based psychology, and also by the entrenched position psychoanalysis held as an alternative to experimentally based therapies. Eysenck's belief in the major role of the genetic component in determining an individual's development has also led him to support the genetic position in the debates about intelligence. He has published several books on this topic (1968, 1975), but has not been an original theorist or researcher in this area as he has in personality. RL

Bibliography

Cattell, R.B. and Kline, P. 1977: *The scientific analysis of personality and motivation.* New York and London: Academic Press.

Eysenck, H.J. 1944: Types of personality: a factorial study of 700 neurotics. *Journal of mental science* 90, 851–961.

—— 1947: *Dimensions of personality*. London: Routledge and Kegan Paul; New York: Praeger.

—— 1964: *Crime and personality*. London: Routledge and Kegan Paul.

—— 1967: *The biological basis of personality*. Springfield, Ill.: C.C. Thomas.

—— 1972: Human typology, higher nervous activity, and factor analysis. In *Biological bases of individual behavior*, eds. V.D. Nebylitsyn and J.A. Gray. New York and London: Academic Press.

—— 1973: *The inequality of man*. London: Temple Smith.

—— ed. 1976: *The measurement of personality*. Lancaster: MTP.

—— 1979: *The structure and measurement of intelligence*. Berlin and New York: Springer-Verlag.

—— 1981: *A model for personality*. Berlin and New York: Springer-Verlag.

—— 1985: *Decline and fall of the Freudian empire*. New York and London: Viking.

—— and Eysenck, M.W. 1985: *Personality and individual differences*. New York and London: Plenum.

—— and Eysenck, S.B.G. 1968: The measurement of psychoticism: a study of factor stability and reliability. *British journal of social and clinical psychology* 7, 286–94.

—— and Eysenck, S.B.G. 1969: *Personality structure and measurement*. London: Routledge and Kegan Paul.

—— and Eysenck, S.B.G. 1975: *The Eysenck personality questionnaire*. London: London University Press.

—— and Rachman, S. 1965: *The causes and cures of neurosis*. San Diego: Knapp; London: Routledge and Kegan Paul.

—— and Wilson, G.D. 1973: *The experimental study of Freudian theories*. London: Methuen.

Other references cited will be found in Eysenck 1967 and 1976.

F

facial expression and emotion The face is the dominant site of nonverbal signaling. The facial skin shows the state of health or the embarrassment or arousal of the individual. Intentions and emotions are conveyed by expressions such as smiles or frowns, which may be used deliberately, or may unwittingly betray states of mind. Primates have facial expressions, but expressions also appear in (e.g.) other animals' snarls. The origin of expressions may be in intention movements such as showing the teeth ready for attack; ritualization may then have turned them into signals (threats). Such a history would lead one to expect a large innate element in the forms of human expressions, since muscular movements which display anger do not seem to have an inherently different signaling function from the white (blood-drained) or red (blood-suffused) faces brought about by action of the autonomic nervous system.

Until recently however it was the differences in expressions across cultures which seemed most striking. Klineberg (1938) looked at the descriptions of emotional expressions (not only facial) in Chinese novels, and found many unfamiliar to westerners. For example stretching out the tongue is an expression of surprise. Attempts to find cross-cultural uniformities seemed generally to founder. This was taken to mean that the use of the face in signaling was a culture-bound affair.

Darwin (1872) however was convinced that non-verbal signals were universal, and collected testimony from missionaries in far-flung places. He asked, for example, whether the natives used the grief muscle as Europeans do, or expressed anger in the same way. There were also studies of blind children, for example by Thompson and by Fulcher in the 1940s, which showed that blind and sighted children used the same facial muscles in posing or making natural faces such as smiles or expressions of fear or anger. Again studies of infant smiling found how early it appears in a recognizable form and how important it is for the bond between the mother and the child. It is unlikely that an expression which has such survival value and which appears within the first month of life could be other than innate. Izard et al. (1980) have produced evidence that other discrete emotional expressions are made by infants in response to the relevant emotion-producing stimuli.

Ethologists in particular tended to support the innateness hypothesis. Eibl-Eibesfeldt (Hinde 1972) found the "eyebrow flash" (raising the eyebrows maximally for about 1/6 second) used in distant salutations all over the world. He also filmed deaf and blind children to see if their patterns of facial expression differed from normals. There seemed to be no such differences, even with blind/deaf thalidomide children who had no arms and could therefore not learn by touch. Support for innateness was also produced by van Hooff, who found chimpanzees using various bared teeth displays in affirmation (open-mouthed) or in appeasement (horizontal display of teeth). He suggested that these expressions may be related phylogenetically to human laughter and smiling.

There are criticisms which can be leveled at the research with blind children, although they become less plausible as the difficulties of learning increase. Clearly ordinary blind children can have learnt their facial expressions (especially to pose them) from proprioceptive information and the labels others use, but this hardly seems true of the elicited, natural expressions of those who cannot hear. Likewise differences in the structure of the face which underlies expressions may undermine direct comparisons between men and chimps. Again there is evidence of a cultural and even possibly human impact on animals' facial expressions. Van Hooff recorded a vertical bared teeth display which he thought possibly "an idiosyncratic trait of this group". Bohlwig reported that baboons in captivity had far more developed "cordial laughter" expressions than in the wild.

The best evidence for innateness therefore remains the cross-cultural comparison, which has been carried on more seriously by Ekman and his colleagues. Their approach was from the work of those interested in emotions which are "basic" i.e. different from each other in facial expression and labeling (e.g. Plutchik 1962). Having decided, on the basis of these studies, to use six basic emotions, viz. happiness, sadness, anger, disgust, surprise and fear, they selected photographs "which showed the facial components they hypothesized to be specific to each". These were shown to people from USA, Brazil, Chile, Argentina and Japan and there was very good agreement about which face went with which emotion. Because these cultures may have a lot in common and the agreement therefore be based on learning, Ekman and Friesen went to New Guinea to the Fore, a preliterate people who had little contact with outsiders. They used stories, such as, "A person's mother has died", and the subject selected the correct photograph (out of three). The fear and surprise expressions were confused, but otherwise the Fore agreed with previous subjects. Other Fore people were also asked to pose expressions to fit the stories. Videotapes of these poses were shown to American students who were fairly accurate in deciphering the expressions, except again the fear and surprise.

There are objections to these studies because they use stereotypes of emotional expressions. The innateness hypothesis claims that particular expressions are produced by emotions, not that particular expressions are seen by others as appropriate to particular emotions. Obviously universality of such conventions of percep-

tion would be difficult to explain unless there were an underlying emotion/expression link. Ekman however has worked with elicited emotion. A film of sinus surgery was shown to Japanese and to American students, who were videotaped while they watched it alone and while talking to a researcher about the experience. When alone both nationalities showed very similar expressions, although they differed in company. The similarity demonstrates that the same stimuli will produce similar expressions in different cultures. Since the Japanese and Americans reported similar feelings and showed similar physiological responses, there is good evidence that their emotions were also the same.

The different expressions in company illustrate Ekman's concept of a display rule. This explains the observed differences between cultures' facial expressions. Japanese expressions are notoriously difficult to interpret, even for the Japanese. Ekman suggests that they, in common with other cultures, have their own rules about the appropriateness of emotional display. Hence there are cultural differences in control of the face. There are also different values in different cultures, so the stimuli which elicit anger, say, or disgust may vary.

The expressions in this study were coded using Ekman's Facial Affect Scoring Technique atlas, which divides the face into three areas (brows, eyes and lower face). These areas are largely motorically independent. They are in all seventy criterion photographs, and the areas of the face can be coded separately by comparison with them. Because expressions are thereby broken down into components, it is possible to see that some expressions are blends of primary emotional expressions showing, for example, a mixture of happiness in one area and surprise in another. There are other possible kinds of blend, such as a rapid sequence of two primary expressions. Ekman says that 'without postulating . . . blended expressions . . . we would not be able to account for the host of complex facial expressions . . . and of emotion words . . .'

Ekman and Friesen (1978) subsequently

developed the Facial Action Coding System (FACS). This catalogs the "action units" which the face is capable of producing, and the muscular movements which underlie them. "Action units" are visible motions of parts of the face; but because the coding system notes the muscles involved, a coder can infer which muscular movements are responsible for any overall facial expression. Coding expressions on the basis of muscle action allows more detailed description, and also brings out the mechanisms which produce blends, as when an expression of fear or disgust is suppressed by the use of extra muscles to counteract those which produce the spontaneous expression. A similar coding scheme has been developed by Izard (1979).

At present the innateness and universality findings seem unassailable (although the small number of cultures used hardly allows Ekman's complete confidence). Other studies which concentrate specifically on the facial muscles also support the view that the face is linked to emotion. Schwartz for instance recorded from electrodes on the surface of four facial muscles. Subjects were instructed to think of happy, sad or angry experiences. No expressions were visible but the electrical readings allowed the types of thought to be distinguished. Laird and Shimoda have separately found that changes in one's facial expression produce changes in one's feelings.

It should be remembered, however, that many uses of facial expression are conventional. The posed smile for a photograph or in greeting mother-in-law are examples. Kraut and Johnston (1979) noted that people smile at others rather than just because of pleasant circumstances. Different neural pathways are involved in the production of voluntary and emotional facial expressions. Voluntary expressions are controlled by the motor strip of the cerebral cortex, from which nerve impulses pass through the pyramidal system. Emotional expressions emanate from the extrapyramidal motor system, an older, mostly subcortical group of neural circuits. Patients with lesions of the motor strip of

the cortex may be unable to pose a facial expression, which they can produce spontaneously. Conversely patients with lesions of the extrapyramidal system may be able to pose expressions which they do not produce as spontaneous expressions of emotion.

Rinn (1984) points out that the cortically mediated behavior is generally flexible, differs cross-culturally, and is under conscious control. Subcortically mediated behavior does not have these features. Rinn, therefore, concludes that 'the influences of display rules are almost certainly organized cortically'. This might be taken to imply that display rules operate at a superficial, conscious level, whereas the "real" universal mechanisms of emotional expression are distinct and more profound. Display might seem to be a matter of *choosing* whether to show an emotion or not, and having no trouble acting on that choice. But clearly a great effort may be needed to suppress spontaneous expressions. A society may have rules that men should not show sadness or fear, and that women should not show anger. Learning to act on these rules may require learning habits which impinge on one's emotional life, and are not comparable to more superficial habits commended by etiquette.

Buck and his colleagues have found that women's facial expressions are more recognizable than men's. Women also verbally acknowledge their emotions, while men do not. Physiological measures appear inversely related to the recognizability of one's expression. In other words, the less emotionally expressive one's behavior, the greater is one's physiological (and therefore perhaps emotional) arousal. This sex difference seems learnt, as there is not one between preschool girls and boys (Buck 1977, 1984). If this shows repression by men, it seems possible that Ekman's display rules may affect the amount of emotion experienced, and hence that culture may interfere more radically in the emotional process than the superficial concept of "display" implies.

The picture Buck provides of the relation between display rules and arousal is clouded by "facial feedback" studies (e.g.

Zuckermann et al. 1981), in which subjects are asked to exaggerate or minimize spontaneous facial expressions. Such studies typically report a *positive* relation between expression, acknowledgement of emotion, and physiological arousal. The explanation offered is that one "interprets" the feedback from one's face. More expression tells one that one has more emotion. There are reasons to doubt the facial feedback interpretation of these data (not least the fact that muscles of expression do not seem to have the spindles which give feedback from other muscles). If it were correct, it would support Darwin's (1872) hypothesis that 'repression of all outward signs softens our emotions', while 'the simulation of a emotion tends to arouse it'. The findings, however, seem to be the opposite of Buck's.

Habitual inhibition of spontaneous expression may clearly have different effects from conscious manipulation of one's facial expressions to please an experimenter. Buck et al. (1974) suggested that the increased arousal of non-expressive people may be due to stress associated with learning to inhibit overt expression, rather than the mere "bottling up" of the emotion. Such stress would not be an active variable distinguishing those instructed to be expressive from those instructed to inhibit expression in a facial feedback study. The different findings only underline the fact that display can refer to a posed smile for the photographer, but also to the very different phenomenon of habitual and painful effort not to show one's feelings. Both Buck's work and the facial feedback data strongly imply that culturally determined display rules affect not only what one does with one's face, but also one's physical arousal and how one experiences the emotions one has.   RL

Bibliography

Buck, R. 1977: Nonverbal communication of affect in preschool children. *Journal of personality and social psychology* 35, 225–36.

——— 1984: *The communication of emotion*. New York and London: Guilford.

——— Miller, R.E. and Caul, W.F. 1974: Sex, personality, and physiological variables in the communication of affect via facial expression.

Journal of personality and social psychology 30, 589–96.

*Ekman, P. ed. 1982: *Emotion in the human face*. 2nd edn. Cambridge and New York: Cambridge University Press.

——— and Friesen, W.V. 1975: *Unmasking the face*. Englewood Cliffs, N.J.: Prentice-Hall.

Hinde, R.A. ed. 1972: *Non-verbal communication*. Cambridge and New York: Cambridge University Press.

Izard, C., Huebner, R.R., Riser, D., McGinnes, G.C. and Dougherty, L.M. 1980: The young infant's ability to produce discrete emotional expressions. *Developmental psychology* 16, 132–40.

Kraut, R.E. and Johnston, R. 1979: Social and emotional messages of smiling. *Journal of personality and social psychology* 37, 1539–53.

Rinn, W.E. 1984: The neurophysiology of facial expression: a review of the neurological and psychological mechanisms for producing facial expressions. *Psychological bulletin* 95, 52–77.

Schwartz, G.E. 1974: Facial expression and depression: an electromyogram study. *Psychosomatic medicine* 36, 458.

Zuckerman, M., Klorman, R., Larrance, D.T. and Spiegel, N.H. 1981: Facial, autonomic and subjective components of emotion: The facial feedback hypothesis versus the externalizer-internalizer distinction. *Journal of personality and social psychology* 41, 929–44.

Other references may be found in Ekman 1982.

factor analysis A method of simplifying data by reducing the number of variables. The technique provides a summary of the intercorrelations among variables in a data set. It may be exploratory to discover underlying patterns, or confirmatory to test whether expected patterns emerge from the data. The starting point is the matrix of correlations among the variables which may, for instance, be subjects' scores on tests or on different items in a personality questionnaire.

The procedure is based on two principles. The first, which was pointed out by GALTON, is that the correlation between two variables equals the products of their correlations with a third hypothetical variable: $r_{ij} = r_{ig}r_{jg}$. In the ideal case in which there was only one factor which accounted for all the variance in the two variables, the partial correlation between the two, after that factor had been controlled for, would be zero. If there are several factors underlying the correlations in the matrix, the correlation between any two variables is the sum of the cross-products of their common factor loadings: $r_{ij} = r_iF_1r_jF_1 + r_iF_2r_jF_2 + \ldots + r_iF_nr_jF_n$ (where i and j are the variables and $F_1 \ldots F_n$ are the common factors). The second factor analytic principle is that the total variance in a set of data is the sum of the variance contributed by the common factors, the specific factors (unique to individual items) plus error. (The error may be calculated from the reliability (see TESTS, RELIABILITY OF)). If the reliability (e.g. correlation between the scores of the same subject on the same item on different occasions or "test-retest reliability") is 0.67, the error of the item is $1 - 0.67 = 0.33$.)

There are two methods for extracting the first factor from the correlation matrix: principal components analysis and classical factor analysis. In principal components analysis the first component is defined as the best linear combination of the variables (i.e. the combination which accounts for more of the variance than any other). The second component is the second best linear combination, under the condition that it is orthogonal to (i.e. uncorrelated with) the first component. This means that it accounts for the maximum amount of the residual variance after the removal of the effect of the first component. Subsequent components are extracted in the same way, until all the variance in the matrix is accounted for. Each accounts for the maximum amount of residual variance and is orthogonal to the already extracted components. Unless at least one variable is entirely predictable from some or all of the other variables, there will be as many factors as there are variables. Each observed variable can therefore be described as a linear combination of the n components: $z_j = a_{j1}F_1 + a_{j2}F_2 + \ldots + a_{jn}F_n$. In this equation z_j is the observed variable, $F_1 \ldots F_n$ are the n components (factors), and $a_{j1} \ldots a_{jn}$ are the factor loadings of the variable j on factors $F_1 \ldots F_n$.

Classical factor analysis is based on the assumption that the correlations are the result of an underlying regularity in the data. Each variable is therefore influenced by common factors which influence other variables, but each variable also contains unique and error variance. Each observed variable can therefore be described as follows: $z_j = a_{j1}F_1 + a_{j2}F_2 + \ldots a_{jn}F_n + d_jU_j$. In this equation everything is the same as in the previous equation except for the addition of the expression d_jU_j. In this expression U_j is the unique factor for variable j, which is orthogonal to all common factors and to all other unique factors; d_j is the factor loading (standardized multiple regression coefficient) of variable j on the unique factor U. Whether defined principal components or inferred classical factors are employed depends on whether there is assumed to be unique variance. At each step in principal components analysis the procedure extracts the maximum of the total variance, regardless of whether it is true or error variance, whereas classical factor analysis makes specific allowance for unique variance and error.

The factors are reference axes and may be rotated for the purpose of interpreting the data. Rotation is to *simple structure* (Thurstone), that is to a position in which each item loads on as few factors as possible. This allows interpretation of the factors. For example, if verbal tests load heavily on one factor and arithmetical tests load heavily on another, they may be defined as a verbal and an arithmetical factor. If, on the other hand, an item loads on more than one factor, it does not help in labeling the factors. Orthogonal rotation retains the lack of correlation between the factors. Oblique rotation allows factors to be moved to positions in which they fall among clusters of items. This may clearly ease the task of interpretation, although it means that factors are no longer accounting for discrete portions of the variance in the data. As Thurstone pointed out, however, there is no reason to believe that useful classificatory dimensions in the real world are unrelated to each other. He used the example of height and weight, which are useful as separate dimensions on which to classify people even though they are correlated. When factors have been rotated obliquely they are correlated with each other. This allows the researcher to extract second-order factors from the matrix of correlations among the factors. It is possible, for instance, to extract second-order factors from CATTELL's 16 first-order personality factors, and the second-order factors include two which are similar to EYSENCK's introversion-extraversion and neuroticism dimensions.

There are many criticisms of interpretations which treat factor analytic results as if they revealed underlying structure (see Lykken 1971). It is true that "you get out what you put in" since the analysis provides a summary of the intercorrelations in a set of data. But a summary may be enlightening when a correlation matrix is not. It is also true that if tests or items are added or taken away from the battery or the questionnaire, the factor structure may change. But again this is only to be expected since the analysis reveals the relationships among the variables which are there. A researcher would infer that factor analysis might be revealing "real" causes of the observed correlations only if the same factors could be reliably extracted from the same tests, and similar factors could be extracted from different tests of a similar kind. Even then a good theory would require that the factors be related to other phenomena (see EYSENCK). A different sort of criticism is offered by Buss and Craik (1985), who point out that traits which do not correlate with others will tend to be overlooked by researchers who use factor analysis since they will not load on any of the main factors. This, however, is a danger with any technique which reduces or summarizes data.   RL

Bibliography

Buss, D.M. and Craik, K.H. 1985: Why *not* measure that trait? Alternative criteria for identifying important dispositions. *Journal of personality and social psychology* 48, 934–46.

Lawley, D.N. and Maxwell, A.E. 1971: *Factor analysis as a statistical method*. London: Butterworth.

Lykken, D.T. 1971: Multiple factor analysis and personality research. *Journal of experimental research in personality* 5, 161–70.

family, the The human group centrally concerned with biological and social reproduction and generally considered a universal unit of social organizations in its nuclear or primary form as constituted by a man, a woman and their socially recognized children. Its broader composition varies with social structural and cultural factors and its meanings reflect its use in psychological as well as in sociological and biological theories. Within psychoanalytic theory the term "family romance" refers to fantasies which distort the subject's relationship with its parents, e.g. that it is an adopted child, but which have their origins in the OEDIPUS COMPLEX. The family and particularly the mother-child relationship is held to be extremely important in early development. Psychological and social development occurring as the result of living in the family is described as primary socialization. (See also ATTACHMENT.)

There is a great deal of anthropological, historical and sociological work on the family in the context of the wider society (see e.g. Anderson 1971), but there has been comparatively little contact between this and the work of developmental psychologists (see Maccoby 1984). Psychologists, however, have not ignored the effects of different family structures on children's development (LeVine 1974). There is now also a fairly substantial body of observational or quasi-experimental studies of family interaction (e.g. Blechman and McEnroe 1985).

Potentially one of the most fruitful approaches to studying the family is that of family therapists, who use ideas drawn from SYSTEMS THEORY and BATESON, and 'focus on the patterns that are developed and maintained in the family through time and that regulate the behavior of system members' (Minuchin 1985). The family, in other words, is treated as a system of which the members are (primarily) interdependent parts, whose behavior is to be understood by reference to the regulatory processes of the system rather than as a product of their individual psyches.   BBL/RL

Bibliography

Anderson, M. ed. 1971: *Sociology of the family.* Harmondsworth: Penguin.

Blechman, E.A. and McEnroe, M.J. 1985: Effective family problem solving. *Child development* 56, 429–37.

L'Abate, L. ed. 1984: *Handbook of family psychology and psychotherapy.* Homewood, Ill.: Dow Jones-Irwin.

LeVine, R.A. 1974: *Culture and personality.* Chicago: Aldine.

Maccoby, E.E. 1984: Middle childhood in the context of the family. In *Development during middle childhood*, ed. W.A. Collins. Washington, D.C.: National Academy Press.

Minuchin, P. 1985: Families and individual development: provocations from the field of family therapy. *Child development* 56, 289–302.

fantasy: Freudian theory An imaginary and organized scene or episode dramatically fulfilling a conscious or unconscious wish, in which the subject appears as one of the actors. English psychoanalysts proposed the systematic use of two spellings and employed fantasy to refer to conscious constructions and phantasy to describe the content of unconscious processes. This distinction has been ignored in American and French writings.

For FREUD fantasies can operate at either a conscious or unconscious level. Unconscious fantasies are intimately tied to repressed infantile desires; they are the structures that underpin such unconscious products as dreams and symptoms. Conscious fantasies include daydreaming and fictions which fulfill wishes that are more accessible to the conscious mind mainly because they are given coherence by the process of secondary revision. Nevertheless in analysis even conscious fantasies can be seen to be connected to unconscious ones and the wishes they articulate.

Fantasy is given a central place in OBJECT RELATIONS theories, particularly in the writings of Melanie Klein. The term comes to mean the person's inner world of unconscious feeling and impulse – the effective source of *all* human behavior. It is believed that these phantasies are the unconscious content and that the content begins in the first minutes of the infant's life when his instinctual demands have to be met by the objects in his environment. The infant's phantasies are also connected with his need to satisfy unmet needs; early phantasies articulate instinctual urges both libidinal and destructive. As the child grows phantasies are elaborated; they are found in both normal and abnormal people and are seen to be *real* to the extent that they shape the person's interpersonal relationships. It is this dynamic reality of phantasies that prompted Isaacs to distinguish conscious fantasies from primary unconscious phantasies.

A connection between conscious mental activity and unconscious wishes is exploited in projective tests which employ a variety of ambiguous stimuli, e.g. inkblots, pictures or clouds, to assess unconscious motivation.   BBL JWA

Bibliography

Laplanche, J. and Pontalis, J-B. 1973: *The language of psychoanalysis.* London: Hogarth; New York: Norton.

Riviere, J. ed. 1952: *Developments in psychoanalysis.* London: Hogarth.

feminism in psychology Over the last fifteen years political feminism has had extensive effects on social science. No social scientist predicted the rise of feminism in the 1960s, but no social science has remained subsequently untouched by it. There has been an explosion of research on women, on sex roles and on sex differences. Social science research has contributed to our understanding of sexual inequality, and has provided support for legislative action. This research has produced an extensive body of new knowledge and, in addition, social scientists in all disciplines have been engaged in a major reconsideration of the concept of "gender" which has had a substantial effect on theory and methodology.

The early feminist-based critiques of psychological practice focused on biases in method – the under-representation of women in sampling, the tendency to generalize to the whole human race from all-male samples, and the fact that social scientists were inclined to ignore many areas of life which are predominantly the domain of women (Dan and Beekman 1972). As research progressed the complexity of the problems became more apparent. Research which suggested the relative unimportance of biological or innate sex differences and undermined simple biological determinism, revealed the conflicts and paradoxes of sex roles. Attention has latterly been paid to re-formulating both cultural and scientific conceptions of masculinity and femininity in the light of inadequacies in the traditional dichotomy, since it has consistently been demonstrated that characteristics which are associated with femininity are devalued by social scientists and by society in general. It seems that Aristotle's view that "we should regard female nature as afflicted with a natural deficiency" dies hard.

The distinction between masculinity and femininity is an essential element in most cultures. Gender is the primary social category and the basis of social classification and of social relationships. We grow up aware that the basic polarity is both antithetical and symbiotic. Recent research has demonstrated that the gender dichotomy is related to many other dichotomies in symbolic classification in western culture; for example active-passive, instrumental-expressive, nature-culture, internal-external, analytic-intuitive and agency-communion (Glennon 1979). Children acquire knowledge of the cultural stereotypes of gender very early; they also learn that gender is associated with anxiety, and that there are different evaluations of masculine and feminine (Ullian 1976). Much recent research has been concerned with the nature and extent of sex stereotypes, and the way in which they affect interpersonal perception, our explanations of others' behavior, and the goals we deem to be personally desirable or unacceptable.

Stereotypical social classifications serve a number of psychological functions; they reduce complexity, they provide convenient definitions of "in" and "out" groups, and they provide simple models for emulation and for self-definition. Stereotypes

can also serve to defuse threat. Clifton, McGrath and Wick (1976), for example, found that the general stereotype of women was sub-divided, particularly by men, into four categories, which they labeled "housewife", "bunny", "careerwoman" and "athlete". The first two of these categories included different aspects of the general "feminine" stereotypes; the latter two involved predominantly "masculine" characteristics. It is tempting to draw parallels with the Greek pantheon, which provided separate and distinct roles for women – Hera and Venus, the "feminine" women who related to men, and Athene and Artemis, representing wisdom and active independence, whose separateness from men was symbolized by their virginity.

The paradoxes, contradictions and evaluative connotations of stereotypical gender classification have been demonstrated in innumerable studies. Broverman, Rosenkrantz and associates found that the characteristics which were regarded as socially desirable and healthy in adults (sex unspecified) were those associated with males, but not those associated with females – a mentally healthy woman was therefore seen to be a mentally unhealthy adult (Broverman et al. 1970). Activity and general competence seem to be incompatible with feminity. If females succeed, observers and agents tend to put the success down to luck or extra effort, whereas male success is due to ability (Feldman-Summers and Kiesler 1974). When females fail, it is from lack of ability; when males do it is from bad luck or laziness.

Many forms of speech have different connotations for each sex (for example swearing, terms of endearment and expressive style), and women switch to a "neutral" form of language when they wish to be taken "seriously" (Lakoff 1973). Men make a similar adjustment when expressing intimacy and tenderness. Some subjects, for example science and technology, are seen as distinctively masculine, and to require the kind of thinking that is associated with a masculine style (Weinreich-Haste 1981).

The pervasiveness of sex stereotypes can

lead to psychological conflicts for both sexes, but particularly for females. Paradoxically while a dualistic culture expects different things from males and females, coping with adult life demands a common set of capacities and skills. Women who conform to stereotypical "feminine" personality characteristics, particularly if they are engaged solely in the most stereotypically feminine activities as wives and mothers, are more prone to depression. Women who enter non-traditional occupations, and women who hold non-traditional sex role attitudes, tend to have personality characteristics and family backgrounds (such as an active or working mother) which have either reduced the impact of social norms in childhood, or have equipped them to resist the social pressures to conform. Many women manifest role conflict; Horner, for example, found that many academically gifted women showed a "motive to avoid success" if they saw achievement to be in conflict with femininity (Horner 1970).

Psychologists have documented the conflicts and contradictions of the female role in parallel with the changes in political attitudes. The political response has been a massive effort towards redefinition of both existing and ideal social roles. The process of redefinition is difficult and painful and, for the individual, involves considerable psychological effort which results in extensive reappraisal of the self and of social and interpersonal relations. The main outcome is that women come to define themselves in autonomous terms, not, as traditionally, in terms of their relationship to men (Goldschmidt et al. 1974). Psychologists have become aware of the extent to which they have uncritically accepted cultural assumptions concerning masculinity and femininity, and (like Thomas Aquinas) have tended to define women as "imperfect men".

Recently our understanding of the traditional symbolic male-female duality has been enlarged by the development of various concepts of ANDROGYNY. Within psychology, there are two distinct formulations of androgyny.

The first is *integrative*. It focuses on the ways in which the sexes are more alike than they are different (cf. the research of Bem (1984) and others). They devised sex role scales which broke with the traditional measures which *polarized* masculinity and femininity. Their scales measure masculinity and femininity separately, so an individual may be identified as "sex-typed" (high on one and low on the other), "androgynous" (high on both) or "undifferentiated" (low on both). It had already been suggested that a balance of masculine and feminine characteristics was desirable, and indeed it emerges from studies using Bem's scale that the androgynous person is mentally and physically healthier and more adaptable (Williams 1979). The implications are that research should be directed to identifying the social origins of gender differentiation, with a view to finding ways of reducing its effects.

The second conception of androgyny is *dualistic and dialectical*. It recognizes that there are important gender differences, in the sense that there are definable "masculine" and "feminine" styles of thought, behavior and social interaction. The main problem is seen to be the under-valuation of the feminine and the failure to acknowledge it as a valid alternative to the currently dominant masculine principle. This model seeks to identify what is specific about the feminine, and about the "feminine" pole of the various other dichotomies. Gilligan (1977), for example, has found that there is a distinctively female way of thinking about moral and personal dilemmas; whereas males focus on issues of rights and justice, females are oriented to the interpersonal and relational. Several studies have specifically addressed Bakan's distinction between *agency* (individual orientation, focus on the self and self-expansion) and *communion* (orientation to others, seeing the self as part of a social whole (Bakan 1966)). This distinction is one which matches the masculine-feminine duality. These studies demonstrate that women tend to have a greater appreciation than men of the interpersonal, and demonstrate better integration of their various biological and social roles.

There is considerable overlap between these two notions of androgyny and in practice the distinction is not always sharp. The aim of both is to provide a more balanced and accurate model of the person. The difference is in their implications for research and policy. The first conception implicitly assumes that a patriarchal society exaggerates and fosters gender differences, and that pointing out their social origins will ameliorate their potentially disastrous effects, clearly an aspect of the nature-nurture debate. The second conception recognizes the reality of gender differences, and aims for a re-evaluation of the feminine, rather than for transcendence of masculinity and femininity. An understanding of the origin of gender differences is less important for this approach. What is at issue is the dynamic relationship between masculinity and femininity within society (in both practical and symbolic forms) and within the individual.   HW-H

Bibliography

Bakan, D. 1966: *The duality of human existence*. Chicago: Rand McNally.

Bem, S.L. 1984: Androgyny and gender schema theory: A conceptual and empirical integration. In *Nebraska symposium on motivation*, ed. T.B. Sondregger. Lincoln: University of Nebraska Press.

Broverman, I.K. et al. 1970: Sex role stereotypes and clinical judgements of mental health. *Journal of consulting and clinical psychology* 34, 1–7.

Clifton, A.K., McGrath, D. and Wick, B. 1976: Stereotypes of women: a single category? *Sex roles* 2, 135–48.

Dan, A.J. and Beekman, S. 1972: Male v. female representation in psychological research. *American psychologist* 27, 1078.

Feldman-Summers, S. and Kiesler, S.B. 1974: Those who are number two try harder: the effect of sex on attributions of causality. *Journal of personality and social psychology* 30, 846–55.

Gilligan, F. 1977: In a different voice: women's conception of self and morality. *Harvard educational review* 47, 481–518.

Glennon, L.M. 1979: *Women and dualism*. London: Longman.

Goldschmidt, J. et al. 1974: The women's liberation movement: attitudes and actions. *Journal of personality* 42, 601–17.

Horner, M.S. 1970: Femininity and successful achievement: a basic inconsistency. In *Feminine personality and conflict*, eds. J.M. Bardwick and E. Douvan. Belmont: Brooks/Cole.

Lakoff, R. 1973: Language and woman's place. *Language and society* 2, 45–79.

Lloyd, B.B. and Archer, J. 1976: *Exploring sex differences*. London: Academic Press.

Ullian, D.Z. 1976: The development of concepts of masculinity and femininity. In *Exploring sex differences*, eds. B.B. Lloyd and J. Archer. London: Academic Press.

Weinreich-Haste, H.E. 1981: The image of science. In *The missing half*, ed. A. Kelly. Manchester: University Press.

Williams, J. 1979: Psychological androgyny and mental health. In *Sex role stereotyping*, eds. O. Hartnett. G. Boden and M. Fuller. London: Tavistock.

field dependence/independence A dimension of individual differences in the perception of self as separate from the environment. The field dependent individual relies heavily on the visual context to establish his or her own spatial orientation, whereas the field independent person relies more on postural and gravitational cues. The dimension was first described by Witkin (1949) who used the rod and frame test (among others), to dissociate visual from gravitational cues. This test requires a rod to be adjusted to the upright position when perceived in a frame, itself at some degrees of tilt from the upright. Witkin found stable differences in adherence to the orientation of the surround (i.e. field dependence) between individuals, between the sexes (with females being more field dependent than males) and with development (with field dependence decreasing with age). There is some evidence that these differences in perception also correlate positively with other personality factors, such as authoritarianism. (See COGNITIVE STYLE.) The other major test used has been the embedded figures test in which the subject must find a simple form in a complex background. Those who find the form more quickly are regarded as field-independent. More recent evidence suggests that the embedded figures test and the rod and frame test do not measure the same thing. McKenna (1984) reviews a number of studies which lead him to conclude that the embedded figures test is a measure of cognitive ability rather than cognitive style.   GEB

Bibliography

McKenna, F.P. 1984: Measures of field dependence: cognitive style or cognitive ability. *Journal of personality and social psychology* 47, 593–603.

Witkin, H.A. 1949: The nature and importance of individual differences in perception. *Journal of personality* 18, 145–60.

field theory A theoretical approach by which investigators have attempted to consider the phenomena under investigation as occurring in a field, that is, as part of a totality of co-existing facts which are conceived as mutually interdependent. In particular, field theory refers to the method of analyzing causal relationships employed by Kurt LEWIN and his students. This method assumes that the properties of any event are determined by its relations to the system of events of which it is a component and that changes of the moment are dependent upon changes in the immediate vicinity at a time just past.

Lewin stressed the need for clear understanding of the formal properties of scientific constructs, and he insisted that the determinants of behavior would have to be represented in mathematical terms if psychology were to become a rigorous discipline. As a result of this conviction Lewin formulated two different psychological geometries – topological space and hodological space – to serve as diagrammatic representations of his theoretical insights.

TOPOLOGICAL PSYCHOLOGY provides a method for diagramming relationships in field theory. Lewin was concerned with the properties of figures that remain unchanged under continuous transformation or stretching. The emphasis is on the qualitative aspects of connection and position: belongingness, membership and part-whole relationships. Concepts explained in topological terms allow one to determine which events are possible in a given life space and which are not. Some of the more important concepts defining topological space are life space, behavior, environment, person, region, differentiation, locomotion and boundary.

The most fundamental construct for Lewin was the LIFE SPACE, or the psychological field. All psychological events (thinking, acting, dreaming, hoping, etc.) are conceived to be a function of the life space, which consists of the person and the environment viewed as one constellation of interdependent factors. Life space equals the psychological field or total situation; it refers to the manifold of coexisting facts which determine the behavior of an individual at a given moment. The emphasis on the interrelatedness of the person and the environment was one of Lewin's major contributions to psychological theorizing. Psychological events, that is, changes in the life space, must be explained in terms of the properties of the field which exists at the time when the events occur. Past events can only have a position in the historical causal chains whose interweaving creates the present situation; they cannot directly influence present events.

Behavior is a function of the life space: $B = f(LS)$. The life space is, in turn, a product of the interaction between the person (P) and his environment (E). In symbolic expression, $B = f(LS) = f(P,E)$. The word "behavior" is employed to refer to any change in the life space which is subject to psychological laws. The characteristics of the life space (or person) are deduced from observed behavior in an observed environment. Lewin also used the word "behavior" to refer to things that are not directly observable but must be inferred, and to refer to observable interaction between the individual and the objective environment.

The word "environment" is used to refer to the objective environment or stimulus situation – the objective situation which confronts the individual at a given moment. However, Lewin also uses the term to refer to the psychological environment, which is conceived to be the environment as it exists for the individual. From this viewpoint, the psychological environment is an interactive product, determined both by the characteristics of the objective environment and by the characteristics of the person.

Lewin employed the term *person* in three ways. First, he used it to refer to those properties of the individual (his or her needs, beliefs and values, perceptual and motoric systems) which in interaction among themselves and with the objective environment produce the life space. In a second usage, Lewin regarded "person" as the equivalent to "life space" (Lewin 1936). Finally, he also used the term to refer to the "person in the life space". The person in the life space or "the behaving self" (Tolman in Parsons and Shils 1951) is the individual as related to the other entities in his life space. "The behaving self" may be thought of as the individual's perception of his relations to the environment he perceives.

Another basic concept is that of *region*, which may be defined as any distinguishable part of the life space (or person). Regions of the psychological environment refer to present or contemplated activities rather than to the objective areas in which activities are linked (Leeper 1943, pp. 92–5). The degree of differentiation of a region refers to the number of subparts within it. Any region which has no distinguished subparts may be called a cell. Human development is expressed as a change of life space towards increasing differentiation. The life space of the newborn child is a field which has relatively few and only vaguely distinguishable areas. There is no time dimension or concept of past experiences in the child at this age.

Any change of position of a region within the life space is conceived to be a *locomotion*. This refers primarily to locomotion of the behaving self rather than to locomotion of parts of the psychological environment. Locomotion from one region to another involves movement of the behaving self from its present to its terminal position through a path of neighboring regions. The boundary of a region consists of those cells in the region for which there is no surrounding boundary that lies entirely within the region.

Direction in the life space is represented through the geometry of *hodological space*. The distinguished path between any two regions is the path along which the individual expects to move if he or she chooses to proceed from one region to another. It is the preferred or "psychologically best" path, determined by its attractiveness rather than its shortness. Direction is influenced by such factors as the degree of differentiation of the space into subregions, the relative prominence of whole versus parts, and the properties of the field at large. It should also be said that direction in the life space is dependent upon cognitive structure. If the individual has no clear knowledge of the sequence of steps necessary to achieve a given objective (i.e. to solve a mathematical problem) he or she does not know the direction of locomotion necessary to obtain that goal. Most new situations are cognitively unstructured, and behavior will be exploratory, trial-and-error, vacillating and contradictory. Lewin utilized the concept of unstable cognitive structure to give insight into the situation of adolescence. He pointed out that the change from childhood to adulthood is a shift to a more or less unknown position (Lewin 1951).

There is an interdependence between Lewin's geometrical concepts and vector psychology, which incorporates the following main dynamic concepts: tension, valence, driving force and restraining force, supplemented by the concept of potency. These dynamic concepts have the function of enabling one to determine which of a set of possible psychological events will occur.

A system in a state of *tension* is said to exist within the individual whenever a psychological need or an intention exists. Tension is a state of a region or system S which tries to change itself in such a way that it becomes equal to the state of its surrounding regions $S_1, S_2, \ldots S_n$; it involves forces at the boundary of the region S in tension. A definite relation exists between the tension systems of the person and properties of the psychological environment. When a goal region which is relevant to a system in tension exists in the psychological environment, one can assert that there is a force propelling the behaving self toward the goal. From the foregoing assumptions it follows that the tendency to recall interrupted activities should be greater than the tendency to recall finished ones (Zeigarnik 1927).

A region within the life space of an individual which attracts or repels is considered to have *valence*: a region of positive valence attracts, a region of negative valence repels. *Potency* is a factor influencing the effective strengths of valences or forces.

The construct *force* characterizes the direction and strength of the tendency to change. In "The conceptual representation and measurement of psychological forces" (1938), Lewin pointed out that the strength of a force can be measured by (1) the strength of opposed driving or restraining forces, (2) the relative persistence of directed activity, (3) the velocity of locomotion or of restructuring. Driving forces correspond to a relation between at least two regions of the life space: the region of present activity and the region of a goal. Driving forces tend to lead to locomotion. Restraining forces, as such, do not lead to locomotion but they do influence the effect of driving forces. Any region which offers resistance to locomotion, that is, any barrier to locomotion, is characterized by restraining forces at its boundary. When oppositely directed forces of about equal strength play upon the person simultaneously, conflict results (Lewin 1935).

As a specific psychological theory, field theory has little current vitality, but it has made its mark on the current general orientation of psychology. Its primary legacy has been a belief that psychological events must be explained in psychological terms; that central processes in the life space (distal perception, cognition, motivation, goal-directed behavior) are the proper focus of investigation rather than the peripheral processes of sensory input and muscular action; that psychological events must be studied in their interrelations with one another; that the individual must be studied in his interrelations with the group to which he belongs; and that important social-psychological phenomena

can be studied experimentally. A discussion of the work of those associated with Lewin may be found in Deutsch (1968).

MDe

Bibliography

Deutsch, M. 1968: Field theory in social psychology. In *The handbook of social psychology*, eds. G. Lindzey and E. Aronson. Reading, Mass.: Addison-Wesley.

Festinger, L. 1957: *A theory of cognitive dissonance*. Stanford: University Press.

Heider, F. 1958. *The psychology of interpersonal relations*. New York: Wiley.

Leeper, R.W. 1943: *Lewin's topological and vector psychology: a digest and a critique*. Eugene: University of Oregon Press.

Lewin, K. 1935: *A dynamic theory of personality*. New York: McGraw-Hill.

—— 1936: *Principles of topological psychology*. New York: McGraw-Hill.

—— 1938: The conceptual representation and measurement of psychological forces. *Contributions to psychological theory* 1, No. 4.

—— 1951: *Field theory in social science*. New York: Harper.

Parsons, T. and Shils, E.A. eds. 1951: *Toward a general theory of action*. Cambridge: Harvard University Press.

Zeigarnik, B. 1927: Über das Behalten von erledigten und unerledigten Handlungen. *Psychologische forschung* 9, 1–85.

Freud, Sigmund (1856–1939) Founder of the branch of psychological theory and psychotherapeutic practice known as psychoanalysis. Born on the 6 May 1856 in Freiberg, Moravia, which was then within the Austro-Hungarian Empire (now Pribor in Czechoslovakia), Sigmund was the first child of the second marriage of a Jewish wool-merchant Jakob Freud, whose two sons by a previous marriage were already grown up; one of them was married and the father of a small boy, so that Freud was an uncle at birth. He had seven brothers and sisters.

The family moved to Vienna when Sigmund was only three, and the half-brothers emigrated to England (Manchester) at this time. Thereafter Freud lived in Vienna for the rest of his life, except for the last fifteen months when he too settled in England (London) after being forced to flee from Nazi persecution at home. Although family finances were very limited, the eldest son's education was fostered, and his intelligence and academic industry won him a place at the local *Gymnasium*. Here, in addition to German literature and some English, he studied mainly the language and literature of the Greek and Latin classics. In his latter years at school he was consistently top of his class, putting to good use an exceptionally retentive visual and auditory memory, and his flair for writing was singled out as unusual by one of his teachers. Formal recognition of his literary achievement as an adult came with the award of the Goethe Prize at Frankfurt in 1930, three years before Hitler ordered his books to be burned in Berlin.

By the time he left school, his career plans had changed from becoming a lawyer to 'desire to eavesdrop on the eternal processes' of nature, as he wrote to his boyhood friend Emil Fluss (Schrier 1969, p.424). In practice this meant registering in the medical faculty of Vienna University to study biology, physiology and anatomy. But Freud did not abandon his earlier interest in cultural and philosophical matters, for during his first few years he also sat at the feet of Franz Brentano whose theories about the object-orientation of mental processes may have influenced his own later psychological formulations. As a third-year student he did laborious work on the reproductive system of the eel, but was later able to concentrate under Ernst Brucke upon neuroanatomy, the field in which he published his first scientific observations (1877). It was Brucke who eventually had to persuade Freud that he could not make a living as a research worker and had therefore better take his medical degree. This he did in 1881.

The need for a financially gainful career became more urgent the following year when he became engaged to Martha Bernays of Hamburg. The next four years, which it took him to establish this career as a basis for marriage, produced an assiduous two-way correspondence which is a rich source for biography as well as for

glimpses of Freud's view of women. The couple were married in 1886 and eventually had six children; the marriage lasted until Freud's death. During his engagement he was working in the Vienna General Hospital, mainly on neurological problems, and trying to make a mark in the medical world. He did so in 1884 with his pioneering paper on the medical and psychotropic properties of cocaine, and he consolidated this success by acquiring in the following year a teaching post at the university (*Privatdozent*) and a traveling scholarship to visit the eminent psychiatrist Jean-Martin Charcot in Paris. Charcot was well known for his particular interest in the pseudo-neurological symptoms (such as anesthesia, amnesia, paralysis, dysphasia) produced by some patients suffering from hysteria, and in using hypnosis for their treatment. He also intuited the sexual component in many of these disturbances. It may almost be said that Freud went to Paris as a neurologist and came away as a psychotherapist. For although, when back in Vienna, he worked for another two years or so in brain pathology (especially with children) and gathered material for an important later monograph (1891) on speech disorders arising from brain damage (aphasia), he soon began to collaborate with Joseph Breuer in the psychological treatment of a number of hysterics. From these case-studies, published in 1895, emerged several hypotheses which have remained central in psychoanalytic theory. The question of the relation between Freud's early neurological preoccupations and his later psychological theories also remains, but at the outset he was certainly concerned to sketch an elaborate and detailed neurological model for his psychological postulates. This seminal *Project for a scientific psychology*, as it is now known in English, was written only four years after the study of aphasia, but not published until 1950 (*Standard edition*, vol. 1).

Some of the crucial ideas to emerge from these first psychotherapeutic researches were (1) that the neurotic symptom, and the pattern of such psychological disturbance as a whole, are a symbolic reaction to an emotional shock; (2) that the memory of this shock, and its associated feelings, are so distressing that they have been banished from conscious recall by the mind's processes of defending itself against anxiety (see REPRESSION); (3) that these repressed elements, now located in "the unconscious", are not dormant but are part of a system of non-rational associations and transformations (the "primary process") which can indirectly influence and disrupt conscious feelings, trains of thought, recollections and perceptions, and which are most clearly evident in dreams.

The greater part of Freud's subsequent work consisted of the investigation, modification and elaboration of these central ideas, and of addressing the questions that they raise not only about the origin and treatment of emotional disturbance but also about normal personality development, motivation, thinking and the organization of mental life in general. For he was after a *general* psychology, whose principles would apply equally to the sick and the healthy, to the individual and to society. The early clinical observations had already suggested to him some more fundamental hypotheses about the structure and processes of the mind.

The idea of an emotional "trauma" in (1) and (2) above, which Freud initially identified with sexual interference by a parent-figure (the "seduction hypothesis" which he soon gave up), raised questions about the origins of ANXIETY, why some anxieties are intolerable, what agency initiates the defense of repression, and whether there are other defenses. Again, the assumptions in (3) compel one to ask how the contents of the unconscious are organized, how this evidently active system is energized, and what principle governs its indirect incursions into conscious mental life. Already by the turn of the century Freud was thinking of a motivating force (*libido*) whose aim is the satisfaction of instinctual drives towards survival, pleasure and the avoidance of pain, and whose psychological manifestation is in wish-fulfillment (see INSTINCT). This libido is in constant tension with an adaptive agency, the EGO, whose function is to regulate our actions according to reason and reality. Since the "reality principle" of the ego often requires us to delay impulse-gratification, it may conflict with the "pleasure-principle" of the libido. The frustration of libidinal gratification ultimately underlies anxiety, he argued, only to revise the idea later; and the philosophically uneasy anthropomorphic and hydraulic metaphors in which Freud depicts the psychobiological interaction between bodily instinct and mental energy are characteristic.

By the turn of the century also, the form taken by infantile sexuality in the OEDIPUS AND ELEKTRA COMPLEXES had been sketched, and he was ready to illustrate in *The interpretation of dreams* (1900; *Standard edition*, vols. 4 and 5), how "latent" unconscious feelings, images and desires are symbolically transformed and organized into the "manifest", wish-fulfilling content of normal dream-life in accordance with the "pleasure-principle".

Freud generalized his concept of libido-motivation in the theory that, in the normal course of development, the growing child gets instinctual gratification from different zones of the body at different age-levels (see PERSONALITY THEORY, PSYCHOANALYTICAL). At about the time that these views were published in *Three essays* (1905; *Standard edition*, vol. 7), the incipient psychoanalytic movement was joined by JUNG from Zurich, who accompanied Freud on a lecturing invitation to Clark University in 1909, but broke away for theoretical and personal reasons some five years later. That was just three years after Adler had done the same (see McGuire 1974 and *Standard edition*, vol. 14, pp. 48–66).

The post-war influenza epidemic killed his beautiful, happy and healthy daughter Sophie, mother of two young children, at the age of twenty-six. Three years later he learned of the cancer of the jaw which kept him in constant pain and frequent surgery for his last sixteen years. The first theoretical revision of his work was to some extent also a consequence of the war. The "pleasure-principle" did not allow him to explain *inter alia* why soldiers who had been traumatized in battle and removed from combat retained their recurrent nightmares. He concluded that there must be a fundamental "compulsion to repeat" which is just as basic as the pleasure-principle, and which is in the service of a more general destructive motive called the "death instinct" or *Thanatos*. A group of constructive motives contend against this. It makes up the "life instinct" or *Eros*. Many of Freud's sympathizers have misgivings about these reformulations in *Beyond the pleasure principle* (1920; *Standard edition*, vol. 18), but are much happier with the "structural" revision of psychoanalytic personality theory in *The ego and the id* (1923; *Standard edition*, vol. 19), which introduce the Id as the reservoir of instinctual impulses, and the SUPEREGO or EGO IDEAL as the source of the evaluative regulation of actions and mental activity in addition to the Ego's controls.

Freud plainly thought that both his theorizing and his therapeutic investigations were "scientific". Doubting critics, however, stress the lack of objectivity in observation and the difficulty of deriving specific testable hypotheses from the theory. On the other hand, there is now a considerable literature, by no means all unfavorable, about the empirical testing of Freudian theory (Kline 1981). Freud died in London on 23 September 1939.   NMC

Bibliography

Cheshire, N.M. 1975: *The nature of psychodynamic interpretation*. London and New York: Wiley.

Freud, E.L. ed. 1961: *Letters of Sigmund Freud, 1873–1939*. London: Hogarth.

Freud, J.M. 1957: *Glory reflected: Sigmund Freud – man and father*. London: Angus and Robertson.

Freud, Sigmund 1895–1938: *Gesammelte Werke*. Frankfurt am Main: S. Fischer. *Standard edition of the complete psychological works of Sigmund Freud*. 24 vols. London: Hogarth; New York: Norton.

*Jones, E. 1961: *The life and work of Sigmund Freud*. New York: Basic Books; London: Penguin (1964).

Kline, P. 1981: *Fact and fantasy in Freudian theory*. 2nd edn. London and New York: Methuen.

McGuire, W. ed. 1974: *The Freud-Jung letters*. London: Hogarth; Princeton, N.J.: Princeton University Press.

Schrier, I. 1969: Some unpublished letters of Freud. *International journal of psychoanalysis* 50, 419–27.

Sulloway, F.J. 1979: *Freud, biologist of the mind*. New York: Basic Books; London: Fontana (1980).

frustration The word frustration has been employed in three different ways in psychological literature, referring either to (1) external circumstances, (2) a fairly general emotional response to circumstances, or (3) specific reactions to a particular external event. Operational definitions following the first usage have involved such things as physical barriers to a goal, the omission of a reward, threats or the actual delivery of punishment, and even insoluble problems. The internal state involved in the second usage has been discussed in terms of a measured physiological arousal or as a hypothetical variable having both energizing and directional properties. Much more specifically, the reactions involved in the third sense of the term have included regression (a return to a less mature form of behavior), fixation (an inability to modify habitual behavior), aggression, and an increased vigor of response (see Cofer and Appley 1964 for a comprehensive discussion). Most contemporary analyses seem to favor the first, external definition. One of the best examples of this usage can be found in the classic discussion of the frustration-aggression hypothesis by Dollard et al. (1939), who formally defined frustration as 'an interference with the occurrence of an instigated goal-response at its proper time in the behavior sequence', but considering the total context, it is clear that the authors were thinking more generally of a failure to obtain an anticipated goal. This is similar to Amsel's conception of frustration as the non-attainment of an expected reward (1962). Whatever the exact definition of the term, frustration must be distinguished from privation or deprivation. Where the latter concepts basically refer to the absence of a common source of gratification, frustration does not exist unless the person had been expecting to reach this particular goal and then finds it cannot be attained.

Several questions have been faced in recent years by investigators interested in the consequences of frustrations. One of these deals with why people often work harder or persist longer in a particular form of behavior after they have been thwarted. According to Amsel (1962) the increased persistence arises when non-rewarded occasions had previously been interspersed with rewarded trials so that the persons had learned to perform in the presence of frustration cues. The relationship between frustration and aggression also continues to attract considerable attention and controversy. Many critics of the 1939 formulation have argued that only illegitimate thwartings generate an aggressive inclination, but there is some evidence that supposedly legitimate frustrations can also evoke an instigation to aggression although this tendency may be suppressed because it seems "wrong" to be aggressive in that situation (see Berkowitz 1969). In line with several other writers (e.g. Ferster 1957), Berkowitz (1978, 1980) has recently held that frustrations elicit an instigation to aggression because of their aversiveness rather than their intrinsic nature as frustrations. (See also AGGRESSION; EMOTION AND SOCIAL BEHAVIOR.)   LB

Bibliography

Amsel, A. 1962: Frustrative nonreward in partial reinforcement and discrimination learning: some recent history and a theoretical extension. *Psychological review* 69, 306–28.

Berkowitz, L. 1969: The frustration-aggression hypothesis revisited. In *Roots of aggression*, ed. L. Berkowitz. New York: Atherton Press.

—— 1978: Whatever happened to the frustration-aggression hypothesis? *American behavioral scientist* 21, 691–708.

—— 1980: *A survey of social psychology*. New York: Holt, Rinehart and Winston.

Cofer, C. and Appley, M. 1964: *Motivation: theory and research*. New York: Wiley.

Dollard, J. et al. 1939: *Frustration and aggression*. New Haven: Yale University Press.

Ferster, C.B. 1957: Withdrawal of positive reinforcement as punishment. *Science* 126, 509.

functional autonomy Habits, skills and behavioral patterns that were originally developed in the past for instinctual satisfaction have a tendency to become, in the normal mature personality, self-motivated and independent from their historical causes.

The term originated with ALLPORT (1937) to dispute the claim held by prominent psychologists such as McDOUGALL (see HORMIC PSYCHOLOGY) and FREUD, that adult conduct was functionally related to and anchored in commonly held instincts, desires and needs.

Allport wanted to account for the uniqueness of each personality and the impossibility of reducing personalities to historically elementary motives. For him motivation is contemporary and independent of the original drive. The term accounts for many phenomena: (i) a human's lasting, stable interest: the mature personality depends upon an inevitable incompleteness to account for lasting interest; (ii) the persistence of habit when the incentive has been removed; (iii) the endless variety of human goals; (iv) compulsive behavior that continues after the original reason has disappeared.

The term is close in meaning to Woodworth's notion that instrumental activity may become an interest in itself – the habit may become a drive.   JWA

Bibliography

Allport, G. 1937: *Personality*. London: Constable.

functionalism (in the social sciences) An approach to society which focuses on the functions performed by customs, beliefs, institutions and other items within the social system as a whole. The term first gained wide currency in connection with the work of the social anthropologists Bronislaw Malinowski (1922) and A.R. Radcliffe-Brown (1922). Later, it spread into sociology, where it was soon used to denote what many took to be the dominant school in the field. The contours of what was denoted, however, have often been left rather fuzzy. Depending on what is supposed to be meant by the "function" of an item, functionalism admits of three main interpretations.

In one interpretation, functionalism simply consists in approaching a society *as a whole*, in studying each part of it in relation to that whole. In contrast to the historical approach from which the first functionalists had to free themselves, it does not focus on isolated customs or beliefs in order to track down their historical origins, but investigates the role each custom and each belief plays in the social system and the function it performs in it. However, as was emphatically stated by Kingsley Davis (1959) in a famous presidential address at the American Sociological Association, the functionalist point of view is nothing in itself and it is therefore unable to form the core of a distinctive approach.

This is not the case with a second interpretation, strongly suggested by some of Radcliffe-Brown's more theoretical essays (1952), which soon became the dominant view. As outlined by the philosophers of science Ernest Nagel (1956) and Carl G. Hempel (1959) and the sociologist Robert Merton (1949), it states that the function of an item basically consists in its contribution to the survival or the good functioning of the system of which it is a part. A functionalist approach to society or to a person, consequently, consists in identifying needs (or functional requirements), i.e. the conditions whose fulfillment is required for the system to survive or to function properly, and in showing how particular customs, beliefs, etc. contribute to the satisfaction of these needs. Identifying the relevant social or psychological system and its needs may often turn out to be a tricky business, but here at least – so it was argued – functional analysis constitutes a distinctive type of inquiry.

The key question, which soon emerged, was whether this type of inquiry can genuinely explain the customs, beliefs, behavior etc. with which it is concerned: a claim unambiguously present in the early functionalists' work. First of all, assuming the existence of a particular need has been established, the item considered may not be indispensable to its satisfaction. In other words, there may be *functional alternatives*. Where this is the case – which is likely to be the rule rather than the exception – showing that the item contributes to the satisfaction of a need of the system could not possibly explain why *it* is present, rather than another member of the class of functional alternatives. Secondly and more fundamentally, even when it is demonstrably indispensable for the proper functioning of the system, be it social or personal, the item considered can still not be said to have been *explained*. The most that can be said is that its presence at a given time is *predictable* from the knowledge of the (if only slightly) later fact that the system is functioning properly. It is therefore very hard to claim that, just by showing that without the item the system would not function properly, one has explained why it is there.

Faced with this fundamental difficulty authors have tended to take one of the following two stances. Many, following Nagel's and Hempel's suggestions, have attempted to give functionalism a *cybernetic* cast. Typical of the goal-directed systems studied by cybernetics is the fact that they are able to bring about, within certain limits, whatever is required to maintain themselves in a particular goal state. If a social or psychological system can be described as a goal-directed system in this sense, with its proper functioning as its goal state, then showing how a particular item contributes to the system's good functioning may be explanatory after all. This solution has been very popular in the most sophisticated theoretical statements of functionalism. But it has a serious drawback. It restricts the relevance of social scientific functionalism to the negligibly small number of situations in which the item to be explained can plausibly be said to be part of such a self-regulating device.

Other authors have attempted to preserve the wide relevance of functionalism by giving up its explanatory claim. This approach is exemplified by Parsons's later work (e.g. 1961) where the functional analysis of a social system essentially consists in classifying the problems it has to solve, within a framework provided by the four fundamental "functions" which any social system must perform: adaptation, goal-attainment, integration and latent pattern maintenance. Along the same lines, functional theory is said to consist, for the most part, in formulating a hierarchy of "reference problems" to be solved by a social system – the ultimate problem being that of "reducing environmental complexity" – and a parallel hierarchy of "equivalence domains", i.e. sets of functionally equivalent solutions to the reference problems. Without engaging in such grand theoretical constructions most functional analyses of particular customs, institutions, etc. have tended to consist of pointing out some of the latter's "beneficial" or "problem-solving" consequences, without pretending thereby to explain *why* those customs, institutions, etc. exist, or *why* they take the form they do.

The first interpretation of functionalism suffered from a lack of distinctiveness. The second interpretation leads to the dilemma just sketched, between giving up functionalism's claim to be widely relevant and abandoning its claim to be truly explanatory. There is still a third interpretation, only recently developed in a systematic way, which avoids both shortcomings. According to this third interpretation, as foreshadowed by Larry Wright (1976) and elaborated by G.A. Cohen (1978) and Phillippe Van Parijs (1981), functional statements typically made by social scientists are by no means concerned with contributions to the so-called "proper functioning" of the social system. They must be understood as causally accounting for the presence of the item to which a function is ascribed, by reference to a *dispositional property* of the item which can be expressed as follows: the situation is such that, if the item (say, a rain ceremony) is or were present, its presence has or would have the consequences referred to as its function (say, the promotion of social cohesion). This move opens up the possibility of further research to justify the attribution of a dispositional property to the item. Functionalism, thus interpreted as

the systematic use of a peculiar type of causal explanation, allows social-scientific functional statements to be explanatory in exactly the same way as biological functional statements advanced against the background of evolutionary theory. It not only makes explanatory sense of the functionalist approach in social anthropology; it is also able to integrate into the same framework, for example, the core of Marx's historical materialism and so-called functionalist diachronic linguistics, thus negating the criticism that functionalism is unfit for the explanation of social change.

Beyond the clarification of the logical structure of functional explanation, however, the key question for functionalism in this third interpretation concerns the nature of the underlying mechanisms: what is it that plays for the social sciences the role played by natural selection in the case of biology? Some, e.g. Cohen (1978), claim that functional explanations may be acceptable even in advance of any detailed knowledge about the mechanism. Others, e.g. Van Parijs (1981), believe that re-inforcement, in a broad sense, provides the required set of mechanisms, and hence a basis for the legitimation of a wide variety of social-scientific functional explanations. Others still, e.g. Jon Elster (1982), think that no such set of mechanisms can be found. Research and argument in this area will strongly influence the future of functionalism.

(See also DARWINISM, SOCIAL; DURKHEIM; HOMEOSTASIS; STRUCTURALISM.)   PVanP

Bibliography

Cohen, G.A. 1978: *Karl Marx's theory of history: a defence.* Oxford: University Press; Princeton, N.J.: Princeton University Press.

Davis, K. 1959: The myth of functional analysis as a special method in sociology and anthropology. *American sociological review* 24, 757–72.

*Elster, J. 1982: Marxism. functionalism and game theory. *Theory and society* 4, 14.

Hempel, C.G. 1959: The logic of functional analysis. In *Aspects of scientific explanation and other essays in the philosophy of science.* New York: Free Press.

Luhman, N. 1974: *Zweckbegriff und System-rationalität.* Frankfurt: Suhrkamp.

Malinowski, B. 1922: *Argonauts of the Western Pacific*. London: Routledge and Kegan Paul.

Merton, R. K. 1949: Manifest and latent functions. In *Social theory and social structure*. New York: Free Press.

*Moore, W.E. 1978: Functionalism. In *A history of sociological analysis*, eds. T. Bottomore and R. Nisbet. London: Heinemann.

Nagel, E. 1956: A formalization of functionalism. In *Logic without metaphysics*. New York: Free Press.

Parsons, T. 1961: An outline of the social system. In *Theories of society*, vol. 1. New York: Free Press.

Radcliffe-Brown, A.R. 1922: *The Andaman Islanders*. New York: Free Press.

—— 1952: *Structure and function in primitive society*. London: Routledge and Kegan Paul.

Van Parijs, P. 1981: *Evolutionary explanation in the social sciences: an emerging paradigm*. Totowa, N.J.: Rowman and Littlefield; London: Tavistock.

Wright, L. 1976: *Teleological explanations*. Berkeley, Calif.: University of California Press.

G

Galton, Sir Francis (1822–1911) A pioneer in the study of individual differences and in the application of statistical techniques to psychological problems. He was born in Sparkbrook, Birmingham, England; apprenticed to study medicine at Birmingham General Hospital, 1838; after a year he went on to King's College, London to continue medicine, but left to go to Trinity College, Cambridge to study mathematics, and took his degree in 1840. His father's death allowed him to give up medicine and undertake exploration in Africa. He went to the Sudan in 1845–46, and to South West Africa in 1850. He married in 1853. His accounts of his travels earned him a gold medal from the Royal Geographical Society in 1854 and election to the Royal Society. For some years he settled to the life of a gentleman, although he did produce *The art of travel*. He subsequently took to a study of the weather, and discovered the anticyclone.

It is common to introduce accounts of Galton by mentioning that he was a (half-)cousin of Darwin. This unfairly implies that this relationship was a main claim to fame. It also however hints at the importance of Darwin's *Origin of species* (1859) in inspiring Galton's interest in anthropology and psychology, although this impact was hardly confined to Darwin's relatives. Galton believed that many human characteristics are transmitted through heredity. He published a magazine article on the inheritance of talent and character in 1865, and *Hereditary genius* in 1869. Using biographical sources, he found that there was a tendency for eminence to run in families, and that relatives were often eminent in the same field of endeavor. He ascribed this tendency to genetic inheritance, and ignored the possible effect of socio-economic status, education, parental encouragement and acquaintance with the right people. He was not of course unaware of the possible effects of the environment, as is shown by his study of the physical characteristics of twins (the first ever twin study) which was published in *Inquiries into human faculty* (1883). Nevertheless in the second edition of *Hereditary genius* (1892) the only thing he regretted about the book was its title, since, as he said, he was not actually looking at genius "in any technical sense, but merely as expressing an ability that was exceptionally high, and at the same time inborn". His belief in the effects of GENETICS and in the consequent hypothesis that it is just as possible to produce a better breed of men as of livestock, led to his founding eugenics, to which certain notorious racialist beliefs and policies have given a bad name.

The work which Galton went on to do after this entitles him to be regarded as the founder of scientific psychology in Britain; his contribution was as important as that of any of the initiators of the subject in other countries. He invented a variety of mechanical devices which enabled him to quantify sensory discrimination and speed in different modalities; for example, ability to distinguish different weights and odors, or to estimate extension, and reaction times to lights and sounds. But he was also interested in individual differences in mental imagery. He produced a questionnaire in which people were asked to imagine that morning's breakfast table, and to answer questions about the clarity of the image, the definition of the objects and the naturalness of the colors. He was surprised to find that his first subjects, who were scientists, denied having any mental imagery, and did not believe that other people had such images either. Other people, however, reported clear images, and were surprised when questioned in a way which implied slight disbelief in the truth of their claims.

In the 1880s Galton started his anthropometric laboratory in which people could pay 3d. and be given a battery of tests. Despite the fact that the subjects paid the experimenters this was never economically viable. In 1883 he published the results of his previous seven years' work on psychometrics in *Inquiries into human faculty and its development*. This is an original *pot pourri* of studies which makes no attempt at unity. Apart from the topics mentioned above, he studied the association of ideas, and conducted experiments on himself, in the course of which he discovered the prevalence of associations deriving from early childhood, and invented the WORD ASSOCIATION TEST. He also noted that a great deal of the mind's operation seems to be going on "below the level of consciousness", and anticipated FREUD's metaphor to distinguish the conscious from the preconscious.

Apart from the fertility of his mind in inventing topics of study and methods of studying them, he laid the foundations of much future work in social science by his applications and discoveries in statistics. Quetelet (1796–1874) had demonstrated that human physical variability is symmetrically (i.e. normally) distributed under a bell-shaped curve, with the majority of people clustered near to and on either side of the mean. Galton found that marks in university exams were distributed about the mean in the same way, and felt that this justified the application of statistics to mental phenomena. His most significant discovery in statistics was of correlations, on which he gave a paper at the Royal Society (1888). He produced graphs to illustrate the basic idea of linear relationships between variables (e.g. taller people tend to have larger chests). He also produced a mathematical formula to work out the degree of relationship, and it was his student Karl Pearson who invented the formula which is still current today (see STATISTICAL METHODS). He wrote an autobiography, *Memories of my life*, but the fullest account of him is to be found in Pearson's four-volume biography

(1914–30), *The life, letters and labours of Francis Galton*.   RL

Bibliography

Galton, F. 1869: *Hereditary genius*. London: Macmillan.

——— 1883: *Inquiries into human faculty and its development*. London: Macmillan.

——— 1888: Co-relations and their measurement, chiefly from anthropometric data. London: *Proceedings of the Royal Society* 15, 135–45.

——— 1908: *Memories of my life*. London: Methuen.

Pearson, K. 1914–30: *The life, letters and labours of Francis Galton*. 4 vols. Cambridge: Cambridge University Press.

galvanic skin response (GSR) A change in the electrical resistance of the skin, related to sweating. The GSR can be produced by a minute electrical current and as such has been widely used as an unconditional response in classical conditioning paradigms. The GSR also occurs in situations which provoke emotion or anxiety. As a result it has become important in lie detection where it is used together with other measures regulated by the autonomic nervous system such as blood pressure and respiratory rate. The underlying assumption is that the individual may be capable of hiding overt expressions of emotion associated with lying, but not the autonomic responses that are beyond voluntary control. While useful in this respect these measures, including GSR, are not always reliable and are usually not admissible as evidence in a court of law.   GWi

Bibliography

Montagu, J.D. and Coles, R. 1966: Mechanism and measurement of the galvanic skin response. *Psychological bulletin* 65, 261–79.

games A term referring to a variety of experimental paradigms used primarily in the study of cooperation and competition and of decision-making under conditions of uncertainty. Typically, subjects are required to choose between sets of response alternatives which can lead to a range of possible costs and benefits to themselves and/or to others with whom they interact.

The original focus of social psychological research on games was on how behavior is influenced by the structural properties of a situation defined in terms of costs and benefits contingent on alternative choices. The analysis of such costs and benefits was based on the mathematical theory of games derived from studies of economic behavior (von Neumann and Morgenstern 1944). More recent research has emphasized the importance of more cognitive variables, particularly trust and interpretation of others' intentions.

Social psychologists have been mainly concerned with games in which two or more people are (supposedly) interacting with each other, and the costs and benefits each receives are contingent both on their own choices and on the choices made by their "partners" in the interaction. By far the most frequently used game of this kind is that called the "Prisoner's Dilemma" (PD). The name refers to an imaginary situation in which two accomplices are awaiting trial, and are each individually offered lighter sentences if they plead guilty and inform on the other. If neither informs, they are likely to get away with moderate sentences. If one informs and the other does not, the informant receives a light sentence, the other a severe one, but if both inform, their sentences will be more severe than if they both kept quiet. The dilemma here is that, *if* you can trust your partner, the best *joint* outcome is for both you and your partner to keep quiet. On the other hand, whatever your partner does, you will be better off *individually* if you inform – except that if your partner thinks the same way, each of you will end up informing on the other.

In the laboratory, this dilemma is represented in terms of a two-person game where each person has a choice of two possible responses. The outcomes for each player depending on his own behavior and that of his partner are represented in terms of a pay-off matrix, as shown in figure 1. The figures above the diagonal in each square of the matrix refer to the outcomes

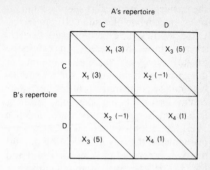

of player A, those below the diagonal represent the outcomes of player B. The numbers in parentheses are examples of a typical PD pay-off structure. For a game to be classed as a PD, the pay-offs must conform to the following rules:
(a) $X_3>X_1>X_4>X_2$; and
(b) $2X_1>(X_2 + X_3) > 2X_4$.

The two response alternatives (labeled C and D) are usually referred to as "cooperative" and "competitive" moves respectively. The PD is an example of a "nonzero sum mixed-motive" game. "Non-zero sum" means that there is at least one cell of the matrix where the sum of A's and B's outcomes does not equal zero. "Mixedmotive" means that the structure could motivate subjects either to cooperate (jointly achieve X_1 rather than X_4 outcomes) or to compete (individually achieve X_3 rather than X_1 or X_4 rather than X_2).

Research on the PD has shown that mutual cooperation is extremely difficult to achieve in the standard situation where subjects respond simultaneously (i.e. without knowledge of the other's choice until after they have made their own) over a series of trials. Typically, the percentage of cooperative responses is no more than about 40 per cent. The main question researchers have asked, therefore, is why cooperation is not higher.

A number of experiments have simulated the behavior of the partner, substituting a pre-programed sequence of responses without the subjects' knowledge (Oskamp 1971). The most effective strategy in improving cooperation is when the simulated "partner" responds cooperatively only when the subject cooperates. Other studies have manipulated the real money value of the rewards and costs in the pay-off matrix, which are often notional or imaginary. Within limits, such manipulations have comparatively little effect. The *relative* sizes of the pay-offs, real or imaginary, however, can be quite effective (Terhune 1968). Other researchers have manipulated the way in which the pay-off matrix is presented to subjects (Pruitt and Kimmel 1977). Such manipulations can have quite dramatic effects on levels of cooperation, even though the pay-offs remain unaltered from a mathematical point of view. In the standard procedure players are unable to communicate with each other, and there are suggestions that this may be one of the most important factors inhibiting cooperation (Nemeth 1972). However, the effectiveness of communication depends on there being a basis of trust.

Much of the early work on the effects of trust used a "trucking game" devised by Deutsch and Krauss (1962), in which the players take the role of owners of trucking firms both needing to use a one-lane road in opposite directions. Using a PD, Kelley and Stahelski (1970) considered the factors which influence subjects to attribute cooperative or competitive intentions to their partner. They point out that, because of the structure of the PD, someone who acts competitively may also force his partner to act competitively out of self-defense. However, they argue, competitive individuals fail to discount the causative influence of their own behavior on that of their partner. Consequently, competitive individuals tend to see their partners as competitive also, whereas cooperative individuals tend to be more varied in the intentions they attribute to their partner. Miller and Holmes (1975) show that the special form of this relationship no longer applies when the structure of the game is "expanded" to include a third response option which enables players to defend themselves without their behavior being interpretable as attempts at exploitation.

Experimental games have been repeatedly criticized for their apparent artificiality and lack of generalizability (e.g. Sermat 1970). However, there may be real-life situations that can also be characterized as "mixed-motive", where short-term individual gains need to be forgone if longer term mutual gains are to be achieved (see Pruitt and Kimmel 1977). Game-theoretical concepts and gaming analogies have been used more widely within social psychology (Thibaut and Kelley 1959), sociology (Goffman 1970) and popular writings on psychotherapy (Berne 1968) (see TRANSACTIONAL ANALYSIS). Laboratory research stresses that in applying such concepts one must be attentive both to the structure of interactions, and to how they are interpreted by the subjects.   JRF.

Bibliography

Berne, E. 1968: *Games people play: the psychology of human relationships*. Harmondsworth: Penguin.

Colman, A.: 1982: *Game theory and experimental games*. Oxford: Pergamon.

Deutsch, M. and Krauss, R.M. 1962: Studies of interpersonal bargaining. *Journal of conflict resolution* 6, 52–76.

Goffman, E. 1970: *Strategic interaction*. Oxford: Basil Blackwell; Philadelphia: University of Pennsylvania Press.

Kelley, H.H. and Stahelski, A.J. 1970: Social interaction basis of cooperators' and competitors' beliefs about others. *Journal of personality and social psychology* 16, 66–91.

Miller, D.T. and Holmes, J.G. 1975: The role of situational restrictiveness on self-fulfilling prophecies: a theroretical and empirical extension of Kelley and Stahelski's Triangle Hypothesis. *Journal of personality and social psychology* 31, 661–73.

Nemeth, C. 1972: A critical analysis of research utilizing the prisoner's dilemma paradigm for the study of bargaining. In *Advances in experimental social psychology*, ed. L. Berkowitz, vol. 6. New York: Academic Press.

Oskamp, S. 1971: Effects of programmed strategies on cooperation in the Prisoner's Dilemma and other mixed-motive games. *Journal of conflict resolution* 15, 225–59.

Pruitt, D.G. and Kimmel, M.J. 1977: Twenty years of experimental gaming: critique, synthesis, and suggestions for the future. *Annual review of psychology* 28, 363–92.

Sermat, V. 1970: Is game behavior related to behavior in other interpersonal situations? *Journal of personality and social psychology* 16, 92–109.

Terhune, K.W. 1968: Motives, situation, and interpersonal conflict within the Prisoner's Dilemma. *Journal of personality and social psychology. Monograph supplement* 8, 1–24.

Thibaut, J.W. and Kelley, H.H. 1959: *The social psychology of groups*. New York: Wiley.

von Neumann, J. and Morgenstern, O. 1944: *Theory of games and economic behavior*. Princeton, N.J.: Princeton University Press.

gaze Reactions to others depend on how they are perceived and how their behavior is interpreted. It follows that how much people look, and when and where they look are crucial for their social performance. Most research treats gaze only as a signal, but it operates primarily as a channel.

Gaze has a social function early in life. By the third week infants smile at a nodding head, and during the fourth week there is mutual gaze between mother and infant. Bruner (1976) found that at six weeks mother-infant interaction involves games like peek-a-boo, which consist basically of making and breaking mutual gaze. The level of gaze declines up to adolescence and then increases again.

These gaze phenomena have been found in all cultures. However, there are cultural differences. "Contact cultures", where people stand closer and touch more, also gaze more. In these cultures social relations could be more intimate (in terms of subjective feeling), or the same signals may simply have different meanings.

In every culture people notice if gaze is incorrect; this indicates the presence of cultural rules. Too much gaze is regarded as intrusive or disrespectful, too little as insincere and cold. Gaze can also vary in meaning between different cultures. Belief in the evil eye is still common in some Mediterranean countries. Certain women or priests, who have squints or deep-set eyes, are thought to cast a curse on people they look at. These ideas perhaps arise out of the discomfort of being stared at by strangers.

It has been suggested that a person will look at someone he or she likes more than at someone disliked. Rubin (1973) found that couples who were more in love engaged in more mutual gaze than couples less deeply in love. Argyle and Dean (1965) suggested that pairs of people reach an equilibrium of intimacy, based on conflicting approach and avoidance forces. This is expressed by a combination of affiliative signals, such as gaze, proximity or smiling. If the equilibrium is disturbed, for example by an increase of distance, compensating signals would be expected, such as more gaze. Their experiments confirmed this and other findings also support it; for example, Exline found less gaze and mutual gaze when intimate topics are being discussed.

Gaze can signal other attitudes besides liking and loving. Submissive or lower status people look more, especially while listening. Hostility can be signaled by a stare, or by aversion of gaze, as when ignoring another person. Deception and embarrassment are accompanied by reduced gaze. Other emotions produce characteristic gaze patterns; for example, depression is shown by gazing downwards. In the main positive attitudes and emotions, such as liking and happiness, are shown by more gaze, and negative ones such as dislike and depression, by less. People look at those they like because the appearance and behavior of the other are rewarding.

People draw inferences from others' gaze. For instance a person looking 15 per cent of the time may be seen as nervous, evasive and defensive while a person looking 85 per cent of the time is seen as self-confident, friendly and sincere. The way the eyes are opened is also used. Emotions can be decoded with above-chance accuracy from photos of the eyes, while for certain mixed emotional states, such as pleasure and anger, this is the most informative area of the face. Although others' gaze can be, and is, interpreted Swain et al. (1982) cast doubt on the expressive function of gaze and suggested that need for information would explain all the replicable findings, such as the greater amount of direct gaze between pairs who are further apart during a conversation.

They found a greater amount of eye-contact between two strangers than between friends or married couples.

People being gazed at have an impression of being the object of the other's attention. In the experience of mutual gaze each person feels that he is open to the other. The general meaning of being gazed at is that the other is attending and interested. But the perceived nature of the other's interest varies.

Gaze may be interpreted as a threat. Ellsworth et al. (1972) found that continuous staring caused motorists to move off more rapidly from stop-lights. Marsh et al. (1978) found that a glance by a rival football fan may start a fight. However, gaze is only seen as a threat under certain conditions. It can lead to help if someone who has collapsed stares at the nearest person.

In conversation, speakers use gaze at the ends of long utterances and at grammatical breaks. This is to see whether the other person has understood, agreed, and so on, or whether the listener is willing to continue listening. But there is much more gaze while listening than when speaking. It has been suggested that this is because speakers' attention is directed towards planning what to say, so they look away to avoid cognitive overload. However, this hypothesis is not supported by La France and Mayo's finding (1976) that North American Blacks look more when speaking than when listening.

During conversation people take turns in speaking and usually manage without much overlap or interruption. This is mainly through nonverbal cues, of which gaze is one. The speaker's final gaze functions as a full-stop signal. If there is no terminal gaze, it is often some time before the other person replies, at least when the conversation is hesitant.

A speaker may also use gaze as an emphasizer, sometimes by a sudden widening of the eyes. A listener indicates his attention and also his approval by looking, nodding and smiling. These glances act as reinforcers, increasing the speaker's tendency to talk about particular topics.

Gaze also plays a part in greetings.

Kendon and Ferber (1973) found that there is a mutual glance in the first stage, the "distant salutation", aversion during approach and another mutual gaze in the third, or close, phase, when bodily contact also occurs. These phases are reversed in partings, again with two mutual glances.

Females look more than males. The difference is greatest for mutual gaze and for looking while talking. Girls attend to faces more than boys do at six months, so there may be an innate difference. But this difference increases, and is greater for adults. Gaze is probably used more for affiliative purposes by females, and their affiliative needs are stronger. Furthermore, being looked at for a female is probably interpreted in terms of affiliation or sexual interest, rather than threat.

In conclusion, people look at each other when they are interested in each other's reactions. This leads to gaze acquiring meaning as a social signal. There may have been evolutionary development of gaze as a ritualized signal whose meaning is innate. Gaze plays a central part in communication, and is closely co-ordinated with speech. The use of gaze can go wrong in a variety of ways: aversion of gaze and staring are common in mental patients.   JMA/RL.

Bibliography

*Argyle, M. and Cook, M. 1976: *Gaze and mutual gaze*. Cambridge and New York: Cambridge University Press.

—— and Dean, J. 1965: Eye-contact, distance and affiliation. *Sociometry* 28, 289–304.

Bruner, J.S. 1976: Early rule structure: the case of peek-a-boo. In *Life sentences*, ed. R. Harré. New York: Wiley.

Ellsworth, P.C., Carlsmith, J.M. and Henson, A. 1972: The stare as a stimulus to fight in human subjects: a series of field experiments. *Journal of personality and social psychology* 21, 302–11.

Exline, R. and Fehr, B.J. 1978: Application of semiosis to the study of visual interaction. In *Nonverbal behavior and communication*, eds. A.W. Siegman and S. Feldstein. Hillsdale, N.J.: Erlbaum.

Kendon, A. and Ferber, A. 1973: A description of some human greetings. In *Comparative ecology and behavior of primates*, eds. R.F. Michael and J.H. Crook. London: Academic Press.

La France, M. and Mayo. C. 1976: Racial

differences in gaze behavior during conversation. *Journal of personality and social psychology* 33, 547–52.

Marsh, P., Rosser, F. and Harré, R. 1978: *The rules of disorder*. London: Routledge and Kegan Paul.

Rubin, Z. 1973: *Liking and loving: an invitation to social psychology*. New York: Holt, Rinehart and Winston.

Swain, J., Stephenson, G.M. and Dewey, M.E. 1982: "Seeing a stranger": does eye-contact reflect intimacy? *Semiotica* 42, 107–18.

Geisteswissenschaftliche Psychologie Originally referred to psychology as it explores the transindividual, objective mind and its products, then its relations to individual, subjective minds whence the alleged foundation of *Geisteswissenschaften* (i.e. the humanities, historical and cultural sciences). It was put forward by E. Spranger, a disciple of Dilthey, as an elaboration of the term *Verstehende Psychologie*, with which it is now used interchangeably.   HUKG

genetics *See* behavior genetics, and below.

genetics, evolution and behavior Genetic and evolutionary influences on human behavior remain controversial areas of study more than a century after Mendel's discovery of particulate inheritance and Darwin's original exposition of evolutionary theory. In the 1970s and early '80s acrimonious debate reached new depths following, for example, Jensen's publication (1969) of a review paper combining the topics of genetics, intelligence, and race, and Wilson's treatise (1975) on behavioral evolution. The current debates often involve heavy doses of polemical politics and *ad hominem* attacks. However, at the same time they often represent attempts by practitioners of academic disciplines such as anthropology, biology, genetics, psychology, and sociology to come to grips with a plethora of new information which crosses their traditional disciplinary boundaries.

Two fundamental approaches have been applied in the study of genetics. One is mechanism oriented and involves Mendelian segregation combined with physiological and cellular studies of genetic influences on the development of the phenotype of individuals. The second is a statistical approach, variously labeled biometrical or quantitative genetics, which attempts to understand the influence of genetic variation on phenotypic variation by analyzing the patterns of distribution of characteristics among the members of populations. Both approaches have been applied to the investigation of psychological phenotypes.

That genetic variation can have profound influences on behavioral phenotypes of humans was unequivocally demonstrated by the discovery and subsequent investigations of phenylketonuria (PKU) beginning in the 1930s. This now-treatable form of profound mental retardation is related to a metabolic block of a particular enzymatic pathway which is itself due to homozygosity for a particular genetic allele at a single autosomal locus. The discovery of a specific genetic etiology for a particular set of retardates constituted a true breakthrough in investigations of the causes of retardation. PKU is now a classic model for a large set of genetically distinct "aminoacidurias" and further single-gene causes of retardation. Another breakthrough in understanding the genetic underpinnings of human variation was the discovery in 1959 that an extra chromosome was the cause of Down's Syndrome. It was only in 1956 that the normal diploid human chromosome number was established to be 46 (44 autosomes plus two sex chromosomes, X and Y). Having 47 chromosomes with the supernumerary being an extra copy of the chromosome labeled number 21, hence "trisomy-21", is the cause of Down's Syndrome. Females having one X chromosome rather than the normal two (45X0) were, also in 1959, discovered to display Turner's Syndrome, the symptoms of which include a specific cognitive deficit and failure to mature sexually. Klinefelter's Syndrome males (47XXY) have an extra X chromosome, and display sexual and personality disturbances. These and many other chromosomal anomalies associated with behavioral symptoms have been discovered in recent decades. At the present time human chromosome studies (cytogenetics) is one of the fastest expanding areas of genetic investigation with implications for psychology. Literally many hundreds of genetic alleles are now known to influence various aspects of psychological function, ranging from sensory abilities to cognition.

The biometrical approach to understanding hereditary contributions to individual differences in human behavior antedates the discovery of Mendelian genetics, having begun with investigations by Sir Francis Galton. Recent advances in methodological sophistication, especially techniques involving path coefficients and utilizing twin and adoptive family data, continue to contribute to an unraveling of the complexities of genetic and environmental influences on psychological individuality. Bouchard and McGue (1981) reviewed 111 studies, many of them recent, containing an aggregate of 526 familial correlations including 113,942 pairings dealing with genetic involvement in intellectual functioning as assessed by IQ tests. The general interpretation of the outcomes of carefully conducted studies has not changed since the inception of IQ tests early in the century; a substantial proportion of the variation in IQ appears to be mediated genetically. However, numerical estimates of the technical heritability statistic, which indexes the proportion of trait variance which is attributable to genetic variance of the population, has changed. Recent large studies point to a heritability of IQ in the vicinity of 0.5, rather than the 0.75–0.8 values which were widely cited in previous decades. Large-scale adoption and twin studies, some utilizing the extensive national records available in some countries (such as Denmark), are being conducted for many psychological variables. An inherited susceptibility or predisposition has been documented for many behavioral dimensions, ranging from smoking and alcoholism to homosexuality and likelihood of criminal activity, as well as diverse psychopathologies and variation

in normal-range personality traits. Although specific mechanisms remain undiscovered, the evidence is unequivocal for a strong genetic dimension in the etiology of both schizophrenia and affective psychoses. Somewhat surprisingly to many, Plomin et al. (1980) point out that when genetic background is taken into account there remains no evidence for an important role of any known environmental variables in the development of schizophrenia. Although the details vary, and in most cases are poorly understood at present, it is perhaps not surprising that genetic individual differences appear to play a role in the development of individual differences on every psychological variable that has been investigated (Whitney 1976). At the present time the rapidly accumulating knowledge of genetic influences on behavior has exceeded its incorporation into general psychological theory.

Although data now outstrip general theory in the realm of psychological genetics, in the realm of human behavioral evolution theoretical speculations greatly exceed empirical data. Phenotypic variation influenced to some degree by heritable genetic variation, combined with differential reproductive success (individual Darwinian fitness or inclusive fitness) is the essence of evolution. While it is clear that heritable variation does influence most (perhaps all) dimensions of human behavior it is usually difficult to relate behavioral variation and concomitant genetical variation, at least within the normal range of variation, to differential reproductive success. Bajema (1971) has drawn together a number of papers which attempt to measure ongoing genetic evolution in contemporary societies. Unfortunately virtually every serious study is met with a wide range of criticism, much of it not scientifically grounded. Nevertheless, theoretical speculation and accounts of plausible possibilities abound in both the technical and popular literature.

Most recent accounts of human behavioral evolution remain at the level of comparisons between species and largely restrict their treatments of human behavior to species-general typological concepts.

This is the case even though natural selection depends on heritable variation among individuals within the species. It has become impolite and exceedingly controversial even to discuss heritable individual differences which could involve human behavioral evolution, and academics tread lightly. Nevertheless possibilities abound, many based on quite extensive data. As an example, phenotypic intelligence as measured by the controversial IQ tests displays many of the characteristics to be expected of an evolutionarily-relevant phenotype. Phenotypic individual differences are large, measurable, and have substantial genetic influence; extreme individuals, at least at the low end of the trait continuum, are severely depressed in reproductive performance; the trait displays inbreeding depression as do many other fitness relevant traits; and a reproductive difference favoring individuals of above average intelligence is demonstrable even within some modern industralized populations. The latter finding, replicated in various independent studies (e.g. Waller 1971), is surprising to many layman who share the common observation that "less bright" people tend to have larger families. The actual data are consistent with that observation. However, a larger proportion of the "less bright" people also have no children at all. When account is taken of the reproductive performance of all the members of a group, including those that do not reproduce, the general outcome has been that higher intelligence is positively related to reproductive performance.

Racial variation is another taboo topic that could shed considerable light on human behavioral evolution. Of course existing biological races of humans display considerable overlap of distribution for many behavioral traits and share many of the same genes. Some geneticists and anthropologists have stated that the vast preponderance of genetic variation is among individuals within a race and not among races, leading to suggestions that investigations of racial subgroups within the species would not be fruitful with regard to evolutionary interests. However Neel (1981) points out that from simul-taneous consideration of only 8 genetic loci one can be correct about 87 per cent of the time in assignment of an individual to race, and greater accuracy can be obtained when dealing with small groups. Races differ in the frequency of many genes, including many of relevance to behavior. Well-known examples include the genes responsible for PKU, which are predominantly found among Caucasians; Tay-Sachs disease which is almost exclusively limited to Jewish populations; and Sickle-Cell Anemia which is most common in Blacks. The incidence of many behavioral phenotypes also differs substantially among races. Examples are many: the distribution of IQ scores have been found in studies from the 1920s through the 1980s to differ among races in an ordering of Americans of Asian ancestry, Americans of European Caucasian ancestry, Americans of Black African ancestry; rates of psychologically relevant phenomena such as homicide, schizophrenia, affective psychoses, and suicide differ substantially among races. Although studies of racial variation within other species have shed much light on the processes of evolution in general, the recent social climate has tended to stifle investigations of human behavioral genetics and behavioral evolution from this potentially informative perspective.   GW

Bibliography

Bajema, C.J. (comp.) 1971. *Natural selection in human populations*. New York and Chichester: John Wiley and Sons.

Bouchard, T.J. and McGue, M. 1981. Familial studies of intelligence: a review. *Science* 212, 1055–9.

Jensen, A.R 1969. How much can we boost IQ and scholastic achievement? *Harvard educational review* 39(1), 1–123.

*Lumsden, C.J. and Wilson, E.O. 1981. *Genes, mind, and culture*. Cambridge, Mass. and London: Harvard University Press.

Neel, J.V. 1981: The major ethnic groups: diversity in the midst of similarity. *The American naturalist* 117, 83–7.

*Plomin, R, DeFries, J.C., and McClearn, G.E. 1980: *Behavioral genetics, a primer*. San Francisco: W.H. Freeman and Company.

*Vogel, F., and Motulsky, A.G. 1979. *Human genetics*. Berlin and New York: Springer-Verlag.

Waller, J.H. 1971: Differential reproduction: its relation to IQ test scores, education, and occupation. *Social biology* 18, 122–36.

Whitney, G. 1976: Genetic considerations in studies of the evolution of the nervous system and behavior. In *Evolution, brain and behavior: persistent problems*, eds. R.B. Masterton, W. Hodos and H. Jerison. Hillsdale, N.J.: Lawrence Erlbaum Associates; London: distrib. by Halsted Press Div., Wiley.

Wilson, E.O. 1975: *Sociobiology: the new synthesis*. Cambridge, Mass.: Belknap Press of Harvard University Press.

gerontology Involves the study of social and psychological mechanisms in aging. It is a complex, wide-ranging and multi-disciplinary subject. No sharp distinction can be drawn between the mechanisms of aging and the mechanisms of chronic degenerative illness. Research and theory in psychosomatics, behavioral medicine and psychoneuroimmunology express a conviction that psychological factors influence not only mental well-being in the sick and the old, but also neuro-endocrine balances, immune system competence and cardiovascular function, and hence an individual's physical fitness and longevity. Evidence has accumulated which shows that the onset and course of almost every form of chronic degenerative illness are susceptible to social influences, many of which become especially acute in the lives of old people.

The main areas of research

(i) *Large-scale epidemiological surveys*: statistical surveys of rates of death and disability among populations of retired people.

(ii) *Quality of life studies*: the study of amenities, living conditions, social services and other environmental and economic factors and their relation to health and longevity in the elderly.

(iii) *Personal contact and social support*: studies of family relations, social networks, isolation and loneliness in the elderly. These involve the use of ad hoc scales as well as interview techniques.

(iv) *Studies of work and retirement*: factors affecting the adjustment of individuals who are retiring from work and descriptive studies of the transition from work to retirement.

(v) *Biographical studies*: based on the idea of life as an unfolding biographical career, this approach sets a value on forming an understanding of an individual's priorities for later life by listening to the accounts given of the path of his or her life history.

All these areas of research share the ultimate objective of prescribing measures to assist the elderly. The wider-scale survey style studies assume such measures to be general and commensurable, the smaller-scale idiographic studies reflect the assumption that caring involves sensitivity to the particular esoteric needs of an individual.

The main theories

(i) *Disengagement theory* (Cumming and Henry 1961): a functionalist theory in which aging is represented as a process of mutual withdrawal of individual and society. The individual necessarily withdraws because of his or her diminished abilities; society withdraws because younger people are needed to fill vacant roles.

(ii) *Activity theory* (Lemon et al. 1972): opposed to disengagement theory in proposing that although role-related activity diminishes with age, level of activity nevertheless correlates with life satisfaction and perhaps health and longevity.

(iii) *Social breakdown model* (Kuypers and Bengtson 1973): aging is characterized by the loss of an identity previously sustained through roles, norms (see NORM), and reference groups (see REFERENCE GROUP), and substitution of the identity "old person", with its connotation of incompetence and social redundancy.

(iv) *Exchange theory* (Dowd 1975): a generalization of economic exchange theory; the decline in power resources associated with age prevents the aged from becoming involved in balanced exchange relationships with other groups.

(v) *Learned helplessness model* (Abramson et al. 1978): the diminished powers of old people give rise to attributions of uncontrollability of important outcomes. This results in a generalized helplessness set, leading to depression and perhaps illness.

GT

Bibliography

Abramson, L.Y., Seligman, M.E.P. and Teasdale, J.D. 1978: Learned helplessness in humans: critique and reformulation. *Journal of abnormal psychology* 87, 49–74.

*Binstock, R. and Shanas, E. eds. 1976: *Handbook of aging and the social sciences*. New York: Van Nostrand.

Birren, J.E., Cunningham, W.R. and Yamamoto, K. 1983: Psychology of adult development and aging. *Annual review of psychology* 34, 543–75.

Cumming, E. and Henry, W.F. 1961: *Growing old*. New York: Basic Books.

Dowd, J. 1975: Aging as exchange: a preface to theory. *Journal of gerontology* 30, 584–94.

Kuypers, J.A. and Bengtson, V.L. 1973: Social breakdown and competence: a model of normal aging. *Human development* 16, 181–201.

Lemon, B.W., Bengtson, V.L. and Peterson, J.A. 1972: An exploration of the activity theory of aging: activity and life satisfaction among inmovers to a retirement community. *Journal of gerontology* 27, 511–23.

gesture The word is used in several senses. Either it is used specifically to refer to communication with the hands or some other part of the body (as in the case of facial gesture) or else it is used generally to refer to communication with the whole body. This section deals only with gesture as a form of manual communication, and the reader is referred to the entry on COMMUNICATION, NON-VERBAL for a discussion of other types of gesture.

The study of manual gesture can be traced back to Cicero and Quintilian, who were concerned with rhetorical uses of the hands in oratory. However it was only during the seventeenth century, with the publication of works such as Bonifacio's *L'Arte dei Cenni* (1616) and Bulwer's *Chirologia . . . Chironomia* (1644), that gesture acquired the status of a subject in its own right. Bonifacio and Bulwer tended to rely on literary sources rather than observation for their evidence, and their treatments were taxonomic rather than functional or pragmatic. Bulwer, however, gave a great deal of attention to gesture as a speech surrogate, and he is generally acknowledged as the first author to recognize the possibility of a codified manual language for the deaf. Since the seventeenth century there has been a growing interest in gesture and its relations to other forms of communication, and it is now possible to identify several areas in which gesture has been studied.

Gesture and the origins of language

It has been seriously proposed that the phylogenetic origins of language are to be found in gesture. The list of authors who have advanced this notion includes such notables as Wundt, Swedenborg, Romanes, Paget and Johannesson. Although there are some variations in the theories that have been offered, the basic idea is that pre-linguistic hominids started by using a gestural form of communication, and that with the development of the brain and the vocal apparatus there was a corresponding shift from a manual to a vocal proto-language, which in turn gave way to vocal language proper. A comprehensive treatment of this topic and the relevant literature can be found in Hewes (1975).

Gesture as a language

Certain societies and groups of people possess extremely elaborate repertoires of gesture. In some cases the repertoire may simply consist of a gestural lexis which does not have the properties of a language, and where the signs are typically employed as isolated units, whereas in other cases the lexis may be associated with a grammar and therefore be a fully constituted language. There appear to be three explanations for the development of gestural systems which have the properties of language. Firstly there are those groups, such as the Cistercian monks (Barakat 1975) and the Australian Aborigines (Kendon 1980), which have committed themselves to silence and eschewed the use of speech for reasons connected with religious belief or social custom, and which have therefore developed a sign language to take the place of speech. Secondly there are peoples such as the North American Plains Indians

(Mallery 1880; Taylor 1975) who have been forced to invent a *mano franca* in order to make themselves intelligible to neighboring peoples who speak another language, and finally there are the deaf who have been deprived of the ability to speak (Stokoe 1980). There are also various other groups, such as racecourse touts, Bushmen hunters, Indian merchants, as well as radio, sawmill and stock exchange personnel, who have developed sign systems because of the need to communicate across great and sometimes noisy distances, but these systems are seldom properly constituted languages. The most elaborate and thoroughly researched case of a gestural language is that of American Sign Language (Klima and Bellugi 1979). However there are other sign languages used by the deaf. These include the Paget system and finger spelling.

Colloquial gestures

Colloquial gestures are those which are not part of a sign language. They can be divided into several categories, according to whether they are iconic or symbolic, whether they accompany speech or function as a substitute for speech, whether they are produced intentionally or unintentionally, and so on (Efron 1941; Ekman and Friesen 1969). The major categories of colloquial gesture include emblems, illustrators or mimic signs and batons.

(a) *Emblems*. An emblem is defined by the fact that its shape bears no obvious relationship to its meaning; like most words in language, the link between sign and meaning is arbitrary. Examples of emblems include gestures such as the Thumbs Up, in which the thumb is extended upwards from the fist, and the Ring sign, in which the tips of the thumb and first finger are brought together to form a circle. The most thorough study of a single emblem is undoubtedly Taylor's investigation of the Shanghai or nose-thumbing gesture (1956). Numerous attempts have also been made to catalogue the emblems used by groups of people, to uncover the origins of these gestures and to explore their geographical distribution and cultural diffusion. Di Jorio (1832), for example,

catalogued the emblems of Naples and traced certain Neapolitan gestures to depictions on Greek vases. Efron (1941) studied the gestural habits of first and second generation Jews and Italians in New York. Saitz and Cervenka (1972) listed and compared some of the emblems used in Columbia and the United States, and Morris et al. (1979) mapped the use and meanings of various emblems across Europe and examined the theories about the origins. Apart from these and other comparative studies, there have also been several investigations of the emblems used within a particular society. Green's (1968) analysis of Spanish gesture and Sparhawk's (1978) work on Persian gestures are examples.

(b) *Illustrators and mimic signs*. These gestures are iconic and representational and are used as a graphic means of illustrating some idea which is or is not encoded in speech. Historically there is some evidence that illustrators and mimic signs, together with onomatopoetic speech, have formed the basis of communication between people who do not share a common language (Hewes 1974). Research in this area has concentrated on the location of illustrative hand movements in relation to speech (Birdwhistell 1970; Ekman and Friesen 1972; McNeil 1979; Kendon 1983).

(c) *Batons*. As their name suggests, batons are those movements of the hands which are used to stress and orchestrate speech. Some attempt has been made to produce a taxonomy of baton postures (Morris 1977), and to examine their cultural distribution (Efron 1941), but by and large this category of gesture has gone largely unnoticed.

Although emblems, illustrators, batons and other classes of gesture can usually be distinguished, problems of classifications do arise, and the field still awaits an exhaustive taxonomic system that is applicable cross-culturally.   PC

Bibliography

*Bauml, B.J. and F.H. 1975: *A dictionary of gestures*. Metuchen, N.J.: Scarecrow Press.

*Critchley, M. 1975: *Silent language*. London: Butterworth.

*Hewes, G. 1974: Gesture language in culture contact. *Sign language studies* 4, 1–34.

*—— ed. 1975: *Language origins: a bibliography*. The Hague: Mouton.

*Kendon, A. ed. 1981: *Nonverbal communication, interaction and gesture*. The Hague: Mouton.

—— 1983: Gesture and speech: how they interact. In *Nonverbal interaction*, eds. J.W. Wiemann and R.P. Harrison. Beverly Hills: Sage.

*Morris, D. et al. 1979: *Gestures: their origins and distribution*. London: Cape.

All the other references referred to in this entry may be found in either Kendon (1981) or Morris et al. (1979). Useful journals to consult are *Semiotica* and *Sign language studies*.

Goffman, Erving

Goffman, Erving A sociologist who has had an enormous influence on thinking and studies of the SELF (and SELF-PRESENTATION), INSTITUTIONALIZATION, ROLES, and SOCIAL INTERACTION. Goffman was born in 1922 in Manville, Alta, Canada, and was educated at the universities of Toronto (graduated 1945) and Chicago (M.A. 1949, Ph.D. 1953). He was a member of the Shetland field research unit in the Edinburgh University department of social anthropology between 1949 and 1951, and did a year's fieldwork at St Elizabeth's Hospital, Washington DC (1955–6). Following this Goffman became assistant, associate and full professor at Berkeley (1958–68), and then moved to be professor of anthropology and sociology at the University of Pennsylvania. He died in Philadelphia in November, 1982.

At Chicago Goffman encountered Blumer (who moved to Berkeley in 1952) and other members of the "Chicago School" of SYMBOLIC INTERACTION. All symbolic interactionists 'share the substantive view that human beings construct their realities in a process of interaction with other human beings'. (Meltzer et al. 1975). Unlike Kuhn and many other interactionists, however, Blumer also regarded the "soft" approach of using biographies, diaries, non-directive interviews and participant observation as proper ways of collecting data. He resisted the concept of roles as fixed positions in the social structure which determine their occupants' behavior, and preferred to see them as frameworks within which there is latitude for creative interaction with other people.

Goffman was clearly influenced by these methodological and conceptual assumptions, as well as the ideas of DURKHEIM, Simmel and Burke. Throughout his career he was preoccupied with the study of face-to-face interaction. Blumer (1972) thought this led to a 'corresponding exclusion of the vast mass of human activity' and felt it was Goffman's weakness. Goffman's (1983) defense was that such interaction is common to all societies and is an aspect of social life which is not dependent upon social structure, even though interactions are affected by presuppositions embedded in the society beyond their immediate context.

Goffman made his name with the very successful book *The presentation of self in everyday life* (1956, 1959). In this he argued that interaction could be compared to drama, not as a completely adequate model, but as a suggestive analogy. As he put it: 'All the world is not, of course, a stage, but the crucial ways in which it isn't are not easy to specify'. This so-called "dramaturgic approach" has been the source of heated debate. It draws attention to the fact that people are dissimulators and hypocrites, or at least act to bolster the impression of their competence and worth when they are performing a legitimate role (e.g. as a doctor). So even if someone is really a competent doctor, Goffman's eye is upon the aspects of his or her performance which are expressive and not primarily functional.

Even earlier than *The presentation of self* Goffman was interested in the "fraudulent" use of status symbols (1951). He argued that symbols 'are better suited to the requirements of communication than are the rights and duties which they signify'. But their separation from what they signify means they can be used for misrepresentation. Using symbols to signify occupational status to which one has no right may bring one up against legal sanctions. But 'legal sanctions cannot be applied against those who represent themselves as possessing a class status which an informed majority would not accord them.' He lists 'devices for restricting misrepresentative use' of symbols, but he also remarks that social mobility increases 'the tendency for signs that symbolize position to take on the role of conferring it'. In other words, the expressive aspects of role and status become the criteria for occupation of the role or status. As he states in *The presentation of self*: 'Society is organized on the principle that any individual who possesses certain social characteristics has a moral right to expect that others will value and treat him in an appropriate way'.

Such an analysis stresses the superficial accoutrements of status, while implying that their superficiality in no way diminishes their importance. It therefore tends to imply that there is something artificial or illusory about much of social life, and that there is a constant, more or less conscious intention on people's part to deceive, or at least manipulate others' beliefs. In fact Goffman admits that some people's self-presentations may be sincere, but expresses this as 'the performer fully taken in by his own act'. He also points out that a performance necessarily incorporates 'officially accredited values'. We may therefore 'look upon it . . . as a ceremony – as an expressive . . . reaffirmation of the moral values of the community'.

Goffman employs a vocabulary derived from his "dramaturgical principles", which produces suggestive metaphors of "performance", "routines", "setting", "props", "front region" and "back-stage". He is able to make the dramaturgic approach more plausible by describing the social actor in the context in which he is part of a team of co-workers who are putting on a performance designed to make a particular impression on an audience (1959). This is clearly analogous to the position of an actor in a theater, and it gives the performer certain duties not to act out of role and thereby upstage his fellow team-members. But in many social situations one is obviously not part of a team, and the audience and the fellow performers are the same people. Goffman, in fact, stresses that

in presenting oneself in a certain light one is implicitly inviting a complementary performance which offers active support for one's pretensions to one's projected role.

On face-work (1955, reprinted in *Interaction ritual*, 1967) gives a detailed account of actions taken by the actor and his audience in order to preserve (or save) his face. Some of these are "preventive practices" and some are "corrective". The preventive practices may be defensive or protective, depending on whether they are the actor's or the audience's. Goffman regards the breakdown and repair of interaction as particularly revealing, and gives them further attention in *Remedial interchanges* (see 1971). After an actor has "taken a line" he must act in a way which is consistent with that line. When things go wrong with a performance the actor must account for what has happened, either by redefining the offense as something other than it appears to be (a joke, for instance), or by accepting his failure, but excusing it or apologizing for it and suggesting that it is not typical of him. When something goes wrong, however, those present may show tact, by accepting the actor's corrective action, and joining in a "round" of interchanges to remedy the fault before it upsets the tacitly agreed definition of the situation. The motivation to do this is partly self-interested, as people have a stake in maintaining these established definitions and avoiding embarrassment. But it is partly at least enlightened self-interest, a tacit contract to respect each other's self-definitions for the benefit of all.

Symbolic interactionism has been described as a product of the flux and egalitarianism of America (Shaskolsky 1970). Goffman's dramaturgical analogy seems to imply a vision of social action which is more rootless, momentaneous and other-directed than that of earlier interactionists. It therefore seems peculiarly the product of a modern urban environment. Yet Goffman frequently illustrates his points with anecdotes about the Shetland crofters. He asserts (1967) that 'societies everywhere . . . must mobilize their members as self-regulating participants in social encounters', and that one way of doing this 'is through ritual'. In other words, the theatrical principles he describes are as applicable to a tight-knit and traditional rural community as to the inhabitants of a modern metropolis.

At the heart of much of Goffman's thinking lies the problem of identity. An implication of the theatrical analogy of interaction is that people do not have any central reality, or "self" beyond the performances which they put on for others. Goffman does not deny that people may believe their behavior is natural and sincere. On the other hand, he describes as 'vulgar' the 'tendency ... to divide the conduct of the individual into a profane and sacred part', in which 'the profane part is attributed to the obligatory world of social roles' while 'the sacred part has to do with ... what an individual is "really" like underneath in all' (*Role distance* in *Encounters*, 1961). He tends to define apparently spontaneous or out-of-role behavior in ways which make it simply part of the theatrical performance. For example (1967) emotions are said to 'function as moves' in interaction. Even a child cries or sulks 'not as an irrational expression of frustration, but as a ritual move'. Another example is "role distance". This is an ironic approach by which people 'convey some disdainful detachment' from a role, and thereby distance themselves from a complete identification with the role they are playing. As such, it is certainly a show of "personal style" and a sign that people are free 'to give way to the wider constraints of their multiple self-identifications'. But it often serves a functional purpose within the role from which one apparently distances oneself, as when a surgeon behaves light-heartedly to control or distract his team during an operation. Expressively, it is a way of demonstrating thorough mastery of a role and a defensive practice to protect oneself from any implications attendant upon over-immersion in inappropriate behavior.

Concern with identity is also prevalent in his work on the handicapped or those labeled in a demeaning way (see *Stigma*, 1963), and appears in his work on insti-tutionalization. *Asylums* (1961) is the result of participant observation of 'the social world of the hospital inmate, as this world is subjectively experienced by him', but it also draws on reports of life in prison and the forces. He calls such institutions "total" because an inmate's whole life is circumscribed by the institution twenty-four hours a day. The institution also controls the inmate's time and invades his sense of identity, involving what Goffman calls 'profanations of self'. From the admission procedure onwards the inmate is stripped of possibilities or simply of objects which define and support his identity. He lacks individuality and privacy, or even 'a margin of face-saving reactive expression'. The inmate is under observation, or even surveillance. He has no back-stage.

In his later work, Goffman continued to be preoccupied with interaction, developing some of his earlier ideas in books such as *Relations in public* (1971). Many of his minute observations (as of "tie-signs" which show off relationships) have great descriptive value even for those who discount their theoretical underpinnings. He also investigated other analogies of social order, such as Ross's (1908) suggestion of traffic codes. But Goffman did not treat this as an analogy so much as a microcosmic example of social order in action. As such he treated it in some detail, since 'Road-traffic rules serve as something of an ideal case in arguments regarding the nature and value of ground rules'.

In *Frame analysis* (1974) Goffman looked further at the social constructions of reality, using the idea that people 'imply . . . (and in effect employ) one or more frameworks or schemata of interpretation' in the face of any event. Despite the cognitive tone, however, Goffman was once again preoccupied with errors: "flubs", "goofs" and "gaffes", and with the 'set of conventions by which a given activity . . . is transformed into ... something quite else'. Such redefinition of the situation occurs in play, as he points out. The creation and re-creation of social reality are primary preoccupations of Goffman's. They are central to apologies and other forms of remedial

145

activity, and may be seen as part of the process involved in role distance.

In *Forms of talk* (1981) he continued with similar ideas. This book concerns itself with types of talk such as radio talk, the lecture etc. Goffman also discusses conversation, and suggests that the second move in a conversation should be seen as a "response" rather than a "reply". This is partly because conversation is interaction, not dialogue. It is a "ritual interchange" and unlike grammar because 'grammars do not have rules for managing what happens when rules are broken'. Over and above that, however, responses may comment on an initial statement and not merely reply to it. The response may 'address aspects of a statement which would ordinarily be "out of frame", . . . for example, the statement's duration, tactfulness, style . . .'. It may therefore serve to deny or modify presuppositions implied in these features (cf. 1971, chapter 4, section 9).

Goffman did not meet with universal acclaim either for his method or his ideas. Certainly both may seem superficial, or to display an obsession with the superficial. He was sensitive to the objections. In *Asylums* he says: 'I did not employ usual kinds of measurements and controls. I assumed that the role and time required to gather statistical evidence . . . would preclude my gathering data on the tissue and fabric of patient life'. In *Frame analysis* he admits that he is using 'anecdotes cited from the press and from popular books in the biographical genre. There could hardly be data with less face value'. But he is using these methods 'not . . . as evidence or proof, but as clarifying depictions'. In *Relations in public*, he grants that he makes 'unsubstantiated assertions', and that 'unsystematic, naturalistic observation . . . has very serious limitations', but he holds that this is the only way 'if a broad attempt is to be made to tie together bits and pieces of contemporary social life in exploratory analysis'. He also challenges the presumptions of some of his critics, who work in laboratories and think 'that if you go through the motions attributable to science then science will result. But it hasn't . . .'. These strictures have not prevented others

from attempting to be more "scientific" in testing Goffman's ideas (see e.g. Semin and Manstead 1983).

The ideological objections include charges of cynicism and conservatism. Goffman accepted something of the view of himself as an upholder of social order (1971), but it is social order for its own sake, not a particular order. Goffman thought things would probably be better if particular changes were made, but 'an order can benefit all of its participants individually . . .'. The claim that his ideas are all cynical or reactionary is a slander. *Asylums* (and *Stigma*) belong to the same liberal tradition as the writings of Laing and Szasz, and embody the same disrespect for institutions and the same respect for their victims. Further, although he seems to have been unattracted by that pious subject, the "real self", his work constantly implies the emancipating aspects of symbolic interaction. Brittan (1973) criticizes Goffman for treating people for being too much at the mercy of their scripts (p.86). But only a few pages later (p.93) he enthusiastically proclaims that Goffman's concept of role distance 'implies the ability to stand aside from the identity that one has been ascribed by the defining others. As agents, therefore, we can stand back and comment on the actual constitutive elements of that process'. The substitution of "responses" for "replies" and the idea that "frames" are not rigid, underline the same message in different contexts.

Inmates of total institutions are obliged to accept others' definitions of their identities without any reprieve. In comparison the play-acting in which people are supposed to indulge may be seen as an expression of their freedom from such constraints. The idea that we are not entirely fixed in social roles, but may create social reality as we go along, and assume the perhaps definitive trappings of social roles for the purposes of interaction seems neither cynical nor uplifting. According to Goffman, one's 'social face . . . is only on loan to him from society; it will be withdrawn unless he conducts himself in a way that is worthy of it'. The attempt to live up to attributes society approves in one makes 'of every man his own jailer' (1967). Irony and detachment may be more of a show than a proof that one is not defined by one's role. But they 'introduce a thin layer ... between what ... men define themselves as and what the institutional scene has defined them as'. It would be a mistake, however, to applaud Goffman as if he had introduced the concept of role distance to allow some chink for freedom to shine through. Expressing that there is more to oneself than one's immediate situated role may be a way of demonstrating and affirming one's freedom. But for Goffman this makes it an interesting and revealing subject for analysis, not a sign of man's inalienable natural rights.

Goffman's published works include: 1956: *The presentation of self in everyday life* (Edinburgh: Edinburgh University Press; rev. edn. New York: Doubleday, 1959); 1961: *Encounters* (Indianapolis: Bobbs-Merrill); 1961: *Asylums* (New York: Doubleday); 1963: *Behavior in public places* (New York: Free Press); 1963: *Stigma: notes on the management of spoiled identity* (Englewood Cliffs, N.J.: Prentice-Hall); 1967: *Interaction ritual* (New York: Doubleday), 1969: *Strategic interaction* (Philadelphia: University of Pennsylvania Press; New York: Ballantine, 1972); 1971: *Relations in public* (New York: Harper and Row); 1974: *Frame analysis* (New York: Harper and Row); 1979: *Gender advertisement* (New York: Harper and Row); 1981: *Forms of talk*. In the UK all were published by Penguin, except *Behavior in public places*, *Strategic interaction* and *Forms of talk* (all Blackwell); and *Gender advertisements* (Macmillan). (See also SYMBOLIC INTERACTION; COMMUNICATION: HUMAN GENERAL). RL

Bibliography

Blumer, H. 1972: Action vs. interaction (review of *Relations in public*). *Society* 9, 50–3.

Brittan, A. 1973: *Meanings and situations*. London and Boston: Routledge and Kegan Paul.

Goffman, E. 1951: Symbols of class status. *The British journal of sociology* 2, 294–304.

—— 1983: The interaction order. *American sociological review* 48, 1–17.

Meltzer, B.N., Petras, J.W. and Reynolds, L.T. 1975: *Symbolic interactionism: genesis, varieties and criticism*. London and Boston: Routledge and Kegan Paul.

Ross, E.A. 1908: *Social control*. New York: Macmillan.

Semin, G.R. and Manstead, A.S.R. 1983: *The accountability of conduct*. London: Academic Press.

Shaskolsky, L. 1970: The development of sociological theory in America – a sociology of knowledge approach. In *The sociology of sociology*, eds. L.T. Reynolds and J.M. Reynolds. New York: McKay.

greeting When two conspecifics meet, their response to one another may be hostile, but if not, and they are positively attracted to each other, they will probably engage in a more or less elaborate series of species-characteristic behavior patterns toward each other. These rituals are referred to as greeting displays. Some birds such as nesting kittiwakes have elaborate greeting ceremonies the object of which is to ensure that the new arrival at the nest is indeed the mated partner of the nest-holder and will feed its own genetic offspring. Such greetings are mostly found in pair-bonded species that separate for feeding and then meet up again.

Among social mammals, greetings are extended to other members of the species as well as mates, and involve highly stereotyped behavior patterns such as the side-by-side, head-to-tail, genital sniffing of dogs. Among primates greetings are most marked in chimpanzees, and occur whenever individuals who know each other meet after a temporary spell of separation. Males frequently touch each others' testicles, while both sexes may kiss, touch hands, or hug each other.

In humans greetings are culturally specified, but the fact that they exist, and often involve hand touching, embracing and kissing indicates that their roots may lie in our primate ancestry. Writers such as LaBarre, however, have emphasized cross-cultural differences in the use of posture and gesture, including those used in greetings (LaBarre 1947). Firth (1970) and Collett (1983) have produced detailed descriptions of greeting rituals in other societies. Both stress the symbolic import of the actions which go to make up the greeting (forms of prostration, sniffing, touching). The most extensive work on greetings in Western society is that of Kendon and Ferber (see Kendon, 1977).

It is clear that greetings (and partings) are highly formalized and include elements such as touching and kissing which may not occur elsewhere in the greeters' relationship and can be seen simply as polite form. Nevertheless, etiquette books stress elements of respect and warmth in discussing greetings, and the ritual necessarily allows the expression of many different degrees of both. GOFFMAN (1971) has pointed out the easily overlooked importance of greetings in displaying willingness to talk or setting the tone for subsequent interaction, as well as their role, even in passing, of reaffirming recognition and friendship after a lapse of time.

VR/RL

Bibliography

Collett, P.C. 1983: Mossi salutations. *Semiotica* 45, 191–248.

Firth, R. 1970: Postures and gestures of respect. In *Échanges et communications*, eds. J. Pouillon and P. Maranda. The Hague: Mouton.

Goffman, E. 1971: *Relations in public*. New York: Basic Books; London: Penguin.

Kendon, A. 1977: *Studies in the behavior of social interaction*. Bloomington: Indiana University; Lisse: Peter de Ridder.

LaBarre, W. 1947: The cultural basis of emotions and gestures. *Journal of personality* 16, 49–68.

(The articles by LaBarre and Firth are reprinted in *Social aspects of the human body*, ed. E. Polhemus. London: Penguin, 1978.)

gregariousness   In ethology, the tendency of individuals to associate in groups. One way of explaining gregariousness relates to its survival value. Two main explanations in these terms have been proposed, relating to advantages accruing to gregarious individuals (or their relatives) in predator avoidance and in food acquisition (Bertram 1978). A quite different type of explanation relates to the causal and developmental basis of gregariousness. In a well-known primate study (1932) Zuckerman proposed that sexual BONDS between adult males and females were the primary factor in group cohesion, but it is now clear that this was incorrect. To say instead that groups cohere because individuals are socially attractive to each other is probably true but circular, and it may be more profitable to investigate relationships and social structures in a detailed way than to search for an overall explanation of gregariousness (Chalmers 1979).   RDA

Bibliography

Bertram, B.C.R. 1978: Living in groups: predators and prey. In *Behavioral ecology: an evolutionary approach*, eds. J.R. Krebs and N.B. Davies. Oxford: Blackwell Scientific; Sunderland, Mass.: Sinauer Associates.

Chalmers, N. 1979: *Social behaviour in primates*. London: Edward Arnold; Baltimore: University Park Press.

Zuckerman, S. 1932: *The social life of monkeys and apes*. London: Kegan Paul; New York: Harcourt Brace.

group polarization   *See* risky shift.

groups   A group may be defined as two or more persons who are interacting with one another, who share a set of common goals and norms which direct their activities, and who develop a set of roles and a network of affective relations. Many other slightly differing definitions are found in the literature, but most of these contain the key element of social interaction, or mutual influence of group members (Shaw 1981). Practically this implies a vague boundary between a group and larger social entities, such as mobs, crowds, masses and collectivities, in which direct mutual influence is not possible. Usually the line is drawn between twenty and thirty members. Most readers will be familiar with several types of groups, such as the couple, the family, playgroups, school classes, social clubs; and with groups having a wide variety of production tasks, decision-making tasks, or problem-solving tasks, such as work teams, crews and committees. Rough estimates indicate that the average person in contemporary Western society belongs to five or six groups at one moment, and that more than 90 per cent of all existing groups have five members or less. Groups of this size with a cognitive task, such as decision-making, or problem-solving, have been studied most intensively in a branch of social psychology usually referred to as "group dynamics" (Cartwright and Zander 1968) or "small group research" (Hare 1976). These are also the main focus of this entry.

In abstract terms, a group may be described as an open system (Bertalanffy 1962) with input, process, and resulting output. On the input side individual factors, group factors and environmental factors can be discerned (Hackmann and Morris 1975). The individual factors include properties of group members, such as biographical and personality character-istics, abilities, skills, knowledge and atti-tudes toward the group goals, the task, other group members, the situation and other relevant topics. They also include the physical and the social positions in the group, which may, for example, be based on the physical place in the communication network, or on age, sex, social status, formal assigned rank or function and job title. The group factors consist mainly of group size and group composition, that is, the distribution and patterning of individ-ual characteristics in the group. An important aspect of group composition is the compatibility of individual character-istics. Generally, high compatibility leads to high group cohesiveness, and improves task performance (Hare 1976). Usually in formal groups, such as committees, the group composition is established explicitly and formally by prescribed roles, such as chairman, secretary, advisor and members. This is one form of group structure. The environmental factors include the physical and social surroundings of the group. Other environmental factors are the characteristics of the task which has to be performed, the nature of the group goal and the obstacles which block the path towards that goal.

In the interaction in groups, a distinction can be made between the pattern and the content of the interaction (McGrath and Kravitz 1982). The pattern of interaction includes the number of participating members, the length of time spent partici-pating and the number of communications sent and received by each member. Gener-ally, group members differ considerably in verbal participation rate, and these dif-ferences increase with group size. In addition, a strong relationship has been observed (Hare 1976; Shaw 1981) between the emitting and receiving of communi-cation. The content of interaction includes the number of task-oriented communi-cations in the whole group or of particular members, such as information or opinion giving, asking for suggestions and goal setting. It also includes social-emotional communications, which may be verbal or non-verbal, such as showing solidarity, agreement and tension release, or showing of antagonism, disagreement and tension.

A breakthrough in the study of the pattern and content of interaction in groups was the development by Bales (1950) of a category system which enabled observers to code (mainly verbal) behavior reliably. Since then, this category system has been modified by Bales (Bales, Cohen and Williamson 1979), or expanded by others. In addition, category systems have been developed for the coding and scoring of non-verbal behavior, such as physical distance, bodily positions, facial postures and GAZE (Argyle 1969).

In many studies which use these cate-gory systems, it has been observed that the enormous variety of interactions in groups reduces basically to four dimensions or factors (Hare 1976). The first and most important dimension is dominance versus submissiveness. Examples of dominant behavior are loquacity, attempts to influ-ence others and seeking status by directing group activity. In contrast, asking for help, or showing anxiety and frustration are examples of submissiveness. The second dimension is positive social-emotional behavior (showing affection or agreement, asking graciously) versus negative behavior (unfriendly disagreement, or showing antagonism). The third dimension is seri-ous, task-oriented behavior versus expressive behavior, such as supporting others regardless of their task performance, and jocularity. The last dimension is CONFORMITY, seeking to be guided by group norms, and revealing the basic nature of the group versus non-conformity, showing tension and withdrawal, and resisting pressures to conform to group norms. Different attempts to influence the behavior, attitudes and cognitions of group members, or efforts to resist these influences usually take the form of conduct at the extreme poles of these four dimensions.

The interaction process in the group over a certain period of time results in several types of outcome. Firstly, the members become (better) acquainted with one another. Feelings of sympathy and antipathy develop, and a more or less stable ATTRACTION structure is formed. Secondly, by virtue of the group composition some members appear to behave more dominantly than others and to contribute more to goal attainment and task performance. If, at the time of group composition, an influence structure, leadership or social power structure has not been established, it will now come into being, but often only after a struggle for power takes place. Sometimes group members take over formal roles from one another, and often formal roles are supplemented by informal roles, such as the "garrulous", the "supporter", the "silent member" and the "joker" (Hare 1976). Thirdly, in task groups the most important output is, by definition, the task performance or goal attainment of the group. This may be judged on several qualitative and quantitative criteria. Fourthly, the resulting structures, and the goal attainment are usually related to the satisfaction or dissatisfaction of personal, social-emotional and task-related needs of the group members, which, in turn, are related to more or less cohesiveness in the group.

As even this rough sketch illustrates, the student of groups has to deal with a variety of input factors, process variables and outcomes, which also have complex unidirectional and bi-directional causal links over a given period of time. This multitude becomes even larger when other types of group with different tasks and goals are considered. Not surprisingly therefore this multitude is matched by a multitude of research questions, theoretical analyses, research methods and empirical results (Cartwright and Zander 1968; Hare 1976; Shaw 1981).

The social psychological study of groups in the twentieth century reflects two trends; namely, the development of social psychology as a science, and the study of the main problems of Western society. Up to the first decades of this century, groups were mainly the object of theoretical or impressionistic analyses in which their linking function between individual and society was stressed. In the next fifteen years what are now considered to be classical studies of groups took place. These were more modest in scope, now concentrated on phenomena such as the attraction structure in groups (Moreno 1934), the development of group norms (Sherif 1936) and social influences in factory groups (Roethlisberger and Dickson 1939). However, the social psychological study of groups was shaped definitively by LEWIN and his school (Zander 1979). Partly inspired by some of the societal problems of the 1940s and '50s, studies were conducted into theoretical and practical problems of LEADERSHIP, productivity, and group discussion. The dominant research form became the controlled experiment with small ad hoc groups in the psychological laboratory. Since then, some phenomena and processes which were originally studied as group phenomena have been studied more and more intensively in their own right (often, even without free interacting groups). Among these are: conformity, cooperation and competition (for example, in the prisoner's dilemma game – see GAMES), affiliation, and interpersonal attraction. Exceptions to this trend are studies on leadership, on processes and outcomes of decision-making groups (Brandstätter, Davis and Stocker-Kreichgauer 1982) partly inspired by the RISKY SHIFT phenomenon, and recent studies on personal relationships (Duck 1982, 1984; Duck and Gilmour 1981).

(See also EMOTIONAL ROLES IN GROUPS; REFERENCE GROUP.)   RWM

Bibliography

Argyle, M. 1969: *Social interaction*. London: Methuen.

Bales, R.F. 1950: *Interaction process analysis: a method for the study of small groups*. Cambridge, Mass.: Addison-Wesley.

——, Cohen, S.P. and Williamson, S.A. 1979: *SYMLOG, a system for the multiple level observation of groups*. New York: Free Press.

Bertalanffy, L. von 1962: General systems theory: a critical review. *General systems* 7, 1–20.

Brandstätter, H., Davis, J.H. and Stocker-Kreichgauer, G. eds. 1982: *Group decision making*. New York and London: Academic Press.

Cartwright, D. and Zander, A. eds. 1968: *Group dynamics: research and theory*. 3rd edn. London: Tavistock; New York: Harper and Row.

Duck, S. ed. 1982, 1984: *Personal relationships*. vols. 4 and 5. New York and London: Academic Press.

—— and Gilmour, R. eds. 1981: *Personal relationships*, vols. 1–3. New York and London: Academic Press.

Hackman, J.R. and Morris, C.G. 1975: Group tasks, group interaction process, and group performance effectiveness: a review and proposed integration. In *Advances in experimental social psychology*, vol. 8, ed. L. Berkowitz. New York and London: Academic Press.

Hare, A.P. 1976: *Handbook of small group research*. 2nd edn. London: Collier Macmillan; New York: Free Press.

McGrath, J.F. and Kravitz, D.A. 1982: Group research. *Annual review of psychology* 33, 195–230.

Moreno, J.L. 1934: *Who shall survive?* Washington, D.C.: Nervous and Mental Diseases Publishing Company.

Roethlisberger, F.J. and Dickson, W.J. 1939: *Management and the worker*. Cambridge, Mass.: Harvard University Press.

Shaw, M. 1981: *Group dynamics: the psychology of small group behavior*. New York and London: McGraw-Hill.

Sherif, M. 1936: *The psychology of social norms*. New York: Harper.

Zander, A. 1979: The psychology of group processes. *Annual review of psychology* 30, 417–51.

guilt and shame Guilt is the condition attributed to a person (including oneself) upon some moral or legal transgression. Shame is occasioned by an object which threatens to expose a discrepancy between what a person is and what he or she ideally would like to be. Thus, a person may be guilty of a crime but ashamed of the self. The degree of guilt is usually proportional to the offense committed: by contrast, the act that precipitates shame is often inconsequential in itself; its importance lies in what it reveals about the self. Both guilt and shame presume internalized standards of conduct, but guilt has a more abstract, judgmental quality than shame (e.g. one can admit to being guilty without feeling guilty, but one cannot be ashamed without feeling ashamed); and guilt is less tied to the threat of exposure. (See EMOTION AND SOCIAL BEHAVIOR). In terms of its experiential immediacy and its close relationship to self-identity, shame may be considered the more fundamental of the two emotions. In western cultures, however, guilt has been the more highly valued because of its implications for autonomous action. This prejudice is reflected in psychological theories, which tend to ignore shame as a phenomenon distinct from guilt. Psychoanalytic theories trace the origins of guilt to internalization of prohibitions imposed by early authority figures (see SUPEREGO); behaviorist theories view guilt as a conditioned emotional response to actions that in the past have led to punishment; and existentialist theories conceive of guilt as a reaction to behavior that impedes the realization of one's full potential, however that potential is defined (biologically, socially, or spiritually).

Evidence suggests that men may be more prone than women to experience guilt, and conversely with respect to shame (Lewis 1971). No single explanation can account for this and other (e.g. socioeconomic) group differences in the tendency toward guilt and/or shame. Social expectations, family dynamics, and child-rearing practices all undoubtedly play a role. Entire societies have been contrasted on the extent to which they foster guilt-like or shame-like reactions as a means of social control. However, cross-cultural comparisons are made difficult by varying conceptions of guilt and shame.

For example, even such cognate terms as *Scham* in German and shame in English have somewhat different meanings, the former connoting modesty as well as shame.

JRAv

Bibliography

Lewis, H. 1971: *Shame and guilt in neurosis*. New York: International Universities Press.

*Smith, R.W. ed. 1971: *Guilt: man and society*. Garden City, New York: Doubleday.

Thrane, G. 1979: Shame. *Journal for the theory of social behavior* 9, 139–66.

H

Heider, Fritz was born in 1896, of Austrian parents, in Vienna. However, his childhood and youth were spent in the university town of Graz, where his father was an architect. Attracted early to painting and sketching, he was a contemplative child, puzzling about the actions and motivations of people. Later, uncertain about a career, he ranged widely in his studies at Graz, eventually veering toward art history, philosophy and psychology. A leading figure there was Alexander Meinong, a pupil of Brentano and a teacher of Christian von Ehrenfels. Graz was the center of a variant of gestalt psychology that preceded the work of the Berlin group.

In 1921 Heider moved to Berlin. There he attended the seminars of Wertheimer, Köhler and Kurt Lewin, forming with the latter a lasting friendship. In 1927 he accepted an assistantship with Wilhelm Stern at Hamburg, where he met among others Heinz Werner, the philosopher Ernst Cassirer, and Martin Scheerer, later to become his colleage in America.

A turning point in Heider's life came in 1930 with his acceptance of a research appointment in the United States at a school for the deaf in Northampton, Massachusetts. This was also the location of Smith College where Kurt Koffka held a professorship. During these years Heider continued to ponder fundamental questions in perception and thinking. It was not however, until he joined the University of Kansas that he gained the leisure for his main work, *The psychology of interpersonal relations* (1958).

This influential book is a wide-ranging phenomenal inquiry, with a dominant functional aim: to explicate how we discern meaning in everyday events, mostly under ambiguous conditions. It focused on interpersonal relations, preferably between a few, say two, people, but even more so on the representation of such relations within a single individual. Heider started from the conviction that an implicit theory under-girds and controls the course of inter-personal events. To lay bare this system became his main goal. He first looked for aid in the ideas of LEWIN, but came to realize that these could not accommodate the predominantly reflective and reflexive interpersonal concepts. One of his more interesting attempts at a different direction was the adoption of Spinoza's propositions in the *Ethics* of the conditions and effects of love and hate; these have an unmistakable intuitive plausibility. Heider also applied Wertheimer's principles of perceptual organization to interpersonal relations. Their promise appears more limited; the conditions were sketchily stated and the interpretations were not uniformly convincing. Here also belong Heider's views concerning the conditions and effects of balance and imbalance between cognitive and affective phenomena. (See COGNITIVE BALANCE; COGNITIVE CONSISTENCY).

One issue that has attracted the lion's share of interest in the work of Heider is that of ATTRIBUTION, an emphasis that follows naturally from his starting point. Attribution is a central notion of everyday experience. It remained for Heider to move it to center stage, to illustrate how inter-personal meanings are largely determined by causal attribution. Thus, was this harmful action directed at me by another person intentional or not? If intentional, what was the underlying reason? Was it due to external events or to conditions within the person? These and innumerable other questions arise, as they have in domains such as jurisprudence. Attribution has spurred an enormous amount of empirical investigation.

The gestalt orientation, indigenous in Heider, was articulated early in this century, but most of the problems he considered had long been, as he himself taught, closely related to earlier views – among others of Spinoza, Adam Smith, Hume, Schopenhauer, Nietzsche, not excluding Aristotle. His topics included the analysis of action, of desire and pleasure, the structure of sentiments, the concepts of ought and value, of request and command, of benefit and harm.

These were problems that students had not realized or had avoided, particularly in America, largely owing to the prevailing behavioristic outlook. Nevertheless investigators came under the spell of a tradition remote to them, probably because they saw empirical questions to be explored (although Heider himself has not been notably enthusiastic about this direction). Heider had unwittingly brought back a tradition that had withered in human psychology. Only the future will tell how far he has succeeded in firmly re-establishing it. His thought opens new – and old – horizons.   SEA

Bibliography

Heider, F. 1944: Social perception and phenomenal causality. *Psychological review* 51, 358–74.

—— 1946: Attitudes and cognitive organization. *Journal of psychology* 21, 107–12.

—— 1958: *The psychology of interpersonal relations.* New York: John Wiley.

Weiner, B. 1980: *Human motivation.* New York: Holt, Rinehart and Winston. chs. 7 and 8.

hermeneutic interpretative theory

The theory of human understanding in its interpretative aspect. In particular, a hermeneutic is a set of practices or recommendations for revealing an intelligible meaning in an otherwise unclear text or text-analogue. Essentially the character of the hermeneutical process consists in introducing into something already partially specified a further degree of specificity, such that what is strange, alien, foreign or unfamiliar is made familiar, or comprehensible, or simply expressible. Whether beyond this it is possible to speak of a single such process, and of a *correct*

interpretation, is a matter for debate – hence the proliferation of theories in this area.

Debate revolves mainly around the following three issues. Firstly, the question of whether interpretation takes place in an already fixed and existing world, or in an evolving one, a world which is already specified to a degree but which remains open to further specification, with each interpretation actively contributing to its further development – a world which, as Hegel and Marx argued, is possibly still progressing towards its own true self-comprehension, but which does not yet possess the appropriate practical social conditions for other than "illusory" understandings of a "false" reality. Secondly there is the not unrelated question as to whether interpretation is a process taking place within a formal system of already existing categories, or whether it is a much more fundamental process, one which works to provide, prior to any explicit understandings, a specific structure of "pre-understanding" (to use Heidegger's term), a structure upon which all our more explicit, categorical understandings must rest. Thirdly, "dualistic" and "monistic" positions may be distinguished, in the sense that the hermeneutical task can be considered as directed either towards grasping a spiritual or objective "inner reality" in people's "outer" expressions, or towards a more practical aim, i.e. attempting to realize concretely the possibilities for further human being implicit in our current structures of pre-understanding – where our current categories of understanding are to be seen as a parochial commitment to a particular, historically determined mode of pre-understanding.

The oppositions set out above emerge in setting the early modern hermeneutics of Schleiermacher and Dilthey over against the later views of Heidegger and Gadamer. The earliest recorded usage (1654) and probably still the most widespread meaning of the term "hermeneutics" refers to canons of biblical exegesis. But the search for a secure method or system by which to divine the true but hidden meaning of a text was clearly active even in Old Testament times. The distinction of first formulating a systematic "historical hermeneutics" with a "psychological" approach to interpretation, *and* of reconceptualizing hermeneutics as concerned with the general problem of human understanding, must go to Schleiermacher (1768–1834). Others (e.g. Wolff 1759–1824; Ast 1778–1841) had previously agreed that the hermeneutical task involved the discovery or reconstruction of a larger unity, lost or hidden within the aggregate of fragments provided by a text or texts. They were clear that in order to render comprehensible what was, owing to its isolation and singularity, impervious to understanding, the hermeneutical process must move perpetually back and forth from the particular to the whole it indicates and back again to the particular, each polarity providing a corrective for the other. Interpretation must work, in other words, within what Ast called "the hermeneutical circle". But to say this was only to describe a part of what people do in their attempts to clarify their understanding. What was still missing was any reference to what Schleiermacher took to be the foundational act of all hermeneutics: the ordinary, everyday acts of understanding in which people come to a direct and immediate grasp of each other's meanings in their discourse with one another. To the existing grammatical and philological canons, Schleiermacher added psychological ones: hermeneutics must accomplish by conscious effort and technique what ordinary conversationalists achieve effortlessly, namely a grasp of the contents of one another's "minds". To do this, hermeneutics must restore what is lost when the immediacy of a direct, living contact between people is lost, i.e. the background, historical context in which people act. The task is to reconstruct the subjective "inner reality" within which historical actors saw their expressions as originally making sense.

Such a view requires, for the purposes of interpretation, that we split reality into two: into an "outer" reality which can be *explained* causally, and an "inner" reality which must be *understood*. Continuing in the same tradition as Schleiermacher (of romantic individualism), Dilthey (1833–1911) attempted to establish this interpretative dualism as the basis for a special methodology for the human sciences (or the *Geisteswissenschaften* as he called them, in his translation of J.S. Mill's term, "the moral sciences") – a methodology radically different from that of the natural sciences. Rather than *erklären* (to explain) their task must be *verstehen* (to understand); where understanding was to be achieved by a psychological re-enactment or imaginative reconstruction of the experience of those to be understood, Dilthey's hermeneutics was, therefore, a hermeneutics of authors not of texts. And the special method of "the sciences of the spirit" worked to reveal (what was inaccessible to the method of the natural sciences) the hidden subjectivity, the intentions and purposes of the historical actors and authors which informed the texts they left behind them (cf. WEBER).

This "subjective" approach is now, however, under attack both in Anglo-Saxon philosophy under the influence of the later Wittgenstein and on the Continent. One strand of this criticism issued from Heidegger (1889–1976). He, like Dilthey, saw in hermeneutics intimations of a more general process, one in which human conduct reveals itself to itself, so to speak. But unlike Dilthey, he emphasized the practical, non-cognitive aspects of understanding, the embodied structures of "pre-understanding" people acquire in the course of their immediate, unplanned encounters with one another (Heidegger 1962). In such activities, people do not simply come to a subjective understanding of something before unknown to them, their very *being* is re-structured. And it is this pre-structuredness of their being which then makes it possible for them to exercise particular modes of understanding upon a subjective or cognitive level – and denies other modes to them. While in previous, more "dualistic" views, people could simply express themselves as they pleased, in Heidegger's view they must *participate* in a communal linguistic process with its own dynamic. Rather than people expressing their *selves* by their language, it is their language which expresses *them* so to speak, for it determines the nature of their being and hence what they find intelligible. In other words, their "reality" is constituted for them by the very language they use in their attempts to describe it. In this "ontological" interpretation of hermeneutics, the task ceases to be that of merely clarifying or evaluating already known data with the aim of conceptual mastery; it becomes that of recognizing and expressing the new possibilities for human being implicitly present but dispersed within the texts and "text" of everyday forms of life. Heidegger's radical deepening of Schleiermacher's concern with the general problem of understanding results ironically in hermeneutics returning to its traditional concern with authorless texts – but with now an ontological rather than an epistemological concern.

Such new "truths of being" – "truth" here being truth as disclosure rather than as correspondence to a pre-existing reality – cannot, however, be revealed methodically, by the use of pre-structured modes of understanding. For strictly, methods can only render explicit the kind of truths already implicit within them. This is the theme of Gadamer's *Truth and method* (1975). Rather than the manipulation and rearrangement of things within categories already thought of, a quite different kind of thought or mental activity is required. Indeed, Gadamer, like Heidegger, is critical of what he sees as our surrender to technological modes of functioning in everything that we do. What is required is a dialectical or dialogical approach, an active participation in the subject matter of the text. In other words, a text is understood, not by attempting to reconstruct the world within which it had its original being, nor by re-living the subjective experience of its author, but by letting the text itself "have its own say", so to speak, by letting it address one in one's own world. The kind of understanding which results here is that described by Wittgenstein (1953) when he says: 'Try not to think of understanding as a "mental process" at all ... But ask yourself: in what sort of case ... do we say, "Now I know how to go on"'. In other words, one's aim is the practical one of

enlarging (and transforming) one's current reality to incorporate a text's message, its subjective strangeness being rendered familiar in the process. *Leben* (or form of life) replaces *Geist* (or mind) as the central focus in this hermeneutics.

But does this mean that, if our interpretations gain a consensus agreement, they are true? That depends, suggests Habermas (1972, 1976) following Marx on whether in fact our current form of life allows the kind of "undistorted communication" required for a properly critical appreciation of the interpretations offered. For unless 'a structure of human life' exists which 'constitutes itself in a self-formative process' (Habermas 1972, p.194) – i.e. unless all a society's newborns are socialized as autonomous *persons*, all able to participate equally in negotiating meanings – the consensus reached is likely to be a false consensus, representing hidden sectional interests.

The current quickening of interest in hermeneutics in Anglo-Saxon philosophy and social theory reflects an interesting convergence between its problems and those raised by the philosophy of the later Wittgenstein. Both reject logical empiricism as an adequate approach to mental phenomena – a rejection currently echoed in psychology by the determination to study the *actions* of *agents* rather than merely *behavior* in general (see ETHOGENICS). In such a context it is not surprising that there is a return to Dilthey's claim that the natural and the human sciences require radically distinct methodologies. Yet remarkably, it is not a claim which has been unreservedly welcomed, and the unity of all the sciences is once again being asserted: but, all are now being claimed to be equally hermeneutical (see for example Bhaskar 1979, p.195)! Duhem (1906) had already noted long ago (around the turn of the century) that natural scientific assertions were not tested one by one against experience, but required interpretation within a theory as a whole. Kuhn (1962), however, has been most influential in this respect, arguing that the proper interpretation of theoretical statements requires reference to the context of scientific traditions and practices within which they have their currency.

But as Taylor (1980) points out, to claim that there is no essential difference between the human and the natural sciences on the grounds that both possess an interpretative component, is to forget that the aim of the natural sciences is to give an account of the world independently of the meanings it might have for individual subjects. This is achieved in the natural sciences by the use of idealizations and formal systems of interpretation which determine, prior to any further investigations the kinds of things being sought. The human sciences, however, cannot so limit themselves. For they must discover not only what kind of activity it is which makes the natural sciences possible, but they must also account for those human activities which make possible their own disciplines. To select a methodology for this task would be to pre-judge the issue; this need not, however, preclude the use of methodologies for other purposes. Controversy about this issue can be expected to continue.   JDS

Bibliography

Bhaskar, R. 1979: *The possibility of naturalism*. Brighton: Harvester Press.

Bauman, Z. 1978: *Hermeneutics and social science*. London: Hutchinson.

Duhem, P. 1906 (1962): *The aim and the structure of physical theory*. New York: Atheneum.

Gadamer, H-G. 1975: *Truth and method*. Revised edn. London: Sheed and Ward.

Habermas, J. 1972: *Knowledge and human interests*. Trans. J. Shapiro. Boston, Mass.: Beacon Press; London: Heinemann (1976).

—— 1976: *Legitimation crisis*. Trans. T. McCarthy. London: Heinemann.

Heidegger, M. 1962: *Being and time*. Oxford: Basil Blackwell; New York: Harper and Row.

Kuhn, T.S. 1962: *The structure of scientific revolutions*. Chicago: University of Chicago Press.

Palmer, R.E. 1969: *Hermeneutics: interpretation theory in Schleiermacher, Dilthey, Heidegger, and Gadamer*. Evanston, Ill.: Northwestern University Press.

Rorty, R. 1980: *Philosophy and the mirror of nature*. Princeton, N.J.: Princeton University Press; Oxford: Basil Blackwell.

Taylor, C. 1980: Understanding in human science. *Review of metaphysics* 34, 3–23.

Wittgenstein, L. 1953: *Philosophical investigations*. Trans. G.E.M. Anscombe. Oxford: Basil Blackwell; New York: Macmillan.

higher-order need strength Based on the work of Hackman and Oldham (1980), this concept is derived from Maslow's theory which asserts that needs exist in a hierarchy of prepotency from lower (physiological: e.g. safety) to higher (social: e.g. SELF-ESTEEM and SELF-ACTUALIZATION) and from Alderfer's modification which posits three levels of needs: existence, relatedness and growth. In the context of work-motivation, Hackman and Oldham argue that employees who have high higher-order need strength will respond more positively to job enrichment (with respect to performance and/or job satisfaction) than will employees who have low higher-order need strength. The results of this prediction have been mixed. White (1978) takes a pessimistic view of the findings, as do Griffin, Welsh and Moorhead (1981). One problem with the research may be that inadequate measures of need strength have been used. Also, from a career growth perspective, job enrichment changes tend to be very modest; they may only involve changing the job so that 60 per cent of the workers' mental capacity is used instead of 30 per cent, so that need strength differences are irrelevant.   EAL

Bibliography

Griffin, R.W., Welsh. A. and Moorhead, G. 1981: Perceived task characteristics and employee performance: a literature review. *Academy of management review* 6, 655–64.

Hackman, J.R. and Oldham, G.R. 1980: *Work redesign*. Reading, Mass.: Addison-Wesley.

White, J.K. 1978: Individual differences and the job quality-worker response relationship: review, integration, and comments. *Academy of management review* 3, 267–80.

historical psychology is concerned with cross-time alterations or transformations in patterns of human conduct and their psychological bases. In principle the historical psychologist is concerned with all patterns of change, ranging from the momentary to the millenial. For example, an historical psychologist might apply a theory of dialectic change with equal facility to momentary shifts within conversations, the development of the individual over a life span, generational change, and to cultural change spanning centuries. Yet, while broadly applicable, the vast share of interest within historical psychology has been devoted to patterns of change exceeding the life span of individuals. In this sense historical psychology has much in common with diachronic linguistics and the kind of historical sociology exemplified by Norbert Elias's *The civilizing process*. Although the concerns of the historical psychologist overlap with those of the historian, the two disciplines tend to differ in (1) the focus of study and (2) the place of theory within the research process. In the first instance traditional historians have typically focused their concerns on incidents within the governmental, economic and military spheres, while the historical psychologist is typically more concerned with common psychological processes (perception, cognition, valuation, etc.) and their manifestations in general social patterns. With respect to theory, traditional historians have tended to leave theoretical predilections unarticulated, while attempting to vindicate a particular descriptive narrative. In contrast, for the historical psychologist theoretical concerns are generally paramount, and often dictate the historical eras to be studied and the particulars of concern within these eras.

The founding of historical psychology is most reasonably attributed to Wilhelm WUNDT. Although Wundt devoted the greater part of his career to the laboratory study of mental structure and its physiological coordinates, the last twenty years of his life were devoted to his ten-volume work, *Völkerpsychologie*. Wundt argued that the laboratory study of isolated, reflex-like events was insufficient for the understanding of more general patterns of human conduct including cultural values and institutions. For such understanding Wundt proposed an historical orientation. From this perspective, understanding of contemporary patterns is achieved by tracing their origins and vicissitudes through history. For example an understanding of contemporary race relations in England would, from this perspective, require that one trace the conditions under which various racial minorities immigrated into the country, their economic and educational experiences within the country since this time, the effects of various civil policies in various periods and so on. Wundt's orientation continued to have an impact on psychology for some years. For example, the Murchison *Handbook of social psychology* (1935) contained four chapters devoted to an understanding of cultural patterns through historical analysis. However, with the hegemony of the positivist orientation in psychology, and its handmaiden behaviorism, historical psychology was largely obscured from view, though scattered works continued to appear. McClelland's analysis (1961) of the dependency of achievement motivation on historical circumstances, van den Berg's study (1961) of the changing character of human nature, Vygotsky's discussion (1934) of the dependency of cognitive process on cultural conditions, and Fromm's inquiry (1941) into the historical basis for fascism, are notable in this respect. However, only within the past decade has historical psychology once again begun to play a significant role in psychological study.

The reasons for this renaissance of interest are many and complex. Among them must be included the general deterioration of confidence in the basic tenets of positivist-empiricist philosophy. This philosophic view favored the stimulus-response form of psychological theorizing, along with the method of experimentation. Psychologists typically believed that through laboratory study they could elucidate the functioning of basic mechanisms or processes. These mechanisms, or processes, it was assumed, stood outside history. It was believed for example that the laws of conditioning operate identically regardless of historical era. Yet, as confidence in the positivist-empiricist meta-theory began to erode, so did corresponding beliefs in the mechanistic character of human conduct, the dependency of human behavior on environmental antecedents, and the capacity of experimentally manipulated conditions to furnish reliable information regarding patterns of human conduct. Theorists could begin to give serious consideration to the possibility that human behavior is largely governed by historically contingent rules as opposed to determinative mechanisms of the mind, that behavior is self-directed as opposed to environmentally determined, and that reactions to laboratory manipulations might have little to do with normal patterns of conduct within society more generally. These latter views have each favored a concern with the historical embeddedness of human activity. One is invited to see contemporary patterns of behavior as embedded within an historical sequence, the contours and implications of which may be altered through scholarly enlightenment.

A second important influence on the re-emergence of historical psychology may be traced to Marxist criticism of capitalist economic principles. As Marx argued, such principles are typically treated as both temporally unbounded in their generality and as value neutral. Yet, as Marx also demonstrated, capitalist economics appeared to be an historical contingent system and capitalist economic doctrine typically served to legitimize and mystify an economic structure which favored the proponents of the doctrine. Such argumentation later became expanded within various treatments of the sociology of science and within critical sociology more generally (Habermas 1971; see CRITICAL THEORY). As a result of such expansion, wide-ranging critical analysis has been directed toward various forms of seemingly general and value neutral theory. Although largely severed from their Marxist origins, critical analyses have focused on the valuational investments or implications of conflict theory, cognitive psychology, stimulus-response models, moral development theory and traditional historical treatments of psychology. Such work has served to enhance consciousness of the historical conditions giving rise to various psychological theories (see Buss 1979), and of the ways in which theories themselves may alter social patterns.

Contemporary inquiry in historical psychology can be divided into three major forms. First, many investigators have focused on psychosocial patterns occurring in differing historical eras. Such work usually attempts to throw into relief the historical contingency of contemporary, taken-for-granted assumptions about human nature, by documenting periods in which differing patterns existed. Exemplars of this approach include Erikson's treatment of perception in the medieval period and Verhave and van Hoorn's discussion (1983) of the self-concept over history. Certain historical treatments, particularly those of the *Les Annales* school are also of interest to such concerns. Badinter's analysis (1981) of the historical vicissitudes of the "maternal instinct" has been of special interest to psychologists.

The second major form of research in historical psychology is employed by theorists arguing for universal principles of human functioning, but simultaneously holding that historical conditions establish the values of variables within the theory. One theory will make differential predictions in differing historical periods. Historical research is used in this case to justify such conclusions. For example Simonton (1979) has used wide-ranging research to argue that certain historical configurations will favor a high creative output. Specifically, if there are numerous role models in the two preceding generations and a period of nationalistic revolt, the period is likely to be a creative one across wide-ranging domains, from science to the arts. Similarly, Secord's research employs gender ratio theory to make predictions about the character of heterosexual relations in various historical climes. This approach is perhaps the most conservative in the historical psychology movement, as researchers remain committed to the view of universal, deterministic theories.

The third major form of research in historical psychology has focused on patterns of change across time. Historical research in this case is typically used to vindicate a particular theory of change. An example of this orientation is Martindale's work (1975) on alterations in aesthetic taste. As he argues, regardless of aesthetic domain, the evolution of aesthetic fashion over time undergoes a similar pattern, which can be largely attributed to basic psychological make-up.

Research in a number of other domains also contributes to the historical psychology movement. Much life span developmental inquiry is concerned with the socio-historical conditions giving rise to various life span trajectories. Research employing cohort analysis has been particularly important in documenting the dependency of such trajectories on the particular age cohort (Baltes and Schaie 1973). Inquiry into biography and psychohistory furnishes insight into the vicissitudes of historical trajectory, sensitivity to temporal background of contemporary pattern, and understanding of the processes of historical construction itself. Finally, historical inquiry in psychology, particularly that which focuses on various ideological inputs into theory and the process of historical accounting bear importantly on the development of historical psychology.   KJG/HFMP

Bibliography

Badinter, E. 1981: *Mother love*. New York: Macmillan.

Baltes, P.B. and Schaie, K.W. 1973: On life span developmental research paradigms, retrospects and prospects. In *Life span developmental psychology: personality and socialization*. New York: Academic Press.

Buss, A.R. ed. 1979: *Psychology in social context*. New York: Irvington.

Elias, N. 1939 (1978): *The civilizing process*. New York: Urizen; Oxford: Blackwell.

Fromm, E. 1941: *Escape from freedom*. New York: Rinehart.

Gergen, K.J. and Gergen, M.M. eds. 1983: *Historical social psychology*. Hillside, N.J.: Erlbaum.

Habermas, J. 1971 (1976): *Knowledge and human interest*. Boston, Mass.: Beacon Press; London: Heinemann.

Martindale, C. 1975: *Romantic progression: the psychology of literary history*. Washington, D.C.: Hemisphere.

McClelland, D.C. 1961: *The achieving society*. New York: Van Nostrand.

Secord, P.F. 1983: Love, misogyny and feminism. In Gergen and Gergen, op. cit.

Simonton, D.K. 1979: Multiple discovery and invention: Zeitgeist, genius, or chance? *Journal of personality and social psychology* 37, 1603–16.

van den Berg, J.H. 1961: *The changing nature of man*. New York: Norton.

Verhave, T. and van Hoorn, W. 1983: The temporalization of the self. In Gergen and Gergen, op. cit.

Vygotsky, L.S. 1934 (1961): *Thought and language*. Cambridge, Mass.: MIT Press.

Wundt, W. 1900–16: *Völkerspychologie*. 10 vols. Leipzig: Engelmann.

historical relativism A consequence of many varieties of HISTORICISM: the abandonment of an absolute standpoint in historical thinking implies the relativity of all norms and values. This relativism poses problems both for philosophy and the *Geisteswissenschaften* which were discussed, first in nineteenth-century Germany by thinkers such as Dilthey and Troeltsch. Against historical relativism it is argued that the relativism of all philosophies and *Weltanschauungen* (conceptions of the world) can only be recognized from an ideal of valid truth. Relativism seems to be a paradoxical position. As a philosophical doctrine, historical relativism was in a sense rehabilitated after the second world war because of developments in the philosophy of science (e.g. Kuhn's thesis of the incommensurability of paradigms) and the philosophy of mind (Wittgenstein's later work). The criticism of opponents (e.g. Popper) remained essentially the same: they maintain that relativism cannot be defended coherently and fear that it leads to scepticism and ultimately to irrationalism.   SJST

Bibliography

Kuhn, T.S. 1970: Logic of discovery or psychology of research? In *Criticism and the growth of knowledge*, eds. I. Lakatos and A. Musgrave. Cambridge: Cambridge University Press.

Popper, K.R. 1962: Facts, standards and truth: a further criticism of relativism. In *The open society and its enemies*, vol. 2. London: Routledge and Kegan Paul.

historicism A term indicating the tendency to regard all cultural phenomena, including philosophies and worldviews, as the result of a historical development. The word historicism (German: *Historismus*) has been used with various meanings since the beginning of the nineteenth century (Schlegel, Von Ranke, Dilthey, Croce, Troeltsch, Collingwood); historicism as an intellectual movement is still older (Vico, Herder). With the growing awareness that the past is fundamentally different from the present, historicism considered itself as a *Weltanschauung* (conception of the world) which recognized the historical character of all human existence. Each age must be viewed through its own values, and attempts by historians of the Enlightenment to measure the past by the norms of their own time were rejected. At the beginning of this century historicism came to mean "historical positivism", an investigation of historical facts for their own sake, without inquiring into their meaning and relation to the present.

K.R. Popper introduced the word in *The open society and its enemies* in a new, critical sense: here, historicism is a general term for all social philosophies (especially that of Marxism) which believe that they have discovered laws of history which enable them to prophesy the course of future events. Popper distinguishes this historicism from "historism": a theory which maintains the determination of common sense and scientific knowledge by history. Popper's distinction is not generally accepted. Historicism is also used to indicate HISTORICAL RELATIVISM.   SJST

Bibliography

Popper, K.R. 1962: *The open society and its enemies*. 2 vols. London: Routledge and Kegan Paul.

Troeltsch, E. 1923: *Christian thought: its history and application*. London.

historicity Refers to the historical contingency of human action. The term is frequently employed by opponents of those traditional forms of psychology that assume the trans-historical stability of behavior patterns. As maintained by the critics, virtually all patterns of behavior are embedded within a particular confluence of historically contingent circumstances and thus subject to alteration or decay over time. It is said that virtually all patterns of human action are subject to historicity. The term has its roots in the longstanding historicist debate within the social sciences more generally. (See also HISTORICISM.) KJG

Bibliography

Gergen, K.J. and Gergen, M.M. eds. 1983: *Historical social psychology*. New York: Erlbaum.

history of social psychology G.W. Allport (1954) stated that, whilst social psychology was firmly rooted in Western, mainly European, traditions of thought its flowering was a peculiarly American phenomenon.

European origins

Wilhelm Wundt (1832–1920) and the origins of psychology as an experimental and social science.

In 1862 WUNDT set himself three tasks in life: the creation of (i) an experimental psychology, (ii) a scientific metaphysics, and (iii) a social psychology. He achieved the first task by writing a *Handbook of physiological psychology* (1874), establishing a laboratory (1879), and founding a journal *Philosophical studies* (1881) in which he published the results of the experimental research carried out in his laboratory. The second of his three tasks must have sounded, to any self-respecting positivist, a contradiction in terms. For a positivist science expands at the expense of metaphysics and so there can be no such thing as a *scientific* metaphysics. The histories of psychology have been written, in the main, by positivists. As history is written by the victors the vanquished received a raw deal at the bar of history. There are, then, gross distortions in the accounts of Wundt's work in the histories of psychology that are available in English. This is what Danziger (1979) refers to as the positivist repudiation of Wundt. The positivists could not easily forgive Wundt for stressing the limitations of the experimental science he had established.

Wundt achieved the third of his three tasks during the final two decades of his life (i.e. 1900–20) when he published, in ten volumes, his *Völkerpsychologie* (henceforth *VPs*, for short). The objects of study in the *VPs* were language, religion, myth, customs, magic and cognate phenomena. These collective representations, which are important for an understanding of higher cognitive processes in the human species were not, Wundt considered, amenable to investigation by means of introspection which was the basis of his laboratory science. For Wundt social psychology (i.e. the *VPs*) was an answer to the limitations of his laboratory science. However, his *VPs* has largely been ignored by the pioneers of psychology in North America and elsewhere and, except for the first two chapters of volume 1, it has not been translated into English. Nevertheless, this work has been influential in the development of social sciences other than psychology. The conception of mind which underlies Wundt's experimental science is a non-social conception. Wundt, then, bequeathed a non-social experimental science and a non-experimental social science.

Individual and collective psychologies

(a) *Durkheim and the emergence of sociology*. DURKHEIM visited various German universities in 1885–86 and was impressed by what he saw there. His distinction between "collective" and "individual" representations (Durkheim 1898) mirrors that between Wundt's *VPs* and his experimental science. For Durkheim, however, this was the distinction between sociology and psychology. He insisted that "social facts", such as suicide rates, could not be explained in terms of mere psychology; the study of collective representations was part of sociology, and he was quite happy to leave the study of individual representations to the psychologist.

(b) *Le Bon and the psychology of crowds*. Le Bon was interested in the heightened suggestibility of individuals when they form part of a crowd. He compared the power of the leader over the crowd to that of a hypnotist over those who fall under his spell. The contrast was between the behavior of individuals *qua* individuals and their behavior when they form part of a crowd. Le Bon's observations on mass phenomena were to influence Freud a great deal.

(c) *Freud's Massenpsychologie*. Like Wundt, FREUD switched from an analysis of individual minds (i.e. his clinical studies) to an analysis of such cultural artifacts as religion, civilization, myths etc. He wrote *Totem and taboo* (1913) to refute Wundt's account of the totemic age. In the 1920s Freud substantially revised his theory of mind to account for observations by Le Bon and others concerning the psychology of crowds and the power of political leaders.

(d) *Two early textbooks of social psychology*. 1908 saw the publication by McDOUGALL of his *Introduction to social psychology*, and by Ross of his *Social psychology*. McDougall set out to identify a limited number of instincts that form the basis of life in society. Ross summarized, for the benefit of his American readers, many of the early forms of collective psychology that had flourished in Europe. One was a psychology of the individual (McDougall), the other a psychology of collective fads and fashions (Ross). Many see here the start of the distinction between psychological and sociological traditions of social psychology.

(e) *McDougall's two-volume social psychology*. McDougall's 1908 book was not itself a social psychology but merely an introduction to one. The second volume, of 1920, was entitled *The group mind*. In this McDougall dealt with differences in national character. He also discussed the characteristics of organized groups such as armies and churches, in contrast to the disorganization of crowds and mobs.

A phenomenological perspective: the emergence, in Germany, of gestalt psychology.

The main rival in Germany to the Leipzig model of experimental psychology was the

Berlin School that developed under Stumpf. They were opposed to the practice of breaking up one's immediate experience of the world into its constituent elements. The whole is more than the sum of its parts considered in isolation. To understand the behavior of others it is first of all necessary to understand the whole *as it appears to them*. This was to become an explicitly social orientation when, with the advent of World War II, they fled from Germany and re-assembled in America where they found themselves in opposition to the dominant tradition of American behaviorism. The historian Ash has written (1982) an excellent account of the history, up to 1920, of the Berlin School of gestalt psychologists.

Transatlantic crossings

Before World War I

Historians estimate that some 10,000 Americans studied in Europe between 1865 and 1914 (Sokal 1981). The tide was stemmed only by the outbreak of war in 1914. Some were attracted by the new academic disciplines that were beginning to emerge in Germany. Psychology was one of those new disciplines. The establishment by Wundt of his laboratory at Leipzig, in 1879, was the watershed between the "long past" of psychology as a branch of philosophy and its "short history" as a scientific discipline. Boring (1929) noted the pioneers of experimental psychology in America who made the pilgrimage to Leipzig. Among the American scholars who flocked to Germany during this period there were three who were to play an important role in the development of social science at Chicago – the philosopher G.H. Mead, the journalist R.E. Park, and the sociologist W.I. Thomas.

After reading philosophy and psychology at Harvard MEAD studied with Wundt at Leipzig in 1888–89 before moving on to Berlin where he studied physiological and experimental psychology with Ebbinghaus and, under Dilthey, started a doctoral dissertation on the relationship between space and vision that he failed to complete before his return to the States in 1891. At Chicago Mead began an annual course of lectures on social psychology which he continued until his death there in 1931. A transcript of his 1927 series was published, posthumously in 1934, as *Mind, self and society: from the standpoint of a social behaviorist*. Mead developed his social psychology from Wundt's concept of the gesture. He produced a natural history account of the origins of mind and of self-awareness in the human species based on a very close reading of Darwin. He interpolated the notion of "self" between those of "mind" (Wundt's experimental science) and "society" (Wundt's *VPs*). Mind implies society (e.g. the notion of "self") but society does not, necessarily, imply mind (e.g. at the level of insects). Mead stressed the discontinuity between man and other species whilst J.B. Watson (who had been one of his junior colleagues at Chicago) stressed the continuity.

When Mead died in 1931 his course of lectures in social psychology was taken over by Herbert Blumer, a sociologist. It was Blumer, not Mead, who gave the name SYMBOLIC INTERACTIONISM to this particular tradition. It is still a flourishing tradition of social psychology within American sociology. It is based (in the view of the writer) on a serious misinterpretation of Mead's philosophy. When the sociologists heard Mead criticize Watson many probably assumed that, like them, he was an anti-positivist. Mead's point was that Watson had not gone far enough i.e. he had not produced a natural history of mind and of self-awareness in the human species.

Park, an American journalist, obtained his doctorate at Heidelberg in 1904 with a dissertation on *Masse und Publikum*. He clearly differentiated the "public" from the "crowd" and the "mass". As a professional journalist he believed there was a degree of rationality in how the public form opinions about issues.

Thomas, a sociologist from Chicago, was a student of Wundt's at Leipzig in 1907–8. With Znaniecki, he published the classic study of *The Polish peasant in Europe and America* (1918–20). He defined social psychology as being "the scientific study of social attitudes." For Thomas, attitudes and collective representations were very closely interrelated (Jaspars and Fraser 1984). This is also evident in the techniques devised by Thurstone, at Chicago, for the measurement of social values and attitudes.

The years between the wars (1919–1939)

It was Americans, rather than Europeans, who began to set the pace during this period. Behaviorism became the dominant force in American psychology. Psychology ceased to be the science of mind and became, instead, the science of behavior. Both behaviorism in America and gestalt psychology in Germany were reactions against the inadequacies of the Leipzig model of experimental psychology. Between the wars it was Europeans who migrated to America. At first it was only a few isolated individuals e.g. McDougall left England for Harvard in 1920. Then as the clouds of war began, once again, to amass over Europe with Hitler's rise to power in Germany, the trickle became a virtual torrent with whole "Schools" of researchers making the transatlantic passage from East to West. Lazarsfeld and some of his co-workers emigrated from Vienna and established the Bureau of Applied Social Research at Columbia (Jahoda 1983). The famous Frankfurt School of social scientists (Adorno, Horkheimer, Marcuse, Fromm et al.) also emigrated, wholesale, to America when Hitler closed down their research Institute. Their monumental study of *The authoritarian personality* (Adorno et al. 1950) became an important landmark in North American social psychology in the post-war era (see AUTHORITARIAN PERSONALITY). Other important refugees of this period were Egon Brunswik, Fritz Heider and Alfred Schutz from Austria and the Berlin group of gestalt psychologists – Koffka, Wertheimer, Lewin and Kohler. This flood of refugees was to play an important role in the shaping of social psychology in North America in the post-war era i.e. that peculiar "flowering" of the discipline that G.W. Allport saw as typically American.

In North America social psychology became both an experimental and a social science during these inter-war years. An important landmark was the publication, in 1924 by F.H. Allport, of his textbook *Social psychology*. He firmly established social psychology as a branch of behavioral science. For Allport the only ultimate reality was the behavior of individuals. He attacked McDougall for appearing, in his book *The group mind*, to assign agency to entities other than individuals. Indeed, due to the fierceness of Allport's attack, this came to be known as "the group mind fallacy". Allport maintained the same model at the level both of the individual and of the collectivity. For him, in fact, the collectivity was a collectivity of individuals. He was an enthusiastic supporter of public opinion polling when this was introduced in the States in the 1930s. The technology of polling was isomorphic with is own theoretical model of the individual. Graumann (1986) has shown how, in the work of Allport, the individualization of the social goes hand in hand with the de-socialization of the individual.

American flowerings

The long past and the short history of social psychology

The Murchison *Handbook of social psychology* (1935) was the high watermark in America of the influence of Wundt's *VPs*. Its various sections, and even the titles of individual chapters, reflected the range and scope of Wundt's *VPs*. Murchison was centrally concerned with identifying the evolution and the historicity of the human mind and the volume was interdisciplinary in character. There was, for example, a quartet of chapters, each written by a distinguished anthropologist, on the social history of the white, red, yellow and black man. Other contributions came from distinguished biologists, sociologists, and even botanists. The volume reflected the scope of a comparative psychology that no longer exists. The methodology was that adopted by Humboldt when he established the science of comparative linguistics at Berlin and by Darwin when he developed his theory of evolution. It is the perfect complement to Wundt's laboratory science where the physical aspects of the experimental situation could be rigorously controlled. In comparative studies one has to work with the varieties of phenomena that exist naturally whether these are species, in the case of Darwin; languages, in the case of Humboldt or cultures in the cases of Wundt and Murchison.

In his classic chapter on the historical background to modern social psychology G.W. ALLPORT (1954) designated Comte as the "founding father" of social psychology. In doing so he set the seal of approval on the attempt, thirty years earlier, by his brother, F.H. Allport, to establish social psychology as a branch of behavioral science (Allport 1924). As Samelson (1974) pointed out Allport also created a false "origin myth" for social psychology. G.W. Allport's historical chapter was written for the first edition of the Lindzey *Handbook of social psychology*. This *Handbook*, and its successive revisions, marks the *modern* era in social psychology. The Allport chapter was the link with the long past of the discipline. The successive *Handbooks*, edited by Lindzey (1954) and by Lindzey and Aronson (1959/60, 1985), record the "flowering" of social psychology as a peculiarly American discipline.

The discontinuity with the past is in clearest focus in the most recent edition of the *Handbook* (Lindzey and Aronson 1985). The editors effectively identify 1935 as being the year that marks the break between the long past and the short history of social psychology. They do this in three ways: (i) by distancing themselves, in their editorial, from the Murchison *Handbook* of 1935; (ii) by including, *for the third time*, Allport's chapter of 1954 on the historical background to *modern* social psychology; and (iii) by commissioning a new chapter (Jones 1985) to cover significant developments in the past five decades (i.e. since 1935). The distinction is now quite clear between the long past of social psychology as part of a Western, mainly European, intellectual tradition, and its short history as a science that is predominantly American and experimental. The watershed is the Murchison *Handbook* of 1935.

There are very powerful individualizing tendencies at work within American culture which can have quite a dramatic effect when they encounter any inherently social forms of social psychology that might emanate from Europe. We have already noted (see *The years between the wars*) the reception accorded to McDougall's book on *The group mind*. In his text of 1924, F.H. Allport also demonstrated how a purely individual model of behavior could explain phenomena at a collective level, without there being any need for a separate collective psychology such as those outlined in the above section *Individual and collective psychologies*. Graumann (1986) has shown how the individualization of the social goes hand in hand with the desocialization of the individual. Whilst G.H. Mead produced an inherently social model of the individual (see *Before World War I*) this has been largely ignored by psychological social psychologists in North America, though it has been of considerable interest to sociological social psychologists.

Jaspars and Fraser (1984) have identified the chapter by G.W. Allport on attitudes, in the Murchison *Handbook* of 1935, as being the turning point in North American social psychology, when attitudes ceased to be collective representations and became, instead, merely individual representations. The successive editions of the *Handbook* also testify to a move away from a concern with collective phenomena, macro-level concepts and broad theoretical orientations to a preoccupation with individual phenomena, micro-level concepts and narrow theoretical models. The best description of the individualizing tendencies at work in American culture is to be found in Ichheiser's monograph (1949) on the IDEOLOGY of success and failure in various Western cultures (see Farr 1986). He portrays the individual as a collective representation in the full Durkheimian sense of that term. It is faintly ironic that the diffusion of his own work in North American succumbed to the ravages of the very representation he portrayed. He produced a sociology of interpersonal relations that, very rapidly, became a mere psychology of interpersonal relations and then disintegrated into a series of unrelated programs of research in attribution theory that had little or nothing to do with interpersonal relations in the real world.

The post-war years

The migration of the gestalt psychologists, immediately prior to the War, had important consequences for the development of a post-war experimental social psychology. LEWIN, in particular, gave impetus to the development of an experimental social psychology and whilst he, himself, did not long survive the War the tradition he helped to establish was carried on by a generation of very talented American graduate students of his who included, amongst others, Festinger, Schachter, Cartwright, Deutsch and Kelley.

In the context of American behaviorism the gestalt psychologists emerged as cognitive theorists. The divergence in perspective between the gestaltist and the behaviorist is comparable to that between the "actor" and the "observer" (Jones and Nisbett 1972). It is, perhaps, clearest in the opposition between Heider and Skinner. In the interests of methodological rigor Skinner ruled out of court any "going beyond the evidence available". From the perspective of self as perceiver, the evidence that is available about others is their behavior. One should, therefore, stick to the behavioral facts. HEIDER observed that lay men and women are always going beyond this evidence when they infer the goals, intentions, motives, opinions and mental states of others. ATTRIBUTION THEORY is the study of these lay rules of inference. Heider helped to inspire experimental research on person perception in the 1950s; on consistency models of attitude change in the 1960s and on attribution theory in the 1970s and into the 1980s.

It was in America, and then only in the context of behaviorism, that many of the gestalt psychologists became, in effect, social psychologists. They were certainly not explicitly "social" psychologists before emigrating from Germany. The chapter by Jones (1985) gives an adequate account of the "flowering" of social psychology in North America in the course of the last half century.   RFa

Bibliography

Adorno, T.W., Frenkel-Brunswik, E., Levinson, D.J. and Sanford, R.N. 1950: *The authoritarian personality*. New York: Harper and Row.

Allport, F.H. 1924: *Social psychology*. Boston: Houghton Mifflin.

Allport, G.W. 1954: The historical background of modern social psychology. In *Handbook of social psychology*, ed. G. Lindzey, vol. 1. Reading: Mass.: Addison-Wesley. pp. 3–56.

Ash, M.G. 1982: *The emergence of gestalt theory: experimental psychology in Germany 1890–1920*. Ph.D. dissertation. University of Harvard. University Microfilms, Order No. 8303408.

Boring, E.G. 1929: *A history of experimental psychology*. New York: Century.

Danziger, K. 1979: The positivist repudiation of Wundt. *Journal of the history of the behavioral sciences* 15, 205–30.

Durkheim, E. 1898: Représentations individuelles et représentations collectives. *Revue de metaphysique et de morale* 6, 273–302.

Farr, R.M. 1986: Self-other relations and the social nature of reality. In Graumann and Moscovici, op. cit.

Graumann, C.F. 1986: The individualisation of the social and the desocialisation of the individual: Floyd H. Allport's contribution to social psychology. In Graumann and Moscovici, op. cit.

—— and Moscovici, S. eds. 1986: *Changing conceptions of crowd mind and behavior*. New York: Springer-Verlag.

Ichheiser, G. 1949: Misunderstandings in human relations: a study in false social perception. *American journal of sociology*. Supplement to September issue. 1–72.

Jahoda, M. 1983: The emergence of social psychology in Vienna: an exercise in long-term memory. *British journal of social psychology* 22, 343–9.

Jaspars, J. and Fraser, C. 1984: Attitudes and social representations. In *Social representations*, eds. R.M. Farr and S. Moscovici. Cambridge: Cambridge University Press.

Jones, E.E. 1985: Major developments in social psychology during the past five decades. In Lindzey and Aronson, vol. 1. 3rd edn., op. cit.

Lindzey, G. ed. 1954: *Handbook of social psychology*. 2 vols. Reading: Mass.: Addison-Wesley.

—— and Aronson, E. eds. 1959–60: *Handbook of social psychology*. 2nd edn., 5 vols. Reading, Mass.: Addison-Wesley.

—— 1985: *Handbook of social psychology*. 3rd edn., 2 vols. New York: Random House.

McDougall, W. 1908: *Introduction to social psychology*. London: Methuen.

—— 1920: *The group mind: a sketch of the principles of collective psychology with some attempt to apply them to the interpretation of national life and character*. Cambridge: Cambridge University Press.

Mead, G.H. 1934: *Mind, self and society: from the standpoint of a social behaviorist*, ed. C.W. Morris. Chicago: Chicago University Press.

Murchison, C.A. ed. 1935: *Handbook of social psychology*. 2 vols. Worcester, Mass.: Clark University Press.

Ross, E.A. 1908: *Social psychology*. New York: Macmillan.

Samelson, F. 1974: History, origin myth and ideology: 'discovery' of social psychology. *Journal of the theory of social behavior*. 4(2), 217–31.

Sokal, M.M. ed. 1981: *An education in psychology: James McKeen Cattell's journal and letters from Germany and England: 1880–1888*. Cambridge, Mass.: MIT Press.

Thomas, W.I. and Znaniecki, F. 1918–20: *The Polish peasant in Europe and America*. 5 vols. Boston: Badger.

homeostasis Literally "staying the same". Living organisms and some self-regulating machines (such as thermostatically controlled heating systems, or automatic pilots) have the ability to resist change, and to keep certain properties or variables constant, even when factors are present which would tend to change them. This is most commonly done by means of negative feedback, an arrangement whereby any small fluctuations of the property in question are detected and messages fed back to an earlier point in the causal chain, where compensatory changes are made to cancel out the original fluctuations; hence the name negative feedback.

Homeostatic mechanisms are responsible for many important aspects of automatic self-regulation in animals, from the stabilization of blood chemistry, to the fine control of motor behavior.

The concept has been used in theories of motivation such as those of FREUD or Hull; organisms are driven to satisfy their appetites and thereby restore their equilibrium.

DDC

Bibliography

Cannon, W.B. 1932: *The wisdom of the body*. New York: Norton.

Weiner, B. 1980: *Human motivation*. New York: Holt, Rinehart and Winston.

homosexuality and lesbianism Sexual interest directed at members of one's own sex. Estimates of prevalence in Western countries vary considerably; high estimates, such as Kinsey's oft-cited one in three, include any homosexual experience whatever, whereas low estimates limit themselves to life-long exclusive homosexuality. Homosexual behavior is no longer illegal in Britain and North America, nor is it regarded as a form of mental illness. Homosexual behavior is permitted in many non-Western societies, but subject to social control. Recent research (e.g. Bell and Weinberg 1978) argues that homosexuals are not an identifiable class apart, but are as varied as heterosexuals, having only their sexual orientation in common. A few vulgar misconceptions about homosexuals still exist: few male homosexuals are effeminate; few females are correspondingly masculine; few homosexuals cross-dress; few molest children.

Theories of the origin of homosexuality fall into two broad classes: the biological and the social. Biological theories look for physical or physiological differences between homosexuals and heterosexuals, and tend to assume an inherited element (see Bell et al. 1981). Social theories are more varied, ranging from the psychoanalytic theory of the unresolved Oedipus complex to McGuire et al.'s (1965) theory of social learning mediated by self-reinforced fantasy (see Storms 1981). Some theories argue that homosexuality is fear of the opposite sex more than a preference for one's own. Homosexual behavior sometimes results from force of circumstance, such as unavailability of the opposite sex rather than from inner dispositions. In some cultures homosexual behavior is required, at certain ages or on certain occasions, so explanations based on individual differences would not apply.　JHC

Bibliography

Bell, A.P. and Weinberg, M.P. 1978: *Homosexualities: a study of diversity among men and women*. London: Mitchell Beazley.

—— and Hammersmith, S.K. 1981: *Sexual preference: its development in men and women*. Bloomington: Indiana University Press.

McGuire, R.J., Carlisle, J.M. and Young, B.G. 1965: Sexual deviations and conditioned behaviour: a hypothesis. *Behaviour research and therapy* 2, 185–90.

Peplau, L.A. and Gordon, S.L. 1983: The intimate relationships of lesbians and gay men. In *The changing boundaries: gender roles and sexual behavior*, eds. E.R. Allsgeier and N.B. McCormick. Palo Alto: Mayfield.

Storms, M.D. 1981: A theory of erotic orientation development. *Psychological review* 88, 340–53.

hormic psychology

Denotes the school of purposive psychology in general, and more specifically William McDougall's theory of instincts on which he based the subdisciplines of differential, clinical and social psychology. The name itself was suggested by T.P. Nunn in derivation from the Greek noun δρμη (impulse, drive). According to McDougall, who argued his theory against the mechanistic approaches of the time (Watson and McDougall 1929), all behavior is rooted in the instinctive endowments of organisms (McDougall 1934). In addition, human behavior is guided by intentionality (McDougall 1912, pp.233–4). Nonetheless, all patterns of behavior, whether animal or human, belong to an unbroken "continuity" (McDougall 1928, pp. 407–8).

Although intended to be purely scientific, McDougall's theory goes beyond the realm of science and merges with that of metaphysics. It conflates methodological purposivism as a device for the identification of the units of behavior and metaphysical purposivism which stresses the reality of spirit.　AM

Bibliography

McDougall, William 1912: *Psychology: the study of behavior*. London: Williams and Norgat.

—— 1928: *An introduction to social psychology*. 21st edn. London: Methuen.

—— 1934: *The frontiers of psychology*. London: Nisbet.

Watson, J.B. and McDougall, W. 1929: *The battle of behaviorism: an exposition and an exposure*. New York: Norton.

human relations school

This school of thought holds that the most important influences on employee performance and satisfaction are relationships among people, specifically intra-group relations, inter-group relations, and supervisory-subordinate relations. Implicit in this view is the premise that job satisfaction leads to high productivity. The school grew out of the well-known Hawthorne studies done at the Western Electric Co. during the 1920s and 1930s (see, for example, Roethlisberger and Dickson 1956). Ironically, these studies were quite poorly designed and were probably widely misinterpreted (Franke and Kaul 1978). Nevertheless the human relations school has had enormous influence. One consequence was the study of LEADERSHIP or supervisory style, which has not proved very fruitful at least with respect to the prediction of work group performance. However, it is widely accepted that leadership as such plays a crucial role in organizational effectiveness (Yukl 1981).

Another outcome was the study of work attitudes. Job satisfaction has not been found to lead to greater productivity, but has come to be studied in its own right as a desirable outcome of work experience. Group dynamics have been widely studied by both psychologists and sociologists. Group norms have been verified as important influences on employee morale and motivation and can serve to enhance or subvert organizational goals. It is now conceded that while social factors are important (Likert 1961), they are only one of many aspects of the job that affect employee productivity and attitudes so that the views of the human relations school are not now accepted in their entirety.　EAL

Bibliography

Franke, R.H. and Kaul, J.D. 1978: The Hawthorne experiments: first statistical interpretation. *American sociological review* 43, 623–43.

Likert, R. 1961: *New patterns of management.* New York: McGraw-Hill.

Roethlisberger, F.J. and Dickson, W.J. 1956: *Management and the worker.* Cambridge, Mass.: Harvard University Press.

Yukl, G. 1981: *Leadership in organization.* Englewood Cliffs, N.J.: Prentice-Hall.

humanistic psychology An approach to psychology which includes love, involvement and spontaneity, instead of systematically excluding them. The object of humanistic psychology is not the prediction and control of people's behavior, but the liberation of people from the bonds of neurotic control, whether these derive from the structure of society or from the psychological condition of individuals.

Humanistic psychology emerged from the confluence of ten different streams: (1) group dynamics, particularly in the area of T-groups; (2) the doctrine of SELF-ACTUALIZATION (Maslow 1968); (3) the person-centered approach to counseling, therapy and education (ROGERS 1961); (4) the theories of Wilhelm Reich and his emphasis on the body; (5) existentialism – particularly as interpreted analytically by Laing (1967) and practically/experientially by Perls (Fagan and Shepherd 1972); (6) the results of the use of mind-expanding drugs – particularly LSD (Stafford and Golightly 1967); (7) Zen Buddhism particularly in its idea of "letting go"; (8) Taoism, particularly in its ideas of "centering" and the yin-yang polar unity; (9) Tantra, particularly in its emphasis on the importance of the body as an energy system; and (10) peak experiences as revelatory and enlightening (Rowan 1976).

Humanistic psychology is not a tidy and coherent body of knowledge, but a way of dealing with human problems by reference to a set of paradigmatic experiences:

(1) A deep and intense group experience resulting in a general realignment of attitudes to self and others.

(2) Ecstatic or peak experiences, with a sense of unity and pattern of both the human and natural world.

(3) The existential experience of complete independence and total responsibility for one's thoughts and actions.

Humanistic psychology is directed strongly to practical ends. The central concepts are *personal growth* and *human potential.* They imply that people can change by "working" on themselves. Humanistic psychology has drawn on a large number of different methods for self-intervention which can be ranged under four headings:

Body methods: Reichian therapy, bioenergetics, rebirthing, Rolfing, Feldenkrais method, Alexander technique, sensory awareness, holistic health, etc.

Feeling methods: encounter, psychodrama, gestalt awareness, primal integration, Rogerian counseling, co-counseling, etc.

Thinking methods: transactional analysis, personal construct approach, family therapy, neuro-linguistic programming, rational-emotive therapy, etc.

Spiritual methods: transpersonal counseling, psychosynthesis, enlightenment intensive workshops, dynamic meditation, sand play, dream work, etc.

It has been understood recently that humanistic psychology entails a new paradigm of how research should be carried out with human beings if it is to yield practical knowledge. The people being studied are recruited as co-researchers, who participate fully in the planning of the research, in its execution, and in making sense of the results. This process yields a more many-layered kind of knowledge than the old paradigm of research could offer, and it is knowledge which can be used immediately (see Reason and Rowan 1981).

Several concepts have been elaborated on the basis of this research:

The real self: Though dropped from some radical psychologies, this is a key concept for humanistic psychology. It is common to Rogers (1961), Maslow (1968), Laing (1967) and many others. It presumes that we can dive beneath the surface appearance of roles and masks to a permanent, underlying self (Shaw 1974).

Some large-scale research studies which bear on this have been put together by Hampden-Turner (1971).

Subpersonalities: This is a concept put forward in various forms by Assagioli and others (Ferrucci 1982). It implies we have a number of subpersonalities, which seem to come from several sources: the collective unconscious (see JUNG); the cultural unconscious; the personal unconscious; long-standing conflicts and problems; long-term roles and social frames; and fantasy images of how we would like to be. The original suggestion, by Ornstein (1972) of two modes of consciousness, has been greatly elaborated in recent studies (see Fadiman and Frager 1976).

Abundance motivation: Most orthodox psychology is based on a homeostatic model, which is deficiency oriented. Action is thought of as initiated by a need or want. Human beings (and animals) however, seek for tension creating and maintaining situations, as well as for tension reduction. Achievement motivation (McClelland 1953) or need for varied experience (Fiske and Maddi 1961) can be comprehended under the concept of abundance motivation. Any kind of action may be done out of abundance motivation. Motivation cannot be inferred from the performance. It is known only to the actor.

Finally, humanistic psychologists believe that attention to one's own states and motives makes possible the avoidance of self-deception and facilitates the discovery of a "real self".   JCR

Bibliography

Fadiman, J. and Frager, R. 1976: *Personality and personal growth*. New York: Harper and Row.

Fagan, J. and Shepherd, I.L. eds. 1972: *Gestalt therapy now*. London: Penguin.

Ferrucci, P. 1982: *What we may be*. Wellingborough: Turnstone Press.

Fiske, D.W. and Maddi, S.R 1961: *Functions of varied experience*. Dorsey Press.

Hampden-Turner, C. 1971: *Radical man: the process of psycho-social development*. London: Duckworth; Cambridge, Mass.: Schenkman.

Laing, R.D. 1967: *The politics of experience*. London: Penguin.

McClelland, D. et al. 1953: *The achievement motive*. New York: Appleton-Century-Croft.

Marrow, A.J. 1969: *The practical theorist*. New York: Basic Books.

Maslow, A.H. 1968: *Motivation and personality*. New York: Harper and Row.

Ornstein, R. 1972: *The psychology of consciousness*. London: Penguin.

Reason, P. and Rowan, J. eds. 1981: *Human inquiry: a sourcebook of new paradigm research*. New York and Chichester: John Wiley and Sons.

Rogers, C.R. 1961: *On becoming a person*. London: Constable; Boston: Houghton Mifflin.

Rowan, J. 1976: *Ordinary ecstasy: humanistic psychology in action*. London: Routledge and Kegan Paul.

Shaw, J. 1974: *The self in social work*. London: Routledge and Kegan Paul.

Stafford, P.G. and Golightly, B.H. 1967: *LSD: the problem-solving psychedelic*. Award Books.

humor Among various entries for "humor" in *The Shorter Oxford English Dictionary* there is reference to the excitement of amusement, the expression of amusement, and temporary and habitual conditions of the mind. In everyday language, therefore, "humor" can apply to a stimulus, a response or a disposition. On the disposition side virtually all respondents in surveys and interviews are reported as rating themselves as "above average" for sense of humor; and Frank Moore Colby, through implication, scarcely exaggerated the importance attached to humor when he said; 'men will confess to treason, murder, arson, false teeth or a wig. How many of them will own up to a lack of humor?'

There is no doubt that in modern times a good sense of humor has come to be regarded as thoroughly healthy and desirable. Historically humor was more typically characterized as base and degenerate, fit solely for the ignorant and foolish. Classical Greek and Roman scholars evidently believed that laughter was rooted in deformity and shabbiness; it was said to be degrading to art, morals and religion. In the Bible humor and laughter are very rarely mentioned, and, less in keeping with the quick than the dead. The present-day Penguin *Dictionary of psychology* defines

"Laughter" anachronistically as 'an emotional response, expressive normally of joy, in the child and the *unsophisticated* adult' (emphasis added).

Until recently psychologists and other social scientists regarded humor and laughter as either taboo or trivial topics for systematic inquiry, while at the same time textbook authors occasionally pointed to their ubiquitous nature. It is only in the last ten years or so that psychologists have begun to contribute significantly to knowledge: there has been a genesis and development of several substantial strands of investigation, although laughter remains a largely unexplored area of research. By and large humor researchers tend to disregard laughter partly because it is seen as an essentially social response and hence a poor index of humor appreciation. It can accompany any number of emotional states, most of them having nothing to do with humor or amusement. Even when contiguous with humor its quality and quantity may be governed principally by the constitution and behavior of the surrounding company. Perhaps more to the point, it is rarely engendered in its explosive or effusive form under contrived and sterile laboratory arrangements. It is likely that humor loses its potency and maybe some of its character under laboratory scrutiny, and laboratories remain the speciously safe haunt of most empirically minded psychologists; as a consequence, much of the research has been truncated and even asocial, and there has been rather a dearth of trenchant empirical work.

Theories abound in the psychological literature but, with few exceptions, they are in effect statements of function or statements of properties: they are descriptive and taxonomic accounts rather than explanations as to *why* humor occurs and *why* laughter is emitted, and remarkably few draw on general principles within psychology. Generally speaking the quest for a grand theory has been abandoned, the consensus being that no single theory could usefully embrace all facets of creation, initiation and reaction. Instead there has been a proliferation of mini-theories in recent years, dwelling separately on aspects of stimulus variables – content, structure and complexity; of individual differences – personality, motivation, physiology, cognitions and psychodynamic reactions; of internal amusement and of expressive responsiveness – subjective ratings and nonverbal reactions; and also dwelling on companionship variables, as well as other social psychological matters.

Previously philosophers and littérateurs had promoted theories on a much grander scale, and the ancestry of many present-day views is readily detected in pre-twentieth century writings. For example, Plato and Aristotle drew attention to the malevolent and invective nature of some humor, and their thoughts were precursors to derision and superiority theories which remain in vogue today. Plato (in the *Philebus*) saw the weak as a justifiable target for humor, and he regarded malice as essential to laughter. Aristotle (in the *Poetics*) maintained that infirmity and ugliness are prime sources of the ludicrous. By the seventeenth century Thomas Hobbes's writings on humor (in *Leviathan* and *Human nature*) incorporated most of the essential rudiments of contemporary superiority theory. Writers in the eighteenth and nineteenth centuries – notably Beattie and Schopenhauer – were the forerunners of contemporary incongruity theorists.

It was Herbert Spencer more than a century ago who first advanced the conception of laughter as a "safety valve" against surplus energy, and at the turn of the century FREUD, synthesizing relief, conflict and incongruity theories similarly saw laughter as an outlet for discharging psychic energy. Then and later Freud described the relief action as operating when the SUPEREGO has effectively censored other uses of built-up energy. Freud discriminated between "the comic", "wit" and "humor" in a manner which only his most ardent followers have done since. The discharge of energy through laughter was said by Freud to be pleasurable because of gratification derived from economic expenditures of thought (in the case of the comic), inhibition (for wit) or feeling (for humor). In humor, potentially damaging events were said to be relegated to lesser significance by the ego assuming an infantile state after energy has been displaced onto the superego.

Before the 1970s most empirical research was centered on Freudian notions but this emphasis has been superseded by widespread attention to cognitive dimensions, and particularly by work in an information-processing vein. A disparity between expectations and perceptions is generally taken to be a necessary but not a sufficient condition for humor. It is this disparity which is termed "incongruity". For humor an incongruity has to be made meaningful or appropriate; or some would say that a cognitive rule has to be found which renders the incongruity explicable within the context of the humor. A partial or complete "resolution" of the incongruity is considered to be an essential component of the humor process.

The salience of the social context is apparent in analyses of infants' humor and laughter where the necessity for a playful mood is emphasized. Developmental psychologists in general see humor as a form of play involving symbols, images and ideas. It is first manifested at about eighteen months of age as the child acquires the ability to manipulate symbols. However, operating according to a different definition of humor, some researchers argue that humor is experienced by children as young as four months: theirs is a broader definition and one which does not embody any reference to symbolism (or capacities for playing games of pretend or make-believe); it merely requires that incongruities can be resolved by the infant, and that particular incongruous events are perceived as safe and playful. It is agreed that incongruity is never sufficient: the perception of something unexpected might lead to laughter but, if there is no playful mood, it may lead instead to fear, curiosity, problem-solving or concept learning.

Humor, through laughter and smiling, can serve a wide variety of social functions. For example, there is already research indicating that it can assist the flow of an interaction, reveal attitudes with relative impunity, communicate allegiances, induce changes in group esteem, form an integral part of a coping strategy, assist in the maintenance of a status hierarchy, and help to test the standing of relationships. It is multi-dimensional and, depending primarily upon content and social context, single instances may cause multiple and diverse effects amongst initiators, recipients and bystanders. The effects on the recipients are mediated in part by the perceived values and motives of the initiator, who in turn is influenced by responses to the humor.

The neglect of expressive responses, particularly laughter and smiling, and the neglect of the social climate will become yet less tenable as humor researchers begin to extend their breadth of inquiries. For no obvious reason, other than convenience, they have so far placed heavy emphasis on *responsiveness* to humor: we still await rigorous and heuristic work on aspects of the creation and instigation of humor. Typically in studies to date the experimenters have selected jokes, cartoons or comedy films and presented them to subjects from whom they then elicit funniness ratings. In this way research has endeavored to focus on the structure, content and psychological functions of humor, and it has ignored behavioral consequences. Also studies of groups have tended to overlook the fact that groups have their own histories and cultures: they are not *ad hoc* assemblies of individuals, and the richness of humor will not become manifest so long as they are regarded as such for laboratory purposes. Fundamental questions about how, why, when and where humor is initiated are not likely to be addressed squarely until humor is recorded as it naturally occurs; and that is usually in social situations, just before laughter.   AJC

Bibliography

Chapman, A.J. and Foot, H.C. 1977: *It's a funny thing, humor*. Oxford and New York: Pergamon Press.

McGhee, P.E. and Chapman, A.J. 1980: *Children's humour*. Chichester and New York: Wiley.

—— and Goldstein, J.H. eds. 1983: *Handbook of humor research*. New York: Springer-Verlag.

I

id Latin word used in English translation of FREUD for *das Es* (literally the "It"). Freud (1923) contrasted it with the EGO and the SUPEREGO. It is the major portion of the UNCONSCIOUS MIND, and the seat of INSTINCT. As such it is the source of energy and desire which the ego must constantly try to control and direct towards realistic possibilities of gratification. (See PERSONALITY THEORY, PSYCHOANALYTICAL.)   RL

Bibliography

Freud, S. 1923 (1961): The ego and the id. In *The standard edition of the complete psychological works of Sigmund Freud*, vol. 19, ed. J. Strachey. London: Hogarth; New York: Norton.

ideal self An image or representation of oneself as one would like to be. Derived from societal values and significant others, the ideal self is composed of wished for (but possibly unattainable) modes of behavior, values, traits, aspects of personal appearance etc. A disparity between the ideal self and SELF-CONCEPT (i.e. image of oneself as one really is) is taken to be a sign of poor mental health, and its reduction a primary goal of psychotherapy (see ROGERS). The self-ideal disparity has consequences for the regulation of behavior since it is intrinsically anxiety producing (see ANXIETY; SOCIAL PSYCHOLOGY). Recent work in experimental social psychology (e.g. Higgins et al. 1985) has sought to explicate these regulative processes by studying the conditions under which a self-ideal comparison is likely to be induced and then subsequently dealt with by the individual. (See SELF AWARENESS, OBJECTIVE; SUPEREGO.)
                                         BRS

Bibliography

Higgins, E.T., Klein, R. and Strauman, T. 1985: Self-concept discrepancy theory: a psychologi-

cal model for distinguishing among different aspects of depression and anxiety. *Social cognition* 3, 51–76.

idealization In the widest sense, this is the process of regarding a person as perfect. It involves overlooking or denying attributes of the person that do not fit the idealized picture and, in this respect, it differs from admiration.

In Freudian psychoanalytic terminology it refers to the mental process whereby objects may be construed as ideally good. The love-object 'is aggrandised and exalted in the subject's mind' (Freud). This over-evaluation involves the transfer or displacement of an excessive quantity of libido from the ego to the object. Identification with idealized objects, especially parents, plays a part in the construction of ideal models that contribute to the formation of character. Some authors emphasize the defensive functions of idealization e.g. Klein's conception of splitting of objects into "good" and "bad" as a defense against anxiety.   WLIP-J

Bibliography

Freud, S. 1953–74: On narcissism: an introduction. *Standard edition of the complete works of Sigmund Freud*, vol 14. London: Hogarth Press; New York: Norton.

Klein, M., 1952: In *Developments in psychoanalysis*, ed. Joan Rivière. London: Hogarth Press.

identification A core concept in psychoanalytic theory denoting the process through which the subject assimilates aspects of others (objects) and constitutes its personality from the resulting products. A legacy of FREUD's use of the term in successive theoretical formulations is a set of related meanings. Noting that the assimilative process may involve extension of the subject's identity into another, a fusing with another or the borrowing of identity from another, Rycroft (1968) lists four types of identification. *Primary identification* in infancy is problematic in that the subject is scarcely differentiated from the other. The sense of the term most widely employed in psychology is *secondary identification*. It functions as a defense best known in the OEDIPUS COMPLEX where assimilation of the parents replaces the ambivalent feelings of love and hostility towards them and leads to the formation of the SUPEREGO. *Projective* and *introjective identification* are also defenses and involve fantasies in which the subject either is inside and in control of another or has taken the object, or part object inside the self. Identification is distinguished from incorporation which is linked with the oral stage of development and fantasies of ingesting the object, and from internalization which denotes the assimilation of relations such as that of the subject to the authority of the father.

Identification is also an important concept in work on group relations (Turner 1984). The basic assumption of social identity theory is that people identify themselves and others by the groups to which they belong, and that people are in consequence motivated to favor their ingroup at the expense of the outgroup (see INGROUP AND OUTGROUP; PREJUDICE).   BBL.

Bibliography

Rycroft, C. 1968: *A critical dictionary of psychoanalysis.* London: Nelson; New York: Basic Books.

Turner, J.C. 1984: Social identification and psychological group formation. In *The social dimension: European developments in social psychology*, ed. H. Tajfel. London: Cambridge University Press.

ideology Any false, and more especially categorically mistaken, ensemble of ideas whose falsity is explicable, wholly or in part, in terms of the social role or function they, normally unwittingly, serve. Among the more discussed ideological phenomena are the representation of sectional or particular

interests as universal; the screening of social conflict and contradiction; the naturalization of the social status quo making it seem eternal; and the creation of the impression that the social order is the product of mere conventions (e.g. in social contract theory).

The term "ideology" was initially coined by Destutt de Tracy (1754–1836) to designate the scientific study of ideas, but was used pejoratively by Napoleon Bonaparte (1769–1821) to refer to the fanciful and impractical schemes of the Enlightenment. This connotation was extended and then transformed by Marx (1818–83) and Engels (1820–95) in *The German ideology* (1845–6) to characterize the mystified and mystifying abstraction of the thought of their contemporaries from the real processes of history. In the schematic topography of historical materialism such ideas were designated as part of the superstructure, ultimately explicable in terms of the economic base; while in Marx's critical work this characteristic pattern of critical explanation was employed to take in not just German philosophy, but utopian socialism, so-called classical political and vulgar economy and mystificatory thought generally, thereby linking up with aspects of the Baconian, Kantian and Hegelian critiques of illusion.

Subsequently the radical historical tradition, in both its Marxian (e.g. Gramsci 1891–1937) and non-Marxian (e.g. Mannheim 1893–1947) avatars, played down the "negative" connotation of false consciousness and emphasized the "positive" notion of ideology as expressing the values or world-view of a particular social group or milieu. More recently there has been a tendency, e.g. within modern structuralism, for ideology to become effectively identified with the entire cultural sphere. Marx's original concept of ideology has clear affinities with Freud's (1856–1939) concept of rationalization, and some writers (e.g. Habermas b.1929) have modeled ideology-critique on depth-analysis. Among the topics of contemporary investigation are the criteria for differentiating ideology from science; the relation between ideologies and systems of domination; and the socio-psychological mechanisms at work in the reproduction and transformation of ideological forms.

RB

Bibliography
Bhaskar, R. 1983: *Philosophical ideologies*. Brighton: Harvester Press.
Larrain, S. 1979: *The concept of ideology*. London: Hutchinson.

imitation This can be defined as placing one's own actions into correspondence with the behavior of others, implying an active process of matching or rendering equivalent behavior. Such a definition stresses the social functions of imitation in maintaining interpersonal relations and group identity.

Imitation may also serve the useful purpose of disseminating knowledge acquired by individuals to other groups or across generations. In the latter case, what is inherited is not the particular, adaptive behavior itself, but a generalized capacity to imitate and thus rapidly benefit from the accumulated learning of others. Recent evidence from developmental studies suggests that the ability to imitate may be innate. It has been shown that babies in the first month of life can imitate movements of the mouth and tongue (Meltzoff 1982). Such an ability may be very useful in helping the infant rapidly to produce the particular sounds of the language into which it is born. (See also SOCIAL LEARNING THEORY.)

GEB

Bibliography
Meltzoff, A.N. 1981 : Imitation, intermodal co-ordination and representation in early infancy. In *Infancy and epistemology*, ed. G.E. Butterworth. Brighton: Harvester Press; New York: St Martin's Press.

implicit personality theory A term used to describe naive observers' assumptions about the co-occurrence of personality traits. Studies in IMPRESSION FORMATION, stimulated by the pioneering work of ASCH (1946), have shown that people often assume personality traits to be present or absent in a person on the basis of limited information about only a few traits. Multivariate analysis of these assumptions (FACTOR ANALYSIS, cluster analysis) shows that people use only a few judgmental dimensions in forming impressions of others. Rosenberg and Sedlak (1972) showed how such analyses can reveal a writer's implicit notions about human personality.

In Kelly's PERSONAL CONSTRUCT THEORY this idea has been developed and elaborated into a cognitive personality theory and an instrument for clinical diagnosis and research.

Recent research in person perception has been influenced by Rosch's work on natural categories. Mervis and Rosch (1981) have suggested that prototypes and basic categories in Rosch's sense play an important role in the development and use of a person's implicit personality theory. A more recent discussion of these ideas appears in Lingle et al. (1984).

JMFJ

Bibliography
Asch, S.E. 1946: Forming impressions of personality. *Journal of abnormal and social psychology* 41, 259–90.
Lingle, J.H., Altom, M.W. and Medin, D.L. 1984: Of cabbages and kings: assessing the extendability of natural object concept models to social things. In *Handbook of social cognition*, vol. 1, eds. R.S. Wyer Jnr and T.K. Srull. Hillsdale, N.J.: Erlbaum.
Mervis, C.B. and Rosch, E. 1981: Categorization of natural objects. *Annual review of psychology* 32, 89–117.
Rosenberg, S. and Sedlak, A. 1972: Structural representations of implicit personality theory. In *Advances in experimental social psychology*, vol 6, ed. L. Berkowitz. New York: Academic Press.
Scheider, D.J. 1973: Implicit personality theory: a review. *Psychological bulletin* 79, 294–309.

impression formation (or person perception) The way in which we "perceive" or understand other persons. Much of the work in the 1940s and early 1950s was on the accuracy of person perception. This work (see Bruner and Tagiuri 1954 and Cook 1979) was undermined by

Cronbach (1955) who pointed out that it had relied on inadequate criteria of accuracy. The primary problem lay in the conception that a subject's ratings were accurate if they agreed with ratings produced by "experts". There were also problems caused by the fact that different people use rating scales somewhat differently. So, even if the definition of "accuracy" was acceptable, there were still intractable difficulties in assessing the agreement between the subjects' and the experts' ratings. Since then there has been a good deal of work aimed at producing a more realistic criterion of accuracy, but the focus of research has shifted to the processes involved in impression formation.

ASCH (1946) initiated this approach in the ten experiments in his paper 'Forming impressions of personality'. In experiment 1, Asch asked subjects to imagine a person who was "intelligent, skillful, industrious, warm, determined, practical, cautious". Other subjects received the same adjectives, with the exception that "cold" replaced "warm". This single change produced differences between the two groups' descriptions of the imagined person, and also their selection of appropriate adjectives in ten of eighteen forced-choice pairs, which included "generous (vs. ungenerous), happy, good-natured, humorous, and sociable". Asch was unable to produce similar contrasts when he substituted "polite/blunt" for "warm/cold". He argued that warm and cold are "central qualities" at least in this array. He also found that forty-nine percent who received "warm" and forty-eight percent who received "cold" ranked these traits in first or second place for their importance in determining their impressions, and he believed that this also suggested that they were "central".

Another of Asch's findings was that a group presented with the list, "intelligent, industrious, impulsive, critical, envious" wrote more favorable sketches and more often checked favorable traits than a group presented with the same list in the reverse order (experiment 6). He concluded that the better impression created by the list

with the favorable initial adjectives was an example of a 'primacy effect' in which the information acquired first sets up 'a *direction* which then exerts a continuous effect on the latter terms'.

There were other interesting results. Experiment 8, for instance, showed that people had no difficulty in constructing a profile of someone from a slightly inconsistent set of trait descriptions, unless they were told that the whole set described a single person after having first been told that some of the adjectives described one person and some described another. In experiment 10, fifty-one percent of the subjects thought that "quick" in the trio "quick, clumsy, helpful" resembled "slow" in "slow, clumsy, helpful" more than "quick" in "quick, skillful, helpful". Asch believed that these ten experiments supported his (gestalt) view that the traits are not summed additively but "integrated" in 'the perception of a particular form of relation between' them, such that 'identical qualities in different structures may cease to be identical' and even have opposed meanings.

Asch remarked on the artificiality of his experimental design, and critics were not slow to agree. In general however, less artificial designs have produced similar results to Asch's. Studies have used descriptive vignettes rather than mere lists of adjectives. Luchins (1957a), who had been one of the earliest critics, used two contrasted paragraphs about a student who was described as behaving in a friendly, outgoing way in one and as behaving in an introverted and unfriendly way in the other. The results showed a clear primacy effect, with subjects judging the character of the student on the basis of the information in whichever paragraph they received first. Warr and Knapper (1968, experiments 10–13) obtained the "warm/cold" effect when they embedded Asch's traits in quite long descriptions of a person.

Other studies have shown these effects even when subjects are not presented with verbal descriptions or asked to juggle adjectives on paper. Gollin (1954) used film of a young woman who behaved considerately in two scenes and promiscuously in two more. The impressions subjects formed sometimes integrated the two kinds of behavior under some superordinate heading ("easy-going"), sometimes simplified by omitting mention of one kind, and sometimes aggregated by mentioning both and leaving it at that. This shows that integration of the kind suggested by Asch may occur when judgment is based on observation. Jones et al. (1968) found a primacy effect when observers judged someone whom they saw solving problems. If success came early and failure later, the person was rated brighter than if the failure was early and the success later. More striking still was Kelley's (1950) demonstration of the "warm/cold" effect. He handed out descriptions of a visiting teacher who was about to lead a class discussion. The whole class were told that the teacher was "industrious, critical, practical and determined", but half were told that he was "very warm", and half that he was "rather cold". Despite the fact that the students had the opportunity to interact with the teacher for twenty minutes, the ratings which the two halves of the class produced after the discussion showed just the same differences as the sketches and trait-choices of Asch's subjects.

Other researchers have attacked the vagueness of Asch's idea of "central" traits, since he does not say which traits should be central in which contexts or why. They have also disagreed with the relational/structural interpretations of his results. Wishner (1960) asked students to use a six-point scale to rate their instructors (anonymously) on fifty-three traits used by Asch. He found that the trait-pairs on Asch's check list which had shown large differences between the "warm" and "cold" groups correlated very highly with "warm" and "cold". He also found that "un-intelligent/intelligent" produced similar check list effects on trait-pairs with which they correlated. He therefore concluded that there was no need for a gestalt explanation of Asch's results, since 'in general, a stimulus trait will have strong effects if the items to be judged are correlated with it, and weak effects if they are uncorrelated'. This certainly seems to explain how the "warm/cold" distinction affects the check list, and implies that similar correlations may also explain the different personality sketches. Other correlational interpretations of trait perception have been put forward in literature on the SEMANTIC DIFFERENTIAL (Osgood et al. 1958) and IMPLICIT PERSONALITY THEORY (Bruner and Tagiuri 1954; Rosenberg and Sedlak 1972).

Wishner (1960) also claimed that order is not as important as Asch had suggested, but the number of studies which have demonstrated a primacy effect tends to show that this is not true. Nevertheless primacy effects can be avoided, as Luchins (1957b) found. Anderson (1965) has argued that, on Asch's interpretation, the effect should not dissipate if more attention is paid to the later information, since the meaning of the later words in a list (or of later observations) should still be affected by the earlier. But the primacy effect can be replaced by a recency effect if attention is focused on later information. This implies that the effect is not the result of the processes proposed by Asch. It is not that the earlier information dictates how the later is understood, but rather that less attention is usually paid to later items.

Anderson (1981) has been a principal opponent of Asch's gestalt interpretation of impression formation. He has produced a good deal of evidence that the overall impression created by a list of traits can be predicted from the values of the individual traits. He has, however, rejected the additive model suggested by Bruner et al. (1958), who claimed that the overall impact was merely the sum of the impacts of the individual items in isolation. Anderson found that the overall impression is an *average* of the values of the individual items. A moderately favorable item paired with a very favorable item does not add to the power of the very favorable item as an additive model would predict, but makes a less favorable impression than the very favorable item on its own. Averaging, however, cannot account for all the findings. Warr (1974), for instance, found that two adjectives which were similarly favorable or unfavorable added to each other's impact to produce a more extreme impression than either did in isolation, whereas two adjectives which were very dissimilar produced an average impression. Warr suggested that similar pairs form a compound that 'is not in need of integration, but rather one single attribute'. He also found that negative information had more impact than positive. Others too have found this. Anderson (1981) has argued that a *weighted average* model fits the various findings best. In this model, not all items of information carry equal weight, so negative and early items are given more weight than positive or later ones.

The implication of both the adding and the averaging models is that trait meanings do not change in different combinations. It might be argued that sufficient disparity in the weighting given to different items would amount to a change of meaning for the lightly weighted items. In this case the configural and averaging models would be indistinguishable. Certainly it is hard to interpret Asch's experiment 10 (in which one "quick" resembled "slow" more than another "quick"), without assuming that trait meanings can change, or at least that different facets of them are called to mind in different contexts. Furthermore studies with a different method suggest that the implications of a description can be changed by "priming" subjects to think about particular topics before they are presented with the description. For instance, subjects primed to think about hostility before reading a description of someone's behavior, rate the person as more hostile than subjects who have not been primed (Srull and Wyer 1980).

The dispute over Asch's configurational models and Anderson's averaging model has been replaced by consideration of the role of "prototypes" or "schemata" in person perception. These concepts have been imported from cognitive psychology, and by and large fit in with Asch's ideas more than Anderson's. One's impressions of others are not thought to be formed simply on the basis of the information given. Rather, one categorizes others on the basis of how well they fit one's established, abstract prototypes or resemble proto-

typical exemplars (e.g. Higgins et al. 1982; see also SOCIAL COGNITION). Since a change of a "central" trait ("warm" for "cold") may obviously call to mind a different type, in which the other trait adjectives do have a slightly different meaning, it appears that central traits may be ones which are decisive in determining to which prototype a target is assimilated. Asch's ideas therefore appear to be supported by recent work.

Ironically, Watkins and Peynircioglu (1984) have shown that Asch's configural model seems to explain the integration of information presented in lists of adjectives (like Asch's own) far less well than the integration processes for a different mode of presentation. They used a sentence to set the context for the critical trait. Recall cued with a synonym of the trait-word was worse when the context-setting sentence was inconsistent with the usual meaning of the word. This implies that the word might not have been encoded in memory with its usual meaning, which implies in turn that the context affected the perceived meaning. There was no difference in recall when the critical trait was preceded by a list of three other compatible or incompatible traits. Such a list is obviously similar to Asch's. They therefore inferred that the result is artifactual in studies like Asch's own, and concluded that 'the meaning change hypothesis applies to some situations but seems not to stretch to the paradigm that has dominated the research seeking its illustration'.

Although the work reviewed above forms the mainstream, there have been attempts to investigate other aspects of impression formation, such as the cues which people actually use in their everyday perceptions of others. There is, for instance, an extensive literature on how people's physical appearance affects judgments others makes of them (see Cook 1979 for a review), and a still more extensive literature about the different impact of different kinds of expressive behavior (see SOCIAL INTERACTION). The equally extensive literature on ATTRIBUTION THEORY also had roots in the investigation of person perception, and retains a central interest in the inferences people make about others, and the mistakes they make in drawing their conclusions (see also SOCIAL PERCEPTION; STEREOTYPES). RL

Bibliography

Anderson, N.H. 1965: Averaging versus adding as a stimulus-combination rule in impression formation. *Journal of experimental psychology* 70, 394–400.

—— 1981: *Foundations of information integration theory*. New York and London: Academic Press.

Asch, S.E. 1946: Forming impressions of personality. *Journal of abnormal and social psychology*, 41, 258–90.

Bruner, J.S., Shapiro, D. and Tagiuri, R. 1958: The meaning of traits in isolation and in combination. In *Person perception and interpersonal behavior*, eds. R. Tagiuri and L. Petrullo. Stanford: Stanford University Press.

—— and Tagiuri, R. 1954: The perception of people. In *Handbook of social psychology*, ed. G. Lindzey. Cambridge, Mass.: Addison-Wesley.

Cook, M. 1979: *Perceiving other people*. London and New York: Methuen.

Cronbach, L.J. 1955: Processes affecting scores on "understanding others" and "assumed similarity". *Psychological bulletin* 52, 177–93.

Gollin, E.S. 1954: Forming impressions of personality. *Journal of personality* 23, 65–76.

Higgins, E.T., King, G.A. and Mavin, G.H. 1982: Individual construct accessibility and subjective impressions and recall. *Journal of personality and social psychology* 43, 35–47.

Jones, E.E., Rock, L., Shaver, K.G., Goethals, G.R. and Ward, L.M. 1968: Pattern of performance and ability attribution: an unexpected primacy effect. *Journal of personality and social psychology* 9, 133–41.

Kelley, H.H. 1950: The warm-cold variable in first impressions of persons. *Journal of personality* 18, 431–9.

Luchins, A.S. 1957a: Primacy-recency in impression formation. In *The order of presentation in persuasion*, ed. C.I. Hovland. New Haven: Yale University Press.

—— 1957b: Experimental attempts to minimize the impact of first impressions. In *The order of presentation in persuasion*, ed. C.I. Hovland. New Haven: Yale University Press.

Osgood, C.E., Suci, G.J. and Tannenbaum, P.H. 1958: *The measurement of meaning*. Urbana: University of Illinois Press.

Rosenberg, S. and Sedlak, A. 1972: Structural representations of implicit personality theory. *Advances in experimental social psychology* 6, 235–97.

Srull, T.K. and Wyer, R.S. 1980: Category accessibility and social perception: some implications for the study of person memory and interpersonal judgments. *Journal of personality and social psychology* 38, 841–56.

Warr, P.B. 1974: Inference magnitude, range and evaluative direction as factors affecting relative importance of cues in impression formation. *Journal of personality and social psychology* 30, 191–7.

—— and Knapper, C. 1968: *The perception of people and events*. London: John Wiley.

Watkins, M.J. and Peynircioglu, Z.F. 1984: Determining perceived meaning during impression formation: another look at the meaning change hypothesis. *Journal of personality and social psychology* 46, 1005–16.

Wishner, J. 1960: Reanalysis of "Impressions of personality". *Psychological review* 67, 96–112.

impression management See self-presentation.

indexical expressions A term used by philosophers and social scientists in referring to expressions, statements or utterances which can be understood only with reference to the context in which they occur. The most obvious examples are words such as "here", "there", "now", "then", "me", "my", "you", etc. But there is a wider sense in which almost any expression whatever can be regarded as indexical. This latter view has been important in the development of ethnomethodology, and a useful discussion of its implications for social scientific research is to be found in Garfinkel (1967, pp.4–7).

One of Garfinkel's main points is that a conceptual distinction between "objective" and "indexical" expressions has been central to most debates about scientific method. Sciences can be viewed as involving determined attempts to transcend or avoid the problems of ambiguity, vagueness, imprecision, subjectivity, etc. that are associated with the use of indexical expressions. Scientific method can thus be conceived as a set of procedures or methods which facilitate the substitution of "objective" expressions for "indexical" ones. But there is no perfect or absolute way of accomplishing this in practice, which means that scientists have to rely on a range of *ad hoc* procedures which enable the substitution to be effected "for all practical purposes". Such methods or practices, however, tend to be largely taken for granted, and have seldom been fully explicated. One of the aims of ethnomethodological inquiries, then, is to identify what these practices are and to describe how they work.

Substituting objective for indexical expressions is not a process which is exclusively confined to the work of scientists. Indexical expressions are encountered by everyone in the course of everyday life. And, while any and every expression they come across may "in principle" be open to a multiplicity of possible interpretations, making sense of any particular expression depends in practice on people making decisions as to which interpretation is to be treated as the "objectively" correct one for the practical purposes at hand, and in the light of what they know about the context in which it occurs, the course of the interaction thus far, the identity, biography and intentions of their co-interactant, etc. In other words, the process of achieving mutual understanding in the course of everyday interaction can itself be viewed as involving participants in repeatedly substituting objective for indexical expressions. In so far as the methods of interpretation used to accomplish this are – like those used in the production of scientific interpretation – largely taken for granted, they too are regarded as part of the subject matter for ethnomethodological investigations. (See also ETHNOMETHODOLOGY; TACIT KNOWLEDGE.)   JMAt

Bibliography

Garfinkel, H. 1967: *Studies in ethnomethodology*. Englewood Cliffs, N.J.: Prentice-Hall.

indigenous psychology The study of man as he conceives himself in terms of his collective representations. The term "indigenous" emphasizes cultural views, theories, conjectures, assumptions and metaphors; draws attention to what is generally available (see SOCIAL REPRESENTATION) to man in his attempts to make sense of and organize his psychological life. On occasion, however, psychologies developed by means of experimental, philosophical and religious inquiry percolate through to the indigenous level.

Among other things, the term "psychology" refers to the manner in which the individual or person is conceptualized, the divisions made within the individual, the powers attributed to the self, the location of controlling agencies (internalized or externalized), the way in which action is conceived, the way in which emotions are classified and evaluated, the properties attributed to dreams, episodes of mental abnormality or unusual states of consciousness, and to the nature of personality judgments.

The United States has recently been described as "the Psychological Society" (Gross 1978). Psychobabble is rife (a nice example is the psychoanalytically oriented dentist who told the *New York Times* that the mouth "acts as a barometer of the personality set of the individual"). Americans use psychology in the course of many daily activities: the salesman who has been taught the value of positive thinking, those who practice the advice contained in books such as *Baby and child care* and *Understanding your dog*. And Americans turn to psychology when they seek explanations of, and responses to, suffering. It is estimated that over seven million receive psychological intervention annually. Tending to assume that suffering is unnatural, the "healthy" but distressed person seeks a cure. Tending also to abnegate self-control and responsibility (on the grounds that the unconscious largely controls what people do and feel), Americans turn to specialists for what used to be called salvation.

The tendency in American culture is away from Riesman's "other directed" man (receiving life cues from outside sources) towards psychologically inspired man. But not only do indigenous psychologies change with time – they also show marked cross-cultural variation. Although there are no societies in which the psychological is not acknowledged at all, a number use allegorical or surrogate ways of talking about the individual, thereby muting comprehension of the autonomous self. The issue here is one of differences in the locus of the psychological (including LOCUS OF CONTROL). We think in terms of our being informed from within, of being able to act on the world, of exercising our will-power and self-control. And our apprehension of ourselves as autonomous beings is encapsulated in the notion "mind": "I make up *my* mind"; "I put *my* mind to it". The Dinka of the southern Sudan, however,

> ... have no conception which at all closely corresponds to our popular modern conception of the "mind" as mediating and, as it were, storing up the experiences of the self. There is for them no such interior entity to appear, on reflection, to stand between the experiencing self at any given moment and what is or has been an exterior influence upon the self. (Lienhardt 1961, p.149.)

In contrast to the Western view, the Dinka individual is the object, and the external world (specifically religious "powers") provide the locus of controlling "mentalistic" agencies. Dinka speak of "memories" being activated by powers, not by the self, as when we say, "I recall to mind the time that . . .".

Despite the pioneering work of Tylor, Lévy-Bruhl and others, the anthropological study of indigenous psychologies is not far advanced. But together with the contributions of cultural historians (going back to Burckhardt and Nietzsche), scholars of English literature, Sinologists, classicists (e.g. Snell 1953), social psychologists (e.g. Wegner and Vallacher 1977), and so on, there is material enough to show that there is remarkably little consistency in the manner in which man's psychological attributes have been envisaged across cultures and through time (see Heelas and Lock 1981 for ethnographic illustrations). But why should psychologists be interested in indigenous psychologies?

At first sight it appears that psychologists have as little reason to attend to the indigenous as astronomers have to take astrology seriously. Indigenous notions generally appear to be culturally contingent, present contradictory claims in any given culture (let alone cross-culturally), and often take a curious if not "erroneous" form (emotions located in the liver, as the Chewong of Malaysia maintain – see Howell 1981). Why should psychologists use such suspect evidence to map the psychological when they can use experimental and quantifiable techniques to explore the psychological as it "really" is?

On looking again, however, one sees that psychologists are not in the position of astronomers, studying objects which exist and function independently of how they are conceived. In Hampshire's words, 'The nature of the human mind has to be investigated in the history of the successive forms of its social expression' (1959, p.234). The psychological culture in which people are raised has a profoundly *constitutive* impact on their psychological performance. At the present time it is not possible exactly to demarcate the extent of constitutive processes, or the extent to which psychological phenomena operate and exist independently of how they might be conceptualized. There does however appear to be a spectrum – between the exogenous (culture dependent) and the endogenous (culture independent) – in terms of which the psychological significance of indigenous psychologies can be assessed.

At one extreme lies, for example, motivation. Rosaldo's aim in *Knowledge and passion* (1980) is to interpret Ilongot (northern Luzon) activities 'from the point of view of self-conceptions – accounts of how and why to act – that must inform the social lives of actors' (p.61). Ilongot headhunting, she argues, is explicable in terms of Ilongot psychological notions, not their religious beliefs: 'Not gods, but "heavy" feelings were what made men want to kill; in taking heads they could aspire to "cast off" an "anger" that "weighed down on" and oppressed their saddened "hearts"' (p.19). Social psychological and anthropological concerns meet when what is under examination is the role of what Hallowell calls the "behavioural environment" (1971, p.87) in sustaining the individual as a social being.

At the other extreme lie psychological processes (such as memory and perception) which largely operate independently of folk "theories". In between the exogenous and endogenous lies more debatable territory. Different theorists of emotions, for example, attach varying degrees of importance to cultural factors. But although there has been something of a shift back to endogenous theories, those who advocate such a shift of emphasis have not generally gone so far as to deny a role to the exogenous component of the cultural appraisal of "emotional" arousal. Given this role, a psychological account of the emotions as they are organized and managed in any particular culture must include consideration of how the emotions are regarded: whether, for example, as with the Chewong, display of most "emotions", including anger and joy, are associated with fear-inducing images – this plausibly indicating that "anger" is colored by "fear" to the extent that participants do not live with the same emotional repertoire as we in the West (see Howell 1981).

It is apparent that the more social the psychologist, and the more "anthropomorphic" the psychologist's model, the greater the attention that should be paid to what is most explicitly anthropomorphic: that is, how man envisages himself. However, indigenous psychologies do not provide comprehensive and automatically reliable paths to psychological nature. Indigenous formulations might be adventitious (see Needham's (1972) argument that "belief" does not describe a universal psychological phenomenon or might well not acknowledge what is actually occurring).

Indigenous psychological notions are of greatest interest to the psychologist when they bear on phenomena which appear to be under the influence of sociocultural constitutive processes.   PLFH

Bibliography

Gross, M. 1978: *The psychological society*. New York: Simon and Schuster.

*Hallowell, A. 1971: *Culture and experience*. New York: Schocken Books.

Hampshire, S. 1959: *Thought and action*. London: Chatto and Windus.

*Heelas, P. and Lock, A. eds. 1981: *Indigenous psychologies*. London and New York: Academic Press.

Howell, S. 1981: Rules not words. In Heelas and Lock, op. cit.

Lienhardt, G. 1961: *Divinity and experience*. Oxford: Clarendon Press.

*Needham, R. 1972: *Belief, language and experience*. Oxford: Basil Blackwell; Chicago: University of Chicago Press.

O'Hare, D. and Duck, S. 1981: Implicit psychology and ordinary explanation. In Heelas and Lock, op. cit.

Rosaldo, M. 1980: *Knowledge and passion*. Cambridge and New York: Cambridge University Press.

Snell, B. 1953: *The discovery of the mind*. Oxford: Oxford University Press.

Wegner, D. and Vallacher, R. 1977: *Implicit psychology*. New York: Oxford University Press.

individual psychology: history of

The name "individual psychology", was used by several founders of the field (Münsterberg 1891; Oehrn 1895; Binet and Henri 1896; Kraepelin 1896). Stern (1911), however, preferred the name "differential psychology" arguing that "individual psychology" referred to all aspects of the psychological life of the individual, including the general psychology of human beings. Besides, "differential psychology" also had as its object the investigation of differences between groups, so the phrase "individual psychology" was misleading and inadequate. On the other hand the reduction of individual persons to mere carriers of inter-individual differences was incompatible with Stern's personalistic philosophy (1911). Individuals conceived as relatively self-contained entities were therefore incorporated in his differential psychology as the converse of the distribution of one or more characteristics over a group of individuals. In other words, according to Stern, one of the basic data of differential psychology was constituted by a matrix of m characteristics exhibited by n

individuals, so that one could concentrate either on the distributions and the correlations of the characteristics or on one or more individuals in whom they jointly occurred. In the latter case, the investigation of a large number of traits manifested by one individual and the analysis of their internal relationships would lead to a "psychography", a term first used by Baade (1908) (see also Ostwald 1909), whereas it would be the task of a *Komparationslehre* to examine how much and in what respects two or more individuals resemble each other. Still, Stern must have felt that he hadn't done full justice to the individual person for he added that, in order to bridge the gap between the nomothetic and the idiographic approach, the individualizing function of psychographies had to be supplemented by biographies. In his view the basic presupposition of biography is the unity of personality whereas psychography takes as its starting point a multiplicity of traits so that both are complementary to each other.

About half a century earlier than Stern's decisive contribution, J.S. Mill (1851) had put forward the idea that character, which had been left out of the picture by association psychology, should become the object of a new science: ethology. For similar reasons, Samuel Bailey (1858) insisted on the necessity of developing a new discipline of individual and personal character which he conceived as separate and distinct from psychology. On the continent J. Bahnsen's plea for a characterology (1867) led to the development of typologies or theories of characterology such as the one championed by L. Klages as the basis of his system of graphology. Most of them remained separated from psychology, or as was the case with Klages, were openly hostile to it. Wundt on the other hand suggested the creation of 'a practical psychology, namely a characterology, which should investigate the basic and typical forms of individual character with the aid of principles derived from a general theoretical psychology'. Other authors who were also acutely conscious of the inability of the psychology of their times to deal with the problem of human individuality pleaded for a science of personality but unfortunately limited their efforts to the coining of new names. Mercier (1911) thought that the new discipline should be called "praxiology" whereas J.C. Smuts (1926) suggested the term "personology" which was later adopted by H.A. Murray (1938).

However, all these new scientific programs remained sterile for their proponents had not clearly spelled out the far-reaching consequences these programs implied. Indeed, in order to realize their objectives nothing less was required than a redefinition of the object of psychology, and the development of new methods of investigation – tasks which they were neither prepared nor willing to undertake. Because he attempted all of them, Stern achieved a major break-through for individual psychology.

At about the time Stern published his second book on differential psychology (1911), A. Adler, who had just broken with FREUD, developed his own theory which he called individual psychology in order to emphasize his conception of the individual as a unified totality. Years later, in 1930, Adler summarized his basic theory thus: 'The fundamental fact in human development is the dynamic and purposive striving of the psyche ... The unity of personality is implicit in each human being's existence. Every individual represents both a unity of personality and the individual fashioning of that unity.'

When through ALLPORT's and Murray's contributions personality psychology had achieved academic status, Adler's theory was already so well known that it had monopolized the appellation of "individual psychology." Consequently various research orientations, clinical and assessment activities which in fact belonged to the field of individual psychology, received other names (case-study; personology; life-history approach; etc.) and the terminological diaspora which ensued prevented the clear delimitation of a specific domain.

The virtual disappearance of personality psychology during the period extending from the end of the 1950s up to the late 1970s eliminated individual psychology almost completely from the field of current concerns. As R. Carlson noted in an important review of 226 articles published in the 1968 volumes of two major journals publishing research on personality: 'Although the literature as a whole has elicited a wide range of potentially important informations about persons, no single investigation either noted or utilized much information about any individual subject. Thus the task performances of subjects in current research remain un-interpretable as personality data in the absence of anchoring information.' And further: 'Not a single published study attempted even minimal inquiry into the organization of personality variables within the individual.'

One of Carlson's major conclusions, was that the goal of studying whole persons had apparently been abandoned. This diagnosis is fully confirmed by the number of individual case-studies referred to in *Psychological abstracts* from 1960 to 1978. During this period only about one per cent of published articles were devoted to the investigation of single persons and no trend whatsoever that could be considered symptomatic of the existence of individual psychology as a specific field was noted. The variety of the studies was so great that Shontz's classification of case-studies (1965) could not be applied. Instead, a new two-dimensional classification emerged based on: (i) the kind of individuals it examined; and (ii) the goals pursued by the investigators. Among the individuals studied, the following groups could be distinguished:

(a) Problematic persons who are the source of assessment or taxonomic problems (e.g. individuals whose personality is difficult to conceptualize within current frameworks or historical personalities).
(b) Well-known individuals posing no diagnostic problems.
(c) Groups of individuals (families, siblings) considered as a unit.

As to the goals of individual case-studies, six groups emerged:

(a) Assessment of an individual's personality and formulation of explanatory hypotheses susceptible to generalization.
(b) Detailed investigation of specific psychological processes.
(c) Illustration of a theory, a technique, a particular kind of therapy or of an interesting or rare case.
(d) Explorative studies.
(e) Theory testing either by confirmatory cases or by falsifying instances.
(f) Biographies and life-histories.

A few clear-cut conclusions can be drawn from the distribution of observed frequencies. First of all the major category of studies is constituted by the illustration of various techniques of behavior-therapy applied to known cases. On the other hand biographies and studies in which the investigation of a single person is regarded as a goal in itself are extremely scarce. Correspondingly, case-studies are concentrated in the field of clinical psychology whereas they are conspicuously absent in personality psychology. As to the methods used, they consist predominantly of TESTS and QUESTIONNAIRES. It is also interesting to note that, with the exception of the increase of publications devoted to behavior therapy, no differences can be observed between the decade preceding and the seven years following Carlson's important paper. In the absence of any explicit and scientifically founded justification of this state of affairs, the evolution of individual psychology is obviously in great need of scrutiny by historians and sociologists of science.   J-PDeW

Bibliography

Adler, A. 1925: *The practice and theory of individual psychology*. Trans. P. Radin. London: Kegan Paul, Trench, Trubner.

Allport, G.W. 1937: *Personality: a psychological interpretations*. New York: Holt.

Baade, W. 1908: Psychographische Darstellungen über normal begabter Individuen. *Zeitschrift für angewandte Psychologie*, 1, 274–7.

Bahnsen, J.F.A. 1867: *Beiträge zur Charakterologie*. Leipzig: F.A. Brockhaus.

Bailey, S. 1858: *Letters on the philosophy of the human mind*. 2nd series. London: Longmans, Green.

Binet, A. and Henri, V. 1896: La psychologie individuelle. *Année psychologique* 2, 411–65.

Kraepelin, F. 1896: Der psychologische Versuch in der Psychiatrie. *Psychologische arbeiten* 1, 1–91.

Mercier, C. 1911: *Conduct and its disorders*. London: Macmillan.

Mill, J.S. 1851: *System of logic*, vol. II. London: J.W. Parker.

Münsterberg, H. 1891: Zur Individual Psychologie. *Zentralblatt für Nervenheilkunde und Psychiatrie* 14, 196–8.

Murray, H.A. et al. 1938: *Explorations in personality*. New York: Oxford University Press.

Oehrn, A. 1895: Experimentelle Studiën zur Individual Psychologie. Diss. Dorpat. *Psychologische arbeiten* 1, 95–152.

Ostwald, W. 1909: *Grosse Männer*. Leipzig: Akademische Verlagsgesellschaft.

Shontz, F.C. 1965: *Research methods in personality*. Century Psychology Series. New York: Appleton-Century-Crofts.

Smuts, J.C. 1926: *Holism and evolution*. New York: Macmillan.

Stern, W. 1911: *Die Differentielle Psychologie*. Leipzig: J.A. Barth.

individual psychology: methodology

Since PERSONOLOGY investigates general aspects of personality, its mode of approach is nomothetic. However, individual psychology is also interested in individuals' personalities and should therefore also proceed idiographically. The question therefore is the relationship between nomothesis and idiography, and more precisely whether a specific idiographic domain exists and more precisely whether a specific idiographic domain exists and, if so, how it is to be characterized. Du Mas (1955) whose important contribution has not received all the attention it merits, proposes that we should regard nomothesis as that method of science which studies data obtained from more than one individual, whereas idiography makes use of data yielded by only one individual. A second assumption is that the basic data of nomothetic as well as of idiographic sciences are observations. Let O denote an observation. According to a third assumption an observation is always made of an entity on a particular occasion. Using here

interchangeably entity and individual, let individuals be denoted by 1, 2, 3, . . . i . . . N and let successive occasions be denoted by 1, 2, 3, . . . k . . . L. A fourth assumption which must be introduced is that an individual always has more than one property which will be denoted 1, 2, 3, . . . j . . . M. The illustration, which corresponds to CATTELL's co-variation chart *(see* Cattell 1950) gives a graphic representation of these assumptions. It also represents all observations collected from every individual in a sample or a population. Thus an observation O (ijk) corresponds to a point at coordinates i, j and k. Group or population studies are made of observations obtained from vertical sections of the cube while single case-studies are made of observations collected from horizontal sections.

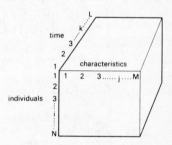

Let K denote that data are collected. Then the collection K(Oijk) means that observations are made and recorded of the jth characteristic, at the kth time, on the individuals 1, 2 . . . N. An observation O(ijk) may be regarded as a point and a specifically defined group as a set or domain. Domain A is identical to domain a if A and a are the same set of points. Domain B contains domain A if the set of points in B includes the set of points of A and one or more additional points. Domain A is contained in domain B, if the set of points of A is included in the set of points of B and B has one or more additional points.

All possible domains of nomothesis (n > 1) and idiography (n = 1) can now be represented within the three-dimensional system that has been outlined. These

	Nomothetic N>1	Domains	*Idiographic* N = 1
	O_{ijk} Basic datum E.g.–Rating of a characteristic	A a A identical to a both contained in all Nomo- thetic and Idio- graphic domains.	O_{ijk} Basic datum E.g.–Rating of a characteristic
Individuals	N $K (O_{ijk})$ i = 1 E.g.–Population distribution and parameters –Scoring system $\left\{ \begin{array}{l} \text{Contains domains A, a} \\ \text{Contained in C, D, E, a} \end{array} \right\}$	B b	L Occasions $K (O_{ijk})$ k = 1 E.g.–Trends and change as a function of time –Reliability and individual variability $\left\{ \begin{array}{l} \text{Contains domains A, a} \\ \text{Contained in C, E, d, e} \end{array} \right\}$
Individuals and Time	L N K $K (O_{ijk})$ k = 1 i = 1 E.g.–Changes in population distribution and parameters due to time factors. –Longitudinal studies S factor-analysis (one test administered to N persons at different times – correlations between persons) and T factor- analysis (one test administered to N persons at different occasions – correlations between occasions). $\left\{ \begin{array}{l} \text{Contains A, B, a, b} \\ \text{Contained in E, e} \end{array} \right\}$	C c	M Characteristics $K (O_{ijk})$ j = 1 E.g.–Configuration of ratings for a single individual. –Cross-sectional study of an individual. $\left\{ \begin{array}{l} \text{Contains domains A, a} \\ \text{Contained in domains} \\ \text{D, E, d, e} \end{array} \right\}$

	Nomothetic N>1	Domains		*Idiographic* N = 1
Characteristics and Individuals	$\begin{array}{cc} M & N \\ K & K \end{array} (O_{ijk})$ $j=1 \quad i=1$ E.g.–Trait intercorrelations –Profiles, clusters, configurations –Cross-sectional studies of population –Q and R factor analyses.	D	d	$\begin{array}{cc} L & M \\ K & K \end{array} (O_{ijk})$ Characteristics $k=1 \quad j=1$ and occasions E.g.–Changes in configurations as a function of time. –Intercorrelation of characteristics in a single individual. –O and P factor analyses.
	$\left\{ \begin{array}{l} \text{Contains domains} \\ \text{A, b, a, c} \\ \text{Contained in E, e} \end{array} \right\}$			$\left\{ \begin{array}{l} \text{Contains domains} \\ \text{A, a, c} \\ \text{Contained in E, e} \end{array} \right\}$
Characteristics and Individuals and Occasions	$\begin{array}{ccc} L & M & N \\ K & K & K \end{array} (O_{ijk})$ $k=1 \quad j=1 \quad i=1$ E.g.–Changes in profiles or configurations due to time factors –Longitudinal studies of configurational changes in the population	E	e	$\begin{array}{ccc} L & M & N \\ K & K & K \end{array} (O_{ijk})$ $k=1 \quad j=1 \quad i=1$ Identical to domain E
	$\left\{ \begin{array}{l} \text{Contains all} \\ \text{Nomothetic and} \\ \text{Idiographic domains} \\ \text{except o identical to} \\ \text{domain c.} \end{array} \right\}$			

domains are represented in the table together with some methods of data collection proper to each domain. In this way five nomothetic and five idiographic domains can be defined among which two are identical: A and a are identical as basic data and E is identical to e because both contain all the available information. Therefore the interesting comparisons to be made concern the domains B,b,C,c,D, and d. An examination of their relations of inclusion produces a few important conclusions:

(1) The three nomothetic domains B,C,D, are richer in information than the three corresponding idiographic domains. Indeed C can account for b and D for c, since b is included in C and c in D. It also looks as if there exists an asymmetry of inclusion between nomothesis and idiography favoring the nomothetic domains C and D. As the data collected in these domains contain information concerning single cases, it would apparently be true that from a nomothetic knowledge of a sample, information could be derived about single cases, whereas from an idiographic knowledge of single cases almost nothing can be inferred about the sample.

But, the first part of this conclusion is wrong because in drawing it one overlooks the fact that the idiographic data are irreversibly included in the nomothetic domains. The treatments to which they are submitted by the methods corresponding to these domains only yield aggregate propositions (Bakan 1967) about collective properties characterizing the group data but which are not applicable to the individuals composing the group. Therefore, once included, the individual data are lost, the methods used for analyzing group data making it impossible to retrieve them.

(2) The question whether there exists a specific idiographic domain must be answered positively. Indeed while d contains A and a (the basic data) and is contained in E and e (the totality of the information available) it is not contained in any other domain. This specific idiographic domain is one in which several characteristics exhibited by one individual on identifiably different occasions are studied.

This conclusion bears out Windelband's intuition that idiography is the approach appropriate for the study of processes and the representation of concrete evolving entities. It also confirms and retrospectively justifies Stern's insistence on supplementing psychography by biography, since his two-dimensional scheme lacked a third dimension along which occasions could be ordered. Still, there is an aspect of the idiographic domain which escaped the attention of both these authors. Indeed, whereas the succession in time of the moments at which observations are gathered refers to the situations in which the observed phenomena take place, it is quite possible to compare a set of situations without taking into account the temporal order in which they occurred. Consequently, the definition of the idiographic domain must be rephrased in order to accommodate the two possibilities covered by the term "occasion". Accordingly the idiographic domain is one in which several characteristics manifested by one individual in identifiably different temporally

ordered *or* unordered situations are studied. Biography is an example of idiographic investigation where consideration of the temporal order of situations is essential. On the other hand, a cross-sectional study of the ways an individual deals with the various situations confronting him, is an illustration of the second kind of idiographic approach. In both cases the objective is to discern patterns of consistency characterizing the individual person.

J-PDeW

Bibliography

Allport, G.W. 1972: The general and the unique in psychological science. *Journal of personality* 40, 1–16.

Bakan, D. 1969: *On method: toward a reconstruction of psychological investigation*. San Francisco: Jossey-Bass.

Cattell, R.B. 1950: *Personality: a systematic theoretical and factual study*. New York: McGraw-Hill.

De Waele, J.P., and Harré, R. 1976: The personality of individuals. In *Personality*, ed. R. Harré. Oxford: Basil Blackwell.

——— 1979: Autobiography as a psychological method. In *Emerging strategies in social psychological research*, ed. G.P. Ginsburg. New York: Wiley.

Du Mas, F.M. 1955: Science and the single case. *Psychological reports* 1, 65–75.

Lamiell, J.T. 1981: Toward an idiothetic psychology of personality. *American psychologist* 36, 276–89.

Shontz, F.C. 1965: *Research methods in personality*. Century Psychology Series. New York: Appleton-Century-Crofts.

Stern, W. 1906: *Person und Sache*. Leipzig: Barth.

——— 1911: *Die Differentielle Psychologie*. Leipzig: Barth.

——— 1919: *Die menschliche Persönlichkeit*. Leipzig: Barth.

Windelband, W. 1894: *Geschichte und Naturwissenschaft*. Strassburg: Heitz.

individuality: conceptual issues

Although Kluckhohn and Murray (1953) were undeniably right in asserting that "every man is in certain respects (1) like all other men, (2) like some other men, (3) like no other men", this often quoted statement reveals the need for an elucidation of the concept of individuality but doesn't provide one. To begin with its adequate explication requires the distinction of two pairs of contrasted concepts in which the term "individual" appears with two different meanings and which are both indispensable to the definition of individual psychology as the study of whole single persons across time and situations.

The first contrast is that between an individual (conceived as a unitary undivided entity) and a totality, population or structure of which it constitutes an identifiable part or element. The origin of this meaning is to be found in the fact that *individuum* is the Latin translation of the Greek *atomos* i.e. that which is indivisible. In spite of its etymological origin, "individual" in the sense of indivisible, unitary entity does not preclude either a multiplicity of attributes or a complexity of structure.

The second contrast involved opposes individual and general (or universal) taken as the extremes of a series of terms hierarchically ordered in kinds and species. Among these the individual occupies the lowest level because it cannot be further divided logically. This lowest term is also called singular. The big question to which very diverging answers have been provided is whether and how the unique entity referred to by a singular term can be an object of scientific knowledge. According to Aristotle, science is the knowledge of the essence of things which finds its formulation in a definition 'per genus proximum et differentiam specificam'. Genus and species belong to the *praedicabilia*, i.e. that which can be predicated of a subject. And as they can be predicated of more than one subject they are said to be universal. Whereas the genus is that part of the essence of anything which is predicable also of other things differing from it in kind, the differentia is that part of the essence which distinguishes it from other species within the genus. Equally included in the praedicabilia is the *proprium* (Greek: *idion*) which is an attribute common to some or all members of a species or to several species but not constitutive of their

essence and therefore not bearing upon their definition. Accidents are also non-essential praedicabilia whose presence or absence leaves unchanged the essential nature of the subject to which they are attributed. A series of terms ordered according to a hierarchy of genera and species exhibits as the lowest step of the differentiation of essence the "infima species" (Greek: *to atomon eidos*, i.e. the indivisible species) below which there are no essential differences left which might define new species. Since the individual or singular term doesn't correspond to a general concept it excludes any further logical division. However as "infima species" it subsumes an undetermined number of individuals which differ only "numero" i.e. by their mere existence in certain numbers, but not "specie" i.e. by the essence proper to their kind. Thus, for Aristotle as well as for his later followers such as A. Arnauld and P. Nicole, the authors of the influential Logic of Port-Royal (1683), there exists only numerical but not qualitative individuality. This theory should not be confused with the indefensible position taken by K. Pawlik (1972) who states that: "representatives of idiographic personality research (such as ALLPORT) understand individuality as the unique *qualitative* characteristic of the individual, whereas representatives of the nomothetic variety (such as Guilford) consider it as the unique *quantitative* characteristic (in the sense of a uniqueness of the individual configuration of factor values in the relevant ability and personality factors)".

Consequently, it is only as a member of the species man that we can know this unique Tom Brown, but not as an individual. For as the schoolmen's saying summarizes the whole matter: "Scientia non est individuorum". This rather formidable limitation resulting from Aristotle's theory inevitably raises the problem of individuation and the search for a principle of individuation which in addition to belonging to a species might confer concrete singular existence on a being. For Aristotle and Aquinas, this principle is "matter" so that Tom Brown and John

Smith can only be distinguished, as individuals, by the "matter" they are made of. To quote the Stagirite 'the skin and bones are different, humanity is the same'.

It is the difficulties inherent in this view as well as the problems of the reality of the *praedicabilia* defining the essence of a thing which during the Middle Ages set in motion the memorable debate between realists and nominalists, a discussion which, although generating less heat, is still going on. In fact it is only for the adherents to a realist conception of universals that there exists a problem of individuation because this view confers priority on the general. For nominalists, on the contrary, individuals are the primary reality and universals have to be abstracted from them and hence exist only "in mente". The nominalists however are confronted by a new problem: how does it come about that individual entities manifest characteristics which, because of their repetition in single instances, are general?

That this problem is still with us is demonstrated by the fact that Burt's four factor theorem concerning the measurement of any individual for any one of a given set of traits (see Burt 1941), reproduces in factor-analytic terminology the four Aristotelian praedicabilia.

Leibniz (see Broad 1975), who attempted to look at the question from a new angle, considered that the differences by which individuals are distinguished from each other are not of a different nature from those which differentiate the species of a same kind, but the analysis of these characteristics would require an infinite process. Still according to this view the existence of complete notions of individuals has to be admitted, i.e. notions which exhibit no indeterminate or variable aspect capable of further determination.

Another leading conception of individuality is to be found in the Hegelian "concrete universal" which is said to be universal because it can be applied to an unlimited number of instances while remaining concrete since it also constitutes a unique and indivisible totality. English idealist philosophers have particularly emphasized this last aspect and Bosanquet

(1912) summarized this conception by defining the individuality achieved by a concrete universal as "macrocosm constituted by microcosms".

From this brief overview of the philosophical issues involved in the concept of individuality several conclusions of interest to psychology can be drawn.

(1) Whatever philosophical position one endorses, the two associated meanings of the concept of individuality must be distinguished because they originate in different operations. The first (the individual as an indivisible unitary entity) results, in principle, from a real division, whereas the second (the individual as the ultimately concrete reality) is generated by a conceptual and logical division.

(2) Provided certain presuppositions are given up, a solution to the problem of individuality can be formulated which is fully consonant with current scientific thinking and practice.

Renouncing idealism which fuses both operations of division is necessary to prevent conflation of the two meanings of individuality in the notion of concrete universal.

If one rejects presuppositions that subject-predicate relation reflects the structure of reality, one no longer needs to invoke subjects that cannot be exhaustively defined by predicates, i.e. substances.

If the separation of essence from existence is replaced by a complementary relationship, the gap between numerical (i.e. existential) and qualitative (i.e. essential) individuality disappears.

The relationship between the general and the individual can then be summarized as follows:

Every real thing or process is individual, but only as a whole and not in its particular determinations.

Each aspect or characteristic of an individual real thing is general because it is common to others; if it didn't repeat itself it would be unknowable. In each and every real thing its various features and relationships combine to form a unique configuration.

As the general features, by combination, do not lose generality, it may be said that the general inheres in the individual. This constitutes the reality of the general and the reason for the inseparability of the individual from the general.

Scientific knowledge is constant oscillation between individualization and generalization which progresses in ever-widening spirals.

(3) It should be borne in mind that the concepts of idiography and nomothesis introduced by Windelband (1894) to designate the polarity constituted in most science by generalizing and individualizing approaches is in fact theoretically neutral. Although the term "idiography" originates in the Aristotelian terminology concerning the *praedicabilia*, the term "nomothesis" is a neologism. Windelband's position on the question of individuality is difficult to ascertain, and neither Stern nor Allport have explicitly stated their views. Allport, having introduced Windelband's and Stern's terminology into Anglo-Saxon personality psychology (1937), has unfortunately added to the existing confusion by giving prominence to the notion of *proprium* which he has defined in one of his later works (1955) as the individual quality of organismic complexity – tracing back the origin of this additional meaning to Swedenborg (ed. Bigelow 1907), who used it in the special sense of selfishness and pride.   J-PDeW

Bibliography

Allport, G.W. 1937: *Personality: a psychological interpretation*. New York: Holt.

—— 1955: *Becomings*. New Haven and London: Yale University Press.

Arnauld, A. and Nicole, P. 1970: *La logique ou l'art de penser*. Paris: Flammarion.

Bosanquet, B. 1912: *The principle of individuality and value*. London: Macmillan.

Broad, C.D. 1975: *Leibniz: an introduction*. Cambridge and New York: Cambridge University Press.

Burt, C. 1941: *The factors of the mind*. New York: Macmillan.

Kluckhohn, C. and Murray, H.A. 1953: Personality formation: the determinants. In *Personality in nature, society and culture*, eds. C. Kluckhohn, H.A. Murray and D.M. Schneider. New York: Knopf.

Murray, H.A. et al. 1938: *Explorations in personality*. New York: Oxford University Press.

Pawlik, K. 1972: Individuality. In *Encyclopedia of psychology*, eds. H.J. Eysenck, W. Arnold and R. Meili. New York: Heider and Heider.

Swedenborg, E. 1907: *Proprium*, ed. J. Bigelow. New York: New Church Board of Publication.

Windelband, W. 1894: *Geschichte und Naturwissenschaft*. Strassburg: Heitz.

information processing: social psychology A term used to describe the encoding, integration, representation and decoding of information in making (social) judgments. ATTRIBUTION THEORY suggests that behavioral information is encoded by making causal inferences about latent, more or less invariant characteristics of the person and/or the situation. Such attributes are then thought to be integrated mainly by a weighted averaging process, which takes into account inconsistency in the information and results in a representation (e.g. IMPLICIT PERSONALITY THEORY) and final (evaluative) judgment or category assignment. Recent research by Nisbett and Ross (1980) and Kahneman, Slovic and Tversky (1982) has revealed many biases in human judgment and has suggested that information processes rely heavily upon simplifying cognitive heuristics in which prototypes play an important role. (See also SOCIAL COGNITION.)   JMFJ

Bibliography

Kahneman, D., Slovic, P. and Tversky, A. 1982: *Judgment under uncertainty: heuristics and biases*. Cambridge and New York: Cambridge University Press.

Mervis, C.B. and Rosch, F. 1981: Categorization of natural objects. *Annual review of psychology* 32, 109–115.

Nisbett, R.E. and Ross, L. 1980: *Human inference: strategies and shortcomings of social judgment*. Englewood Cliffs, N.J.: Prentice-Hall.

ingroup and outgroup Sumner (1906) was the first to use the terms "ingroup", "outgroup" and "ethnocentrism", but the concepts are used mainly in research and theorizing which concern intergroup relations. Quite literally a person's ingroup is the group to which he sees himself as belonging, and the outgroup the group to which he does not see himself as belonging. Numerous experiments have shown that the mere act of categorizing people into groups can lead them to discriminate in favor of their ingroup and against their outgroup. However, ingroup and outgroup allegiances may change if the ingroup ceases to contribute to the individual's sense of positive social identity. (See also PREJUDICE.)

AF

Bibliography
Sumner, W. 1906: *Folkways*. New York: Ginn.

initiating structure A term used to refer to the task-oriented behavior of a leader of a small group. It refers to the extent to which a leader defines his own role, specifies the duties of group members, indicates procedures and standards to be used, and evaluates group achievements. In combination with measures of the extent to which leaders show concern for the feelings and welfare of their group, measures of initiating structure have been used to identify different leadership styles and to explore their effects on productivity and satisfaction. See LEADERSHIP; MANAGEMENT.

FHMB

instinct: in general and human psychology Those patterns of experience and behavior which – as universally distinctive among the members of a species as their anatomical features – emerge within the process of maturation, are adapted to normal environmental conditions, and are inherited (not learned, though learning is significantly related to them). They comprise: (a) specific neurophysiological conditions, and elements of (b) perception (sign stimuli), (c) conation (drive), motivation, exploratory and appetitive behavior, (d) consummatory acts (fixed pattern reactions and associated reflexes) and (e) emotion attendant upon fulfillment or thwarting. Their maturational order marks critical periods of development and learning (e.g. imprinting, the effects of which seem enduring and irreversible). The presence of instinct does not signify the absence of intelligence or learning (a common misunderstanding), its degree of flexibility being related to the degree of complexity of the species-organism. Before, in, and after the work of Darwin, instinctual experience and behavior has been held to exist in man, though here the element of drive in particular, and flexibility in relation to learning, are emphasized. Also, man's biological inheritance being always overlaid by a cultural heritage, the accommodation of the one to the other leads to the establishment of *sentiments*, entailing non-rational as well as rational elements. The significance of instinct for sentiment-formation, learning, personality and character development, and the operation of cultural influences has entered psychological and sociological theories in many ways. Examples are: McDougall (Social Psychology); Shand (Foundations of Character); Freud (see INSTINCT; PSYCHODYNAMICS); Cooley and Mead (the importance of primary group communications during the early years of family and play-group experience in the growth of the "self" in society); Pareto (regarding the instinctual dispositions of the human mind as "residues" exerting continual and powerful influences of a "non-logical" kind in the many theories ("derivations") which men construct about the world and society, and in the struggles between elites); and Westermarck (*The origin and development of the moral ideas*). Always criticized in its application to man, the concept of instinct remains important in the human sciences.

RF

Bibliography
Cooley, C.H. 1902 (1964): *Human nature and the social order*. New York: Schocken.
—— 1909 (1962): *Social organization*. New York: Schocken.
Fletcher, R. 1968: *Instinct in man*. London: Allen and Unwin.

McDougall, W. 1908: *An introduction to social psychology*. London: Methuen.

Shand, A., P. 1914: *The foundations of character.* London: Macmillan.

Westermarck, E. 1903: *The origin and development of the moral ideas*. 2 vols. London: Macmillan.

instinct: psychodynamics

A term which refers both to innate and fixed behavior patterns common to most members of a species and to a motivational force usually distinguished by its goal. In his writing FREUD used the German word *Instinkt* for the former and *Trieb*, sometimes translated as drive, for the latter. He developed his theory of instinct (*Trieb*) in the context of his psychoanalytic investigations of sexuality. Freud described an instinct as having a source within the body and a pressure or quantity of energy which was seeking release, related both to its somatic source and to its object. A subject's choice of object and method of gaining satisfaction or aim are constructed in the course of development and represented psychologically. Freud viewed instinct as 'a borderline concept between the mental and the physical' (Freud 1915). In a wider sense Freud was a dualist, initially placing EGO or self-preserving, and sexual or species perpetuating, instincts in competition, but in his final formulations opposing *eros* (love, both self and sexual instincts) and *thanatos* (instinct of death and disorder).   BBL

Bibliography

Freud, S. 1915 (1957): Instincts and their vicissitudes. *Standard edition of the complete works of Sigmund Freud*, vol. 14. London: Hogarth Press; New York: Norton.

institutions and institutionalization

In the broader sociological sense, the term "institution" or "social institution" refers to the major organized systems of social relationships in a society. Institutionalization refers to the process whereby norms, values and ways of behaving are transformed into enduring, standard and predictable patterns.

In psychology, however, and in everyday language, the term "institution" has a much narrower and more specific meaning. It refers to certain specialized organizations and establishments for processing or changing people. The goals of such institutions include reform, treatment, re-education, re-socialization, punishment and rehabilitation. The people who find themselves in such institutions are usually called inmates, patients or clients and usually belong to one or other deviant or dependent group. Examples of such institutions are prisons, mental hospitals, old people's homes and children's homes. Being sent to these places is often referred to as "being institutionalized".

An important subgroup of such institutions has become known as "closed" or (following GOFFMAN) "total" institutions. These are places where 'a large number of like-situated individuals, cut off from the wider society for an appreciable period of time, together lead an enclosed, formally administered round of life' (Goffman 1961). Time spent in a total institution might be an enforced form of punishment or treatment (prisons, mental hospitals), a voluntary retreat from the world (convents, monasteries) or a process of education or service (army barracks, boarding schools).

The immediate and long-term psychological effects of prolonged experience of these regimes and communities is usually described as "institutionalization". In psychiatric terms, the effect is seen as pathological – "institutional neurosis" (Barton 1966) – and is characterized by withdrawal, lethargy, childlike dependency and (at the extreme) an inability to survive outside the institution. Sociologists tend to see institutionalization (and specific forms such as "prisonization") not solely as pathological, but as a form of secondary socialization. The inmate learns gradually how to adjust to the regime and its deprivations, particularly by taking on the norms of the informal inmate SUBCULTURE. This process often subverts or undermines the formal aims of the organization. These learnt strategies of "making out" or survival may or may not facilitate later adjustment outside and (as certain studies have shown e.g. Cohen and

Taylor, 1981) will depend in form and intensity on the inmate's pre-institutional identity.   SCoh

Bibliography

Barton, R. 1966: *Institutional neurosis*. Bristol: John Wright.

Cohen, S. and Taylor, L. 1981: *Psychological survival: the experience of long term imprisonment*. Harmondsworth: Penguin.

Goffman, E. 1961: *Asylums: essays on the social situation of mental patients and other inmates*. New York: Doubleday; Harmondsworth: Penguin (1968).

institutions, rationality of Standards or criteria against which reasoning practices within particular cultural and organizational settings are deemed adequate. Social life can be thought of as a complex of activities in which people are continually interpreting, explaining, understanding and categorizing features of their environment, which include the actions of others, their own actions and the objects and events around them. In short, people are continually making sense of their world. Traditionally, the notion of rationality implies the existence of criteria by which the adequacy of these sense-making activities can be assessed: such criteria are assumed to exist independently of the context or setting of the reasoning practice; and the reasonableness of action is thought to be indicated by the extent to which individuals match up to these criteria. By contrast, the notion of rationality of institutions

(1) holds that criteria of adequacy in reasoning are institutionally circumscribed; and

(2) suggests that these criteria are best regarded, not as a pre-existing independent set of procedural rules, but as an argumentative resource drawn upon by participants.

The implication of (1) is that what counts as adequate will depend on the particular INSTITUTION in which reasoning is being adjudged. Thus the empirical findings of research influenced by ETHNOMETHODO-LOGY demonstrate that the adequacy of

sense-making is contingent upon the immediate practical purposes of actors in the organizational environment. For example, the accuracy of medical records is not a matter for analysis of correspondence between documents and the "actual facts of the matter", but a question of whether the records are "good enough" for the immediate use to which they will be put (Garfinkel 1967).

Although "rationality" clearly varies between different environments, it is not clear to what extent particular forms of rationality can be ascribed to particular institutions. On the one hand there is the general argument that certain forms of rationality characterize whole social institutions; for example, that what counts as the correct use of evidence is characteristic of the law. On the other hand the implication of (2) above is that forms of rationality should not be attributed in this way. Such is the interpretive flexibility of any procedural criterion that what counts as rational practice can vary with each occasion of use. From this "radical situationist" point of view, the emphasis switches from an attempt to discern which forms of rationality are peculiar to an institution, to an attempt to document the ways in which different notions of rationality are used by participants as a means of characterizing both their own and others' practices.

In certain institutions, questions about adequacy of procedure are especially lively for participants themselves. For example, practitioners in science, the law and psychiatry often reveal explicit concern with the adequacy of reasoning practices. Science, in particular, is sometimes thought to embody the most stringent and well-defined criteria of procedural adequacy. However, ethnographic investigation of scientific practice suggests that even in science what counts as adequate depends crucially on the practical exigencies of the laboratory situation (Latour and Woolgar 1979). The construction of scientific facts thus arises out of a series of localized, contextual and highly variable criteria as to procedural adequacy. In the course of such work various abstract canons of scientific procedure are invoked by scientists, but these feature as an evaluative resource in the post hoc characterization of practice rather than as a principle which guides that practice.   sww

Bibliography

Garfinkel, H. 1967: *Studies in ethnomethodology.* Englewood Cliffs, N.J.: Prentice-Hall.

Latour, B. and Woolgar, S. 1979: *Laboratory life: the social construction of scientific facts.* Beverly Hills, Calif.: Sage.

intergroup discrimination *See* prejudice.

internalization In social psychological terms the adoption of attitudes or behavior patterns by an individual. Indeed much of socialization and education is involved with encouraging the individual to internalize the behavioral norms, morals and values of his or her group. A child's behavior is shaped or guided by example, encouragement, rewards and punishments, and hence directed into particular channels by external instruction and intervention. However, as the child develops he or she becomes able to give him or herself these instructions. Full internalization is reached when the behavior takes place not just because it is rewarded or punished, but because it is seen to be correct or appropriate. In psychoanalytic theorizing the term is often used synonymously with introjection or identification and describes the process by which objects or norms in the external world are molded into permanent mental representations. The ego defense mechanism of IDENTIFICATION is the way in which an individual attempts to take on the characteristics of someone who is more important than himself. Identifications may be made on the basis of guilt feelings, the need for punishment, or strong emotional attachments.   AF

interviewing A personal interview is a face-to-face discussion between two people, directed towards some specific purpose. This may, for example, be assess-ment of suitability for a job, or giving advice about a problem.

In a selection interview the aims are first to match the candidate's qualifications with job requirements, and second to predict to what extent he or she is likely to work hard and be successful. The interview usually follows a biographical approach: starting from the written information on the application form, the interviewer asks the candidate to highlight the main events in his or her upbringing, education, employment, and leisure activities to date, and also to explain why he or she has applied for the job. The interviewer should follow up in depth any points which seem important. Non-verbal interaction between the two parties, smiling, nodding etc, may also have a considerable influence on what they think of each other (see Argyle 1983).

One of the greatest pitfalls of the interview is "halo effect", the tendency when meeting another person to form a general impression, favorable or otherwise, and to allow this general impression to affect all other judgments. One way of guarding against this is to use an interview rating form. Specimen forms are presented in Anstey (1977). Using a form of this kind compels the interviewer to make separate assessments of each aspect of personality before arriving at a final overall assessment, and to weigh the factual evidence obtained from the interview itself and from other sources, before making a decision.

Interviewing needs to be studied as a science, to be practiced as an art. There are three stages in developing the skills of interviewing:
(1) The casual, unplanned approach typical of many untrained interviewers.
(2) The careful, systematic approach of the interviewer who has received some training, but is still preoccupied with asking the right questions of the candidate rather than with interpreting the answers.
(3) The development of sensitivity to a candidate's attitudes and feelings as well as the content of his or her replies; in a word, establishing rapport. Once rapport has been achieved the actual questions matter less, and the

interview is likely to yield reasonably reliable information. An experienced interviewer may hope to achieve rapport in about 75 per cent of personal interviews.

Though one-to-one interviews are the most common, board or panel interviews are often used by large organizations when filling senior appointments. A panel of three is usually most cost-effective, preferably with members varied in age, sex, and experience. Subjectivity is reduced through pooling different impressions, but because of the shorter time available to each member for questioning it is harder to achieve rapport than in a personal interview.

Widely used though the interview is, it is still a subject of considerable controversy. Views on interviewing are affected by two contrasting views of human personality. The first holds that a person's intelligence and other basic characteristics are largely innate and enduring, and also capable of measurement. In the 1950s and 1960s such writers as Eysenck (1953) and Mayfield (1964) published evidence that these basic characteristics are measured more accurately by written tests of intelligence or temperament than by interview. It should be noted, however, that nearly all the interviewers involved had been given little or no training in how to interview, and this fact may well have had a bearing on the results obtained. According to this school of thought, interviewing is so subjective and unreliable that it should be used only as a last resort.

The opposite view is that even intellectual abilities are greatly affected by early upbringing and changes in environment. Written tests measure abilities at a point of time. On the other hand, interviewers can, by studying how an individual has progressed relative to the opportunities available to him or her, make reasonable predictions of likely future development. Interviewing, for all its obvious limitations, has the merit of two-way contact and of considering the individual in the round.

Each point of view deserves some respect. Even the strongest advocates of interviews should reinforce them by other

means. Due note must be taken of academic, professional or technical qualifications where these are relevant. When selecting for any job in which a particular skill is required it is obviously sensible first to administer the relevant test, and to interview only those who reach the qualifying standard.

Promotion interviews differ from selection interviews in that solid information is available about a candidate's record within the organization, usually in the form of a series of written reports on performance. These written reports can be used in conjunction with interview information to predict how far the candidate could develop to meet the responsibilities of higher grade work.

Appraisal interviews were first generally recognized as a desirable ingredient in improved personnel management policy in the late 1950s (see Maier 1958). The purpose of an appraisal interview is for a manager to discuss a subordinate's performance with him or her, and consider how this performance can be improved and the subordinate's potential developed. Most of the early appraisal schemes failed to fulfill the hopes expected of them, mainly because they were introduced without adequate explanation or training, and because interviewers tended to adopt too authoritarian an approach. A second wave of appraisal schemes introduced in the late 1960s achieved much better results. More emphasis was placed on preparation and training for the interviews, on a problem-solving approach, on directing the interview towards specific limited objectives which were capable of achievement, and on regular feedback of information on how the scheme was working. For the outcome of research into the factors making for success or failure in appraisal schemes, see Anstey, Fletcher and Walker (1976). If, and only if these conditions are fulfilled, the general consensus now is that appraisal interviews can make a worthwhile contribution towards making the best use of staff and maintaining their morale.

Since the interview is directed towards a specific purpose its usefulness will depend critically upon both parties knowing this purpose and preparing accordingly. In selection it is up to the employer to disseminate accurate information about requirements for the job and how selection will be made. It is up to an applicant to study this information carefully, to learn about the organization, and to prepare replies to questions likely to be asked at interview. In appraisal, it is up to the manager to review the subordinate's performance over the past year and previous discussions between them. It is up to the subordinate to consider any difficulties which may have prevented him or her from achieving more.

Training for interviews is critical. Talks on how to interview are almost useless unless followed immediately by practice interviews in which students can try out the suggestions made. The best training courses include at least two practice interviews, giving each student an opportunity to improve performance during the course, reinforcing good points and learning from mistakes, sometimes by watching video-tape feedback. Advice on selection training is given in Goodworth (1979), and on appraisal training in Anstey et al. (1976). Advice to interviewees is equally important. Fletcher (1981) provides guidance in self-preparation and presentation.

Another kind of interview is the counseling interview, in which the interviewer gives guidance about choice of career, about problems with people, or about personal or financial problems. While a counselor can sometimes make positive suggestions, the most important function is often to listen sympathetically and, by offering factual information or impartial comments, help the client to make up his or her own mind on which course to follow.

There are also survey or market research interviews in which the sole function of the interviewer is to elicit opinions on political or other topics, or on the relative merits of various products.

Finally, in all occupational interviews, the possibility of unfair racial or sexual discrimination is assuming increasing importance. In both the USA and the UK this is theoretically prohibited by law, but "Discriminating fairly" (1980) lists some common sources of bias which can lead to unfair discrimination. One example (p.16) is "the tendency of the employer to recruit in his own image", and hence unwittingly to prefer someone of the same race and color, and possibly also from the same social background. Where members of ethnic minority groups are involved it is even more important that sound interviewing principles should be resolutely enforced, and that interviewers should supplement their interview impressions wherever possible by reference to objective data.   EA

Bibliography

Anstey, E. 1977: *An introduction to selection interviewing.* London: H.M. Stationery Office.

—— Fletcher, C. and Walker, J. 1976: *Staff appraisal and development.* London: Allen and Unwin.

Argyle, M. 1983: *The psychology of interpersonal behaviour.* 4th edn. London and Baltimore: Penguin.

Discriminating fairly: a guide to fair selection. 1980: London: Runnymede Trust; Leicester: British Psychological Society.

*Downs, C.W. et al. 1980: *Professional interviewing.* New York: Harper and Row.

Eysenck, H.J. 1953: *Uses and abuses of psychology.* London and Baltimore: Penguin Books.

Fletcher, C. 1981: *Facing the interview.* London: Allen and Unwin.

Goodworth, C.T. 1979: *Effective interviewing for employment selection.* London: Business Books.

*Higham, M. 1979: *The ABC of interviewing.* London: Institute of Personnel Management.

Maier, N.R.F. 1958: Three types of appraisal interview. *Personnel* March, 27–40.

Mayfield, E.C. 1964: The selection interview: a reevaluation of published research. *Personnel psychology* 17, 239–60.

*Moffat, T.L. 1978: *Selection interviewing for managers.* New York: Harper and Row.

introversion *See* Eysenck; Jung; type.

J

Jung, Carl (1875–1961) The contributions to personality theory of the Swiss psychiatrist C.G. Jung were developed over a period of more than fifty productive years and now reside in the twenty volumes of his collected works (ed. Read, 1953–79). None of these, however, is devoted to a systematic discussion of what has come to be known as Jungian theory, nor do any of these volumes present an entire theory in brief outline. The task of systematizing the work was left to others. The better-known attempts have been offered by Jacobi (1962), Fordham (1966) and Hall and Nordby (1973).

Jung's earliest interest in the study of personality stemmed from his attempt to understand the dynamic relationship between conscious and unconscious processes (*CW* vols. 1, 2; 1961). This work led to an alliance with Sigmund FREUD in the early development of psychoanalysis as a theory of personality and as a method of therapy. His defection from the psychoanalytic school founded by Freud, after five years of intense participation, was occasioned by his dissatisfaction with Freud's pansexual explanation of the origins of personality development and Freud's reluctance to approach the deeper layers of the unconscious which he feared would be associated with mysticism.

The publication in 1912 of Jung's book, *Symbols of transformation*, heralded his departure from the psychoanalytic ranks and he began a lonely, tortuous path, largely unaided by others until later life, to understand the nature of personality. In this book, in which the spontaneous fantasy productions of a single individual are analyzed, much of the material that constituted the basis for a lifetime of original work are to be found in nascent form.

In general outlines Jung thought of the personality as a series of interacting bipolar energic subsystems whose undifferentiated potentialities existed at birth in a vast realm he labeled the "collective unconscious". The encounter with life forced a differentiation of the inherently dominant poles into consciousness to shape and form conscious experience. The path through life was guided by the ultimate pull to make the potential actual, to reconcile or balance the opposites, to make available to consciousness the implicit potential latent in the original structure. This life-long process he designated as "individuation". Energy was inferred from change created by the tension of opposites.

From a structural point of view Jung described personality as consisting of two dynamic, interacting realms, consciousness and the unconscious. Within consciousness he delineated two structures, the ego and the persona. The ego he designated as the center of the conscious field, the experiencing "I" or "me", the source of the individual feeling of identity and continuity. Surrounding the ego is the persona, the individual's "face to the world", the constellation of roles, attitudes and behavior by which a person presents who he or she is to the world in response to societal demands. The ego, of necessity allied with the persona, must guard against an over-identification with this public mask to the exclusion of the expression of inner promptings from unconscious sources. Such an imbalance leads to tension resulting in psychological distress.

Jung divided the unconscious into its personal and collective aspects. The personal unconscious consists largely of experiences that were once either dimly conscious or too painfully salient to maintain a consistent persona image. Through repressive kinds of mechanisms they are kept from easy access to consciousness. Some semblance of order is postulated to exist in the personal unconscious through the formation of complexes, an adherence of relevant experiences around an attracting nucleus. Thus all repressed thoughts, feelings, memories and wishes relating to experience with one's mother are described as part of a "mother complex".

The deeper layers containing the primal, universal material without which the ultimate aspects of personality cannot be forged are thought to reside in the collective unconscious, a concept unique to Jungian psychology. He conceived of mind as being capable of generating images prior to and independent of conscious experience, similar in form in all people, prototypical or archetypal in nature. In and of themselves they are the raw materials which often appear in dreams, fantasies and other creative human products, usually called forth by the imbalances caused by the demands of conscious existence. When intuitively factored they reflect the central themes with which human beings have struggled throughout history. These include good and evil, gender, power and mortality among many others. Jung personified these clustered images by giving them various names. The gender archetypes Anima and Animus referred to the hidden opposite side of the male and female, respectively. The Wise Old Man and the Great Mother were names assigned to the authoritative power figures appearing in unconsciously derived imagery. Archetypal figures or structures are all collective but not necessarily unconscious. The ego and the persona are archetypal in structure yet largely conscious in content while the "shadow", a collective term which includes all that is primitive and all that is hidden about personality, contains a large segment of material that was once conscious. The flow of psychological life is conceived as a continuous engagement between consciousness and the unconscious within the confines of a relatively closed system. The development of personality, although influenced by the outside world, is pictured basically as an internal struggle.

In the search for an operating framework in which to describe the manifestations of personality, Jung settled on a typological schema which because of its empirical possibilities has had more impact in academic psychological circles than any other aspect of his theoretical work. In his classic volume *Psychological types* (1933), Jung attempted to bring order into the diversity presented by individual differences in personality through the delineation of a conceptual model which included two basic attitudes and four essential psychological functions common to humankind. The attitudes were termed "introversion" and "extraversion", probably biologically determined, which influenced the direction of energy, or interest, in the psyche. In introversion the focus of interest was centered on the internal, subjective, intrapersonal aspects of psychic life; in extraversion, on the external objective, interpersonal side. As in all major Jungian concepts, a bipolarity is intended. The functions were described as thinking and feeling – a rational pair, and sensation and intuition – a perceptual pair. Thinking and feeling are evaluative or judgmental functions, the former emphasizing the use of cognitive and intellectual information, the latter relying upon affective cues. The data they utilize are in the service of settling value issues, such as whether something is good or bad, liked or disliked. The perceptual functions are concerned with the processes related to the identity of things rather than their value. Sensation operates as the function concerned with facts or the apparent, concrete nature of the world. Intuition is directed toward the elaboration of the possibilities or relational aspects of perceptual data.

In describing personality Jung assumes that both attitudes and all four functions are part of the inherent endowment of all human beings. During the course of development, as a result of the mix of individual propensities, familial and more general cultural pressures, one of the attitudes and one of the functions are most clearly differentiated and become the conscious, operating framework of the personality. Thus, as a first approximation, personality may be described by the combination of the dominant attitude and the first function. For any person this would result in one of eight possibilities, either introversion or extraversion in tandem with one of thinking, feeling, sensation and intuition. Further complexity is added by the differentiation into consciousness of an auxiliary function, one of the pair of functions orthogonal to the first function. An individual would then have as descriptors of personality three identifying features; a dominant attitude, a first function and an auxiliary function. The general schema that emerges is a sixteen category typology. The behavioral and imaginal characteristics of each type are elaborated in the work of Isabel Briggs-Meyers (1962) whose Type-Indicator represents the most sophisticated attempt to measure individual type structure.

The concept of development, although central to Jung's teleological view of personality, focused little on the problems of early childhood and socialization. Initially he was content to adopt the Freudian view. In later years the contributions of Frances Wickes (1966) and Michael Fordham (1947) related Jung's ideas to the experiences of childhood. Jung's picture of development remained at a much more global level. He conceived of the progression of life as basically divided into two parts. The first half, roughly marked by the end of the fourth decade, was directed toward the adaptational problem of establishing one's position or place in the world. This he saw proceeding through the development of the dominant attitude and the first function and all that such development intended in the essential choices of occupation, object attraction, mate selection, values and more general interests. As a result of this necessarily one-sided emphasis, there grows over time a pressure for expression of the neglected, more unconscious aspects of the personality contained in the opposite attitude and the fourth function, the polar opposite of the first. The occurrence of this psychological unrest may be related phenomenologically to what is commonly termed the mid-life crisis, a mark of entry into the period Jung called the second half of life. During this stage the adaptational problem

shifts from finding one's way into the world to that of finding one's way out, the ultimate confrontation with mortality. In a poetic vein Jung described the entire process as an exploratory trek of traversing a mountain in which the initial energy is devoted to reaching the summit with limited concern for what lies beyond. When the peak is reached, a set of new problems is revealed in how to descend and negotiate all that is involved in concluding the task.

Thus the path of personality development is directed toward an ultimate outcome which Jung called "individuation". In its most general sense the process of individuation mirrors the sequential progression of physical existence. The templates of the physical structures are given at conception, differentiate at different rates, are strengthened or impeded by different experiences and form different integrations with each other at various times in the life history. The ultimate outcome under positive circumstances is a well-articulated, smooth-functioning physical system equipped to do in the species sense what it is capable of doing. This model Jung basically used for psychological individuation. He delineated the essential system parts (consciousness and the unconscious), the structural units within those parts (the archetypes), the stylistic framework in which these structural units operated (the attitudes and functions), and provided a dynamic rule of order by which the system and its parts were governed (the law of opposites). The energic aspects of the interaction of the system parts were guided by the principles of equivalence and entropy borrowed from the laws of thermodynamics.

In yet another vein Jung described the individuation process as directed toward the achieving of selfhood. Since the self in Jungian thought represents the totality of psychic life, we must interpret that statement as meaning the achievement of the most differentiated and integrated state of psychological development. In a metaphoric sense, as in alchemy, when the primal ingredients are put together in an appropriate mix, there will emerge an ultimate substance which will be greater than the sum of its parts. For Jung the press toward individuation is accelerated in the second half of life largely as a result of the imbalances created by the necessary adaptations during the first half of life. He identified the essential steps in the achieving of selfhood. These included relinquishing an absolute identification with the ego, accepting the power of the collective unconscious aspects of the psyche, making all the functions and the non-dominant attitude conscious and thus available for use, and similarly integrating the archetypes of the collective unconscious into conscious experience. The successful result of such a continuing set of efforts is largely ideal and hardly permanent. It creates a state of internal harmony through which both the immediate problems of living and the larger problems of life may be filtered.

While Jung thought of individuation as a universal human process, he also pointed out that the path did not necessarily resolve into an individual human struggle. Institutionalized, symbolic, non-conscious forms have emerged in the development of culture to deal with these very problems. Religious systems and their ritual practices may speak directly to these issues. Jung saw the individual need to "know oneself" as both an affliction and a blessing in that the progress of humankind is reflected in the expansion of consciousness which involves pain as part of the price of achievement.

IEA

Bibliography

Fordham, F. 1966: *An introduction to Jung's psychology*. Harmondsworth: Penguin.

Fordham, M. 1947: *The life of childhood*. London: Kegan Paul.

Hall, C.S. and Nordby, V.J. 1973: *A primer of Jungian psychology*. New York: New American Library.

Jacobi, J. 1962: *The psychology of C.G. Jung*. New Haven: Yale University Press.

Jung, C.G. (1921) 1933: *Psychological types*. New York: Harcourt.

—— 1961: *Memories, dreams, reflections*. (Recorded and edited by Aniela Jaffé.) New York: Pantheon; London: Routledge and Kegan Paul (1963).

Meyers, I.B. 1962: *The Meyers-Briggs type indicator*. Princeton: Educational Testing Service.

Read, H. et al. eds. 1953–79: *The collected works of C.G. Jung*. Princeton: Princeton University.

Wickes, F. 1966: *The inner world of childhood*. Rev. edn. New York: Appleton-Century.

K

Kelly, George A. (1905–1966) This physicist, mathematician, sociologist, educationalist and eventually clinical psychologist, influenced psychology with one major work: *The psychology of personal constructs* published in 1955. Jerome Bruner in his review of the two volumes described it as 'the greatest single contribution of the past decade to the theory of personality functioning' and as 'a genuine new departure and a spirited contribution to the psychology of personality'. Few would quarrel with those words thirty years later, but they underestimate the significance of Kelly's ideas for psychology.

Kelly saw the person as being the central concern of psychology. *Person*ality is thus equivalent to "psychology" and not just one aspect of it. The whole nature of the discipline would change were PERSONAL CONSTRUCT THEORY its point of departure (for a detailed discussion see Bannister and Fransella 1986).

The *Fundamental Postulate* states that 'A person's processes are psychologically channelized by the ways in which he anticipates events' and is elaborated by eleven *Corollaries*, every word of which is defined. No one person has direct access to "the truth" of these events (although reality does exist). The best we can do is to act "as if" our construing of the world were true. Formally stated as the philosophy of Constructive Alternativism it asserts 'We assume that all of our present interpretations of the universe are subject to revision or replacement.' None of us need be trapped by our past, although we may become a victim of how we *construe* our past. This philosophy stems from the "new" as opposed to the "old" (Newtonian) physics. It acknowledges that, amongst other things, the experimenter changes the very nature of that which he is investigating by his very intervention. All we can strive

for in research is the best explanation of events at the moment.

Since there is no "truth" we can lay our hands on, Kelly suggests psychologists might look at everyone "as if" each were a scientist peering at the world through a system of discriminations (constructs) built up through the years. Some of these discriminations have verbal symbols attached to them, many do not. These constructs, or mini-theories, are our bases for predicting the outcome of events facing us. Behavior is the experiment we conduct to test out our current construing (predictions) about the world. In Kelly's theory behavior becomes the independent and not the dependent variable.

The reflexive nature of the theory sees psychologists and "subjects" alike as forms of motion, acting upon and not just responding to the world. To assist in the understanding of a person's construing of the world, Kelly described the *repertory grid* to quantify the relationships between the units of his theory – constructs.

Studying the person as a whole within a single theoretical framework eliminates the chapter headings commonly found in most psychology textbooks. For instance, motivation relates mainly to the *Choice Corollary*, learning to the *Experience Corollary*, unconscious processes to differing levels of awareness, and emotion to an awareness that our construing is in a state of transition. But there can be no learning without feelings and behavior. Construing is experiencing. There can be no cognition without affect or *vice versa*. In their struggle for an orderly discipline, psychologists have tried to place personal construct theory within the "cognitive" category. But, as Kelly says: ' ... personal construct theory is no more a cognitive theory than it is an affective or conative one. There are grounds for distinction that operate in one's life that seem to elude verbal expression' (Kelly 1970, p.15).   FF

Bibliography

Bannister, D. and Fransella, F. 1986: *Inquiring man*. 3rd edn. Beckenham: Croom Helm.

Kelly, G.A. 1955: *A psychology of personal constructs*. New York: Norton.

—— 1970: A brief introduction of personal construct theory. In *Perspectives in personal construct theory*, ed. D. Bannister. London: Academic Press.

L

labeling theory A perspective on deviance, which tends to see the deviant as a victim of a society which categorizes him as criminal or mad in an arbitrary or despotic way. The classic text is Becker's *Outsiders* (1963, 1973). According to Becker, 'Deviance is not a quality of the act a person commits, but rather a consequence of the application by others of rules and sanctions to an "offender". The deviant is one to whom the label has successfully been applied; deviant behavior is behavior that people so label.' This approach has been concerned with those who are labeled as addicts, delinquents or mentally ill. It recognizes that behavior is counted as deviant because of others' reactions to it. Intoxication with alcohol is not regarded as abnormal; intoxication with cocaine is. Nevertheless, the implication that the matter is arbitrary, and that *any* behavior may be labeled as deviant has not received unanimous support (Schur 1971). The examples often cited, such as sexual practices, drug use, or the different labels attached to killing in different contexts (murder of a fellow citizen; heroic defense of the realm by a soldier), do not really go to show that the labels are arbitrary, nor that someone might suddenly and surprisingly find himself labeled deviant for behavior he had thought quite normal.

Whether actions are labeled as deviant may be open to negotiation and may depend on the power of the agent. Certainly such labeling will differ from culture to culture, because norms are not universally the same. Lofland (1969) regarded power as crucial, suggesting that groups who have it impose the deviant label on those who do not. It is clear, however, that the values and normative expectations of the groups are important (Schur 1971).

Lemert (1967) distinguished "primary" and "secondary" deviance. Acts of primary deviance may often not be considered deviant by the agent. Subsequently, however, he or she may be labeled by others, perhaps in a "ceremony of status degredation" such as a trial. Having once been labeled a person will suffer social pressures which maintain deviant identity. A convicted criminal, for example, will meet other convicted criminals in prison and be affected by their attitudes and assumptions. After release he may find it hard to get a job because he has been labeled criminal. Even without such ceremonial labeling someone who has done something primarily deviant, such as a homosexual act, may come to see him- or herself as deviant. Whether the deviant identity is publicly or privately endorsed it is likely to lead to other deviant acts, which result from the deviant label, and are therefore defined as examples of secondary deviance.

The perspective has been quite persuasively applied in elucidating the processes and effects of diagnoses of mental illness (Scheff 1974), and received some striking empirical support from Rosenhan (1973). In general, however, empirical support for the approach is not strong. For a review see Gove 1975.   RL

Bibliography

Becker, H.S. 1963: *Outsiders: studies in the sociology of deviance*. New York: Free Press. (Rev. edn. 1973.)

*Gove, W.R. 1975: *The labeling of deviance: evaluating a perspective*. New York: Wiley.

Lemert, E.M. 1967: *Human deviance, social problems, and social control*. Englewood Cliffs, N.J.: Prentice-Hall.

Lofland, J. 1969: *Deviance and identity*. Englewood Cliffs, N.J.: Prentice-Hall.

Rosenhan, D.L. 1973: On being sane in insane places. *Science* 179, 250–8.

Scheff, T.J. 1974: The labeling theory of mental illness. *American sociological review* 39, 444–52.

Schur, E.M. 1971: *Labeling deviant behavior: its sociological implications*. New York: Harper and Row.

leadership By "leadership" we mean the direction, supervision, or management of a group or an organization. Leaders are ubiquitous. They may be "emergent" (informally acknowledged); elected by the group; or appointed by the organization of which the group is a part. A leader may thus be a gas station manager, the chief executive officer of a multinational company, or the person who happens to be most influential in a group. Although the topic of leadership has been a focus of interest since the dawn of recorded history, its scientific examination began only in 1904, and did not get into its stride until the second world war.

Emergent leadership

Early investigations were preoccupied with the question of how one attains a leadership position and, in particular, whether there are certain personality attributes or traits which enable a person to become a leader, or to be effective as a leader. We usually identify emergent leaders by means of sociometric scales, that is by asking such questions as "Whose opinion do you value most in this group?" "Whom would you most like to have as your leader?"

Various studies have shown that emergent leaders do not differ markedly from their followers in personality attributes or traits. They tend to be slightly more intelligent, slightly larger, more visible and socially adept than other members. Their leadership status seems to derive more from the group members' perception that a person is able to provide the needed skills, economic or political resources to help the group to achieve its goals, than from personality.

Moreover, almost everyone is a leader of at least some groups and a follower in innumerable others. It is difficult to see, therefore, how a particular trait could identify a leader.

Leadership effectiveness

The many attempts to find leadership traits and attributes which would distinguish effective from ineffective leaders have had similarly limited success. Nevertheless, Kenny and Zaccaro (1983) showed that in a rotation design study (where each person must deal with different situations and personnel) between 49% and 82% of variance among leaders' performances could be accounted for by some stable personal characteristic. It is of interest to note that there is a wide divergence between practitioners and theorists in their treatment of personality attributes and characteristics.

In practice, the most commonly used predictors of leadership performance, e.g. in hiring or assigning managers, are intellectual abilities, technical competence and leadership experience. On the other hand, the major contemporary theories of leadership practically ignore these cognitive abilities and knowledge: McGregor's Theory X/Y (1960); Likert's System 1–4 (1967); House's Path Goal Theory (1971); Fiedler's Contingency Model (1967); or Vroom and Yetton's Normative Decision Model (1974), etc., either do not discuss the role of intellectual abilities or experience as important elements in their formulations, or mention them only in passing. Instead, their main focus is on such socioemotional variables as managerial attitudes or philosophies, participative management and leadership style.

The concern with socioemotional behavior was also embodied by a groundbreaking study by LEWIN, Lippitt and White (1939). It investigated the effect of democratic, laissez-faire, and autocratic leaders on group climate, participation and member involvement. Boys' clubs were organized under leaders who were instructed to behave in a predetermined manner. The study was interpreted as showing that a democratic, participative style produced better results than either of the others. Above all, this study demonstrated that leadership phenomena could be examined in laboratory experiments and became the model for most empirical leadership research for the next two decades.

The Lewin studies were part of a humanistic, employee-centered movement in management thinking which championed personal growth, employee self-actualization, and participative management practices. These theories, proposed by such leading figures as McGregor, Likert, Maslow and Mayo, had considerable impact on management thinking but neither the theories nor training programs based on them have been consistently supported by empirical research.

Leaders' behavior

A major theme, beginning in the 1940s, was a concentrated effort to identify behavior associated with effective performance. The research, most prominently associated with a group at Ohio State University, found two important factors: "Consideration" (socioemotional, expressive behavior indicating concern for the opinions, feelings, and welfare of subordinates) and "Structuring" (assigning roles and tasks to group members, setting standards and evaluating performance). These behavior factors have played a major part in understanding the leader's role in shaping the group interaction. They did not identify practically useful differences between effective and less effective leaders. Considerate leaders had more satisfied group members and in some studies, leaders who were both structuring and considerate tended to be somewhat more effective than leaders who were not considerate or structuring. Other studies did not find these results (Korman 1967).

Contingency approaches

The Contingency Model of Leadership Effectiveness (Fiedler 1967) led to the abandonment of the notion that there was one best leadership style or behavior for obtaining effective performance. The theory classifies leaders as motivated primarily by the need to accomplish assigned tasks or to develop close and supportive relations with members of their group. The situation is classified as giving a high, moderate or low degree of power, influence and control to the leader. Situational control indicates, in essence, the proba-

bility of being able to accomplish the task. The theory and supporting research showed that task-motivated leaders perform best in high-control and in low-control situations; relationship-motivated leaders perform best in moderate-control situations.

The Contingency Model has generated considerable controversy. Some feel that it has been extensively validated (Strube and Garcia 1981) while others are less convinced (Vecchio 1983). The theory implies that leader effectiveness can be improved by changing either personality or situational factors, and that it is considerably easier to change the latter. A training program was therefore developed to teach leaders how to modify critical components of the leadership situation (e.g. leader–member relations, task structure, position power). The effectiveness of this "Leader Match" method has been demonstrated in a variety of evaluation studies in military and civilian settings (Fiedler, Chemers and Mahar 1976; Fiedler and Mahar 1979).

Path–goal theory

Involves the interaction of behavior and situation and was developed by House (1971). It states that the leader must motivate the subordinates by (a) emphasizing the relationship between subordinates' own needs and the organizational goals, and (b) clarifying and facilitating the path which will enable them to fulfill their own needs as well as the organization's goals.

The theory predicts that structuring behavior (i.e. coaching, direction, specifying goals) will have positive effects when the job is unclear; considerate behavior (support, warmth, concern) will have beneficial effects when the job is boring or aversive. Research supports the theory's prediction of employees' job satisfaction and subordinates' motivation; predictions on performance have not been well supported.

Normative decision model

Vroom and Yetton's (1974) model prescribes the conditions under which leaders should make decisions autocratically, in consultation with group members, or with group members fully participating in the decisions. The theory assumes that (a) individual decisions are more time-effective than group decisions, (b) subordinates are more committed to a decision if they participate in its formulation and (c) complex and ambiguous tasks require more information and consultation for reaching high-quality decisions. The model prescribes the way in which decisions are to be made under various conditions. Up to now, tests of this theory have been based on retrospective reports, and further research is required to evaluate the predictive validity of the theory.

Transactional approaches

These theories deal with the way in which leaders interact with subordinates. Hollander (1978) showed, for example, that the leaders' status increases in proportion to their contribution to the group goal. Leaders must prove their worth by competence and commitment to group values for which they then receive "idiosyncracy credits". These credits allow the leader to diverge from accepted group norms and standards, to strike out in new directions, or to be forgiven for minor transgressions.

Cognitive approaches

Leadership theorists have returned increasingly to the study of cognitive processes. In studies of leader judgments Green and Mitchell (1979) found that leaders attribute more blame when a subordinate's behavior had adverse consequences than if the same behavior had no negative consequences. These and similar studies show why leaders reward certain types of behavior and punish others.

A series of studies (Fiedler et al. 1979) showed that military leaders effectively utilized their intellectual abilities but not their experience when they had relatively stress-free relations with their boss. They effectively utilized their job-relevant experience, but not their intellectual abilities when stress with their boss was high. These studies suggest that intelligence and job-knowledge were prematurely abandoned by leadership theorists.

Task characteristics and formal rules

and customs, as well as technologies, may guide worker activities, and therefore substitute for leadership. These phenomena have been studied by Osborn and Hunt (1975). Leadership research is likely to focus to an increasing extent on the role of task characteristics and on the cognitive components of the leadership process. FEF

Bibliography

Fiedler, F.E. 1967: *A theory of leadership effectiveness*. New York: McGraw-Hill.

—— Chemers, M.M. and Mahar, L. 1976: *Improving leadership effectiveness: the Leader Match concept*. New York: Wiley.

—— and Mahar, L. 1979: The effectiveness of contingency model training: validation of Leader Match. *Personnel psychology* 20, 1–14.

—— et al. 1979: Organizational stress and the use and misuse of managerial intelligence and experience. *Journal of applied psychology* 64, 635–47.

Green, S.G. and Mitchell, T.R. 1979: Attributional processes of leaders in leader-member interactions. *Organizational behavior and human performance.* 23, 429–58.

Hollander, E.P. 1978: *Leadership dynamics: a practical guide to effective relationships*. New York: Free Press.

House, R.J. 1971: A path-goal theory of leader effectiveness. *Administrative science quarterly* 16, 321–38.

Kenny, D.A. and Zaccaro, S.J. 1983: An estimate of variance due to traits in leadership. *Journal of applied psychology* 68, 678–85.

Korman, A. 1967: "Consideration", "Initiating Structure", and organizational criteria. *Personnel psychology* 18, 349–60.

Lewin, K., Lippitt, R. and White, R.K. 1939: Patterns of aggressive behavior in experimentally created social climates. *Journal of social psychology* 10, 271–301.

Likert, R. 1967: *The human organization*. New York: McGraw-Hill.

McGregor, D. 1960: *The human side of enterprise*. New York: McGraw-Hill.

Osborn, R.N. and Hunt. J.G. 1975: An adaptive reactive theory of leadership: the role of macro variables in leadership research. In *Leadership frontiers*, eds. J.C. Hunt and L.L. Larson. Carbondale: Southern Illinois University Press.

Peters, L.H., Hartke, D.D. and Pohlmann, J.T. 1985: Fiedler's contingency theory of leadership: an application of the meta-analysis procedures of Schmidt and Hunter. *Psychological bulletin* 97, 274–85.

Strube, M.J. and Garcia, J.E. 1981: A meta-analytic investigation of Fiedler's contingency model of leadership effectiveness. *Psychological bulletin*, 90, 307–21.

Vecchio, R.P. 1983: Assessing the validity of Fiedler's contingency model of leadership effectiveness: a closer look at Strube and Garcia. *Psychological bulletin* 93, 404–8.

Vroom, V.H. and Yetton, P.W. 1974: *Leadership and decision-making*. New York: Wiley.

Lewin, Kurt German psychologist. Born 9 September 1890 in Mogilno (Posen) and died 12 February 1947 in Newton (Massachusetts, USA). Lewin studied psychology in Berlin from 1909–14. In 1922 he became *Dozent* and in 1927 Professor of Psychology at the same university, as one of the younger representatives of gestalt psychology. He emigrated to the US in 1933 and was first at Cornell, then moved to the University of Iowa in 1935. After the second world war he became the director of the Research Center for Group Dynamics at the Massachusetts Institute of Technology.

Lewin has had a great influence in many areas of psychology. His work formed in various ways a bridge between gestalt psychology, the study of personality and motivation and social psychology. He was the founder of field theory in psychology, which regarded behavior primarily as a function of the person and the present situation. Lewin attempted to formalize this theory by making use of topology, but this work has been less influential than his research in group dynamics. For details of his ideas see CONFLICT; FIELD THEORY; LIFE SPACE; TOPOLOGICAL PSYCHOLOGY.

His main works are: *A dynamic theory of personality* (1935); *Principles of topological psychology* (1936); *Resolving social conflicts* (1948); *Field theory in social science* (1951).

JMFJ

life events The jargon term "life events" covers all significant social changes and sudden adversities which people may experience. Rigorous standards of assess-

ment are necessary to test the hypothesis that change, particularly if stressful, can lead to various physical and mental conditions. Two methods have been developed, the inventory (Holmes and Rahe 1967) and the interview schedule (Brown 1974). Each method has its particular problems (Bebbington 1985).

In general, an excess of life events is reported before the onset of many physical diseases (Birley and Connolly 1976) and mental conditions such as schizophrenia and depression and especially before suicide attempts.

However, the association is fairly weak. Modifying factors and, in particular, the mediating mechanisms are unclear. Moreover, the association may not arise because events cause the disorder in question. Insidious illness can itself generate such events. The subject and the researcher may share the bias that stress has important effects. Finally psychiatric disorders, particularly depression, have a significant bearing on the way in which we view and report our experiences. Dohrenwend et al. (1984) showed that many so-called "life events" would be categorized as symptoms of psychological disorder.

PBe

Bibliography

Bebbington, P.E. 1985: Psychosocial etiology of schizophrenia and affective disorders. In *Psychiatry*, ed. R. Michels. Philadelphia: Lippincott.

Brown, G.W. 1974: Meaning, measurement and stress of life events. In *Stressful life events: their nature and effects*, eds. B.S. and B.P. Dohrenwend. New York: John Wiley.

Dohrenwend, B.S. et al. 1984: Symptoms, hassles, social supports, and life events: problem of confounded measures. *Journal of abnormal psychology* 93, 222–30.

Holmes, T.H. and Rahe, R.H. 1967: The social readjustment rating scale. *Journal of psychosomatic research* 11, 213–18.

Tennant, C., Bebbington, P.E. and Hurry, J. 1981: The role of life events in depressive illness: is there a substantial causal relation? *Psychological medicine* 11, 379–89.

life space Refers to the psychological field, and was employed by LEWIN (1936) to indicate the manifold of co-existing facts which determine the behavior of an individual at a given moment. This is the most fundamental concept in Lewin's theoretical system; and the emphasis on the interrelatedness of the person and the environment has been one of his most important contributions to pyschology.

The life space is a product of the interaction between the person (P) and his environment (E). Person in Lewin's terminology may be used in three ways: as equivalent to the "life space" itself; in reference to the individual in the life space, the "behaving self"; and, finally, as a direct reference to the psychological properties of the individual. In the last sense, "person" is extended to incorporate the needs, beliefs, values and perceptual and motoric systems which in interaction among themselves and with the objective environment produce the life space (see FIELD THEORY).

Lewin used the word environment to refer both to the objective and the psychological environment. The psychological environment, or the environment as it exists for the individual, is a part of the life space. Its properties are determined by the characteristics of the person as well as by the characteristics of the objective environment. A "region" (i.e. area of psychological activity) of the psychological environment may often be considered attractive or repulsive by the individual when this particular quality is absent in the objective environment.

During development the life space changes towards increasing differentiation. One of these changes involves a time dimension. Plans extend further into the future along with an increased tolerance of delay, and activities of increasingly long duration are organized as one unit. There is also an increasing differentiation of a reality-irreality dimension. Irreality, which corresponds to fantasy, is a more fluid medium and more closely related to the central layers of the person. For instance a daydream has less reality than an action; a faraway "ideal" goal is less real than a goal which determines immediate action.

Since Lewin's introduction of life space and other field theory concepts, the idea that it is pointless to speak of behavior without reference to both the person and the environment has become commonly accepted. To understand behavior requires not only a knowledge of the person's past experience, but also a knowledge of present attitudes, capabilities and the immediate situation.   MDe

Bibliography

Lewin, K. 1936: *Principles of topological psychology*. New York: McGraw-Hill.

lifespan psychology The lifespan perspective in personality development is relatively recent. The study of development began in the nineteenth century as the study of growth-related change in infancy, childhood and adolescence. Maturational changes were thought to occur in a universal ONTOGENETIC SEQUENCE, paralleled by universal stages in psychological development. For example it is reasoned that while there is some variation in the age at which walking or talking begins, or the age of first menstruation, both sequence and timing are relatively predictable within broad bounds. Furthermore, in a given culture, it can be expected that children or adolescents will, at any given age, be working on the same set of developmental tasks, tasks representing the intersection of biological readiness and social institutions. For example, six-year-olds in one culture may be starting school, in another learning to hunt.

The lifespan perspective recognizes the need to search for a general sequence of change over the entire life course, notwithstanding the absence of maturational markers (the menopause in women is considered the only universal maturational change in adulthood), and the diversity of social roles in a pluralistic age-graded system. One cannot become a parent, for example, before puberty, nor contract a marriage independent of parental consent before reaching the age of political majority. Child labor laws restrict the participation of the young in the labor force, and mandatory retirement in certain occupations excludes the elderly.

Within these very broad bounds, however, there is much possible variation and no single sequence of roles. First marriage and parenthood may occur at twenty or earlier, at thirty, at forty, or later; the peak of a career will occur early for those in certain fields (for example professional athletes, musicians and mathematicians) and later in others (art, literature, the social sciences). The sequence of roles is not invariant: a first marriage may be followed by a second; career peaks may be followed by career changes. Consideration of the entire life cycle is complicated by the fact that the maturational timetable of the first portion of the life span is absent in adulthood, and the range of variation so great.

The scientific study of the life span began in the 1940s, building on such bases as G. Stanley Hall's book *Senescence: the last half of life*, published in 1922; Charlotte Buhler's distinction between the biological and the biographical life curves, published in 1933; and Else Frenkel-Brunswik's studies of the life span, begun in Berkeley during the 1930s. The concept of developmental tasks was developed by Robert Havighurst at the University of Chicago during the 1940s, combining the drive toward growth, or maturational timetable, of the individual with the constraints and opportunities in the social environment. In 1950 Erik Erikson published *Childhood and society*, widely considered to be the most influential book of the period and an introduction for many readers to the concept of development over the life cycle.

Although Erikson's work built on that of others, his model of eight stages of the life cycle was the first widely received model of development extending the notion of developmental stages into adulthood. Paralleling FREUD's ontogenetic sequence for the first part of the life cycle, Erikson poses the following "nuclear crises" or stages in psychosocial development:

Stage	Approximate age	Freudian equivalent
basic trust vs. mistrust	infancy	oral
autonomy vs. shame and doubt	toddler	anal
initiative vs. guilt	preschool	phallic/oedipal
industry vs. inferiority	school age	latency
identity vs. role confusion	adolescence young adulthood	none
intimacy vs. isolation	young adulthood	genital
generativity vs. stagnation	middle adulthood	none
ego integrity vs. despair	later adulthood	none

Erikson's theory is an extension of Freud's in the following ways: first, he expands the concept of stages of development to embrace the entire life cycle; second, he recognizes more explicitly the interaction of the individual with the social context; third, the content of those stages for which there is no Freudian equivalent adds new substance to our understanding of development over the life span. The stage of identity vs. role confusion is the stage at which the young adult finds a place in society; generativity vs. stagnation marks the stage of responsibility for the next generation, not only through parenthood but through any form of care and concern for the young; the stage of ego integrity vs. despair marks the point when one's one and only life cycle is accepted, when one can look back over the life course without despair.

Recognition of personality development in adulthood was greatly enhanced by the work of Bernice Neugarten and her colleagues at the University of Chicago in the Kansas City Study of Adult Life, carried out over the decade 1954–64. Although she found a regular progression toward increased interiority of personality, there was no comparable regularity of change in social behavior. On the basis of these findings, she challenged the disengagement theory of Cumming and Henry, suggesting that life satisfaction was associated with sustained activity throughout the life cycle. A major contribution of Neugarten's work is expanded understanding of the developmental changes in middle age, hitherto thought to be a period of stability. Her work marks the beginning of a lifespan perspective, uniting child developmental studies at one end of the life cycle with GERONTOLOGY at the other.

Since its beginnings in the study of personality development over the life course, lifespan psychology has seen major advances in the study of family and intergenerational relations, cognitive development, age grading and the social system, and social policy. Not only does lifespan psychology encompass the life course of the developing individual, but the broader social and political context in which the individual's development occurs. There are a number of recent texts on lifespan development. For further reading see Honzik 1984.   ND

Bibliography

*Baltes, P.B. and Schaie, K.W. eds. 1973: *Life-span developmental psychology: personality and socialization*. New York and London: Academic Press.

Datan, N. and Ginsberg, L.H. eds. 1975: *Life-span developmental psychology: normative life crises*. New York and London: Academic Press.

*―――― and Lohmann, N. eds. 1980: *Transitions of aging*. New York and London: Academic Press.

*Erikson, E.H. 1963: *Childhood and society*. 2nd edn. New York: Norton; Harmondsworth: Penguin.

Goulet, L.R. and Baltes, P.B. eds. 1970: *Life-span developmental psychology: research and theory*. New York and London: Academic Press.

*Honzik, M.P. 1984: Life-span development. *Annual review of psychology* 35, 309–31.

*Neugarten, B.L. ed. 1968: *Middle age and aging*. Chicago and London: University of Chicago Press.

locus of control A concept first developed by Phares (1957) relating to beliefs about internal versus external control of reinforcement. It is assumed that individuals develop a general expectancy regarding their ability to control their lives. People who believe that the events that occur in their lives are a result of their own behavior and/or personality characteristics are said to have an "expectancy of internal control", while people who believe events in their lives to be a function of luck, chance, fate, powerful others or powers beyond their control or comprehension are said to have an "expectancy of external control".

Various questionnaires have been devised to measure this belief system, of which the best known are the Rotter (1966) I-E scale, the Levenson (1974) IPC scale, and the Collins (1974) scale. Each of these has been criticized on psychometric grounds. There have also been constant conceptual disagreements. A primary dispute has been about the number of dimensions which underlie control beliefs. Collins suggested four, Levenson three. Rotter holds that there is one unitary set of beliefs and therefore only one dimension. Factor analytic studies of his scale have not entirely supported his view, since they have tended to find that it has several factors. Not all studies, however, produce this kind of result. Some continue to imply that the unidimensional model could be right (e.g. Ashkanasy 1985). Conceptual disputes also continue about the relationship of locus of control to other constructs such as Seligman's learned helplessness model of depression. The concept has been widely used and applied in cross-cultural studies, on health beliefs and behavior, investigations of mental illness and many other areas of research. See Palenzuela (1984) for a review. Lefcourt (1981) provides a representative sample of the research.

AF/RL

Bibliography

Ashkanasy, N.M. 1985: Rotter's internal-external scale: confirmatory factor analysis and correlation with social desirability for alternative scale formats. *Journal of personality and social psychology* 48, 1328–41.

Collins, B. 1974: Four components of the Rotter internal-external scale: belief in a difficult world, a just world, a predictable world and a politically responsive world. *Journal of personality and social psychology* 29, 381–91.

Lefcourt, H.M. ed. 1981: *Research with the locus of control construct*. New York: Academic Press.

Levenson, H. 1974: Activism and powerful others: distinctions within the concept of internal-external control. *Journal of personality assessment* 38, 377–83.

Palenzuela, D.L. 1984: Critical evaluation of locus of control: towards a reconceptualization of the construct and its measurement. *Psychological reports*, Monograph I–V 54.

Phares, F. 1957: Expectancy changes in skill and chance situations. *Journal of abnormal and social psychology* 54, 339–42.

Rotter, J. 1966: Generalized expectancies for internal versus external control of reinforcement. *Psychological monograph* 80, No. 1.

longitudinal research A method of study which involves repeated measures on the same individuals over a period of time. This is one of several methods by which developmental change is studied. Longitudinal research measures change over time in a particular sample. CROSS-SECTIONAL RESEARCH compares different age groups at the same point in time. The cross-sequential method, a method by which different age groups are studied longitudinally, allows the researcher to distinguish cohort effects from age effects. "Cohort effect" refers to the effect of being born at a particular time and into a particular historical context. "Age effect" refers to the effect of chronological age. Both contribute to developmental change.

ND

Bibliography

Baltes, P.B., Reese, H.W., and Nesselroade, J.R. 1977: *Life-span developmental psychology: introduction to research methods*. Belmont, Calif.: Brooks Cole.

Wolman, B.B. ed. 1982: *Handbook of developmental psychology*. Englewood Cliffs, N.J.: Prentice-Hall.

love An act of full attention and giving that accepts and attaches to someone as he or she is, thereby enhancing the potential of what that person can become. Research into love has not been extensive and according to Reik, FREUD said at the conclusion of his career 'we really know very little about love' (1976). However, in the past twenty years some useful research on certain aspects of the subject has taken place.

ATTACHMENT and bonding in early development have been studied by Harlow (1959), Bowlby (1969) and Klaus and Kennell (1976). Harlow's research with monkeys revealed that attachment to a maternal figure is vital to healthy development and socialization. Bowlby's studies of institutionalized infants showed common patterns of pathological reaction to separation from the mother, such as apathy and unresponsiveness. Klaus and Kennell have looked at bonding (the close physical and emotional interaction after birth) as a sensitive period which evokes strong attachment behavior between mother, father and child.

Kaplan (1979) describes the feelings of oneness in early attachment, and the moulding of mother's and child's bodies into one. What follows is the opposite pole of separateness, and the baby's need to sense the body as a mode of self-definition and as an expression of the fear of losing self by merging with the mother. According to Fromm (1956) the attachment phase carries with it the sense of love as being loved, and with the struggle for separateness the universal paradox manifests 'that two beings become one and yet remain two'.

Psychoanalytic theory describes the attachment phase as the setting for NARCISSISM. Narcissism in this sense does not refer to love of self, in contrast to love of others; Geller and Howenstine in Pope (1980) describe it as our first erotic disposition in the sense that before we know that other bodies exist or what it is to like other bodies, we direct our libido towards our own bodies. This understanding of narcissism parallels Piaget's definition (1936) of EGOCENTRISM as a failure to discriminate external objects in the child's environment. Some psychologists maintain that throughout life the struggle between narcissism and object love characterizes all erotic relationships. Object love refers to the later ability to differentiate between another's needs and one's own.

The FAMILY is the setting for the early stages in the development of love. The young child experiences a prolonged and intense emotional attachment to a parent, who is associated with the gratification of needs. The limited perspective of the child leads to the belief that this relationship is the most important, and perhaps the only one, in which the parent is involved. The growing child soon learns that not all needs can be fulfilled in that relationship, and that he or she has to compete with another adult for the desired parent's affection. In most families the marital relationship, the incest taboo, and the process of maturation prevent the child from becoming too dependent, thus leading him or her to look for fulfillment elsewhere.

According to the Freudian conception (see PERSONALITY THEORY, PSYCHOANALYTI-CAL), one of the major characteristics of romantic love that distinguishes it from early attachment and mature love is IDEALI-ZATION. The child develops an idealized fantasy relationship with the parent of the opposite sex, who is of course not completely possessible. Idealization is seen as a result of the unfulfilled need to possess the parent. This tension is partly resolved by identifying with the same sex parent. The child achieves partial gratification through identifying with the person who is most highly regarded by and who is seen to possess the desired parent. Hero worship is another variant of romantic idealization which also combines with identification. A child may idealize a popular sports figure, but then, consistent with the motive for identification, subsequently tries to become like this idealized person. From a developmental viewpoint, idealization and fantasy can be seen as precursors of a more mature love for another person, because they lead to greater discrimination of someone beyond oneself. However, development may be retarded if idealization and fantasy become substitutes for genuine gratification in real relationships.

In adolescence feelings of tenderness largely experienced in the family can become blended with the newly emerging sexual feelings when focused on an individual outside the family. Falling in love is experienced when there is a combination of sexual attraction and intimacy. Having crushes from a distance may substitute for actual involvement if the person is tentative about approaching another individual. Crushes can be likened to practice emo-tions which prepare a person for later interpersonal contact. Similarly "chum" relationships, which play an important part in emotional development, are intimate same-sex friendships. Both types of re-lationships involve loving someone like oneself and they represent a mid-point between the stages of loving oneself and loving another person. (See Sullivan 1953; Farber in Pope 1980.)

Erikson (1968) emphasized that adol-escence is a time for defining one's identity. He maintained that a stable sense of identity is a prerequisite to establishing loving intimacy. Yet the attainment of a stable identity is closely connected with the ability to communicate with others in an intimate manner. People who avoid falling in love may have fears of loss of self or being engulfed by others.

Love in adulthood and the decision to marry are among the most important choices a person makes. There is little likelihood that a love relationship can survive without a supporting framework of interpersonal skills, mutual interests, and occupational skills. Mature love, according to Fromm (1956) is active rather than passive. For the child, love means being loved, and many adults continue to expect this from their spouses. For the mature person, love means giving love, as well as receiving it. It is an act rather than an affect. Many people identify love with intense feelings (Berscheid and Walster's (1978) "passionate love"). When the intensity subsides they may wonder whether the love has gone. In doing this they miss the more essential dimension of love as an action, of which feelings are a byproduct (see Rubin 1973). Also many partnerships get stuck in a need-bartering phase of "I'll do this for you if you'll do that for me" which can lead to a destructive struggle to get something from the partner. It is also asserted that people who come to psychotherapy with complaints about not being loved fre-quently discover that they themselves are not giving love.

Much of the research on love has focused on definitions of the concept and the psychosocial dimensions of the experi-ence. Current research methodology has in general proved inadequate in investigating the phenomenology, or inner experience of loving. But questionnaires about love, although blunt instruments, have included questions about feelings (see Sternberg and Grajek 1984).

Csikszentmihalyi (Pope 1980) investigated people's experience of enjoyment in sport, chess, mountain climbing and loving. A common pattern emerged which he called the "flow experience". The flow experience is satisfying in itself and involves a sense of oneness between the individual and his activity. The attention is focused and feedback from the situation is clear. There is a balance between the challenges of the activity and the skills developed to meet them. Loving is seen by Csikszentmihalyi as an investment of attention in another person, with the intention of realizing that person's goals or those that are shared by both partners. The growth and enjoyment of the love relationship depend upon the development of interpersonal and other skills to meet the challenges that arise in the pursuit of shared goals.

Sadler (1969) describes loving as a dual mode of experience in which the sense of "we" is greater than the sense of "me". Theorists who employ explanatory concepts of EQUITY and EXCHANGE do not accept that the rewards and costs experienced by each partner individually ever cease to be major determinants of the satisfaction and success of their relationship (see Kelley 1983). But Kelley and Thibaut (1978) also argue that 'in relationships of high interdependence' it is mutually beneficial to care about one's partner's needs, and about joint welfare as well as one's own.

A major problem for adult relationships in Western society is presumably that the passionate, exhilarating, and emotionally involving kind of love has been culturally sanctioned as the desirable kind, and a proper basis for commitment and marriage (see Sarsby 1983). Apart from the probability of disappointment or gradual loss within marriage of the relationship's apparent *raison d'être*, this cultural ideal may obscure the varieties of love and loving relationships of which people are capable.

Certainly there may be more than one type of love. Lee (1977) distinguished six major types in fictional and non-fictional accounts of love. Kelley (1983) suggested three distinct models (passionate, pragmatic and altruistic), although he thought that, 'in actual close relationships love is typically a blend of the different forms.' Sternberg and Grajek (1984) factor analyzed people's reports of their own experiences over a range of relationships (including more than one heterosexual relationship), and found one major general factor with several much weaker specific factors. This implies that different experiences of love in different relationships have much in common with each other. They argued that what they had found was 'a set of affects, cognitions, and motivations' which made not a "unity" but a "composite", which could be 'decomposed into a large number of underlying bonds that tend to co-occur ... and that in combination result in the global feeling that we view as love'.

The study of love and RELATIONSHIPS which are generally assumed to be founded on love is now beginning to increase, and is greatly needed. The development of an effective understanding of how people learn to love and to preserve relationships would have practical benefits as well as removing our surprising ignorance of an aspect of people which we are supposed to think both fascinating and valuable. TCK

Bibliography

Berscheid, E. and Walster, E. 1978: *Interpersonal attraction*. 2nd edn. Reading, Mass.: Addison-Wesley.

Bowlby, J. 1969: *Attachment and loss*. London: Hogarth Press, New York: Basic Books.

Erikson, E.H. 1968: *Identity: youth and crisis*. New York: Norton; London: Faber and Faber.

*Fromm, E. 1956: *The art of loving*. New York: Harper and Brothers.

Harlow, H.F. 1959: Love in infant monkeys. *Scientific American*. 200(6), 68–74.

Kaplan, L.J. 1979: *Oneness and separateness*. London: Jonathan Cape.

Kelley, H.H. 1983: Love and commitment. In *Close relationships*, ed. H.H. Kelley et al. New York: Freeman.

—— and Thibaut, J.W. 1978: *Interpersonal relations; a theory of interdependency*. New York: Wiley Interscience.

Klaus, M.H. and Kennell, J.H. 1976: *Maternal-infant bonding*. Saint Louis: C.V. Mosby Company.

Lee, J.A. 1977: A typology of styles of loving. *Personality and social psychology bulletin* 3, 173–82.

Piaget, J. 1936 (1966): *The origins of intelligence in children*. New York: International Universities Press.

*Pope, K.S. et al 1980: *On love and loving*. San Francisco, Washington and London: Jossey-Bass.

Reik, T. 1976: *Of love and lust*. New York: Pyramid Books.

Rubin, Z. 1973: *Liking and loving: An invitation to social psychology*. New York: Holt, Rinehart and Winston.

Sadler, W.A. 1969: *Existence and love*. New York: Charles Scribner.

Sarsby, J. 1983: *Romantic love and society*. Harmondsworth: Penguin.

Sternberg, R.J. and Grajek, S. 1984: The nature of love. *Journal of personality and social psychology* 47, 312–19.

Sullivan, H.S. 1953: *The interpersonal theory of psychiatry*. New York: Norton.

M

Machiavellianism A personality factor characterized by the ability to manipulate others through flattery, threat and deceit which is named after Machiavelli, on whose political advice in *Il Principe* research is based. The Machiavellian scale devised by Christi and Geis (1970), correlates it with sex (males score higher), urban background, age (young people score higher) and professional status (people-oriented professions score higher). Machiavellianism is also related to success in bargaining, and Machiavellians are more successful at resisting the influence of others. They violate conventional moral standards more often, by stealing and coolly denying this when accused. Even at the age of ten, differences in Machiavellianism appear to have an effect, in the successful manipulation of other children. Machiavellian children appear to have Machiavellian parents. In later life occupational success is related to Machiavellianism, particularly among women and those who have had a college education.

JMFJ

Bibliography

Christi, R. and Geis. F.L. eds. 1970: *Studies in Machiavellianism*. New York: Academic Press.

Machiavelli, N. (1532) 1891: *Il principe*, ed. A. Burd. Oxford: Oxford University Press.

McDougall, William (1871–1938) Born at Chadderton in Lancashire and died in Durham, North Carolina, McDougall achieved the distinction – rare for a psychologist – of election to a Fellowship of the Royal Society. He trained as a physician before turning to problems of physiological psychology. He was a member (1898) of the famous Cambridge Anthropological Expedition to the Torres Straits where psychological tests were administered for the first time in a cross-cultural setting. In 1900 McDougall was appointed as part-time director of the psychological laboratory at University College, London – a post he later combined with the Wilde Readership in Mental Philosophy at Oxford (1904–20). He helped to found the British Psychological Society in 1901. In World War I McDougall served as a psychiatrist specializing in the treatment of shell-shock. In 1920 he emigrated to America where he held appointments first at Harvard (1920–27) and then at Duke University (1927–38).

There were two separate though interrelated elements to McDougall's social psychology. The first was a psychology of the individual (*An introduction to social psychology, 1908*), in which he outlined the biological basis of life in society and introduced his theory of human sentiments. The second was a psychology of the collectivity (*The group mind, 1920*), in which he tackled such issues as the morale of armies, nationalism as a moral sentiment and national character. Together, the two constituted his social psychology. Both books were controversial – especially with behaviorists; the first because McDougall relied on instincts to account for human behavior (a concept described as HORMIC PSYCHOLOGY), and the second because he appeared to assign agency to entities other than individuals. In 1924 he and J.B. Watson met to debate their differences at the Psychology Club in Washington DC before an audience of a thousand people, with McDougall being adjudged the winner. McDougall's views were often sound. In many ways he was ahead of his time, though his views did not win general acceptance. This may have been due in part to his combative nature. When, in the 1920s, Freud began to revise quite radically his theory of the human mind

McDougall saw this as a strong vindication of his own approach to social psychology in 1908. McDougall's views on the instinctive basis of human behavior received support in the later work of ethologists. His critique of behaviorism and his insistence on the purposive nature of all human striving is highly compatible with the viewpoints of modern cognitive science. McDougall was, in many ways, a progenitor of modern SOCIOBIOLOGY.   RFa

Bibliography

Farr, R.M. 1986: The social psychology of William McDougall. In *Changing conceptions of crowd mind and behavior*, eds. C. Graumann and S. Moscovici. New York: Springer-Verlag. pp. 83–95.

McDougall, W. 1908: *An introduction to social psychology*. London: Methuen.

——— 1920: *The group mind*. Cambridge: Cambridge University Press.

management Attempts at definitions of management are problematical. They range from the common sense (getting things done through people, arranging for needs to be met), to the complex. The problem is that any definition reflects an explicit or implicit underlying view of the nature of organizations. An economic view would cast the manager in the role of rational economic decision-maker. Structural/functional views of organizations cast the manager as the receiver of objectives and delegator of sub-objectives, with associated activities of monitoring, controlling, reporting, etc. Certain "systems" views of organizations interpret managers as nodes in a network of information flows and decision points. More "political" interpretations of organizations as arrangements for working together cast managers as middlemen in a trade of power and influence, continuously involved in finding a way forward through compromise and negotiation. Interactionist views of organizations interpret managers as involved in the creation and maintenance of the organization's meanings, and through this, of its structures and processes.

There is an empirical tradition of research in this area (e.g. Mintzberg 1973; Stewart 1967). Such research often produces valuable insights but it is caught in the paradox of needing a prior definition of management to decide whom to study, and some observational categories with which to work. These categories inevitably carry certain assumptions about the nature of management.

Fascinating questions arise from the various definitions of management. For example, is it an entity, a function, a social class or a process? Is it a social definition that can be applied in certain situations or is it a process present by definition in all organizations? What is to be made of the many kinds of organization that do not have explicit "management" activities, roles or functions (professional partnerships, universities, churches, the military, etc.)? The idea of management, both in theory and as a social label for a practical activity is time-bound and has a history (Child 1969) in which the meaning has changed in a changing historical and social context. In different cultures too, there is an enormous variation in conceptions of management.

The concept of "management" is clearly going to remain problematical for everyone, from those concerned to serve it with psychological technology through to those who suspect it of having an insidious and possibly malign influence on how psychological questions are framed and addressed. Addressing the issue of management is likely to be an activity in which psychologists will find themselves alongside members of other social sciences and the intellectual consequences of this are potentially very exciting.   JGB

Bibliography

Burrell, G. and Morgan, G. 1979: *Sociological paradigms and organizational analysis*. London and Exeter, N.H.: Heinemann.

Child, J. 1969: *British management thoughts: a critical analysis*. London: Allen.

Heather, N. 1976: *Radical perspectives in psychology*. London and New York: Methuen.

Mintzberg, H. 1973: *The nature of managerial work*. New York and London: Harper and Row.

Stewart, R. 1967: *Managers and their jobs*. London: Macmillan.

Yuhl, G.A. 1981: *Leadership in organizations*. Englewood Cliffs, N.J.: Prentice-Hall.

marketing psychology The psychology of economic choice, and in particular the analysis of consumer behavior.

A marketplace is simply a forum in which economic exchange takes place. As such, it lends itself to behavioral analysis: economic choices are made daily by everyone; the choices are observable; experimentation is easy; and data describing, for example, the brand choice sequences of households, are plentiful. Indeed, markets are one of the richest natural laboratories in which to develop and test theories of human behavior.

It is, of course, the laboratory in which economists work and its most influential product is the concept of rational economic man. This is a model of man, particularly as he appears in the neo-classical mainstream of economic theory, that is unashamedly behavioristic and deterministic.

Man's rationality resides in his omni-science and infallibility. Psychologically, for example, he is transparent both to himself and to others (who are, themselves, equally transparent): he knows his own values, needs and tastes; and the world he inhabits, including the full range of options open to him, is an open book. Nothing holds any surprises for him. So completely is his behavior guided by informed reason that, in effect, his choices are made for him by the logic of the particular situation in which he finds himself. In short, economic man has no personality and no choice. He has been stripped of any psychological identity, complexity or realism.

To predict his behavior, all that need be known are the combinations of economic options between which he is indifferent. To quote Pareto (1906), 'the individual can disappear, providing he leaves us his photograph of his tastes'. And Shackle (1977) asks the rhetorical question, 'If "choice" is a *mere* response to tastes and circumstances, both kinds being given and known, does "choice" originate anything?'

Psychological interest in the market as an object of study represents, for the most part, a reaction against what is increasingly seen as an excessively narrow and sterile view of rational choice. The development of a more substantively psychological model of economic behavior has been an attempt to give back to economic man his individuality and his freedom. For example the Austrian school of economists, borrowing heavily from psychological theory, has stressed the necessity of including inter-personal *differences* in knowledge, beliefs and expectations in any explanation of economic behavior. For this school of thought, economic man is characterized by: *imperfect* knowledge of his own tastes and the options available to him; *fallible* interpretations of his own situation, including the actions of others; *speculative* forecasts of events and actions in the future; and *inquisitive* alertness to novel opportunities, and inventiveness in seeking them out.

Here, economic behavior is quintessentially a process of discovery and co-ordination, not of instantaneous adjustment to prevailing conditions Man is now the *subject* – the originator of states of affairs – and not simply an object. Indeed, Hayek (1952), the leading modern Austrian economist, has argued that "it is probably no exaggeration to say that every important advance in economic theory during the last hundred years was a further step in the consistent application of subjectivism."

In marketing literature, a whole range of psychological theories has been imported and synthesized to give conceptual support to this subjectivist stance and thereby lend greater realism to the models of consumer behavior originally inherited from economics. For example, one class of models (Nicosia 1966; Howard and Sheth 1969) has aimed at presenting an integrated view of how the consumer processes inputs (information) into outputs (choices). Looking into the "black box" between input and output researchers have drawn upon concepts and findings in the psychological literature of perception, evaluation, motivation and learning to map the stages through which consumers pass to reach a purchasing decision. For example, theories of selective attention, perceptual distortion, concept formation, symbolic encoding, hierarchical memory, attitude structure and stability and habituation are all shown to have direct application to understanding the behavior of consumers.

JOG

Bibliography

Engel, J.F., Blackwell, R.D. and Kollatt, D.T. 1978: *Consumer behavior.* 3rd edn. New York: Holt, Rinehart and Winston.

Hayek, F.A. 1952: *The counter-revolution of science.* New York: The Free Press of Glencoe.

Howard, J.A. and Sheth, J.N. 1969: *The theory of buyer behavior.* New York: Wiley.

Nicosia, F.M. 1966: *Consumer decision processes.* Englewood Cliffs, N.J.: Prentice-Hall.

Pareto, V. 1906 (1971): *Manual of political economy.* New York: A.M. Kelly.

Shackle, G.L.S. 1977: New tracks for economic theory, 1926–39. In *Modern economic thought*, ed. S. Weintraub. Philadelphia: University of Pennsylvania Press; Oxford: Basil Blackwell.

*Tuck. M. 1976: *How do we choose? A study in consumer behavior.* London and New York: Methuen.

Marxian personality psychology

A psychological meta-theory deriving its assumptions from Marx's materialist philosophy of history and applied to the historical development and social basis of personality. It derives from historical materialism. Unlike other materialist philosophies this does not allot a central role to nature or the mind. Its starting point is "production", which is just as material as is nature, and just as creative as mind.

Rubinstein (1959) derived four principles from this philosophy. These principles were to be applied both to a Marxian activity psychology and to personality psychology. They are: (1) the principle of objectivity – mental phenomena refer to objects in the material world; (2) the principle of activity – mental dispositions develop in the activity they regulate; (3) the principle of historicity – mental states bear the marks of their history; and (4) the principle of sociality – mental characteristics are socially determined.

None of these principles, considered separately, is a unique characteristic of Marxian psychology. It is their combination which is peculiar to the psychological meta-theory derived from historical materialism. This combination is brought about by a particular interpretation of each principle:

1. A manufactured object is conceived as produced by an activity of men and as reciprocally influencing men. Marx (*Economic and philosophical manuscripts*) claims the world of manufactured objects is the "inorganic body" of man.
2. Activity is pictured as a necessary everyday cycle of production and reproduction. The cycle is interrupted occasionally by moments of free creation in which new values are introduced. But these are then incorporated in subsequent everyday cycles of activity.
3. History is conceived as composed of autonomous human acts restricted by social laws. These social laws are actualized in the autonomous acts of others.
4. Society is pictured as based upon and as establishing property relations (Marx, *Grundrisse*).

Rubinstein did not apply his four principles in their entirety. He considered the personality as an internal mediator of external determinants and as originating from other external determinants internalized in the past. According to his metaphor the personality of a man is his "socially determined nature".

This pattern is highly typical of allegedly Marxist personality psychologies. The personality psychology outlined by Rubinstein turned out to be an amalgam of a social cognitivism and a social behaviorism. It describes the emergence of personality through socialization and the social functioning of a personality through attitude (or the similar but not identical central notion of set in Uznadse's theory), through social interaction, communication, etc.

None of these points is particularly characteristic of a Marxist approach. In fact the application of some of the above principles in isolation from others results in a kind of psychoanalytic personality theory. The central tenet of a psychoanalytic personality theory with Marxian underpinning is the interdependence of the personality structure and the structure of society.

For Reich (1970) the structure of a repressive society creates an AUTHORITARIAN PERSONALITY structure through sexual repression in family education. Fromm (1963) claims that a competitive society based on private property frustrates a need for secure relationships with others and fixes the personality at an immature and dependent level. József (1972) states that the distortion of the personalities of both the capitalist and the worker is determined by the fundamental distortion of the capitalist society. While society as a whole is both the subject and the object of socialization and production (that is, in the process of production it reproduces itself), the worker is only the subject of production and the object of socialization. The only subject of socialization is the capitalist. This produces neurotic rather than rounded personalities.

In contrast, for Marcuse (1962) it is not the structure of an actually given social relation (e.g. between capitalists and workers in a capitalist society) that more or less distorts the structure of a personality. Still less does it depend on how repressive or liberal a society is. "Civilization" as such is opposed to "Eros" and transforms it by repression into aggression. A group of followers of Lacan and Althusser (Bruno et al. 1973) hold that besides nature the only reality is discourse (or symbolic interaction) between people. This interaction results in the formation of shared systems of beliefs, or ideologies. These provide people with set ways of understanding the world which may distort their perceptions and their personalites. The ideology is produced by those who occupy the dominant place in the established structure, but may present itself either as corresponding to an objective reality or as a mere subjective belief system of a set of individuals.

It was in controversy with such theories as well as the humanistic philosophy (Garaudy) going back to the early Marx that Lucien Sève (1969) advanced his psychological meta-theory of personality. He rejected the basic thesis of the theories of Reich, Marcuse and so on, sketched above, that the personality is distorted by social relations and loses the intrinsic, specifically human essence (*Gattungswesen*) given in advance of any social relations. Nevertheless he argued that there is an essence of human personality. It is neither intrinsic nor given in advance but is borne by the historically developed totality of relations of production. Furthermore, it is neither generic, nor intimately characteristic of a given individual. Each class has its own essential personality. For example, the human essence that characterizes a worker in a capitalist society is defined by the relations in which his personal power has a concrete use value which produces abstract exchange value for the capitalist and, at the same time, has an abstract exchange value which produces concrete use value for the worker himself.

Garai and his team (1979) tried to extend such a production-centered approach to those aspects of the historical development and social relationship of personality which are not directly connected with production as such. For that purpose they adopted Vygotsky's idea (1978) of analyzing a mental context according to a paradigm derived from an economic context. Vygotsky's basic argument was that man utilizes as mental tools signs that are mental products of his previous activity and, as such, constitute a special (i.e. mental) category of means of production brought into being as products of production. Leontjew (1969) set out from a psychology describing man's activity as oriented to such mental objects taken both as a means and a product, and attempted to derive from it a personality psychology that describes the agent of that activity with his characteristic hierarchy of motives.

Garai took it that personality could be analyzed according to a paradigm obtained from another economic context, i.e. that of class relations (Garai 1977). The main paradigmatic point of class relations is claimed to be the representation of the common law of different classes by only one of them. Neither the detection of personality differences nor finding out general laws of the functioning of personalities interests Marxist personality psychology. It investigates how, during its development, a personality establishes its differences and similarities according to or in contrast with a common pattern represented by someone significant to the person. At the beginning the elaboration of nuances of similarity and difference into categorical identities (see SOCIAL CATEGORIZATION) is not the result of a series of conscious acts but takes place by means of an elaboration of physical differences such as sex, height or color (as well as all kinds of body activity) into signs. These unconsciously symbolize, by the identities and differences of their structures, the parallel elaborated identities and differences of social structures (Köcski and Garai 1978). The emergence of the conscious self is then mediated by the confrontation between the personality's self-definition and general laws represented by others.

A further point stressed by a Marxist personality psychology is related to the economic fact that the means of production may be expropriated by a class that becomes, by virtue of its property, the class which represent the common pattern for all the classes. This has implications for personality development: (1) the way in which physical objects become signs that mediate the unconscious mental elaboration of the social world is determined by property relations; (2) so is the emergence of the conscious self since it is mediated by the confrontation between the personality's (unconscious) self-definition and the roles which society allots. Personality development in socialization depends upon the individual's privileged or under-privileged position, whether this privilege is strictly economic or not. The main non-economic privilege is being able to frame a law or pattern of socially approved personality. This privilege is self-perpetuating since the laws are designed to protect the position of those who make them (Garai 1977). Those in an under-privileged position can ensure their personality unconstrained development only by

introducing radical changes into their social world.

Personality development is not conceived by Marxist personality psychology as a joint effect of biological maturation and a social shaping process on a passive individual. Instead, it is seen as the result of an individual's activity, which is all a form of work activity: need-motivated cycles of production are interrupted by life crises which may provoke creative inventions and these become patterns to be reproduced in renewed cycles by the force of a specifically human need for a need-free activity.

The production-centered meta-theory of Marxist personality psychology is the same as that applied in Marxist activity psychology. Hence there is a real possibility of basing an integrated psychology on this meta-theory instead of reproducing the traditional distinction between a "scientific" (*naturwissenschaftliche*) and a "humanistic" (*geisteswissenschaftliche*) psychology.

LG

Bibliography

Althusser, L. 1969: Freud and Lacan. *New left review* 55, 48–65.

Bruno, P. et al. 1973: La psychologie sociale: une utopie en crise. *La nouvelle critique* 62, 72–8; 64, 21–8.

Fromm, E. 1963: *Marx's concept of man.* New York: F. Ungar.

Garai, L. 1977: Conflict and the economical paradigm. *Dialectics and humanism* 2, 47–58.

——— et al. 1979: Towards a social psychology of personality: development and current perspectives of a school of social psychology in Hungary. *Social science information* 18(1), 137–66.

József, A. 1972: Hegel, Marx, Freud. *Action poétique* 49, 68–75.

Köcski, M. and Garai, L. 1978: Les débuts de la catégorisation sociale et les manifestations verbales. Une étude longitudinale. *Langage et société* 4, 3–30.

Leontjew, A. 1969: *Problems of mental development.* Washington: Joint Publications Research Service.

Marcuse, H. 1962: *Eros and civilisation.* New York: Random House.

Reich, W. 1970: *The mass psychology of fascism.* New York: Simon and Schuster.

Rubinstein, S. 1959: *Principles and ways of mental*

development. (In Russian). Moscow: Publishing House of Soviet Academy of Sciences.

*Sève, L. 1969: *Marxisme et la théorie de la personnalité*. Paris: Editions Sociales.

Vygotsky, L. 1962: *Thought and language*. Cambridge: MIT Press.

———— 1978: *Mind in society. The development of higher psychological processes*. Cambridge, Mass.: Harvard University Press.

Marxist activity psychology

The concept of object-related activity (*gegenständliche Tätigkeit*) is the main concept of Marxist psychology. It is the part of human behavior which relates man to his social and natural environment, to other persons and to himself. (In German and Russian the words *Tätigkeit* and *dejatelnost* have different meanings from the words *Aktivität* and *aktivnost*. The English word activity does not mean what *Tätigkeit* or *dejatelnost* mean in Marxist psychology).

Man is the subject of his activity. The activity of the individual is characterized by its sociohistorical determination, its relation to an object (*Gegenständlichkeit*), its goal-directedness, the goal-oriented organization of its components, and consciousness (Marx, *Capital* vol. II).

The attribute "object-related" designates the pivotal feature; 'in fact the very notion of activity implicitly contains the notion of an object of activity ... objectless activity has no sense' (Leontjew 1972, p.152). On the one hand, the object is 'an independently existing entirety subordinating activity of the subject' (p.152). On the other hand, the mental representation of the object is a result of activity, which in turn regulates activity.

Different categories of activity may be distinguished by means of the dominating type of motivation, especially affective or impulsive activity, instinctive activity and voluntary activity (Lewin 1926). Marxist activity psychology mainly deals with voluntary activity. The development of voluntary activity, from a phylogenetic and historical point of view, is connected with the development of work.

Marxist activity psychology tries to overcome the barrenness of the controversy between mentalist and behaviorist approaches. A main methodological principle is the unity of mental phenomena (processes, states and traits) and activity. All these mental phenomena develop and realize themselves in the kind of activity in which they are necessary for orientation and regulation. The key function of mental phenomena within activity is regulative. The development of mental phenomena within and by means of activities reveals a dialectical nature: on the one hand, mental phenomena are the results of activities; on the other hand, individuals will develop mental phenomena which are then realized in man-made objects and settings (e.g. toys, tools, towns). Mental phenomena may be analyzed only in activity. The principle of the unity of mental phenomena and activity has broad consequences for the methodology of research and for psychodiagnostics. The decisive role of activity in the development of mental processes, states and traits was elaborated in two empirically based theoretical approaches:

(a) The Galperin approach of the stepwise interiorization from complete overt object-related actions up to mental processes (1972). According to this view, mental processes develop in a child from his or her movements being verbally interpreted by adult speakers; they then pass through many increasingly abbreviated sensorimotor steps up to the "pure idea" of an object or process, i.e. mental representation. Such steps of abbreviation and interiorization are, for instance, talking loudly with oneself and internal talking while manipulating an object (Vygotsky 1962).

(b) The "assimilation hypothesis" of Leontjew (1969), in which the decisive link in the development of mental representations (especially perceptions) is a "motor copy" of the object or process perceived, formed by kinesthetic feedback of the muscles in the sense organs or used by them. The modality-specific information of the specific sense organs is integrated into these motor copies. Leontjew analyzed these relations, referring *inter alia* to the role of the activity of the voice muscles for precise hearing.

The psychologically relevant chunk of activity is *action*. Actions include *operations*. In the Leontjew approach (1969), activities are separated from one another by motives, and actions by their different goals. Operations are subordinate means of achieving the goals of action; often they are sensori-motor skills, which do not need conscious mental regulation. "Action" is therefore a main concept in the Marxist psychology of activity. Actions are the smallest psychologically relevant units of voluntary activities. Actions are defined by their goals, i.e. in anticipation of the future results. This anticipation is combined with the intention of bringing about the anticipated result (Luria 1973). Mental representations of goals are the most important mental regulators of action. Further categories of such representations are those of the initial states (e.g. of raw materials) or of the possible transformations between such initial states and the anticipated results (Hacker 1980). Each action includes cognitive processes (perceptions, decisions, mental reproduction), motivation (goal-setting), and sensori-motor processes. So action is a psychomotor process.

Goal-directed actions simultaneously present a cyclic feedback structure and a hierarchical organization (Bernstein 1967). Units consisting of goals, action programs, and feedback or control processes are nested into one another. Although this hierarchical feedback structure seems to be common to all actions, their individual structures depend on the task, defined by the individual's goal, on the subjective significance of this goal, and on its conditions of realization.

The psychological analysis of actions is not limited to the obvious "surface" sequence of motions, but includes the regulating mental "deep structure". Main aspects of this psychological analysis of action are (Tomaszewski 1978):

(a) goal setting;
(b) working out how to achieve the goal;
(c) designing or producing the necessary means;
(d) deciding to employ one means rather than another, if there is any choice;
(e) controlling the implementation by comparing the procedures and results with the program and the goal.

The last four processes may not all be equally conscious. Intellectual processes are conscious in so far as they are verbalized or represented symbolically. Sensori-motor processes are predominantly unconscious. Perceptive processes regulating actions have an intermediate or limited consciousness.   WH

Bibliography

Bernstein, N.A. 1967: *The co-ordination and regulation of movements*. Oxford and New York: Pergamon.

Galperin, P.J. ed. 1972: *Probleme der Lerntheorie*. Berlin: Volk und Wissen.

Hacker, W. 1980: Objective and subjective organization of working activities. In *The analysis of action*, eds. M. von Cranach and R. Harré. Cambridge: Cambridge University Press.

Leontjew, A.N. 1969: The significance of the concept of reflection for scientific psychology. In *The XVIII International Congress of Psychology*. Moscow: International Union of Scientific Psychology Organizing Committee.

———— 1972: On the importance of the notion of object-activity for psychology. In *Short communications prepared for the XX International Congress of Psychology*, ed. B.F. Lomow. 146–64. Moscow: USSR Society of Psychologists.

Lewin, K. 1926: Untersuchungen zur Handlungs- und Affektpsychologie: Vorbemerkungen über die psychischen Kräfte und Energien und über die Struktur der menschlichen Seele. In *Psychologische forschung* 7.

Luria, A.R. 1973: *The working brain: an introduction to neuropsychology*. London: Penguin; New York: Basic Books.

Tomaszewski, T. 1978: *Tätigkeit und Bewusstsein. Beiträge zur Einführung in die polnische Tätigkeitpsychologie*. Weinheim: Beltz.

Vygotsky, L.S. 1962: *Thought and language*. Cambridge, Mass.: MIT Press.

Mead, George Herbert (1863–1931).

An American philosopher and social psychologist whose most influential work is *Mind, self and society* (1934). His greatest insight: if an individual, by its gesture, calls out in itself the *same response* that it evokes in another participant in a social act, then that gesture is a linguistic gesture or a significant symbol, and it has the same meaning to both the one who makes it and to the other. A gesture is a stimulus and its meaning is the response it evokes. There are nonlinguistic (bodily) gestures and linguistic gestures. A nonlinguistic gesture evokes an overt response directly whereas a linguistic gesture evokes, first, the meaning of an overt response, or it makes one aware of the general form of an overt response. The meaning of a linguistic gesture is the universal, the conception of the nature of particulars belonging to the same class. If A says to B, "close the door", and if B understands A, both have the meaning, the idea, of closing a door. However, the specific way in which B may close it is not indicated, but only the general, universal form of the act. Both A and B have the same concept; they grasp the meaning of a symbol. Hence for A to call out in himself, by his gesture, the *same response* that he calls out in B means that both have the same concept, a covert, mental response. This provides a basis for a clear definition of both mind and language. Sharing meanings or concepts with other members of a group is essential if an individual is to have a mind and a self. Since lower animals do not use significant symbols Mead contends they have no minds and no selves.

Selves and minds emerge out of social behavior. To have a self an individual must respond implicitly to its own behavior as another does overtly. Contrary to the claim of many previous psychologists as well as to the Hobbesian social contract theory, Mead holds that social behavior is a necessary condition for the emergence of selves and minds. The mind has two fundamental components; the social and the personal. The social component consists of beliefs, attitudes and ways of responding to objects that are shared by other members of one's community, the "generalized other". This requires that one be able to take the role of the other or to take the attitude of the community toward his own linguistic gestures and his overt behavior. One thereby becomes conscious of oneself 'as an object or individual, and thus develops a self or personality' (Mead 1934). This is the "me" component of the

self. The personal or private component of the self is the "I", the actor, performer, the evaluator, the decider. It encounters conflicts between customary traditional ways of behaving that do not answer effectively to new experiences and new situations. At the juncture of conflict reflective intelligence sets in, which consists of a conversation, by an individual, between the "I" and the "me". Because of such conflicts the individual has the freedom to construct new hypotheses, new ways of responding, which, if accepted by the community, becomes a part of the attitude of the community. Hence the newly created idea becomes objective and is no longer confined to the private perspective of the individual.

Accordingly, no self can exist apart from society, mind cannot be separated from behavior, and the "I" cannot exist apart from the "me". Mead is not a social determinist and he explains that an individual's freedom depends upon the social component of the self. The "me" is servant to the "I" in its creative constructive operation. To practice individualism is to be neither anti-social, as is claimed by certain traditionalists, nor an isolationist of the Henry Thoreau type.

Mead is a behaviorist, but not of the Watson-Skinnerian kind, who either denies the existence of the internal mental process (more recently called SYMBOLIC INTERACTION) or reduces it to overt observable behavior. Mead explains that the mental process is a phase of the act of adjustment, that even as the individual and society are functionally related, so are mind and conduct, and by this thesis he evaded Cartesian dualism. DLM

Bibliography

Hewitt, J.P. 1984: *Self and society: a symbolic interactionist social psychology*. 3rd edn. Boston: Allyn and Bacon.

Mead, G.H. 1934: *Mind, self and society*, ed. C.W. Morris. Chicago: University of Chicago Press.

―――― 1938: *The philosophy of the act*. Chicago: University of Chicago Press.

Strauss, A. ed. 1956: *George Herbert Mead on social psychology: selected papers*. Chicago: University of Chicago Press.

mechanistic theory The description of behavior exclusively through causal concepts employed in traditional natural (Newtonian) science, where a complete account of things is attempted through the use of material causes (the substance comprising things) and efficient causes (the impetus moving things). No use is made of purpose or intention. To use these would require that the "formal" cause (a pre-existing pattern of meanings) or final cause (selection of meanings that are to be achieved in action) be used as basic principles of explanation. Since mechanistic theory holds that the same natural laws which move inanimate events move the behavior of living organisms, a uniformity and predictability is achieved suggestive of a machine-like process taking place throughout nature. Thus, people are said to behave due to such underlying systematic (mechanistic) processes without meaningful understanding or choice. JFR

Bibliography

Ayer, A.J. 1967: Man as a subject for science. In *Philosophy, politics and society*, 3rd series eds. P. Laslett and W.G. Runciman. Oxford: Blackwell.

meme A term introduced by Dawkins (1976) in his proposed analogy between biological and cultural evolution, to refer to the hypothetical cultural counterpart of the gene – a "unit" of cultural inheritance. Suggestions that socio-cultural change has some of the properties of biological evolution have been made repeatedly, and early ones have long been discredited. Recently, however, a number of subtler models have been proposed and debated (see Plotkin and Odling-Smee 1981). Some schemes suggest that cultural traits change in frequency according to their effects on the biological fitness of their bearer, but Dawkins's idea differs in suggesting that memes change frequency simply according to their capacity for cultural transmission from one individual to another. Dawkins (1982) also distinguishes between memes (units of information residing in the brain) and meme products (their outward and perceptible manifestations). This speculative scheme has stimulated a continuing debate (see Dawkins 1982; Staddon 1981; Harré 1979). RDA

Bibliography

Dawkins, R. 1976: *The selfish gene*. Oxford: Oxford University Press.

―――― 1982: *The extended phenotype: the gene as the unit of selection*. Oxford and San Francisco: W.H. Freeman.

Harré, R. 1979: *Social being*. Part IV. Oxford: Basil Blackwell; Totowa, N.J.: Littlefield Adams.

Plotkin, H.C. and Odling-Smee, F.J. 1981: A multiple-level model of evolution and its implications for sociobiology. *Behavior and brain science* 4, 225–68.

Staddon, J.F.R. 1981: On a possible relation between cultural transmission and genetical evolution. In *Perspectives in ethology, 4: advantages of diversity*, eds. P.P.G. Bateson and P.H. Klopfer. New York and London: Plenum Press.

mere exposure effect The fact that repeated exposure to a neutral stimulus is sufficient to induce positive reactions to that stimulus. Zajonc (1968), who was the first to discover this effect, has presented a good deal of evidence in support of it. The effect is not restricted to interpersonal ATTRACTION. Repeated exposure also affects our evaluation of verbal, visual and auditory stimuli of various kinds (words, symbols etc.) and can provide, at least in part, an explanation for early attachment in animals. Recently Zajonc has shown that such preferences can develop without conscious recognition or discriminations (Zajonc 1980).

In many circumstances other factors may, of course, have a much stronger effect on liking, attitudes or attractions and overshadow the effect of mere exposure. JMFJ

Bibliography

Zajonc, R. 1968: Attitudinal effects of mere exposure. *Journal of personality and social psychology*. Monograph supplement 9, 127.

―――― 1980: Feeling and thinking: preferences need no inferences. *American psychologist* 35, 151–75.

MMPI, the The Minnesota Multiphasic Personality Inventory is an objective personality inventory developed as an aid in assessing clinical problems. It is the most widely researched personality measure with substantial validity studies supporting its use. The information available on its scales has encouraged the broad use of automated (computer-based) interpretation. The MMPI clinical scales were devised according to a strategy of empirical scale construction. Items which validly discriminated the clinical group from normals were included in the scale. Scales were devised to assess hypochondria, depression, hysteria, psychopathic deviation, psychasthenia (obsessive-compulsive behavior), schizophrenia, and mania. In addition, there are several validity scales to alert the clinician to deviant response attitudes such as lying (L Scale), faking (F Scale) and general defensiveness (K Scale).   JNB

Bibliography

Dahlstrom, W.G. and Dahlstrom, L. 1980: *Basic readings on the MMPI*. Minneapolis: University of Minnesota Press.

Lanyon, R.I. 1984: Personality assessment. *Annual review of psychology* 35, 667–701.

multidimensional scaling (MDS) refers to a growing family of psychometric techniques concerned with the representation of structure in similarity data. The central assumption is that psychological distance, or similarity (between stimuli, constructs, traits, concepts, etc.) can be effectively represented and analyzed in terms of Euclidean (or other) distance formulations. Through the geometric modeling of psychological relationships, MDS can be an important tool of description, quantification, classification and even discovery by providing a sensitive, multidimensional representation of otherwise complex and elusive psychological domains.

Input to MDS normally consists of a matrix of measures of similarity between all the elements to be scaled. The objective is to produce an optimal representation of this similarity structure in a limited number of dimensions. The problem is, generally stated, to find "n" points whose interpoint distances represent the (dis)similarities between "n" objects (Kruskal 1964). While earlier, fully metric MDS methods required some fairly rigorous assumptions about the data (Torgerson 1965), later so-called non-metric methods were able to produce metrically invariable solutions when given only ordinally invariant solutions (Shepard 1974). Another group of techniques (e.g. Carroll and Chang's (1970) INDSCAL program) greatly expanded the psychological utility of MDS by also allowing the study of individual differences between input units (subjects, occasions, situations, etc.). Non-metric MDS, and individual differences MDS (either metric or non-metric) have been the most frequently used procedures in psychology. An early review of the psychological uses of MDS is contained in Shepard et al. (1972), while Carroll and Arabie (1980) offer a more recent summary.

MDS may be used to achieve a variety of scientific objectives in social research. The discovery of hidden structures, for example of cognitive representations about social stimuli, is one major area of application (Shepard 1974, p.374). A second application of MDS is the parametric representation of otherwise inaccessible data. For example, the way people implicitly think about social episodes may be studied using MDS to construct an "episode space" mapping all encounters within a particular subculture (Forgas 1982). MDS is also a useful tool for the construction of empirical taxonomies of psychological domains, as Smithson, Amato and Pearce's (1983) MDS study of the helping or altruism literature showed. Through the quantified representation of previously unquantifiable data, MDS has frequently been used as a preliminary step before subsequent hypothesis testing procedures can be applied. Some research strategies, such as Guttman's facet theory, place a major emphasis on MDS and related procedures for empirical evaluation of formalized research hypotheses.

The use of MDS techniques usually

involves a number of logical steps. The definition of the stimulus domain to be studied (interaction episodes, relationship scripts, political leaders, person prototypes, personality traits, etc.) comes first. Next, the index(es) of similarity between elements in the stimulus domain need to be defined, and the appropriate data collected. Measures of similarity may be based on correlation coefficients, temporal and spatial co-occurrence frequencies, similarity judgments, number of shared features, profile distances on bipolar scales, category sorting tasks, etc. Because of the ubiquity of the similarity dimension, almost any domain of interest to psychologists is potentially accessible to MDS analysis. Input to MDS consists of one or more similarity matrices. The user normally needs to specify the maximum and minimum dimensionality of the expected solution, and/or some criterion measure of goodness of fit between the input data and the output representation. MDS programs, for example Carroll and Chang's (1970) INDSCAL, then produce a multidimensional spatial map of the elements scaled, and a second "subject space" indicating the differences between subjects in their weighting of each of the dimensions. In deciding the optimum number of dimensions, usually the mininum number of necessary and sufficient dimensions are selected in terms of such criteria as proportion of variance accounted for, meaningfulness and interpretability. MDS axes may also be labeled, either intuitively, or through the establishment of empirical links between each of the MDS axes and a number of bipolar "hypothesis" scales using regression or similar techniques. A simple and non-technical summary of the steps involved in using MDS programs and some of the problems involved is provided in Forgas (1979), and many of the key background texts have been collected in Davies and Coxon (1983). A particularly useful collection of programs is the MDS-X package, which uses the SPSS control language.

MDS analyses have been successfully used in a variety of fields. Research on cognitive representations of complex social phenomena (e.g. implicit perceptions of interaction situations, relationship scripts, aggressive encounters, political leaders and parties, etc.) is one popular application. Taxonomic studies on person perception, helping behavior, implicit personality theories, person prototypes, stereotyping, emotional experiences, or group structure have also successfully used MDS methods. In more macro-social contexts, MDS has been an important tool for describing and quantifying domains such as occupational status, conflict-resolution strategies, social networks, perceptions of nations and ethnic groups, and cross-cultural differences in cognitive representations. However, as with most descriptive methods, great caution must be exercised in the interpretation of MDS results, particularly when interpreting axes, or the quantitative analysis of individual differences (Forgas 1979).

In conclusion, MDS is clearly a most useful method in the social sciences. It allows the quantified empirical description of complex and elusive stimulus domains, it can greatly help in the construction of taxonomies, it can be used as a preliminary to subsequent statistical analyses based on the coordinate structures, and it can help in the critical evaluation of pre-formulated structural hypotheses. In cognitive social psychology in particular, MDS is one of the most promising techniques for the detailed analysis and study of implicit cognitive representations of the social world.   JPF

Bibliography

Carroll, J.D. and Arabie, P. 1980: Multidimensional scaling. *Annual review of psychology* 31, 607–49.

Carroll, D.J. and Chang, J.J. 1970: An analysis of individual differences in multidimensional scaling via N-way generalization of Eckart-Young decomposition. *Psychometrika* 35, 283–319.

Davies, P.M. and Coxon, A.P.M. eds. 1982: *Key texts in multidimensional scaling*. London: Heinemann.

Forgas, J.P. 1979: Multidimensional scaling: a discovery method in social psychology. In *Emerging strategies in social psychology*, ed. G.P. Ginsburg. Chichester: Wiley.

———— 1982: Episode cognition: internal

representations of interaction routines. In *Advances in experimental social psychology*, ed. L. Berkowitz. New York: Academic Press.

Kruskal, J.B. 1964: Non-metric multidimensional scaling: a numerical method. *Psychometrika* 29, 115–29.

Shepard, R.N. 1974: Representation of structure in similarity data: problems and prospects. *Psychometrika* 39, 373–421.

—— Romney, A.K. and Nerlove, S.B. eds. 1972: *Multidimensional scaling: theory and application in the behavioral sciences*. New York: Seminar Press.

Smithson, M., Amato, P.R. and Pearce, P. 1983: *Dimensions of helping behavior*. Oxford: Pergamon.

Torgerson, W.S. 1965: Multidimensional scaling of similarity. *Psychometrika* 30, 379–93.

N

narcissism After the Greek myth of Narcissus, either (i) a sexual perversion in which a person treats his or her own body as the preferred sex-object, or (ii) in Freudian theory any investment of libido in, and hence cathexis of, aspects of the self as opposed to external objects (see PERSON-ALITY THEORY, PSYCHOANALYTICAL). In the latter sense narcissism is not necessarily pathological, since some positive self-regard may be both intrinsically healthy and also necessary to forming stable relationships with other people (Freud 1917, ch. 26).

Hence (a) narcissistic "object-choice", where an object is chosen because of its similarities to oneself; (b) "narcissistic hurt", which is a blow to self-esteem or morale; (c) "narcissistic supplies", which are the reassuring feedback as to their own worth which infants and young children seek from their mothers as a basis for forming their own identity (individuation); and later any affection or attention from any source which enhances self-esteem (Kohut 1971).   NMC

Bibliography

Freud, S. 1917: Introductory lectures, part 3. *Standard edition of the complete psychological works of Sigmund Freud*, vol. 16. London: Hogarth Press; New York: Norton.

Kohut, H. 1971: *The analysis of the self*. New York: International University Press.

negotiation A verbal interchange aimed at reaching a joint decision. More recent uses include the negotiation of identity or of accounts of past conduct (see Semin and Manstead 1983); but more commonly "negotiation" refers to interactions between parties who perceive that their interests diverge on the issue(s) under consideration. Other procedures for making decisions under such circum-stances include unilateral pre-emptive action, coercion, norm following, tacit bargaining, and decision by higher authority. Multiple parties may be invol-ved, though most theory and research concerns the two-party case. Negotiation is found in all realms of society including the family, workplace, marketplace, and the arenas of labor management and inter-national relations. It can be viewed as a mild form of conflict which often results in genuine conflict resolution and which, so long as it continues, has the potential for averting more serious struggles.

Theoretical and empirical contributions to the study of negotiation are found in most branches of social science. The earliest work was done by economists, who developed several formal models (see Young 1975). More recently, significant contributions have been made by socio-logists (e.g. Bacharach and Lawler 1981), political scientists (e.g. Zartman 1978), anthropologists (e.g. Gulliver 1979), industrial relations specialists (e.g. Walton and McKersie 1965), international rela-tions scholars (e.g. Ikle 1964), and social psychologists (e.g., Drucknan 1977; Pruitt 1981; Rubin and Brown 1975).

Sometimes only one issue (e.g. the price of an antique) is under consideration in negotiation. But more often there are multiple issues creating a problem of cognitive overload. This problem can be handled by (a) developing an agenda; (b) placing more fundamental issues early in the agenda so that a simple formula or "framework agreement" can emerge as a guide for later, more detailed discussions; and (c) parceling out issues among several representative committees. These proce-dures help organize decision-making but add to the complexity of the task by producing still more issues requiring joint agreement.

Positional bargaining

Research has shown that negotiators who make higher demands and slower concessions usually achieve more favorable outcomes for themselves if agreement is reached, but their agreements are reached more slowly and they are less certain to reach agreement. High demands and slow concessions are made to the extent that (a) negotiators have high levels of aspiration, (b) they have attractive alternatives to reaching agreement, (c) they expect the other party to make large concessions in the long run, (d) they have the capacity to mount effective threats, (e) time spent in negotiation is not costly to them, and (f) a deadline for reaching agreement is not imminent. Also, representatives tend to make higher demands and slower concessions than do individuals negotiating on their own behalf, especially when they are highly accountable to, distrusted by or under the surveillance of their constituents.

Negotiators defend their proposals by means of competitive (or, as they are sometimes called, "distributive") tactics, such as (a) presenting arguments that favor their demands, (b) committing themselves not to moderate their demands so that the other party must accept them if agreement is to be reached, (c) imposing a deadline, and (d) threatening to punish the other party for not agreeing to their terms. Though often successful in eliciting concessions, competitive tactics tend to be resented and are frequently answered in kind, starting a conflict spiral.

Prominent solutions

Sometimes a single alternative stands out in a negotiator's thinking as the most proper or most likely solution to an issue; for example, a 50–50 division of a prize, a mediator's suggestion about an appropriate hourly increase, a river or historical boundary in a border dispute. If the same alternative stands out in the other party's thinking, and each party knows that this is true of the other, a "prominent solution" is said to exist (Schelling 1960). Research suggests that the existence of a prominent solution increases the likelihood that

agreement will be reached, speeds concession making, thus reducing the time spent in negotiation, and dampens the impact of other determinants of demand level and concession rate. However, if different alternatives stand out in the two parties' thinking, concessions are probably slower than they otherwise would be and agreement is likely to be jeopardized.

Problem solving

While capable of establishing some of the boundary conditions that will delimit the final agreement, positional bargaining is often incapable of producing agreement (Fisher and Ury 1981). Prominent solutions sometimes emerge to fill this gap, but they are by no means a certain development. Hence, there is often a need for problem solving or mediation. An example of joint problem solving would be a frank discussion between the two parties in which they reveal the interests underlying their proposals and their priorities among these interests and then brainstorm in search of a way to reconcile those interests that seem to be opposed.

Activities of the kind just described are quite risky in the sense of producing high potential cost if the other party is not genuinely interested in problem solving but is intent on extracting as many concessions as possible (Pruitt 1981). Problem-solving activity may make one appear weak (i.e. willing to make extensive future concessions) and may reveal information that can be used by the other party to devise effective threats and locate alternatives that are just barely acceptable. In addition there is a danger that the other party will treat one's tentative proposals as concessions that provide a starting point for further negotiation. Hence, parties who wish to engage in problem solving but do not trust the other's intentions often employ less risky tactics. These include sending conciliatory signals, transmitting messages through disavowable intermediaries, and attending unofficial "backchannel" meetings with the other party. All these procedures can be employed on an exploratory basis while maintaining a rigid competitive stance in the formal negotiation.

There are many advantages to employing problem solving in addition to or instead of positional bargaining. As mentioned earlier, agreement is more likely to be reached. The agreement reached is often better for both parties (i.e. more "integrative") because it reconciles their separate interests. However positional bargaining cannot usually be avoided altogether, because it is encouraged by self interest. Rather, a two-step process is frequently found, in which positional bargaining is pursued until a deadlock is reached, followed by problem solving to agreement.

A desire to engage in problem solving is encouraged by freedom from constituent surveillance during negotiation. Constituent surveillance must be distinguished from accountability for the ultimate agreement to constituents. The latter encourages firmness about one's interests and, hence, in the context of problem-solving activity, can lead to the development of agreements that provide high benefit to both parties.

Mediation

Problem solving is not always possible or successful, and mediation by third parties is often essential for reaching agreement in negotiation. Mediators can take either a process approach, a content approach, or both (Rubin 1981). Process mediation involves encouraging problem solving, reconciling the parties to one another, improving communication, educating the parties about the dynamics of conflict, etc. Content mediation involves suggesting possible agreements, providing decommitting formulas, providing incentives for particular concessions, etc. The most effective mediators are those who have rapport with both parties, a condition that often but not always requires impartiality between the parties. Timing is important in mediation, in that third party assistance is most welcome when the negotiators become aware that they cannot solve the problem on their own or that uncontrollable forces (e.g. escalation of the conflict) threaten the future of negotiation. Mediation must be distinguished from arbitration, in which the third party imposes a settlement. Arbitration encourages rapid, cost-effective conflict resolution. But since it takes decision-making out of the hands of the conflicting parties it runs the danger of overlooking opportunities for the development of mutually beneficial agreements.

DGP

Bibliography

Bacharach, S.B. and Lawler, E.J. 1981: *Bargaining: power, tactics, and outcomes*. San Francisco: Jossey-Bass.

Druckman, D. ed. 1977: *Negotiations: social-psychological perspectives*. Beverly Hills, Calif.: Sage.

Fisher, R. and Ury, W. 1981: *Getting to YES: negotiating agreement without giving in*. Boston: Houghton Mifflin.

Gulliver, P.H. 1979: *Disputes and negotiations: a cross-cultural perspective*. New York: Academic Press.

Ikle, F.C. 1964: *How nations negotiate*. New York: Harper.

*Pruitt, D.G. 1981: *Negotiation behavior*. New York: Academic Press.

*Rubin, J.Z. ed. 1981: *Dynamics of third party intervention: Kissinger in the Middle East*. New York: Praeger.

—— and Brown, B.R. 1975: *The social psychology of bargaining and negotiation*. New York: Academic Press.

Schelling, T.C. 1960: *The strategy of conflict*. Cambridge, Mass.: Harvard University Press.

Semin, G. and Manstead, A.S.R. 1983: *The accountability of conduct*. London: Academic Press.

*Walton, R.E. and McKersie, R.B 1965: *A behavioral theory of labor negotiations: an analysis of a social interaction system*. New York: McGraw-Hill.

Young, O.R. 1975: *Bargaining: formal theories of negotiation*. Urbana, Ill.: University of Illinois Press.

Zartman, I.W. ed. 1978: *The negotiation process*. Beverly Hills, Calif.: Sage.

neo-Freudian theory A term used of the approach of psychoanalytic theorists who have rejected, added to, or modified significant portions of Freud's original theory. The term is used by different writers with varying levels of specificity. In its most general sense it can apply to a wide range of psychoanalytically-orientated psychologists whose theories diverge from Freud's in greater or lesser degrees: in this sense for example, Carl JUNG, Erik Erikson, Otto Rank and object relations theorists could all be considered neo-Freudians, even though Erikson accepts the basic premises of Freudian analysis while Jung rejects many of them. Usually, however, the term neo-Freudian is reserved for a smaller group of psychoanalysts whose theories share two core features: (1) they reject Freud's "libido theory", his view that the primary motivators in personality are innate biological instincts of sexuality and aggression which are specific to childhood; and (2) they correspondingly emphasize the importance of social needs, the influence of cultural and interpersonal factors and the role of the self in personality development.

The four theorists most frequently described as neo-Freudians in this more restrictive sense are Alfred Adler, Karen Horney, Erich Fromm and Harry Stack Sullivan. The following brief discussion first describes the major contributions of these thinkers and then summarizes what their theories have in common.

Alfred Adler was born in Vienna in 1870. He was a member of the original small group of psychoanalysts which met at Freud's house to discuss analytic theory, and was the first president of the Vienna branch of the Psychoanalytic Society. He came to reject some basic tenets of Freud's theory, however, including the notion that sexual trauma is the basis for neurosis, and resigned from the society in 1911 to form his own school which he named INDIVIDUAL PSYCHOLOGY. Adler sees the person as a united whole, indivisible, responsible for his actions, free and striving towards conscious goals. The major tenets of his theory are contained in six key concepts: (1) *fictional finalism*, the notion that people are motivated not primarily by past events, but by their images and expectations for future possibilities; (2) *striving for superiority*, the individual's innate tendency to develop his capacities to the full and to strive for perfection; (3) *inferiority feelings*,

which Adler sees as the normal response to the realization of being less than perfect and which motivate all efforts towards self-actualization; (4) *social interest*, the innate tendency to be interested in other people and in the social group, manifested in cooperation, empathy, altruism and, ultimately, the desire for a perfect society; (5) *style of life*, the different unique forms in which individuals strive for perfection; and (6) the *creative self*, the active, constructive center of personality which interprets experience and chooses a response to it.

Karen Horney was born in Germany in 1885. She was associated with the Berlin Psychoanalytic Institute from 1918 to 1932, then emigrated to the USA where she founded an association and a training institute. Horney saw herself as remaining within the Freudian tradition, though she tried to correct what she saw as the limitations of Freud's approach: his biological and mechanistic orientation. She accepted Freud's notions of psychic determinism, unconscious motivation and the importance of irrational emotional experience. The root of neurosis for Horney is the childhood experience of basic anxiety and the strategies adopted in response to it. The helpless, totally dependent child encountering rejection, inconsistency or harsh treatment from its parents, feels that its safety and fundamental security are threatened. The child can adopt various strategies to cope with this, and these can become permanent features of personality and eventually take on the status of needs in their own right. Horney catalogues ten of these neurotic needs; they all mirror needs of normal people, but in an unrealistic, exaggerated and insatiable form: for example, the need for perfection, for total love, for complete control. Horney does not believe that the experience of basic anxiety is an inevitable part of development; it can be avoided if the child is treated with love, respect and consistency.

Like Horney, Erich Fromm was born in Germany and emigrated to the United States in the early 1930s. Fromm's work was influenced by the writings of Karl Marx and by existentialism as well as by psychoanalytic theory. He calls himself a "dialectical humanist". The central notion in Fromm's theory is his description of the human condition. Humans, he says, are animals and thus part of nature; however, because of their distinctively human nature they are also more than an animal and experience a separation between themselves and the natural world and between themselves and other people. This separateness from the natural order gives human beings the freedom to choose their lives; this freedom gives human life its meaning and potential, but it also gives rise to anxiety. As a result, people often try to relinquish their freedom through conformity or submission to authorities. Like Freud and Adler, Fromm believes that there is a species-specific, innate human nature which is independent of culture. However he has also emphasized the role that social context plays in determining the way in which the individual deals with basic human needs. Different societies and different groups within society create particular types of "character". Moreover Fromm judges societies on the basis of how well they meet the basic human needs of their members; he argues that no present society makes an adequate job of this task, and calls the form of society that he believes would do so "Humanistic Communitarian Socialism".

More than any of the other neo-Freudians, Harry Stack Sullivan moved away from Freudian theory and articulated a model of personality that is thoroughly social and interpersonal. In fact Sullivan claims that the notion of personality, conceived in terms of the single individual, is hypothetical, an illusion. Personality, he argues, consists in the relatively enduring patterns of interpersonal relations which are manifested in our lives – our relations both with real others and with the imagined others which make up the content of our thoughts, feelings and fantasies. He was strongly influenced by social psychology and anthropology, particularly by George Herbert MEAD and other theorists at the Chicago School of Sociology. He was born in 1892 in New York and trained as an analyst. Sullivan described six stages in personality development, each of which represents a new interpersonal constellation. In *infancy* the child relates to the mother via its oral activity towards the nipple and develops notions of the good and bad other, and the correct and the wrong other. In *childhood* with the beginning of language, the child begins to relate to playmates and to form more cognitive representations of others. In the *juvenile* period (first school) the child learns to relate to the peer group and to authorities outside the home. In *pre-adolescence* "chum" relations with same sex peers are central for learning cooperation, mutuality, reciprocity and intimacy. The development of patterns of heterosexual relationships become the focus in *early adolescence*, as puberty brings the beginning of the lust dynamism and this becomes differentiated from companionship and intimacy. Finally, in *late adolescence*, a long period of education in varying social roles and relations brings about the transition to the complexity of adult social living and citizenship.

All four theorists share several core orientations which characterize the neo-Freudian approach. First, they all take a more positive and optimistic view of human nature than does classical psychoanalysis; they stress the striving for self-actualization, for active adaptation to the environment and for social relatedness and harmony, in contrast to Freud's emphasis on antisocial impulses of sexuality and aggression. Where Freud sees the individual as in inevitable conflict with the society which demands restriction of his impulsive acts, the neo-Freudians propose a more harmonious relationship between the individual and society. They see social life as a fulfillment of basic human nature, not a repression of it. In addition, these writers pay as much attention to the role of conscious conflicts and experiences in adolescence and adulthood as to unconscious conflicts in early childhood. Finally, they stress the effects of the social milieu in determining personality. (See also COGNITIVE PERSONALITY THEORY; PERSONALITY THEORY, PSYCHOANALYTICAL.)

SB

Bibliography

Adler, A. 1927: *The practice and theory of individual psychology*. New York: Harcourt, Brace and World.

Ansbacher, H.L. and R.R. eds. 1956: *The individual-psychology of Alfred Adler*. New York: Basic Books.

Fromm, Erich 1941: *Escape from freedom*. New York: Rinehart.

—— 1947: *Man for himself*. New York: Rinehart.

—— 1955: *The sane society*. New York: Rinehart.

Hall, C.S. and Lindzey, G. 1978: *Theories of personality*. 3rd edn. New York and Chichester: John Wiley.

Horney, K. 1942: *Self-analysis*. New York: Norton.

—— 1950: *Neurosis and human growth*. New York: Norton.

Munroe, R.L. 1955: *Schools of psychoanalytic thought*. New York: Dryden Press.

Sullivan, H.S. 1953: *The interpersonal theory of psychiatry*. New York: Norton.

norms: social psychology A norm is a rule or standard for action. Social norms are shared definitions of desirable behavior. They can be enforced in various ways. To the extent that a norm is effective, it leads to uniformity of behavior, but as a standard for evaluating behavior a norm does not necessarily describe the most common actual behavior. As such the term should be distinguished from concepts like statistical measures of central tendency, customs, folkways or mores.

Norms play an important role in social influence processes which are manifested in the general tendency towards conformity. Although compliance with norms depends to some extent upon the enforcement of positive and negative sanctions, the sheer unanimity with which a norm is endorsed by members of a group is in itself a factor which can induce compliance with a norm. As Moscovici (1976) has shown, the effect of active minorities in this respect is different from the effects of a dominant majority. Nevertheless, although Moscovici has found evidence that minorities within groups may have a more profound SOCIAL INFLUENCE than majorities, it appears that minority influence is comparatively ineffective when it runs counter to the norms (or *Zeitgeist*) of society at large (see Maass et al. 1982).

Deviation from norms and the origin and maintenance of norms have mainly been studied by sociologists. In social psychology the related concept of rules has become more important in recent research.

JMFJ

Bibliography

Maass, A., Clark III, R.D. and Haberkorn, G. 1982: The effects of differential ascribed category membership and norms on minority influence. *European journal of social psychology* 12, 89–104.

Moscovici, S. 1976: *Social influence and social change*. London and New York: Academic Press.

O

obedience As a technical term the word became popular in psychology through the work of Milgram (1974), who wrote: 'Obedience is the psychological mechanism that links individual action to political purpose. It is the dispositional cement that binds men to systems of authority. Facts of recent history and observation in daily life suggest that for many people obedience may be a deeply ingrained behavior tendency, indeed, a prepotent impulse overriding training in ethics, sympathy and moral conduct' (p.1).

Obedience, in this special psychological sense, may be defined as a particular form of compliance where behavior is performed in response to a direct order. Social psychologists have done extensive research into compliance, conformity, persuasibility and obedience, particularly obedience and conformity. Yet, as Milgram noted, obedience and conformity may be distinguished in the following ways: (i) Hierarchy: whereas conformity regulates the behavior of equal status subjects, obedience links one status to another; (ii) Imitation: whereas conformity is imitation, obedience is not; (iii) Explicitness: in obedience the prescription for action (an order) is explicit whereas in conformity the requirement for going along with the group is implicit; (iv) Voluntarism: because conformity is a response to implicit pressure, the subject interprets his or her own behavior as voluntary, but as obedience is publicly defined as a situation devoid of voluntarism, the subject can use the public definition of the situation as a full explanation of his or her action.

Milgram's studies on obedience have been criticized in terms of ethical problems, experimental artifacts, lack of generality, and conceptual confusion. (See also SOCIAL INFLUENCE.)   AF

Bibliography

Milgram, S. 1974: *Obedience to authority*. London: Tavistock.

object relations A term used frequently by contemporary psychoanalytic writers, its shades of meaning reflecting a theoretical movement away from a model of the subject as isolated and biologically (instinctually) motivated toward a view which encompasses the subject's interactions with its surroundings – its interpersonal relations. Use of the word *object* to refer to persons derives from the commitment of psychoanalysts to an instinct theory. The object through which instinctual gratification is held to be achieved is usually a person, an aspect of a person or a symbolic representation of a person toward which the subject directs its actions or desires. Technically "object relations" refers to the mental representations of the self and other (the object) which are an aspect of ego organization and not to external interpersonal relationships. (See also INSTINCT.)   BBL

Bibliography

Greenberg, J.R. and Mitchell, S.A. 1983: *Object relations in psychoanalytic theory*. Cambridge, Mass.: Harvard University Press.

Klein, M. 1948: *Contributions to psychoanalysis*. London: Hogarth.

observational methods A distinctive feature of ETHOLOGY from its origins, and one which has proved more durable to the present day than some of its specific theories, has been its insistence on the importance of observation (see Tinbergen 1963; Thorpe 1979; Blurton Jones 1972). This does not imply avoidance of experimentation or of laboratories: rather it reflects a stress on meticulously detailed observational descriptions of behavior, whatever the context. Ethologists also try to ensure that the categories used for describing observed behavior are objective – that is, that they refer to its observable form and consequences, and are capable of consistent use over time and between observers. Ethologists do recognize, however, that objectivity in this sense is not perfectible, and also that the actual designation of behavior categories studied is invariably selective (see Reynolds 1976). Errors which ethologists hope to avoid in their descriptions include choosing behavior categories that are too crude to be useful and describing behavior in ways that do not distinguish clearly between observation and interpretation.

For much of ethology's development, observational methods have largely been based on prolonged immersion in observation and becoming a "good observer", compiling a behavior catalog or ethogram, extended recording of observations, and analysis in predominantly verbal terms. In recent decades, however, the emphasis has shifted towards quantification and the use of computer and other technology in both the recording and analysis of observed behavior (see e.g. Bramblett 1976).   RDA

Bibliography

Blurton Jones, N. ed. 1972: *Ethological studies of child behavior*. Cambridge and New York: Cambridge University Press.

Bramblett, C.A. 1976: *Patterns of primate behavior*. Palo Alto, Calif.: Mayfield.

Reynolds, V. 1976: The origins of a behavioural vocabulary: the case of the rhesus monkey. *Journal for the theory of social behaviour* 6, 105–42.

Thorpe, W.H. 1979: *The origins and rise of ethology: the science of the natural behaviour of animals*. London, Melbourne: Heinemann; New York: Praeger.

Tinbergen, N. 1963: On aims and methods of ethology. *Zeitschrift für tierpsychologie* 20, 410–33.

Oedipus and Elektra complexes

After the Greek legends in which, respectively, King Oedipus inadvertently killed his father, and Elektra avenged the murder of her father by assisting in the murder of her mother, these terms refer in PSYCHOANALYTICAL PERSONALITY THEORY to two clusters of mainly unconscious feelings and ideas which set in at the "phallic" stage of psychosexual development. The child's attachment to the opposite-sex parent becomes sexualized, so that the child wishes to possess him or her and get rid of the other parent. The boy's rivalry with the father produces "castration anxiety", the female parallel of which is "penis envy". The child deals with the associated anxieties by eventually "identifying" with the same-sex parent (see DEFENSE MECHANISM) and "introjecting" his or her prohibitions as a basis for the primitive SUPEREGO, and his or her positive values as EGO IDEAL (Freud 1917, ch. 21). Some non-clinical studies of dreams and PROJECTIVE TESTS do seem to support some of the constituent hypotheses of these complexes (see Kline 1981, ch. 6).   NMC

Bibliography

Freud, S. 1917: *Introductory lectures*, part 3. *Standard edition of the complete psychological works of Sigmund Freud*, vol. 16. London: Hogarth Press; New York: Norton.

Kline, P. 1981: *Fact and fiction in Freudian theory*. 2nd edn. London and New York: Methuen.

ontogenetic sequence A concept typified by the Freudian model of psychosexual development, derived by analogy from the epigenetic development of embryology, in which each organ or organ system undergoes a critical period of rapid growth and differentiation at a specific time and in a particular, fixed sequence. Failure to develop during the critical period dooms the organ or organ system, and thus the organism, to developmental defects. FREUD considered the psychosexual development of the individual to undergo a similar series of critical periods, or stages: the oral stage, the anal stage, the oedipal stage, the latency period, and the genital stage. Failure or fixation at any stage endangered the subsequent stages and the individual's development.   ND

Bibliography
Freud, S. (1916–17) 1963: *Introductory lectures on psychoanalysis*. Part 3. Trans. J. Strachey. London: Hogarth.

operant behavior Behavior that is instrumental in obtaining reinforcement. The concept of operant behavior was introduced by the American psychologist B.F. Skinner, who described it as being emitted in the sense that it resulted from no external stimulation, and as operating on the environment to produce consequences (the reinforcement) capable of modifying the behavior. Many psychologists regard operant behavior as akin to voluntary behavior.

The process by which animals learn to modify their behavior to obtain reinforcement is often called *operant conditioning* and is regarded by some psychologists as a form of learning different from classical or Pavlovian conditioning. Operant conditioning techniques are widely used in laboratory studies of animal behavior, in training animals to perform circus tricks etc., and in the modification of human behavior for clinical or teaching purposes.

DJM

Bibliography
Mackintosh, N.J. 1983: *Conditioning and associative learning*. Oxford and New York: Oxford University Press.

Skinner, B.F. 1938: *The behavior of organisms*. New York: Appleton-Century-Crofts.

P

peer group The concept is used in two different senses: first, as a term for a small group of friends or associates who share common values, interests and activities; second, as a term for virtually all persons of the same age, a definition which reflects the fact that schools tend to be age-graded. Peer group influence can therefore be the influence that friends exercise on one another or the influence exerted by a much wider category of age-mates. The term "peer-group influence" is generally restricted to discussions of young people or adolescents, despite the fact that there is little evidence that peer group influence among adolescents is either highly distinctive or greater than among other age groupings. Using the first sense of the term, educational researchers have drawn heavily on the theory of group dynamics in social psychology. The sources and effects of influence are related to concepts such as LEADERSHIP, conformity and SELF-CONCEPT. Using the second sense of the term, researchers have been more interested in youth subcultures within any one of which many smaller friendship groups can be contained. The differences between subcultures are usually explained with reference to the broader social class subcultures in society.

In some studies, such as Coleman's classic account (1961), the different senses of peer groups and their influence are brought together. In most studies there is a tension, as yet not adequately clarified, between two ideas: on the one hand pupils come to school already sharing subcultural values which influence attitudes to school and educational achievements; on the other hand the school itself plays an active role in the formation of subcultures and friendship groups, perhaps especially in the formation of oppositional (or counter-cultural) groups who are alienated by their school experience, and these peer groups then influence educational attitudes and aspirations. A further unresolved problem is that of determining the relative power of family and peer group to influence adolescents (see Youniss 1985).

The SUBCULTURE varies with age-level. In childhood, when dependence on parents is high, the peer group serves as an extension of the socialization mediated by the family and peer associates are likely to be governed by parents. In ADOLESCENCE its quality and functions change as orientation shifts away from the family. The adolescent peer group may be part of a subculture that is at variance with the parental culture although generally its influence is congruent with parental values. The extent to which the peer group is relied upon by the adolescent depends on the degree of estrangement from parents, parental attitudes to the peer group and the nature of the dilemma, since adolescents perceive parents and peers as useful guides in different areas (Brittain 1968). During adolescence the peer group plays an important part in providing social support and identity, although some of its pressures e.g. for conformity and social acceptability, may generate difficulties. Its effects may be important in the development of antisocial behavior and DELINQUENCY although they are difficult to estimate.

It is now widely recognized that research has hitherto focused excessively on peer groups which are male, working-class and deviant at the expense of groups which are female or middle class or non-deviant. This bias is being corrected in current research.   DHH/WLIP-J

Bibliography

Bany, M.A. and Johnson, L.V. 1964: *Classroom group behaviour*. London and New York: Collier-Macmillan.

Brake, M. 1980: *The sociology of youth culture and youth subcultures*. London and Boston: Routledge and Kegan Paul.

Brittain, C.V. 1968: An exploration of the basis of peer-compliance and parent-compliance in adolescence. *Adolescence* 2, 445–58.

Coleman, J.S. 1961: *The adolescent society*. Glencoe Ill.: Free Press.

Conger, J.J. 1977: *Adolescence and youth: psychological development in a changing world*. New York: Harper and Row.

Youniss, J. 1985: *Adolescents: their parents and friends*. Chicago: University of Chicago Press.

person: concept of Though SELF-CONCEPT, a system of beliefs an individual comes to form about him- or herself, and social identity, the social category to which people assign themselves and to which they are assigned by others are well established in psychology, the concept of "person" has mainly attracted the attention of philosophers. This is unfortunate since such a concept is heavily involved in theorizing about others (see ATTRIBUTION THEORY) and in the making of moral judgments.

Philosophical interest in the concept of person centers on whether the concept refers to a primary, indecomposable entity or to a secondary conglomerate of more basic units. In the Cartesian tradition persons are composite beings requiring the union, though not the fusion, of a mind and a body. This conception of a person has been bedevilled by two main problems; how do these disparate components interact (the mind-body problem)? and since we are aware only of the bodily envelope of others, how do we know that they too "have" minds (the problem of other minds)? (See also SELF: PHILO-SOPHICAL.)

A more satisfactory concept of person has recently been identified by Strawson (1959). In his view persons are basic beings, publicly identified by the possession of a cluster of different kinds of attributes, some bodily, some behavioral and some mentalistic. The key step in the argument for adopting this concept of person is the suggestion that though our grounds for attributing states and conditions to ourselves and to others may be different, the meaning of first person and other person attributions is the same. Though there has been considerable critical discussion of this proposal (Ayer 1964) it has much to recommend it. Latterly it has appeared in the theory of human cognitive development as a public-collective model for the acquisition of an individual's sense of personal identity (Harré 1983).

The concept of "person" has been problematic in psychology partly because human beings are not to be distinguished as persons in virtue of their physical characteristics. Being a person, suggests Abelson (1977), is to have a special *status* bestowed upon one by one's fellow agents. Persons assign to one another the *right*, not only to make first-person avowals, such as "I like you", "I am hungry", "I have changed my mind", but also to have them taken seriously, i.e. acted upon. However, such a privilege may be lost if one cannot at the same time fulfill a *duty*: that of monitoring what one says and does to ensure that it is acceptable in socially shared terms. While the concept of person includes that of SELF, it is not identical to it. Personhood is a cultural universal (Geertz 1973), while selves may exhibit different forms: the western "individualistic" self; the "impersonal" self of the Eskimo; the "bifurcated" self of the Javanese with an "inside" and an "outside" self; the "player" self of the Balinese and so on (Geertz 1975). Although the ability to make reference to self-knowledge is essential to being a person, that ability develops only slowly. However, this cannot mean that human beings in society have first to qualify as persons before being treated as such. Indeed, the facts of psychological development are that human beings only develop the appropriate self-referential abilities by being treated as if already possessing them. This interdependency – of people relying upon one another for their personhood – has been termed "psychological symbiosis" by Spitz (1965). Such an interdependency also allows for the possibility of *depersonalization*: if people's actions are treated by others as lacking significance, they can experience themselves as not present in the world of ordinary, everyday life, and may lose their sense of agency (see e.g. Goffman 1961).

RHa/JMS

Bibliography

Abelson, R. 1977: *Persons: a study in philosophical psychology*. London: Macmillan.

Ayer, A.J. 1964: *The concept of a person*. London: Macmillan.

Geertz, C. 1973: *The interpretation of cultures*. New York: Basic Books.

———— 1975: On the nature of anthropological understanding. *American scientist* 63, 47–53.

Goffman, E. 1961: *Asylums: essays on the social situation of mental patients and other inmates*. New York: Doubleday; Harmondsworth: Penguin (1968).

Harré, R. 1983: *Personal being*. Oxford: Basil Blackwell.

Spitz, R.A. 1965: *The first year of life: a psychoanalytic study of normal and deviant development of object relations*. New York: International Universities Press.

Strawson, P.F. 1959: *Individuals*. London: Methuen; Atlantic Highlands, N.J.: Humanities Press (1960).

person perception *See* impression formation.

person/situation controversy A rather unfortunate title for the debate over whether people do or do not have consistent personality TRAITS. Although the topic is not at all new (see e.g. Ichheiser 1943), it has aroused a good deal of interest since the publication of Mischel's book *Personality and assessment* in 1968. The importance currently attached to this debate is demonstrated by the fact that a whole issue of the *Journal of personality* (vol. 51, no. 3, 1983) was devoted to concerns which has arisen from Mischel's book. This recognition was underlined by the space given to the controversy in the *Nebraska symposium on motivation*'s personality issue (1982), and in Pervin's (1985) review of recent research in personality.

Mischel (1968) argued that if people have traits, as psychologists such as ALLPORT, CATTELL, and EYSENCK have claimed, they must be seen to display consistent behavior in different situations. In other words, if we describe a person as "honest" or "friendly" we imply that he or she is consistently more honest or friendly than average. According to Mischel, however, there is no evidence that such traits of "honesty" or "friendliness" exist. He claimed that the ratings of people's behavior on such traits seldom produced a cross-situational correlation of more than 0.3. Because there is no consistency of the necessary kind he argued that such traits do not exist.

Throughout Mischel's argument there is a degree of fuzziness over the concept of consistency. Someone's behavior is obviously not literally identical in different situations (since that would be somewhat maladaptive). It is therefore possible that even in a well-designed study in which a person's friendliness is rated on the basis of criterion behavior (such as saying "hello" to people met in a corridor, or striking up a conversation with someone with whom one is in a waiting-room), there may be some dispute about the degree to which the types of behavior chosen really are manifestations of the same trait in different contexts. Nevertheless the fact that it might be difficult to *say* whether any particular behavior is relevant to the attribution to someone of a trait, does not weaken Mischel's argument. A more serious failing is his reliance on the study of Hartshorne and May (1928), in which it was found that the honesty of children in one situation (e.g. cheating on a test) bore little relation to their honesty in another (e.g. telling lies). From this evidence Mischel concluded that the children behaved in a way "to suit the situation", and that honesty cannot be regarded as a trait. Even if this were a justified conclusion one could not infer from it that there are no traits at all. However, Mischel's reliance on this study to show that honesty is not a trait is misplaced. The work of Piaget and of Kohlberg on moral development suggests that children do not develop any consistent moral sense until they are in their teens (although this has been challenged). The fact that the Hartshorne and May children did not display consistent moral behavior can therefore not be used as evidence that adults do not do so.

Nevertheless the problem of consistency was taken seriously by other psychologists, and there have been numerous attempts to explore consistencies and inconsistencies of behavior in the years since Mischel's book came out. In 1968 he proposed a simple stimulus-response model of behavior, saying, 'behavior depends on stimulus situations and is specific to the situation'. By 1973, however, Mischel suggested a SOCIAL LEARNING THEORY approach to personality. His claim was that people are not the passive puppets of either inner states or outer stimuli, but are able to organize their behavior 'in the absence of, and sometimes in spite of, immediate external situational pressures'. Behavior was still seen to be 'controlled to a considerable extent by externally administered consequences' and, although people are "self-regulating", the standards to which they adhere are set 'for conduct in a particular situation'. Mischel has therefore predicted that a person's behavior will be consistent over time in the same situation, but that behavior in one situation gives us no grounds to expect similar behavior in a different situation. Latterly (*Journal of personality* 1983), Mischel has strenuously denied the identity of social learning theory and situationism, and has shown himself more sympathetic to those who are interested in stability or predictability of personality. But his conclusions about cross-situational consistency have not altogether changed (see Mischel and Peake 1982).

If Mischel's claims are true, we need an explanation of why people are thought to be consistent when they are actually inconsistent. A possible explanation is that consistency is in the eye of the beholder. Shweder (1977), for example, suggested that belief in consistency might be "magical thinking". To demonstrate this, he used the results of a study by Newcomb (1929), in which retrospective assessments of boys' introversion or extraversion did not tally with the daily descriptions of their behavior. Shweder had a group of students rate the "conceptual similarity" of the twenty-six check-list terms used by Newcomb for both the daily records and the final assessments. He found a high correlation (r = 0.84) between the perceived similarities and the final assessments of Newcomb's raters, while there were smaller negative correlations between both and the daily records. He concluded that the memory of one example of extraversion would lead to the attribution of other extravert characteristics, even though few or none had actually been seen. Shweder and D'Andrade (1979) reviewed seven studies which showed lack of behavioral consistency, but high ratings of consistency which paralleled the similarities of meaning in the descriptions used.

Work in ATTRIBUTION THEORY has also suggested that personality traits might lie in the eye of the beholder. Other people's behavior is frequently explained by reference to their dispositions (although these may be momentary rather than consistent dispositions) rather than to the circumstances in which it occurred. Ross (1977) referred to this tendency as "the fundamental attribution error". He also produced evidence about other errors which people make in judging their own and others' behavior, such as persevering in their assessment of ability even after learning that the evidence on which the assessment was based was wholly worthless. Such perseverance is reminiscent of the "primacy effect" found in IMPRESSION FORMATION, while Shweder's work is reminiscent of earlier ideas about IMPLICIT PERSONALITY THEORY (i.e. beliefs about which characteristics are found together in the same person). It seems likely that we do assume that someone's observed behavior is an expression of his or her personality, that similar behavior may therefore be expected in future, and inferences may reasonably be made about other probable behavior as well. In other words we assume that others have consistent personalities, if only because, as Ichheiser (1943) said, most people we meet are encountered in 'certain stereotyped situations, performing the same stereotyped roles'. In fact, as Kelley and Stahelski (1970) noted, we may overlook the degree to which we ourselves (perhaps consistently) elicit particular behavior from others in our company.

Mischel's criticisms met with various objections. In 1973 Bowers considered the results of eleven studies in which it was possible to look at the impact of personality, the situation, and their interaction on feelings or behavior. Means derived from analyses of variance performed in each study showed that while only 12.71% of the variance could be accounted for by personality, only 10.17% could be accounted for by the situation, 20.77% was accounted for by the interaction of the two. Bowers argued that any form of situationism was circular because the ambiguity involved in the definition of the situation meant that if behavior was the same in two different situations, the situationist would simply take this as evidence that the two were in fact the same situation. If, on the other hand, behavior did differ in two different situations, this would be taken as supportive evidence for the claim that behavior is not cross-situationally consistent. Bowers concluded that behavior is best regarded as determined by an interaction of the situation and the personality.

It is certainly true that some people are made anxious by one situation, some by another. In this sense reactions are determined by both the person and the situation. In most situations not everyone is anxious. Furthermore, a particular person will not be made anxious by every situation. So knowing either what the situation is, or that the person involved has been anxious in other situations need not give a good prediction of how he and she will react. On the other hand, knowing about the person's reactions in previous situations of this kind may allow an accurate prediction. The common sense of this point led to a spate of research on "interactionism", apparently aimed at clarifying the degree to which behavior could be predicted from the person, the situation, and the interaction of the two (see Magnusson and Endler 1977). This pursuit has hardly produced profound discoveries, or even led to greater clarity about the issues involved. On the one hand, the interactionist claim is a truism, as it appears perfectly obvious that different people do behave and react differently in the same context, and that the same person behaves and reacts differently in different contexts. No one presumably thought that this was not so. Eysenck, for instance, explicitly described the interactionist position as a "non-issue" (Pervin 1984). On the other hand, interactions have not been easy to investigate. Researchers have found that person and situation both overshadowed interaction effects, or have concluded that interactions are not replicable or meaningful (see Golding 1975). The work on interactionism would have had greater value if it had produced more conceptual clarity, or more accurate predictions of behavior.

There have of course been those who have denied that people are inconsistent. They have frequently criticized the objective measures (observed behavior) which have been used as criteria, and have argued for the greater realism of interviews and questionnaires. A more powerful argument has been that aggregation over many tests, rather than reliance on one or two, would produce much higher correlations (see Rushton et al. 1983; articles by Block and by Epstein in Magnusson and Endler 1977; and by Epstein in the Nebraska Symposium and the *Journal of personality* mentioned above). Another criticism of the behavioral measures used is that they overlook the degree to which people choose their situations, and may therefore have the opportunity to make their behavior more consistent than it can be in situations which are controlled by the experimenter (see Bowers 1973).

An alternative approach to the issue of consistency was that of Bem and Allen (1974). They conducted a study in which they showed that people who claimed to be consistently conscientious seemed in fact to be so, whereas those who did not claim to have such consistency were not rated as conscientious by parents and peers, or observed to be conscientious on behavioral measures such as neatness and punctuality.

They found a similar but stronger effect in the case of friendliness. Consistency is therefore a "moderator variable", in that for any given trait some people may be consistent and some not. If this were true it would help to explain (especially in conjunction with Ichheiser's point) why people are thought to be consistent, but often turn out not to be.

In Bem and Allen's view a person's consistency in one characteristic would be unrelated to his or her consistency in another. Snyder, on the other hand, suggested the more global moderator variable, self-monitoring (Snyder and Monson 1975). This is sensitivity to social cues and eagerness to fit in with the requirements of any social situation. According to Snyder some people are more highly self-monitoring than others. They therefore display inconsistency across situations, or at least social situations. Those who are not highly self-monitoring tend to be much more consistent in their social behavior. This implies that someone who was consistent in one characteristic should be expected to be consistent in another. However, research on self-monitoring has shown that high self-monitors may in some cases be more consistent than low self-monitors (Lippa 1978), so there is no straightforward consistent/inconsistent distinction. Furthermore, doubt has been cast on the validity of the self-monitoring construct (see SELF-MONITORING). This seems in itself to show that self-monitoring does not currently provide a satisfactory solution to the issue of consistency.

Nevertheless, the idea that some people are consistent and others are not is intuitively appealing, and a number of researchers have followed Bem and Allen's lead. Their studies have often used observation of naturally occurring behavior in a wide variety of contexts, and have therefore overcome some of the objections mentioned above about the artificial experimental control of the situation, and the superior consistency demonstrable from aggregation. Their results reinforce the view that self-monitoring is an inadequate moderator variable, as they suggest that consistency on one trait is unrelated to consistency on another. Kenrick and Stringfield (1980) tried to go further than Bem and Allen by giving subjects the opportunity to say on which of Cattell's sixteen personality traits they were most consistent, and also "how publicly observable" they considered their behavior to be on each trait. They used only self-ratings and ratings by others (parent and peer), and did not include any behavioral measures. Their results were in line with Bem and Allen's, but covered a larger number of traits. The average correlations between own and others' ratings was 0.26 overall, but when they used only the traits which the subjects rated as their most consistent, the correlations were 0.61, while for the self-rated least consistent traits they were 0.16 (own vs. parent's) and 0.12 (own vs. peer's). If the most consistent trait was "publicly observable", the correlations were higher still.

Despite this kind of success, Chaplin and Goldberg (1985) have cast considerable doubt on the moderator variable approach. They used Bem and Allen's traits of friendliness and conscientiousness, as well as six others. They had subjects rate their own consistency in three ways. Two of these had been used by Bem and Allen (a direct question about each trait, and a questionnaire which covered several criterion types of behavior for each trait and asked whether one would act in that way in a particular context). They also used six self-report measures, and the ratings of a larger number of other people than the earlier studies. In addition there were various objective, behavioral measures for each trait. With all this care they managed to draw almost a complete blank. First of all the three consistency measures did not intercorrelate. They pointed out that Bem and Allen never reported the correlation between their two measures, and that one of them (the simple question) worked for friendliness, while the other (the questionnaire) worked for conscientiousness. These findings therefore suggest that "consistency" is not a unitary construct. Using each of their three consistency measures separately, and looking at the mean intercorrelations among the ratings and objective measures for each trait, Chaplin and Goldberg found that the high and low consistency groups did not differ. The only result which directly replicated Bem and Allen's was the significantly greater correlation for the the highly consistent conscientious group defined by Bem and Allen's questionnaire.

Studies in this tradition have done nothing to suggest that there are high correlations between different ratings of people's personality, or between these ratings and (possibly questionable) behavioral measures. It may be that aggregation provides a solution to the problem of consistency, although Chaplin and Goldberg used many measures and did not produce high mean correlations among them. At present the case for consistency does not seem proven, but the problem does not appear to be soluble by recourse to either the Snyder or the Bem and Allen version of the claim that some people are more consistent than others.   RL

Bibliography

Bem, D.J. and Allen, A. 1974: On predicting some of the people some of the time: the search for cross-situational consistencies in behavior. *Psychological review* 81, 506–20.

Bowers, K.S. 1973: Situationism in psychology: an analysis and a critique. *Psychological review* 80, 307–36.

Chaplin, W.F. and Goldberg, L.R. 1985: A failure to replicate the Bem and Allen study of individual consistency in cross-situational consistency. *Journal of personality and social psychology* 47, 1074–90.

Golding, S.L. 1975: Flies in the ointment: methodological problems in the analysis of the percentage of variance due to persons and situations. *Psychological bulletin* 82, 278–88.

Hartshorne, H. and May, M.A. 1928: *Studies in the nature of character*, vol. 1. *Studies in deceit*. New York: Macmillan.

Ichheiser, G. 1943; Misinterpretation of personality in everyday life and the psychologist's frame of reference. *Character and personality* 12, 145–52.

Kelley, H.H. and Stahelski, A.J. 1970: Social interaction basis of cooperators' and competitors' beliefs about others. *Journal of personality and social psychology* 16, 66–91.

Kenrick, D.T. and Stringfield, D.O. 1980:

Personality traits and the eye of the beholder: crossing some philosophical boundaries in the search for consistency in all people. *Psychological review* 87, 88–104.

Lippa, R. 1978: Expressive control, expressive consistency and the correspondence between expressive behavior and personality. *Journal of personality* 46, 438–61.

Magnusson, D. and Endler, N.S. eds. 1977: *Personality at the crossroads: current issues in interactionist psychology*. Hillsdale, N.J.: Erlbaum.

Mischel, W. 1968: *Personality and assessment*. New York and London: Wiley.

——— 1973: Toward a cognitive social learning reconceptualization of personality. *Psychological review* 80, 252–83.

——— and Peake, P.K. 1982: Beyond *déjà vu* in the search for cross-situational consistency. *Psychological review* 89, 730–55.

Newcomb, T.M. 1929: The consistency of certain introvert-extrovert behavior patterns in 51 problem boys. Teachers' College, Columbia: *Contributions to education*, no. 382.

Pervin, L. 1984: *Personality: theory and research*. 4th edn. New York: Wiley.

——— 1985: Personality: current controversies, issues and directions. *Annual review of psychology* 36, 83–114.

Ross, L. 1977: The intuitive psychologist and his shortcomings: distortions in the attribution process. *Advances in experimental social psychology* 10, 173–219.

Rushton, J.P., Brainerd, C.J. and Pressley, M. 1983: Behavioral development and construct validity: the principle of aggregation. *Psychological bulletin* 94, 18–38.

Shweder, R.A. 1977: Likeness and likelihood in everyday thought: magical thinking in judgments about personality. *Current anthropology* 18, 637–58.

——— and D'Andrade, R.G. 1979: Accurate reflection or semantic distortion? A reply to Block, Weiss, and Thorne. *Journal of personality and social psychology* 37, 1075–84.

Snyder, M. and Monson, T.C. 1975: Persons, situations, and the control of social behavior. *Journal of personality and social psychology* 32, 637–44.

personal construct theory In 1955 George A. KELLY proposed a total psychology of the person. He employed the model of the individual as a "scientist", trying to predict and gain control over a personal world. This model has since aroused interest internationally.

Kelly's psychology focuses on how individuals construe events. He suggests that our understanding of and interactions with others are based on "getting inside" their psychological world. He sees people's feelings, thoughts and actions as intimately bound up with their system of constructs. Kelly's theory is therefore not strictly a cognitive one.

All this stems from Kelly's model of the person as a scientist. He argues that it need not only be professionals conducting experiments who are scientists. He suggests it might be useful to look at people "as if" they were all developing theories about events, and deriving hypotheses from those theories which were then put to the test. The more their predictions or anticipations are proved correct, the better control they have over their personal world.

An unusual feature of Kelly's psychology is that behavior becomes the experiment. It is by behaving that people test their conceptions or constructs. If they do not like the answers they get from their behavioral experiments they may change constructs – and then their subsequent behavior.

The philosophical theme of constructive alternativism runs through personal construct theory and its practical applications. Kelly proposes that *one should assume that all present interpretations of the universe are subject to revision or replacement*. There are alternative ways of looking at any event. There is no fact that is "true". There is an objective reality "out there", but no one has direct access to it. All that is possible is to interpret it. This leads to a science that does not concern itself with the accumulation of facts, but with the testing of hypotheses which account best for events as currently understood. At some later date an alternative construction will emerge giving rise to new questions and the search for new answers.

Personal construct theory is formally stated in a fundamental postulate that a person's activities are determined psychologically and controlled by the ways in which he anticipates events. This is then elaborated by eleven corollaries.

This psychology is essentially about individuals in action. There is no need to explain why people act since, as living creatures, they are "forms of motion". What needs explaining is why people do what they do. Motivation is partly built in to the idea that to construe is to anticipate. A construct is a discrimination in which some events are seen as sharing qualities which, in turn, make them different from other events. Construing a person as "friendly" means one predicts certain responses and not others from him, and acts accordingly.

A child's interminable questions about the nature of its environment are attempts to form constructs. By questioning, it eventually determines where similarities in, say, various "floors", lie and what makes them different from pavements or walls. The child now anticipates that, whenever something is construed as a "floor" it will be relatively flat and safe to walk on and, conversely, will *not* suddenly shift to a position above its head.

The construct "floor-not floor" is, of course, a very simple one. But invalidation of those descriptions of the physical world that are taken for granted creates great confusion. This may happen in some forms of interrogation. For instance, invalidation of "time" by alteration of clocks and the day/night ratio, results in great confusion and anxiety.

It is here that Kelly brought emotion into his theoretical system. People experience emotion whenever they are aware that their system of constructs is in a state of change or that their ways of construing the world are inadequate. The person who finds he is unable to anticipate that day regularly follows night and that hours are precisely the same length, will experience anxiety because he will be aware that the events with which he is confronted lie outside the range of convenience of his construct system.

Kelly, who started life as a physicist and mathematician, outlined two techniques to help gain insight into another's personal world. The repertory grid assesses the relationship between constructs. It has been developed in a variety of ways and is particularly widely used in research and the clinic (see Fransella and Bannister 1977). The self-characterization invites people to describe themselves in the third person, as if sketching a character in a play. Both techniques are widely used for personal exploration and in psychotherapy.

It is important to emphasize that the words people use are not necessarily the same as the construct to which they are attached. Indeed, some constructs have no verbal labels at all. Kelly did not feel that the distinction implied in the use of the term unconscious (see FREUD) was sufficiently comprehensive to encompass the complexities of construing. He preferred to use the term "levels of awareness". There is preverbal construing. This refers to those ways in which the young child has come to discriminate between events in its environment but which have no words attached to them. Those not verbalized before adulthood can result in behavior which is inexplicable to the agent himself. If, on meeting strangers, you take an instant dislike to them and 'feel in your guts they are no good', you are probably using a preverbal construct.

Everyone does not experience events in the same way; people differ from each other in the construction of events (Individuality Corollary). However, to the extent that one person employs a construction of experience which is similar to that employed by another, his psychological processes are similar to those of the other person (Commonality Corollary). Here is an example of Kelly's use of the bi-polarity of constructs. Personal construct psychologists typically focus on individual constructions in, say, psychotherapy and on shared constructs when studying cross-cultural differences. Repertory grids can be used in either context.

Merely sharing constructions with another does not guarantee a successful relationship. For that one needs at least to make some effort to see things through the other's eyes. Communication is dependent on the extent to which one person construes the construction processes of another (Sociality Corollary). This is the central point at which social psychology comes into Kelly's theory.

Personal construct theory has been found useful in many areas of psychology, but particularly the clinical field. Kelly felt that the psychotherapeutic setting was where his theory was centrally applicable. Here one individual struggles to step into another's shoes so as to look at the world through the other's eyes. Only in this way is it possible to understand why a person is experiencing problems. Fixed role therapy is an example he gave of how his theory might be applied in a practical context. Here a character sketch is written based on a person's self-characterization. The new character is not the opposite of the existing one, but different in a number of ways. The person is then encouraged to live the life of this person for a specified time. Implicit in fixed role therapy is the idea that people can recreate themselves and have already created the person they currently are.

Personal construct psychology is truly reflexive. It accounts for the psychotherapist's conceptions as much as for the client's. Equally it accounts for Kelly's formulation of his theory as it does for the unique human being that is you or I. The full range of application of personal construct theory is far from being determined. But wherever there are individuals to be understood, whether by psychologists, priests, sociologists, historians or friends, the personal construct model can be, and is being, found useful.   FF

Bibliography

Bannister, D. and Fransella, F. 1986: *Inquiring man.* 3rd edn. Beckenham: Croom Helm.

Fransella, F. and Bannister, D. 1977: *A manual for repertory grid technique.* London and New York: Academic Press.

Kelly, G.A. 1955: *The psychology of personal constructs.* New York: Norton.

Landfield, A.W. and Leitner, L.M. 1980: *Personal construct psychology: psychotherapy and personality.* New York: Wiley.

personality development Personality is defined as those characteristics of an individual which determine the unique adjustment he makes to his environment.

Development begins at birth and continues throughout the lifespan.

Published work on the development of personality deals mainly with children. It is useful to distinguish two main approaches to this area. One emphasizes measurement at the expense of theory. A typical study uses data from assessments of the individual's personality throughout infancy or childhood in an attempt to discover regularities and continuities in development. The other approach deals mainly with the theory of personality development and systematic observation of behavior is less important. FREUD's well-known theory (Freud 1910) of psychosexual development is an excellent example of this type of theory.

Freud believed that instinctual forces, primarily sexual in nature, were the basis of all human behavior. He termed these forces "libido". Libido is sexual in a very broad sense, and during infancy and early childhood libidinal energy is associated with the various orifices of the body. The first stage is associated with the mouth and is known as the *oral* stage. Freud assumed that the extent to which libidinal drives are gratified or frustrated by the environment may lead to *fixation* at that stage. This means that a disproportionate amount of libidinal energy will be invested in a particular bodily zone. Those fixated at the oral stage are expected to develop personalities which make them compulsive eaters, smokers, talkers, etc.

Following the oral stage is the *anal*. Freud assumed that the baby derives pleasure from the process and products of his own excretions and that this pleasure is opposed by those who socialize him. If fixation occurs at this period, Freud expected that the child would develop later problems with relationships to authority and the need for self-control. The third stage is called *phallic*. Here, the child is said to engage in specifically sexual play and to show sexual curiosity. It shades into the final or *genital* stage of early psychosexual development. During this stage, the boy's feelings and fantasies toward his mother (the primary libidinal object from the beginning) assume a specifically sexual

character. (See OEDIPUS COMPLEX.) According to Freud, this is a very important period for children from both sexes because many anxieties and conflicts have to be dealt with. Freud claimed that most of the individual's later patterns of traits and defenses are determined by the particular ways in which the genital conflicts are resolved.

Freud, therefore, saw personality as fully developed or at least determined by about the age of four years. His critics often reject this view and, in addition, point out that he overinterpreted as universal and instinctual certain aspects of human nature which were specific to the time and place in which he worked. Even modern theorists generally sympathetic to his views have almost rejected the emphasis on sexual drives and paid more attention to the social and interpersonal aspects of personality development. Erikson (1963) and Sullivan (1953) are both influential theorists of the psychoanalytic school who constantly stress interpersonal relationships across the individual's lifespan as determining the capacity for other personal adjustment and development. Nevertheless, four characteristics of Freud's theory have persisted and influenced modern work on personality development. Firstly, interaction with a social environment is necessary for each successive stage to unfold. Secondly, adult personality is largely a function of interactions likely to occur within a nuclear family. Thirdly, early personality development often occurs as a resolution of internal conflicts and is likely to be unobservable (and therefore difficult for the behaviorist to "understand"). Fourthly, events in early childhood determine personality to a greater extent than do later events.

Observational studies, as mentioned earlier, lay little stress on theory and seek instead to sample the activities of individuals (usually from birth) with the object of discovering regularities and continuities in personality. There is a limited range of activities engaged in by the newborn but observations have been made of the frequencies of sucking and crying and on the lengths of periods of sleep and wakefulness. (Korner et al. 1981) Such observations are made of the same children at regular intervals. Results suggest that most individuals show an unstable pattern of behavior in early life (0–6 months) and only moderately stable patterns thereafter (Thomas et al. 1963). The extent to which these inconsistencies are due simply to problems of measurement is not clear. There are obviously problems both in sampling individual behavior properly and in relating behavior in infancy to later behavior (Nunally 1973). Despite these problems certain consistencies have been found. Some of the main discoveries are that (a) locomotor activity level is moderately consistent in infancy and childhood and there is a link between high activity and lack of self-control in adulthood (Escalona and Heider 1959); (b) passivity and submissiveness tend to be consistent characteristics (Honzik 1964); (c) dominance is a consistent characteristic during childhood and adolescence (Bronson 1967). Other longitudinal studies (e.g. Kagan 1960) for age periods from infancy to twenty years indicate that individuals tend to have a consistent approach to social situations. At the same time, there are instances in these and other longitudinal studies which show that personality development involves large and abrupt adjustments to the environment. Many personality traits seem not to be fixed in the individual but changeable throughout the life span.

Although it is interesting simply to describe and to assess personality, it is also important to try and specify its origins and the causes of permanence and change. Efforts have been made to determine the extent to which personality characteristics are inherited. Such studies of inheritance have not met with conspicuous success either in identifying the traits most likely to be inherited or the degree to which any such traits are inherited. Research into the personalities of monozygotic and dizygotic twins (e.g. Goldsmith and Gottesman 1981) yield moderate estimates of the heritability of "extraversion", "anxiety", "persistence" and "fearfulness". However, because twin data are used, even these moderate heritabilities are likely to be overestimates. The evidence that personality traits owe little to inheritance probably goes against popular belief. Prenatal experience is another variable which is widely expected to influence personality development. Yet, here again the data are poor and no clear trends can be reported.

The best researched and most fruitful investigations into the causes of individual personality development are concerned with the impact of specific early experiences. Most work here has been done in an attempt to refine the statements of Bowlby (1951) on maternal deprivation in early infancy. In his widely quoted and influential book, Bowlby declared that 'mother love in infancy and childhood is as important for mental health as are vitamins and proteins for physical health'. Bowlby and others offer evidence that a child deprived of proper mothering in the first two years of life will be poorly adjusted psychologically and be unable to develop close affectional ties with others.

Bowlby's body of evidence has been carefully dissected during the past twenty years (Rutter 1981). Bowlby (heavily influenced by Freud) appears to have exaggerated the irreversibility of deprivations in infancy and early childhood. Although infantile experiences are still held to be important, the effects of early deprivations of attachment can be reversed if opportunities for long-term attachments are offered in childhood and adolescence. Furthermore, experiences at all ages can probably have a profound influence on personality development. However, there is a shortage of evidence available on adult personality development and thus it is not yet possible to evaluate this idea fully. Some work which has been done suggests that personality is not fixed from one period to another (see, for example, Neiner and Owens 1982). On the other hand, there are studies which support the idea that there are consistencies over considerable periods (for example, Conley, 1984).

Our grasp of this area is still tentative. Nevertheless, certain basic facts are emerging. These are:

(a) The organization of personality into traits probably takes place after birth:

evidence for the heritability of global and organized characteristics is poor.

(b) Individual differences in personality and its development are strongly influenced by the processes of caretaking and socialization.

(c) Many personality characteristics develop as a result of internal psychological conflicts which are unobservable.

(d) Later socialization experiences, even those in adulthood, can greatly modify earlier trends. Early experience is not as fundamental to the later course of personality development as was once thought.

RMcH

Bibliography

Bowlby, J. 1951: *Maternal care and mental health*. Geneva: World Health Organization.

Bronson, G.W. 1967: Adult derivatives of emotional expressiveness and reactivity control: developmental continuities from childhood to adulthood. *Child development* 38, 801–15.

*Clarke, A.M. and Clarke, A.D.B. 1976: *Early experience: myth and evidence*. London: Open Books.

Conley, J.J. 1984: Longitudinal consistency of adult personality: self-reported psychological characteristics across 45 years. *Journal of personality and social psychology* 47, 1325–33.

*Erikson, E.H. 1963: *Childhood and society*. 2nd edn. New York: Norton.

Escalona, S.K. and Heider, G.M. 1959: *Prediction and outcome*. New York: Basic Books.

Freud, S. 1910: Infantile sexuality. Three contributions to the sexual theory. *Nervous and mental disease monographs*, no. 7.

Goldsmith, H.H. and Gottesman, I.I. 1981: Origins of variation in behavioral style: longitudinal study of temperament in young twins. *Child development* 52, 91–103.

Honzik, M.D. 1964: Personality consistency and change: some comments on papers by Bayley, Macfarlane, Moss, Kagan and Murphy. *Vita humana* 7, 139–42.

Kagan, J. 1960: The long term stability of selected Rorschach responses. *Journal of consultational psychology* 24, 67–73.

Korner, A.F., Hutchinson, C.A., Koperski, J.A., Kraemer, H.C. and Schneider, P.A. 1981: Stability of individual differences of neonatal motor and crying patterns. *Child development* 52, 83–90.

Neiner, A.G. and Owens, W.A. 1982: Relationships between two sets of biodata with 7 years separation. *Journal of applied psychology* 67, 146–50.

Nunally, J.M. 1973: Research strategies and measurement methods for investigating human development. In *Life-span developmental psychology: methodological issues*, eds. J.R. Nesselroade and H.W. Reese. New York: Academic Press.

*Rutter, M. 1981: *Maternal deprivation reassessed*. 2nd edn. Harmondsworth and New York: Penguin.

Sullivan, H.S. 1953: *The interpersonal theory of psychiatry*. New York: Norton.

Thomas, A. et al. 1963: *Behavioral individuality in early childhood*. New York: New York University Press.

personality questionnaires or inventories consist, in the main, of sets of items, usually questions or statements about behavior to which subjects have to answer or state their agreement or disagreement. They are essentially, therefore, self-reports of or introspections about feelings and behavior.

They are widely used as personality tests because they have a number of advantages: it is relatively easy to make them highly reliable and it is simple to standardize them and build up valuable normative data. This makes them useful in applied psychology (educational, industrial and clinical) although there are considerable problems concerning their validity.

Amongst the best known of these tests are the Minnesota Multiphasic Personality Inventory (MMPI); the Cattell 16 Personality Factor Test (16 PF Test); the Eysenck Personality Questionnaire (EPQ), and Jackson's Personality Research Form (PRF).

To understand fully the advantages and disadvantages of personality questionnaires it is necessary to understand how they are constructed. Personality questionnaires fall into two categories from their method of construction. There are criterion-keyed inventories and factor-analytic or item-analytic tests. This is a critical distinction for these two types of test have very different characteristics.

In criterion-keyed tests items are selected if they can discriminate members of a criterion group from controls. The

MMPI is the outstanding example of a test thus constructed. Items were written which seemed relevant to abnormal personality and were administered to different groups of neurotics, psychotics and controls. An item was retained in a scale if it could discriminate the relevant group from the others. For example items in the Manic scale all discriminate manics from controls and the other neurotic groups.

The problem with this type of scale is that such groups may differ on a variety of variables so that the psychological meaning of a set of items which discriminate a group is by no means obvious. This lack of psychological homogeneity makes the interpretation of results of such tests highly dubious.

FACTOR ANALYSIS and the computationally more simple but less elegant item analysis are used to construct tests which will be univariate. It cannot be too strongly emphasized that tests should be unitary. If two factors run through a test, scores are not necessarily comparable. For example, a score of 10 can be made up of 5 and 5, 6 and 4 and so on.

Factor-analytic test construction ensures that each test loads only one factor. Normally this factor should be identified not simply from the nature of the items which is no more than face validity, but by relating the factor to external criteria, by experimental methods or by relating it to other known marker factors. Because the factor analysis of items is beset by technical problems often resulting in low loadings, item analysis (correlating each item with the total score) can be used to select items which can then be factored. Item and factor analyses usually produce virtually identical results.

Of tests constructed by factor analysis the best known and validated are CATTELL's 16 PF test which measures 16 factors; EYSENCK's EPQ which measures 3 factors – extraversion, neuroticism and psychoticism – and the tests of Guilford and Comrey. To some extent these measure different factors and a continuing problem in the field is to reconcile the different findings. Other variables which seem to have considerable psychological import-ance and which are measured by questionnaires are authoritarianism (see AUTHORITARIAN PERSONALITY), sensation seeking and obsessional personality.

A number of problems have proved difficult to overcome in using personality questionnaires, especially in applied psychology. Their validity is often obscured by response sets such as *acquiescence* – agreeing with items regardless of content, and *social desirability* – responding to an item in terms of how desirable the behavior is. In the applied setting conscious distortion becomes a problem and questionnaires are easy to fake.

It is clearly difficult to establish the validity of the kind of variables personality tests measure. One method is to attempt to locate all factored tests in factor space by a common factor analysis. This solves the conundrum that there seem to be as many sets of factors as factorists. Many of the sets align themselves and clearly are similar. Others drop out because they were the product of poor factor-analytic techniques – incomplete rotations, too many or too few factors extracted – as Cattell has argued.

A recent comparison of all factor-analytic personality questionnaires has revealed that reliably only three factors can be found – extraversion, neuroticism or anxiety, and psychoticism. These first two are, of course, found by Cattell at the second-order. Recently these higher-order factors have been broken down into somewhat narrower components, e.g. sociability, impulsivity, but the value of this has yet to be shown. Authoritarianism, the social emanation of obsessionality seems an important factor, but others appear to be of small variance.

In summary personality questionnaires can be reliable and well standardized but are too easy to fake to be highly valuable in many applied settings. The validity of many of these measures has not been demon-strated, but Eysenck's EPQ would appear to measure broad, higher-order factors with some validity. Of the others, the Cattell 16 PF test is probably still the best despite the fact that not all the factors emerge as clearly as they should (see Walsh 1978). PK

Bibliography

Cattell, R.B. 1973: *Personality and mood by questionnaire*. New York: Jossey-Bass.

Kline, P. 1970: *Psychometrics and psychology*. London: Academic Press.

—— 1983: *Personality measurement and theory*. Hutchinson: London.

—— and Barrett, P. 1983: The factors in personality questionnaires among normal subjects. *Advances in behavior research and therapy* 5 (3/4), 141–202.

Nunnally, J.O. 1977: *Psychometric theory*. New York: McGraw-Hill.

*Vernon, P.E. 1963: *Personality assessment*. London: Methuen.

Walsh, J.A. 1978: Review of the 16 PF test. In *The eighth mental measurements yearbook*, ed. O.K. Buros. Highland Park, N.J.: Gryphon.

personality research: methodology

Personality research is the study of common characteristics which distinguish between people, or of the structure of a person's thoughts, feelings and behavior. The methods of inquiry must meet the criteria of reliability and validity (see TESTS, RELIABILITY; TESTS, VALIDITY).

The information gathering methods in personality research include naturalistic observation; content analysis; interview; questionnaires; personality tests, including the assessment of the biopsychological system; and the experimental method. Since human subjects are involved in the research, ethical and moral considerations involving the rights, safety and comfort of the potential subjects must be scrutinized (see American Psychological Association, Committee on Ethical Standards in Psychological Research 1973).

Systematic observation in everyday settings is particularly useful in the exploratory phase of inquiry. Darwin (1859) devoted five years to the careful, detailed field observations of thousands of plants and animals during the preparation of *The origin of species*. Piaget (1926) studied his own children. Modern ethologists attempt to follow Darwin's lead (see ETHOLOGY). Another approach is participant observation (see GOFFMAN) in which the observer becomes part of a group and observes the other members. There is a good deal of observational work on children (Blurton-Jones 1972), but this and the participant work is not typically aimed at elucidating individual differences, since the observations are made in a limited number of contexts (and sometimes with a very small sample). It is therefore the characteristics of contexts or types of interaction which are brought into focus (Goffman 1967).

Clinical observation is also regarded by some as a similar activity. FREUD, who was greatly influenced by Darwin, spent years observing a wide range of behavior, dreams, fantasies, physical illnesses and emotional difficulties which led to insights into individual behavior and provided clues to the structure and function of personality in general. Often, however, the clinician believes that he can understand the individual without reference to more general laws of human behavior and without attempting to test or establish such laws. The approach is therefore "idiographic" rather than "nomothetic" (see INDIVIDUAL PSYCHOLOGY).

Observations in natural settings do not distort life as laboratory observation may and do not require the subject to have descriptive skills or even assume that he or she is willing to respond. It is clear, however, that even in non-directive therapy (see ROGERS), therapists do not merely observe. They prompt the client. In addition, their tone of voice and other non-verbal communication will tend differentially to reinforce, and hence shape the client's responses (see SOCIAL INTERACTION; also Argyle 1983). Furthermore Frank (1971) claims that the rationale offered to the client to explain his or her problem is an important factor in therapy, regardless of the actual content of that rationale. For clinical success, therefore, the therapist must guide the client and interpret what is said. Clinical interviews cannot therefore be seen as straightforward observations.

The observational approach itself cannot control irrelevant variables or use precise measures. Precision can be improved, however, through the use of trained, reliable observers, unbiased recording techniques (e.g. Bales 1950), the development of coding techniques which focus on critical behavior, and sampling behavior across time.

Content analysis involves categorizing behavior, specifically oral and written communications, including conversations, speeches, diaries, photograph albums, recorded fantasies and even archival materials such as census reports and crime statistics. As in naturalistic observations, the subjects need not be aware of the analysis. For example, Winter (1976) analyzed the announcements and speeches of several 1976 presidential candidates for various components of motivation such as achievement, affiliation and need for power. The procedure involves the selection of the material to be analyzed, the type of communication whose content is to be analyzed, selecting the unit of analysis such as word, sentence, or paragraph, categorizing the units of analysis such as the use of "I" or "we" as indicating self as opposed to other orientations and finally summarizing the information through quantification such as the relative length of speeches of political candidates. There is now a substantial literature in this area, some quantitative and some qualitative (e.g. Howe 1982; Simonton 1981; see also ARCHIVAL METHOD; PSYCHOHISTORY.)

Interviews and questionnaries involve systematically asking people about themselves. Interviews are probably most useful when we are interested in learning about someone's thoughts, feelings and goals. The process consists of the following steps: (1) formulating objectives; (2) deciding on a format, developing questions; (3) conducting pilot tests with preliminary instruments, and (4) revising and refining the instruments. The process may also involve the use of non-verbal responses such as asking the subject to take a set of photographs which reveal something about him or her (Ziller 1981) followed by open-ended questions about the meaning of the photographs and a content analysis of them. A major concern of the interview approach is avoiding bias through the nature of the questions.

Questionnaires, when administered anonymously, can evoke a greater degree of honesty than the face-to-face interview, though responses may be colored by the respondents' attempt to present themselves favorably and are subject to error of response sets such as stylistic tendencies to agree or disagree regardless of the nature of the question (see QUESTIONNAIRES). They may be open-ended or closed. For example, an open-ended question may ask 'What does the "good life" mean to you?' A closed questionnaire presents a series of alternative responses from which the respondent selects, as in the Rotter LOCUS OF CONTROL questionnaire (Rotter 1966), which requires a choice between two alternative statements, or the EYSENCK Personality Questionnaire (Eysenck and Eysenck 1975), in which the respondent answers questions by marking either "Yes" or "No".

The investigator often sets out to demonstrate a relationship between variables, either to try to find possible causes of individual differences, or to assess how one such difference may be the result of another. For example, a relationship between a child's self-esteem as measured by a personality test may be related to reading achievement or the way his parents treat him (Coopersmith 1967). Instruments designed to measure facets of personality are involved in most personality research. These may include biopsychological assessment, behavioral approaches to assessment, and objective and projective techniques.

Biopsychological assessment concerns the relation of bodily characteristics to personality. How do our daily cycles of bodily functioning affect our behavior; what are the effects of drugs on behavior; how is behavior related to the dominance of the left or right brain hemisphere? In investigating these areas the researcher has recourse to a vast array of equipment and techniques such as the electroencephalograph (EEG) which records "brain wave" rhythms or the polygraph, popularly known as the "lie detector" which along with measures of changes in the GALVANIC SKIN RESPONSE, respiration, blood pressure and heart rate may be used to study reactions to stress (see e.g. Eysenck 1967; Eysenck and Eysenck 1985).

In the behavioral approaches to assessment, observers record a person's behavior. For example, interactions within the family of a delinquent child are recorded with a specific emphasis on aversive statements or negative remarks directed at the child. Observations are made over a one-month period to establish the "baseline" of behavior which is to be changed in order to facilitate an atmosphere conducive to personal growth and development (see e.g. Wahler 1980).

In objective tests of personality which are often carried out in laboratory experiments 'the subject does not know on what aspect of his behavior he is really being evaluated' (Cattell 1965). CATTELL has used over 400 varieties of such tests, while Eysenck has investigated differences between extraverts and introverts in learning, perception and fatigue on motor tasks (Eysenck 1967). There are other perceptual tests, such as picture completion tasks or the rod-and-frame test (see FIELD DEPENDENCE; Witkin 1967). Scores on such tests, or batteries of them, are claimed to correlate with personality traits or factors as measured by other means.

Projective tests are more disguised and ambiguous procedures using a wide variety of stimuli and evoking a variety of responses. The technique derives from psychoanalytic theory and requires the interpreter to view the results as a sign of underlying personality dynamics. The Rorschach has been the most widely used projective technique (see Exner 1974). It requires the subject to describe various ink blots in terms of what he or she sees. Its validity has not been established.

Doubts exist about all the techniques mentioned, and all provide their own problems, although clearly a battery of different kinds may eliminate some of the difficulties peculiar to individual tests (see Bray 1982; Eysenck and Eysenck 1985). (See also INDIVIDUAL PSYCHOLOGY: METHODOLOGY; PERSON/SITUATION CONTROVERSY; PERSONALITY QUESTIONNAIRE; TRAITS; TYPE.)

RCZ

Bibliography

Argyle, M. 1983: The psychology of interpersonal behavior. 4th edn. Harmondsworth: Penguin.

Bales, R.F. 1950: *Interaction process analysis.* Cambridge, Mass.: Addison-Wesley.

Blurton-Jones, N. ed. 1972: *Ethological studies of child behavior.* Cambridge and New York: Cambridge University Press.

Bray, D.W. 1982: The assessment center and the study of lives. *American psychologist* 37, 180–9.

Cattell, R.B. 1965: *The scientific analysis of personality.* Harmondsworth: Penguin.

Coopersmith, S. 1967: *The antecedents of self-esteem.* San Francisco: Freeman.

Darwin, C. 1859 (1936): *The origin of species.* New York: Random House.

Exner, J.E. 1974: *The Rorschach: a comprehensive system.* New York: Wiley.

Eysenck, H.J. 1967: *The biological basis of personality.* Springfield, Ill.: Thomas.

—— and Eysenck, S.B.G. 1975: *Manual for the Eysenck personality questionnaire.* London: Hodder and Stoughton.

—— and Eysenck, M.W. 1985: *Personality and individual differences.* New York: Plenum.

Frank, J.D. 1971: Therapeutic factors in psychotherapy. *American journal of psychotherapy* 25, 350–61.

Goffman, E. 1967: *Interaction ritual.* New York: Doubleday; Harmondsworth: Penguin.

Howe, M.J.A. 1982: Biographical evidence and the development of outstanding individuals. *American psychologist* 37, 1071–81.

Piaget, J. 1923 (1926): *Language and thought of the child.* London: Routledge and Kegan Paul; New York: Harcourt, Brace.

Rotter, J. 1966: Generalized expectancies for internal versus external control of reinforcement. *Psychological monograph* 80, no. 1.

Simonton, D.K. 1981: The library laboratory: archival data in personality and social psychology. *Review of personality and social psychology* 2, 217–43.

Wahler, R.G. 1980: Behavior modification: application to childhood problems. In *Emotional disorders in children and adolescents,* eds. P. Sholevar, R.M. Benson and B.J. Blinder. Lancaster: M.T.P.; New York: Spectrum.

Winter, D.G. 1976: What makes the candidates run? *Psychology today* 10.

Witkin, H.A. 1967: Cognitive studies across cultures. *International journal of psychology* 2(4).

Ziller, R.C. 1981: Self, social, environmental orientation through auto-photography. *Personality and social psychology bulletin* 7, 338–43.

personality theory, psychoanalytical There are two main strands to personality theory in the Freudian tradition, and the relation between them still poses problems. One is a "dynamic" theory of an instinctual drive whose satisfaction or frustration at different stages of a child's development gives rise to particular TRAITS or DISPOSITIONS; the other is a "structural" description of how various mental functions are organized and interact.

(1) Personality is shaped by the way in which a person deals with instinctual drives, and with the anxieties associated with them. This part of the theory is about the form taken by those drives (known as "libido") and by the anxiety produced when libido is blocked, and about the defense mechanisms used by the ego to reduce psychic tension and preserve a balance of forces consistent with adaptive action. Libido is satisfied or discharged mainly through bodily pleasure associated with the meeting of biological needs; it is therefore "sexual" in Freud's revised technical sense of 'obtaining pleasure from zones of the body' (1938, *Standard edition*, p.152). But since successful ego-functioning is necessary for some pleasures to be possible, such as self-preservation and self-esteem, the ego must have its own instinctual energy which is known as "narcissistic libido" (see NARCISSISM). The process by which an instinct latches onto an appropriate object, whether material or psychological, as a medium for its discharge, is "cathexis"; so that a person, place, activity etc. which has become a source of pleasure is said to have been "cathected" or invested with libido. Obstruction of cathexis, and hence of libidinal discharge, produces tension which is experienced as anxiety, unless the libido can be "displaced" onto a substitute object serving the same purpose. Displacement onto abstract, intellectual or cultural-aesthetic objects is called SUBLIMATION.

In the course of normal psychological development, libido is concentrated successively on different zones of the body, and its satisfaction or frustration at each stage is accompanied by particular emotional reactions. (See PERSONALITY DEVELOPMENT.) Those that are particularly intense or preponderant become consolidated as habitual dispositions. Too much of either satisfaction or frustration at a particular stage may lead to libido becoming "fixated" there, so that personality is dominated by the traits associated with that level and psychosexual maturity is not achieved. The young baby's emotional gratification centers on oral activities such as sucking, swallowing, spitting and biting. The first two of these responses mediate pleasure, acceptance, security and affection, and are conducive to an attitude of "basic trust" (Erikson 1963, ch.7): the latter two express rejection, hurtfulness and destructiveness, characteristic of "basic mistrust". The question whether traits allegedly arising from oral satisfaction (e.g. optimism, generosity, tolerance) do cluster together, and separately from those attributed to oral frustration (e.g. jealousy, impatience, hostility), has been statistically analyzed by Kline and Storey who demonstrated two separate factors, "oral optimism" and "oral pessimism", closely resembling Erikson's trust and mistrust above (Kline 1981, pp.41–6).

At the time of toilet-training, libido is focused on the anal zone and its processes, and this is when the infant 'is first obliged to exchange pleasure for social respectability' (Freud 1917, *Standard edition* vol. 16, p.315). Tension-reduction must be confined to approved times and places; and this learning of impulse-control is a seed of ego-development. The issues are retention-release, giving-withholding, mess-cleanliness, obstinacy-flexibility, approval-shame. The significant grouping of associated traits known as the anal triad (orderliness, meanness and obstinacy – Freud 1905, *Standard edition* vol. 7) has also been confirmed statistically (Kline 1981, ch.3).

From about the fourth year, the phallic part of the genitalia, i.e. penis or clitoris, becomes the focal zone, representing for the child physical prowess, competence and worth (or their apparent absence). Necessarily the theory diverges for the sexes, and it also asserts that the child's feelings about parents are now intensified in the OEDIPUS AND ELEKTRA COMPLEXES whose dominant anxieties are castration-fear and penis-envy. Associated phallic personality features are recklessness, self-confidence and courage, but these have not been validated in the way oral and anal traits have. But the existence of a latency period, between the Oedipal stage and pre-puberty, in which sexual and aggressive fantasies are relatively dormant, has been given some support by Friedman (Kline 1981, p.134).

The final genital phase is characterized by a move away from mere self-satisfaction toward a pleasure-giving relationship with an opposite-sex partner, with the aim of reproduction. Psychological correlates are group activities, social awareness and constructive and protective schemes. The relative security and dominance of this stage in the mature personality depends upon how much libido has been shed at the pregenital stages, like troops left behind to fortify precarious positions (in Freud's own simile, 1917, *Standard edition* vol. 16, p.341). The stage at which the strongest force was left is that to which a person most readily "regresses" under stress (see DEFENSE MECHANISMS).

(2) From the structural point of view (Freud 1923, *Standard edition* vol. 19), the mental apparatus is seen as made up of three main systems: id, ego and superego. The concept of an ID (*das Es*) was borrowed immediately from Groddeck (1923), but has a longer history as a murky, mysterious and sinister realm of the mind. For Freud it is specifically the reservoir of biological instincts and primitive emotions which press non-rationally for gratification according to the pleasure-principle. It forms a major part of the UNCONSCIOUS MIND. The EGO, by contrast is rational and realistic, and has developed out of the id as the young child learns to delay and adapt his demands in the light of physical and social realities (chewing before swallowing, waiting for the potty before defecating). It is the ego that checks whether and how

satisfaction of a particular wish, fantasy or impulse would be consistent with reality-constraints ("reality-testing"), and to do this it is equipped with "perceptual-consciousness". Freud had realized, some thirty years before Pavlov, that early reality-learning is achieved especially through auditory verbal conditioning and therefore gave the ego a "hearing-cap" (i.e. an auditory lobe) in his notorious diagram (1923, *Standard edition* vol. 19, p.24). The extent to which a person can "keep his head" and regulate his actions adaptively on the basis of perception, learning and memory, even when under emotional pressure, is consequently called "ego strength" and has been independently confirmed as a valid personality trait by CATTELL (1965, pp.71–5).

Behavior is checked and steered not only by reality factors but also by evaluative considerations as to what actions, thoughts, feelings etc. are good, bad, right and wrong. This is the work of the SUPEREGO. A process fundamental to the formation of both ego and superego is IDENTIFICATION. In "primary identification", which pre-dates the ego developmentally, the neonate does not distinguish perceptions of himself from perceptions of the mother, and in that sense is identified with her. But "secondary identification", which presupposes individuation and a sense of separate objects, refers to building into one's own personality, for some emotional reason, the perceived characteristics of another. In "goal-oriented" identification, it is done in order to gain for oneself the pleasure that the other has from that characteristic; it has something in common with "projective identification" in Kleinian theory (Segal 1979). Thus a person might dress or talk in the same way as another who is perceived as happier, cleverer, more attractive, stronger etc.

(3) Personality is also described in psychoanalysis by reference to clinical conditions whose features or dynamics a personality shows on a small scale without being clinically disturbed (because those dynamics are under "ego-control"). An obsessional personality takes pleasure in (i.e. has "cathected") precision, order-

liness, rules, regularity, cleanliness, safety, punctuality etc., and is irritated by their absence. But that person's general psychological functioning is not disrupted by washing-rituals or by catastrophic anxiety about untidiness, as in an obsessional illness. The same goes for "depressive", "hysterical', "paranoid" and "schizoid" personality (see also CONSTITUTIONAL PSYCHOLOGY).

Non-orthodox followers in the broad Freudian tradition have gone in two contrasted directions: whereas the Kleinians have placed even greater emphasis on very early sexual-aggressive phantasies in infants, the NEO-FREUDIANS have held that Freud exaggerated the part played by early instinctual factors in personality development, and have given more weight to the ego's role both in shaping personality through later social learning and in overcoming emotional problems in therapy.

As a result of applying psychoanalytic principles to the therapeutic interpretation of young children's play, Melanie Klein produced an account of personality development in which emotional OBJECT-RELATIONS, and especially unconscious phantasies about them, are crucially formative from the earliest months (Segal 1979). The infant conceives of the source of pleasurable experiences as separate from that of unpleasant ones, and therefore constructs in phantasy a good and a bad object. He loves and takes in (incorporates) emotionally the "good" object, but rejects and attacks the "bad" one; he also fears that the one he hates and attacks will attack him back. Here we have the basis of "schizoid" (splitting) and "paranoid" dynamics, and the infant is in the "paranoid-schizoid position". But half-way through the first year, the baby realizes that the objects of his love and hate are not two but one and the same, so that he is after all attacking and destroying the one he loves. Guilt and the "depressive position" set in. From this he emerges only by recognizing that he can make up for the hurt he is causing the loved object by acts of "reparation" such as cooperating with toileting. In this view, personality is determined by the quality of

these object-relations, and by the anxieties and phantasies they arouse, and personality structure is understood as an "inner world" of internalized objects whose qualities and relationships a person tends to "project" more or less appropriately onto the outside world in which he lives.

(4) Two contemporaries of Freud whose personality theories also diverged from his were Carl JUNG and Alfred Adler (see NEO-FREUDIAN THEORY). Both rejected Freud's picture of childhood sexuality, but Jung retained the notion of libido as a general psychological life-force while Adler substituted a kind of will-to-power as the basic motivating drive.

Jung elaborated the theory that there are two constitutionally determined "psychological types": introvert and extravert. In the former, the libido is mainly turned inward upon the person's thoughts, feelings, plans, imagination; in the latter, it is turned outward via perception to the material world and other people (Jung 1921). There are, therefore, in the manifest personality (known as the personal) two sets of traits which characterize the two types in descriptive behavioral terms. (See JUNG.) The introvert tends to be reflective, cautious, solitary, emotionally reserved and controlled, while the extravert is more active, emotionally spontaneous, confident and impulsive. The validity of the behavioral distinction is experimentally endorsed by EYSENCK (1967). For Jung, as for Freud, the libido passes through maturational stages in childhood; however such stages are concerned with feelings about growth and are given much less importance. There is also a "dark" side of the personality, known as the "shadow", which inhabits the "personal unconscious" and consists of uncivilized wishes, feelings and images rejected from the persona. At a still deeper level there is an unconscious counterpart to a person's dominant sexual identity: for a man the "anima", for a woman the "animus". Apart from the difference of "types", personality differences depend upon which of the four "functions" – thought, feeling, intuition and sensation – a person uses predominantly to relate adaptively to the world.

Since for Adler the basic motivating drive is a wish to be powerful, dominant and superior to others, it follows that the fundamental source of anxiety is feelings of inferiority; and that characteristics of personality are formed by situations and perceptions which induce such feelings, and by the defense mechanisms used to combat them. Reality-factors which induce anxiety will therefore include actual physical limitations, such as poor eyesight, speech-defect, conspicuous nose, short stature, and these are said to give rise to "organ-inferiority". Intellectual, social and emotional inadequacies (as well, of course, as imagined limitations) can similarly become the focus of inferiority-feelings. A person may give in to these feelings by becoming over-dependent and a "chronic complainer", or he may compensate by striving to demonstrate power in other areas.

Everybody experiences as a child the reality of being inferior, both physically and psychologically, so the structure of the "family-constellation" is a fundamental determinant of personality. The eldest child, for example, although for a while physically and mentally superior to his or her siblings, is inferior to the parents and will have had the unsettling experience of being "dethroned" from exclusive possession of the parents by the next-born. This tends to encourage early identification with adults, and (in theory) a mature, conservative, independent personality. The last-born is inferior on all sides, and is therefore the most likely candidate for a "chronic complainer" or for intense, potency-demonstrating compensation. A typical youngest-male fantasy is that one day he will have the rest of the family at his mercy, so that they are dependent upon him. For Adler the biblical story of Joseph and the many-colored coat is an example of just such a fantasy having passed into legend (Adler 1928, chs.5 and 8). Much subsequent empirical research has confirmed the influence of birth-rank and family-size, but the latter is perhaps more important than the former; and, although Adler seems to have been right about the conservatism and caution of first-borns in relevant cultures, he was wrong about their emotional independence (Schachter 1957; Grinder 1978, pp. 259–63). NMC

Bibliography

Adler, A. 1928: *Understanding human nature*. Trans. W.B. Wolfe. London: Allen and Unwin.

*Brown, J.A.C. 1961: *Freud and the post-Freudians*. Harmondsworth: Penguin.

Cattell, R.B. 1965: *The scientific analysis of personality*. Harmondsworth: Penguin.

Erikson, E.H. 1963: *Childhood and society*. 2nd edn. Harmondsworth: Penguin.

Eysenck, H.J. 1967: *The biological basis of personality*. Springfield, Ill.: Thomas.

Freud, S. 1895–1938: *Standard edition of the complete psychological works of Sigmund Freud*. 24 vols. London: Hogarth Press; New York: Norton.

Grinder, R.E. 1975: *Adolescence*. 2nd edn. New York: Wiley.

Groddeck, G.W. 1923 (1949): *The book of the Id*. Trans. V.M.E. Collins. London: Vision Press.

Jung, C.G. 1921 (1971): *Psychological types*. Trans. H.G. Baynes. London: Routledge and Kegan Paul.

Kline, P. 1981: *Fact and fantasy in Freudian theory*. 2nd edn. London and New York: Methuen.

Schachter, S. 1957: *The psychology of affiliation*. London: Tavistock.

Segal, H. 1979: *Klein*. London: Fontana.

*Storr, A. 1960: *Integrity of the personality*. London: Heinemann.

personality theory and astrology
Astrology provided some of the earliest personality theories, with origins dating back to pre-historic times. Today we have an abundance of overlapping and even contradictory theories which link the positions of the sun, moon and planets at the moment of our birth with character development and destiny. With regard to the signs of the zodiac, the first positive demonstration that there might be some truth in the claimed link between the cosmos and life on earth came using a conventional personality questionnaire. With a sample of over 2,000 people, it was found that outgoing extraverted types tended to be born during the odd-

numbered signs (such as Aries) while reserved introverted types tended to be born during the even-numbered signs (such as Taurus). This finding was consistent with the astrological personality descriptions laid down by ancient Greek astrologers. Subsequent research, however, has indicated that the results were due to a self-fulfilling prophecy. People answering a questionnaire tend to be influenced by their knowledge of astrology; a person born during Aries is more likely to endorse such questions as, "Are you bold and energetic?" if he happens to know that these attributes are traditionally associated with Aries. The hypothesized link between signs of the zodiac and personality is not apparent when research subjects are carefully screened for knowledge of astrology. Other claims of astrology have been investigated by numerous researchers, the most noteworthy being Geoffrey Dean, and almost without exception the claims are found to be false or, at best, not proven.

The strongest support for astrology has emerged from the work of the French psychologist, Michel Gauquelin, who discovered that many eminent people had been born when one of the major planets was just above the horizon or just past the point of upper culmination. For famous actors it was Jupiter, for celebrated scientists Saturn, and for international sportsmen Mars. The sports finding has been the subject of independent research. For each group studied, and there are now five sets of samples ranging from 100 to 1,500 sportsmen, the results are similar. The combined probability that such a pattern is due to chance is many millions to one against. Research has also revealed that it is eminent people with personalities typical of their profession who are most likely to have been born "under" the astrologically appropriate planet. Independent ratings of personality descriptions taken from their biographies show that those with predominantly extraverted traits tend to be born "under" Mars or Jupiter while introverted types tend to be born "under" Saturn. In general, these findings are consistent with ancient Greek astrology: Mars as the god of war is associated with bold and assertive traits, Jupiter with joviality and Saturn with a saturnine temperament.

The evidence for this obtained link between planetary positions at the moment of birth and personality has been rigorously checked and evaluated, so far without any flaws being detected. The findings cannot be explained in terms of knowledge of astrology and self-fulfilling prophecies since very few people know the positions of the planets at the moment they were born. We are left with evidence of planetary effects, for which chance is a highly unlikely explanation, and for which there is no known physical or causal mechanism. As in the case of extra-sensory perception, psychokinesis and other apparently demonstrable para-normal phenomena, the effects are at present outside the realm of scientific possibility.   DKBN

Bibliography

Dean, G.A. et al. 1977: *Recent advances in natal astrology*. UK: Recent Advances, 36 Tweedy Road, Bromley, Kent; USA: Para Research, Rockport, Mass.

Eysenck, H.J. and Nias, D.K.B. 1982: *Astrology: science or superstition?* London: Temple Smith; New York: St Martin's Press.

personology Authors such as Korchin (1976) use the word "personology" to refer to the study of the internal structuring and the psychodynamic patterns of the individual. In this way personology can be roughly delimited from the vast and ill-defined field of differential studies focused on variables of personality in populations of subjects. However, it would be completely inappropriate to restrict the field of personology to the internal organization of the person at a given time. The person in which personology is interested is situated in a life-world of its own in which it acts and relates to other persons who recognize each other as such. Besides, it possesses a history which is always in the making so that at any moment of its life it appears as the joint product of its history and of its projects. Besides personology does not address an immutable entity rooted in an unchangeable human nature. Indeed, the study of historically determined forms of personal individuality as they can be found in various past and present-day socioeconomic conditions with their particular cultures and ideologies also belongs to the field of personology.

At the present day, personology is a little-practiced discipline, and whatever personological researches are being performed are difficult to summarize because the kind of data used and the theoretical and methodological orientations are so divergent as to suggest a state of complete disarray. The most useful overview of personology that can be given can only consist of an enumeration of its most pressing tasks.

Among these the first concerns the conceptual analysis of personhood and the logical as well as genetical reconstruction of the kind of structured and functional whole a person is conceived to be. It is indeed too often forgotten that definitions of personality, abundant as they are, far from replacing, in fact presuppose a definition of the notion of person, i.e. of personhood. Even if the formulation of the necessary and sufficient attributes of personhood may seem too ambitious a task, mention of some necessary conditions can help to dispel current confusion on this subject.

Consciousness with its basic characteristic of intentionality (Searle 1983) is a first candidate without which the whole realm of the self is inconceivable. Next comes "personification" as the process which, proceeding through the successive stages of initially non-reciprocal and ultimately reciprocal attributions of intentionality issues in the social construction of the person. Rule-governed and value-oriented activities with their alternatively corresponding and antagonistic technical-instrumental and social-interactional processes are another basic aspect of personhood which find their expression in dramaturgically staged ROLES and SELF-PRESENTATIONS, and in RELATIONSHIPS regulated by principles of SOCIAL EXCHANGE. Personhood also implies the production

and communication of meanings not only through linguistic means but also on the level of action. One of the most potent meaning-structures associated with personhood is represented by an individual's more or less coherent IDEOLOGY on which his basic accounting schemes are founded.

Consideration of structural aspects is also relevant to the definition of personhood. The various degrees of unity which a person is capable of manifesting is a first question that must be dealt with. Identity, directly experienced as well as socially defined is another basic category of personhood. Much less conspicuous but nonetheless important is the notion of the delimitation of the person, i.e. of its boundaries which do not necessarily coincide with those of the body. Unity, identity and delimitation of the person are not fixed once and for all. They are achieved through successive constructions and reconstructions imposed by the fact that in any situation at any time, it is never the whole person which is involved, although a person's unity and identity, as well as the outline of its boundaries constitute basic characteristics pertaining to it as a whole. Consequently, changes instigated by internal organic causes or originating in situational requirements will inevitably lead to successive readjustments in the structure of the person.

The analysis of personhood is not the only task of personology. Besides knowing what persons are and how they can be distinguished from non-persons, a question which has scarcely been asked must be answered: Why do persons exist? In other words, what are the relationships between the development of persons and the functions they fulfill? Answers to this question can be found in authors as widely divergent in their ideological commitments as Gehlen (1940) and Galperin (1980). The atrophy of instinctive mechanisms, the extraordinarily high degree of cephalization, the slowness of development through maturation and learning and the length of life following the reproductive phase are closely related aspects of the biological constitution of human beings which make it both possible and necessary for them to become part of a process of self-domestication through early, intensive and extensive forms of SOCIALIZATION. Thereby new action-structures emerge, the most crucial of which is work which enables man to produce his means of subsistence. Within this context of new competences – including language – which for their performance require an ensemble of social relationships, action patterns no longer depend on configurations of stimuli triggering off innate behavior-mechanisms sensitized by varying internal states. Needs and situations are now mediated by cognitive processes, activities and their affective regulations whose coordination and organization within the network of existing social relations constitute the functional foundation of personhood. In other words, according to this view, the person is the socially structured organization which, in the course of anthropogenesis, substitutes itself for the innate organization of instinctive mechanisms.

The person is so closely bound up with social relationships that it cannot possibly be reduced to either a superstructural or infrastructural component of social structure. In fact, to use Sève's happy expression (1975), it can best be described as manifesting a "juxtastructural" articulation with the basic components of social structure. Within the framework of historical materialism this means that the basic attributes of personhood entering into the construction of the person are technical-instrumental activities (belonging to productive forces), social-interactional and interpersonal relationships (corresponding to social relations of production) and the interpretation and justification of the latter under a form of *Weltanschauung* (derived from the ideological superstructure).

The emergence of a developed person through a series of reorganizations imposed on the structure of its social relations and its world-view by the latter's growing technical-instrumental competencies, is made possible by the peculiarities of human ontogeny and the resulting duration of the human life-span as it unfolds in a historically determined socioeconomic formation. This means that at any moment a person can be understood only as the product of its biography and that, considering the totality of its temporal extension, it is identical with it.

As Conrad (1963) has shown, linking the development of personality to the highly specific characteristics of human ontogeny also offers the possibility of explaining the origin of individual differences in certain mental and physical traits as resulting from differential growth patterns. Thus, he was able to derive a corrected version of Kretschmer's typology from the duality of a conservative and a progressive growth tendency each of which favors the body proportions proper to different developmental stages. (See TYPE.)   J-PDeW

Bibliography

Conrad, K. 1963: *Der Konstitution typus*. Berlin: Springer.

Galperin, P.J. 1980: *Zu Grundfragen der Psychologie*. Pahl-Rugenstein.

Gehlen, A. 1940 (1950): *Der Mensch*. Bonn: Athenäum Verlag.

Korchin, S. 1976: *Modern clinical psychology*. New York: Basic Books.

Searle, J.R. 1983: *Intentionality: essays on the philosophy of mind*. Cambridge and New York: Cambridge University Press.

Sève, L. 1975: *Marxisme et théorie de la personalité*. 4th edn. Paris: Editions Sociales.

phenomenology: in philosophy

The word phenomenology came into use in philosophy with the publication in 1807 of Hegel's *Phenomenology of the spirit*. This was an introduction to his vast metaphysical system, designed to trace the evolution of consciousness as the recipient of phenomena or appearances, from the simplest to the most complex form.

Phenomenology did not become a kind of philosophy in its own right, however, until the works of Edmund Husserl (1859–1938). Husserl acknowledged great debts to Franz Brentano (1838–1917) whose course of lectures on Descriptive Psychology, delivered in Vienna in 1888, had "Phenomenology" as its alternative title. Brentano distinguished between introspection, deliberate self-examination which was subject to error, and inner perception, the direct awareness of our own psychic phenomena – an awareness which he claimed accompanied all experience and was infallible. The fundamental function of consciousness was to represent. Judging and feeling emotions were both dependent on representation. Consciousness must be consciousness of something. This function he called Intentionality. Phenomenological philosophy was dependent on the description of the objects of consciousness as they appeared, that is, as representations.

According to Husserl, then, philosophy was concerned with the description of pure phenomena, with the experiences, regardless of whether they referred to concretely existing objects, to fictions, or to themselves. Purity was ensured by the deliberate refusal of the philosopher to make any assertion of existence about any of the phenomena in question. To pursue this course the philosopher had to undertake a "reduction" (epoche). He had to put aside (in brackets) all that is known, or normally assumed, about the objects of perception or thought in order to analyze them as appearing in experience.

In addition to being the bearer of experience, in Husserl's theory consciousness also had a creative role. Our consciousness constructs the objects of our experience out of what, without it, would be a mass of chaotic, indescribable, non-recurring data. (At this point the influence of Kant is clear. Consciousness has the role of the imagination in Kant.) It would be completely impossible to produce an accurate psychological description of these raw data in the mind. Even the purest of pure phenomena is already imbued by us with sense, or meaning, in terms of which we understand what we experience as part of the universe we inhabit. Intentionality, in Brentano the essential feature of consciousness, now comes to mean that aspect of consciousness which creates or discovers meanings.

The discovery of meaning in experience is connected with the discovery of universality, or essences. Husserl thought that there was a special kind of immediate experience in which universal or general essences were grasped. In seeing a particular white object, for example, and concentrating on the experience of it, one is experiencing whiteness itself. Every particular item in experience points beyond itself. If you listen to a sustained note you cannot hear each separate moment of it, without hearing it as pointing to the same note in the past and in the future. This is what the particular momentary experience means. What I hear at any given moment is not wholly "in" the mind. Because it points to more than can be heard at that moment, it is not "immanent" but "transcendent".

So in concentrating on immediate experience, shorn of assumptions or presuppositions phenomenological philosophy discovered more in it than mere experience. The consciousness grasps essences in perception. This grasping was called *Wesensschau*, and was meant to be scientific, the source of true systematic knowledge. The method invited us to put the world in brackets and as it were dismember things ordinarily taken as objects in the world, in order to show how they were constructed as objects for us. And so their meaning for us will be revealed.

Phenomenology was the dominant philosophy in Germany from its beginnings until the 1930s. Husserl's most famous successor was Martin Heidegger (1889–1976), but in his hands, the philosophical method changed, and Heidegger is not to be thought of as a true phenomenologist. The search for meanings, "hermeneutics", nevertheless continued to be his primary concern, but without the limitation to the immediate objects of consciousness which marks phenomenology itself.

Phenomenology was introduced into France by Jean-Paul Sartre, and both he and Maurice Merleau-Ponty owe a great debt to Husserl, though their philosophy had no pretensions to being scientific and indeed was if anything hostile to the methods of science. But even in Sartre's later philosophy, for example in *The question of method* (1957), the influence of Husserl and phenomenology can be seen in the proposal that Existentialism should "interiorize" Marxism. It should concentrate on the question of how the worker experiences his world, and what meanings he gives it.

In England, in a different way, both Ryle in *The concept of mind* (1949) and Wittgenstein in *The philosophical investigations* (1953) show the influence of phenomenology.   MW

Bibliography

Pivčevič, E. 1970: *Husserl and phenomenology*. London: Hutchinson.

Ryle, G. 1949: *The concept of mind*. London: Hutchinson; Totowa, N.J.: Barnes and Noble (1975).

Spiegelberg, H. 1965: *The phenomenological movement*. The Hague: Mouton.

Wittgenstein, L. 1953: *Philosophical investigations*. Oxford: Basil Blackwell; New York: Macmillan.

phenomenology: in psychology

The analysis of the person-world relationship in terms of its intentionality. Phenomenologically, intentionality means that any human experience or action has an object which is conceptually distinct from that experience or action, and may or may not exist independently. The house which I see over there, the pain which I feel in here, or the Pythagorean theorem which I hold to be true – are all objects of my present mental acts of seeing, feeling, believing, and as such they are said to be "intended" by these mental acts. The relationship between phenomenology and the human sciences has always been a case of selective exposure. It has been well documented by Merleau-Ponty (1973), Natanson (1973), Schütz (1962), Spiegelberg (1972) and Strasser (1963). What we gather from these sources is: (a) what phenomenological philosophers learnt from the human sciences, mainly psychology; and (b) what human scientists could have learnt from phenomenology. What we hardly find at all is: (c) what human scientists did take from phenomenology; and (d) what phenomenologists could have learnt from the human sciences.

The assessment, accordingly, is ambiguous. Spiegelberg (1972, xli), for example says: 'in this century phenomenology has influenced psychology and psychiatry more than any other movement in philosophy', but (p.364), 'phenomenology is the concern of only a small and unrepresentative minority'. Similarly, in the 1950s, Merleau-Ponty (1973, p.50) assumed that what psychologists think about phenomenologists would be humiliating for the latter. He, nevertheless, believed that 'it is in the problems and difficulties [that psychology] has encountered that we shall find both an influence of phenomenology and a harmony of two parallel investigations into common problems of the time' (ibid).

The fact is that from phenomenology the human sciences took different things at different times in a very selective manner, a state of affairs facilitated by changing emphases in phenomenological research. Four such emphases may be considered important, at least for their impact on psychology.

(1) From the beginning, phenomenology has been interpreted as the *method of faithful description of phenomena* in order to get "to the things themselves" (*zu den Sachen selbst*). Psychologists familiar with Brentano and Husserl considered the unbiased description of psychological phenomena the most elementary lesson to be learnt. Phenomenological descriptions have been given of the world of things (of colors, of touch), of inner experience, later, albeit rarely, of behavior. The methodological claim has been to place description first in the process of scientific investigation, before experimental or other forms of data reduction take place. Historically, however, it has been ethnomethodologists and related sociologists and anthropologists, even human ethologists, rather than psychologists who followed suit. (See ETHNOMETHODOLOGY; ETHOLOGY.)

(2) *Phenomenology as a critical science* is another aspect which was taken up by psychologists. The criticism meant here is closely connected with the descriptive aspiration: to be critical with respect to one's own assumptions as a prerequisite of unbiased description. Husserl warned the investigator 'not to hunt deductively (*von*

oben her) after constructions unrelated to the matter in question (*sachfremd*), but to derive all knowledge from its ultimate sources ... not to be diverted by any prejudices, by any verbal contradictions or indeed by anything in the whole world, even under the name of "exact science", but to grant its right to whatever is clearly seen ...' (quoted from Spiegelberg 1960, I, 128). Robert Macleod (1974, p.194) later expected social psychologists to adopt 'an attitude of disciplined naiveté. It requires the deliberate suspension of all implicit and explicit assumptions ....'

(3) *Phenomenology as the science of meaning.* This is less a procedural than a substantive aspect resulting from the central role of the conception of intentionality. Every experience of reality is an experience of unities of meaning. For Husserl and, mainly, Schütz the "life-world" is a universe of significations, a framework of meaning which we incessantly interpret. This challenge was taken up by interpretive sociology, but largely ignored by mainstream psychology after VERSTEHENDE PSYCHOLOGIE was discontinued. Although the problem of meaning was recognized by behaviorists as well as by gestaltists, it was not solvable in terms of conditioning or organization; nor will it be under the spell of the computational metaphor, i.e. in terms of information-processing. In contrast the alternative ETHOGENIC approach (Harré 1979) explicitly deals with the social constitution of meaning.

(4) *Phenomenology as the science of the life-world.* In the history of phenomenology the analysis of the life-world came late. After Husserl's *Crisis* it was mainly Schütz's work which focused on the life-world as the correlate of our natural attitude, the unquestioned basis of all human (including scientific) activities. While a (positivistic) preference for laboratory experimentation shielded psychology from everyday life, recently at least everyday (or "naive") conceptions and "implicit theories" have become topics of research (Wegner and Vallacher 1977). However, the structure of everyday situations is hardly analyzed. Exceptions,

i.e. examples of a phenomenologically oriented psychology, are rare.

In conclusion, the major phenomenological emphases for psychological research are as follows:

(a) 'Psychology is the scientific study of the situated person' (Linschoten 1953, p.246). While psychology traditionally focuses on the individual, phenomenological psychology is *situation-centered*. The first emphasis, therefore, is on the intentional person-world relationship in the context of individual or social *Umwelten*. That is, things and events, as intentional correlates, have meanings and values, and as such bear reference to actual or potential behavior. We encounter them less as "data", than as "agenda", i.e. something to be dealt with. To analyze the person-world relationship in terms of its intentionality makes explicit what Merleau-Ponty (1973, p.176) calls the "human dialectic".

(b) If we focus on a person's world phenomenologically it is revealed as *Umwelt*, as inhabited place. No analysis of behavior is complete without an adequate description of the place in which and with respect to which behavior "takes place". This *spatiality* of human existence is the infrastructure which facilitates or inhibits behavior.

(c) Its correlate is the *bodily* nature of the behaving subject. Whether a person perceives or acts, the world is encountered within the potentialities and limits of the body, articulated in perspectives, within or beyond our reach, etc. (Schütz 1962).

(d) Equally, the intentional relationship is to be understood as *temporal* reference. Intentional correlates may be present as perceived, past as remembered, future as anticipated. Phenomenologically more important is the fact that what we experience as being there now, as a rule, impresses us as having been there before we looked, and still being there when we turn away. Things and persons appear to have a history of their own, yet related to ours.

(e) We are born into a world of other people and of things which we have learnt to name and to handle by the mediation of others. Even the world of things carries social meaning as a world of man-made or, at least, man-ordered objects. Again, many of these things serve as media for interpersonal communication. This *sociality* of our experience and behavior is another phenomenologically essential feature of human existence. To remind psychologists of the essentially social, historical, spatial and bodily condition of the situated person has for a long time been the critical function of phenomenology in psychology. Judging from the present state of psychology this phenomenological critique has had little impact so far.   CFG

Bibliography

Harré, R. 1979: *Social being.* Oxford: Basil Blackwell: Totowa, N.J.: Littlefield Adams.

*Husserl, E. 1936: *The crisis of European sciences and transcendental phenomenology.* Evanston, Ill.: Northwestern University Press (1970).

Linschoten, J. 1953: Naaword. In *Persoon en wereld.* Utrecht: Bijleveld.

Macleod, R.B. 1974: The phenomenological approach to social psychology. *Psychological review* 54, 193–210.

Merleau-Ponty, M. 1973: *Phenomenology and the sciences of man.* In Natanson, op. cit. vol. 1, 47–105.

Natanson, M., ed. 1973: *Phenomenology and the social sciences.* 2 vols. Evanston, Ill.: Northwestern University Press.

*Schütz, A. 1962–6: *Collected papers.* 3 vols. The Hague: Nijhoff.

Spiegelberg, H. 1960: *The phenomenological movement.* 2 vols. The Hague: Nijhoff.

——— 1972: *Phenomenology in psychology and psychiatry: a historical introduction.* Evanston, Ill.: Northwestern University Press.

Strasser, S. 1963: *Phenomenology and the human sciences.* Pittsburgh: Duquesne University Press.

Wegner, D.M. and Vallacher, R.R. 1977: *Implicit psychology – an introduction to social cognition.* New York: Oxford University Press.

positivism Auguste Comte, 1798–1857, was the founder of the original school of positive philosophy (1844). He divided the history of mankind into three stages, the theological, the metaphysical and the positive or scientific. Science alone yielded knowledge and anything that could not be put on a scientific basis should be discarded.

The Logical Positivists, who flourished in Vienna between the 1918 and 1939 wars, took over Comte's promotion of science and rejection of metaphysics and developed it as a theory of meaning. They maintained that our sensory contact with the material world gives us not only all our knowledge of truth, but also all our understanding of meaning. This empirical theory of meaning was not new: the novelty was its systematic development, begun by Ernst Mach (1900) and continued by the philosophers of the Vienna Circle, who first called themselves "Logical Positivists". The motto of this school was the Verification Principle: the meaning of a proposition is the method of its verification. The idea was developed in different ways by Rudolph Carnap (1935), Friedrich Waismann (1965), Karl Popper (1959) and A.J. Ayer, who adapted it and imported it into English philosophy (1936). The two main variables were the choice of a particular empirical basis for the theory of meaning – should the basic propositions be about sensations or about things in the physical world? – and the method of building the superstructure of language on the chosen basis. What was common to all versions of the theory of meaning was a ruthless pruning of all the more tender and adventurous shoots of language and thought.   DP

Bibliography

Ayer, A.J. 1936: *Language, truth and logic.* London: Gollancz. 2nd edn. with a new introduction by the author, 1946.

——— ed. 1959: *Logical positivism.* Glencoe, Ill.: London: Allen and Unwin.

Carnap, R. 1935 (1937): *The logical syntax of language.* London: Kegan Paul.

Comte, A. 1844: *Discours sur l'esprit positif.* Paris.

Mach, E. 1934: *Die Analyse der Empfindung.* Jena.

Popper, K. 1934 (1959): *The logic of scientific discovery.* London: Hutchinson.

Waismann, F. 1965: *The principles of linguistic philosophy,* ed. R. Harré. London: Macmillan.

power semantics The study of power semantics is concerned with the use of language in maintaining and consolidating differential power in a society and the manipulation of people by means of language.

The principal areas of study include address pronouns (Lambert and Tucker 1976), sex-related speech differences, political indoctrination (O'Barr and O'Barr 1976) and advertising.

An example of how differential power is expressed in language is the use in a number of European languages of a T (from French *TU*) pronoun by masters to address their servants, whilst the servants address their master with the V (from French *VOUS*) pronoun.

The study of power semantics is closely related to that of linguistic relativity as proposed by Whorf.   PM

Bibliography

Lambert, W.E. and Tucker, G.R., eds. 1976: *Tu, vous, usted: a socio-psychological study of address patterns*. Rewley, Mass.: Newbury House.

O'Barr, W.M. and J.F. eds. 1976: *Language and politics*. The Hague: Mouton.

practical syllogism That form of reasoning running from premises which state an intention or consensual belief to a conclusion involving an action. In his *Nicomachean ethics*, Aristotle described it as having a universal premise (e.g. "Everything sweet ought to be tasted"), a particular premise (e.g. "This thing before me is sweet"), and a conclusion pertaining to an action. Aristotle's treatment leaves two questions unanswered: Is the practical syllogism formally valid? and, Does the conclusion assert a truth-claim about an action, reflect a decision whether to act, or constitute the performance of an action? Aristotle was aware of the problematic relation between the premises and the action prescribed: he specified that 'the man who *is able* and *is not prevented is bound* to act accordingly at once' (1147a, Martin Ostwald, trans. emphasis added). The qualifiers "able" and "not prevented" are external to the syllogism. Further, the term "is bound to act" seems qualitatively different from the logical necessity of a valid syllogism. The action entailed by the premises of the practical syllogism is somehow different from the proposition that one *should* act. In Lewis Carroll's words, practical necessity does not 'take you by the throat and *force* you to do it'.

Modern commentators have responded in four ways. Perelman and Olbrechts-Tyteca (1969) assume that the "power of deliberation" may be usefully applied to domains in which exact calculation, experiment and logically valid deduction are impossible. The result is "rhetoric" or "argumentation": the methods of proof used to secure adherence about logically uncertain or contingent matters. Kenny (1966) developed criteria for demonstrating the validity of practical reasoning leading to propositions prescribing that one *should* act. Aune (1977) argued that the conclusion of the practical syllogism is neither the performance of an action nor a proposition about an action but a decision about an action. As such, practical reasoning may be evaluated from the perspective of Bayesian decision theory in addition to logical standards. For social scientists, the work by Anscombe (1963) and von Wright (1971) is the most useful of these modern treatments of practical reasoning. Their key move is the treatment of action as intentional, interpreted events within the context of language-games and forms-of-life which provide explanatory frames. Within these contexts, the practical syllogism provides a structure for organizing the reasoning actors *use* in deciding what to do and the reasons actors and/or observers *give* when explaining actions. Anscombe (1963, p.84) argued that intentional acts are distinguished by the "form of description" which are applied to them. Those which are described using the practical syllogism are judged by the speech community as "intentional". von Wright (1971) championed the practical syllogism as the structure of explanation for those branches of social science which envision humans as purposive. von Wright (1978) cautioned that the practical syllogism in which the first premise is written in the first person (e.g. "I want X") should not be taken as an accurate representation of the reasoning which "causes" a person to act. However, he argued that the syllogism in which the first premise is written in the third person can be used "retrospectively" to identify premises which justify or explain actions, and "prospectively" to predict subsequent actions. In both instances, the result is "understanding", or the locating of an action as appropriate within the language games of the community. In von Wright's formulation, the practical syllogism has this form:

A intends to bring about Y;
A knows that Y will not occur unless he does X;
Therefore, A sets himself to do X.

At least five lines of social science research employ or are consistent with the practical syllogism as the structure of explanation. Harré's "ethogeny" (1977) is the most philosophically sophisticated of a number of "dramaturgical" or "interpretive" schools of thought which analyze 'both the social force and explanatory content of the speech produced by social actors as a guide to the structure of the cognitive resources required for the genesis of intelligible and warrantable social action by those actors' (Harré 1977, p.284). Harré argues that social interaction is a social product of intentional acts based on cognitive templates. The product of ETHOGENIC research is a description of those templates and the manner in which persons achieve intelligibility in their performance. 'Competent people "contain" templates' (ibid. p.289), although they probably cannot articulate them fully. Ethogenists can identify a number of different types of templates, including "plans", formal causes of nonstandard action pattern, and "rules", formal causes of the structure of standard action sequences. These templates are that which is designated as "Y" in the first premise of the practical syllogism. Actions are justified or interpreted by showing their connection to the template. The statement of that connection is the warrant for the minor premise.

A less transparent use of the structure of the practical syllogism can be found in Jackson's "Return Potential Mode" (1966, 1975). Jackson assumes that a person's intentions are clear and powerful, but there are various means by which they could be realized. He locates the necessity or imperative force of the practical syllogism in 'the distribution of potential approval and disapproval by Others for various alternatives of Actors' behavior ...' in a given defined situation (Jackson 1966, p.36). "Intensity" represents the deviation of the mean response from "indifference", while "crystallization" expresses the degree of consensus of the group. The quantitative measures of intensity and crystallization provide measures of the force of the necessity from the practical syllogism which impinges upon the relevant action. If intensity or crystallization are either or both low, then practical force will be low, expressed in a premise such as "a person A knows that if he does X, Y may or may not occur".

Pearce and Cronen's (1980) theory of "the coordinated management of meaning" postulates "logical force" as the "necessity" explaining patterns of social action. Persons seldom if ever act capriciously; they perceive their actions necessarily entailed because of the actions of others, their own concept of self, the demands of a situation, their intentions, etc. Pearce and Cronen treat these "perceived entailments" as scalar variables, the combination of which comprises a "logic of meaning and action" which has variable force. The entailments from preceding acts or previously established meanings is described as "prefigurative force"; the entailments from an act to subsequent acts by self or other and to meanings to be established subsequently are described as "practical force." The implications of this move are to make the practical necessity of performing an entailed action a measurable force as perceived by actors rather than an attribute of the arrangement of propositions in a syllogism; and to subsume practical necessity within an explanatory framework which includes prefigurative force.

Pearce and Cronen treat communication

as a process of creating/maintaining interpretations during attempts to coordinate activity with others. This process is inherently problematic since individuals can never be certain that they have accurately perceived the other's interpretations. Researchers can develop a "portrait" of social episodes by graphing the way the logical forces of the actors intermesh. Such portraits have usefully described the occurrence of recurring patterns known to and unwanted by the actors, violence in families, and difficulties in intercultural communication. WBP

Bibliography

Anscombe, G.E.M. 1963: *Intention*. 2nd edn. Ithaca: Cornell University Press.

Aune, B. 1977: *Reason and action*. Dordrecht, Holland and Boston: D. Reidel.

Harré, R. 1977: The ethogenic approach: theory and practice. In *Advances in experimental psychology*, vol. 10, ed. L. Berkowitz. New York: Academic Press.

Jackson, J. 1966: A conceptual and measurement model for norms and roles. *Pacific sociological review* 9, 35–47.

—— 1975: Normative power and conflict potential. *Sociological methods and research* 4, 237–63.

Kenny, A. 1966: Practical inference. *Analysis* 26, 65–73.

Pearce, W. B. and Cronen, V. 1980: *Communication, action and meaning*. New York: Praeger.

Perelman, C. and Olbrechts-Tyteca, L. 1958 (1969): *The new rhetoric: a treatise on argument*. Notre Dame, Indiana: Notre Dame Press.

Schwartz, S.H. 1973: Normative explanations of helping behavior: a critique, proposal, and empirical test. *Journal of experimental social psychology* 9, 349–64.

—— 1974: Awareness of interpersonal consequences, responsibility denial, and volunteering. *Journal of personality and social psychology* 30, 57–63.

von Wright, G. 1971: *Explanation and understanding*. Ithaca New York: Cornell University Press.

—— 1978: On so-called practical inference. In *Practical reasoning*, ed. J. Raz. Oxford: Oxford University Press.

praxis The Marxist conception of human activity or production, embedded within and simultaneously creating socio-historical conditions.

Marx specifically emphasized praxis as uniquely characterizing the human mode of production in the sense that, although itself a part of nature, the human being is able to transcend nature through his or her productive activity. In attempting to meet his or her physical needs, the individual engages in labor, and through labor recreates these needs into cultural and social activities. For example, the needs for food, shelter and procreation are recreated or transformed into agriculture, property, and family which in turn initiate more complex activities. These activities constitute both society as a progressive process of social relations and the way through which human capacities and potentialities are actualized. In this sense praxis aims both at the transformation of the world (e.g. economic, material, historical conditions) and at the individual's own self development (Janoušek 1972). It exemplifies the Marxist belief in the unity of individual and society, thought and action, and recognizes their fusion in human experience or in the human mode of production itself (see DIALECTIC THEORY; MARXIAN PERSONALITY PSYCHOLOGY). MG

Bibliography

Janoušek. J. 1972: On the Marxian concept of praxis. In *The context of social psychology: a critical assessment*, eds. J. Israel and H. Tajfel. London: Academic Press.

Marx, K.: German ideology: economic and philosophical manuscripts. In *Karl Marx: selected writings*, ed. D. McLellan. Oxford: Oxford University Press (1977).

predation A concern with the nature and implications of predatory behavior has arisen in the heated debate over the extent to which AGGRESSION is biologically determined. Writers such as Ardrey (1979), following Dart (1953) have argued that Man's instinctive hostility to his fellows derives from his emergence as a predatory hominid. His use of primitive weapons for the killing of prey were also used in conflicts with other hominid rivals and, coupled with territoriality, led to the evolution of a "killer" species. Montagu (1976), on the other hand argues that predation in Man has been overemphasized and is largely irrelevant in the discussion of the origins of aggression. Many have argued that aggression and predation should be seen as quite separate processes – hunting behavior being quite different in form from patterns of conspecific fighting and display in both animals and humans. Marsh (1978) suggests that the unique ability of Man is to manipulate symbols and thereby *dehumanize* his rivals. Where others can successfully be demoted to the role of prey, typical predatory acts are then, and only then, manifested.   PEM

Bibliography

Ardrey, R. 1979: *The hunting hypothesis.* London and New York: Methuen.

Dart, R. A. 1953: On the predatory transition from ape to man. *International anthropology and linguistic review.*

Marsh, P. 1978: *Aggro: the illusion of violence.* London: Dent.

Montagu, A. 1976: *The nature of human aggression.* Oxford: Oxford University Press.

prejudice The term "prejudice", as used in psychology, is in some ways broader and in some ways narrower than its definition in the *The Concise Oxford Dictionary* as a 'preconceived opinion, bias (against, in favor of, person or thing)'. Prejudice in psychological usage is broader because it includes not only biases of beliefs or opinions but also their evaluative and emotional connotations. It is narrower for two reasons. The first is that it is generally applied to people's views about social groups and their members rather than more generally to "persons" or "things". The second is that, in practice, the term has been mainly restricted in psychological theory and research to hostile or unfavorable views about human groups other than one's own ("outgroups"). It has been used by psychologists in the context of intergroup hostility, conflicts, persecution or discrimination.

Prejudice is therefore, in psychology, an

ATTITUDE which has two aspects: the *cognitive*, which consists of the nature and contents of the opinions, beliefs and views about certain social groups; and the *affective* which consists of the associated emotions and values. These attitudes must be distinguished from the actual behavior towards certain groups or their members which is often referred to as "discrimination". Prejudice against a group may sometimes be present without the existence of clear and objective marks of discrimination. This may be so for a variety of reasons, such as legal or moral prohibitions, political and economic motives, etc. Conversely, there may be forms of discrimination against a group which are not necessarily associated with prejudice. For example, some people may propose restrictions on immigration without necessarily harboring hostile attitudes towards the groups upon which they wish to impose limitations of this kind. But these theoretical distinctions often do not work in practice. Attitudes of prejudice which remain for long without being capable of some form of expression in behavior tend to weaken. Discrimination against certain groups which may start from an absence of hostility often ends up as discrimination accompanied by prejudice.

Several trends of thought and research can be distinguished in the history and the present directions of the study of prejudice in psychology. An excellent review of the earlier work can be found in Allport (1954). Looking back a quarter of a century later, it appears that a twofold general distinction can be made: between research and theory concerned with prejudice as an outcome of certain individual psychological processes; and research and theory starting from the individuals' group membership and looking at its effects upon behavior and attitudes towards other groups (see Tajfel and Fraser 1978, chs. 16 and 17).

Some of the "individual" conceptions of prejudice focused upon its motivational or affective aspects; others were more concerned with the nature and contents of the beliefs about outgroups, i.e. the cognitive aspects of prejudiced attitudes.

Most of the conceptions about individual

motives determining prejudice have been powerfully influenced, directly or indirectly, by ideas deriving from the Freudian theory. There is not room here for details of the theoretical links which FREUD established between his general theories of human personality and his "group psychology" (see e.g. Freud 1922), particularly as his conceptions about these links changed from the earlier to the later period of his work. His two basic ideas relevant to prejudice were: the inevitability of outgroup hostility, and its function in holding the group together. As he once wrote: 'It is always possible to bind together a considerable number of people in love, as long as there are other people left over to receive the manifestations of their aggressiveness' (1930, p.14).

These views were very much a part of the *Zeitgeist*. The ingroup-preserving functions of aggression against other groups fitted in with the general conceptions of SOCIAL DARWINISM and were not very different from the ideas expressed earlier by social scientists, such as Sumner (1906), who first popularized the terms "ethnocentrism", "ingroup" and "outgroup" and who also felt that the cohesion and survival of the "we-group" depended upon the availability of external enemies. Freud derived his views from certain transpositions to group attitudes and behavior of the emotional entanglements through which, according to him, each individual human being had to go in his or her (mainly his) early childhood. Sumner's ethnocentrism was an "umbrella concept" principally derived from what appeared to him to be the universal and undeniable features of social reality.

These ideas found strange bedfellows in some versions of behaviorism popular in the 1930s. A book on *Frustration and aggression* published in 1939 by Dollard and his colleagues, a group of Yale behaviorists, started from a theoretical sequence very different from that postulated by Freud and finished with very similar conclusions. Although these views later underwent a number of revisions, in which some concessions about their general validity had to be made, the basic sequence was a stark and simple one: all AGGRESSION is preceded by FRUSTRATION; all frustration is followed by aggression. When aggression against the agent of the frustration cannot be "discharged" directly because it is inhibited by external or internal impediments, it becomes displaced, i.e. directed towards a substitute target which happens to be available. In the case of relations between social groups, the outgroups and their members provide often the most convenient target for this displaced aggression. The frustration-aggression hypothesis was later revised and modified by e.g. Berkowitz (1962) who extended the concept of "frustration" in a cognitive direction through including in it the "failure of expectancies", denied the inevitability of the frustration-aggression sequence, and tried to describe, more clearly than was possible from the earlier versions of the theory, the nature of the processes guiding the choice of a particular target of aggression. But the basic idea behind all this work, from before Freud until the 1960s and later, remains that prejudice against outgroups can be accounted for by the inevitability of individual hostile motivations which somehow are joined together to create the socially shared phenomenon of prejudice. The major difficulty with such a view is its assumption that very large numbers of people happen to find themselves in a similar motivational state which sometimes lasts for very long periods of time, since in many cases prejudice against certain groups goes on for generations or even centuries (see Billig 1976).

The horrors and systematic massacres of the second world war and the persistence in its aftermath of hostile attitudes towards certain minorities in the United States led a group of refugees from Nazi Germany to attempt to answer the question: what kind of people were they who either did or potentially could commit acts of that nature? The result was the large and influential study *The authoritarian personality* published in 1950 by a team which included refugees from the Frankfurt Institute for Social Research and their American colleagues (Adorno et al. 1950). As in the ideas about prejudice described earlier, here again the influence of psychoanalytic theory (in a much modified form) was clearly visible. The sociopolitical background of the Frankfurt exiles led them to focus their attention upon the links between family structure and its wider framework in the surrounding society. Their conviction that psychological processes had to be taken into account in the understanding of intense hostility against outgroups made them look at the psychological effects of early emotional experiences in certain kinds of family relationships of which a rigid authoritarianism was the hallmark. The result of all this was the concept of an AUTHORITARIAN PERSONALITY (see ADORNO). Such personalities were, according to the authors, characterized by the need to work out their inner problems and difficulties by transposing them into hostility towards the weaker, the alien, the unusual and the "different". The F ("fascist") and E ("ethnocentric") scales were among the empirical outcomes of this work; the scales were claimed to measure predispositions to hostile attitudes and actions towards certain outgroups. The validity of these scales, their reliability and their capacity to encompass the wider aspects of prejudice, by no means always associated with certain personality "types", led to many controversies, some of which are still with us today.

It could be said that the research on authoritarian personality was mainly concerned to find out why some people hate or dislike "alien" groups under most conditions, rather than why most or many people are capable of developing long-lasting prejudiced attitudes towards outgroups in some conditions. In addition to the "motivational" theories discussed earlier, three other recent trends of research focused upon the latter of these two questions. One of them was mainly concerned with the cognitive aspects of prejudice, i.e. with the systems of beliefs about outgroups which hostile attitudes towards them usually include. The other two took as their point of departure the psychological effects of various forms of conflict or competition between social groups.

The systems of beliefs about outgroups in which unwarranted (and often unfavorable) generalizations are made about groups as a whole or their individual members are known in psychology as social STEREOTYPES. ALLPORT (1954) was one of the earliest authors to insist that the functions served by these stereotypes had to be understood in the more general context of the human activity of categorizing the environment, both physical and social. These categorizations consist of systematizing the world around us in terms of classes of objects and events. Items within each of the classes are considered as approximately equivalent for purposes of action or of understanding the complexities of what happens around us. Thus, social categories segment our social environment into groups of people who (we assume) can be considered similar in terms of their common characteristics and of the attributions of causality concerning their actions, intentions, personal traits, and individual and collective behavior. Because of the usefulness that these preconceived ideas have both in simplifying the social world around us and in preserving intact our value systems, we tend to select, interpret and accentuate the information we receive about other people in accordance with what we know or think we know about the categories to which they belong. The stronger our emotional involvement in separating between sheep and goats on certain social criteria, the stronger will be the tendency to "filter" accordingly the relevant information. This leads to a number of clear-cut effects on judgments of other people which are determined by the social category to which they are assigned (see Tajfel 1981).

These social categorizations become particularly salient and effective in conditions of conflict or competition between a group to which we belong and other groups. The classic studies on the psychological effects of such conflicts were conducted over the years by Sherif and his collaborators and summarized by him in a book published in 1966. It was found that a conflict (manipulated by the psychologists) between two groups of boys in a holiday camp, which was based on several competitions in which only one of the groups could win, led to all the usual manifestations of intergroup prejudice and hostility, including the development of ingroup rituals and of unfavorable stereotypes about the outgroup, and also, in some cases, the breakdown of previously existing individual friendships between boys who found themselves in opposing camps.

A number of more recent studies have shown, however, that biases in favor of one's group (and correspondingly, unfavorable treatment of, or ideas about, an outgroup) can develop even in the complete absence of an explicit conflict of interests or competition between groups (see Tajfel 1981; Turner and Giles 1981). Membership of some groups is important; it includes commitment and an emotional involvement in the group. Salient aspects of our self-concepts or self-images are then tied in to the image of the group as a whole. In turn, the favorable or unfavorable connotations of these collective images acquire most of their significance when comparisons of the ingroup are made with certain selected outgroups. In other words, the quality and significance of the social or group identity of individuals are largely derived from the ways in which their groups can be compared in certain important respects with other groups which, because of the nature of their relations with the ingroup, invite comparability. Many of the present-day industrial conflicts about "differentials", as well as the multiplicity of social and political movements concerned with ethnicity, are based on an interaction between the pursuit of the "objective" interests of the groups involved and these psychological processes of social identity and social comparisons. Prejudice against selected outgroups is one aspect of this interaction. The development and functioning of hostile intergroup attitudes cannot be understood in isolation from their historical, social, political and economic background; but their proper understanding requires in addition an analysis of the complex social psychological processes which also form an indissoluble part of our social reality.   HT

Bibliography

Adorno, T.W. et al. 1950: *The authoritarian personality*. New York: Harper.

*Allport, G.W. 1954: *The nature of prejudice*. Cambridge, Mass.: Addison-Wesley.

Berkowitz, L. 1962: *Aggression: a social psychological analysis*. New York: McGraw-Hill.

*Billig, M. 1976: *Social psychology and intergroup relations*. European Monographs in Social Psychology, no. 9. London: Academic Press.

*Brewer, M.B. and Kramer, R.M. 1985: The psychology of intergroup attitudes and behavior. *Annual review of psychology* 36, 219–43.

Dollard, J. et al. 1939: *Frustration and aggression*. New Haven: Yale University Press.

Freud, S. 1922 (1976): Group psychology and the analysis of the ego. *Standard edition of the complete psychological works of Sigmund Freud*. London: Hogarth; New York: Norton.

—— 1930 (1976): Civilization and its discontents. *Standard edition*, op. cit.

Sherif, M. 1966: *In common predicament: social psychology of intergroup conflict and cooperation*. Boston: Houghton Mifflin.

Sumner, W.G. 1906: *Folkways*. New York: Ginn.

*Tajfel, H. 1981: *Human groups and social categories: studies in social psychology*. Cambridge and New York: Cambridge University Press.

*—— and Fraser, C., eds. 1978: *Introducing social psychology*. London: Penguin Books.

*Turner, J.C. and Giles, H. eds. 1981: *Intergroup behavior*. Oxford: Basil Blackwell; Chicago: University of Chicago Press.

projection A DEFENSE MECHANISM in which persons have no awareness of some anti-social impulse in themselves, instead attributing it erroneously to others. Like other defense mechanisms, projection serves to protect persons from the anxiety and guilt they would feel if they were to become conscious of their underlying anti-social impulses. As described by FREUD and his followers, projection is regarded as relatively immature (being characteristic of the developmental stages of the first two years of life). When projection forms a major part of an adult's character structure, it is a sign of a fixation (or arrest of development) having taken place early in life. Fixations are likely when parents are either over-indulgent or over-punitive with their children. The form of projection in which the persons around one are typically perceived as having aggressive designs is often regarded as an aspect of latent HOMOSEXUALITY. SRM

Bibliography
Freud, A. 1937: *The ego and the mechanisms of defence*. London: Hogarth.

projective tests Psychological tests devised to measure global aspects of personality and personality dynamics. They include a range of instruments such as the Rorschach, Thematic Apperception Test (TAT), Sentence Completion, and Draw-A-Person Test, which provide generally vague, ambiguous stimuli and require the subject to respond with his or her own constructions. The individual's response, since it cannot be attributed to the stimulus itself, is believed to reflect the individual's basic personality make-up. Projective tests have been popular instruments in clinical settings as a means of gaining understanding about the patient's psychodynamics. Recently, however, projective tests have waned in popularity partly as a result of their generally low reliability, questionable validity and the increased emphasis upon behavior treatment in clinical settings. (See also TESTS, RELIABILITY; TESTS, VALIDITY.) JNB

Bibliography
Lanyon, R.I. 1984: Personality assessment. *Annual review of psychology* 35, 667–701.
Wiener-Levy, D. and Exner Jnr, J.E. 1981: The Rorschach EA-ep variable as related to persistence in a task frustration situation under feedback conditions. *Journal of personality assessment* 45, 118–24.

proxemics Study of the ways in which people use space and physical environment in the course of their social interactions. Originally: 'the study of how man unconsciously structures microspace – the distance between men in the conduct of daily transactions, the organization of space in his houses and buildings, and ultimately the layout of his towns' (Hall 1963). Proxemic research is concerned with: (a) the phenomenon of personal space and the body buffer zones which people establish when dealing with each other and with objects; (b) the cultural patterning of sensory (visual, acoustic, tactile, olfactory) interlock during social encounters; (c) the spatial architecture (postures, spaces, distances, orientations) of face-to-face interactions; (d) the spatial distribution, placement, and orientations of people in the indoor and outdoor settings; and (e) interactional properties of semi-fixed (e.g. furniture) and fixed (e.g. walls, partitions) environmental features. Proxemics has made major contributions to studies in human communication, territoriality, crowding and privacy and constitutes an important source of data to architects and environmental designers. (See COMMUNICATION, NON-VERBAL.) TMC

Bibliography
Hall, E.T. 1963: A system for notation of proxemic behavior. *American anthropologist* 65, 1003–26.

psychoanalysis A subject linked inextricably with the name of its originator, Sigmund FREUD. Freud (1916) pointed out that the word as he used it referred to three subjects: a general psychology, a treatment (a form of psychotherapy), and a research methodology. It is difficult to consider any one of these aspects without at the same time considering the other two. The problem of definition is still more complex because over the passage of time psychoanalysis has also come to refer to a highly organized movement which, apart from being involved in training, treatment and research into psychoanalysis, is a quasi-political organization in the sense that it attempts to influence the training of psychiatrists, clinical psychologists and social workers. In addition, and despite a specific denial of this from Freud, psychoanalysis has become part of general culture. ('As a specialist science, a branch of psychology

... it is quite unfit to construct a *Welt-anschauung* of its own.'). It has become an influence within sociology (Parsons 1965), anthropology, literary criticism (Faber 1970) and philosophy (Wollheim 1974) and, especially in certain circles, it has become an intrinsic part of intellectual attitudes and verbal currency. Because psychoanalysis has been in existence for nearly 100 years, because of the many highly speculative and imaginative aspects of its writings and, above all, because of its widespread and imprecise applications, definitions of the essence of the subject, are extremely difficult. The following five features have been organized as "the basic assumptions" (Sandler, Dare and Holder 1972) and summarize many disparate attempts to encapsulate its nature.

The first assumption is that despite its origins in the consulting rooms of a psychotherapist in private practice in Vienna at the turn of the nineteenth century, psychoanalysis is a general psychology and not solely a psychopathology: a continuity between the mental functioning of "normality" and "abnormality" is assumed, just as there is central belief in a causal continuity between mental states in infancy, childhood and adulthood. Within these continuities the function of motivational instinctual drives and conflict of motivation affecting all aspects of mental life are extremely important and are mentioned later.

Secondly, and this embodies a particular view of the philosophical issue of the body/mind relationship, psychoanalysis supposes the existence of a "mental apparatus", a construct implying a mental system in interaction, that is, making an input to and having an output from the physiological systems such as the cardiovascular and the nervous systems. The mental apparatus is discussed in terms of structures (that is to say with processes whose rate of change is slow) and with non-structural elements which are experiential. This latter is a very crucial notion, for the basic topic of psychoanalysis is that of subjective experience rather than the observable actions, behavior, or verbal communications themselves which are the source of information about subjective experience.

Thirdly, the concept of psychological adaptation is embodied in all versions of psychoanalytic psychology. Adaptation is always assumed to be an attempt to reach a "steady" state (by analogy with the physiological notion of homeostatic equilibrium) in the face of pressures from external, environmental sources; from internal, physiological sources and from equally important and powerful sources within the mental apparatus itself. Here again it can be seen that conflict is regarded as inevitable as an organizer of psychoanalytic psychology. DEFENSE MECHANISMS, postulated as omnipresent in the control and modification of conflicting motivational tendencies, are constant elements in the psychoanalytic understanding of short-term and long-term adaptational processes. The adaptational change of mental functioning over the course of psychological development, leading to the persisting imprint of many such adaptations at different stages of life, is an important part of the psychoanalytic view of the mental world.

Fourthly, psychoanalysis is based upon an assumption of what is somewhat confusingly called determinism. Because of philosophical controversies current at the time of his education it was necessary for Freud to take a strong stand as to the possibility of finding causes for all mental activity without resort to elements either of divine inspiration or governance or of chance. Psychoanalysts still hold to this view, although it seems much less necessary to argue the case at length, and the concept of psychic determinism has become combined with the principle of overdetermination, whereby most mental events are believed to become outwardly expressed because of their origins in multiple, converging psychological processes.

Fifthly, and of extreme importance, psychoanalysis is built on the assumption that mental life can be thought of as progressing both in ways that can be brought into consciousness and at levels of functioning quite inaccessible, as a rule, to introspective awareness. The unconscious aspects of thought which are for the largest part inaccessible to the conscious mind, are described as being dynamically unconscious. They are thought to become consciously registered only under specific circumstances such as dreams, in some psychotic states, or are implied by the symbolic meanings of symptoms, parapraxes and slips of the tongue and, above all, can be constructed by the process of the clinical method of psychoanalysis.

The five assumptions underlie the different models of mental functioning which were developed by Freud and have been extended and modified by the generations of psychoanalysts since. There has been an increasing move away from an emphasis upon sexual drives as the major motivational system. First there has been the inclusion and integration of an aggressive drive paralleling the sexual drive ("the libido"). Until the 1950s there was little challenge from within psychoanalysis of Freud's suggestions of sexual and aggressive drives as specific sources of particular mental energies. Over recent years, however, this has no longer been thought to be the case. Experiences in the early stages of life are consolidated to interact with innate tendencies for the infant to be orientated toward the mother and attendant caretakers. The mental apparatus is now thought to be structured by the pressure to remain close to and to enact specific relationship needs. The psychoanalysts who have developed these ideas are referred to as the "object relations" school (e.g. Klein 1965; Winnicott 1965; Balint 1952; Bowlby 1969, 1973, 1980).

The change away from a model emphasizing the impingement of specific drives toward an accentuation of the object-attaching quality of the thrust of mental life, can be seen as the outcome of a hundred years of psychotherapeutic practice, which remains the major field of activity of psychoanalysts.

Initially Freud saw himself as reconstructing features of the patient's unconscious mental life by the constructions he was able to put upon the patient's

encouraged flow of thoughts ("free associations"). Symptoms, casual thoughts and dreams were the principal stimuli for freely expressed thoughts, and interpretation of the psychoanalyst's understanding of the unconscious meaning of the stream of thought was held to be therapeutic by a process of enlightenment. The balance of conflicting forces within the mind was thought to be changed. Over time, however, Freud came to realize that the main interest of the psychoanalytic provision of confidentiality and reliability in frequent (usually daily) sessions, lay in revelations about the nature of the patient's thoughts and beliefs, attitudes and longings, hatred and loves concerning the analyst. These complex feelings ("transferences") demonstrated the many experiences structured by the infantile and juvenile mind in relation to crucial people in the patient's earlier life. The provision of a new, ambiguous but reliable relationship with the analyst, combined with a careful discussion with the patient of the meaning of the unconscious mental orientations toward the psychoanalyst, has become the major activity of psychoanalytic psychotherapy; it is believed to be the source of the therapeutic improvement in the patient's abilities to make satisfactory relationships outside the therapy and to develop realistic life goals.

The analysis of the therapeutic relationship can be seen to be likely to direct the theoretical thinking of the psychoanalyst toward relationship models (OBJECT RELATIONS theory) of the mind. It can also be seen to be related to the application of psychoanalytic ideas to therapy in stranger groups (group analysis or family therapies).

The peculiar nature of the psychoanalytic treatment setting consists in the unusual feature of the communications. The patient is encouraged to speak simply and as completely as possible the thoughts that come into his mind. The psychoanalyst gives no commitment to speak or respond in any way, other than to facilitate the flow and understanding of the supposedly underlying meaning of the thoughts. Questions from the patient are unlikely to be regularly answered and requests for reassurance about the patient's present condition or its future course will not, usually, elicit a response. Yet the psychoanalyst expresses a concerned and detailed interest in all aspects of the patient's life and devotes up to 200 hours a year to helping the patient. This devotion, combined with the unpredictability and peculiarities of the timing of the psychoanalyst's responses and the rule of free association, give a very special quality to the nature of the material expressed by the patient. The uniqueness of the communications, within the setting, constitute the research interest of psychoanalysis. Using the psychoanalytic method gives particular and special insights into the nature of mental life in differing psychological states. CD

Bibliography

Balint, M. 1952: *Primary love and psycho-analytic technique*. London: Tavistock.

Bowlby, J. 1969, 1973 and 1980: *Attachment and loss*. 3 vols. London: Hogarth Press; New York: Basic Books.

Faber, M.D. ed. 1970: *The design within: psychoanalytic approaches to Shakespeare*. New York: Science House.

Freud, S. 1913: New introductory lectures on psycho-analysis. Reprinted in *Standard edition of the complete psychological works of Sigmund Freud*, vol. 22. London: Hogarth; New York: Norton.

—— 1915–16: Introductory lectures on psycho-analysis. Reprinted in *Standard edition*, vols. 15 and 16.

Klein, M. 1965: *Envy and gratitude and other works 1946–1963*. London: Hogarth Press; Boston, Mass.: Seymour Lawrence.

Parsons, T. 1965: *Social structure and personality*. Glencoe, Ill.: Free Press.

Sandler, J., Dare, C., and Holder, A. 1972: Frames of reference in psychoanalytic psychology. III. A note on the basic assumptions. *British journal of medical psychology* 45, 143–7.

Winnicott, D.W. 1972: *The maturational processes and the facilitating environment*. London: Hogarth Press; New York: International Universities Press.

Wollheim, R. ed. 1974: *Philosophers on Freud*. New York: Jason Aronson.

psychohistory In a strict etymological sense a form of history in which the empirical and theoretical discoveries of psychology are explicitly used to explain past events. By current practice, however, psychohistory entails the more specialized application of psychoanalytic theory to the interpretation of historical events and, especially, historical personalities. Psychohistory includes both psychobiographies of specific historical figures and the highly reductionistic "group-fantasy" analysis that treats whole cultures or collections of individuals – though some practitioners, most notably deMause (1982), tend to reserve the term for the PSYCHOANALYSIS of groups. Since psychohistorians themselves may be either trained psychoanalysts or professional historians, psychohistory may be classed as an interdisciplinary enterprise.

The practice of psychoanalyzing historical people began with the father of psychoanalysis, Sigmund FREUD, whose analysis of Leonardo da Vinci (1910) has become a classic of its kind. Freud also produced analyses of Dostoyevski and Woodrow Wilson (the latter in collaboration with William C. Bullett). However, Freud's work was often criticized for being excessively ahistorical; a Renaissance personality such as Leonardo's is placed on a modern, and rather procrustean, psychiatrist's couch without due reference to the peculiarities of the time and place in which that artist lived. In contrast, Erikson's more truly psychohistorical inquiries into the lives of Martin Luther and Mahatma Gandhi took more care to embed the analysis in the proper historical setting (see e.g. Erikson 1958). Furthermore by not confining himself to the tenets of orthodox Freudianism Erikson broadened the theoretical basis of the discipline. The interest of historians in this form of historical explanations was accelerated when Langer delivered his presidential address "The Next Assignment" to the American Historical Association (1958). Journal articles and books purporting to be psychohistories of major personalities, such as American presidents, have now become commonplace. Moreover, the advent and development of group-fantasy analysis, particularly in the hands of deMause, the founding president of the International Psychohistorical Association, has immensely expanded the aims of some psychohistorians. The long-standing desire to explain the psychological motivations of past historical actors is often complemented if not replaced by an oracular fascination with the interpretation of contemporary events and the prophecy of their future course. As a result it is fair to say that psychohistorians vary greatly in professional respectability, some being true academics who impose some self-restraint while others veer closer to the excesses of "pop psychology".

Psychohistory must be distinguished from those methodologies in psychology which also make successful use of historical or archival data (see Simonton 1981). In particular it should be separated from what is sometimes called "historiometry", a methodology represented by such classics as Cox's study of 301 geniuses (1926). Unlike historiometry, which is merely interested in using historical data to test scientific hypotheses about human behavior (e.g. the relationship between intelligence and achieved eminence), psychohistory is committed to applying already discovered psychological principles to historical events and persons (e.g. the role of the Oedipus conflict in Leonardo's extraordinary investigative curiosity). Where historiometry advances inductively from the particular to the general, psychohistory proceeds deductively from the general to the particular. In this sense psychohistory is more an applied than a pure or basic science. Or, more precisely, its stress on explicating the particular rather than enlarging the store of psychological laws renders it more akin to history than to science; specific and somewhat standardized psychoanalytic concepts merely supplant the common sense psychology formerly used by historians to understand the motives of their subjects. Of course in so far as psychoanalytic therapy can be considered a science, or at least a technology, psychohistory may be viewed in similar terms, a historic patient merely taking the place of a contemporary nonentity. In any event, since psycho-historians must begin their deductive procedure with some theoretical basis, they have no choice but to commit themselves to some theory a priori, that theory invariably being psychoanalytic since it was the only broad-scope theory of human behavior available when psychohistory first emerged as an intellectual discipline. In contrast, historiometry is not obliged to make any such theoretical commitments; it is solely engaged in testing theoretical propositions. The historiometric method can even be used to test predictions derived from psychoanalytic theory. Moreover, these two rival psychological methodologies go about using historical data in contrary ways. On the one hand psychohistory, like its parent psychoanalysis, is clearly devoted to qualitative analysis, to logical and often imaginative disquisition. Historiometry, on the other hand, is explicitly involved in the quantitative analysis of historical data using established measurement and statistical techniques. This makes historiometry more the cousin of psychometrics and cliometrics. Accordingly, where the psychohistorian would be intrigued with identifying the course of Leonardo's Oedipal conflict, a historiometrician would want to assess Leonardo's IQ (at least 150) and his eminence (52nd out of Cox's 301), repeat the process for the remaining 300 geniuses sampled, and then determine the statistical relationship between the two variables. As this example suggests, psychohistory is prone to take the individual case as the basis for analysis, whereas historiometry groups numerous historical personages together as part of a search for the nomothetic principles (or natural laws) of human behavior. Consequently, though superficially similar and sometimes confused with one another, psychohistory and historiometry pertain to two distinct, even rival disciplines.

Practically ever since its conception, psychohistory has come under severe attack both as history and as science (see Barzun 1974; Stannard 1980). The most frequently heard criticisms may be summarized as follows: (i) the historical record is not sufficiently complete, especially with regard to key childhood experiences, to provide a firm basis for psychoanalytic explanation; (ii) the psychohistorian all too often compensates for this dearth of fact by loosely surmising the existence of undocumented childhood events from adulthood personality and then, in a subtle form of circular reasoning, uses these inferences as actual facts for interpreting adulthood motivations; (iii) like psychoanalysis generally, psychohistory tends to be a highly subjective intellectual exercise whose interpretations are vulnerable to many equally plausible alternative accounts; (iv) despite all corrective efforts, psychohistory remains ahistorical, especially in its disregard for the possibility that psychoanalytic theory may be both era- and culture-bound and therefore inapplicable to other times and places; (v) psychoanalytic theory itself is not a validated scientific theory, nor even a successful foundation for therapy, and consequently its use to explicate history is premature; (vi) even if psychoanalytic theory were sound in the restricted sphere of its origins, there is no assurance that principles derived from clinical practice and introspective self-analysis will have applicability to non-psychiatric populations; and (vii) even if this extrapolation were justified, psychoanalytic theory, as a model primarily of unconscious motivation, may be simply irrelevant to our understanding of a good many historical events, such as those that concern attribution, decision making, or group-dynamic processes. To such arguments most psychohistorians respond that psychoanalytic theory, particularly if suitably revised, does indeed offer a scientifically valid and universally applicable framework for historical explanation whenever it is feasible to obtain adequate materials on early childhood conditions. Nonetheless, some psychohistorians have suggested that it may be time to forfeit any strict allegiance to psychoanalytic theory. As an alternative, psychohistorians could be more eclectic, freely exploiting any psychological discovery that has explanatory value. Psychohistory might even find it advantageous to utilize more fully the growing number of generalizations that have emerged from the historiometric analysis of past creators and leaders. If the theoretical basis of the discipline were enlarged, the word psychohistory could be used in a way which was etymologically more correct to refer to studies that have only a historical, not a logical link with psychoanalytic theory. Whether psychohistory will move in this direction remains to be seen.   DKS

Bibliography

Barzun, J. 1974: *Clio and the doctors: psychohistory, quanto-history, and history*. Chicago: University of Chicago Press.

Cox, C. 1926: *The early mental traits of three hundred geniuses*. Stanford, Calif.: Stanford University Press.

deMause, L. 1982: *Foundations of psychohistory*. Planetarium Station, New York: Creative Roots.

Erikson, E.H. 1958: *Young man Luther: a study in psychoanalysis and history*. New York: Norton.

Freud, S. 1910 (1957): Leonardo da Vinci and a memory of his childhood. Trans. A. Tyson. *Standard edition of the psychological works of Sigmund Freud*. London: Hogarth; New York: Norton (1964).

Langer, W.L. 1958: The next assignment. *American historical review* 63, 283–304.

Simonton, D.K. 1981: The library laboratory: archival data in personality and social psychology. In *Review of personality and social psychology*, vol. 2, ed. L. Wheeler. Beverly Hills and London: Sage Publications.

*Stannard, D.E. 1980: *Shrinking history: on Freud and the failure of psychohistory*. New York and Oxford: Oxford University Press.

Q

questionnaires Also known as surveys and self-report inventories, questionnaires include a number of "instruments" such as check-lists (simple lists of items which the respondent understands and "checks-off" his or her response to), rating scales (usually attitude statements or people that are rated on a number of carefully chosen and independent 3-, 5- or 7-point rating scales) and inventories (usually longer questionnaires which have a number of rating scales on which the respondent is asked to respond in a particular way and which give a single score or a number of subscores). Respondents are usually required to read various questions themselves and provide some sort of written answer (a tick, a sentence etc), although the questions are occasionally given orally as in public opinion poll surveys. They are used to assess everything from attitudes to personality traits, and values to behavioral patterns. Although some questionnaires are open-ended in the sense that the respondent is relatively free in the quality and quantity of his or her responses, most questionnaires in psychology have pre-determined response categories which, though restricting variety, facilitate coding and analysis.

In order for a valid, reliable and unambiguous questionnaire to be devised a number of decisions have to be made and considerable pilot work done. Oppenheim (1966) has noted three major decisions that have to be made in the initial phase. Firstly there is the decision about the methods of data collection such as interview, mailed questionnaires and self- or group-administered questionnaire, each of which has particular problems associated with it. Secondly there are problems of question sequence and question type such as the use of filter questions (which start with broad issues and progressively narrow the scope of the questions onto specific points), the proportion of open and closed questions, how to ask tricky or sensitive questions and how to code the answers. Finally there are decisions to be made as to how to cope with missing data or lost information.

One of the most problematic aspects of questionnaire design relates to the wording of questions. Factual, rather than attitudinal or opinion questions are usually easier to phrase but are not without their problems. Oppenheim (1966) for instance points to the problem involved in the simple question "When do you usually have tea?" which in England can mean a beverage, a light meal in the afternoon or an evening meal. Loaded, leading, double-barreled or double-negative questions should always be avoided and instructions should be clear and concise.

It has long been established that all self-report questionnaires are open to a range of specific response biases (Furnham and Henderson 1982). These biases include: *faking good* or a social desirability/prestige bias where respondents reply in the manner that they believe is expected of normal well-adjusted people and hence present themselves in a socially acceptable way; *faking bad* in which respondents intentionally give an answer which will give a bad (deviant, amoral, sick) impression of themselves and hence present themselves in a socially unacceptable way; *acquiesence* or yea-saying in which respondents have a tendency to agree or say yes to questions irrespective of their content; *opposition* or nay-saying where respondents have a tendency to disagree or respond negatively to all questions irrespective of their content; *"mid-point" response set* where respondents tend to choose mid-point or neutral responses to all questions; and *carelessness, inconsistency* and *incomplete answers*. Because these response biases threaten the validity and reliability of results, numerous strategies are used to overcome them. Some questionnaires include a measure of response bias (a lie scale) which may be used to detect unreliable subjects; some questionnaires are administered along with a social desirability questionnaire of which there are quite a number; some attitude or personality questionnaires include factual or intelligence questions to check that the respondent is reading the questions; some questionnaires have "trick" or "repeated" questions so that some reliability may be tested; and still others have been deliberately subjected to experiments where respondents have been asked either to fake good or to fake bad and the results compared with those of a control group.

Most questionnaires are concerned with measuring ATTITUDES. There are four principal scaling methods for the measurement of attitudes, each of which has certain advantages and disadvantages. (1) The method of *equal-appearing intervals* (Thurstone) in which judges compare all items, two at a time, judging which of the pair was more positive or negative in order that all the items may be scaled in relationship to one another. This enables the tester to assign a value to each item and place each respondent on a continuum according to the median scale value of the item endorsed. (2) The method of *summated ratings* (Likert) in which subjects place their answers on a continuum from strongly agree to strongly disagree. These are given simple linear weights (e.g. from 1 to 7) and then totaled. (3) *Social distance scaling* (Bogardus) in which subjects are required to indicate to what extent they are willing to accept a close degree of relationship with another nationality or group (e.g. "Would you let your daughter marry a young socialist?"). (4) *Cumulative scaling* (Guttman) which is a procedure that allows the investigator to determine from a respondents' score exactly which items he or she has endorsed. With careful preparation items in the scale are ordered and cumulative so that one can determine to what extent respondents' attitudes deviate from an ideal scale pattern.   AF

Bibliography

Anastasi, A. 1982: *Psychological testing*. 5th edn. New York and London: Macmillan.

Furnham, A. and Henderson, M. 1982: The good, the bad and the mad: response bias in self-report measures. *Personality and individual differences* 3, 311–20.

Oppenheim, A. 1966: *Questionnaire design and attitude measurement*. London: Heinemann.

R

reference group Reference group theory, according to Merton and Kitt (1950), who gave the term prominence in sociology and social psychology 'aims to systematize the determinants and consequences of those processes of evaluation and self-appraisal in which the individual takes the values or standards of other individuals and groups as a frame of reference.' The concept of reference group was first employed by Hyman (see Merton 1957) in studying the psychology of status and by Newcomb (see Merton 1957) in the well-known Bennington College study. Stouffer (see Merton 1957) used the related notion of 'relative deprivation' to explain the relatively high degree of dissatisfaction of soldiers in the US army, which appeared to depend on the perceived level of the groups to which they compared themselves rather than any absolute level. Symbolic interactionists have been concerned with the extent to which 'reference categories have major importance in the development and maintenance of the self' (Kuhn 1964). Some such as Hewitt (1984) use "reference group" to mean, for example, a higher social class to which one aspires, and whose standards one therefore adopts. Kuhn suggests that a reference group may be a category of persons with whom one is comparable for some purposes (and to which one may actually belong) but which does not necessarily provide a salient part of one's self-definition.   JMFJ

Bibliography

Hewitt, J.P. 1984: *Self and society: a symbolic interactionist social psychology*. 3rd edn. Boston: Allyn and Bacon.

Kuhn, M.H. 1964: The reference group reconsidered. *Sociological quarterly* 5, 6–21.

Merton, R.K. 1957: *Social theory and social structure*. New York: Free Press.

—— and Kitt, A.S. 1950: Contributions to the theory of reference group behavior. In *Continuities in social research: studies in the scope and method of the American soldier*, eds. R. Merton and P.F. Lazarsfeld. Glencoe, Ill.: Free Press.

regression In common use, the appearance of behavior appropriate to an earlier life stage, triggered by stress. Examples include the adolescent who "regresses" to whining or tantrums when parental demands are imposed; the young child who "regresses" to bedwetting or thumbsucking with the birth of a younger sibling. The term derives from FREUD's ontogenetic model of development, in which the individual passes through a series of developmental stages. Ideally, progress requires a balance of gratification and frustration; either excessive frustration or excessive gratification leads to fixation. In reality, normal development inevitably entails a less than perfect balance, and earlier stages leave residues in the form of minor fixations. Regression represents a return to an earlier stage, commonly a stage at which gratification was experienced. ND

Bibliography

Freud, S. (1916–17) 1963: *Introductory lectures on psychoanalysis*. Part 3. Trans. J. Strachey. London: Hogarth.

regression, in statistics is used in two distinct ways. In regression analysis values of a dependent variable are predicted from a linear function: $y = bx + a$, where y is the value of the dependent variable, b is a constant by which values of the independent variable x are multiplied, and a is a constant which is added in every case. We are therefore able to predict how much increase or decrease in the value of the independent variable x will produce a stated increase or decrease in the value of the dependent variable y. In multiple regression the values of the dependent variable y are predicted from the values of several independent variables $x_1 \ldots \ldots x_j$ rather than one.

The other use of the word "regression" is in the phrase "regression to the mean". This was a phenomenon noted by GALTON, who found that the children of two tall parents tend to be shorter than their parents, although still taller than average. This seemed to imply that the population was continuously getting closer to the mean. But this was clearly not happening. The solution to this conundrum lies in the fact that in a normally distributed population the majority of members have heights (or weights, or abilities) which are close to the mean. The probability of any individual deviating far from the mean is therefore very small. Hence it is very unlikely that any child of two extremely tall parents would also be extremely tall.   RL

Bibliography

Winer, B.J. 1962: *Statistical principles in experimental design.* New York: Holt, Rinehart and Winston.

relationships were very little researched by psychologists until the 1980s, but since then the study of personal relationships has proved to be one of the fastest growing areas in social and personality psychology. Some of the most striking indicators of this growth are a five-volume series of research chapters produced from 1981 to 1984, a new international and cross-disciplinary *Journal of social and personal relationships* first published in 1984, a series of monographs on practical applications of relationship research started in 1986, three International Conferences on Personal Relationships held between 1982 and 1986, the foundation of an International Society for the Study of Personal Relationships in 1984, and the preparation of a *Handbook of research in personal relationships* for publication in 1986.

Such developments have surprised those social and personality psychologists who correctly identified work on relationships before 1979 with laboratory studies of ATTRACTION to strangers. In the past, work focused primarily on such initial attraction. Relationships research now concerns the joint social action that makes a relationship actually work. Thus it explores the taxonomizing, description and explanation of the different forms of naturally-occurring personal relationships (e.g. friendship, parent-child relations, courtship, adolescent relations) and examines the reasons for their breakdown and the best means for their repair. Although the social psychological origin of the research on real-life human interactions was from reactions to and improvements on the work on attraction, the area best dates from the seminal analysis by Hinde (1979) who brought together the common themes of work carried out in ETHOLOGY, developmental psychology, clinical psychology and social psychology. Hinde pointed out that social psychologists had founded theories of attraction on an inadequate descriptive base, whilst ethologists had descriptive categories but few theories, and presented a system for understanding relationships. He noted that social psychologists had concentrated almost exclusively on liking as an attitude, without developing systematic approaches to the ways in which liking was expressed in the relationship, nor to the means by which intimacy was negotiated in extended encounter. The different styles of behavior that differentiated one recognizable form of relationship from another were also neglected. Hinde (1981) proposed eight categorical dimensions by which relationships could be investigated and differentiated:
(a) the content of interactions (i.e. what the participants do together);
(b) the diversity of interactions (whether solely one type or several types of interaction);
(c) the qualities of interactions (the ways in which participants do what they do);
(d) the relative frequency and patterning of interactions;
(e) the extent to which the relationship is based on reciprocity (where partners,

for example, do the same thing alternately) or complementarity (where partners do different things which nonetheless complement one another to serve a common goal);

(f) the degree of intimacy;

(g) the interpersonal perceptions held by the partners about each other and their relationship;

(h) the degree of commitment of the partners to the relationship.

Although basing his work on a call for greater description of relationships on some of the dimensions outlined above, Hinde stresses that the ultimate goal is not the description of relationships but the understanding of their dynamics which springs from such a descriptive base.

A valuable part of Hinde's (1979, 1981) contribution has been the demonstration of some ways in which an interdisciplinary science of human social relationships can be built, despite the different interests and viewpoints on the total problem – an approach now embodied in the *Journal of social and personal relationships*.

From the social psychological point of view, however, the greatest importance is attached to the *growth* of liking and the expression of intimacy. In part the ripeness of the time for Hinde's suggestion is found in methodological advances in research on acquaintance and methods for keeping daily records of relational events and experiences (Duck and Miell 1986).

An excellent survey of methodological points in this area has been provided by McCarthy (1981) who identifies the strengths and weaknesses of much past and present research on relationship growth. Specific examples of innovative work are provided by Huston and his co-workers (e.g. Huston et al. 1981) who have adopted a new approach to courtship development based on couples' retrospective accounts of the trajectory of their courtship from first meeting to marriage. This team has subsequently identified different pathways to sexual intimacy (Christopher and Cate 1985); different attributions associated with turning points in the decision to wed (Surra 1986); and the extent to which premarital conflict predicts or interferes

with success of the marriage (Kelly et al. 1985).

In part also the growth of the area has become possible because of theorists' growing recognition of the importance of COMMUNICATION in developing acquaintance, not only in terms of the ways in which partners self-disclose and indicate the geography of their selves to one another (Duck and Perlman 1985) but also because changes in the form of communication actually serve to define and develop the relationship (Morton and Douglas 1981). These last authors have thus studied and been able to tie together several different lines of research on information processing, exchange and communication.

An extremely wide range of issues is studied under the aegis of the term relationships, as might be expected, given the interdisciplinary origins of its study. Whilst some workers are concerned to study and explain the effects of the social context in which particular relationships occur, others are concerned with their conduct and the consequences of the relative patterns of equity in partners' behavior (see EQUITY THEORY) whilst a third category of workers has studied different types of relationships, for instance, sexual relationships, relationships in marriage and the family, and relationships at work (see Duck and Gilmour 1981a). More recently many researchers have turned their attention to the breakdown of relationships (Baxter 1984; Lee 1984) and to their repair and re-establishment (Duck 1984). Issues here focus largely on the SOCIAL SKILLS of relating but also on knowledge of social rules and NORMS.

Several other major areas concern the development of relationships with age and disordered personal relationships in clinical and prison populations. In the first category, work focuses mostly on mother-infant relationships and their role in the development of subsequent social relationships (Pawlby 1981). The folly of ignoring the role of father-child relationships and the friendships of children with their peers has been noted by Parke (1981) and by La Gaipa (1981). Despite its social importance, work on the relationships of adults, especially elderly adults, has been very little studied and the role of relationships in preventing illness or premature death is only just being researched (Gottlieb 1985).

A further field that is full of social importance concerns the disorders that occur to relationships and the relationships of disordered people. Most research has so far been devoted to the study of marital disruption and divorce (e.g. Hagestad and Smyer 1982), but the larger problems of loneliness and social isolation have recently been addressed by Peplau and Perlman (1982) who suggest a new theory of loneliness. Their suggestion is that loneliness cannot sensibly be seen as mere absence of friends but as a discrepancy between desired and achieved levels of social interaction. By relating these ideas to ATTRIBUTION, Peplau and Perlman are able to make a number of testable hypotheses about the effects and antecedents of loneliness. A collection of reports of successful programs for treating loneliness as well as full details of the physical as well as mental difficulties that it has now been shown to have can be found in a recent *Sourcebook on loneliness* (Peplau and Perlman 1982).

Dissolutions of relationships is a topic which has recently received growing attention from researchers beyond those working in marital dissolution (Duck 1982, 1984). It is now clear that breakdown of relationships cannot be seen simply as the mere reverse of the growth of liking and the development of relationships; the processes involve not only disaffection with a partner, but also social consequences in terms of the responses of significant others, of friendship networks, and the like. Another major element is the accounts that people produce as a face-saving device to explain the dissolution of their relationships and their own role in it. To make useful inroads into the complexities of relationships greater study is needed on the processes of development of relationships; to make inroads into social problems, the research of dissolution and repair of relationships is more urgent.

SWD

Bibliography

Baxter, L.A. 1984: Trajectories of relationship disengagement. *Journal of social and personal relationships* 1, 29–48.

Christopher, F.S. and Cate, R.M. 1985: Premarital sexual pathways and relationship development. *Journal of social and personal relationships* 2, 271–88.

Duck, S.W. 1982: *Personal relationships 4: Dissolving personal relationships*. London: Academic Press.

—— 1984: *Personal relationships 5: Repairing personal relationships*. London: Academic Press.

—— and Gilmour, R. 1981a: *Personal relationships 1: Studying personal relationships*. London and New York: Academic Press.

—— 1981b: *Personal relationships 2: Developing personal relationships*. London and New York: Academic Press.

—— and Miell, D.E. 1986: Charting the development of relationships. In *The emerging field of personal relationships*, eds. R. Gilmour and S.W. Duck. Hillsdale, N.J.: LEA.

—— and Perlman, D. 1985: The thousand islands of personal relationships: a prescriptive analysis for future research. In *Understanding personal relationships*, eds. S.W. Duck and D. Perlman. London: Sage.

Gottlieb, B.H. 1985: Social support and the study of personal relationships. *Journal of social and personal relationships* 2, 351–76.

Hagestad, G.O. and Smyer, N. 1982: Dissolving long-term relationships: patterns of divorcing in middle-age. In Duck 1982, op. cit.

Hinde, R.A. 1979: *Towards understanding relationships*. London and New York: Academic Press.

—— 1981: The bases of a science of interpersonal relationships. In Duck and Gilmour 1981a, op. cit.

Huston, T.L., Surra, S., Fitzgerald, N. and Cate, R. 1981: Mate selection as an interpersonal process. In Duck and Gilmour 1981b, op. cit.

Kelly, C., Huston, T.L. and Cate, R.M. 1985: Premarital relationship correlates of the erosion of satisfaction in marriage. *Journal of social and personal relationships* 2, 167–78.

La Gaipa, J.J. 1981: Children's friendships. In Duck and Gilmour 1981b, op. cit.

Lee, L. 1984: Sequences in separation: a framework for investigating endings of the personal (romantic) relationships. *Journal of social and personal relationships* 1, 49–74.

McCarthy, B. 1981: Studying personal relationships. In Duck and Gilmour 1981a, op. cit.

Morton, T.L. and Douglas, M.A. 1981: The growth of relationships. In Duck and Gilmour 1981b, op. cit.

Parke, R. 1981: *Fathering*. New York: Fontana.

Pawlby, S. 1981: Infant-mother relationships. In Duck and Gilmour 1981b, op. cit.

Peplau, L.A. and Perlman, D. 1982: *Loneliness: a sourcebook of current theory, research and therapy*. New York: Wiley.

Surra, C. 1986: Attributions about turning points in the decision to wed. *Journal of social and personal relationships* 3, in press.

religion: psychology of The psychological study of religion can: (1) provide descriptive accounts of devotional, mystical, conversion or other experiences reported as "religious"; (2) discover the degree of correlation, if any, between various elements of religiosity, such as religious practices, beliefs, moral preferences and intense experiences; (3) identify background or personality factors that may shape these religious elements; (4) trace out the consequences and functions for an individual or a group, of any of the religious elements; (5) contribute to or borrow from philosophical or theological reflections on human nature. Psychologists pursue these studies with quantified empirical data, case studies, field studies, culling of historical and biographical materials and with armchair reflections.

In principle psychologists aspire to generalizations that would apply universally to human experience of religion. In practice, studies are usually limited to available groups (e.g. clinic patients, university students, church members) in mainstream Western religions.

It is convenient to distinguish broadly between three approaches. The first tends to define religion in terms of behavior that is *distinct*, sometimes dramatically so, from other behavior. Church affiliation is sharply distinguished from other institutional participation, with assumed distinct psychological meaning and function – a belief in God which is distinguishable from other beliefs and attitudes, and

prayers and mysticism which are unlike other intense introspective experiences, etc. The second approach regards such behavior as *illustrative* of whatever psychological principles apply to any membership, belief, etc. Religion might be cited as an example in any chapter in a psychology textbook, but would not warrant a chapter of its own. This approach tends not to produce any distinctive "psychology of religion", and will therefore drop out of further discussion in this article. In the third approach, religion is defined not in terms of behavior, but as a more subjective and fundamental dimension or orientation of personality and human existence, as the way a person or group deals with such issues as trust and mistrust, commitment, evil, ideals and their frustration, with personal wholeness, fragmentation, and shortcomings, and with death.

The first and third of these approaches, to be termed here simply "objective" and "subjective", will provide the framework for the rest of this article. The distinction corresponds to a fundamental distinction made by religious persons, roughly between "conservatives" and "liberals": whether religious importance is attached primarily to objective creeds, forms and institutions (which liberals term "literalism") or to existential pilgrimage wherever, as they see it, God is at work (which conservatives term "secularism"). The distinction is recognized by what is undoubtedly the most cited terminology in the field, ALLPORT's categories of "extrinsic" and "intrinsic" religion, and accounts for the persistent popularity of these terms, despite their patent conceptual and empirical shortcomings (see Batson and Ventis 1982, Dittes 1969; but, for a different view, see Donahue 1985).

The "objective" approach favors substantive definitions of religion as "belief in God", participation in public worship or private devotions etc. It often assumes the uni-dimensional nature of religion, i.e., intercorrelation and interchangeability among these various indices, and often assumes one such index sufficient to assess the degree of a person's religiousness. Among researchers (e.g. Argyle and Beit-

Hallahmi 1975) using quantifiable empirical data with relatively large samples, the typical study correlates religion with social or personality variables, similarly defined "objectively". Typical and repeated findings are that religion is "greater" among women, young adolescents and those past middle age, among the less educated and less intelligent (when class differences are held constant), among the middle class, and among those who have more conservative attitudes on social questions, more racial prejudice and more authoritarianism. The findings suggest to some that religion encourages socially dysfunctional behavior and attitudes, to others that religion attracts those who feel most marginal, i.e. those who "need" it. Some studies attempt to connect religion with identifiable effects, such as desirable behavior or improved mental health.

The question of uni-dimensionality, i.e. the intercorrelation among the several indices, has been answered empirically, largely through factor analyses. Religion appears as a single factor when respondents and questionnaire items are religiously unsophisticated; "religion" then appears as an undifferentiated cluster, with the church building the most visible marker. But when respondents are limited to more religiously experienced persons and when questionnaire items permit differentiation, multiple factors appear and different elements of religion are seen to play different roles.

The "subjective" approach favors functional definitions. Religion is whatever yields trust, reduces guilt, integrates personality, increases social responsibility or helps people to cope with death etc. As is apparent, some such functions are more conventionally identifiable to psychologists than others. This approach does not assume uni-dimensionality of religion but examines behavior, whether conventionally regarded as "religious" or other kinds. This approach is not limited to clinical or field studies (e.g. Erikson 1958) but is also used by empiricists with quantifiable data (e.g. Batson and Ventis 1982, Yinger 1970). It is also more closely connected to

the thought of theologians (e.g. Tillich 1953).

Risks or accusations of "reductionism" are especially rife in the psychology of religion because it is thought that the reality of the religious belief or practice, as understood by the practitioner, is challenged or denied by the demonstration of psychological motives or functions, especially motives not consciously recognized by the practitioner. Logically there should be no problem. The truth or correctness of religious belief and practice is determined by philosophical or theological inquiry and by criteria entirely independent of psychological analysis. True or false belief can be equally motivated; or, to put it theologically, God may or may not use psychological processes. The "genetic fallacy" has been soundly disclaimed by every major writer in the psychology of religion, including Freud (1927) who carefully defined "illusion" as he applied it to both religion and to science, to refer to certain wish-fulfilling functions, not to objective validity. But logic aside, believers are often threatened by analysis, feeling, in effect, "I believe *either* because it is true, *or* because I need to", and analysis is sometimes used as a hostile attack on religion. Such behavior probably deserves its own psychological study.

Historically, the psychology of religion has been prominent from the beginning of modern psychology. Empirical techniques (especially sophisticated scaling and factor-analytic methods) and personality theories have not only been applied readily and promptly to religion but have been developed in part in order to deal with the elusive and dramatic phenomena of religion. The earliest book to bear the title *Psychology of religion* appeared in 1899 (Starbuck). During the early decades of this century church institutions and theological schools encouraged psychology of religion as an aid to the task of religious formation and religious education, but in the middle of the century this gave way to a preoccupation with the adaptation of therapeutic and counseling skills for clergy. More recently, especially in the US, the rapid growth of non-doctrinal, objective and analytic "religious studies" particularly in secular universities, has again encouraged the discipline. The principal organization for psychologists and sociologists of religion is the Society for the Scientific Study of Religion which has published a quarterly journal since 1960.   JED

Bibliography

Argyle, M. and Beit-Hallahmi, B. 1975: *The social psychology of religion*. Boston: Routledge and Kegan Paul.

*Batson, C.D. and Ventis, W.L. 1982: *The religious experience: a social-psychological perspective*. New York and Oxford: Oxford University Press.

*Dittes, J.E. 1969: Psychology of religion. In *Handbook of social psychology*. 2nd edn, eds. G. Lindzey and E. Aronson. Boston: Addison-Wesley.

Donahue, M.J. 1985: Intrinsic and extrinsic religiousness: review and meta-analysis. *Journal of personality and social psychology* 48, 400–19.

Erikson, E.H. 1958: *Young man Luther*. New York: Norton.

Freud, S. 1912 (1953): *Totem and taboo. Standard edition of the complete psychological works of Sigmund Freud*, vol. 13. London: Hogarth Press; New York: Norton.

——— 1927 (1961): *The future of an illusion. Standard edition*, vol. 21, op. cit.

James, W. 1902: *The varieties of religious experience*. New York and London: Longman.

Starbuck, E.D. 1899: *The psychology of religion: an empirical study of the growth of religious consciousness*. New York: Scribner.

Tillich, P. 1953: *The courage to be*. New Haven, Conn.: Yale University Press.

Yinger, J.M. 1970: *The scientific study of religion*. New York and London: Macmillan.

repression The principal DEFENSE MECHANISM in psychoanalytic theory. The process by which a wish, idea etc. is kept out of consciousness because it is unacceptable either to the EGO (because maladaptive) or the SUPEREGO (because offensive to moral precepts). "Primary" repression is what prevents the idea of an instinctual impulse from ever emerging into consciousness, so that much of the UNCONSCIOUS MIND consists of ID-impulses; while "secondary" repression rejects from consciousness also ideas associated with, or symbolic of, such an impulse (Freud 1915). Repression differs from inhibition in that in the former the energy of the impulse is opposed by a counter-force, whereas in the latter the energy of the impulse itself is withdrawn. If repression is excessive, impulses find indirect expression in neurotic symptoms rather than in constructive sublimitations, and normally repressed material is expressed in disguised form in dreams or in the mild disruption of everyday psychological functioning.   NMC

Bibliography

Freud, S. 1915 (1957): Repression. In *Standard edition of the psychological works of Sigmund Freud*, vol. 14, pp. 143–58. London: Hogarth Press; New York: Norton.

reticular activating system The AROUSAL of the brain is the function of the reticular activating system (RAS) (see figure). The reticular formation consists of a diffuse collection of neurons located in medial regions of the brain stem. This formation extends from the medulla through the pons and mid-brain to the thalamus. Lesions of this brain region produce persistent sleep, while electrical stimulation of the reticular formation will arouse a sleeping animal. Not only does RAS activation lead to awakening, but it also produces increased levels of arousal once awake. All sensory pathways to the cortex send branches to the RAS. Although this sensory information is very non-specific, it serves to stimulate the RAS which, in turn, activates the cortex so that the incoming message can be interpreted. Additionally, there are descending neural pathways from the cortex that may excite the RAS which will, in turn, more fully activate the cortex. EYSENCK associates differences in arousal, and RAS activity with differences between people on the fundamental personality dimension introversion-extraversion (Eysenck 1967).

               RAJ

Bibliography

Eysenck, H.J. 1967: *The biological basis of personality*. Springfield, Ill.: Thomas.

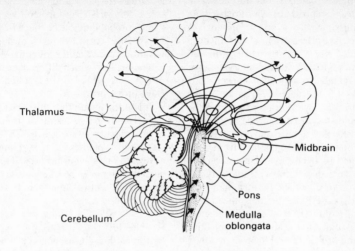

Thalamus

Midbrain

Pons

Cerebellum

Medulla
oblongata

The reticular formation is the shaded area.

risk-taking There are two conceptual specifications of this sort of action, one emerging from social psychology and the other from the psychology of decision theory: (1) risk-taking behavior occurs if the risk-taker places something at stake, where a stake exists only if both positive and negative outcomes are possible, *and* if the risk-taker recognizes that something is or will be at stake, *and* if the risk-taker takes action which by its nature and context makes the stake irreversible and in the normal course of events will lead to some outcome (Blascovich and Ginsburg 1978); (2) risk-taking entails choosing among options which are associated with outcomes that will be of benefit or harm, but for any option the occurrence of one or the other of its set of outcomes is uncertain. A gamble is an archetypal case of each definition; so are most forms of investment, provided the returns are not guaranteed.

The social psychological study of risk-taking became extremely active in the wake of a counter-intuitive finding that individuals in a group setting take greater risks than they do when acting on their own. The phenomenon came to be known as the RISKY SHIFT, and hundreds of studies were conducted under that rubric (see Dion,

Baron and Miller 1970 for a review of the early material). Considerable effort was devoted to experimental assessment of competing theories of the underlying mechanisms, which included proposals of a risk-taking norm, the role of persuasive arguments, various social comparison processes, and the spread of responsibility. Eventually it became apparent that most (but not all) of the research had little if anything to do with risk-taking, and the findings became re-interpreted as instances of group polarization, in which there is a 'group produced enhancement of a prevailing individual tendency' (Lamm and Myers 1978, p.146) and has no necessary connection to risk-taking. The immense popularity of the risky shift as a research topic was due in part to its counter-intuitive nature; in part to its potential relevance to a wide range of important decision contexts, such as medicine and surgery, emergencies, and judicial sentencing; and in part to the existence of a simple questionnaire – the choice dilemmas questionnaire CDQ – as the criterion measure of risk-taking. Unfortunately the CDQ was a personality measure and not a measure of risk-taking behavior, which made irrelevant the 80 per cent of the studies that had used it. The absence of an adequate conceptual analysis of risk-taking made possible the adoption of such a measure (see Blascovich and Ginsburg 1978; also see Cartwright 1973 for an historical review and commentary).

Risk-taking has not been consensually defined in the decision-making arena either, but the criterion task by which the "risk" being taken is measured is the choice by the risk-taker of one from among two or more options. Risk-taking from the standpoint of decision-making has been conceptualized within a framework of rational choice, which in turn had emphasized a criterion of the maximization of expected utility (EU) – or of subjective expected utility, in the absence of objective values and probabilities. However, it now is clear that the choices which people make do not necessarily conform to the technical requirements of the EU model (see Coombs and Huang 1976) and more realistic models have been proposed. One of these is prospect theory (Tversky and Kahneman 1981) which takes into account individual differences among risk-takers in the environmental information which they take into account and in the ways in which they integrate and weight that information. The EU maximization model holds that a rational individual will choose among risky options so as to maximize the expected utility of the choice, which in turn is construed as a product of the probability p of occurrence of the outcome associated with that choice and the value v of that outcome. The prospect model assumes that each person has a changeable, neutral reference point, and that outcomes are evaluated as positive or negative deviations from that reference point. Moreover, people differ in the importance attributed to various probabilities; usually, small probabilities have greater impact on decisions than high or moderate probabilities. This is reflected in a weighting factor, Π, and in the use of the "decision weight" Πp instead of simple probability p as in EU. Thus, in the prospect model of risky choice, outcomes are evaluated as deviations from a reference point, which itself may be a desired state, a current state,

a feared state, an earlier state, the state of some comparison group, and so on; and some probabilities can be given more importance than others through the weighting factor; and sequential decisions can be made in which different criteria and different weights can be applied at each stage of the process.

It is unfortunate that the social psychological study of risk-taking has ceased to be of investigative interest, because the decision theory models of risky choice have advanced to a stage where social processes and conditions can be taken into account. A blend of the two approaches would be synergistic.   GPG

Bibliography

Blascovich, J. and Ginsburg, G.P. 1975: Conceptual analysis of risk-taking in "risky shift" research. *Journal for the theory of social behavior* 8, 217–30.

Cartwright, D.A. 1973: Determinants of scientific progress: the case of research on the risky shift. *American psychologist* 28, 222–31.

*Coombs, C.H. 1975: Portfolio theory and the measurement of risk. In *Human judgment and decision processes*, eds. M.F. Kaplan and S. Schwartz. New York and London: Academic Press.

—— and Huang, L.C. 1976: Tests of the betweenness property of expected utility. *Journal of mathematical psychology* 13, 323–37.

Dion, K.L., Baron, R.S. and Miller, N. 1970: Why do groups make riskier decisions than individuals? In *Advances in experimental social psychology*, vol. 5, ed. L. Berkowitz. New York and London: Academic Press.

Lamm, H. and Myers, D.G. 1978: Group-induced polarization of attitudes and behaviors. In *Advances in experimental social psychology*, vol 2, ed. L. Berkowitz. New York and London: Academic Press.

Myers, D.G. 1983: Polarizing effects of social interaction. In *Group decision processes*, eds. H. Brandstatter, J.H. Davis and G. Stocker-Kreichgauer. London: Academic Press.

Tversky, A. and Kahneman, D. 1981: The framing of decisions and the psychology of choice. *Science* 211, 453–8.

risky shift A term which describes the fact that groups often take riskier decisions than the individual members of the group would take. This phenomenon, which counters the popular belief that groups are more conservative than individuals, was first put forward in an unpublished dissertation by Stoner in 1961. Many studies have used a choice dilemma questionnaire, developed by Kogan and Wallach (1967), in which a person or a group is asked to estimate what the odds for success would have to be in order to recommend the more risky and more valuable course of action in a two-choice situation. More recent research has shown that groups can also be more conservative than the average individual and hence the term "group polarization" has replaced the term "risky shift". The direction of the polarization depends first of all upon the initial positions of the individual members. The group decision shifts in the direction of the majority. Although various explanations have been offered for group polarization it appears that informational influence, based on the availability of more arguments in one direction rather than the other, explains the phenomena (Lamm and Myers 1978). JMFJ

Bibliography

Kogan, N. and Wallach. M.A. 1967: Risk taking as a function of the situation, the person and the group. In *New directions in psychology*, vol. 2, eds. G. Mandler et al. New York: Holt, Rinehart and Winston.

Lamm, H. and Myers, D.G. 1978: Group induced polarization of attitudes and behavior. In *Advances in experimental social psychology*, vol. 2, ed. L. Berkowitz. New York and London: Academic Press.

ritual and ritualization In anthropology, ritual refers to a prescribed formal pattern of cultural behavior, usually symbolic and often religious or ceremonial in character (see Keesing 1981).

In ethology, by an intended analogy, ritual refers to a pattern of animal behavior, such as reproductive display, which has a distinctively stylized quality: and ritualization is the evolutionary or developmental process which brings a ritual into existence (see Immelmann 1980). Hypothetically, evolutionary ritualization originates with a non-ritual movement such as

feeding, and proceeds by a gradual modification of the movement in which it also acquires the function of a social signal. The modified form of the movement may be exaggerated, formalized and repetitive, and may include the display of conspicuous colors or structures: these changes are considered to enhance the clarity of the communication involved.

Discussions between ethologists, anthropologists and others (e.g. Hinde 1972) have raised many issues of interest, but have also demonstrated that the different disciplines use "ritual" and "ritualization" in very different senses. RDA

Bibliography

Hinde, R.A. ed. 1972: *Non-verbal communication*. Cambridge, New York and Melbourne: Cambridge University Press.

Immelmann, K. 1980: *Introduction to ethology*. New York and London: Plenum Press.

Keesing, R.M. 1981: *Cultural anthropology: a contemporary perspective*. 2nd edn. New York and London: Holt, Rinehart and Winston.

Rogers, Carl Ransom The proponent of "client-centered therapy" (nondirective counseling) and the "father of humanistic psychology". Rogers was born in Illinois in 1902. His family were farmers with, according to Rogers himself (1959) 'almost fundamentalist' religious beliefs. He went to agricultural college at the University of Wisconsin (1919), but decided to become a minister. Rogers graduated from the Union Theological Seminary in New York in 1924. After that he attended the Columbia University Teachers College where he studied clinical psychology (Ph.D. 1931). He was an intern at the psychoanalytically oriented Institute for Child Guidance in New York, and from 1928 to 1940 he was a psychologist in the child study department of the Society for Prevention of Cruelty to Children in Rochester, and its replacement the Rochester Guidance Center. During this period Rogers recognized the patient's (or, as he would say "the client's") capacity to gain insight into his or her own problem and to find a solution. He argued that listening to the client is better than guiding.

In 1939 he published *The clinical treatment of the problem child* and in 1942 he published *Counseling and psychotherapy*, which contained the transcript of the tapes of an eight-session therapy.

In 1940 Rogers became a professor at Ohio State University but in 1945 he joined the University of Chicago as professor of psychology and head of the counseling center. He now argued that the SELF-CONCEPT is central in the organization of the personality (1947), and that the recognition and clarification of feelings are basic to therapy. During this period he worked out his ideas about the best approach for therapists to take. His views (1957, 1966) were that beneficial change would occur if the therapist was able to provide "congruence" (genuineness), unconditional positive regard, and empathic understanding. The genuine therapist can be him- or herself without putting on an act. Rogers believed that the client is "likely to sense" that put-on concern is false. The "positive regard" for the client is a (genuine) display of care by the therapist, which is not conditional on the client behaving in any particular way. The therapist must also display EMPATHY and show that he understands the client's feelings and takes them seriously. There is evidence that these characteristics do distinguish inexperienced therapists from good therapists, regardless of theoretical orientation (Frank 1971).

In 1957 Rogers became professor of psychology and psychiatry at the University of Wisconsin. He went on to the Western Behavioral Sciences Institute in La Jolla, California in 1964. He and several colleagues set up the Center for the Study of Persons in 1968. In doing this he dissociated himself from academic psychology, declaring himself 'rather turned-off by the ... methods of studying (people) as objects for research' (1972).

Rogers is considered important not only as a theorist (and practitioner) of psychotherapy, but also for his ideas about the SELF. His conceptions of personality and therapy revolve around these ideas. He believes in the 'fundamental predominance of the subjective', and that 'Man lives essentially in his own personal and subjective world' (1959). In Rogers's view the individual has an organized set of perceptions of his or her own self and its relationship to others. The self-concept is not fragmented, but a gestalt with a coherent and integrated pattern. It is also conscious. Rogers's experience with the sudden reversals of clients' self-concepts during therapy persuaded him that 'the alteration of one minor aspect could completely alter the whole pattern' (1959; cf. ASCH).

In addition to the self-concept the individual has an IDEAL SELF, i.e. what one would like or thinks one ought to be. Rogers takes the discrepancy between the self-concept and the ideal self as a measure of maladjustment, but the evidence does not entirely support this suggestion. Katz and Zigler (1967), for example, found that older and more intelligent children had greater discrepancies, and argued that this was because they had higher ideals and were more realistic about themselves. On the other hand some of the findings on TYPE-A PERSONALITY, Burger's (1984) work on need for control and Higgins et al.'s (1985) work on self-discrepancy, imply that a belief that one is not living up to one's ideals may be a risk factor in mental and physical illness. Rogerians consider that support for the discrepancy model of maladjustment is provided by evidence that discrepancy is reduced by non-directive counseling (Butler and Haigh 1954). This, however, only shows (at best) that after this kind of therapy recovery is associated with such a reduction.

The only motive recognized in Rogers's theory is the "basic actualizing tendency", i.e. 'the inherent tendency of the organism to develop all its capacities in ways which serve to maintain or enhance the organism' (1959). This tendency 'expresses itself ... in the actualization of ... the self'. In Rogers's description of the development of his ideas about the self he says that from what his clients said "it seemed clear that in some odd sense (a client's) goal was to become his real self". Self-actualization has never become a conceptually clear or empirically useful idea.

According to Rogers, there is frequently a discrepancy between the concept of oneself and the reality. He calls this "incongruence". People are vulnerable to anxiety when their self-concepts do not tally with reality. If experience does not support one's view of oneself, one is likely to employ various DEFENSE MECHANISMS such as distortion or denial. In therapy, on the other hand, clients appear to revise their self-concepts. Rogers believes that 'psychological adjustment exists when the concept of the self is such that all the . . . experiences of the organism are . . . assimilated . . . into a consistent relationship with the concept of self' (1951). The maintenance of consistency has, of course, been proposed as a major motive by many psychologists and has led to a great deal of empirical research (see COGNITIVE CONSISTENCY).

Apart from the "basic actualizing tendency" Rogers also thinks everyone has a secondary or learnt "need for positive regard" (i.e. to be valued for him- or herself). This has already been mentioned as a necessary element in client-centered therapy. Rogers also has the more general belief that acceptance of oneself and high SELF-ESTEEM are the result of being brought up in a family which shows such positive regard (1951). Coopersmith (1967) provided evidence that children have high self-esteem when their parents have an attitude of acceptance, which is neither too cloying nor too detached, and which does not preclude control or punishment.

Rogers's ideas developed in the practice of therapy and the things he says (as well as the things he does) show that he has remained suspicious of many of the presumptions of academic psychology. This has possibly produced a tension between his systematic theorizing self and his pastoral self. He effects a reconciliation by claiming that 'research is not . . . an activity in which one engages to gain professional kudos. It is the persistent, disciplined effort to make sense and order out of the phenomena of subjective experience'. Rogers has clearly been of major importance in advancing understanding of psychotherapy. His theories about the self

are more difficult to evaluate. Although they often seem to have appealed more to the enthusiastically woolly-minded, they have had sufficient strength and empirical support to provide a valuable counter to some of the more reductive and bizarre assumptions about human psychology which have been popular in Rogers's lifetime. RL

Bibliography

Burger, J.M. 1984: Desire for control, locus of control, and proneness to depression. *Journal of personality* 52, 71–89.

Butler, J.M. and Haigh, G.V. 1954: Changes in the relation between self-concepts and ideal concepts consequent upon client centered counseling. In *Psychotherapy and personality change*, eds. C.R. Rogers and R.F. Dymond. Chicago: University of Chicago Press.

Coopersmith, S. 1967: *The antecedents of self-esteem*. San Francisco: Freeman.

Frank, J.D. 1971: Therapeutic factors in psychotherapy. *American journal of psychotherapy* 25, 350–61.

Higgins, E.T., Klein, R. and Strauman, T. 1985: Self-concept discrepancy theory: a psychological model for distinguishing among different aspects of depression and anxiety. *Social cognition* 3, 51–76.

Katz, P. and Zigler, E. 1967: Self-image disparity: a developmental approach. *Journal of personality and social psychology* 5, 186–95.

Rogers, C.R. 1939: *The clinical treatment of the problem child*. Boston: Houghton Mifflin.

—— 1942: *Counseling and psychotherapy*. Boston: Houghton Mifflin.

—— 1947: Some observations on the organization of personality. *American psychologist* 2, 358–68.

—— 1951: *Client-centered therapy*. Boston: Houghton Mifflin.

—— 1957: The necessary and sufficient conditions of therapeutic personality change. *Journal of consulting psychology* 21, 95–103.

—— 1959: A theory of therapy, personality, and interpersonal relationships, as developed in the client-centered framework. In *Psychology: a study of a science*, vol. 3, ed. S. Koch. New York and London: McGraw-Hill.

—— 1966: Client-centered therapy. In *American handbook of psychiatry*, ed. S. Arieti. New York: Basic Books.

—— 1972: My personal growth. In *Twelve therapists*, ed. A. Burton. San Francisco: Jossey-Bass.

role ambiguity, conflict and overload

Role ambiguity exists when an individual has inadequate information about his or her role, where there is a lack of clarity about the objectives associated with a role (especially at work), about others' expectations of the role, and about its scope and responsibilities. Role conflict exists when an individual in a particular role is torn by conflicting demands or troubled by having to undertake tasks which he or she does not want to do. There is also inter-role conflict when an individual occupies two or more roles which have mutually conflicting demands (see also ROLES: SOCIAL PSYCHOLOGY).

In the work setting, French and Caplan (1973) have differentiated between quantitative and qualitative overload. Quantitative refers to having "too much to do", while qualitative overload involves work that is too difficult. (See also WORK STRESS.)

In general, there is a debate about whether occupancy of multiple roles is a strain (Goode 1960) or a benefit to the individual (Marks 1977). The former position emphasizes that people have limited energy and that each of their roles demands more than they can give. The latter emphasizes the privileges roles confer. Thoits (1983) found a positive correlation between the number of roles one occupies and psychological well-being, which supports the benefit hypothesis.

CLC/RL

Bibliography

French, J.R.P. and Caplan, R.D. 1973: Organisational stress and individual strain. In *The failure of success*, ed. A.J. Marrow. London: Amacon distr. Graham and Trotman Ltd.

Goode, W.J. 1960: A theory of strain. *American sociological review* 25, 483–96.

Marks, S.R. 1977: Multiple roles and role strain: some notes on human energy, time and commitment. *American sociological review* 41, 921–36.

Thoits, P.A. 1983: Multiple identities and psychological well-being: a reformulation and test of the social isolation hypothesis. *American sociological review* 48, 174–87.

role-rule theory

An approach to the analysis and explanation of the more formal kinds of social interaction. It is an integral part of the ETHOGENIC method in social psychology. In many of their social interactions people can be seen as performing in roles. The basic notion of role is taken from the stage but it has been developed in various different ways, so that the term is now to some extent ambiguous. A role may be simply a way of referring to some regular pattern in the way people of a certain category behave. We might, for instance, speak of "woman's role". There are no specific rules which need to be followed to create the role, and roles of this sort are usually associated with expectations. A more tightly defined notion of role has been used in the analysis of the way in which people behave in institutional settings. In this context role behavior is related to structural features of institutions, which locate roles in terms of the relations between functional units of the institution. For instance, in a hospital there may be distinctive roles for doctors, nurses, patients etc. In so far as these roles are officially defined they are associated with systems of rules which specify the behavior appropriate to this or that role.

The use of role-rule theory to analyze and explain other kinds of social interaction draws on the psychological features of institutional role behavior. In particular it assumes that the number of routine forms of interaction is greater than one might expect. Further, by extending the notion of role, role-rule theory proposes a hypothetical mechanism which could produce conforming, coordinated interaction between people, and so provides a necessary basis for explaining that behavior. "Role" is used in the analysis of social interactions and "rule" in the explanation of the regularities and patterns found by means of that analysis.

In studying institutional interactions microsociologists (particularly GOFFMAN 1969, pp.37ff) have used the notion of role to identify a number of psychologically interesting phenomena. When a person is so located in an institution that more than one set of rules (and reciprocally of expectations) seems to be in play, they may experience "role-conflict", uncertainties as to the relative priorities to be given to each rule-system. In certain institutions the solemnity of role-fulfilling actions is sometimes a bar to the very best performance, and the leader of a team may sometimes reveal a "human side" by taking "role-distance", that is by acting in a way inconsistent with full immersion in his or her role.

Doubts have sometimes been expressed (Lindsey 1977) about the justification for using the rule metaphor to explain the regularity of the actions people produce in fulfilling the demands of their roles, whether it be in the looser or the stricter sense of "role". A somewhat similar doubt has also been expressed about using the notion of "grammatical rule" in the explanation of the ability of native speakers to produce grammatically correct sentences. Clearly there are many occasions on which people act in a coordinated and regulated way without reference to explicitly formulated rules. However, the use of the rule metaphor has been justified by the argument that any cognitive process by which patterned action is produced must draw on some body of knowledge or belief, whether this is done consciously or not. The fact that this body of knowledge often has normative force, and that when it is explicitly formulated it is often expressed in the form of rules, justifies the use of the rule-metaphor to describe it.   RHa

Bibliography

Biddle, B.J. 1979: *Role theory: expectations, identities and behaviors*. New York and London: Academic Press.

Collett, P. ed. 1977: *Social rules and social behavior*. Oxford: Blackwell; Totowa, N.J.: Rowman and Littlefield.

Goffman, E. 1969: *Where the action is*. London: Allen Lane.

Harré, R. 1979: *Social being: a theory for social psychology*. Oxford: Basil Blackwell; Totowa, N.J.: Littlefield Adams.

Lindsey, R. 1977: Rules as a bridge between speech and action. In Collett, op. cit.

roles: social psychology The term role is usually defined as the behavior which is associated with a particular position in a social system. A social role implies that the person who holds this particular position enacts the associated behavior, but it also carries expectations held by others about the behavior that is appropriate for the occupant of the position. The concept of "position" is often associated with STATUS within a fixed social structure. Biddle (1979), however, pointed out that many roles are entirely determined by the context. A person "takes" or "plays" a particular role on a particular occasion (e.g. "guest" or "host") and the role ceases when the occasion ends. Other roles (e.g. "mother" or "teacher") are more permanent.

Within SYMBOLIC INTERACTION one school of thought (Kuhn 1954) sees individuals' behavior as determined by the roles they are allotted by society. Another (Blumer 1953) sees roles as providing frameworks within (and perhaps between) which individuals have a good ideal of room for choice and maneuver.

Role theory has developed a considerable literature devoted to elucidating and employing its key concepts of "position", "expectation" and "identity", and to drawing out the implications of the role model. The role vocabulary has been developed to cover phenomena such as ROLE AMBIGUITY, ROLE CONFLICT, ROLE OVERLOAD (see previous entries); as well as "role integration" – when different actors' roles fit each other (Warren 1949); "role discontinuity" – when there is a lack of coherence between the roles an individual performs in sequence (Benedict 1938); and "role distance" – when an actor behaves in a manner designed to show he or she is not involved in a current role (Goffman 1961).

The concept of role recently gained some importance for psychology due to the dramaturgical model of man advocated by GOFFMAN (1959), and taken up by writers such as Harré (1979) (see ROLE-RULE THERAPY.) It also gained empirical significance in the psychological study of social situations by Argyle et al. (1981). In general, however, the concept of role has been more important in sociological than in social psychological analyses (see also GOFFMAN). JMFJ/RL

Bibliography

Argyle, M., Furnham, A. and Graham, J.A. 1981: *Social situations*. Cambridge: Cambridge University Press.

*Biddle, B.J. 1979: *Role theory: expectations, identities, and behavior*. New York and London: Academic Press.

Blumer, H. 1953: Psychological import of the human group. In *Group relations at the crossroads*. New York: Harper.

Harré, R. 1979: *Social being*. Oxford: Basil Blackwell; Totowa, N.J.: Littlefield Adams.

Kuhn, M.H. 1954: Factors in personality: Socio-cultural determinants as seen through the Amish. In *Aspects of culture and personality*, ed. F.L.K. Hsu. New York: Abelard-Schuman.

Other references may be found in Biddle, op. cit.

S

self: philosophical usage The dominant theory of self in Western philosophy is plain enough: each of us is an incorporeal self or mind; all of our psychological states are states of this self; and each of us has absolutely certain, though private, knowledge of it and its states whenever they occur.

This view, given embryonic form by St Augustine (*De quantitate animae*, chs. XIII–XIV; 400–22, bk. X; 413–26, bk. XI), owes its popularity to Descartes who defended it with fascinating though perhaps specious arguments. A famous rationale emerges from Descartes's search in several works, for something he could know without any risk of error. It will be a convenience to adopt his terminology, and classify all our multifarious mental processes and states as forms of thinking (*cogitationes*). Accordingly, if someone feels chilled, experiences disappointment, indulges in phantasies, doubts something, seems to perceive objects – when objects are on display or when he is hallucinating or dreaming – then we say he is thinking. Descartes's reasoning proceeds approximately as follows: I could be mistaken if I assumed the existence of any material thing, including the body I call "mine". For instance, I might be dreaming when I believe, apparently on the basis of conclusive evidence, that my hand is here under my gaze. But even if I am constantly deluded, I cannot be wrong when I suppose that I am thinking – however erroneous or muddled my thinking is. More important, I cannot be wrong in supposing that I exist. Descartes goes on to draw four exciting but debatable conclusions: (i) I *know* that this "I" or self exists and thinks; (ii) specifically, I have some kind of direct experience or *introspective* knowledge of it and its operations; (iii) because I may be deluded about everything else, I do *not* know whether this

"I" or self has any characteristics besides thinking; so the safe course is to say that it *only* thinks; (iv) inasmuch as I could be mistaken regarding my body, I do not know whether it exists; yet since I know my self exists, self and body must be distinct, and self non-bodily.

This concept of self was taken over, with appropriate additions by many subsequent theorists of personal identity. Their main further contentions were: (v) I manage to remain one and the same individual because my self endures uninterruptedly and unaltered throughout my career; (vi) I know that it does this because I periodically introspect my self. Bishop Butler evokes this enriched theory when he declares that 'our . . . bodies are no more ourselves, or part of ourselves, than any other matter around us'. As for the *bona fide* self, he says: 'upon comparing the consciousness of one's self . . . in any two moments, there . . . immediately arises to the mind the idea of personal identity . . . reflecting upon . . . my self now, and . . . my self . . . years ago, I discern they are . . . the same self' (1736, ch. 1, dissertation 1).

Hume undermined most of this doctrine by examining claims (ii) and (vi) – asking, in effect, what Butler's "consciousness of one's self" might be like. What is one conscious *of*? In Hume's jargon: we seem to have no 'idea of *self* . . . For, from what impression could this idea be derived?' (1739, bk. I, part IV, sec. VI). But it might be argued that episodes of thought must belong to something? These and other "perceptions" are, however, 'separable from each other . . . and have no need of anything to support their existence'; we have no idea 'after what manner . . . they belong to self', how they are 'connected with it'. So Descartes suggested that we know with the greatest possible certainty that our self exists. But Hume's request for details about it and our supposed knowledge of it casts doubt on the whole theory, and should make us wonder whether the Cartesian term self is even intelligible. Of course Hume admits that his own proposal, that "the mind" or self is 'nothing but a bundle ... of different perceptions', is barely cogent.

Some of Hume's successors adamantly reasserted the Descartes-Butler analysis. Thomas Reid insisted that the 'self or I, to which [my thoughts] belong, is permanent, and has the same relation to all the ... thoughts ... which I call mine' (1785, Essay III, ch. IV). Kant agreed with Hume that there is no introspective or other knowledge of a self, but he argued that we necessarily regard our thoughts as belonging to a self – which we consider but do not know to be distinct from our bodies (1787, B157, B404–8). Finally, some twentieth-century philosophers – Russell, the early Wittgenstein, and Moritz Schlick – tried to develop a variant of Hume's "bundle": the "no-ownership" theory of self (for references and criticism see Strawson 1958).

One cannot help inquiring, incidentally, why nearly all these debaters serenely ignored the way in which people carry on everyday discourse with the pronoun "I" and the noun "self". This might have shaken some theorists' confidence, for example, that the "I" or self must be a ghostly mind exclusively given over to thought and other supposedly ethereal pursuits. When people bathe themselves, dress themselves, look at themselves in a mirror, paint portraits of themselves, feed or starve themselves, could the self in question be a mind? The self they wash, etc., surely is a flesh and blood human being. Even when people pity themselves, condemn themselves, or betray themselves, more than a Cartesian phantom is involved. The noun "self" may turn up when no mental phenomena are in question. Some flowers are self-pollinating, some engines self-lubricating and some watches self-winding. Overall, then, the traditional account ignores many of the ordinary uses of the word "self". Against this the objection can of course be raised

that people regard some aspects of their selves as more fundamental than others, and the parts of themselves they wash or offer to their fathers to be spanked are not necessarily as central as some of the inner states they cherish as their essential "selves". Naturally the slippery uses of words such as "self" in everyday speech can be a dangerous guide for philosophers. Cathy and Heathcliff in *Wuthering Heights* seemed to consider, somewhat romantically, that they had a sort of common self, while some people are said to experience affronts to their friends or property as literal affronts to themselves.

Nevertheless, many recent philosophers have assumed that everyday uses of language are at once a torch and something to be elucidated. Drawing on their novel insights into the logic of common speech they have replaced the immaterial thoughtful self with an embodied person who takes vigorous physical action and reasons out loud, at length and in public. But a new enigma has developed about how to analyze such a person's self-referential cognition, talk and purposive behavior. Suppose I am N.N., until yesterday chieftain of the local Mafia organization. Chagrined that I did not win re-election, I consider shooting myself. I announce my morbid thoughts, and then act on them. What does "myself" mean in this story? One cannot substitute my name, "N.N.", or a description that only fits me, "the recently deposed local Mafia chieftain". I might not recall that I am N.N. or the outgoing capo, although I can hardly have any difficulty in identifying the self which is myself. It is also, and obviously, not necessarily the case that *if* one were planning to do away with N.N. or the last Mafia leader, one would be planning to do away with himself. In a novelette one could hire a killer to murder someone described in a particular way without realizing that the description fitted oneself, or would do so by the time the killer got to work. It is certainly possible that one might misidentify an individual who is the object of one's hostile thoughts, exactly by misdescribing him. But while one might also misdescribe oneself one cannot so readily mis-identify oneself and prescribe the wrong self. This is the sort of problem considered to be important by many modern philosophers who write about the self (see Perry 1979 and essays 1–5 of Diamond and Teichman 1979).

The relevance of such discussions to psychological theories of the self is that they frequently treat a person's self in terms of his SELF-CONCEPT (see Mischel 1977). This is the sum of descriptions one would take to be true of oneself. According to many psychologists such descriptions necessarily situate one in a social world, as a person among persons. They do this because they are learnt from others and are not logically only applicable to oneself. What can truly be said of oneself can also, in principle, be truly said of someone else. But these modern philosophical discussions suggest that though one may describe and misdescribe oneself and others using similar terms and with similar liability to error, one's ability to identify oneself is necessarily not reliant on these descriptions in the way that one's ability to identify others may be. Hence, for all its vulgar embodiment, a person's relation to and cognition of himself does seem to have certain unique features, and these features do seem to be connected with incorrigibility and certainty. This of course was the point, although not the issue, at which Descartes began.   IGT

Bibliography

Augustine, St. (1950): De quantitate animae (On the greatness of the soul). *Ancient Christian Writers*, vol. 9. Trans. J.M. Colleran. New York: Paulist-Newman Press.

—— (1950): De trinitate (On the trinity). *Fathers of the Church*, vol. 45. Trans. J.J. O'Meara. Washington: Catholic University Press.

—— (1963): *De civitate dei (The city of God)*. Trans. J.J. Wand. Oxford: Oxford University Press.

Butler, J. 1736 (1897): The analogy of religion. In *Works of Bishop Butler*, ed. W.E. Gladstone. Oxford: Oxford University Press.

Diamond, C. and Teichman, J., eds. 1979: *Intention and intentionality*. Brighton: Harvester Press; Ithaca, N.Y.: Cornell University Press.

Hume, D. 1739 (1888): *A treatise of human nature*, ed. L.A. Selby-Bigge. Oxford: Oxford University Press.

Kant, I. 1787 (1929): *Critique of pure reason*. Trans. Norman Kemp Smith. London: Macmillan.

Mischel, T. ed. 1977: *The self: psychological and philosophical issues*. Oxford: Blackwell; Totowa, N.J.: Rowman and Littlefield.

Perry, J. 1979: The problem of the essential indexical. *Nous* 13, 3–21.

Reid, T. 1785 (1941): *Essay on the intellectual powers of man*, ed. A.D. Woozley. London: Macmillan.

Strawson, P. 1958: Persons. In *Minnesota studies in the philosophy of science*, vol. 2, eds. H. Feigl et al. Minneapolis: University of Minnesota Press.

self: psychological usage A person's framework of self-referential meaning – cognitive and affective perceptions of self-as-object, arising from innate dispositions and social interactions across a lifetime, characterized by thought, feeling and action relative to a social structure of roles, rules, norms and values.

From the moment of birth onward the child is committed to a world of socially interpreted and evaluated action. The child exhibits an inborn propensity for development from the biological to the social and the symbolic (Cooley 1922). Through a stream of behavior it is engaged in a complex blend of innately pre-adapted actions directed at the development of physical, social and psychological extension beyond mere survival. The human infant attends selectively to its own kind, to human features and human speech. It is not only sensitive to but also actively participates in interaction characterized by temporal sequencing. This sequencing – including turn-taking – is the logical and practical basis of communicating meaning, which minimally requires the acknowledgment, assignment and acceptance of mutually dependent roles of addressor and addressee. Reciprocal exchanges of verbal and non-verbal gestures, and patterns of gesture, founded upon a mutual recognition of identity and role enable successive approximation directed at the demonstration and derivation of meaning (see Bruner 1978).

There appears to be a social imperative to seek out and embark upon dialogue. The child acts in the role of agent or initiator, an implicit "I" with an inbuilt propensity for social outcomes which will cast it in the role of recipient, the incipient "me". Interaction with dialogue makes possible the progression from recognition of reciprocal role to self-consciousness to consciousness of one's self. From simple sensation arises primitive perception in the form of SELF-AWARENESS of "me" – an identity based upon realization and interpretation of physical separation and differentiation.

Primitive perception yields to complex conceptions communicated, albeit approximately, through the expressive symbols of GESTURE and play (MEAD 1934). The path from babbling through the idiosyncratic proto-language of the toddler, inevitably abandoned for adult language with its greater capacity to be comprehended, constitutes an extended experiment in the symbolic expression of experience with respect to social ROLES and rules. Play extends this process. The child enacts, through partial performances, the roles of observed others – particularly of parents and other family members. These performances in play, as in non-play contexts, reflect rules of relationship, of interdependent roles, attitudinally supported by norms and values.

From these processes of symbolization and performance a concept of self arises – a system of self-referential meaning, a synthesis of imagined notions of "me", culturally emergent and defined in social interaction (ALLPORT 1961). Interaction, therefore, engenders a global sense of identity, comprising "I", the experiencing aspect of self as knower, and "*me*", the empirical aspect of personal experience, the knowledge of self as object or self as known (see SELF-CONCEPT).

Attempts at systematic or economic description of the self-concept are destined to be condemned as artificial, impoverished, impersonal and unreal. Self-theorists agree, however, that the self-concept evolves across a lifetime and does not change with the transition from adolescence into adulthood. It can be viewed as a continuing attempt to synthesize many *selves* or multiple facets of a single *self*. James (1890) spoke of three constituents of the empirical self: the *material self* deriving from bodily awareness, clothing, family, home and property; the *social self*, in effect a conglomeration of social selves which reflect two aspects of the individual's imaginations – on the one hand, perceptions or images of the individual that he assumes are held by other individuals, or groups of individuals, who are significant because their views of the individual are important to the individual; and, on the other hand, social values and norms couched in shared views of such issues as shame and honor; finally the *spiritual self*, the awareness of one's own frailties, disposition and one's own existence, that aspect "me" as self-knowledge which is closest to the current experience, the subjective judging thought of "I".

Research into the self-concept of individuals at various ages supports the early descriptive efforts of James. The young child actively constructs the social world of others and self relative to others in terms of sex, appearance, age, kinship, social role, possessions and actions. From puberty onwards construing becomes more psychological, where persons are perceived and conceived in terms of personality (Livesley and Bromley 1973).

Self-evaluation and the evaluation of others emerge as crucial aspects of the evolving self-concept. They contribute to SELF-ESTEEM, when success and failure enter awareness as a notion of worth, reflecting the degree of congruence between pretensions and achievement, the similarity between self-evaluation and the regard or value placed upon oneself by others (Snygg and Combs 1949). It has been suggested that the need to be viewed positively is a universal need, which becomes even more compelling than SELF-ACTUALIZATION, the need to assert or realize fully one's identity. Significant others are important in the generation and maintenance of a sense of continuity and coherence reflecting positive self-evaluation. Although these contributors to the individual's self-esteem change from parents to peers within the period of primary socialization and in the secondary socialization of adulthood include many diverse sources, common requirements foster a sense of high self-esteem. Irrespective of age or socio-economic status, self-esteem emerges as a function of a secure, accepting environment, in which initiative is encouraged within clearly defined bounds of behavior (Coopersmith 1967).

Closely related to descriptive abstractions of self based upon self-evaluation, self-esteem, positive regard and self-actualization is the IDEAL SELF – suggested to be that concept of self which the individual would most like to realize, being the one upon which the highest value is placed.

Perceptions of incongruity between what one is or is becoming and what one wishes to be, create anxiety which can assume pathological proportions. Incongruence between self as knower and self as known, disparity between the "real", "true", or "inner" self and the "unreal", "false" or "outer" enacted self, can lead to distortion, dissociation or disorganisation of the stream of experience and the self-concept (Laing 1960). Such responses serve to emphasize that by the application of the self-concept, events within the social structure, involving persons and personal actions relative to the individual, have the potential to be rendered meaningful. The social world of self and others is comprehensible in terms of anticipated replication and outcome, identification and identity, acceptability and acceptance, evaluation and value.

Several self theorists indicate that the self-concept operates as a guide to behavior and a criterion for conduct (e.g. ROGERS 1961). This assertion needs to be approached with caution. The study of the self-concept can render the student self-conscious and blind to the fact that as a system of self-referential meaning generated in a myriad of interactions across the lifespan, at any given time its contents of internalized roles, status, norms and values are bound to be mutually exclusive and contradictory. The very vagueness of the individual's multifaceted self-concept can be seen as an effective mechanism for coping with co-existent illogicality (but cf. Linville 1985). The extent to which the self-concept exerts an influence on personal conduct at any given time is necessarily a function of the content and degree of self-awareness – the amount and axis of attention focused upon self and performance (see Carver and Scheier 1981).

For the major part of daily life the individual's concept is accessed, edited and implemented preconsciously. Many, if not most, of its constituent constructs of individuality and sociality exist and operate at the pre-verbal level of emotion, "felt" disposition and action itself (see Epstein 1983). Attempts to intellectualize these by raising them to consciousness and expression, to the level of logic, language and thought are necessarily fraught, revealing the mutually exclusive and contradictory. All attempts to gain access to the self-concept, to "measure" it by self-report techniques, are by definition destined to be equivocal. This is because the researcher seeks to render manifest that which for the most part is enacted preconsciously and which, by excluding the incongruous, the contrary and the ambiguous, ensures stability. Recognizing this allows methodological problems of reliability, validity, social desirability and the acquiescence commonly found in self-concept research, to be placed into a sensible, self-conscious phenomenological perspective. Nevertheless it has recently been proposed that the self-concept may function as a schema or prototype which can be used in processing information, particularly about other people (Markus and Smith 1981). This implies that one's self-concept is readily available to one and that others may be categorized by comparison with oneself (see Lewicki 1984).

The whole of issue no.3 of the *Journal for the theory of social behavior* 15, 1985 is devoted to new developments in theorizing about the self.   EWS

Bibliography

Allport, G.W. 1961: *Pattern and growth in personality*. New York: Holt, Rinehart and Winston.

Bruner, J. 1978: Learning how to do things with words. In *Human growth and development*. eds. J. Bruner and A. Garton. Oxford: Oxford University Press.

Burns, R.B. 1979: *The self concept: theory, measurement, development and behavior*. London: Longman.

Carver, C.S. and Scheier, M.F. 1981: *Attention and self-regulation: a control theory approach to human behavior*. New York and Heidelberg: Springer.

Cooley, C.H. 1922: *Human nature and the social order*, rev. edn. New York: Scribner.

Coopersmith, S. 1967: *The antecedents of self-esteem*. San Francisco: Jossey-Bass.

Epstein, S. 1983: The unconscious, the preconscious and the self-concept. In *Psychological perspectives on the self*, vol. 2, eds. J. Suls and A. Greenwald. Hillsdale, N.J.: Erlbaum.

Gergen, K.J. 1971: *The concept of self*. New York: Holt, Rinehart and Winston.

James, W. 1890 (1950): *The principles of psychology*. New York: Dover.

Laing, R.D. 1960: *The divided self*. London: Tavistock; Harmondsworth: Penguin (1965).

Lewicki, P. 1984: Self-schema and social information processing. *Journal of personality and social psychology* 47, 1177–90.

Linville, P.W. 1985: Self-complexity and affective extremity. *Social cognition* 3, 94–120.

Livesley, W.J. and Bromley, D.B. 1973: *Person perception in childhood and adolescence*. London and New York: Wiley.

Markus, H. and Smith, J. 1981: The influence of self-schema on the perception of others. In *Personality, cognition and social interaction*, eds. N. Cantor and J.F. Kihlstrom. Hillsdale, N.J.: Erlbaum.

Mead, G.H. 1934: *Mind, self and society*. Chicago: University of Chicago Press.

Rogers, C.R. 1961: *On becoming a person*. Boston: Houghton Mifflin.

Snygg, D. and Combs, A.W. 1949: *Individual behavior: a new frame of reference for psychology*. New York: Harper.

Suls, J. ed. 1982: *Psychological perspectives on the self*. Hillsdale, N.J.: Erlbaum.

self: social psychology of

Social psychology recognizes the interpersonally determined, and consequently malleable nature of the SELF while sometimes ignoring or rejecting the stabilizing and unifying qualities attributed to it in psychoanalytic and humanistic formulations. This view owes much to GOFFMAN's (1959) theatrical analogy, and other SELF-PRESENTATION models of social behavior (but see Schlenker 1980). Goffman himself was an heir to the symbolic interactionist school. Earlier ideas in that tradition do point up the impact of others on the SELF-CONCEPT. There was in particular Cooley's (1902) conception of the "looking glass self" which refers to the self as a construction built up of other people's attitudes toward us. For MEAD (1934) this process of "reflection" develops into one of "self-reflexivity": what constitutes human selfhood is the capacity to take ourselves as objects of our own consciousness to which we make indications and respond. In Mead's theory, a major precondition to the development of self which marks it as an incipiently social phenomenon is the ability to take the role of the other, so that his attitudes toward us may be appraised and internalized. Nevertheless these writers were concerned with the socialization of the child, and the way in which a comparatively stable self-concept is constructed through social influences. A stable self-concept may obviously direct a person's behavior (see SELF-CONSISTENCY).

If the self is constructed within the social context, rather than being an autonomous substance or an internal propulsion, it is subject to change with changes in social stimulation. Research has shown that people attend to cues from their own and others' behavior in order to infer such important components of their own self-systems as motives, emotions, beliefs, values, desires etc. (see Gergen 1977, for a review). Moreover, the functions for which a homuncular self was originally postulated are in the social psychological tradition seen to be largely illusory: the apprehension of personal identity over time is rather construed to be a reconstruction over time in terms of the end arrived at, and trans-situational consistency is regarded as the exception rather than the rule (see

PERSON/SITUATION CONTROVERSY). Conceiving of the self as a wholly inter- rather than intrapsychic phenomenon can lead to an extreme situationism. But recent trends in SOCIAL LEARNING THEORY (Mischel 1983) stress the role of standards in resistance to situational pressures. Still more recent trends in SOCIAL COGNITION (Markus et al. 1985) underline the role of stable beliefs about the self (self-schemata) in determining people's perceptions of their social world.   BRS/RL

Bibliography

Cooley, C.H. 1902: *Human nature and the social order.* New York: Scribner.

Gergen, K. 1977: The social construction of self knowledge. In T. Mischel, op. cit.

Goffman, E. 1959: *The presentation of self in everday life.* New York: Doubleday; Harmondsworth: Penguin (1969).

Markus, H., Smith, J. and Moreland, R.L. 1985: Role of the self-concept in the perception of others. *Journal of personality and social psychology* 49, 1494–512.

Mead, G.H. 1934: *Mind, self and society.* Chicago: University of Chicago Press.

*Mischel, T. ed. 1977: *The self: psychological and philosophical issues.* Oxford: Basil Blackwell; Totowa, N.J.: Rowman and Littlefield.

Mischel, W. 1983: Alternatives in the pursuit of the predictability and consistency of persons: stable data that yield unstable interpretations. *Journal of personality* 51, 578–604.

Schlenker, B.R. 1980: *Impression management.* Monterey: Brooks Cole.

*Wegner, D.M. and Vallacher, R.R. eds. 1980: *The self in social psychology.* New York and Oxford: Oxford University Press.

self-actualization

The inherent tendency towards self-fulfillment, self-expression and the attainment of autonomy from external forces. It is a process rather than an end state. A self-actualizing individual is deemed to be realistic, spontaneous and demonstrative, able both to engage and to transcend problems, being particularly resistant to social pressures.

According to Goldstein (1939) and ROGERS (1951) self-actualization is the sole motive, with drives such as sex, hunger and achievement as aspects, or modes of this fundamental force. Although universal and innate, its expression varies in individuals, who differ in genetic endowment, environment and cultural background. Maslow (1954) considers self-actualization to be the highest level of need. The prospect of fulfilling the highest needs (meta-needs) such as beauty, goodness and wholeness, cannot arise until lower needs such as physiological deficiencies are satisfied. These also include a need for safety, love and esteem. Maslow believes that very few individuals achieve a degree of self-actualization. This is akin to JUNG's view that self-actualization cannot come about until a person has fulfilled all of his or her capacities, and is individuated and whole.

                                    EWS

Bibliography

Goldstein, K. 1939: *The organism.* New York: American Book Co.

Maslow, A. 1954: *Motivation and personality.* New York: Harper.

Rogers, C.R. 1951: *Client-centered therapy.* Boston: Houghton Mifflin.

self-awareness

The capacity to think in terms of one's SELF-CONCEPT, focusing attention, processing information and acting with regard to this concept. The content of self-awareness can be classified according to accessibility – those conscious aspects of self-information incorporating the open (public) self known also to others, and the hidden self known only to the individual. These contrast with the blind self known only to others, and the unknown self known to no-one, though its existence can possibly be inferred. Consciousness of self, open or hidden, as level of self-awareness, varies. It is low in situations seen to be routine or ritual and heightened when circumstances are viewed as enhancing, eroding, or demanding a revision of, the self-concept.

Objective self-awareness (Duval and Wicklund 1972) is the directing of attention inward so that consciousness is focused on the SELF, its reflex being "subjective self-awareness" wherein consciousness is focused on events external to the self. Duval and Wicklund assert that the former attentive condition generates self-evaluation by setting up an automatic comparison between the individual's current state or level of performance and an ideal state. The larger the perceived discrepancy between the two states the higher the degree of negative self-evaluation, an intrinsically uncomfortable affect which the individual seeks to avoid or dispel either by changing his or her present state towards the ideal or by reverting to the subjectively self-aware condition. Objective self-awareness may be induced by any cues which serve to remind one of oneself (e.g. mirror, tape recording of one's voice, comparison with others). Gibbons (1983) reports that induced self-awareness increases the accuracy of self-report, and the predictive validity of attitude scales. He and others have also found that increasing self-awareness (with a mirror) reduces suggestibility and eliminates a placebo effect. An extension of the theory was the discovery of stable individual differences in chronic objective/subjective self-awareness, or what has been termed "private and public self-consciousness" (Fenigstein et al. 1975). Private self-consciousness is awareness of one's inner states. Public self-consciousness is awareness of oneself as a social object. The two show a slight positive correlation.

Meditation, hypnosis, drugs (particularly alcohol), and provision of simultaneous or recorded feedback, particularly visual, can markedly affect self-awareness, self-concept and social performance. Indeed, it is believed that some degree of self-awareness is basic to all interpersonal behavior and the emergence and application of values and norms. Recent research indicates that self-awareness is not a uniquely human attribute. BRS/EWS

Bibliography

Duval, S. and Wicklund, R.A. 1972: *A theory of objective self awareness.* New York and London: Academic Press.

Fenigstein, A., Scheier, M.F. and Buss, A.H. 1975: Public and private self consciousness: assessment and theory. *Journal of consulting and clinical psychology* 43, 522–7.

Gallup, G.G. 1979: Self-awareness in primates. *American scientist* 67, 417–21.

Gibbons, F.X. 1983: Self-attention and self-report: the "veridicality" hypothesis. *Journal of personality* 51, 517–42.

Kleinke, C.L. 1978: *Self-perception: the psychology of personal awareness.* San Francisco: W.H. Freeman.

*Wicklund, R.A. and Frey, D. 1980: Self-awareness theory: when the self makes a difference. In *The self in social psychology*, eds. D.M. Wegner and R.R. Vallacher. New York and Oxford: Oxford University Press.

self-concept One of many terms (self-identity, self-image, self-ideal, perceived self, phenomenal self) relating to self-perception. To illustrate this, Allport (1965) wrote:

> Suppose that you are facing a difficult and critical exam. No doubt you are aware of your high pulse rate, and of the butterflies in your stomach (*bodily self*): also of the significance of the exam in terms of your past and future (*self-identity*); of your prideful involvement (*self-esteem*); of what success or failure may mean to your family (*self-extension*); or your hopes and aspirations (*self-image*); of your role as solver of problems on the examination (*rational agent*) and of the relevance of the whole situation to your long range goals (*self striving*).

MEAD (1934) wrote of the social construction of the self-concept which is altogether a reflection of the opinions and attitudes communicated by significant others. In this sense, it is argued that society provides a looking-glass in which people discover their image or self-concept.

The related concepts of EGO and SELF form the core of many controversial areas of modern thinking in psychology. The two major approaches concern the self as the person perceives it (self as object), and the self as the agent of activity (self as subject). The self is seen as central for the integration and direction of the individual towards various forms of interaction with persons and objects.

Some of the more interesting questions

on this topic are discussed by Epstein (1973). He is concerned with the functions of the self-concept. He thinks these are to 'optimize the pleasure/pain balance of the individual over the course of a lifetime'; to 'organize the data of experience'; and to help with 'the maintenance of self-esteem'.

The second, cognitive function has recently been stressed by Markus (1977; Markus et al. 1985), who defines the self-concept as 'a set of self-schemas that organize past experiences and are used to recognize and interpret relevant stimuli in the social environment'. In a series of studies she has shown that self-schemas (clear general beliefs about oneself) do affect the way information about oneself and others is encoded, organized and used. This is one of the major areas in which the self has re-emerged in social psychology. Markus's work marries ideas typified by Snygg and Combs's (1949) claim that the self is a 'frame of reference in terms of which other perceptions gain their meaning', and the recent importation of concepts such as "schema" from cognitive psychology (see SOCIAL COGNITION).

The fact that the self-concept can be changed in interaction has been urged as a possible reason for not exaggerating its stability as a cognitive frame (Rhodewalt and Agustsdottir 1986).   AF/RL

Bibliography

Allport, G. 1965: *Pattern and growth in personality*. New York: Holt, Rinehart and Winston.

Epstein, S. 1973: The self-concept revisited: or a theory of a theory. *American psychologist* 28(5), 404–16.

Gergen, K. 1971: *The concept of self*. New York: Holt, Rinehart and Winston.

Markus, H. 1977: Self-schemata and processing information about the self. *Journal of personality and social psychology* 35, 63–78.

———Smith, J. and Moreland, R.L. 1985: Role of the self-concept in the perception of others. *Journal of personality and social psychology* 49, 1494–512.

Mead, G.H. 1934: *Mind, self and society*. Chicago: University of Chicago Press.

Rhodewalt, F. and Agustsdottir, S. 1986: Effects of self-presentation on the phenomenal self. *Journal of personality and social psychology* 50, 47–55.

Snygg, D. and Combs, A.W. 1949: *Individual behavior: a new frame of reference for psychology*. New York: Harper.

Wylie, R.C. 1974, 1979: *The self concept*. 2 vols. Lincoln: University of Nebraska Press.

self-consistency The stability of the SELF-CONCEPT across situations and time. Stability of the self-concept provides a point of reference within a changing environment and a point of projection of the self into the future. The idea was developed by Lecky (1945), and taken up by Rogers (1951), who held that people wish to actualize or maintain their selves, and therefore tend to behave in a way which is consistent with their self-concepts. According to Rogers, when one experiences oneself in a way which does not fit one's self-concept, one is in a state he calls "incongruence", and one suffers inner tension (see ROGERS; and cf. COGNITIVE DISSONANCE).

A variety of other reasons are given for wanting self-consistency, including the provision of a sense of personal control or the ability to regulate change, the economy in the organization of perceptions, the reduction of conflict among concepts, and avoidance of cognitions with conflicting implications for action. The pressure for change of the self-concept usually emerges from information from others which is inconsistent with the relevant facets of the self as perceived by the person. In response to the inconsistent information, the person may avoid or change his or her evaluation of those who provide the information, change the conception of the self as in therapy, or, as Swann and Ely (1984) suggest, resist. Swann uses the term "self-verification" for the process whereby people get others to treat them in a way which fits their self-concept. This effect is stronger if they are certain of their self-concept. Baumeister (1982) also proposes a consistency motive in social interaction. He uses the term "self-construction" to refer to the attempt to present oneself in a way which is consistent with one's IDEAL SELF (see SELF-PRESENTATION). (See also SELF-ESTEEM.)   RCZ/RL

Bibliography

Baumeister, R.F. 1982: A self-presentational view of social phenomena. *Psychological bulletin* 91, 3–26.

Jones, S.G. 1973: Self and interpersonal evaluations: esteem theories versus consistency theories. *Psychological bulletin* 79, 185–99.

Lecky, R. 1945: *Self-consistency*. New York: Island Press.

Rogers, C.R. 1951: *Client-centered therapy*. Boston: Houghton Mifflin.

Swann, W.B. and Ely, R.J. 1984: A battle of wills: self-verification versus behavioral confirmation. *Journal of personality and social psychology* 46, 1287–302.

self-control The ability to defer immediate instinctual pleasure and gratification to attain a future, usually socially valued, goal. The person who exercises self-control shows that innate needs have been socialized, that the culture's values are more significant than his or her desires and urges (see also SUBLIMATION). The term implies another way of stating the problem of the relationship between the idiosyncratic personality confronting the collective's need for conformity and the social rewards that can accrue from delaying instinctual satisfaction.

Self-control can be accounted for at two opposing levels. (i) Consciously the person is aware of future goals and rewards and can plan and structure behavior for future goals. A person's commitment must also be a part of self-control. (ii) For behaviorism self-control is explained by the Law of Relative Effect in that the delay of behavior is accomplished by the relative size of the reward in the future. Organisms will distribute their behavior (responses) according to the relative gains connected with each action. The organism is for the most part unaware of this process.

The social learning theorist, BANDURA, regards self-control as both external and internal. The person can reward himself and actively shape the external environment so as to be more rewarding. This is done through gaining control over reinforcements, and doing this is seen as a sign of maturity.   JWA

Bibliography

Bandura, A. 1982: Self-efficacy mechanism in human agency. *American psychologist* 37, 122–47.

self-disclosure Revealing facts about oneself to others. Self-disclosure has been implicated as an important process in the growth of RELATIONSHIPS, as it increases as relationships develop and it is a sign of attraction (Altman and Taylor 1973; Gelman and McGinley 1978). Laboratory studies however have shown that there are conventions about disclosure. Disclosing intimate details does make one more attractive, but only if the disclosure is well-timed. Those who disclose intimate secrets on first meeting are liked less than those who allow a period to become acquainted (Derlega and Grzelak 1979). Self-disclosure also has a norm of reciprocity. People who give details about themselves and receive none in return are likely to feel affronted (see Cozby 1973). This may be one reason why early disclosure is not attractive, since it imposes upon the recipient an implied demand (either for sympathy or for reciprocal disclosure) and the demand may not be welcome.

Another convention is that pairs of females disclose to each other more than pairs of males do (Rubin and Shenker 1978). This fits in with the model of women as highly affiliative. Men who do disclose intimate details to strangers are disliked more than women who do so (Kleinke and Kahn 1980).

Altman and Taylor (1973) distinguished *breadth* (i.e. range of topics) and *depth* (i.e. intimacy or privacy) of self-disclosure. Increase in both is associated with greater intimacy. Tolstedt and Stokes (1984), however, found that in couples who were having difficulties with their relationships, the decline in closeness was associated with decline in breadth, but *increase* in depth of self-disclosure to each other. They suggested that this might be because negative or undesirable feelings were being disclosed, or because couples in crisis engage in obsessive self-analysis. Their findings, however, seem to show that there is no simple positive relation between self-disclosure and contented intimacy. RL

Bibliography

Altman, I. and Taylor, D.A. 1973: *Social penetration: the development of interpersonal relationships.* New York: Holt, Rinehart and Winston.

Cozby, P.C. 1973: Self-disclosure: a literature review. *Psychological bulletin* 79, 73–91.

Derlega, V.J. and Grzelak, J. 1979: Appropriateness of self-disclosure. In *Self-disclosure*, ed. G.J. Cheleene. San Francisco: Jossey-Bass.

Gelman, R. and McGinley, H. 1978: Interpersonal liking and self-disclosure. *Journal of consulting and clinical psychology* 46, 1549–51.

Kleinke, C.L. and Kahn, M.L. 1980: Perceptions of self-disclosers: effects of sex and physical attractiveness. *Journal of personality* 48, 190–205.

Rubin, Z. and Shenker, S. 1978: Friendship, proximity, and self-disclosure. *Journal of personality* 46, 1–22.

Tolstedt, B.E. and Stokes, J.P. 1984: Self-disclosure, intimacy, and the depenetration process. *Journal of personality and social psychology* 46, 84–90.

self-esteem 'The evaluation that the individual makes and customarily maintains with regard to himself; it expresses an attitude of approval or disapproval and indicates the extent to which the individual believes himself to be capable, significant, successful and worthy' (Coopersmith 1967). Rosenberg (1965) more succinctly defined it as 'a positive or negative attitude towards . . . the Self'.

James's brief (but vague) 'self esteem = success divided by pretensions' (1890) draws attention to possible causes: one will be satisfied with oneself if one perceives one's achievements to measure up to one's aspirations. A similar idea has been crucial in ROGERS's theorizing about the SELF-CONCEPT and IDEAL SELF. "Self-concept discrepancy theory" (Higgins et al. 1985) proposes that disparities between one's beliefs about what one is, and what one ought to be, or what one would ideally like to be, are associated with agitation and dejection. James suggested that one could increase one's self-esteem by increasing achievement *or* reducing aspiration, but Higgins et al. found that individuals with low self-esteem were less inclined than those with high self-esteem to believe that they set 'personal goals and standards as high as possible'. This might imply that the people with high self-esteem are as satisfied with their standards as with their success in living up to them.

The relation between self-esteem and beliefs or thought processes has found a (foster) home in work on the possible causal connection between depression (typically associated with very low self-esteem) and cognition (e.g. Beck 1967; Peterson and Seligman 1984). The literature on self-esteem, however, covers the majority of the empirical work on the self, and much of it is concerned with the manifest external causes and effects of self-esteem. Rogers (1951) suggested that high self-esteem comes from an upbringing in a family which does not make love conditional on one's obedience or success. Beck (1967) believed that depression is often associated with an upbringing in which affection is conditional on meeting one's family's high standards. Coopersmith (1967), in a study of 1700 boys (10–12 years old), found that the parents of those with high self-esteem showed warmth and interest, did set high standards, but were fair though firm in enforcing them, and used rewards rather than punishments as an incentive. Boys with low self-esteem had permissive parents who showed comparatively little interest in their children, but could sometimes be punitive and unfair. The parents of the boys with high self-esteem had high self-esteem themselves, and wanted their children to be self-confident and independent. Rosenberg (1965), studying 5000 adolescents, found that high self-esteem was associated with a closer, warmer relationship with parents. Two assumptions are often made about these findings: (1) that the family relationship causes the high or low self-esteem; (2) that the self-esteem is something one acquires in one's upbringing and is then stuck with. It is obviously possible that neither of these assumptions is true.

Experimental studies have shown that self-esteem can be manipulated. This supports the idea that the cause of self-esteem lies in experience, but it does not support the idea that self-esteem is stable. Videbeck (1960), for example, found that people who were rated by an "expert" changed their beliefs about the rated ability and other aspects of their ability. Haas and Maehr (1965) found a similar effect, and also that the change persisted after six weeks. It is impossible to generalize from such studies, however, as the subjects were judged by "experts" on specialized tasks (reading to a speech expert, and performing motor tasks for a physical education expert). The subjects may, therefore, have given undue weight to a single view because they had little other evidence and the rater was a credible expert. Nevertheless, other studies with different designs also suggest that self-ratings can be raised or lowered by another person's responses to one's claims (Gergen 1965), or that a job-applicant's self-ratings can be affected by sharing a waiting-room with a more unlikely or more likely candidate for the job (Gergen and Morse 1967).

There are, however, other studies which show that it is not always easy to change self-esteem. If plenty of people agree with one's own estimate of oneself, one is less likely to respond to attempts to change it (Backman et al. 1963). Shrauger and Lund (1975) found that if high self-esteem subjects were negatively evaluated, they were inclined to say they doubted the evaluator's competence. Stotland et al. (1957) found that those with high self-esteem tended to rate their failures more positively than those with low. These results imply that a failure or criticism will not affect someone's high self-esteem. This tallies with Coopersmith's finding that high self-esteem boys were independent and not sensitive to criticism. Such reactions may, of course, be seen as defensive (Schneider and Turkat 1975), and possibly not expressions of belief.

It is not surprising that people play down evidence which might undermine their self-esteem (or the good impression they make on others). Various writers have held that people have a 'basic need for self-regard' (Rogers 1959), and therefore a need to enhance their self-esteem or protect it from damage (Allport 1937). Others, such as GOFFMAN (1959) have stressed the need to make a good impression. Unsurprisingly, low self-esteem subjects often, but not always, prefer positive evaluation and praise to derogation and criticism (see Jones 1973). This has been seen as evidence that people are generally motivated by need for self-esteem rather than need for SELF-CONSISTENCY. But finding praise pleasant (and praisers more attractive than derogators, as in Jones et al. 1962) does not make one believe the praise. Furthermore, as Swann (1985) points out, most "low self-esteem" subjects are students with only comparatively low self-esteem, about which they are anyway probably rather uncertain. A glance at the work on depression shows that it is difficult to get people with a genuine, chronic lack of self-esteem to re-evaluate themselves more positively.

If one's level of self-esteem is related to one's beliefs about one's effectiveness and competence, it will also be reflected in one's actions and one's interpretations of events. Those with high self-esteem, for example, persevere longer on difficult tasks (Shrauger and Sormon 1977). This parallels the findings in ATTRIBUTION THEORY that belief that one can secure success through effort leads to one making more effort and hence, perhaps, succeeding (Weiner 1980; cf. Bandura 1982). One's expectations are therefore likely to be self-fulfilling. Furthermore, if a depressed or low self-esteem person thinks he or she cannot succeed by effort or ability, a success may be attributed to luck, or the ease of the task, and such successes will therefore do little to modify the self-concept or self-esteem, while failures will simply confirm the beliefs (see Peterson and Seligman 1984). One's self-esteem will obviously be difficult to change if the beliefs associated with it affect the evidence available and the way in which one interprets that evidence.

Self-esteem is also believed to have effects on aspirations, creativity and relationships with others (see Coopersmith

1967; Rogers 1959). Manipulating self-esteem can certainly affect social judgments and social behavior. In a study of Walster (1965) a handsome male stooge chatted to, and dated individual girls who had just filled in personality questionnaires. The girls were then given (false) favorable or unfavorable evaluations of their personalities. The stooge seemed retrospectively more attractive to those whose evaluations were poor. This may show simple thirst for recognition and approval, or that those whose confidence in their personalities had been shaken were doubtful of finding such approval elsewhere. In a more elegant victimization of students, Kiesler and Baral (1970) took male students one at a time. The student's self-esteem was raised or lowered. Then he was introduced to a girl and left alone with her. If her dress and make-up were attractive, the men with raised self-esteem were very sociable. If her dress and make-up were unattractive, the men with lowered self-esteem were the sociable ones. Need for approval may be involved here, but expectation is clearly playing a crucial role. The low self-esteem students probably expect success with the plain girl rather than the attractive one. The high self-esteem students may expect success with both, or they may be prepared to take a risk. Either way they seem only to be tempted by the greater prize (another example of the higher aspirations of those with high self-esteem).

One thing wrong with many of these studies, or at least their interpretation, has been the apparent assumption that "self-esteem" is a global favorable or unfavorable attitude to oneself. Dissatisfaction with one aspect of oneself need not generalize to other aspects, although it may lead to compensatory efforts in other activities. Another problem is that different measures of self-esteem do not intercorrelate with each other. Wylie (1974) stated that: 'Factor-analytic studies of instruments purporting to measure "overall" self-esteem . . . lead one to believe that either there is no such measurable dimension . . . or at least that some of the scales . . . are doing a poor job'. Wells and Marwell

(1976) also concluded that 'orthodox verbal self-ratings' of self-esteem are inadequate. Demo (1985) found that self-ratings and observer-ratings fall on two distinct factors, which he labeled "experienced" and "presented" self-esteem.

Clearly self-reports and behavior are both open to distortion, not least by strategies of SELF-PRESENTATION (while observers' reports have problems of their own; see PERSON/SITUATION CONTROVERSY). Given these empirical problems, and the underlying difficulties which they reveal, it is hard not to accept Demo's (1985) conclusion that, 'At present . . . we lack a sufficiently clear . . . conceptual framework for understanding self-conception, or even self-esteem'. RL

Bibliography

Bandura, A. 1982: Self-efficacy mechanism in human agency. *American psychologist* 37, 122–47.

Beck, A.T. 1967: *Depression: causes and treatment.* Philadelphia: University of Pennsylvania Press.

Burns, R.B. 1979: *The self-concept.* London and New York: Longman.

Demo, D.H. 1985: The measurement of self-esteem: refining our methods. *Journal of personality and social psychology* 48, 1490–1502.

Gergen, K.J. and Morse, S.J. 1967: Self-consistency: measurement and validation. *Proceedings of the American Psychological Association* 207–8.

Higgins, E.T., Klein, R. and Strauman, T. 1985: Self-concept discrepancy theory: a psychological model for distinguishing among different aspects of depression and anxiety. *Social cognition* 3, 51–76.

Peterson, C. and Seligman, M.E.P. 1984: Causal explanations as a risk factor in depression: theory and evidence. *Psychological review* 91, 347–74.

Swann, W.B. 1985: The self as architect of social reality. In *The self and social life*, ed. B.R. Schlenker. New York: McGraw-Hill.

Weiner, B. 1980: *Human motivation.* New York: Holt, Rinehart and Winston.

Wells and Marwell, G. 1976: *Self-esteem: its conceptualization and measurement.* Beverly Hills: Sage.

Wylie, R.C. 1974, 1979: *The self-concept.* 2 vols. Lincoln: University of Nebraska Press.

All other references may be found in Burns (1979) and Wylie (1974, 1979).

self-monitoring A concept introduced by Snyder (1974), who defined it as 'self-observation and self-control guided by situational cues to social appropriateness' in expressive behavior and SELF-PRESENTATION. He suggested that it is a fundamental dimension along which individuals differ in their social behavior. Highly self-monitoring people are said to be distinguished from low self-monitors on five dimensions:

1. they are concerned to behave appropriately in different social settings;
2. they attend to others' behavior and use it as a guide for their own;
3. they are in control of their expressive behavior, and able to adapt their self-presentation to fit different social demands;
4. they use this ability to create the impression they desire;
5. they are therefore inconsistent in their social behavior.

Snyder developed a self-monitoring questionnaire, which includes items such as "in different situations and with different people, I often act like very different persons" or "I may deceive people by being friendly when I really dislike them". Highly self-monitoring individuals endorse these statements.

Snyder claims that his questionnaire taps an aspect of people which differs from social desirability, MACHIAVELLIANISM, inner-other directedness, and various other individual differences. He validated his questionnaire to some extent by showing that students' self-reports tallied with the descriptions of them offered by their peers. It also successfully distinguished criterion groups. Hospitalized psychiatric patients came out as significantly lower self-monitors than Stanford University students, who in turn came out significantly lower than professional actors (1974). He also found high self-monitors better at role-playing emotions, while Lippa (1976) found them better at role-playing introversion/extraversion.

In another study (Snyder and Monson 1975) high self-monitors reported more inconsistency in their own generosity,

honesty and hostility, and actually behaved differently in two group discussions depending on whether they thought that the discussion was being videotaped or not. Low self-monitors, in contrast, behaved the same. Snyder therefore suggested that self-monitoring is an important mediating factor to take into account in disputes about consistency of personality, as some people may be more consistent than others (see PERSON/SITUATION CONTROVERSY). This is not to say that the control of high self-monitors necessarily leads to inconsistency. Lippa (1978) found them more consistent than low self-monitors in their (role-played) expressive behavior when such consistency was appropriate.

Despite these and other interesting results (see Snyder 1979) some studies using the construct have not been supportive (e.g. Santee and Maslach 1982). FACTOR ANALYSIS (e.g. Briggs et al. 1980) of the questionnaire usually produces three factors (acting ability, extroversion, and other-directedness or social anxiety) which do not match the five features proposed by Snyder. Furthermore, the three factors do not seem to be highly intercorrelated. It is therefore unclear what a high self-monitoring score means, as it may show extraversion and confidence or shyness and lack of confidence. Either might lead to inconsistency.

In a series of studies Lennox and Wolfe (1984) attempted to create a more satisfactory scale than Snyder's by discarding and writing in items. Factor analysis produced two factors which covered all Snyder's features except ability to control expressive behavior (Snyder's dimension 3). Both factors correlated highly with neuroticism on the Eysenck Personality Questionnaire (EPQ) and with self-reported social anxiety. They argued that anxious 'concern for appropriateness' is not the basis of skilled self-presentation, so not a proper part of the original self-monitoring construct. They therefore discarded these items (including cross-situational inconsistency of which Snyder makes so much). Acting ability was a separate factor on its own, and was discarded because (*pace* Snyder) this implied that stage acting is not the same as control of expressive behavior in everyday life. All that was left of Snyder's original dimensions was the ability to control expressive behavior. This correlated with EPQ extraversion and not with neuroticism or social anxiety, and therefore fits the original construct. Lennox and Wolfe added items about sensitivity to others' expressive behavior. They hoped that these two factors might fulfill some of Snyder's expectations for his original construct and questionnaire, but the removal of the cross-situational inconsistency could make this purer self-monitoring scale less useful in the controversy about consistency of personality traits.   RL

Bibliography

Briggs, S.R., Cheek, J.M. and Buss, A.H. 1980: An analysis of the self-monitoring scale. *Journal of personality and social psychology* 38, 679–86.

Lennox, R.D. and Wolfe, R.N. 1984: Revision of the self-monitoring scale. *Journal of personality and social psychology* 46, 1349–64.

Lippa, R. 1976: Expressive control and the leakage of dispositional introversion-extraversion during role-playing teaching. *Journal of personality* 44, 541–59.

—— 1978: Expressive control, expressive consistency and the correspondence between expressive behavior and personality. *Journal of personality* 46, 438–61.

Santee, R.T. and Maslach, C. 1982: To agree or not to agree: personal dissent amid pressure to conform. *Journal of personality and social psychology* 42, 690–700.

Snyder, M. 1974: The self-monitoring of expressive behavior. *Journal of personality and social psychology* 30, 526–37.

—— 1979: Self-monitoring processes. In *Advances in experimental social psychology*, vol. 12, ed. L. Berkowitz. New York: Academic Press.

—— and Monson, T.C. 1975: Persons, situations, and the control of social behavior. *Journal of personality and social psychology* 32, 637–44.

self-perception theory

A theory, proposed by Bem (1972) which suggests that people have no direct knowledge of their own internal states but infer their existence from observations of their own behavior. In Bem's view there is no essential difference between actor and observer in gaining access to one's internal state of mind. Bem's theory, which is a more precise revival of the James-Lange theory of emotion, attracted a good deal of attention by reinterpreting Festinger and Carl-smith's famous experiment in COGNITIVE DISSONANCE. According to Bem, a larger attitude change for a smaller bribe is what one would infer from the behavior of the subjects in the experiment. Bem's re-interpretation has been criticized on various grounds and the evidence appears to be equivocal. Nevertheless Bem's theory has served in many ways to renew interest in a classical problem of psychology. Research in ATTRIBUTION THEORY has shown that significant differences exist between actors and observers in making inferences about internal states. This suggests that self-perception cannot be an exact analysis of the perception of others.   JMFJ

Bibliography

Bem, D.J. 1972: Self-perception theory. In *Advances in experimental social psychology*, vol. 6, ed. L. Berkowitz. New York: Academic Press.

Monson, T.C. and Snyder, M. 1977: Actors, observers, and the attribution process: toward a reconceptualization. *Journal of experimental social psychology* 13, 89–111.

self-presentation

A concept often used synonymously with impression-management to refer to the numerous strategies that people employ to control and manage their outward images and the impressions of themselves which they present to other people. William James, C.H. Cooley, and G.H. MEAD all stressed the idea that in social discourse and interaction people present different selves to different people usually in order to show their best profile or make a good impression.

Self-presentation is at the center of the work by GOFFMAN (1959, 1963, 1967), who uses the theatrical analogy for social interaction. For Goffman each person (actor) attempts to maintain an image appropriate to the social situation and hence to be positively evaluated. Furthermore the rules of social life ensure that each participant will attempt to keep all members of the interaction "in face" or playing an acceptable role through appropriate self-presentation. Everyone therefore has a range of self-presentational images and tactics which he or she uses to sustain social interaction and a positive self-image. Self-presentation obviously seems to imply insincerity, but Goffman (1959) accepted that one may play a role sincerely or come to identify with a role. Experimental work (e.g. Rhodewalt and Agustsdottir 1986) supports this view. Presenting oneself as a certain kind of person may lead to one subsequently thinking (or saying that one thinks) of oneself as being that kind of person.

The idea of self-presentation has greatly influenced the work of Harré (1979) and Snyder (1979). The latter has extended this idea to the concept of SELF-MONITORING, which refers to the extent to which people can and do exercise control over their verbal and non-verbal self-presentation. High self-monitors (those skilled in self-presentation) regulate and control their non-verbal and verbal behavior to make it situationally appropriate. Conversely low self-monitors (those not skilled in self-presentation) do not.

Baumeister (1982) has argued that self-presentation and "self-construction" will explain many findings in research on topics such as ALTRUISM, CONFORMITY, AGGRESSION, and the expression of ATTITUDES. He regards self-presentation as 'pleasing the audience', and "self-construction" as a self-presentational strategy 'guided by the desire to make one's public image equivalent to one's ideal self'. If some people were generally motivated by self-constructive aims and others by a desire to please their audience, the distinction would be equivalent to that between high and low self-monitors, although people's motivations are not interpreted in the same way. In Baumeister's view even self-constructors have self-presentational motives, whereas Snyder suggests that low self-monitors do not feel a strong desire to make an impression on others. It is not made clear whether everyone is both a self-constructor and a self-presenter, nor

in which circumstances people might be motivated to be one rather than the other.

Self-presentational theories are sometimes in danger of explaining all behavior as self-presentation, and therefore losing their power to explain *differences* in behavior in different contexts by the presence or absence of self-presentational motives. Furthermore, the distinction between what one "really" is and what one pretends to be is important and not wholly intractable. This is shown, for instance, in studies of the so-called "self-serving bias" in ATTRIBUTION, i.e. the tendency to attribute one's successes to one's own qualities and one's failures to circumstances. Writers have differed over whether this is a cognitive error (Miller and Ross 1975) or a motivated distortion (Weary Bradley 1978). If the latter, it is theoretically, as well as morally, worthwhile to know whether the process involves unconscious DENIAL to save one's SELF-ESTEEM or conscious denial to save one's face. In other words, are these attributions examples of self-presentation (i.e. lies) or self-deception?

Weary Bradley (1978) pointed out that subjects always made self-serving attributions when under observation, which would imply self-presentation. But Riess et al. (1981) found that subjects who were led to believe that they were wired up to a reliable lie-detector made self-serving attributions as much as subjects who were not. The assumption behind the use of phony lie-detectors (so called "bogus pipelines") is that people will tell the truth when wired to them for fear of being caught out lying. These subjects' self-serving attributions must therefore be assumed to be sincere (though possibly self-deceiving) and not self-presentations. It therefore seems possible to invent tests to distinguish what is and is not self-presentation. Nevertheless, those who like the label "self-presentation" may describe sincerity as self-presentation for which the 'audience . . . is oneself' (Greenwald and Breckler 1985).   AF/RL

Bibliography

Baumeister, R.F. 1982: A self-presentational

view of social phenomena. *Psychological bulletin* 91, 3–26.

Goffman, E. 1959: *The presentation of self in everyday life*. Harmondsworth: Penguin.

—— 1963: *Stigma: notes on the management of spoiled identity*. Englewood Cliff, N.J.: Prentice-Hall.

—— 1967: *Interaction ritual: essays on face-to-face behavior*. Garden City: Doubleday.

Greenwald, A.G. and Breckler, S.J. 1985: To whom is the self presented? In *The self and social life*, ed. B.R. Schlenker. New York: McGraw-Hill.

Harré, R. 1979: *Social being*. Oxford: Basil Blackwell; Totowa, N.J.: Littlefield Adams.

Miller, D.T. and Ross, M. 1975: Self-serving biases in the attribution of causality: fact or fiction? *Psychological bulletin* 82, 213–25.

Rhodewalt, F. and Agustsdottir, S. 1986: Effects of self-presentation on the phenomenal self. *Journal of personality and social psychology* 50, 47–55.

Riess, M., Rosenfeld, P., Melburg, B. and Tedeschi, J.T. 1981: Self-serving attributions: biased private perceptions and distorted public descriptions. *Journal of personality and social psychology* 41, 224–31.

Snyder, M. 1979: Self-monitoring processes. In *Advances in experimental social psychology*, vol. 12, ed. L. Berkowitz. New York: Academic Press.

Weary Bradley, G. 1978: Self-serving biases in the attribution process: A reexamination of the fact or fiction question. *Journal of personality and social psychology* 36, 56–71.

self-schema A 'cognitive generalization about the self, derived from past experience, that organizes and guides the processing of self-related information contained in the individual's social experiences' (Markus 1977). Rogers et al. (1977) found that subjects who were presented with words and were asked "Does this word describe you?" recalled more words than those asked questions about the meanings of the words. These results were explained in terms of the SELF-CONCEPT being a set of schemata or prototypes (see SOCIAL COGNITION) which facilitate the processing and storage of relevant information. Markus (1977) suggested that people differ from each other in the degree to which their beliefs about aspects of

themselves are organized and elaborated. She referred to people as "schematic" or "aschematic" depending on the comprehensiveness of their schemata in any particular domain. She found that schematic subjects were more consistent in picking words to describe themselves. She also found that they would not accept bogus assessments of their personalities, whereas aschematics would accept such assessments of themselves. These findings have been regarded as ambiguous by critics, because Markus did not distinguish the *importance* someone attaches to a particular self-description from the *extremity* of his or her self-rating on that dimension. Markus et al. (1985), however, point out that there is a strong positive correlation between how important one thinks a characteristic is, and how extreme one's self-rating on that characteristic is.

There has been great interest in the supposed effect of self-schemata on perception of other people. There is good evidence that people use the same characteristics to describe themselves and others (e.g. Lewicki 1983); but this obviously does not prove that one's beliefs about oneself affect one's perceptions of others. One may simply use various categories in thinking about people and apply them equally to oneself and to others. Nevertheless the importance or extremity of one's self-ratings on a characteristic are a good guide to whether one will use that characteristic in describing other people and will notice aspects of their behavior which are relevant to that characteristic (Markus et al. 1985).   RL

Bibliography

Lewicki, P. 1983: Self-image bias in person perception. *Journal of personality and social psychology* 45, 384–93.

Markus, H. 1977: Self-schemata and processing information about the self. *Journal of personality and social psychology* 35, 63–78.

——, Smith, J. and Moreland, R.L. 1985: Role of the self-concept in the perception of others. *Journal of personality and social psychology* 49, 1494–1512.

Rogers, T.B., Kuiper, N.A. and Kirker, W.S. 1977: Self-reference and the encoding of personal information. *Journal of personality and social psychology* 35, 677–88.

selfishness In human psychology the word is used with its normal meaning, but evolutionary biologists sometimes use it in a technical sense: selfish behavior increases the welfare of the individual at the expense of the welfare of others. "Altruistic" behavior is the opposite. A third technical term is sometimes defined in a similar way: a "spiteful" act is one that harms the perpetrator, but harms some other individual(s) even more. Mathematical models suggest that spite is unlikely to evolve in nature. Whether ALTRUISM is likely to evolve depends upon how welfare is defined. If it is taken to mean survival, ordinary parental care qualifies as an altruistic act. But if welfare is taken to mean Darwinian fitness or reproductive success, parental care is not necessarily altruistic since a parent only achieves reproductive success through the survival of its offspring. Much the same can be said of apparent altruism towards other close genetic relatives. The history of the Darwinian study of altruism has been, in a sense, a process of explaining away apparent altruism at the level of the individual by showing that it follows from a more fundamental genetic selfishness. This has no connection with another kind of "explaining away" in the field of human motives: we may dismiss an apparently altruistic man as secretly selfish, doing good for his own ends. Darwinian explanations of selfishness at the genetic level make no reference to subjective motives. They are concerned solely with the effects of actions. RD

Bibliography

Dawkins, R. 1976: *The selfish gene*. Oxford: Oxford University Press.

semantic differential A measurement instrument, consisting of a number of carefully selected pairs of adjectives for eliciting the affective meaning of words and concepts. Developed by Osgood et al. (1957), it has been widely used in psycho-

logical research. Factor analysis has shown that semantic differentiations in this sense can be reduced to some extent (20 to 80 per cent of the total variance depending upon the domain from which words and concepts are chosen) to three independent dimensions of affective judgment: evaluation (good-bad), potency (strong-weak) and activity (fast-slow). Osgood has shown in a large number of cross-cultural studies that these dimensions are nearly universal. Semantic atlases which give the affective meaning of scores for a large number of concepts have been based on these and other studies. JMFJ

Bibliography

Osgood, C.E., Suci, G.J. and Tannenbaum, P.H. 1957: *The measurement of meaning*. Urbana: University of Illinois Press.

separation A term derived from psychoanalytic theory to describe the anxiety held to be generated by the absence of a person believed necessary for survival (prototypically the mother) and to denote a major developmental process – separation-individuation (Mahler, Pine and Bergman 1975). Mahler and her co-workers described sub-phases of differentiation, practising and rapprochement to account for development from a symbiotic phase in the middle of the first year when the infant and mother are still primarily a unit, to the autonomy or separation of the three-year-old from its mother. More widely known are the three phases – protest, despair and detachment – described by Bowlby as the young child's response to separation from its primary caregiver and his hypothesis relating maternal loss or deprivation and psychiatric illness. Research in the past thirty years has supported and clarified this proposed relationship but also shown the need to distinguish between bonding failure and bond disruption, between qualitative differences in care and their effects on intellectual, social and emotional factors, between long- and short-term effects and the influence of individual differences on outcomes (Rutter 1981). (See also ATTACHMENT.) BBL

Bibliography

Mahler, M.S., Pine, F. and Bergman, A. 1975: *The psychological birth of the human infant.* London: Hutchinson; New York: Basic Books.

Rutter, M. 1981: *Maternal deprivation reassessed.* 2nd edn. Harmondsworth and New York: Penguin.

sequential analysis A family of research methods which detect and summarize the regularities with which one event or behavior follows another. The commonest techniques begin by calculating transitional probabilities, the conditional probabilities with which each type of event occurs given the types of immediately preceding events. In the simplest case a Markov chain is formed – a sequence of events having as its defining regularity a fixed pattern of probabilities of occurrence for each event, conditional only upon the one event immediately before.

Such methods require three assumptions to be met, which may frequently be a problem with real behavioral data: stationarity (meaning that the transitional probabilities are fixed parameters of the pattern); homogeneity (meaning that the probabilities have not been produced by the unwitting mixture of several different behavior patterns); and order (meaning that probabilities have been used which are conditional on the appropriate number of preceding events).

Other approaches to sequential analysis include methods based on the rule systems of generative grammar and the methods of time series analysis which is used with continuous variables. DDC

Bibliography

Clarke, D.D. 1983: *Language and action: a structural model of behavior.* Oxford and New York: Pergamon.

sex: social and personality psychology The study of sexual behavior and its relationship to other variables such as personality, ATTITUDES and gender. In the past psychologists and sociologists concerned themselves with sexual ATTRACTION, courtship and marriage, which are certainly examples of sex-related attitudes and behavior. They could, however, be studied without prying into intimacy. But the so-called "sexual revolution" and the *in vivo* study of sexual activity by Masters and Johnson (1966) made questions about attitudes to or experience with sex almost wholly respectable.

Kinsey (1948, 1953) carried out his famous interview survey nearly forty years ago. But finding out about sexual behavior by questionnaire grew very popular in the 1970s with surveys such as Hunt's (1974) and the Hite Report (1976). The popularity of such studies is itself presumably a symptom of changed attitudes towards sex. They sometimes seem insufficiently serious, and suffer from the self-selection of their respondents (who often encountered the questionnaire in a magazine, and who may well not have been a representative or honest sample). Well-designed studies such as Farrell's (1978), in which over 1500 teenagers were interviewed, do support the idea that there has been a change in attitude and (claims about) behavior. She compared her data with Schofield's (1965), which were also collected in Britain, and concluded that her sample were more "permissive". However, they disapproved of promiscuity and, in her opinion, were more conservative than popular reports suggest. In the USA Glenn and Weaver (1979) found that younger adults had more permissive attitudes than older adults. Such comparisons suggest the same process of liberalization, but are less clear-cut than Farrell's comparison of data collected at different periods.

Many questionnaire and interview studies have collected only sets of facts, but psychologists have typically been concerned to relate respondents' answers about sex to their gender or personality, or to religious beliefs, other attitudes, or SELF-ESTEEM. For example, EYSENCK (1976) carried out a questionnaire study of British university students, and found differences between men's and women's attitudes to sex, with women less interested in premarital or impersonal sex, and less easily excited. Women, however, seemed generally more satisfied with their sex lives. The conservatism of women's sexual attitudes has been a general finding since Kinsey's work, but in the 1970s there was some evidence of a convergence of male and female attitudes in the USA (Hunt 1974; Singh 1980). This appeared to be due to the attitudes of women "catching up" with those of men, by becoming more permissive more rapidly. Such changes obviously lead to different expectations, which may cause as much frustration as less libertarian beliefs. In the *Redbook* survey for instance, women who did not have orgasms quite often expressed anger and frustration, since they thought that they should have them (Sarrel and Sarrel 1980). There is now some evidence of a resurgence of conservatism, especially among women. Hendrick et al. (1985) found very similar attitudinal sex differences in University of Miami students to those of Eysenck's students and many earlier surveys.

In his study Eysenck was more concerned with the relationship of personality differences to sexual attitudes and behavior. Assessing personality on the three dimensions of introversion/extraversion, neuroticism, and psychoticism (see EYSENCK; TYPE), he found various predictable differences. In comparison with introverts, extraverts claimed to have had sex earlier in life, more often and with more partners. In general, in fact, the typical extravert was satisfied with sex, and lacked guilt or prudishness, whereas the typical introvert was more timid, less satisfied, and did not approve of promiscuity or experimentation. Neurotics had strong feelings of hostility and guilt, were highly excitable but very inhibited, and had sexual problems. "Psychotic" people were the most sexually outgoing, curious and experimental, but also recorded hostility to their partners and dissatisfaction. The introvert/ extravert difference seems to be paralleled by other findings which use different personality measures. Wilson (1973), for instance, found a general "conservative" tendency distinguishes those who feel threatened and resist novelty and change from those who actively seek stimulation and adventure. This difference is mirrored in sexual attitudes and (reported) sexual

behavior (Thomas 1975). Jessor et al. 1983 produced parallel findings that boys and girls who have sex at the earliest age are independent, irreligious, not close to their parents, do not value academic achievement, and do drink alcohol and use drugs. This seems to be an extravert, sensation-seeking and non-conservative profile.

There has been plenty of work on the impact of pornography, both on sexual arousal and on AGGRESSION. Fantasizing about sex has been shown to increase excitement, and subsequent sexual activity (e.g. Eisenman 1982), but most studies on erotic imagery have used external stimuli presented visually or aurally. Cattell et al. (1972) found that married couples were more likely to have intercourse after viewing erotic slides. The effect declines rapidly when erotic material is viewed over a number of days. The experience of seeing the *same* movie every day diminishes arousal and becomes increasingly unpleasant (Kelley 1982). Zillman and Bryant (1983) found that students of both sexes who were shown a series of thirty-six sex films over a six-week period became less aroused (indicated by self-report and physiological measures) and broader-minded in their views about deviance. Males tended to have become more callous in their attitudes to women.

There is no evidence that pornography generally increases aggression. Sex criminals seem often to have had sexually repressed childhoods and less than average contact with erotica in adolescence (Goldstein et al. 1974). Arousal, due for example to exercise, may be misattributed to a provocation and increase aggression. Zillmann (1971) found that arousal by erotica increased aggression. Baron, however, (1974) reported that exposure to erotica reduced aggression. It appears that mild erotica, such as *Playboy* nudes, produce low levels of arousal and good feelings which reduce aggression, whereas explicit depictions of sexual acts produce high levels of arousal and negative feelings which increase aggression (Zillmann et al. 1981). Furthermore violent erotica certainly do seem to increase aggression against women, especially if the erotic scenes show a woman who is attacked *enjoying* the sexual assault (see Malamuth and Donnerstein 1983).

There has been other interesting work on topics such as HOMOSEXUALITY AND LESBIANISM, incest (see Soothill 1980), contraception, and the spread of sexually-transmitted diseases (see Armytage 1980). The last topic is hardly psychological, although AIDS provides an example of labeling (see LABELING THEORY). Calling AIDS a veneral disease, and specifically a homosexual one, probably affects the response to sufferers and the actions bureaucracies take to cope with the disease (Seale 1985).

Studies of the (lack of) use of contraceptives and the steps which can be taken to eliminate the number of unwanted pregnancies provide a good example of how the psychologists' study of sexual behavior may have important practical applications (as does the clinical work on sex therapy; see, e.g. LoPiccolo and LoPiccolo 1978). Ignorance about contraception is probably the major reason why people fail to use contraceptives. The younger one is when one first has intercourse, the less likely one is to use any contraception (Cvetkovitch and Grote 1983). On the other hand, guilt about sex, and unwillingness to discuss sexual topics seem also to cause people to avoid contraceptives (Gerrard 1982). Unsurprisingly guilt about sex tends to be associated with less sexual activity, but it does not eliminate it! Gerrard et al. (1982) therefore compared the effects of merely giving girl students information designed to remove misconceptions with the effects of changing their negative attitudes as well as giving information, and found that the latter produced a greater improvement in their contraceptive practices.   RL

Bibliography

Armytage, W.H.G. 1980: Changing incidence and patterns of sexually transmitted diseases. In Armytage et al. 1980, op. cit.

—— Chester, R. and Peel, J. 1980: *Changing patterns of sexual behavior*. London and New York: Academic Press.

Byrne, D. and Fisher, W.A. eds. 1983: *Adolescents, sex, and contraception*. Hillsdale, N.J.: Erlbaum.

Cvetkovitch, G. and Grote, B. 1983: Adolescent development and teenage fertility. In Byrne and Fisher 1983, op. cit.

Eysenck, H.J. 1976: *Sex and personality*. London: Open Books.

Gerrard, M., McCann, L. and Geis, B. 1982: The antecedents and prevention of unwanted pregnancy. In *Social and psychological problems of women: prevention and crisis intervention*. eds. A. Rickel, M. Gerrard and I. Iscoe. New York: McGraw-Hill.

Hendrick, S., Hendrick, C., Slapion-Foote, M.J. and Foote, F.H. 1985: Gender differences in sexual attitudes. *Journal of personality and social psychology* 48, 1630–42.

Malamuth, N.M. and Donnerstein, E. eds. 1983: *Pornography and sexual aggression*. New York: Academic Press.

Seale, J. 1985: How to turn a disease into VD. *New scientist*, June 20, 38–41.

Soothill, K.L. 1980: Incest: changing patterns of social response. In Armytage et al. 1980, op. cit.

Thomas, D.R. 1975: Conservatism and premarital sexual experience. *British journal of social and clinical psychology* 14, 195–6.

Wilson, G.D. ed. 1973: *The psychology of conservatism*. London: Academic Press.

Zillmann, D. and Bryant, J. 1983: Effects of massive exposure to pornography. In Malamuth and Donnerstein 1983. op. cit.

Other references may be found in the bibliographies of Armytage et al., Byrne and Fisher, Hendrick et al., and Malamuth and Donnerstein.

sex differences in development A field of study concerned with the measurement and explanation of differences in the behavior of males and females as they appear throughout the lifespan. These differences embrace aspects of intellectual functioning, temperament and interests relating to work and leisure. The psychological study of differences is not directly concerned with primary sexual characteristics such as those involving hormones and reproduction or such secondary characteristics as size and bone structure. Psychological differences are often uncovered incidentally when experimenters compare the performance of males and females before combining scores for the two groups. The lack of systematic study is reflected in the variety of reported differences. Not surprisingly controversy surrounds the conclusions which have been drawn from the empirical evidence and conflicting theoretical accounts are offered to explain alleged differences.

Maccoby and Jacklin's landmark survey (1974) of over 1,600 studies reported reliable differences in only four areas and challenged many stereotypic beliefs. They concluded that the evidence supported the belief that females have greater verbal skills although it was unclear whether these are present in early childhood or emerge shortly before puberty. Males were found to have higher visual-spatial and mathematical abilities; these appear reliably in adolescence. In addition boys displayed more aggression both physical and verbal; differences could be observed in the play of toddlers. On the other hand Maccoby and Jacklin concluded that the evidence failed to support beliefs that girls are more sociable or suggestible, that girls are better at simple tasks and rote memory while boys are better able to deal with complex intellectual tasks or those requiring analytical thinking, that girls lack ACHIEVEMENT MOTIVATION and SELF-ESTEEM, that boys are visually orientated while girls are auditorially orientated, or that boys are more responsive to environmental factors while girls' development is more influenced by heredity. They noted that the evidence was inconclusive concerning sex differences in tactile sensitivity, anxiety and fear, activity level, competitiveness, dominance, compliance and nurturance.

Although Maccoby and Jacklin have provided a starting point for much further study their survey has been attacked both for the limited nature of its conclusions and for its lack of stringency (Block 1976; Fairweather 1976). Block argues that the fortuitous reporting of differences in studies which were not designed to reveal them and the reliance on subjects from a restricted age range (over three-quarters of the studies reviewed by Maccoby and Jacklin were of children below the age of thirteen years) challenges the conclusions which are drawn. In addition she questions

Maccoby and Jacklin's decision procedures, for example giving equal weight to statistically weak and powerful studies, omitting some significant reports and failing to achieve conceptual clarity in their own analysis. Block believes that the evidence can just as well support many of the differences which Maccoby and Jacklin reported as unproven and is often clearer than they indicated. In contrast Fairweather, examining studies of intellectual ability, challenged the evidence for differences in verbal and mathematical skills although he supported the view that males and females differ in their visual-spatial abilities.

This lack of consensus has not deterred psychologists from seeking and providing explanations for the differences they believe they have found. These explanations are generally not derived directly from psychological theory but are as wide-ranging and controversial as the evidence they attempt to explain.

Common-sense accounts of sex differences link psychological traits to biological differences of form and reproductive function. Psychological explanations often reveal their origins in naive accounts. So pervasive has the common-sense view been that Victorian scholars sought women's alleged intellectual inferiority in their smaller absolute brain size. This belief has been discredited; when comparisons of intelligence are made across species the ratio of the mass of the brain to the total mass of the individual is employed. Even this alleged relationship is doubtful.

The contemporary and competing naive explanation of differences in terms of social conditioning has gained impetus from the women's movement. It emphasizes that the differences which we are trying to trace reflect the roles which men and women in our society are expected to fulfill – the preparation of girls for motherhood and undemanding low status work and of boys for achievement and competition for society's most prestigious positions. These expectations and aspirations are believed to be differentially inculcated by conditioning, a term which owes little to Pavlov but is used in everyday speech to explain the learning of social rules and values.

Psychologists acknowledge the influence of both biological and environmental factors in development but many emphasize the former at the expense of the latter. Typically, volumes reviewing theories and evidence of sex differences in intellectual ability devote one section to social factors but one each to the effects of genes, hormones and the brain (Wittig and Petersen 1979).

In discussing genes, spatial ability has been linked to a recessive gene on the X chromosome. The evidence for such an inheritance pattern is not strong nor is that for the variability hypothesis which suggests that male heterozygosity (X and Y chromosomes) results in greater extremes in the male on a variety of traits. Hormones which have been shown to affect reproductive behavior in rats are often implicated in explaining temperamental differences as well as intellectual ability. Varying effects of greater lateralization of the right or the left hemisphere of the brain have been used to account for differences in verbal and spatial abilities. None of these explanations has gone unchallenged.

The superior performance of males in educational and occupational domains involving mathematical and visual-spatial abilities has enlivened the debate. There is fairly wide consensus concerning the contribution of biological factors to differences in spatial ability (McGee 1979) and the relation of these to mathematical achievement (Sherman 1978), although more recent analyses have not supported this relationship (Meece et al. 1982). However, psychologists such as Sherman argue for including the impact of sex-role factors in any account of differential performance in mathematics. She has measured children's beliefs about their chances of being successful in mathematics, about the usefulness of it in their lives and about their parents' evaluations of their achievement and shown that they influence performance as much as visual-spatial ability. Sherman's explanation is interactive in that mathematical achievement is shown to reflect biological and social processes. Although

interactional explanations of many varieties are widely considered they are still challenged. A recent study of almost 10,000 adolescents of superior mathematical ability in the United States demonstrated a male superiority and its authors ascribed this difference to inherent factors which distinguished males and females (Benbow and Stanley 1980, 1983).

The vehemence of the controversy focuses attention on the nature of the differences being explained. Primary sex characteristics such as genital structure yield categorical differentiations: males and females show no overlap; while psychological traits are distributed along a continuum, most average differences are small and there is much overlap. The magnitude of difference in visual-spatial abilities is medium to large yet 25 per cent of females perform better than the male average.

Categorical differentiation based upon genitals may be important in subtle ways. Maccoby and Jacklin reported few differences in the socialization of boys and girls but by the time children begin to speak they correctly label themselves. Both social learning and cognitive-developmental theory offer explanations: the former in terms of rewards and punishment as well as imitation and learning through observation and the latter according to the child's developing understanding of the social world and its place in the sex role system (Mischel 1970, Kohlberg 1966).

Undoubtedly the processes described by social learning theorists contribute to the acquisition of differences in behavior. A particular advantage of the cognitive-developmental approach is its emphasis on the child's active participation in constructing its own identity. A new approach to sex differences, which derives from ethno-methodology, begins by attacking the term "sex" and by noting that the processes through which individuals are categorized as male or female are social and problematic in their precise operation (Kessler and McKenna 1978). To mark the social construction of the categories "man" and "woman" the term "gender" is being used increasingly to designate psychological differences and sex is reserved for reference to biological distinctions. The introduction of the term "gender" provides no explanation in itself but accentuates the need for caution before accepting exclusively biological accounts of psychological differences. In addition it stresses that the very situations in which differences are recorded, be they surveys or experiments are recorded, be they surveys or experiments are social situations differently interpreted by men and women. The explanation of psychological differences observed in them will require understanding of these situations as well as of biological and intrapsychic phenomena (Deaux 1976, 1985).   BBL

Bibliography

*Archer, J. and Lloyd, B. 1982: *Sex and gender in society*. Harmondsworth: Penguin.

Benbow, C.P. and Stanley, J.C. 1980: Sex differences in mathematical ability: fact or artifact? *Science* 210, 1262–4.

—— 1983: Sex differences in mathematical reasoning: more facts. *Science* 222, 1029–31.

Block, J.H. 1976: Issues, problems and pitfalls in assessing sex differences: a critical review of "The psychology of sex differences". *Merrill-Palmer quarterly* 22, 283–308.

Deaux, K. 1976: *The behavior of men and women*. Belmont, Calif.: Wadsworth Publishing Company.

—— 1985: Sex and gender. *Annual review of psychology* 36, 49–81.

Fairweather, H. 1976: Sex differences in cognition. *Cognition* 4, 231–80.

Kessler, S.J. and McKenna, W. 1978: *Gender: an ethnomethodological approach*. New York: Wiley.

Kohlberg, L. 1966: A cognitive-developmental analysis of children's sex role concepts and attitudes. In *The development of sex differences*, ed. E.E. Maccoby. Stanford, Calif.: Stanford University Press; London: Tavistock Publications (1967).

Maccoby, E.E. and Jacklin, C.N. 1974: *The psychology of sex differences*. Stanford, Calif.: Stanford University Press; Oxford: Oxford University Press (1975).

McGee, M.G. 1979: Human spatial abilities: psychometric studies and environmental, genetic, hormonal and neurological influences. *Psychological bulletin* 86, 889–918.

Meece, J.L. et al. 1982: Sex differences in math

achievement: toward a model of academic choice. *Psychological bulletin* 91, 324–48.

Mischel, W. 1970: Sex-typing and socialization. In *Carmichael's manual of child psychology*, vol. III. 3rd edn., ed. P.H. Mussen. New York: Wiley.

*Sherman, J.A. 1978: *Sex related cognitive differences: an essay on theory and evidence*. Springfield, Ill.: Thomas.

Shields, S.A. 1975: Functionalism, Darwinism, and the psychology of women: a study in social myth. *American psychologist* 30, 739–54.

Wittig, M.A. and Petersen, A.C. 1979: *Sex-related differences in cognitive functioning: developmental issues*. New York and London: Academic Press.

sex roles A repertoire of attitudes, behaviors, perceptions and affective reactions which are more commonly associated with one sex than the other. Over the last fifteen years, social scientists have documented the content of sex roles and considered their implications for the treatment of men and women by various social institutions such as education, mental health, criminal justice and the labor force.

Ancillary but separate from the study of sex roles is the investigation of sex differences (or gender differences) in human performance. Empirical studies suggest that the most reliable sex differences are to be found in IQ tests (with males performing on average higher on spatial-mathematical subscales, females higher on verbal subscales; see previous entry) and aggressive behavior (males on average displaying spontaneously higher levels). The interaction of sex differences and sex roles has been variously explained by different disciplines. Some anthropologists (e.g. Tiger 1970) have argued that originally small morphological and neuro-anatomical differences between the sexes were augmented by early bifurcation of social responsibilities; men's hunting behavior leading to increases in aggression and spatial discriminations, and women's child-rearing resulting in increased verbal ability and decreased aggression. Neuroendocrine bases of sex differences have been documented by Gray and Buffery (1971) and related to evolutionary processes. Other anthropologists and sociologists have stressed the mutability of sex roles, noting cultures in which men perform "women's" work (Mead 1935), and the way in which economic and social changes have altered the prevailing notions of appropriately "feminine" activities (Rowbotham 1973).

Developmental psychologists have pursued three major approaches to sex role acquisition in children. The psychoanalytic school directs attention to the OEDIPUS COMPLEX and its successful resolution as crucial for appropriate identification, while at the same time positing the passive and active nature of women and men respectively as relatively fixed (Strachey and Richards 1973). Social learning theorists (see SOCIAL LEARNING THEORY) believe that behavior appropriate to sex role results from differential positive reinforcement (Mischel 1970). Cognitive developmentalists suggest that only after the acquisition of the concept of permanence can the child understand the immutability of gender which is a prerequisite for sex role learning (Kohlberg 1966).

Studies of sexually anomalous babies by Money and Erhardt (1972) have shed more light on the plasticity of sex role learning. One of two male identical twins had his penis amputated as a result of a surgical accident. The child received plastic surgery and endocrine treatment resulting in an appearance of femininity although remaining genetically male. While exhibiting heightened levels of rough-and-tumble play more characteristic of a male, the child's behavior by the age of four-and-a-half years was significantly different from the brother's, and virtually indistinguishable from other females. This indicates the importance of socialization in sex role development. Critics of such an interpretation would point to animal experiments in which opposite-sex behavior is produced by administration of the appropriate hormones soon after birth (Edwards 1968; Levine and Mullins 1966). The critics' case might also be supported by Bancom et al. (1985), who found that self-report sex role among women was related to testoterone levels in saliva, less

"feminine" women having higher levels of this male hormone.

Most recent theorists agree that human behavior is malleable even when they argue for biological causation in sex differences (Daly and Wilson 1983). AC

Bibliography

Bancom, D.H., Besch, P.K. and Callahan, S. 1985: Relation between testosterone concentration, sex role identity and personality among females. *Journal of personality and social psychology* 48, 1218–26.

Daly, M. and Wilson, M. 1983: *Sex, evolution and behavior.* Boston: Grant Press.

Edwards, D.A. 1968: Mice: fighting by neonatally androgenized females. *Science* 161, 1028.

Gray, J.A. and Buffery, A.W.H. 1971: Sex differences in emotional and cognitive behaviour in mammals including man; adaptive and neural bases. *Acta psychologica* 35, 89–111.

Kohlberg, L. 1966: A cognitive developmental analysis of children's sex role concepts and attitudes. In *The development of sex differences*, ed. E.E. Maccoby. Stanford, Calif.: Stanford University Press.

Levine, S. and Mullins, R.F. 1966: Hormonal influences on brain organization in infant rats. *Sciences* 152, 1585–92.

Maccoby, E. and Jacklin, C.N. 1974: *The psychology of sex differences.* Stanford, Calif.: Stanford University Press.

Mead, M. 1935: *Sex and temperament in three primitive societies.* New York: Morrow.

Mischel, W. 1970: Sex typing and socialization. In *Carmichael's manual of child psychology*, vol. I, ed. P.H. Mussen. New York: Wiley.

Money, J. and Erhardt, A.A. 1972: *Man and woman, boy and girl.* Baltimore, Md: Johns Hopkins University Press.

Strachey, J. and Richards, A. eds. 1973: *New introductory lectures on psychoanalysis.* Harmondsworth: Penguin. (Lectures by Freud 1925 and 1931.)

Tiger, L. 1970: *Men in groups.* New York: Random House.

Weitz, S. 1977: *Sex roles.* New York: Oxford University Press.

situationism *See* person/situation controversy.

social behavior A term used synonymously with interpersonal behavior and

SOCIAL INTERACTION to denote the subject matter of social psychology. The study of social behavior may include the study of such things as attitudes, values and beliefs, which are taken to influence overt behavior, as well as the study of such things as face-to-face interaction.   AF

social categorization

Has been suggested as an important and fundamental process in intergroup behavior (see PREJUDICE). Tajfel (1982) has argued that social categorization leads to an accumulation of perceived between-group differences and assimilation of within-group differences. Research has confirmed the first of these two hypotheses but there is as yet no clear evidence with respect to assimilation. Tajfel has also argued that social categorization is a sufficient condition for discrimination; but so-called minimal group studies show that people use discrimination of outgroup members only as a means of achieving a positive self-evaluation where discrimination is the only way in which a positive identity can be achieved.   JMFJ

Bibliography

Billig, M. 1985: Prejudice, categorization and particularization: from a perceptual to a rhetorical approach. *European journal of social psychology* 15, 79–103.

Tajfel, H. 1982: Social psychology of intergroup relations. *Annual review of psychology* 33, 1–39.

social cognition

The cognitive processes involved in understanding, and perhaps in guiding social behavior. In general the field has been taken to include people's perceptions and judgments of others. It is not, therefore, a "social psychology of cognition", or a study of how cognitive processes, such as thinking or memory, are influenced by other people or social events if those people or events are not being thought about or remembered. There is a broad and a narrow category of ideas and studies which are recognized to cover topics in social cognition. The narrow category includes primarily recent work which derives from general cognitive

psychology. The broad category includes the study of anything which is both social and cognitive rather than purely affective or behavioral.

Social psychology has always retained a central interest in cognition. There are topics which are not intrinsically bound up with thought and belief, such as non-verbal communication. But even though ritualized display and the expression of emotion may be studied without much reference to cognitive processes, the recognition of and reaction to them is far harder to treat behavioristically. A list of the topics in one book on social cognition, or cognitive social psychology, contains ATTITUDES, SOCIAL PERCEPTION and IMPRESSION FORMATION, ATTRIBUTION THEORY, ATTRACTION, COGNITIVE DISSONANCE, EQUITY THEORY and even GROUPS (Eiser 1980). A more recent text, while retaining "attitudes" and several chapters on "attribution", has "person memory" rather than "person perception", and introduces such cognitive topics as "attention" and "social schemata" (Fiske and Taylor 1984). The former list seems to cover most of social psychology. The study of attitudes, including PREJUDICE and STEREOTYPES, has been regarded as the central social topic, although since World War II the literature on person perception and its offspring, IMPLICIT PERSONALITY THEORY, and attribution, has been equally if not more extensive. Attitude studies have been concerned with people's beliefs, how these are acquired and changed, and how they influence behavior. Studies of impression formation and attribution have concerned themselves with cognitive *processes*, and are therefore closer in spirit to general cognitive psychology and more recent work in social cognition.

Social psychology, therefore, has its own cognitive tradition, which was fostered particularly by the ideas of various European-born psychologists, such as LEWIN, HEIDER and ASCH. Lewin's FIELD THEORY contains cognitive elements, but it is reasonable to claim that Asch and Heider were the seminal figures in establishing social psychology's interest in information-integration and thought processes. Both worked in the USA from the 1930s (and

Asch was brought up in New York), but both were heavily indebted to the ideas of German gestalt psychology, which stressed that the nature of complex entities cannot be explained by the nature of their constituent parts. Such a belief might be expected to be congenial to social psychologists. Although Asch believed that persons are not perceptible in the same way as other entities, and that therefore social psychology cannot be reduced to individual psychology (see ASCH), neither he nor Heider made a serious attempt to erect a theory of irreducible social entities or social facts as DURKHEIM had done.

Nevertheless, social psychology also has its roots in sociology which has shown consistent interest in people's values and beliefs, even when explaining them as products of historical, societal forces beyond the individual's comprehension and control. More particularly the American tradition of SYMBOLIC INTERACTIONISM led to studies of interaction and of the SELF. Interaction can, of course, be studied without reference to the participants' thought processes, as laboratory and ethological work demonstrate. The symbolic interactionists, however, have regarded the interactants' interpretation (or, in Thomas's terms "definition") of the situation as crucial to the entire process of interaction. This is central to the ideas of GOFFMAN and ETHNOMETHODOLOGY. Goffman (1983) went so far as to assert: 'At the very center of interactive life is the cognitive relation we have with those present before us, without which relationship our activity, behavioral and verbal, could not be meaningfully organized'. Cooley and MEAD fostered the view that the self and the self-concept are fundamental to an understanding of social life and behavior. This belief has been a basis for work as dissimilar as that of Kuhn and Goffman, and has also been absorbed into different approaches such as ROGERS'S. Conceptions of the self have been another major topic in recent studies of social cognition (Markus et al. 1985; see also SELF-CONCEPT).

Social cognition in its modern, narrower meaning, became popular in the 1970s. By the early 1980s it had gained institutional recognition. In 1980 the *Journal of personality and social psychology* named one of its sections 'Attitudes and social cognition'. In 1982, there was a new journal called *Social cognition*. The initial editorial stated that 'any article that focuses on the perception of, memory for, or processing of information involving people or social events falls without our purview', but that they should 'deal with the effects of social variables on the *process* of thinking rather than the products of thought'. Books began to appear in the late 1970s, such as Wyer and Carlston 1979, and Eiser 1980. The latter of these covers a very wide range of topics (see above). The former is far narrower, and applies models derived from cognitive psychology to topics of social inference and attribution. In this book, as Ostrom (1984) remarks, 'The term "person memory" appears to be regarded as synonymous to (sic) social cognition'.

Research on memory has provided the background, and many of the tools of research in social cognition. The second volume of the *Handbook of social cognition* (Wyer and Srull 1984) is devoted to memory. The first volume has papers on such topics as the relationship between social cognition and cognition in general, and the applicability of the concepts derived from cognition studies to social phenomena. Three papers are about the use of "prototypes" and "schemata" in social cognition. These concepts again come from the study of memory, although they have been more extensively applied to the question of categorization of objects.

Their meaning is not entirely uncontentious. Bartlett (1932) used the concept of "schema" in investigating how memories of a folk-tale seemed to be reshaped over time in a way which produced interpretation of awkward detail, and assimilation to pre-existing beliefs. Subsequently the term was used by Piaget and by Oldfield to mean an abstract, general construct applicable to a range of cases whose non-common features are not specified in the schema. "Prototype" has been used by Posner (1969) to mean a representation of an entity which possesses the average or most typical features which define the category to which it belongs. "Prototype" has also been used to mean an exemplar, or member of a category which defines the category as a best case. Rosch and Mervis (1975), for instance, believe that category-inclusion is a matter of "family resemblance" (a term borrowed from Wittgenstein) to central or prototypical members of the category. The words "schema" and "prototype" have been taken up in social psychology. Kelley (1972) refers to beliefs about general patterns of cause and effect as "causal schemata" (see ATTRIBUTION THEORY). Both words have also been adopted in discussions of categorization processes related to person perception and the self (Cantor and Mischel 1979; Markus et al. 1985).

Cognitive studies on person perception or the self are frequently concerned with the way in which beliefs about the self operate as a "mnemonic device" in recall (e.g. Bellezza 1984), or the way in which different variables affect memory of persons (even if at the encoding stage). Hamilton et al. (1980), for example, found that subjects who were told to form an impression of a person from given information recalled more of the information than other subjects who were told to memorize it. This appears to be good evidence in support of Asch's conception of the active processes involved in impression formation. The obvious interpretation of the superior recall of the impression-forming group is that in order to form a coherent impression, they must think about the information and organize it by fitting individual items into an integrated framework, and this has the effect of making them easier to recall.

The principal studies on social cognition which are not heavily influenced by concepts derived from work on memory concern inferences (and particularly mistaken inferences) people draw from information about others (Kahneman et al. 1982; see SOCIAL PERCEPTION). The domain of such studies clearly overlaps attribution, and there are several papers on attribution in the Kahneman et al. volume. Ideas derived from non-attributional studies of inference have found their way into recent work on social explanations (e.g. Leddo et al. 1984).

A development closely related to work on categorization (but having a bearing on inference) is the concept of *script*. This is a representation (schema) of a stereotypical sequence of events. Schank and Abelson (1977), who developed the idea, use the example of a "restaurant script", in which the sequence of the customer's (and others') behavior when visiting a restaurant follows a highly predictable pattern. The important thing about scripts is that they are shared SOCIAL REPRESENTATIONS of typical, predictable sequences. When a story brings to mind such a script, people remember details which are part of the typical sequence, but are not actually described (Bowers et al. 1979). The script concept has been used a great deal in social and non-social cognitive psychology (Abelson 1981). For example, scripts contain typical means-end sequences, which suggest that people may draw on scripts in making attributions about others' behavior (Lalljee and Abelson 1983).

Cognitive psychologists concern themselves with how incoming information is organized by people's established ways of categorizing their world, or by their immediate purposes (Higgins et al. 1982). This is nothing new in social psychology. The way in which people think about their social world and themselves has clearly provided plenty of mileage for it in the past. Work on attitudes, impressions and stereotypes has shown consistent interest in the relationship between beliefs and new information, although much of attribution theory might be criticized for having deliberately avoided serious consideration of expectation and belief in favor of an inductive model of the attribution process. The cognitive approach, however, differs from much of this work (but not from that of the equally "Kantian" gestalt group) in stressing that incoming information is actively processed or worked on rather than just inscribing itself on an inert *tabula rasa*. Cognitive studies set out to investigate these processes in detail. Typical experiments (such as Hamilton et al. 1980, mentioned above) investigate how different cues produce different recall of the same information, on the assumption that this shows how cognitive sets affect the storage or retrieval of memories. Other typical experiments attempt to study the unobservable mental operations by recording reaction times, on the assumption that (with certain qualifications) a longer time is a sign of more processing. Ostrom et al. (1980), for instance, have used reaction times to investigate impression formation. They have thrown new light on the issue of primacy by finding that the length of processing time suggests that, after an initial judgment has been made, the judgment, rather than the information from which it was derived, becomes the basis for subsequent judgments. (For a review of these kinds of social studies see Srull 1984).

Social psychology has sometimes seemed to have no subject matter of its own, or to be concerned with processes which have to be understood by reference to simpler, non-social processes which are their building-blocks. Cognitive psychology suggests how more inclusive, higher-order processes may determine the character of processes lower in a hierarchy. This, of course, echoes the gestalt psychologists' view that a whole is not determined by its parts. It also implies that complex thought processes, which may be common in thinking about ourselves and other people, need not be comprehensible in terms of simpler lower-order processes. This in turn implies that complex, social-cognitive processes are not reducible to lower-order non-social processes. So social cognition seems able to provide social psychology with its own irreducible subject matter. One complex process, however, may be very much like another. But even if there is nothing peculiarly social about the processes involved in social cognition, the fact that they are examples of complex cognitive phenomena makes them of central importance to any adequate cognitive psychology.

Others have gone much further in their claims for social cognition. Drawing from work on the development of social cognition in children (e.g. Hoffman 1981), and

work which shows that phenomenal causal relations among objects are described in metaphors derived from descriptions of human action (Heider and Simmel 1944), Zajonc (1980) and Ostrom (1984) have claimed that social cognition has primacy and is the "general case", while non-social cognition is a secondary "special case". RL

Bibliography

Abelson, R.P. 1981: Psychological status of the script concept. *American psychologist* 36, 715–29.

Bartlett, F.C. 1932: *Remembering: a study in experimental and social psychology*. Cambridge: Cambridge University Press.

Bellezza, F.S. 1984: The self as a mnemonic device: the role of internal cues. *Journal of personality and social psychology* 47, 506–16.

Bower, G.H., Black, J.B. and Turner, T.J. 1979: Scripts in memory for text. *Cognitive psychology* 11, 177–220.

Cantor, N. and Mischel, W. 1979: Prototypes in person perception. In *Advances in experimental social psychology* 12, ed. L. Berkowitz. New York: Academic Press.

Eiser, J.R. 1980: *Cognitive social psychology*. London and New York: McGraw-Hill.

Fiske, S.T. and Taylor, S.E. 1984: *Social cognition*. Reading, Mass.: Addison-Wesley.

Goffman, E. 1983: The interaction order. *American sociological review* 48, 1–17.

Hamilton, D.L., Katz, L.B. and Leirer, V.O. 1980: Organizational processes in impression formation. In *Person memory: the cognitive basis of social perception*, eds. R. Hastie et al. Hillsdale, N.J.: Erlbaum.

Heider, F. and Simmel, M. 1944: An experimental study of apparent behavior. *American journal of psychology* 57, 243–59.

Higgins, E.T., McCann, C.D. and Fondacaro, R. 1982: The "communication game": goal-directed encoding and cognitive consequences. *Social cognition* 1, 21–37.

Hoffman, M.L. 1981: Perspectives on the difference between understanding people and understanding things: the role of affect. In *Social cognitive development: frontiers and possible futures*, eds. J. Flavell and L. Ross. Cambridge: Cambridge University Press.

Kahneman, D., Slovic, P. and Tversky, A. eds. 1982: *Judgment under uncertainty: heuristics and biases*. Cambridge and New York: Cambridge University Press.

Kelley, H.H. 1972: Causal schemata and the attribution process. In *Attribution: perceiving the causes of behavior*, eds. E.E. Jones et al. Morristown, N.J.: General Learning Press.

Lalljee, M. and Abelson, R.P. 1983: The organisation of explanations. In *Attribution theory: social and functional extensions*, ed. M. Hewstone. Oxford: Blackwell.

Leddo, J., Abelson, R.P. and Gross, P.H. 1984: Conjunctive explanations: when two reasons are better than one. *Journal of personality and social psychology* 47, 933–43.

Markus, H., Smith, J. and Moreland, R.L. 1985: The role of the self in the perception of others. *Journal of personality and social psychology* 49, 1494–1512.

Ostrom, T.M. 1984: The sovereignty of social cognition. In Wyer and Srull, op. cit.

——— Lingle, J.H., Pryor, J.B. and Geva, N. 1980: Cognitive organization of person impressions. In *Person memory: the cognitive basis of social perception*, eds. R. Hastie et al. Hillsdale, N.J.: Erlbaum.

Posner, M.I. 1969: Abstraction and the process of recognition. In *The psychology of learning and motivation*, vol. 3, eds. G.H. Bower and J.T. Spence. New York and London: Academic Press.

Rosch, E. and Mervis, C.B. 1975: Family resemblances: studies in the internal structure of categories. *Cognitive psychology* 7, 573–603.

Schank, R.C. and Abelson, R.P. 1977: *Scripts, plans, goals, and understanding: an inquiry into human knowledge structures*. Hillsdale, N.J.: Erlbaum.

Srull, T.K. 1984: Methodological techniques for the study of person memory and social cognition. In Wyer and Srull, op. cit.

Wyer, R.S. and Carlston, D.E. 1979: *Social cognition, inference, and attribution*. Hillsdale, N.J.: Erlbaum.

——— and Srull, T.K. 1984: *Handbook of social cognition*. 3 vols. Hillsdale, N.J.: Erlbaum.

Zajonc, R.B. 1980: Cognition and social cognition: a historical perspective. In *Retrospectives on social psychology*, ed. L. Festinger. Oxford and New York: Oxford University Press.

social comparison Festinger (1954) has suggested that we use other people as sources for comparison in order to evaluate our own attitudes and abilities when comparison with objective standards is not possible. The theory predicts a preference for associating with others who hold similar attitudes or have slightly superior abilities because such interactions provide the most informative social comparisons (see Gruder 1971).

Social comparison processes also play an important role in the development of a positive social identity, as suggested in Tajfel's (1982) theory of intergroup differentiation.

A similar notion can be found in the primus-inter-pares (p.i.p.) principle, which suggests that social interaction is in part governed by the desire to be similar to others and at the same time different from others, which results in the paradoxical finding that on average we feel ourselves to be superior to the average other. This tendency has been suggested as a possible explanation for group polarization (see RISKY SHIFT). People who take more extreme views in discussion may perhaps be underlining the difference between their own and others' similar views (see Myers 1983). JMFJ

Bibliography

Festinger, L. 1954: A theory of social comparison processes. *Human relations* 7, 117–40.

Gruder, C.L. 1971: Determinants of social comparison choices. *Journal of experimental social psychology* 7, 473–89.

Myers, D.G. 1983: Polarizing effects of social interaction. In *Group decision processes*, eds. H. Brandstatter, J.H. Davis and G. Stocker-Kreichgauer. London: Academic Press.

Tajfel, H. ed. 1982: *Social identity and intergroup relations*. Cambridge and New York: Cambridge University Press.

social exchange Entails reciprocal giving and receiving between individuals, between individuals and groups, or between individuals representing groups. At its most basic, social exchange expresses the reciprocal rule: that an individual gives and another returns, in some measure, what is given. An imbalance between what is given and received may reflect differences in status or resources between donors and recipients, thus placing one or other in debt and so assuring the continuity of the reciprocal relationship. Social exchange theory is a body of explanations having as their core principle that much of social interaction involves exchanges of material things, of behavior or of ideas.

Exchange can be studied at the individual level of strategies and consequences, or at the level of interdependency of two or more individuals, but it would be mistaken to conceptualize social exchange only as a matter of individual motivations. It may involve some calculation and rational planning of relative rewards and costs by each party, but the form and content of the exchange itself (how much, of what, and how frequently) are influenced or even determined by social conventions and norms prevailing within given societies and groups. Studies of social exchange have often brought a close focus to bear on individual motivations but much of the vast literature on this topic also recognizes that the questions of *why* and *with whom* exchanges take place and the manner in which they do take place, are socially determined issues.

Social exchange attracts research and discussion from an interdisciplinary range that spans social anthropology, sociology, social psychology and evolutionary biology. This gives some warning also that it is no easy matter to attempt to compress the currently existing theory of social exchange explanations into a few representative statements. There is a variety of possible interpretations depending on whether social exchange is discussed by anthropologists, sociologists, psychologists or biologists. These differing interpretations can be summarized as follows: social anthropologists tend to emphasize the classification of the exchanges, their non-material implications and the symbolic meanings of the exchanges that permeate a given society; sociologists tend to interpret social exchange within the context of groups and power relations; social psychologists focus on the interpersonal significance of reciprocal behavior and place some emphasis on motivation; sociobiologists seem influenced also by this latter interpretation, conceptualizing some forms of animal social behavior especially in primates and carnivores in reinforcement terminology.

Together with this variety of interpretations there are large differences in methodology: anthropologists using descriptively based analyses, sociologists using survey methods and taking up the critical discussion of theory, social psychologists following experimental research models and sociobiologists referring to ethological field studies. The result of this variety of approaches is a formidable empirical and theoretical literature on social exchange, much of the latter consisting of critical appraisals contributing to further developments in the theory (Chadwick-Jones 1976). Social exchange explanations have been remarkably well criticized and have survived the criticisms remarkably.

Explanations of social behavior in terms of social exchange first emerged substantially from the work of anthropologists – Mauss, Malinowski, Lévi-Strauss (see Turner 1978) whose work has been influential in sociology but much less so in social psychology. Here the major starting point was provided by George Homans (1961) who applied reinforcement hypotheses, borrowed from experimental studies of learning, to a broad range of empirical evidence and research illustrations. In addition to reinforcement concepts, Homans used analogies from economics and notions of profit and loss, gain and cost. From these analogies what tended to emerge was a model of human motivation in terms of cost/benefit, rational behavior. Homans, however, introduced a superb qualification to this type of conclusion – the Aristotelian principle of distributive justice. Clearly, it had to be admitted that there is no social exchange that does not involve some consideration of justice and there can be no justice if not to resolve some issue of social exchange. (This area of theory in social psychology is sometimes labeled "exchange-equity" theory.) Further questions arise over what *kind* of justice should operate – equity or equality, distributive justice or social justice?

These issues were discussed in a richly illustrative text by Blau (1964), whose discussion of exchange and power, while sharing the emphasis on reinforcement motives and economic analogies, at the same time broadened the area of the explanations to comprise competing social groups, innovations in society and the forms of social exchange that can be observed in loving relationships and in families. In the latter context, critics of social exchange theory have often raised questions implying its basic weakness, such as: how can the giving of love and care to children be explained in terms of calculating returns? On the contrary, family studies provide useful instances of the highly moral aspects of social exchange involving rights and obligations.

The operation of social exchange in the interdependency between two persons was explored very extensively by Thibaut and Kelley (1959). They interpreted exchange as a pattern of behavior rather than merely as an exchange of material values. These two authors contributed a fascinating range of conjectures, using matrices adapted to social psychology from earlier game-theory formats. Thibaut and Kelley, while not themselves claiming a major interest in social exchange, do much to explore the nature of interdependency between individuals. Their work has influenced a very large number of experimental studies on negotiation, trust, bargaining and on the effects of threats and other inducements in producing agreement over the sharing of outcomes between individuals.

Tendencies towards a reductionist view of social behavior are apparent in some introductory textbooks (a rather similar tendency to the simplification and smoothing-over of theories in economics textbooks) in which the label "exchange theory" appears to refer only to "the individual's" opportunist orientations to gains or losses and completely ignores any broader reciprocal scope of social exchanges: for example, their expression of important symbolic meanings, sustaining social structures and, in Sahlins's words (1972) 'provisioning society'. It might, of course, be observed that behavior, in many situations, is influenced by its consequences but this assumption seems no more than commonplace and what is much more problematical is why some consequences are considered important and others disregarded; and how, in different

social groups, do certain consequences come to be valued more than others?

Sahlins's analysis of pre-market, primitive societies provides a historical perspective on social exchange (see also Ekeh 1974). So much so that social exchange, as the expression of reciprocal relations in society, seems to have universal relevance. Lévi-Strauss (1969), in particular, argued along these lines. Nevertheless, within a given society there may be many forms of social interaction including exploitation and coercion that do not bear out either the rational or the reciprocal rule. The boundaries or limits of a social exchange explanation and the circumstances under which behavior becomes more calculating and less trusting seem to provide an especially interesting topic for research.

One of the features of this body of theory is the expression of its influence through a great variety of research designs. Gergen, Greenberg and Willis (1980) provide excellent examples of the creative diversity of both theoretical and research approaches; a chapter by Befu, "Structural and motivational approaches to social exchange" gives a discussion of the moral compulsions in social exchange. Burgess and Huston's useful collection of essays (1979) includes a view from SOCIOBIOLOGY, as expounded in Alexander's "Natural selection and social exchange". Important contrasts between economic and social exchange are brought out by Foa and Foa (1974) whose ideas have continued to inspire largely supportive research (Brinberg and Castell 1982). The work of John and Jeanne Gullahorn on computer modeling of social exchange sequences (see Chadwick-Jones 1976) is a further example of the many possibilities involving a very broad scope of experiments, observational studies and theoretical enquiry as is the large quantity of work on who chooses which principle of fairness, and the contexts in which different choices occur (e.g. Greenberg 1983).   JKC-J

Bibliography

Blau, P.M. 1964: *Exchange and power in social life.* New York: Wiley.

Brinberg, D. and Castell, P. 1982: A resource

exchange theory approach to interpersonal interactions: a test of Foa's theory. *Journal of personality and social psychology* 43, 260–9.

*Burgess, R.L. and Huston, T.L. eds. 1979: *Social exchange in developing relationships*. New York and London: Academic Press.

*Chadwick-Jones, J.K. 1976: *Social exchange theory: its structure and influence in social psychology*. London and New York: Academic Press.

Ekeh, P.P. 1974: *Social exchange theory: the two traditions*. Cambridge, Mass.: Harvard University Press.

Foa, U.G. and E.B. 1974: *Societal structures of the mind*. Springfield, Ill.: Thomas.

*Gergen, K.J., Greenberg, M.S. and Willis, R.H. 1980: *Social exchange: advances in theory and research*. New York and London: Plenum Press.

Greenberg, J. 1983: Self-image vs impression management in adherence to distributive justice standards. The influence of self-awareness and self-consciousness. *Journal of personality and social psychology* 44, 5–19.

Homans, G.C. 1961: *Social behavior: its elementary forms*. New York: Harcourt Brace Jovanovich; London: Routledge and Kegan Paul.

Lévi-Strauss, C. 1969: *The elementary structures of kinship*. 2nd edn. Boston: Beacon.

Sahlins, M.D. 1972: *Stone age economics*. Chicago: Aldine.

Thibaut, J.W. and Kelley, H.H. 1959: *The social psychology of groups*. New York: Wiley.

Turner, J.H. 1978: *The structure of sociological theory*. Homewood, Ill.: Dorsey Press.

social facilitation The first experimentally discovered effect in social psychology indicating that the presence of another person has a motivational effect upon the performance of a subject by enhancing dominant responses (Triplett 1897). Initial research led to seemingly contradictory findings because performance is sometimes improved, and sometimes affected negatively, by the presence of others. Zajonc (1965) argued, however, that these contradictory findings could be reconciled by assuming that the presence of another person increases the drive of the subject, as formulated in the Hull-Spence behavior theory. This would lead to improved performance when

correct responses are dominant and worse performance when errors are dominant (as in the early stages of a learning process).

Other research, however, has suggested that the presence of another person is not in itself sufficient to produce social facilitation. Cottrell et al. (1968) found that an audience (of two) who were interested in the subject's performance had an impact on it, whereas the presence of two other persons who wore blindfolds did not! It was therefore suggested that "evaluation apprehension", or worry about how one will be judged by others, produces social facilitation. The demonstration that the effect occurs in other species such as chickens and cockroaches tends rather to undermine this idea.

To account for such findings Sanders (1981) proposed that social facilitation may be the result of arousal caused by the conflict between attending to the "task" and attending to the audience. Such a distraction model certainly offers a possible explanation for the difference between the effects of an attentive audience and those who are present but not attending. On the other hand, while an audience may certainly distract a performer, it is less clear how Triplett's original example of the incremental effect of a pacemaker on a cyclist's performance could be regarded as a case of distraction. Worse for the theory is the fact that others who are imperceptible, and therefore presumably not distracting, do affect performance (Bond and Titus 1983). At present there appears to be a fairly robust phenomenon with no completely clear explanation(s).   JMFJ/RL

Bibliography

*Bond, C.F. and Titus, L.J. 1983: Social facilitation: a meta-analysis of 241 studies. *Psychological bulletin* 94, 265–92.

Cottrell, N.B., Wack, D.L., Sebrack, G.J. and Rittle, R.H. 1968: Social facilitation of dominant responses by the presence of an audience and the mere presence of others. *Journal of personality and social psychology* 9, 245–50.

Sanders, G.S. 1981: Driven by distraction: an integrative review of social facilitation theory and research. *Journal of experimental social psychology* 17, 227–51.

Triplett, N. 1897: The dynamogenic factors in pacemaking and competition. *American journal of psychology* 9, 507–33.

Zajonc, R.B. 1965: Social facilitation. *Science* 149, 269–74.

social influence Any change which a person's relations with other people (individual, group, institution or society) produce on his intellectual activities, emotions or actions. We usually think that others are free, that they weigh up alternatives and carry out their choices rationally. Everyone seems to be his own master. In reality this is only a Western belief. It utterly denies that fundamental phenomenon of social life which we call influence. This is one of the most important concepts in social psychology. Usually we are not even conscious of such influence and we do not know why or how it takes place.

In the late nineteenth century, when hypnosis was a popular object of public curiosity and scientific development, influence was considered a consequence of hypnotic suggestion under which one was transformed into something like a robot: one's conduct under the control of someone else who can restrict one's awareness and destroy one's critical faculties and independence. Tarde believed that individuals were in a state of hypnotic suggestion whenever they are together. This produced imitation, the mechanism by which everything individual became social, thereby creating the uniformity common to all societies. Le Bon believed that openness to mutual influence, accompanied by a loss of sense of responsibility and of normal intellectual capacities, causes a spread of ideas through emotion and thereby produced mental unity in a group. This conception of social life as a regression to more primitive states of mind is no longer popular in France. It was badly received in the United States where social psychology was developing on a more optimistic and matter-of-fact basis.

In 1936, Sherif experimentally investigated how groups construct shared rules and norms. He made such rules the criterion of the passage from individual functioning to social functioning. He chose an ambiguous situation in which individuals did not have established rules at their disposal. Using a visual illusion, the autokinetic effect (the impression that a fixed point of light is moving when it is seen in total darkness) he showed how members of groups come to agree in their estimation of the displacement of the light until their shared opinion remains stable even if they are subsequently asked to do the experiment on their own.

Even though he was a fugitive from Nazism, ASCH wanted to show that influence has not necessarily the power of suggestion, that the individual can resist, at least if he knows that the influence is misleading. He did not believe that people imitate blindly; whether alone or in a group the individual adopts the opinions of others deliberately and rationally, and can remain independent if circumstances permit. Nevertheless Asch's experiments did not confirm this criticism. On the contrary, they demonstrated the power of pressures to conform, and the tendency of the group to follow blindly even to the extent of denying objective reality. To conform to a majority made up of confederates of the experimenter who give false responses, the subject declares against all the evidence that unequal lines are the same length. From this experiment onwards, social influence *in* a group was confused with individuals' conformity *to* the group, seen in its extreme form in the blind OBEDIENCE displayed in Milgram's famous experiments where more than 60 per cent of subjects did not hesitate to give someone apparent electric shocks on the orders of the experimenter.

Festinger showed that the individual is defenseless in the face of shared beliefs. To attain an objective vision of things he needs to rely on others. In a situation of uncertainty or ambiguity it is necessary to arrive at a collective definition, to create a social reality. Error can only be individual while truth is social and spontaneously imposes itself on the majority. Everyone's adherence to the same belief produces a majority effect creating an influence which never needs to manifest itself as such.

There is no sign of constraint or overt pressure. Everyone accepts the collective belief and all share collectively in the same social reality. If this pressure to uniformity proves ineffective the group can get rid of deviants.

If, in this model of majority influence, groups effectively eliminate deviants and obtain support for the majority view-point, it is not clear how social change could occur, even if only to maintain contact with reality. It seems a fundamental contradiction that a group's uniformity is detrimental to the group's success and adaptation. So groups must be capable of reacting against the rigid forces of conformity. To understand innovation we must assume minority influence. Innovation then becomes, in the face of conformity, a fundamental form of impact which individuals have on each other and on their group. The problem of influence is to understand how the norms of a society are maintained or overturned. Within this framework, majorities and minorities can both exercise an influence in different areas.

Every society functions on the basis of agreements about fundamental principles, i.e. consensus. The power of the minority lies in its ability to refuse the consensus. Certainly the group will bring pressure to bear to re-establish its homogeneity. But the more it knows that exclusion is unusual or even impossible, the more the minority can resist. The group must then resign itself to negotiating with this uncooperative minority and that is where the process of influence begins. Besides, deviance is not necessarily the bogey suggested by the psychology of conformity. Eccentric or unusual behavior has an undoubted attraction.

For a minority to have an influence it must prove its determination by its behavioral style. It is the combination of behavior and its context that produces its instrumental and symbolic significance. It is consistency in the minority's behavioral style which initially determines its power of persuasion. A consistent style is assertive. It demonstrates the individual's involvement and independence to the extent that, even in a hostile environment, it displays his assurance and his determination not to modify his own point of view. Even if perceived as aggressive this style of behavior exercises an incontestable and complex influence.

First it was necessary to prove that minority influence really exists. This was demonstrated by Moscovici, Lage and Naffrechoux (1969). They projected blue transparencies to groups of two confederates and four naive subjects. The confederates systematically judged transparencies to be green. The subjects' threshold of discrimination between blue and green changed: among the intermediate tones between pure blue and pure green they perceived green earlier. In this case, consistency lay in repeating the same response. This demonstrated a refusal to change and an indifference to others' responses. In experiments more specifically concerning attitudes (Mugny 1982; Paicheler 1976) consistency is shown in a firm, coherent statement of an unchanging viewpoint and a refusal to be influenced by others. These experiments again demonstrate the effectiveness of minority influence in conjunction with the persuasiveness of a consistent behavioral style.

The effectiveness of a minority influence comes from the handling of the conflict caused by the disagreement between the source and the target of the influence. This conflict acts as a "thaw". It causes individuals or groups who are open to the influence to question their own positions. The resolution of conflict with a majority comes through passive acceptance or "compliance" expressed in a change of public response but an unchanged private belief. The resolution of conflict with a minority involves re-examining the object itself. While not expressing itself in a modified public response this may operate more indirectly or latently, whether through a halo effect or a profounder modification of the structure of response.

A minority or deviant group and its influence may often be explicitly rejected. Equally, this influence may be avoided by tracing unusual behavior to mental disturbance (Mugny 1982). Nevertheless a consciously rejected influence can develop underground and have unexpected results. Mugny (1982) demonstrates how minority influence acts not on its explicit concerns but on connected issues. Subjects do not have an impression of giving way to a minority influence. Yet, while they "forget" or deceive themselves about the influence's source, because the source is a minority it is more effective. This is found after a lapse of time, in the minority "sleeper-effect". It is also found in the modification of perception apparent in judgments of after-images in a replication of the blue-green experiment. An after-image is the complementary color seen when one looks at a white screen after staring at a color for several seconds. Moscovici and Personnaz (1980) demonstrated that there is no modification of the after-image under majority influence, but under minority influence the subject's after-image is displaced towards the complement of green. Attempts to replicate this particular experiment have not, however, been successful. For a review of the minority influence literature see Maass and Clarke, 1984; and for an attempt to produce a formal model which unites the data see Tanford and Penrod 1984.

Majorities and minorities have distinct influences. Majority influence helps maintain social uniformity. Minority influence introduces processes of social change, processes of differing complexity which are difficult to discern. This claim has been largely supported over a fifteen-year period, notwithstanding some contradictory findings (e.g. Wolf 1985).   SMo/GP

Bibliography

Maass, A. and Clark, R.D. 1984: Hidden impact of minorities: fifteen years of minority influence research. *Psychological bulletin* 95, 428–50.

Moscovici, S., Lage, E. and Naffrechoux, M. 1969: Influence of a consistent minority on the responses of a majority in a color perception task. *Sociometry* 32, 265–79.

——— and Personnaz, B. 1980: Studies in social influence, v. minority influence and conversion behavior in a perceptual task. *Journal of experimental social psychology* 16, 270–82.

Mugny, G. 1982: *The power of minorities*. London: Academic Press.

Paicheler, G. 1976: Norms and attitude change I: polarization and styles of behavior. *European journal of social psychology* 6, 405–27.

Tanford, G. and Penrod, S. 1984: Social influence model: a formal integration of research on majority and minority influence processes. *Psychological bulletin* 95, 189–225.

Wolf, S. 1985: Manifest and latent influence of majorities and minorities. *Journal of personality and social psychology* 48, 899–908.

social interaction The social behavior between two or more people at the level of verbal utterances and non-verbal signals. Utterances alternate, apart from interruptions, while non-verbal signals are sent continuously and simultaneously. The two kinds of messages however are closely linked. It is useful to distinguish between encounters like interviewing and teaching where one person is in charge, two-sided encounters like discussion and negotiation where each side is pursuing certain goals, and casual encounters where each person responds mainly to what happened last. Social interaction occurs with or without other activities such as work, games, eating and drinking. There may be a task, or the meeting can be primarily social.

Events in social interaction can be categorized, for example, as "suggestions" or "questions" as is done in interaction recording. The twelve categories devised by Bales have been used in a variety of settings, but it has been found that special categories are needed for the kinds of interaction which occur in particular settings such as psychotherapy or management-union bargaining. In addition special activities take place, for example, in doctor-patient interviews and when playing games. On the other hand the repertoire of non-verbal communication is much the same in all settings.

Verbal utterances of the kind just described play an important part in most social interaction, but non-verbal communication (NVC) is also important. Non-verbal communication consists of social signals conveyed by facial expression, GESTURES and bodily movements, GAZE, spatial position, TOUCH, appearance and tone of voice. Some are fairly slow or static like proximity, others are fast-moving such as gestures, and may be closely coordinated with speech. The sender encodes an emotional or other state into a non-verbal (NV) signal, which is decoded by the receiver. Often encoding is unconscious and decoding conscious, but both may be below the threshold of awareness, as with pupil dilation which is a signal for sexual attraction, or with signals governing the synchronizing of speech. The meaning of a NV signal can be found by seeing how states of the sender are encoded, and how signals are decoded, or how they affect others' behavior.

NVC conveys several different kinds of message. It is the main way of indicating interpersonal attitudes, such as like-dislike; the author and others have found that NVC is much more powerful than words for this purpose. NVC is the main channel for expressing emotions; these are often concealed, though there may be "leakage" to less controlled areas, such as the voice or feet. It plays an important part in conversation – completing and elaborating on utterances, for example by gesture and tone of voice; providing feedback from listeners, for example showing surprise or annoyance in the face; and controlling the synchronizing of utterances by means of glances and head nods. NVC is the main method of self-presentation, via appearance and by manner of speaking, and it plays an important part in greetings and other rituals.

One way of analyzing sequences of interaction is to find the probability that one kind of social act leads to another. This produces "adjacency pairs" of which the commonest is question-answer; others are joke-laugh, accuse-deny, request-comply. There are also pairs linking two acts by the same person, such as accept-thank. Another important short sequence is response matching, for example of head nods, smiles or jokes. Reinforcement by agreement, smile, head nod etc. increases the frequency of the behavior reinforced, while negative reinforcement reduces it, usually without much awareness on either side. There are rules governing two-step sequences: for example an utterance should be relevant to what has just been said, and also add something new to it. Longer sequences than two can be discovered by further statistical analysis. This has been quite successful in the study of stereotyped non-verbal sequences like greetings and partings, but less successful for conversation. One case in which two-step links do build up to longer sequences is in the formation of repeated cycles. For example part of a class in school may consist of a repeated cycle of interaction, for example, teacher explains — teacher asks question — pupils reply. This illustrates a limitation of interaction recording, since the repeated cycles would consist of a continuous build-up of complexity, and not a repetition of the same questions and answers. Part of the difficulty of this approach to conversation is that there is often embedding, so that question and answer may be separated, for example by another question and answer. In addition, interactors may be looking ahead to the intended goal of the interaction. Encounters divide into a number of partly independent phases, with different sequences of interaction in each, though the phases themselves come in a certain order, as in the different parts of a selection interview, a doctor-patient encounter, or a dinner party.

A model which has helped with the interpretation of longer sequences is the motor-skill model, which uses the similarity between social behavior and the performance of motor skills. In each case the performer is trying to attain some goal, and makes corrections to his behavior as the result of feedback. This suggests a basic four-step sequence, for example interviewer asks question — respondent gives unsatisfactory answer — interviewer repeats, clarifies or sharpens question — respondent gives useful answer. As in motor skills, there is a hierarchical structure, in which larger plans consist of smaller ones. The motor-skill model fits one-sided encounters, like interviews, though in other cases both interactors can be found to be pursuing plans and taking corrective action at the same time. This model makes use of two-step sequences, such as the effects of reinforcement. However there are several differences between social and motor skills, so that the model needs some elaboration. It is essentially a one-way model, and does not fully describe the interaction of two independent interactors; it does not incorporate the rules of sequence or the properties of different social situations; interactors have elaborate cognitive structures which enable them to consider another's point of view, knowledge of rules of sequence, and of moral or other principles.

A model of interaction which takes more account of the independent but coordinated activity of different interactors is the game model. GAMES, including competitive and aggressive ones, are not possible unless both sides keep to the same rules, and the same is true of social interaction. Every kind of encounter is like a kind of game, with particular goals, repertoire and rules. As with games, although there may be competition and conflict of interests, there must also be cooperation to keep the rules. Interactors must work out a pattern of interaction which is agreeable to both, including a degree of intimacy, dominance relations, activity, topic of conversation, timing of speech, etc. The relationship between two people greatly affects the game and the nature of the social interaction, depending on whether they are in love, enemies, of different status, and so on.

Socially skilled behavior depends on the mastery of patterns of social interaction. Failures of social competence show aspects of interaction which most people can perform unthinkingly. These include lack of rewardingness, failure to initiate interaction, inaccurate perception of the other, inability to see the other's point of view, failure to master conversation sequences, failure to deal with the rules or other properties of situations. These basic skills are needed for all kinds of social encounter; to make friends and influence people, to be a teacher or doctor, further interaction skills are needed. Social skills training is given to mental patients with social difficulties, to members of the public in the

form of assertiveness and heterosexual training, to managers, teachers and others, and for those going to work overseas. A number of methods are in use, and follow-up studies show that role-playing, with video-tape playback, modeling, coaching, and "homework" is the most effective.

(See also COMMUNICATION, NON-VERBAL.)

JMA

Bibliography

Argyle, M. 1969: *Social interaction*. London: Methuen.

——— in press: *Bodily communication*. 2nd edn. London: Methuen.

——— 1983: *The psychology of interpersonal behaviour*. 4th edn. Harmondsworth: Penguin Books.

——— Furnham, A. and Graham, J.A. 1981: *Social situations*. Cambridge and New York: Cambridge University Press.

Bellack, A.S. and Hersen, M. 1979: *Research and practice in social skills training*. New York and London: Plenum.

Clarke, D.D. 1983: *Language and action*. Oxford and New York: Pergamon.

Fraser, C. and Scherer, K. eds. 1982: *Advances in the social psychology of language*. Cambridge and New York: Cambridge University Press.

Knapp, M.L. 1978: *Nonverbal communication in human interaction*. 2nd edn. New York: Holt, Rinehart and Winston.

Morris, D. 1977: *Manwatching*. London: Cape.

Singleton, W.T., Spurgeon, P. and Stammers, R.B. eds. 1979: *The analysis of social skill*. New York and London: Plenum.

social learning theory An attempt to explain various examples of human behavior and aspects of personality by reference to principles derived from experiments on learning. The first systematic effort in this direction was that of a group of Yale psychologists, in particular John Dollard and Neal Miller. In a series of books (Dollard et al. 1939; Miller and Dollard 1941; Dollard and Miller 1950) they used the learning theory of Clark Hull, who was also at Yale, to illuminate the development of normal and abnormal human behavior. Both Dollard and Miller received training in PSYCHOANALYSIS in

Europe, and Dollard had taught anthropology and sociology during the 1930s. Their declared intention (1950) was to create 'a psychological base for a general science of human behavior'. To do this they tried to integrate the "three great traditions" of Freudian theory and therapy, academic experimental psychology and "social science". Their aim, as they said, was 'to combine the vitality of psychoanalysis, the rigor of the natural-science laboratory and the facts of culture'.

Much of Dollard and Miller's effort was spent on trying to explain phenomena pinpointed by Freud as the products of mechanisms suggested by Hull. They believed that there are innate *primary drives*, such as sex, hunger or pain. A drive is a stimulus which is strong enough to lead to action. Behavior is a means of reducing drives. They also believed that there are acquired *secondary drives*. These are conditional stimuli whose drive-force is the result of their association with primary drives. An important example of a secondary drive is anxiety (or fear) learnt from the experience of the primary drive, pain. These associative mechanisms, and the supposed force of secondary drives are the building blocks of complex behavior and motivation.

As in other BEHAVIORAL THEORIES OF PERSONALITY reinforcement (reward and punishment) plays a major role. This acts as the equivalent of the "pleasure principle" in Freud's theories since animals, including humans, presumably pursue pleasure and avoid pain. Animals learn "instrumental responses", such as turning a wheel to avoid shock, because these are associated with the increase of pleasure or reduction of pain. In this way complex behavioral repertoires are gradually built up. Such behavior may be normal or abnormal, since the contingencies of reinforcement will lead to the repetition of behavior associated with reward, and thereby establish habits which may as easily be bad as good. Neurotic or deviant behavior is therefore thought to develop through exactly the same learning processes as normal, socially acceptable behavior.

Dollard and Miller paid some attention to imitation (1941) which they saw as a factor in socialization. They explained it by the reinforcements a person (or animal) gains from the successful achievement of an outcome after imitating someone else. They also made important contributions to theorizing about conflict, aggression and psychotherapy. Miller (1944) worked out the concept of APPROACH-AVOIDANCE CONFLICT in which the same object is desired and feared. As one approaches the object the tendency to approach increases, but so does the tendency to avoid, and the latter increases faster. One is therefore baulked at some distance from the goal, driven both to go on and to go back (see Brown 1948). They claimed that aggression was caused by frustration i.e. interruption of a sequence of goal-directed behavior. The amount of aggression was taken to depend on the amount of frustration, which in turn depended on the strength of the drive to make the frustrated response, and the amount and scope of the interference. The psychotherapeutic ideas centered on the role of conflict and anxiety in psychopathology, and the possibility of the patient learning new responses or to discriminate threatening from non-threatening situations.

The second phase of social learning theory is associated with the work of ALBERT BANDURA and his colleagues from the late 1950s to the present. They too have used ideas derived from laboratory studies of learning, but have proceeded in a more piecemeal fashion, not basing their approach on a particular theory such as Hull's. In fact the primary idea behind much of their work seems to have been the rejection of either Freudian or behaviorist conceptions of human behavior. As Bandura (1977) put it, 'People are neither driven by inner forces nor buffeted by environmental stimuli. Rather, psychological functioning is explained in terms of a continuous reciprocal interaction of personal and environmental determinants. Within this approach, symbolic, vicarious, and self-regulatory processes assume a prominent role'.

Bandura, Walters and other colleagues conducted a famous series of experiments on aggression in children (see Bandura 1973). Their interest was in observational learning (which they called "modeling"). They found that frustration was unnecessary for aggressive behavior, since a child would imitate an adult's aggression in free play without any preliminary upset or frustration. Furthermore, contrary to the views of Dollard and Miller, such imitation occurred without any incentive or reinforcement. Bandura believed that observational learning must be a basic process in human development. As he said (1977), 'One does not teach children to swim . . . and novice medical students to perform surgery by having them discover the appropriate behavior through the consequences of their successes and failures . . . Apart from the question of survival, it is difficult to imagine a social transmission process in which the language, lifestyles, and institutional practices of a culture are taught to each new member by selective reinforcement of fortuitous behaviors . . . '. They showed that such observational learning took place even when the actions of the adult model were punished. Children who had seen this, but were subsequently offered an incentive, proved just as ready and able to produce an accurate imitation as children who had seen an aggressive model rewarded (Bandura 1965). The children therefore *learn* regardless of the reinforcement contingencies. Whether they act on their learning is influenced by reinforcement. Bandura distinguished observational learning from imitation because people do not simply ape others' behavior. They extract general rules about how to affect their environment, and put these into effect when they expect them to produce a desirable outcome. Modeling has proved useful in the treatment of anxiety and phobia (Bandura 1969).

The role of expectations of success and failure has been a major consideration for Bandura and other social learning theorists. Bandura (1982) has been interested in "self-efficacy" beliefs (i.e. beliefs about whether one can act effectively to achieve what one wants) especially, but not solely, as they affect patients in psychotherapy or recovering from physical illness such as heart disease. Mischel (1973) has attempted to build a model of personality based on the assumption that people's behavior is determined by the cognitive processes illustrated in Bandura's experiments. Mischel argues that 'behavior is controlled to a considerable extent by externally administered consequences', but that people also control their own behavior 'by self-imposed goals (standards) and self-produced consequences . . . The essence of self-regulatory systems is the subject's adoption of *contingency rules* that guide his behavior in the absence of, and sometimes in spite of, immediate external situational pressures'. (See also PERSON SITUATION CONTROVERSY.)

The latter-day social learning theorists differ from Dollard and Miller in playing down the importance of motivational (drive) factors such as frustration and in playing up the importance of cognitive factors. States of anxiety are explained in terms of beliefs about self-efficacy rather than as conditioned secondary drives. Above all, reinforcement is seen as neither necessary nor sufficient to explain learning or even behavior. Learning by observation without reward or punishment is taken to be the central process of human socialization. Because this involves the abstraction of rules which are stored for future as well as immediate guidance, observation and curiosity allow people to set themselves practical and moral standards. Naturally, as the passages above show, these writers do not deny the effects of reward and punishment, nor do they suppose that learning is not frequently a result of explicit instruction. The principal direction of their work has been towards the rejection of the model of human beings as *driven* either from without (by "reinforcement") or from within (by "drives"). The impulse to take this direction may be an ideological commitment to an alternative model of humans as free and self-determining. Nevertheless the laboratory experiments (with people, not animals) have demonstrated the inadequacy of the mechanisms suggested by the earlier theorists and others who have relied on behavioristic conceptions derived from the animal laboratory. RL

Bibliography

Bandura, A. 1965: Influence of models' reinforcement contingencies on the acquisition of imitative responses. *Journal of personality and social psychology* 1, 589–95.

—— 1969: *Principles of behavior modification*. New York: Holt, Rinehart and Winston.

—— 1973: *Aggression: a social learning analysis*. Englewood Cliffs, N.J.: Prentice-Hall.

—— 1977: *Social learning theory*. Englewood Cliffs, N.J.: Prentice-Hall.

—— 1982: Self-efficacy mechanism in human agency. *American psychologist* 37, 122–47.

Brown, J.S. 1948: Gradients of approach and avoidance responses and their relation to level of motivation. *Journal of comparative and physiological psychology* 41, 450–65.

Dollard, J., Doob, L., Miller, N.E., Mowrer, O.H. and Sears, R.R. 1939: *Frustration and aggression*. New Haven: Yale University Press.

—— and Miller, N.E. 1950: *Personality and psychotherapy*. New York: McGraw-Hill.

Miller, N.E. 1944: Experimental studies of conflict. In *Personality and the behavior disorders*, vol. 1, ed. J.M. Hunt. New York: Ronald Press.

—— and Dollard, J. 1941: *Social learning and imitation*. New Haven: Yale University Press.

Mischel, W. 1973: Toward a cognitive social learning reconceptualization of personality. *Psychological review* 80, 252–83.

social perception The term social perception is used in at least two different ways in social psychology. On the one hand it refers to the social determinants of perception, on the other to perception of the social environment. The main emphasis of research during the past decades has been on perception of the social environment, especially the judgment of other people's characteristics.

The term perception is used here in a broad and extended sense. It includes processes of inference which are often classified as cognition rather than perception.

The traditional areas of research have been the judgment of emotions from facial and other forms of expression; the judgment of personality characteristics from various external signs and the formation of impressions of the personality of other people. In the first two areas of research initial results were interesting, statistically significant and exasperatingly inconsistent. The contradictory results in earlier studies of the accuracy in recognizing emotional expressions have largely been resolved by the obvious discovery that errors recognizing emotion are a function of the psychological distance between emotions and the context in which they are expressed. More recent work by Ekman (1982) has shown the universal nature of a small number of emotional facial expressions.

The study of the accuracy of person perception gave way to an interest in studying the process of IMPRESSION FORMATION, after it had been shown that many of the early findings were artifacts of the procedures used.

Asch (1946) proposed that impression formation is a gestalt-like process in which information about another person is integrated in a complex way, taking into account its specific configuration (sequential and otherwise). Asch was opposed to the view that information integration processes in social judgment are predominantly additive. Anderson (1965, 1978) has produced evidence that the ascription of two bad qualities to a person may result in the person being rated better than if he is said to have only the worse of the two qualities. In other words the integration of the information is achieved not by adding but by averaging processes. Recent research has shown that social judgment is largely based on simple cognitive heuristics (rules of thumb), such as the representativeness and availability of information, which might explain the many shortcomings of human judgment. (Kahneman, Slovic and Tversky 1982; Nisbett and Ross 1980). Related to this approach is the suggestion by Rosch (Mervis and Rosch 1981) that prototypes play an important role in impression formation (see Lingle et al. 1984).

One of the aspects of information integration which has attracted a good deal of interest during the last two decades is the effect of inconsistency of the available information (see COGNITIVE CONSISTENCY). In general it appears that inconsistency does affect social judgment processes but the effect is much less strong and less general than was originally suggested (see Eiser 1980).

Impressions of other people are often based on observed behavior. But HEIDER has argued convincingly that final judgments are arrived at by inferring more or less invariant underlying or latent dispositions of the person and/or situation from observed or assumed variations in behavior. ATTRIBUTION theories have been concerned with the cognitive processes in making such inferences and in general with the explanation of our own and other peoples' behavior.

In addition to the study of attribution and integration processes, research in person perception has also studied the cognitive representations which result from these processes. The study of IMPLICIT PERSONALITY THEORIES analyzes the associations which the observer assumes to exist between inferred personality traits. The same idea has been extended to the study of emotional states, social episodes and social behavior.

A neglected area of research has been the relationship between social cognition and SOCIAL BEHAVIOR. Although social perception has been studied in the context of NON-VERBAL COMMUNICATION and SOCIAL INTERACTION, the results of these studies have so far not been integrated with the more cognitively oriented INFORMATION PROCESSING approach in social perception.

JMFJ

Bibliography

Anderson, N.H. 1965: Averaging versus adding as a stimulus-combination role in impression formation. *Journal of experimental psychology* 70, 394–400.

—— 1978: Progress in cognitive algebra. In *Cognitive theories in social psychology*, ed. L. Berkowitz. New York: Academic Press.

—— 1981: *Foundations of information integration theory*. New York and London: Academic Press.

Asch, S.E. 1946: Forming impressions of personality. *Journal of abnormal and social psychology* 41, 258–90.

*Eiser, J.R. 1980: *Cognitive social psychology*. London and New York: Methuen.

Ekman, P. ed. 1982: *Emotion in the human face*. 2nd edn. Cambridge and New York: Cambridge University Press.

Kahneman, D.G., Slovic, P. and Tversky, A. 1982: *Judgment under uncertainty*. Cambridge and New York: Cambridge University Press.

Lingle, J.H., Altorn, M.W. and Medin, D.L. 1984: Of cabbages and kings: assessing the extendability of natural object concept models to social things. In *Handbook of social cognition*, vol. 1, eds. R.S. Wyer and T.K. Srull. Hillside, N.J.: Erlbaum.

Mervis, G.B. and Rosch, E. 1981: Categorization of natural objects. *Annual review of psychology* 32, 89–115.

Nisbet, R.E. and Ross, L. 1980: *Human inference: strategies and shortcomings of social judgment*. Englewood Cliffs, N.J.: Prentice-Hall.

social power Although social power has been characterized as a fundamental concept in the social sciences, it has not been exhaustively studied in social psychology. Perhaps this is due to the lack of clarity in defining social power and in separating it from related concepts such as leadership, dominance, influence and control.

FIELD THEORY defines power as the maximum resultant force that a person A can bring to bear on another person B with respect to a particular region of B's life space. According to French and Raven (1959), the power of A over B can be based on the mediation of rewards by A for B, coercion, legitimacy, identification and expertness. Other authors, who are mainly concerned with decision making, have equated power and influence, suggesting that power is manifested by changes in the probability of eliciting a response from another person B. In the context of game theory (see GAMES) power has been defined as the ability to affect the quality of the partner's outcome.

The Dutch psychologist Mulder (see Ng 1980) has developed and tested an exhaustive theory which maintains in essence that social power is a basic form of motivation which by itself leads to satisfaction. It is addictive and leads less powerful persons to attempt to reduce the power distance from the more powerful, but the more they succeed the stronger this tendency tends to become.   JMFJ

Bibliography

French Jr, J.R.P. and Raven, B.H. 1959: The bases of social power. In *Studies in social power*, ed. D. Cartwright. Ann Arbor: University of Michigan Press.

Huston, T.L. 1983: Power. In *Close relationships*, eds. H.H. Kelley et al. New York: Freeman.

Ng, S.K. 1980: *The social psychology of power*. London and New York: Academic Press.

social representation The concept of social representation as developed during the last twenty years, mainly by French researchers, has its theoretical origins in the notion of "collective representation" introduced by DURKHEIM (1897, 1951) to refer to the characteristics of social thinking compared to individual thinking.

Further study of this genuinely social psychological phenomenon was delayed by the dominating influence of two main scientific currents: behaviorism in psychology and the positivistic tradition in the philosophy of science.

The social representations approach, stressing their symbolic function as well as their role in the construction of reality, was introduced by Moscovici, who defines them as 'systems of values, ideas and practices with a two-fold function; first, to establish an order which will enable individuals to orient themselves in and master their material social world, and second, to facilitate communication among members of a community by providing them with a code for naming and classifying the various aspects of their world and their individual and group history' (Moscovici 1981).

The concept differs from related concepts such as opinion, ATTITUDE or image which constitute a response to an external stimulus and thus a preparation for action. A social representation defines both the stimulus as well as the response it evokes. More than a simple guide to behavior, the social representation remodels and reconstitutes the elements of the environment in which the behavior will take place; this gives the behavior meaning and integrates it into a larger behavioral and relational system.

The notion of social representation implies simultaneously a process and a content. The latter can be analyzed according to different dimensions: the attitude, the information and the field of representation concerning a given social object.

Comparative studies of the content and coherence of these dimensions may consider the division between groups in terms of their social representations. It is possible to determine the boundaries of a group through its vision of the world.

The way in which a social representation is produced and functions depends on two main processes: objectification and anchoring.

The process of objectification gives material reality to an abstract entity. First, objectification implies the strengthening of the iconic aspect of an ill-defined idea or being; that is, it matches the concept with the image. From the mass of information in circulation regarding the object of representation certain aspects are selected. Drawn from their original context the selected elements are arranged in a specific structure. This figurative model – "iconic cast" – reproduces in a nearly visual manner a certain abstract organization. It constitutes the central part of the representation. Second, the process of objectification "naturalizes" the abstract concept: the figurative model is reified. For the group it has become a category in language; and as such it is identified as objective reality.

Objectification thus involves two converging processes: the first leads from the concept to its image, the second from the image to the social elaboration of reality.

Through the process of anchorage the social object is classified within the society's network of categories. Fitting it into the existing hierarchy of social norms, values and productions, society transforms the object of representation into a serviceable instrument.

This implies that a social representation is a mode of knowledge peculiar to a particular society and irreducible to any other mode.

In sum, the role of the representation is to make the strange familiar. The mode of reasoning underlying this process is characterized by the conclusion controlling the premises. This is true of social thinking in general and it is the opposite of the mode of reasoning that science observes or tries to observe. But social thinking and scientific thinking are not only opposed. The way in which they are complementary, the way in which they nourish each others' productions appears in the orientation of scientific advance as well as in the diffusion of science in society.

Numerous experimental studies have illustrated the close relationship between social representations and behavior. It appears that different representations of the same object (task, partner, situation, group, etc.) determine different types of behavior.

More complex and dynamic functions of social representations have also been addressed by experimental studies. In the field of intergroup relations Doise (1978) investigated the functioning of anticipatory and justificatory representations: they are determined by group interaction which they in turn influence.

The empirical studies of social representations concern mostly very broad or complex objects (psychoanalysis, culture, illness, childhood, body, education, among others). Observing the processes of generation and evolution of social representations, the correspondence between their production and their function, or their role in communication and social behavior, these studies suggest the generality and the relevance of the phenomenon.

EF SMo

Bibliography

Abric, J.C. 1971: Experimental study of group creativity: task representation, group structure, and performance. *European journal of social psychology* 1–3.

Chombart de Lauwe, M.J. 1971: *Un monde autre: l'enfance. De ses représentations à son mythe.* Paris: Payot.

Codol, J.P. 1974: On the system of represen-

tations in a group situation. *European journal of social psychology,* 4–3.

Doise, W. 1978: *Groups and individuals: explanations in social psychology.* Cambridge and New York: Cambridge University Press.

Durkheim, E. 1897; 1951: *Le suicide: étude de sociologie.* Paris: Alcan. (*Suicide.* Trans. J.A. Spalding and G. Simpson. Glencoe Ill.: Free Press; London: Routledge and Kegan Paul. 1951, 1952.)

Farr, R.M., and Moscovici, S. eds. 1984: *Social representations.* Cambridge and New York: Cambridge University Press.

Gorin, M. 1980: *A l'école du groupe. Heurs et malheurs d'une innovation éducative.* Paris: Dunod.

Herzlich, C. 1973: *Health and illness: a social psychological analysis.* London: Academic Press.

Jodelet, D. 1984: The representation of the body and its transformations. In *Social representations,* eds. R.M. Farr and S. Moscovici. Cambridge and New York: Cambridge University Press.

——— 1984: Représentations sociales: phénomènes, concept et théorie. In *Manuel de psychologie sociale,* ed. S. Moscovici. Paris: Presses Universitaires de France.

Kaes, R. 1968: *Images de la culture chez les ouvriers français.* Paris: Éditions Cujas.

Moscovici, S. 1976: *La psychanalyse, son image et son public.* Paris: Presses Universitaires de France.

——— 1981: On social representation. In *Social cognition,* ed. J.P. Forgas. London: Academic Press.

——— 1982: The coming era of representations. In *Cognitive approaches to social behavior,* eds. J.P. Codol and J.P. Leyens. The Hague: Nijhoff.

social skills A concept widely but loosely used to describe the skills employed when interacting at an interpersonal level with other people. Attempts have been made to define social skills in both behaviorist and intentionalist terms. For instance, social skills have been defined as 'the ability to emit both positively reinforcing behavior toward others and to avoid emitting behavior that involves punishment by others' (Libert and Lewisohn 1973), and as 'the extent to which a person can communicate with others in a manner that fulfills one's rights, requirements, satisfactions or obligations to a reasonable degree without damaging the other person's similar rights ...' (Phillips 1978). The concept has been used synonymously with "social competence", "social adequacy", and even "assertiveness" though each is associated with a particular theory of social interest. Talking of "skills" rather than "skill" emphasizes the complexity and variety of the kinds of actions that can be performed completely or partially. Van Hasselt's definition of social skills (1979) highlights three main elements which are seen to be crucial: social skills are situation-specific; they are acquired capacities to display appropriate responses, both verbal and nonverbal; and they should enable people to behave in a way which does not hurt or harm others. Continuing ambiguity as to the definition and empirical realizations of social skills means that social skills training subsumes a huge variety of techniques which range from behavior therapy to non-directive counseling, and have been aimed at widely different kinds of behavior.

AF

Bibliography

Bellack, A.S. 1983: Recurrent problems in the behavioral assessment of social skill. *Behaviour research and therapy* 21, 29–41.

Libert, J. and Lewisohn, P. 1973: Concept of social skills with special reference to the behavior of depressed persons. *Journal of consulting and clinical psychology* 40, 304–12.

Phillips, E. 1978: *The social skills bases of psychopathology*. London: Grune and Stratton.

Van Hasselt, V., Hersen, M., Whitehill, M. and Bellack, A. 1979: Social skills assessment and training for children: an evaluative review. *Behaviour research and therapy* 17, 417–37.

social skills training A practical procedure by means of which new forms of social behavior can be learned, or existing behavior modified. The aim of social skills training is to help clients to organize or improve their social skills, namely behavioral sequences which conform to social NORMS and which enable people to achieve desired social goals more efficiently and acceptably. Social skills training has been developed and scientifically tested by many university, hospital and business based research teams, and has acquired variable support (modest to good) for its effectiveness. The training consists of instruction (description of applicable skills); modeling or demonstration by competent others; imitation and rehearsal by the client; teaching and feedback from others or from video-recordings; reinforcement for achieving set standards; homework practice in which the client applies the new skill in a real-life situation. Such techniques are used for training psychiatric patients, as well as managers and other industrial and business personnel, teachers, social workers, doctors and other professionals. Social skills training is also used for improving intercultural communication.

PET

Bibliography

Trower, P. ed. 1984: *Radical approaches to social skills training*. London: Croom Helm.

——— Bryant, B.M. and Argyle, M. 1978: *Social skills and mental health*. London: Methuen.

socialization A term used to describe the process of growing up, in which children learn the norms of their society and acquire their own distinctive values, beliefs and personality characteristics. In a broad sense it refers to any form of social development; in a specific sense it is particularly concerned with moral development. Early studies were to some extent influenced by PSYCHOANALYSIS. Traditionally, questions relating to sex differences, the ordinal position of the child in the family, maturation, critical periods, the effects of deprivation and child-rearing practices received a great deal of attention. Under the influence of the work of Piaget and Kohlberg, recent research has concerned itself more with moral development.

Anthropology and cross-cultural psychology have contributed in many ways to the comparative study of socialization processes. Sociology and political science have focused in particular on adult (re)socialization.

JMFJ

Bibliography

Jahoda, G. 1982: *Psychology and anthropology: a psychological perspective*. New York and London: Academic Press.

Triandis, H.C. and Heron, A. 1981: *Handbook of cross-cultural psychology*, vols 1–6. Boston: Allyn and Bacon.

socialization, occupational The influence process by which an individual is taught and learns the NORMS, VALUES, ATTITUDES and behavior appropriate for success in an occupational role. Socialization generally proceeds through a series of stages: anticipatory (before entering the occupational role), encounter (or initial entry) and adaptation. Occupational socialization is a continuous process, but it may be highly intensified at certain points, e.g. on initial entry, on promotion to a higher level. Some writers (Katz 1977) draw a distinction between the socialization of newcomers and the resocialization of veterans making some kind of an occupational change, such as a transfer to a different job.

An organization has various means, such as induction programs, at its disposal to bring about the socialization of employees. Early socialization experiences, and the part in them played by the individual's immediate supervisor, are important for later career success. Not all socialization is the result of formal, organizationally directed activities. The informal social influence of the work group has a particularly powerful effect. To the extent that most occupational roles exist within an organizational setting of some kind, the term organizational socialization is sometimes preferred. RSW

Bibliography

Katz, R. 1977: Job enrichment: some career considerations. In *Organizational careers: some new perspectives*, ed. J. Van Maanen. London, New York, Sydney, Toronto: Wiley.

Louis, M.R. 1980: Surprise and sense making: what newcomers experience in entering unfamiliar organizational settings. *Administrative science quarterly* 25, 226–51.

sociobiology The study of the biological basis of social behavior. Although the word was being used in the early 1960s (Altmann 1962), the birth of sociobiology as a discipline is clearly identified with the publication of Wilson's major review (1975).

The field is derived from two separate biological traditions, evolutionary biology and ethology. Sociobiology is properly concerned with the causation and development of social behavior, as well as with functional and evolutionary questions which ask how specific traits serve as adaptations. Research on the causation and ontogeny of social behavior is reviewed by Hinde (1970). However the impetus for Wilson's "new synthesis" came from theoretical considerations of apparent evolutionary anomalies.

Natural selection acts on individuals and results in changes of population gene frequencies. Genes which cause the fitness of their bearers to be enhanced are selectively favored. A tradition in ethology, evident in the writings of Lorenz, has been the belief that animals behave for the benefit of the group or the species rather than in their own individual interests. Selection among groups was seen as a potent evolutionary force. Wynne-Edwards (1962) was explicit about the importance of group selection as a force moulding social behavior. He argued that animals restrict their population density and rate of reproduction so that the maximum sustainable yield is maintained from the available food supplies. He postulated the existence of epideictic displays which allow members of a population to assess the density of the population. Although group selection *is* an evolutionary force, it is a weak one compared with individual selection: biologically unacceptable models of population structure have to be envisaged for group selection to outweigh the importance of individual selection (Maynard Smith 1976).

If animals are generally selected to behave in their own selfish interests, why is altruism such a common component of many animal societies? Although both Fisher and Haldane anticipated his result, Hamilton (1964) described a mechanism whereby genes coding for altruistic behavior would be selectively favored: an individual helping a close relative may be favoring the spread of its own genes because kin are particularly likely to share copies of the altruist's genes through identity by descent. Indeed, parental investment might be seen as one manifestation of such kin selection theory. Another may be that the peculiar kind of inheritance found among some social insects (the hymenoptera – ants, bees and wasps) whereby sisters share more genetic material than do mothers and daughters, predisposes these animals to develop societies founded on altruistic behavior. Not all cases of altruism result from kin selection. Trivers (1971) suggested that under certain conditions reciprocal altruism may evolve in which one animal helps another to its own disadvantage in the expectation that the altruism may be reciprocated later. This process is distinct from mutualism where there is no delay between giving and receiving help.

The currency of sociobiology is units of fitness. Since the advantages of social behavior will result from the summation of individual interactions it is important to understand that the best strategy for an animal to adopt in a social context will depend upon the behavior of others. This realization has led to the identification of the *evolutionarily stable strategy*.

Sociobiologists cannot assume that patterns of behavior are inherited (see BE-HAVIOR GENETICS). Many will be learned or culturally transmitted. Since it is often impractical to determine the heritability of variation in social behavior among animals sociobiologists normally recognize adaptation by a difference between two phenotypic traits which leads to a difference in fitness between the individuals possessing them. The animal with the higher fitness is said to be more adapted than the other. This reasoning does not imply that adaptations necessarily have genetic causes since adaptation is defined by its effects rather than its causes.

The scientific methodology used by sociobiology has been criticized by Lewontin (1979). In addition to cautioning against genetic assumptions he argues that hypotheses are too often accepted without test, and points out that a functional

approach to the interpretation of social behavior and the difficulty of testing hypotheses may lead to the "imaginative reconstruction" of evolutionary scenarios which are later accepted as facts. Furthermore he claims that if the results of tests, when made, do not closely fit predictions the hypotheses are not discarded but merely modified since animals are thought to optimize their behavior. Lewontin calls this technique "progressive ad hoc optimization".

Functional explanations for patterns of variation in social behavior often claim some degree of generality and are, therefore, testable. When similar selective forces act on independently evolving lineages we might expect convergent evolution to produce traits that are correlated in similar ways within different taxonomic groups. This is the nub of the comparative method that was extensively used by Darwin to test functional evolutionary hypotheses. Constellations of functionally related characters are expected to recur in similar ecological circumstances among different taxonomic groups. For instance, in different mammalian families group structures correlate with the distribution of resources. In turn males respond to and influence grouping patterns in their attempts to gain mating access to females. The breeding systems that result correlate with differences in morphology between the sexes (Clutton-Brock & Harvey 1978).

However, there is a tendency among sociobiologists to treat all behavioral differences as adaptive. This is an unfounded assertion, and Lewontin (1979) lists several causes for non-adaptive evolution. One of the major methodological problems facing sociobiologists (and evolutionists in general) is that although it is often possible to demonstrate the adaptive nature of a character difference, it is not possible to be sure that a particular difference is non-adaptive. PHH

The scope and definition of work of human ethologists, especially those who considered themselves to be working in the wider framework of evolutionary biology and the adaptiveness of human behavior, shifted markedly in the 1970s with the growing influence of sociobiology. The adaptive value of behavior was seen no longer in terms of species survival, but in terms of individual and inclusive fitness. Observational and traditional ethological methods became only one of many ways of studying this. The sociobiological assumption of genetic influences on behavior, applied to the human case, has led to vigorous attacks and controversy. It has been stressed by those objecting to this assumption that many of the fundamental processes of human interaction are based on the expectations of individuals about each other which in turn are based on rights and duties embodied in human institutions. These are held to be man-made, and not subject to genetic influence. Such objections are directed against what may be called naive (genetic) sociobiology. For a balanced review see Ruse (1979).

General expositions of human sociobiology include Wilson (1978) and Alexander (1980). Among numerous areas of human behavior approached from a sociobiological perspective are the following: marriage systems: the rareness of polyandry, and the relation of monogamy/polygyny to resource ecology and parental care, sexuality and sexual dimorphism, different reproductive strategies of males and females; kinship terminologies and unilineal and bilineal descent: their relationship to sexual strategies and to paternity and certainty; choice of marriage or mating partners: for example the effects of early co-socialization on later incest avoidance; altruism, reciprocity and exchange: their relationship to kinship; territoriality and aggression: for example circumstances predicting human tribal warfare; parental care and investment: for example the occurrence of preferential female infanticide in highly stratified societies, and adoption of kin and non-kin.

Human sociobiology, even more than human ethology, has the potential to bring together a variety of disciplines other than psychology – notably anthropology, sociology, politics, economics and history (Chagnon and Irons 1979), as well as population genetics and demography.

However, in so doing it is likely to be transformed into a wider theory of gene-culture evolution and the interaction of both genetic and cultural factors in human behavior. Recent attempts to consider such interaction are typified by Lumsden and Wilson (1981). In general such approaches lead to the conclusion that human behavior will not always be adaptive in the way that naive human sociobiology would predict, not only because the human environment has changed so much from that of our hominid ancestors, but also because culture itself can be considered an evolutionary process, embodying selection, variation and retention, which may co-evolve with but can also conflict with the pressures of biological evolution.   PKS

Bibliography

Alexander, R.D. 1980: *Darwinism and human affairs*. London: Pitman; Seattle: University of Washington Press.

Altmann, S.A. 1962: A field study of the sociobiology of rhesus monkeys, *Macaca mulatta*. *Annals of the New York Academy of Sciences* 102, 338–435.

Chagnon, N.A. and Irons, W. 1979: *Evolutionary biology and human social behavior: an anthropological perspective*. Massachusetts: Duxbury Press.

*Clutton-Brock, T.H. and Harvey, P.H. 1978: Mammals, resources and reproductive strategies. *Nature* 273, 191–5.

Eibl-Eibesfeldt, I. 1979: Human ethology: concepts and implications for the sciences of man. *Behavioral and brain sciences* 2, 1–57.

Hamilton, W.D. 1964: The genetical evolution of social behavior. *Journal of theoretical biology* 7, 1–52.

Hinde, R.A. 1970: *Animal behaviour: a synthesis of ethology and comparative psychology*. New York: McGraw-Hill.

*Lewontin, R.C. 1979: Sociobiology as an adaptationist program. *Behavioral science* 24, 5–14.

Lumsden, C.J. and Wilson, E.O. 1981: *Genes, minds and culture*. Cambridge, Mass.: Harvard University Press.

Maynard Smith, J. 1976: Group selection. *Quarterly reviews of biology* 51, 277–83.

Ruse, M. 1979: *Sociobiology: sense or nonsense?* Dordrecht, Holland: D. Reidel.

Smith, P.K. 1983: Human sociobiology. In *Psychology survey*, vol. 4, eds. B.M. Foss and

J. Nicholson. Leicester: British Psychological Society.

Trivers, R.L. 1971: The evolution of reciprocal altruism. *Quarterly reviews of biology* 46, 35–57.

*Wilson, E.O. 1975: *Sociobiology, the new synthesis*. Cambridge, Mass.: Harvard University Press.

—— 1978: *On human nature*. Cambridge, Mass.: Harvard University Press.

Wynne-Edwards, V.C. 1962: *Animal dispersion in relation to social behaviour*. Edinburgh: Oliver and Boyd; New York: Hafner.

sociolinguistics The study of the relationship between linguistic and social phenomena. It began to establish itself as a sub-discipline of linguistics in the 1960s as a result of the realization that many linguistic patterns cannot be studied without also studying the users of such patterns (i.e. there is an indexical aspect to linguistic signs) and that social interaction is carried out, to a significant extent, through the medium of language.

The various subdivisions that are found within sociolinguistics relate to developments within linguistics and sociology and to differential emphasis on social and linguistic phenomena.

The principal directions within sociolinguistics, in their order of development, are: the language and society approach, embracing the study of linguistic codes, the relationship between language and culture etc; variation theories of language; and the communicative competence approach. PM

Bibliography

Grimshaw, A.D. 1978: Language in society: four texts. Review article. *Language* 54, 156–69.

Neustupny, J.V. 1974: Sociolinguistics and the language teacher. *Linguistic communications* 12, 1–24.

sociotechnical system The conceptualization of organizations as the integration of a social component (the organization of people and work) and a technical component (equipment and the production process layout). The concept originated with the Tavistock Institute's study of production problems arising from technological changes in British coal mining (Trist and Bamforth 1951). They concluded that different work tasks and technical requirements have different psychological and social consequences. Even with similar work technologies, alternative social structures may exist, each with a unique impact on people. With its concern for the social component of organizations, the sociotechnical approach has provided an impetus for the HUMAN RELATIONS SCHOOL and many organization development projects. SGH/NMT

Bibliography

Trist, E.L. and Bamforth, K.W. 1951: Some social and psychological consequences of the long-wall method of coal-getting. *Human relations* 4, 3–38.

speech act A term introduced by Bühler (1934) and subsequently taken up by Austin (1962) who stresses that in saying things speakers are actually doing things. According to Austin, we perform three kinds of acts in speaking a language: (i) Acts *of* saying something i.e. *locutionary acts*, or more precisely, phonetic acts of uttering noises; phatic acts of uttering certain words of a certain vocabulary and in a certain grammatical form; and rhetic acts of using those variables with a certain sense and reference. (ii) Acts *in* saying something i.e. *illocutionary acts* such as "asking questions", "giving orders", "making promises". (iii) Acts *by* saying something i.e *perlocutionary acts* of producing certain intended or unintended effects upon the feelings, thoughts or actions of other persons such as "persuading" or "convincing". How an utterance has to be interpreted and what we achieve with speech therefore depends on the illocutionary force of the utterance and its perlocutionary effects. Research has mainly focused on illocutionary acts which can be *direct* or *indirect*. The illocutionary force of direct speech acts corresponds to the literal meaning of the sentence/utterance. For indirect speech acts the force of a literal interpretation is inappropriate and the analyst has to rely on contextual information. It is therefore essential to establish the rules constituting specific speech acts i.e. constitutive rules (Searle 1969, Kreckel 1981). MK

Bibliography

Austin, J.L. 1962: *How to do things with words*. Cambridge, Mass.: Harvard University Press.

Bühler, K. 1934: *Sprachtheorie: die Darstellungsfunktion der Sprache*. Jena: Gustav Fischer.

Kreckel, M. 1981: *Communicative acts and shared knowledge in natural discourse*. New York and London: Academic Press.

Searle, J.R. 1969: *Speech acts*. Cambridge and New York: Cambridge University Press.

statistical methods Procedures for the planning of data collection in experiments and surveys together with techniques for describing and summarizing sample data so that inferences may be made about populations from which the samples were taken. They offer a rigorously based approach to the design and analysis aspects of investigations. Methods for analysis are usually pre-determined by the particular experimental or survey design employed and its implementation. Knowledge of (a) the design and its characteristics, (b) the methods of analysis which may be associated with the design, (c) the amount of precision required for estimation and (d) the variation in the population may be used to determine the sample sizes which will be necessary for a satisfactory investigation.

Following the collection of statistical data the first requirement is usually a description. In the light of the nature of the variables, whether they are nominal, ordinal, interval or ratio in character, appropriate graphical methods are used for presentation. For the first two types of variable a bar chart, pie chart or pictogram is normally used whereas for the last two a histogram or a frequency diagram suffices. Certain probability distributions may be confirmed by plotting sample frequencies on special graph paper. Multivariate data is treated by plotting scatter diagrams or frequency contours for two variables at a time. Graphical methods are used for exploratory data analysis and residual analysis which allow the validity of assumptions made by classical methods to be examined and appropriate action taken.

Following graphical descriptions, statistical measures are calculated from the observations to provide estimates of population characteristics. These may be quantities which describe the distribution of the values of a variable in the population in terms of its location (e.g. mean, median, mode, mid-range) or its dispersion (e.g. standard deviation, mean deviation, range, semi-interquartile range) or its shape (e.g. skewness, kurtosis). Where single values are calculated to represent these population characteristics, the estimates are called "point estimates". More useful are "interval estimates" which consist of two values between which the true value of the population parameter in question will be expected to lie with some stated probability. Such intervals are known as "confidence intervals".

Whereas it is possible to proceed to make inferences about hypotheses involving population parameters using confidence intervals, it is more common to compute "test statistics" for this purpose. These are quantities calculated from samples which are standardized so that their distributions over repeated samples can be derived theoretically and "critical values" obtained and tabulated for use in statistical tests.

Statistical tests are said to be "parametric" if they refer to the form of the underlying distribution of the observations and "nonparametric" or "distribution-free" if they do not. Parametric tests are concerned with hypotheses which mention the population values of parameters of this underlying distribution. The most common parametric tests are based on the sample mean and test a hypothesis regarding the population mean (e.g. normal z-test, Student's t-test) whereas non-parametric tests often use the ranked sample values for testing a hypothesis about the population median (e.g. Mann-Whitney U-test, Wilcoxon test, sign test). The advantage of the latter is that the specific test used will be more valid over a wide range of underlying distributions and the main disadvantage, where both may apply, will be a loss of power. Parametric tests often assume that the sample values follow a normal distribution, or at least that the sample mean is approximately normally distributed and this is true in practice unless the sample sizes are very small because of the Central Limit Theorem.

Non-parametric tests are used for testing the goodness-of-fit of an observed distribution to a theoretical one or may compare two observed distributions. The chi-square (χ^2) test and the Kolmogorov-Smirnov tests are both suitable for these purposes with the latter being more sensitive to the largest deviation between two distributions. Where individuals are classified into categories by two attributes the resulting contingency table may be analyzed using a chi-square test for association between the attributes. Fisher's exact test is used in this situation for small frequencies. Where the samples are correlated, another non-parametric test, McNemar's, is used to test for a difference between the proportions in the categories.

Tests of means for a single population or for two populations are based on the standard normal z- or the t-distribution according as the variance in the population sampled is known or unknown. Tests for proportions use a test statistic which is taken to be approximately normal for large samples. Where there are more than two populations, an analysis of variance is applied using an F-statistic for difference between means or a chi-square statistic for a difference between proportions.

As well as providing for the testing of means of several samples, the analysis of variance, due to R.A. Fisher, is used to test for the effects of several factors which are varied in a systematic way in the same experiment. Such uses of the analysis of variance are examples of linear models which describe the measured response in terms of a sum of effects due to the factors and the interactions between them. For a single factor the simplest design is known as the "completely randomized" design in which the levels of the factor (or treatments) are applied randomly to the experimental units. Where these units are arranged in groups or "blocks" and complete sets of treatments are applied in each block the design is known as a "randomized block design". This very commonly used design allows for independent testing of treatment and block effects by means of an analysis of variance.

Whereas the randomized block design may be seen to exploit the heterogeneity of experimental units in one dimension, an extension of the design known as the "Latin square" design caters for two dimensions. If the two dimensions are thought of as "rows" and "columns" then the rows constitute blocks within which all treatments appear and the columns likewise. This balanced but restricted design allows for independent tests of the "rows", "columns" and treatments factors. Extensions of the randomized block design provide for additional treatment factors and for incomplete blocks containing subsets of the available treatments. The latter include confounded designs in which main effects are estimated with full precision and only those interactions which are of interest are deliberately estimated in the analysis. In balanced incomplete designs, some of the interactions may be estimated with lower precision than main effects. This is also achieved by "split-plot" designs in which less important factors are applied at the level of plots within blocks and more important factors are applied to sub-plots which are formed by splitting main plots. Whereas factorial designs in which all levels of all factors appear in every possible combination are known as "crossed" designs, the split-plot design is an example of a "hierarchical' or "nested" design.

The analysis of variance F-tests are based upon underlying assumptions that the observations are normally distributed and have equal variance within groups. When these assumptions are untenable recourse is made either to transformation of the variable to restore the desired properties or to ranking and a non-parametric test. In the single factor experiment the Kruskal-Wallis test is used and for several factors, Friedman's test for matched samples is applied for each factor separately.

Where the factors may be expressed in the form of quantitative variables, the analysis of variance may be used to test the significance of the trend or response function. The levels of a factor may be equally spaced on an appropriate scale and it is then convenient to consider the response function by fitting orthogonal polynomials. For a factor with two levels, a linear component is tested, with three levels, a quadratic component, etc. If there are several factors of this type operating simultaneously, interactions between these components are investigated also.

As well as the response variable, a concomitant variable is sometimes measured. Adjustment for the effect of this concomitant variable is by an analysis of covariance. This procedure is able to deal with several concomitant variables.

Regression and correlation methods are applied to investigate the relationships between two or more variables. In the case of simple regression, one variable which is statistically varying is seen to depend upon another mathematical variable which is not subject to statistical variation. There are applications, however, where both variables involved are statistical but the "dependent" variable is subject to more variation than the "independent" one. The form of the relationship is most often linear but can also be a higher degree polynomial or exponential or any other mathematical continuous function. Correlation refers more generally to the relationship or interdependence between two variables and therefore applies to situations where regression may be inappropriate. Measures of correlation include the "product-moment correlation coefficient" which measures the degree of linear correlation between two continuous variables and, for ranked variables, Kendall's "tau" and Spearman's "rho".

Multiple linear regression is a method for fitting a relationship in which the "dependent" variable is a linear function of several "independent" variables. Multiple correlation refers to the degree of interdependency between variables in a group. This is often calculated as a coefficient in the multiple regression context where it represents the measured correlation between observed values of the dependent variable and the values predicted by the multiple regression equation.

Factor analysis and associated techniques in multivariate analysis seek to explain the relations between the variables in a set, using the correlation matrix for the set. Principal component analysis establishes a set of uncorrelated combinations of the original variables which explain in decreasing order of magnitude the variation in the sample. Ideally, most of the variation is accounted for by the first few components and the remainder may be discarded. Where the set of original variables is structured with two subsets, one "regressor", the other "independent", canonical analysis is relevant. Discriminant analysis deals with the problem of a single set of variables which have different mean values but identical correlations in two or more populations. A discriminant function is estimated using individuals from known populations and then used to classify unknown individuals. Other techniques such as multi-dimensional scaling and cluster analysis are employed to explore the structural relationships between individuals for whom multiple observations are available.

Some research workers prefer to incorporate "prior" information with experimental evidence in a formal way when making inferences. Bayesian inference, which originates from a theorem of Thomas Bayes on inverse probability, provides for this by requiring a specification of the prior distribution of parameters. This can involve some complicated mathematics and non-Bayesians are concerned by the difficult and arbitrary choice of this prior distribution. The arguments for Bayesian analysis are that it generalizes the inferential procedure so that nothing of the conventional approach is lost, that it encourages the formulation of prior knowledge and that it provides a decision-theoretic approach which is relevant to many situations. Bayesians and non-Bayesians all use prior information and mostly arrive at the same conclusions despite the differences in approach.   RWH

Bibliography

Fisher, R.A. 1935: *The design and analysis of experiments*. Edinburgh: Oliver and Boyd.

Guilford, J.P. and Fruchter, B. 1956: *Fundamental statistics in psychology and education*. New York: McGraw-Hill.

Marriott, F.H.C. 1974: *The interpretation of multiple observations*. London: Academic Press.

Siegel, S. 1956: *Non-parametric statistics for the behavioral sciences*. New York: McGraw-Hill.

Winer, B.J. 1962: *Statistical principles in experimental design*. New York: Holt, Rinehart and Winston.

status The extent to which a person or group is esteemed, admired or approved of by other people and groups. Status is essentially the rank or position of an individual in the prestige hierarchy of a group or community. Nearly all societies have status systems such as class or caste and these status systems significantly determine the social environment and power of the individual.

Psychologists have studied status differences in terms of conformity to group NORMS, openness to change (social mobility), LEADERSHIP, organizational structure etc. Ideas of social status and related concepts appear in Tajfel's theory of intergroup relations. For instance when groups of unequal status interact, they may each show different degrees of intergroup discrimination as a function of their perceptions of the legitimacy and stability of the difference in status. Social and group status is often marked by status symbols which are visible marks serving as cues that enable the members of a group or organization to perceive the status of other members accurately and hence as guides to appropriate behavior. In time, status symbols come to be admired and prized in their own right as symbols of success.   AF

Bibliography

Benoit-Smullyan, E. 1944: Status, status-types and status-interrelations. *American sociological review* 9, 151–61.

Cohen, E. 1984: The desegregated school: problems in status power and interethnic climate. In *Groups in contact: the psychology of desegregation*, eds. N. Miller and M.B. Brewer. San Diego: Academic Press.

stereotypes Usually considered to be oversimplified, rigid, and generalized beliefs about groups of people in which all individuals from the group are regarded as having the same set of leading characteristics. Stereotypes of members of a national, religious or racial group may affect the impressions people form of individuals who are identifiable members of that group. Stereotypes were defined by Lippman (1922), and were first studied empirically by Katz and Braly (1933).

There are individual differences in stereotypes, which form part of a person's IMPLICIT PERSONALITY THEORY. Stereotypes, however, tend to be widely shared by members of a given society. In general, whereas stereotypes of other groups (to which one does not belong) are simplistic and homogeneous, the stereotypes of one's own group are complex and highly differentiated. Stereotypes may lead to distortions of reality by overestimation of the differences between groups, as well as by underestimation of the variation within a group, and thereby to justification of hostility or oppression (Campbell 1967).

Although usually considered undesirable because they tend to sustain prejudice, stereotypes often contain a "grain of truth" and are therefore useful in predicting others' behavior. Occasionally they may be very accurate. In fact McCauley, Stitt and Segal (1980) suggest that 'what is wrong with stereotyping is no more and no less than what is wrong with human conceptual behavior generally.' Even people who are the targets of negative stereotypes may agree with the facts upon which they are based.

The extensive research on stereotypes has mainly been restricted to the study of beliefs about national characteristics. Recent research, however, has gone beyond the adjective check lists of Katz and Braly. In line with the idea of McCauley et al. that stereotypes are themselves typical generalizations, psychologists have looked at the cognitive processes which might lead to mistaken beliefs about group-members' common characteristics, and also at the effects of stereotypes on other cognitive processes. The work of Hamilton and his colleagues is prominent in the former group. They have shown that distinctive events or variables are likely to be perceived as co-occurring even when they do not. Extreme behavior is therefore likely to be expected of a minority, as both the behavior and the minority are distinctive or unusual (see Hamilton, Dugan and Trolier 1985). Work on the effects of stereotypes typically focuses on their impact on judgment and memory (e.g. Bodenhausen and Wyer 1985).

There has been comparatively little work on the social causes of stereotypes, or on their relation to ATTITUDES or behavior.

AF/RL

Bibliography

Bodenhausen, G.V. and Wyer Jr, R.S. 1985: Effects of stereotypes on decision making and information-processing strategies. *Journal of personality and social psychology* 48, 267–82.

Campbell, D. 1967: Stereotypes and the perception of group differences. *American psychologist* 22, 812–29.

Hamilton, D.L., Dugan, P.M. and Trolier, T.K. 1985: The formation of stereotypic beliefs: further evidence for distinctiveness-based illusory correlations. *Journal of personality and social psychology* 48, 5–17.

Katz, D. and Braly, K.W. 1933: Racial stereotypes of one hundred college students. *Journal of abnormal and social psychology* 28, 280–90.

Lippman, W. 1922: *Public opinion*. New York: Harcourt, Brace.

McCauley, C., Stitt, C.L. and Segal, M. 1980: Stereotyping: from prejudice to prediction. *Psychological bulletin* 87, 195–208.

structuralism A contemporary theory attempting to identify universal organizing principles underlying the surface of cultural, social, psychological, linguistic and literary expressions. Although structural analyses have existed since classical philosophy the contemporary approach developed since the second world war on the Continent, particularly in France, has had its greatest impact in the English-speaking world over the past decade or so.

Two forms of structuralism have become prominent in the United States and Britain since 1945; they warrant distinction. One form of structural analysis conceives of the repetitive patterns of interaction among persons codified into the institutions of social life as a structuralism. The myriad visible social institutions which individuals, by means of their interactions, create and in which they live their lives, such as the family, polity, economy, etc., are the foci of these structural analyses. This structuralism is identified with anthropological and sociological structural-functionalism, and American empiricism and symbolic interactionist analyses.

The second type of structuralism is more Platonic, seeking form and not content, bypassing institutional, cultural, and linguistic variation in order to establish universal sources for content. It is the focus upon, and search for, these invariant structures and the lack of involvement with surface appearances which separates this school from the previous one and gives it the appellation structuralism. This is the structuralism to which the term is now most commonly applied. The authors whose works are associated with this structuralism include for example, Althusser, Lévi-Strauss, Foucault, Freud, Lacan, Piaget, de Saussure and Derrida.

The apparent inconsistency in the suggestion that structuralism has had its greatest influence in Britain and the United States in the last ten years and the inclusion of Marx, Freud and Saussure among the structuralists is explained by the knowledge that the contemporary structuralists attribute their intellectual heritage to these earlier thinkers or continue to develop their structuralism through a dialogue with, and reinterpretation of, these nineteenth- and early twentieth-century theorists. Shared epistemological principles harking back to these earlier theorists unite their interests.

348

Sigmund Freud's psychoanalysis can help to illustrate some of these unities.

FREUD formulates two realms of psychic activity, one observable the other not. Regarding the observable realm it is possible to become witness to particular mental processes such as those in conscious thinking, dreams, slips of the tongue, symptoms, etc. The contents of these observable activities varies from person to person across a societal population and from society to society. However, there is another, more fundamental psychic reality, a shared structure which exists across populations, societies, and cultures. This reality is the unobservable realm of unconscious activity. This is the realm of the organization of psychic drives and defenses which makes up every individual's unconscious mental life. It is this structure which determines and unites the varieties of observable, and sometimes conscious, mental life of individuals and societal populations. Despite the variety of observable psychical and mental processes, and their content, they are unified by a shared and universal psychic structure present in every individual. The particularity of observable psychical activity is the result of the unique combination of the unobservable factors but in every individual the structural factors combined are the same. These structural universals for Freud are such as the ID, EGO and SUPEREGO, the OEDIPUS COMPLEX, etc.

A coherence among structuralists' approaches to knowledge can be extrapolated from this illustration of Freudian theorizing. There is a shared assumption among structuralists that the determining reality exists at an empirically unobservable level; scientific knowledge cannot be induced from observable manifestations, it can only be inferred from theoretical knowledge of this deeper reality. Thus, the structuralist theorists cut through the observed reality to formulate a more fundamental one. In this assumption also resides structuralism's criticism of naive empiricism.

While surface or conscious subjectivity of persons, such as in conversations, kinship descriptions, descriptions of symptoms, etc., are data for structuralists they are only signs of deeper invariant underlying structures. For example, Lévi-Strauss (1963) suggests that diametrically opposite incest systems are expressions of the same underlying organizing principle, i.e., the need for the reciprocal exchange of women for marriage among clans. Structuralists do not build their theories upon subjective report but by imaginative conceptual leaps which goes beyond subjective expression, so structuralists' analyses bypass human subjectivity, subjective consciousness.

Cultural idiosyncracy is treated similarly. Cultural variation, so influential in relativistic cultural anthropology, is dealt with by structuralists as forms of manifest or surface appearances; culture is the temporal and spatial expression of the unique organization of underlying structural reality. Thus, cultural variation is relegated to secondary importance in structuralism.

Similar to structuralism's denigration of cultural influences, its conception of causation denies the importance of historical influences. Structuralism distinguishes synchronic from diachronic causation, emphasizing the former. Synchronic causation suggests that surface appearances are understood best in terms of the interaction of the factors which create them at the particular point in time. This type of causal analysis is achieved without regard to the historical evolution of the structural factors which create appearances. Diachronic analyses stress the historical development of causal factors; that is, the history of causal factors in shaping the appearance of the phenomena. Thus, within the framework of structuralist analyses, it can be said of the example from psychoanalysis, that while historical factors in personal biography are crucial in the development of an individual's character, however for an individual's public display of personal characteristics, such as symptoms, cognitive abilities, etc. at a particular time, the structure and process of unconsious drives and defenses, at that moment, are determining. Although, the theoretical distinction between synchronic and diachronic causation has been drawn sharply by structuralists it has not always been possible for them to maintain it in their empirical analyses.

Structuralists also posit a complex relation between appearances and causation. This aspect of causation structuralists refer to as overdetermination. By overdetermination structuralism means that a phenomenon is determined by many factors; surface appearances are the product of several causes at once. Accordingly, in psychoanalytic theory the appearance of a personal attribute, e.g. symptom, may have its origins in the effects of an early fixation, an unconscious organizational residue of an early biographical relationship and simultaneously may be caused by the effects of a personal relation in the present. The symptom is the result of the psychic residue and the effects of the immediate relationship operating synchronically.

Althusser offers another example of overdetermination from political action. He suggests that revolutions do not result from a simple conflict between opposing classes, that is, the struggle between workers and the capitalists, but, he writes (1969, p.99), 'if this contradiction is to become "*active*" in the strongest sense, to become a ruptural principle, there must be an accumulation of "circumstances" and "currents" so that whatever their origins and sense (and many of them will *necessarily* be paradoxically foreign to the revolution in origin and sense, or even its "direct opponents"), they "fuse" into a *ruptural unity* . . .' (emphasis in the original). For Althusser this "ruptural unity" is overdetermined and it causes class revolutions.

Lévi-Strauss's writings stand out in contemporary structuralism for their priority and popularity. His work is significant too because it represents the confluence of a number of influences and in turn has been exceedingly influential in the structuralist movement.

Lévi-Strauss's theorizing developed at the intersection of the two contemporary forms of structuralism. He draws upon the writings of Émile DURKHEIM, an armchair anthropologist whose theoretical, epistemological and substantive focus upon social order influenced structural-functionalism and structuralism alike. Simultaneously, Lévi-Strauss claims as his intellectual forefathers (with proper adjustment to his own thinking) Marx, Freud and Saussure. In addition, Lévi-Strauss is a critic of, and his theorizing developed in reaction to, post-second world war French subjectivist and humanist philosophy of the Sartrean and Bergsonian types.

Lévi-Strauss's structural analysis is based on two principles; the polarity of binary opposites and homology or analogy. By polarity Lévi-Strauss means that underlying any society are sets of opposing linguistic and psychological formulations acting as organizing principles. The polar opposites are such as sacred-profane, pure-impure, male-female, superior-inferior, etc. Further, these opposites are divisible into homologous groupings. The result being that pure, sacred, male, superior, etc. constitute one set and the other homologous group is constituted by the opposites. It is the object of Lévi-Straussian analysis to describe these polar-homologous groupings and to explain the way they achieve their underlying coalescence which is expressed in the visible organization of the particular society. Lévi-Strauss supposes that the principles of this simple scheme underlie all surface appearances. Thus, he uses similar classificatory schemes to analyze poetry, Greek myths and preliterate societies' attitudes to food.

An additional impulse unites Lévi-Strauss, Althusser and other structuralists; this is their desire to develop, at last, a truly scientific theory of human phenomena – one that cuts through all human diversity and is everywhere applicable. But despite their unities in approach to knowledge and in their mission, there are disagreements among them too. For example, Althusser has accused Lévi-Strauss of undermining Marxist materialism with his idealism. And Piaget has been critical of his fellow structuralists (1970). However, structuralism has received special ire not from within but from humanists outside its gates. Humanists have suggested that structuralism's epistemology eliminates from theorizing exactly what is constitutive of humanity – its consciousness, its cultural and historical development, influences, uniqueness. Humanists suggest that there can be no science of humanity without theoretical provision for these characteristics of social life. The result is a continuing controversy between humanists and structuralists and nowhere is this controversy more intense than between the Marxists on both sides of these issues (Thompson 1978; Williams 1977).   GMP

Bibliography

Althusser, L. 1969: *For Marx*. Trans. B. Brewster. New York: Pantheon.

Barthes, R. 1979: *Images, music, text*. Essays selected and translated by Stephen Heath. New York: Hill and Wang.

Derrida, J. 1976: *Of grammatology*. Trans. Gayatri Spivak. Baltimore: Johns Hopkins University Press.

—— 1978: *Writing and difference*. Trans. A. Bass. Chicago: University of Chicago Press.

Foucault, M. 1972: *The archaeology of knowledge*. Trans. Sheridan Smith. New York: Pantheon.

Glucksmann, M. 1974: *Structuralist analysis in contemporary social thought: a comparison of the theories of Claude Lévi-Strauss and Louis Althusser*. London: Routledge and Kegan Paul.

Harrari, J.V. 1971: *Structuralists and structuralism: a selected bibliography of contemporary thought (1960–1970)*. Ithaca, New York: Diacritics.

Lacan, J. 1978: *The four fundamental concepts of psychoanalysis*. Trans. A. Sheridan. New York: Norton.

Lévi-Strauss, C. 1963: *Structural anthropology*. Trans. C. Jacobson and B. Grundfest Schoef. New York: Basic Books.

Miller, J.M. 1981: *French structuralism: a multidisciplinary bibliography with checklist of sources for Louis Althusser, Roland Barthes, Jacques Derrida, Michel Foucault, Lucien Goldmann, Jacques Lacan and an update of the works on Claude Lévi-Strauss*. New York: Garland.

Piaget, J. 1970: *Structuralism*. Trans. C. Maschler. New York: Basic Books.

Saussure, F. de 1959: *Course in general linguistics*. Trans. by W. Baskin. New York: McGraw-Hill.

Seung, T.K. 1982: *Structuralism and hermeneutics*. New York: Columbia University Press.

Thompson, E.P. 1978: *The poverty of theory and other essays*. New York: Monthly Review.

Williams, R. 1977: *Marxism and literature*. Oxford. England: Oxford University Press.

subculture A subdivision of the culture of the whole population or a major section of it at a particular period, consisting of persons who share special concepts and mores whilst adhering to the dominant characteristics of the wider culture. Significant subcultures are determined by social class, racial and religious affiliations. Their emergence is explicable in terms of mutual facilitation and support in groups facing common problems that cannot be solved by traditional methods (Cohen 1955). By sharing beliefs, objectives and ways of behaving, a sense of corporate identity is created, distinctive perspectives about values are provided and role strain, caused by conflict between ideology and role expectations, is reduced. The protective effect of subculture variation on early socialization is especially important. This is mediated initially through the family, then the PEER GROUP. Deviant subcultures have been related to the occurrence of DELINQUENCY in certain geographical areas, although it is more adequately understood in the context of intrafamilial and small group processes.   WLIP-J

Bibliography

Brake, M. 1980: *The society of youth culture and youth subcultures*. London: Routledge and Kegan Paul.

Cohen, A.K. 1955: *Delinquent boys: the culture of the gang*. Chicago: The Free Press of Glencoe, Ill.

McClelland, K.A. 1982: Adolescent subculture in schools. In T.M. Field et al., *Review of human development*. New York: Wiley.

sublimation The most mature form of defensiveness, according to FREUD and his followers, in that only the object of the instinct is altered, permitting considerable instinctual gratification to take place without ensuing anxiety or guilt. In psychoanalytic theory sublimation is the major defensive operation of the genital (or most mature) stage of psychosexual development. For example the true object of an adult male's sexual instinct may be his mother (who was the first female he loved when his sexual instinct was maturing sufficiently to involve his sexual organs *per se*). But the knowledge of, and action upon this would provoke intolerable anxiety and guilt. Therefore, the male sublimates by substituting for the true object another female (not related to him, and available for marriage) who resembles his mother in some fashion he does not consciously recognize. In having sexual relations with this other woman, he gains satisfaction for his originally incestuous impulse in a socially acceptable manner. Achieving this sublimation involves the interplay of various DEFENSE MECHANISMS.   SRM

superego In PSYCHOANALYTIC PERSONALITY THEORY that part of the mind from which emanate evaluative and moralistic prohibitions or recommendations about actions and mental life. These directives have been internalized from childhood experience of (or perhaps rather fantasy about) parental controls. It cannot be equated with "conscience" because its activity is often unconscious, and because these continuing pressures may actually be at odds with the person's conscious values. The severity of those pressures also reflects the strength of the person's own aggressive impulses, and therefore does not reflect the actual severity of parents. In Freudian theory the superego develops out of the EGO as a result of the OEDIPUS AND ELEKTRA COMPLEXES, and is especially apparent in obsessional neuroses. Although FREUD places such development in the fourth-fifth years of life Kleinian theory (Segal 1979) puts it earlier. Since the superego's pressures are essentially non-rational, and at least partly unconscious (hence totems and taboos), psychoanalytic treatment aims at bringing them more under ego-control. (See also EGO IDEAL.)   NMC

Bibliography

Freud, S. 1923: The ego and the id. *Standard edition of the complete psychological works of Sigmund Freud*, vol. 19. London: Hogarth Press; New York: Norton.

Segal, H. 1979: *Klein*. London: Fontana.

superstition An irrational belief or practice. Usually employed in a pejorative sense to refer to the apparently irrational beliefs and/or practices of others. Superstition was a word frequently used by nineteenth-century writers to refer to the religions of pre-literate people. This was normally the result of failure to appreciate the premises on which such religious ideas were based. With a deepening understanding of such practices and beliefs the use of superstition to describe them has fallen into disuse among social scientists. However, individuals will admit to being superstitious and will avoid certain things. Members of certain occupations, sailors for example, are often regarded as more superstitious than others. It is sometimes possible to explain superstitions of this sort in practical terms, but more often not. Most superstitious avoidances are likely to be only peripheral to a major belief system and thus difficult to explain in terms of it.   PGR

Bibliography

Jahoda, G. 1970: *The psychology of superstition*. Harmondsworth and Baltimore: Penguin.

symbolic interaction A theoretical perspective on social life which emphasizes the meaningfulness of human life and action. The perspective additionally emphasizes the pluralistic and conflictual nature of society, the relative openness of social life, the indeterminancy of social structure, the importance of subjective interpretations, the cultural and social relativity of moral and social rules, and the socially constructed nature of the self. The direct intellectual antecedents of the interactionist perspective are commonly traced to the turn of twentieth-century America, and its first empirical researches done at the University of Chicago between 1900–30. One way to appreciate the distinctive nature of symbolic interactionism is to understand its long-standing opposition to many of the central tenets of scientific positivism. This includes the rejection by symbolic interactionism of the organic analogy, scientific hypothesis formulation and testing, cause and effect relationships, universalistic laws of the social world, and the positivist version of scientific objectivity. By contrast, symbolic interactionism has stressed naturalism, analytical induction as a general methodology, indeterminate relationships, culturally and socially specific laws or rules, and an empathic understanding gained from participation or immersion in social life.

The direct philosophical antecedents of symbolic interactionism can be found in the works of the early pragmatists in America, especially those of Charles Sanders Peirce (1839–1914), William James (1842–1910) and John Dewey (1859–1952). Peirce developed an early pragmatic maxim concerning the meaningfulness of human action, namely, that one should not see meanings as being inherent in the objects or relationships themselves, but rather as being displayed in specific, concrete social situations. Furthermore, one must know the practical consequences of a given action in order to know its meaning for the human actor. For William James, who avowed clinical and therapeutic interests in addition to scholarly ones, meaning was even more individualistic and subjective than as conceived by Peirce. James's *Principles of psychology* (1890) articulates his version of pragmatism and its implications for psychology, and in it he asserts that a person has as many social selves as there are other people who carry around some conception or definition of that person. John Dewey further extended many of these ideas, and emphasized the inevitability of pluralism in society as a result of these continuing processes of human interpretation and meaning. Dewey stressed the processual nature of reflective experience, meaning that human existence is necessarily and inevitably open-ended and "incomplete", as individuals continually reflect on, reconstruct, and thereby modify all "past" actions and behavior, preparing the scene for future actions. Dewey was responsible for bringing George Herbert MEAD to the University of Chicago, where they enjoyed a long friendship. For many, Mead's name is associated with the early origins of interactionism in sociology and social psychology.

Early symbolic interactionism flourished at the University of Chicago, where three scholars are of central importance, William I. Thomas (1863–1947), Charles Horton Cooley (1864–1929) and George Herbert Mead (1863–1931). The last is seminal in the development of early interactionism, and the one most responsible for taking the abstract philosophical ideas of the pragmatists and grounding them in empirical, social reality. Mead's student Herbert Blumer is the one responsible for creating the term symbolic interactionism.

Charles Horton Cooley tried to combine hereditary factors with environmental (social) factors, and emphasized the role of emotion in human meanings. He is known for his idea of the "looking glass self", which means that individuals try to imagine the impression they are making on others by their actions and, according to Cooley, try to imagine some judgment of their actions, and then experience an emotional reaction to this perceived evaluation by others. From this early idea it is possible to see the beginnings of a central tenet of interactionism, that the meanings of an act for the individual emerge in the context of interactions with other people, that individuals perceive and take into account others' perceptions and judgments of an act. William I. Thomas formulated another idea which is akin to this, concerning an actor's definition of the situation. The Thomas Theorem states 'if men define situations as real, they are real in their consequences'. This well-known theorem is one of the central ideas of symbolic interactionism, and highlights the extent to which human actions and meanings are framed by the situation or context in which they occur.

Mead regarded the individual as the basic unit of analysis for interactionism, and emphasized the role of language and symbols in the creation of human meaning. The human mind, for Mead, was not a fixed, organic entity, but rather a continuous process of interpretation, reflection, and judgment of experience. Individuals act towards other individuals and physical objects because of the symbolic meaning those have for the individual. These meanings are not fixed, however. They are not given by the nature of culture or society. They are open-ended, and may change in specific situations of human social interaction. When the meaning of a given gesture or communication is shared between a sender and receiver, then a significant symbol is involved, says Mead, and humans are distinguished from animals precisely because they can share, build on, change, and communicate such symbolic meanings through a shared language and interactional competence.

Recent decades have seen the emergence of three distinct branches of symbolic interactionism. These are the neo-Chicago school which has centered around Herbert Blumer, the Iowa school which is associated with the work of the late Manfred H. Kuhn, and the dramaturgy popularized by Erving Goffman and his students. These three branches of symbolic interactionism are distinct, but they share several basic assumptions about human social life. They agree that individuals do things because of the meanings their actions have, and that these meanings must be central to any scientific understanding of behavior. They agree that the central focus of attention is in social interaction, when two or more individuals come into each other's presence, either actually or potentially. Blumer's emphasis tends to be on the fluid, situational, contextual nature of meaning. He views meaning as something which arises when two or more persons come into interaction. Humans are essentially rational, says Blumer, and when they encounter a social situation they engage in a process of interpretation, to discover the intentions of the other, and the meaning of his or her action. By contrast, Kuhn's work tends to emphasize the more stable, unchanging, unproblematic aspects of social life. His work expresses a close affinity with several key positivist assumptions about human life and the nature of science. Both Blumer (1969) and Kuhn (1970) are concerned about the nature of the SELF, what individuals think about their selves, how they arrive at such definitions, and what this means when thrust into an interactional context. Again, the work of Blumer and his followers tends to emphasize the openness of self-definitions and human experience more generally, whereas the work of Kuhn and his followers tends to emphasize the relative stability of social life and the unproblematic nature of human interactions.

The work of Erving GOFFMAN is significantly responsible for the sustained vigor of interactionist thought in sociology and social psychology. His early work *The presentation of self in everyday life* (1959) utilized theatrical metaphors to capture certain important aspects of social life, namely, the devices, strategies, tactics, and procedures used by individuals, either separately or in unison, to present to others the *appearance* of order, normality, and rationality in social situations. He contrasted back-stage preparations with front-stage appearances in social life, and his unique perspective is called dramaturgy, as key theatrical and performative notions are brought to interpret everyday, mundane social scenes. For Goffman, there is an inherent conflict between individuals and the social forms of communication and interaction, and his work concentrates on the many ways individuals present their selves to others, and how they influence each other in face-to-face interaction. Goffman's book *Behavior in public places* (1963) extends these dramaturgical ideas, and together with the essays in *Asylums* (1961), form the crucial early statements of LABELING THEORY in the sociology of deviant behavior. According to this view, no actions are inherently deviant or abnormal, but such definitions emerge in the context of face-to-face interaction. This insight has produced an entire genre of innovative research in the field of deviance.

In the late 1970s and early 1980s symbolic interactionism remains a vigorous and creative perspective and research program. To some extent this results from the emergence of creative research and theoretical work in other disciplines, those which share some or all of the theoretical concerns of symbolic interactionism. These include PHENOMENOLOGY, ETHOGENICS, ETHNOMETHODOLOGY, existential sociology, HUMANISTIC PSYCHOLOGY, conversational analysis, ATTRIBUTION THEORY, sociolinguistics, and the sociology of emotions. Through many discussions and debates, symbolic interactionists have incorporated many key ideas from these other disciplines. The interactionism of today is a more complicated, empirically grounded, scientific perspective than that which began in Chicago during the 1890s.

JMJ

Bibliography

Blumer, H. 1969: *Symbolic interactionism*. Englewood Cliffs, N.J.: Prentice-Hall.

Goffman, E. 1959: *The presentation of self in everyday life*. Garden City, N.Y.: Doubleday.

—— 1961: *Asylums*. Garden City, N.Y.: Doubleday.

—— 1963: *Behavior in public places*. New York: The Free Press.

Hewitt, J.P. 1984: *Self and society: a symbolic interactionist social psychology*. 3rd edn. Boston and London: Allyn and Bacon.

James, W. 1890: *Principles of psychology*. New York: Holt.

Kuhn, M.H. 1970: Self-attitudes by age, sex, and professional training. In *Social psychology through symbolic interaction*, eds. G. Stone and H. Farberman. Waltham, Mass.: Xerox Publishing Co.

*Manis, J.G. and Meltzer, B.N. eds. 1980: *Symbolic interaction*. Boston, Mass.: Allyn and Bacon.

*Rosenberg, M. and Turner, R.H. eds. 1981: *Social psychology: sociological perspectives*. New York: Basic Books.

Schafer, R.B. and Keith, P.M. 1985: A causal model approach to the symbolic interactionist view of the self-concept. *Journal of personality and social psychology* 48, 963–9.

systems theory An aggregate of theories about the structures and functions of systems and methods to understand them. Many different classes of systems (e.g. mathematical, physical, chemical, biological, psychical, social, economic, linguistic) have been analyzed. Many variants of systems theory were advanced mainly in the second half of the twentieth century. The concept of "system" is central to them all. It means an aggregate of interrelated and interconnected elements which form a whole.

The concept of "system" has a very long history. The thesis that the whole is more than the sum of its parts was formulated in antiquity. In the course of the philosophical development beginning with Plato, Aristotle, Euclid and others much attention has also been paid to the interpretation and elaboration of specific features of systems of knowledge. Stoics interpreted system as the universal order. In modern times the encyclopedic views of Leibniz have played an outstanding part in our understanding of the ontology of systems. The system character of cognition was especially stressed by Kant (1781):

This completeness of science cannot be accepted with confidence on the guarantee of its existence in an aggregate formed only by means of repeated experiments . . . [but] only because of their connection in a system . . . The sum of its knowledge constitutes a system determined by and comprised under an idea; and the completeness and articulation of this system can at the same time serve as a test of the correctness and genuineness of all the parts of knowledge that belong to it.

This line was developed further in the works of Schelling and Hegel. The latter wrote, in particular (1817): 'Unless it is a system, philosophy is not a scientific production. Unsystematic philosophising can only be expected to give expression to personal peculiarities of mind, and has no principle for the regulation of its contents'. From the seventeenth to the nineteenth centuries in different special sciences some types of system (geometrical, mechanical, etc.) were subjected to investigation. Marxism, leaning upon a materialist and dialectical tradition in philosophy, formulated general philosophical and methodological foundations for the scientific understanding of integral developing systems. Dialectical materialism presupposes:
(1) integrity of objects of the external world and those of knowledge;
(2) the interrelation of the parts of an object, and that object with others as the parts of yet other objects;

(3) the dynamic nature of any object;

(4) functioning of any object caused by its interaction with its environment, although the inner laws of the object's functioning and development have primacy over those of its environments.

At the beginning of the twentieth century special analytic methods were developed in Bogdanov's tectology, gestalt psychology, and various other biological and psychological theories, but it was during the late 1940s that the Austrian biologist L. von Bertalanffy advanced a program for general systems theory. The main objects of this were:

(1) to formulate general principles and laws of systems independent of their special type, or the nature of their components and the relations between them;

(2) to establish strict laws by analysis of biological, social and behavioral systems;

(3) to build a basis for a synthesis of modern scientific knowledge by establishing the isomorphism of the laws of different spheres of reality (von Bertalanffy 1971).

Cybernetics and a family of scientific disciplines connected with it were of a great importance in understanding the mechanisms of control systems. The methods of elaborating and controlling complex and supercomplex sociotechnical systems have become successively more complete. These were: systems engineering (1950s–60s), operational research (1960s–70s) and systems analysis, which has gradually become widely accepted over the last fifteen to twenty years. Simultaneously in recent years research in the theoretical and methodological foundations of the systems approach, systems modeling and general systems research have been in the process of development.

A system is characterized not only by the connections and relations between its components (its organization), but also by the mutual interactions of the system and its environment. It is in the latter relation that a system expresses its integrity. Usually any system can be regarded as an element of a higher-level system, while for some problems its elements can be repre-sented as systems of a lower level. Invariant aspects of a system are defined by its structure. The morphology, structure and behavior of a system and its functioning are of a hierarchic, multi-level character. Integral functioning comes about as a result of the interaction of all the levels of the hierarchy. Natural, technical and social systems are characterized by their processes of information and control. Some of the most complex systems are goal-orientated systems, and self-organizing systems capable of changing their organization and structure while functioning.

In the twentieth century there has been a development of systems research methods and a widespread use of these methods for solving applied problems of science and technology (for instance, in the analysis of various biological systems, in the construction of transport systems, and in the organization of systems of industrial control). This has demanded the elaboration of strict formal definitions of the concept of "system". Such definitions are being constructed with the help of set theory, mathematical logic, cybernetics, etc. Summing up the main approaches to the definition of the concept, a system may be understood as a class of sets $S = \{M_s^\alpha\}$ for each pair of which a many-to-one correspondence $Yd\beta: M_s^\alpha \rightarrow M_s^\beta$ is established. Specific interpretations are given to set class elements depending on the problems concerned (Shreider 1971; Sadovsky 1974).

Psychology is one of the scientific disciplines in which methods and principles of systems theory are widely and effectively applied. Psychological functioning represents a typical example of a system, but of course psychology has only adopted this approach in the twentieth century. The first stages of psychology's development in the experimental psychology of WUNDT, in associationism and classical behaviorism were marked by the dominance of an "atomistic" viewpoint. For research purposes some components of mental functioning were isolated from the general context of man's mental activity. Reflexes were regarded as the elements of mental functioning and thought to be irreducible into simpler components. At the same time this approach was regarded as the only one which was compatible with the rigorous demands of a scientific psychology. The rise of different forms of reductionism – physiological, sociological and, later, cybernetics – has been a consequence of this approach, and has led not only to the loss of any specifically "psychological" object of research, but also to a belief that this represents a deep crisis in the science of psychology.

Psychology has overcome this crisis as a result of the acceptance (for the most part unrecognized) of a systems view of both its subject-matter and its research methods. Vygotsky said, as long ago as 1930: 'The most essential achievement of psychology in recent years is that the analytical approach to psychological processes has been replaced by a holistic or structural approach ... The essence of this new viewpoint consists in the fact that the concept of the "whole" has moved into the foreground. The "whole" possesses its own attributes and defines the attributes and functions of the objects which constitute it" (Vygotsky 1962). The first steps in this direction were connected with William James's doctrine of the stream of consciousness and more particularly with gestalt psychology. Upholders of this view based their theories on the *Gestalt-Qualitäten* discovered in 1890 by Ch. von Ehrenfels. *Gestalt-Qualitäten* are perceptible structures of objects as wholes which cannot be explained solely on the basis of knowledge of the attributes of the elements which constitute these structures. Gestalt psychologists systematically and holistically interpreted various mental functions (perceptions, thinking, etc.) in accordance with their basic methodological credo: 'There are relations which lead to a state in which the causes and nature of the processes of the whole cannot be learned from the knowledge of its elements which exist allegedly in the form of separate pieces, later put together and interconnected. On the contrary any behavior of a part of the whole is governed by the inner structural

laws of the whole' (Wertheimer 1945). Having decided that mental structures were systems of this kind, gestalt psychologists simply made this an a priori assumption. That is why their work was not a complete success.

Essential progress in the comprehension of the systems nature of genetic psychology was made by J. Piaget and by L.S. Vygotsky. Piaget claimed, on the basis of an enormous amount of empirical data collected over more than fifty years, that intellect is a system of reversible and coordinated operations. He stressed that the operations of inner thought derive from the child's actions on external objects. He singled out the successive stages in the formation of intellect and other mental functions, i.e. the stages in the formation of successively more complicated operational systems. The essence of his anti-elementarist approach to research is expressed in his assertion that 'an isolated operation could not be an operation, because the essence of operations is to form systems' (Piaget 1947).

The ideas advanced by Vygotsky during the late 1920s and early 1930s utilized systems principles in the description of human development. Within this framework Vygotsky and his disciples from the 1940s onwards succeeded in:
(1) singling out and describing the main levels in the holistic development of mental structures;
(2) showing how these structures grew from an interaction between biological peculiarities and culture;
(3) showing how essential the use of signs is in higher functions;
(4) working out a general scheme to describe how actions are "internalized" to form the basis of internal, intellectual functions.

In the course of the development of psychology over the last thirty to forty years the systems structure of the mind has been understood first of all as a result of the "activity" approach in psychology. The concept of activity was one of the key concepts in German classical philosophy. It was interpreted from a dialectical-materialistic viewpoint in Marxist philosophy. Activity is a specific human form of behavior directed to the transformation of an object. "Activity" as a special system includes the elements of subject and object to which the actions of the subject are directed. These two components are not completely separated from each other (as they were in the psychology of the nineteenth century and earlier). There is a fixed systems structure belonging not only to each of them separately (as was supposed in most psychology of the first half of the twentieth century), but also to them both together as they form an organic unity. The conception of the coordination of movements worked out by Bernstein (1967) is an excellent example of a systems analysis of a psychophysiological object and it demonstrates the value of such an analysis. In modern psychology the systems approach appears in various forms: e.g. the theory of the psychological field (see FIELD THEORY); the psychological theory of activity (see MARXIST ACTIVITY PSYCHOLOGY); the conception of activity and psychological unity (Rubinstein 1957); theories of personality (e.g. Allport 1961); and psycholinguistics. In the last fifteen to twenty years the systems approach has been widely used in applied psychology, in the psychology of learning for example, and ergonomics, and also in science connected with psychology e.g. psychiatry (Gray, Duhl and Rizzo 1969).

In modern psychology a systems integrated interpretation of cognitive processes is embodied in the consideration of them as forms of information processing (Neisser 1967). Practically all cognitive processes, from finding stimulation to decision making are best treated as part of a complex and intricate interaction.   VNS

Bibliography

Allport, G.W. 1961: *Pattern and growth in personality*. New York and London: Holt, Rinehart and Winston.

Bernstein, N. 1967: *The coordination and regulation of movements*. Oxford: Pergamon.

Bertalanffy, L. von 1968: *Organismic psychology and systems theory*. Worcester, Mass.: Clark University Press.

Blauberg, I.V., Sadovsky, V.N., and Yudin, E.G. 1977: *Systems theory: philosophical and methodological problems*. Moscow: Progress Publishers.

*Emery, F.E. ed. 1981: *Systems thinking*. 2 vols. Harmondsworth: Penguin.

Gray, W., Duhl, F.J., and Rizzo, N.D. eds. 1969: *General systems theory and psychiatry*. Boston: Little Brown; London: Churchill.

Kornblum, S. ed. 1973: *Attention and performance IV*. New York: Academic Press.

Marx, M. and Hillix, W. 1973: *Systems and theories in psychology*. New York: McGraw-Hill.

Mead, G.H. 1934: *Mind, self and society*. Chicago: Chicago University Press.

Neisser, U. 1967: *Cognitive psychology*. New York: Appleton-Century-Crofts.

Piaget, J. (1946) 1950: *The psychology of intelligence*. New York: Harcourt Brace.

Rubinstein, S.L. 1957: *Being and consciousness*. Moscow (in Russian).

Sadovsky, V.N. 1974: Problems of a general systems theory as a metatheory. *Ratio* 16 (1), 33–50.

Shreider, Y.A. 1971: On the definition of system. *Nauchno-tekhicheskaya informatsiya*. Series 2, No. 7, 5–8 (in Russian).

Vygotsky, L.S. 1962: *Thought and language*. Cambridge, Mass.: MIT Press.

—— 1978: *Mind in society: the development of higher psychological processes*. Cambridge, Mass. and London: Harvard University Press.

Wertheimer, M. 1945: *Productive thinking*. New York and London: Harper.

T

taboo A word of Polynesian origin quickly adopted into the English language in the eighteenth century to refer to behavior (involving people or objects) which is socially disapproved of or forbidden, although not necessarily legally prohibited. In a more technical sense the word is used by anthropologists to refer to relationships to which danger adheres. Failure to observe the conditions of a taboo is regarded as resulting in automatic mystical or supernatural sanctions. For example the breach of the incest taboo is thought to result in some retribution falling on the culprits themselves or perhaps on the whole community.

A precise definition of taboo has never been agreed upon, and even within Oceanian languages its meaning shifts from one society to another. Accordingly its status as an analytic category is questionable, and in recent anthropological literature the term has often been replaced by the word pollution.   PGR

Bibliography

Steiner, F.B. 1967: *Taboo*. Harmondsworth and Baltimore: Penguin.

tacit knowledge: social psychological

A term used to refer to the wide variety of things a person has to know or assume in order both to make sense of other peoples' utterances and activities, and to produce ones that are intelligible to others.

The view that orderly social interaction can be produced only when participants tacitly share a range of common background expectancies that normally remain unexplicated and taken for granted has been particularly important in the development of phenomenological sociology and ethnomethodology. A series of experiments by Harold Garfinkel (1967),

for example, demonstrated how easily various mundane interactions (such as greetings sequences) could be dramatically disrupted if one party began to ask questions about things that are normally assumed or taken for granted. One general conclusion that can be drawn from this and similar studies is that it is necessary to develop an approach to the analysis of social behavior that comes to terms with the "seen but un-noticed" ways in which tacit knowledge features in its production and interpretation.

(See also ETHNOMETHODOLOGY; INDEXICAL EXPRESSIONS.)   JMAt

Bibliography

Garfinkel, H. 1967: *Studies in ethnomethodology*. Englewood Cliffs, N.J.: Prentice-Hall; Cambridge: Polity Press (1984).

Schutz, A. 1962: *Collected papers I: the problem of social reality*. The Hague: Nijhoff.

tests: normative- and criterion-referenced

Norm-referenced tests utilize the performance of some reference group as a standard against which the performance of an individual can be compared. An "above average IQ" is an abbreviated description for a score obtained by an individual which is above the average of the scores obtained by comparable individuals on the same test.

Criterion-referenced tests use as their basis for comparison or reference a specified set of performances or actions, the criteria. The purpose of the test is to quantify or describe in some standard systematic way, the extent to which the individual has achieved or possesses the criterion behavior. The immediate aim of the test is to describe an individual's behavior or competence rather than to draw a comparison with some reference group. Such a test might for instance be developed to index knowledge of basic arithmetic skills, or self-sufficiency among handicapped people. Self-sufficiency, for example, would be defined in terms of a number of components (able to cope with eating, or dressing unaided) which would then be broken down further into a hierarchy of unitary subskills, such as holding a fork or doing up buttons. Criterion-referenced testing would then involve ascertaining which of the component skills were present, and thereby the extent to which the individual had achieved the criterion of self-sufficiency.

It should be noted that "errors" of measurement can be identified fairly precisely in normative- but not in criterion-referenced tests, where the tester's own notional standards are used.   MBe

Bibliography

Anastasi, A. 1982: *Psychological testing*. 5th edn. New York: Macmillan.

tests: personality Personality is a term used in different ways by different psychologists and can include in its definition intelligence, physique, skills, and, more commonly, emotional and social qualities, interests and attitudes. The study of personality is concerned with individual differences, specifically those which seem to particular theorists to be most essential for understanding and predicting idio-syncratic behavior. Some personality tests aim to identify and measure TRAITS (sociability, anxiety, impulsiveness, honesty, etc.). Others are concerned with TYPES (clusters of traits which tend to occur together).

A variety of procedures is used to index these characteristics, including interviews, self-ratings or the judgments of others, specially devised QUESTIONNAIRES, direct observation of behavior, and projection techniques. The last mentioned may involve the use of abstract pictures – such as "ink blots" – or semi-structured pictures which the individual is asked to describe. It is assumed that the person being tested will

"project" his or her own personality into the descriptions, thereby making "it" accessible to the tester.

Personality tests are sometimes used to complement other information for clinical or guidance purposes, in trying to reach a fuller understanding of the patient. It is claimed, for instance, that better predictions about educational accomplishment can be achieved by using personality tests in addition to intelligence tests. There are many theories of personality and many tests available. The particular procedure chosen will be strongly influenced by the theoretical orientation of the user.

Tests have been devised to quantify a great variety of human characteristics such as creativity, anxiety, impulsivity, styles of thinking, motivation to achieve, interests, and there are batteries (a standard collection) of tests for vocational and career guidance. The standard compendium of psychological tests has been compiled by Buros (1978).   MBe

Bibliography

Buros, O.K. 1978: *The eighth mental measurement yearbook*. New Jersey: Gryphon Press.

tests: reliability of The extent to which a measure is free from random error. An observed score on any measure (including, of course, psychological tests) consists of two parts, one of them random (chance events) and the other systematic. A reliability estimate shows the relative size of these two parts. Methods for estimating the reliability of scores involve studying their consistency on a single occasion or their stability over two of more occasions.

The most straightforward way of testing reliability is to correlate the scores of the same people on the same test on two occasions (test-retest reliability). The more reliable the test, the higher will be the correlations (although clearly the length of time between the occasions is likely to affect the strength of the correlation).

Another method is to use two different forms of a test (alternate-form reliability) and correlate the same people's scores on the two. Alternate-form reliability also requires a time-interval between one testing and the next.

A third method of assessing reliability is to correlate scores on one half of a test with scores on the other (split-half or internal reliability). The whole test is done at once, so this method does not require a time interval. It therefore has the advantage that random factors associated with differences between two occasions cannot intrude. A common way of dividing the test in half is to compare odd items with even items. This eliminates effects of warm-up and fatigue.

Two final methods of estimating reliability use the standard deviations of total scores, and either the number of people who "pass" or "fail" each item (Kuder-Richardson) or the sum of the variances of each item (Cronbach's alpha). The latter can be used on tests with a Likert (several point) scale answer format whereas the Kuder-Richardson is designed for tests with a pass/fail or yes/no marking.

Different methods might give different estimates, depending on which components of the score are regarded as random and which are regarded as systematic. The systematic portion of the score may be composed of a single component or of several independent effects which are added together in a composite. For example, if a mathematics examination is given to a group of people on two occasions, some portion of the score on the second occasion will consist of the examinee's memory of answers to the questions on the first occasion. The memory component would be a systematic effect, and from the researcher's viewpoint it may or may not be desirable. In any event it is not random, so it increases the systematic or reliable portion of the score. MDH/RL

Bibliography

Anastasi, A. 1982: *Psychological testing.* 5th edn. New York: Macmillan.

Campbell, J.P. 1976: Psychometric theory. In *Handbook of industrial and organizational psychology*, ed. M.D. Dunnette. Chicago: Rand McNally.

Cronbach, L.J. 1951: Coefficient alpha and the internal structure of tests. *Psychometrika* 16, 297–334.

Kuder, G.F. and Richardson, M.W. 1937: The theory of estimation of test reliability. *Psychometrika* 2, 151–60.

tests: validity of The extent to which scores on tests or other measures are justified or supported by evidence. Validity refers to the relationship between a test and what it is purported to measure or predict. Researchers gather evidence for the validity of a measure from three different angles: content, criterion, and construct.

A test has content validity when it contains relevant items. For example, an exam must have questions which test all relevant knowledge and skills. There are obvious problems of adequate coverage and due weight being given to different skills and topics. Content validity must not be confused with "face validity". A test has face validity when it *appears* to cover a domain. In test construction items are often included because they seem likely to measure what one is interested in. But they may have to be discarded if they turn out not to. Such items have face validity only.

Criterion validity is the most clear-cut. A test has criterion (or experimental) validity if it relates appropriately to an external standard. For example, IQ scores should be positively correlated with academic achievement, and questionnaire measures of introversion/extraversion should relate to introverted and extraverted social behavior. Criterion validity may be concurrent, as with a diagnostic test supposed to reveal the present state of affairs, or predictive, as with selection tests for courses or jobs. The validity coefficient is the correlation between a test and its criterion.

Construct validity (Cronbach and Meehl 1955) is a more complicated concept. It is not always possible to establish a criterion against which to rate a test. But a test may be useful in confirming relationships derived from a theory. For example EYSENCK's arousal theory of introversion-extraversion leads to a range of predictions about concentration, conditionability, wakefulness and fatigue on motor tasks, as well as predictions about sexual preferences and probable social behavior. If a test proves useful in picking up a distinction predicted by the theory and correlates with other tests and observations, it has construct validity. A complex theory comes to be accepted through a gradual accumulation of data from different sources. New tests may have higher construct validity than established ones because they make finer or richer distinctions, or more accurately distinguish between groups the theory predicts will be distinct.

Campbell and Fiske (1959) discuss methods of ensuring that a test has both convergent validity and discriminant validity, i.e. that it correlates with variables which the theory predicts it will, and does *not* correlate with variables which the theory predicts it will not. Until recently it has been believed that validity evidence is specific to the research setting in which it was gathered. However, Schmidt and Hunter (1977) and many others have reported investigations showing that under some circumstances validity evidence may be generalized to new settings.   MDH RL

Bibliography

Anastasi, A. 1982: *Psychological testing*. 5th edn. New York: Macmillan.

Campbell, D.T. and Fiske, D.W. 1959: Convergent and discriminant validation by the multitrait-multimethod matrix. *Psychological bulletin* 56, 81–105.

Cascio, W.F. 1982: *Applied psychology in personnel management*. 2nd edn. Reston, Virginia: Reston Publishing Company.

Cronbach, L.J. and Meehl, P.E. 1955: Construct validity in psychological tests. *Psychological bulletin* 52, 281–302.

Schmidt, F.L. and Hunter, J.E. 1977: Development of a general solution to the problem of validity generalization. *Journal of applied psychology* 62, 529–40.

topological psychology The psychological geometry formulated by LEWIN (1936) to represent diagrammatically certain structural concepts of field theory. Its psychological applications were suggested by the complex mathematical discipline of topology, which deals with the properties of figures that remain unchanged under continuous transformation or stretching. In other words, one can say that mathematical topology deals with the qualitative relationships of connection and position. Mathematicians have not always been able to see the relationship between their geometric precepts and the topology developed by Lewin. However, despite less rigorous mathematical constraints, Lewin's topology investigates spatial relations in a psychological sense, particularly such relationships as "part-whole", "belongingness" and membership characteristics.

The most basic concept in Lewin's topological system is that of the LIFE SPACE, which is the psychological field or total situation. It encompasses the totality of facts which determine the behavior of an individual at a given moment. Any distinguishable part of the life space or person is defined as a region, and this refers to present or contemplated activities rather than to any objective area in which these activities might occur. A region may contain various degrees of differentiation, a term referring to the number of subparts within a region.

Locomotion refers to any change of position of the behaving self within the life space. Movement from one region to another involves locomotion through a path of neighboring regions. Two regions are considered neighboring if they have a common boundary but are otherwise foreign to each other. The boundary of a region is formed by those cells in the region for which there is no surrounding boundary that lies entirely within the region. Finally, Lewin introduced hodological space in an attempt to develop a geometry whose basic spatial concepts could be integrated with dynamic concepts. In hodological space, the distinguished path between any two regions is the preferred or psychologically best path; it is the path the individual expects to take if he chooses to proceed from one region to another.

These are the major concepts of Lewin's topology, and they function within his theoretical framework to allow one to determine which events are possible in a given life space and which are not. In order to determine which of the possible events will occur in a given case, it is necessary to refer to Lewin's dynamic concepts.   MDe

Bibliography

Lewin, K. 1936: *Principles of topological psychology*. New York: McGraw-Hill.

touch in social interaction contact between adults usually implies intimacy and warmth, but there are different kinds of contact, some of which are aggressive. Among non-aggressive touches not all are affiliative, nor are all mutual. Some manual touches are controlling. A distinction must also be made among parts of the body touched and among parts used to do the touching. Jourard (1966) found that females reported being touched far more than males did, a result also found in 1976 by Rosenfeld. Henley too found that women were touched more than men. Henley argued that since superiors and those who might be trying to control others would touch inferiors and those being controlled, the accessibility of women to touch symbolized inferior social status. Argyle however has argued that the sex difference may not symbolize power differences. Men and women are more likely to tell women significant or intimate secrets. Hence women's role as recipients of touch and secrets may reflect society's expectation that women will be warm and supportive, and it may have little to do with control. For a recent review see Stier and Hall (1984).

Touch is also perceived rather differently by men and women. Fisher and others (1976) found that students who had been touched by a librarian, sometimes without knowing it, liked the librarian (and even library) more than did the untouched. The effect was greater among women. Whitcher and Fisher (1979) found greater sex differences in a hospital. Touch from a nurse before an operation lessened women's anxiety and their blood pressure, but the effects were the opposite for men. This perhaps supports the connection with control, though not necessarily status. Men

may have been unhappy about the symbol of loss of control. Nguyen and others (1975, 1976) investigated the perception of receiving different kinds of touch (pat, squeeze, brush and stroke) on different body areas from someone of the opposite sex. Women distinguished touches signaling desire from those signaling love, whereas men did not. But married women and unmarried men found sexual touching "warmer" than married men and unmarried women. Among women touch may increase liking for a man when there are other reasons to like him, but decrease it when there are not (Touhey 1974).

Contact may also be formalized, as in handshakes and other greetings, but contact greetings tend to imply more intimacy than non-contact ones, as Victorian distinctions between bowing and hand-shaking show. There are also cultural differences. "Contact cultures" such as Arabs and Southern Europeans seem to have more touch than "non-contact cultures" such as Northern Europeans and Indians. Jourard reported that couples in cafes touched 180 times per hour in Puerto Rico, 110 times in France, twice in America, and not at all in England. It is unclear whether such differences are caused by differences in friendliness or merely in conventions. Italians appear to use gestures and touch to control conversations and conversational turn-taking where English and Americans use GAZE and intonation.   RL

Bibliography

Heslin, R. and Alper, T. 1983: Touch: a bonding gesture. In *Nonverbal interaction*, eds. J.M. Wiemann and R.P. Harrison. Beverly Hills: Sage.

*Knapp, M.L. 1978: *Nonverbal communication in human interaction*. New York: Holt, Rinehart and Winston.

*Montagu, A. 1978: *Touching*. 2nd edn. New York: Harper and Row.

Stier, D.S. and Hall, J.A. 1984: Gender differences in touch: an empirical and theoretical review. *Journal of personality and social psychology* 47, 440–59.

Touhey, J.C. 1974: Effects of dominance and competence on heterosexual attraction. *British journal of social and clinical psychology* 13, 22–6.

Whitcher, S.J. and Fisher, J.D. 1979: Multi-dimensional reaction to therapeutic touch in a hospital setting. *Journal of personality and social psychology* 37, 87–96.

All other references will be found in Knapp.

traits A trait is a characteristic of a person or animal which varies from one individual to another. Traits may be physical (e.g. height, eye color) or psychological (e.g. intelligence and aggressiveness). The concept is one of particular relevance to personality psychology because the major effort in recent years has been directed at establishing the main dimensions of temperament on which people differ as a first step towards explaining these individual differences. Traits are conceived as reasonably stable and enduring attributes, distinguishing them from *states*, which are temporary behavioral predispositions. Because a person is anxious in the dentist's chair this does not mean he or she is necessarily anxious in general.

It has been estimated that there are about 4500 trait-descriptive adjectives in the English language, many of which are heavily overlapping (e.g. pompous, vain, arrogant, conceited, presumptuous, ego-tistical, snobbish, smug and haughty). The first task of the psychologist, therefore, is to reduce the list to manageable proportions and identify those that are of central importance. A statistical method for doing this is called FACTOR ANALYSIS. This is a technique of classification which starts with a matrix of correlations among test items and looks for the simplest patterns that might account for it. Not uncommonly a hierarchial pattern emerges; a large number of trait clusters are found at what is called the *primary factor level* which, because they are themselves inter-correlated, may be reduced to a smaller number of more independent *higher-order factors*. Some critics of factor analysis claim that the method yields contradictory results on different occasions, but this is usually not true; apparent contradictions arise because researchers favor solutions at different levels of generality. American psychologists, notably CATTELL, have generally concentrated upon the primary factor level (the *Sixteen Personality Factor Questionnaire* being a well-known measuring instrument) whereas European psychologists, such as EYSENCK, have preferred to work with a more general but reliable higher-order level.

Eysenck stresses the importance of three major dimensions which are largely independent of one another: extraversion versus introversion, neuroticism versus stability and psychoticism versus empathy. These are the three scales provided in the Eysenck Personality Questionnaire. If three dimensions seems a very small number within which to describe the many different personalities that we encounter it is worth remembering that all of the 25,000 or so colors we can distinguish may be identified by their positions in relation to just three variables: hue, saturation and brightness. Indeed, research has shown that the multi-trait profiles yielded by many personality tests such as the MMPI can be reduced to three scores with little loss of information.

Eysenck has devoted a great deal of research to the question of the biological basis of these three main dimensions. His theory of extraversion concerns the level of AROUSAL typically prevailing in the cerebral cortex, which in turn depends upon the physiological functioning of the brain-stem reticular activating system. Introverts are believed to have a higher level of chronic arousal than extraverts, who are therefore less in control of their impulses and more sensation-hungry in their behavior. Neu-roticism is thought to be related to the degree of lability of the emotional midbrain (which controls the autonomic nervous system and therefore factors such as fearfulness and irritability). Psychoticism is assumed to have some kind of biochemical basis that is as yet unknown but involves the balance of sex hormones or the chemistry of synapses. Jeffrey Gray has proposed a rival theory that anxiety and impulsiveness are basic temperamental variables, relating at the neurological level to pain avoidance and reward-seeking mechanisms respect-ively. Both theories have assembled considerable experimental support but there are many issues still to be settled.

Other personality variables that have been widely researched because of their theoretical and practical significance are authoritarianism, dogmatism, internal versus external control, aggressiveness, achievement motivation and field dependence. Within the clinical field there are other particularly relevant variables, such as depression, obsessionality, anxiety and thought disorder.

Measurement of traits is most commonly undertaken with questionnaires and adjective check-lists, although there are many other techniques that may be used for special purposes, such as behavioral observation and ratings, projective devices and performance in laboratory tasks. All such measures are samples of behavior that have direct or theoretical relevance to the trait in question. Color preferences, for example, may be used as a clue to extraversion since it is known that extraverts tend to choose bright, garish colors while introverts prefer subtle, reserved colors.

In recent years, some psychologists, such as W. Mischel, have questioned the usefulness of the trait concept, claiming that situational factors are much more important determinants of behavior. They illustrate this argument by referring, among others, to a 1928 study by Hartshorne and May which found that dishonesty in school children did not generalize greatly from one situation to another. Thus a child who cheated in exams would not necessarily steal from a shop or lie to his parents. Since only low correlations are found among such behaviors Mischel has argued that behavior is very largely situation-specific.

Trait theorists such as Eysenck reply that the low correlations occur because these different situations place variable degrees of stress on the child's honesty and that a whole battery of such items is needed before stable and valid trait measurement is achieved. They cite the parallel case of intelligence in which a child may pass one IQ test item and fail another because one is more difficult than the other. This does not mean that intelligence does not exist as a trait, merely that a large number of problems are needed to comprise a satisfactory IQ scale.

The specificity theory gained considerable popularity among American psychologists because it was consonant with the environmentalist *Zeitgeist* of the 1960s and '70s (see PERSON/SITUATION CONTROVERSY). Today, however, it is recognized that although situational factors need to be considered in a full account of human motivation and behavior, the measurement of temperamental traits is also a necessary exercise for many purposes. Developmental studies have confirmed that emotional tendencies, strongly predictive of similar characteristics in later childhood, can be identified in infants within a few weeks of birth.

Another criticism of the trait approach is the argument that every individual is totally unique and therefore it is not possible to classify people with respect to preselected factors. This is a misunderstanding of the nature of scientific thought, which depends heavily upon classification and generalization. It is true that nobody is perfectly duplicated, not even by their identical twin, but such a statement is utterly unhelpful. Every banana is unique, but it is sometimes useful to classify bananas as large or small, straight or bent, green, ripe or bad. The unique individual may be of interest to the novelist, dramatist or clinician, but it would be difficult even to describe him without resort to higher order (summary) concepts.

Trait measurement is of particular interest in the field of behavioral genetics, where concern is with the degree of heritability of factors such as height, intelligence, musical ability, and psychoticism. Modern techniques of genetic analysis based on comparisons of identical and fraternal twins can also reveal the approximate number of different genes that are involved in determining the individual's position on a trait and whether the family or other aspects of the environment are the more influential in modifying it. The old, naive heredity versus environment argument has given way to a comprehensive partitioning of variance of a trait into different kinds of genetic and environmental influence (see also BEHAVIOR GENETICS).

Among the complications of genetic analysis are assortative mating, dominance and epistasis. *Assortative mating* refers to the fact that humans tend to marry or pair on the basis of similarity on a great number of traits such as height, intelligence, attractiveness and political conservatism. This causes a certain degree of polarization within the population on the trait in question and an increase in the kinship correlations that has to be put into the equations of the behavioral geneticist.

Dominance refers to the fact that some genes predominate over others (called recessives) in terms of the degree to which they are manifested in body or behavior. The best-known example is eye color, in which brown is dominant over blue. In the field of behavior it is found that most of the genes determining high IQ are dominant (some evidence for this being seen in the phenomena of *inbreeding depression* and *hybrid vigor*), but neither end of the extraversion-introversion dimension predominates over the other. It is likely that this reflects the fact that high extraversion and introversion are roughly equally adaptive to the individual in evolutionary terms.

Epistasis refers to the fact that the expression of a gene may be modified by the action of a non-coinciding gene, possibly even one that is located on a different chromosome. Since the effect of this is to lower all kinship correlations except those for identical twins, epistasis is often difficult to distinguish from dominance. It may, however, account for some part of the variance in IQ and other traits that has previously been attributed to the environment.

Trait psychology (and indeed the science of psychometrics) may be said to have originated in the last century when GALTON took a variety of anatomical and behavioral measurements on a large sample of visitors to the great Crystal Palace Exhibition in Kensington and sought to intercorrelate them. We have come a long way since then in terms of measurement techniques, experimental procedures and genetic analysis, although there are problems yet to

be solved. Criticisms of the trait concept have had little impact on this progress and, with the decline of psychoanalytic approaches to the explanation of behavior, the psychology of personality has increasingly come to be regarded by many writers as synonymous with the study of traits.

GDW

Bibliography

Blass, T. ed. 1977: *Personality variables in social behavior*. Hillsdale, N.J.: Lawrence Erlbaum.

Eysenck, H.J. and Eysenck, M.W. 1985: *Personality and individual differences*. New York: Plenum.

Lynn, R. 1981: *Dimensions of personality*. Oxford and New York: Pergamon.

Mischel, W. 1968: *Personality and assessment*. New York and London: Wiley.

transactional analysis (TA) A theory of personality and social behavior, used as a vehicle for psychotherapy and more general social change. It was born out of Eric Berne's early interest in intuition (1949) and his desire to produce a language of behavior which would be universally understood (1972).

Central to TA is the concept and practice colloquially known as "stroking" – the process of stimulating and giving recognition to fellow human beings. Stroking patterns form a common theme in the main sub-sections of TA.

Personality structure is formed by the interrelationship of Parent, Adult and Child. These labels do not bear their common meaning but denote "egostates", coherent systems of external behavior and internal process. They are formed from the early beginnings of human development. The Parent egostate is based on limit-setting and nurturing as modeled by an individual's own parent figures. The Adult comprises reality testing and probability computing. The Child is an expression of feelings, creativity or adaptations which were originally experienced during actual childhood. TA prescribes methods for achieving a balance of energy among the egostates which is held to be essential for the well-being of the individual, the family or the organization.

Communication is defined as a series of stimuli and responses from the egostates between individuals. TA pays particular attention to the stimuli and responses which occur at a psychological level, usually non-verbally and outside the awareness of the participants. These are "ulterior" transactions and it is believed they decide the real outcome of an exchange. They are the powerful means which we adopt to influence each other.

Games, arguably the most original construct in TA (Berne 1964), are created by a regular use of ulterior transactions leading to a conclusion in which all participants lose. They are played from the psychological roles of Persecutor, Rescuer or Victim and constitute set routines to structure time, provide excitement and avoid intimacy. They can range from low-level teasing to criminal involvement and occupy a large part of everyday activity.

Feelings analysis is focused on the possible repertoire of anger, fear, sadness and joy or those feelings like guilt, hurt, boredom or jealousy which are compounds of two or more of the basic four. They can be experienced as reactions – appropriate contemporary responses; as "rubberbands" – old feelings reactivated by a trigger in the present; or as "rackets" – favorite permitted or displaced feelings generated as a background accompaniment to living.

Script analysis examines plans decided upon in early childhood under parental influence, which are intended to shape the most important aspects of life. They consist of myths arising out of messages received about self and the world and are perpetuated by games and rackets. They fall into the main categories of "winner" – breeding success, "non-winner" – which is tolerable but unsatisfying and "loser" – which presents problems of varying degree. Scripts may be changed through redecisions which will replace old internal frames of reference with a realistic and more accurate world view.   CT

Bibliography

Berne, E. 1949: The nature of intuition. *Psychiatric quarterly* 23, 203–26. Reprinted in E. Berne. 1977: *Intuition and egostates*. San Francisco: TA Press.

—— 1964: *Games people play*. New York: Grove Press; London: André Deutsch (1966).

—— 1972: *What do you say after you say hello?* New York and London: André Deutsch (1974).

Woollams, S. and Brown, M. 1978: *Transactional analysis*. Michigan: Huron Valley Press.

twin studies The comparison of genetically identical with genetically similar humans, with a view to establishing the interaction between biological and environmental factors that give rise to behavior.

The usual method involves comparisons between monozygotic (identical) twins and dizygotic (fraternal) twins. Where both sets have been reared in similar environments the lesser variability of behavior between identical twins is taken to reflect their greater genetic similarity for that trait. Various measures of heritability (some controversial) for different TRAITS have been derived. Heritability is the proportion of variance in behavior due to genetic factors that appeared over generations, when environmental factors were held to be constant. The best-known example concerns the intelligence quotient for which heritability estimates vary between 0.4 and 0.8.

Other methods compare identical twins reared together with those reared apart, to establish more precisely the role of the environment in behavioral development. It is generally found that adopted monozygotic twins reared apart are nevertheless more similar to each other (and to their biological parents) than to their adoptive siblings (or adoptive parents). Although this does not rule out a general contribution of a common human environment to development, it suggests that specific effects of the environment as in the development of particular interests or aspects of personality, may occur only in relation to genetic predispositions shared by parent and child.

Another method has been to compare identical twins who are dissimilar (discordant) for a particular trait. This has proved very useful in establishing that environmental factors are crucial to the etiology of schizophrenia. GEB

Bibliography

Mittler, P. 1971: *The study of twins*. Harmonds-worth: Penguin.

Nance, W.E. 1978: *Twin research*. New York: A.R. Liss.

Stevenson, J. and Fielding, J. 1985: Ratings of temperament in families of young twins. *British journal of development psychology* 3, 143–52.

type A word used in personality theory. It is usually contrasted with TRAIT, but the basis of the contrast is not always the same. In everyday usage there is often no contrast beyond the linguistic one, that a hostile type of person is someone who has a trait of hostility. Some people (e.g. Feshbach and Weiner 1983) regard the character sketches of Aristotle and his successor, Theophrastus, as descriptions of person-ality types. These sketches pick out a few aspects of the behavior taken to typify a particular kind of person. Some of this behavior is part of the definition of that type, and some is more superficial. For example, Aristotle's description of the "magnanimous" man includes the reference to his dignity and beneficence, but also to the way in which he speaks and the speed of his gait.

It is more common to regard more systematic and reductive approaches to personality as type theories. The principal example of this sort of approach which is usually cited is the doctrine of the four humors. This doctrine goes back to the Hippocratic writings of the fifth century B.C. and is thoroughly worked out by Galen (130–200 A.D.). Temperament was supposed by these Greek writers to depend on the prevalence of one of four bodily fluids (Latin *humores*), blood, phlegm, yellow bile and black bile. The tem-peraments corresponding to these humors are sanguine (optimistic), phlegmatic (calm), choleric (irascible) and melancho-lic. The idea that there are four types of temperament has retained its popularity right up until the present. References to the humors are found in medieval and renais-sance literature. The doctrine of tem-peraments (without the attendant physiology) was adopted by Kant, and also by WUNDT (1903), usually thought of as the father of modern psychology.

Another typological theory of personality was Kretschmer's (1921, 1925). He sug-gested that different body builds are associated with different temperaments. He divided body-build into "pyknic" (short and stocky), "athletic" (strong and well-proportioned), "leptosomic" (tall and slender) and "dysplastic" (a mixture). This idea was taken over by Sheldon (Sheldon and Stevens 1942). His triad was the endomorph (soft and round) who is relaxed and sociable and loves eating, the meso-morph (muscular) who is energetic and courageous, and the ectomorph (long and fragile) who is restrained, introverted and artistic. Kretschmer claimed that schizo-phrenics are usually leptosomic, while manic-depressives are usually pyknic (i.e. at the other end of the physical spectrum). This is now thought simply to be because the age of onset of schizophrenia is much earlier than that of manic-depression, and people tend to get fatter as they get older! Sheldon claimed that there was evidence for the relation between the personality types and the body builds. The evidence, however, was very poor as his method consisted in photographing people and having the photographs sorted according to body-type. The personalities of the people were then rated by untrained observers. Such a procedure probably draws on the STEREOTYPES of the observers, who are inclined to see short fat people as jolly, and tall thin people as artistic. When specific behavior is recorded rather than global ratings of personality, no correlations are found between body-build and personality (see Mischel, 1968).

It is often said that the concept of types requires a categorical distinction, such that a person is either one type or another, and cannot be a mixture of two. This presents a clear contrast with the concept of traits, which are taken to be continuous. A person can have more or less of any trait. One does not possess (all) the trait or not possess it at all. Kretschmer, however, clearly thought that there could be a dysplastic body build, which was a mixture of the other three types, while Wundt and EYSENCK (1947) adopted a dimensional view of personality, despite acknowledging the basic correctness of the fourfold typology of Galen. Wundt argued that two of the temperaments (choleric and melancholic) are highly emotional, while the other two are not. People may therefore be said to differ on a continuous dimension of emotionality. Again Wundt pointed out that two of the temperaments (choleric and sanguine) involve highly changeable behavior, while the other two do not. People may therefore be said to differ on a second continuous dimension of changeability. Because the emotionality dimension contrasts the choleric and melancholic with the sanguine and phlegmatic, while the changeability dimension contrasts the choleric and sanguine with the phlegmatic and melancholic, it is clear that they are orthogonal (uncorrelated) dimensions. In other words the fact that someone is highly emotional tells us nothing about how changeable he or she is.

JUNG in his book *Psychological types* (1921, 1923) also used the type concept, suggesting that *introversion and extraversion* were the two principal types of personality. Eysenck (1947) suggested that introversion-extraversion is a continuous dimension, and corresponds to Wundt's "changeability". Jung had suggested that different kinds of neurotic illness are found in introverts and extraverts (psychasthenia and hysteria respectively). Eysenck took up this point and inferred from it that since there are neurotics at both ends of the introvert-extravert, spectrum, neuroticism must be a second dimension orthogonal to introversion-extraversion. Using the same logic he drew on Kretschmer's idea that there are psychotics at both ends of the normal spectrum, and argued that schizophrenics are introverts while manic-depressives are extraverts. Hence, since tests which discriminate normals from neurotics do not discriminate normals from psychotics, he suggested that there must be a third dimension of psychoticism (see Eysenck and Eysenck 1968). He refers to these dimensions as personality types.

They are therefore contrasted with traits, but in rather a different way from the category vs. continuum contrast outlined above.

Eysenck in fact regards types as second-order factors obtained from FACTOR ANALYSIS. He proposes that the personality is organized hierarchically. At the bottom level there are specific responses to specific stimuli. At the next level there are habitual responses. Above that are the traits, such as sociability and impulsiveness. The evidence for their existence comes from the observed intercorrelations between different kinds of habitual response. At the highest level are the types (i.e. the three dimensions), the evidence for their existence coming from observed intercorrelations between traits. He regards such a "type" approach to personality as superior to the trait approach of CATTELL, because of its greater simplicity, reliability and theoretical grounding in physiology and genetics. (For further treatment of this issue see TRAITS).   RL

Bibliography

Aristotle (1925): *Nicomachean ethics*. Trans. D. Ross. Oxford: Oxford University Press.

Eysenck, H.J. 1947: *Dimensions of personality*. London: Routledge and Kegan Paul; New York: Praeger.

Eysenck, S.B.G. and Eysenck, H.J. 1968: The measurement of psychoticism: a study of factor stability and reliability. *British journal of social and clinical psychology* 7, 286–94.

Feshbach, S. and Weiner, B. 1982: *Personality*. Lexington, Mass.: D.C. Heath.

Jung, C.G. (1921), 1923: *Psychological types*. Trans. H.G. Baynes. London: Kegan Paul; New York: Harcourt Brace.

Kretschmer, E. 1925: *Physique and character*. New York: Harcourt Brace.

Mischel, W. 1968: *Personality and assessment*. New York: Wiley.

Sheldon, W.H. and Stevens, S.S. 1942: *The varieties of temperament: a psychology of constitutional differences*. New York: Harper.

Wundt, W. 1903: *Grundzüge der physiologischen Psychologie*. Leipzig:

type-A personality Friedman and Rosenman (1974) observed a statistically significant relationship between certain behavior patterns and the prevalence of coronary heart disease (CHD). Individuals significantly at risk were referred to as exhibiting "the coronary-prone behavior pattern, Type A" as distinct from Type B (low risk of CHD). Type A people showed the overt behavioral syndrome or style of living characterized by "extremes of competitiveness, striving for achievement, restlessness, hyper-alertness, explosiveness of speech, tenseness of facial musculature and feelings of being under pressure of time and under the challenge of responsibility". Type Bs possess the opposite extremes of the attributes above.

In the early studies, persons were designated as either Type A or Type B on the basis of clinical judgments by doctors and psychologists or through peer ratings. These studies found higher incidence of CHD among Type A than Type B. Many inherent methodological weaknesses were overcome by the classic Western Collaborative Group Study (Rosenman, Friedman and Strauss 1964, 1966). This was a prospective national study of over 3,400 men free of CHD. All these men were rated as Type A or B by psychiatrists after intensive interviews, without knowledge of any biological data about them and without the individuals being seen by a cardiologist. Diagnosis was made by an electrocardiographer and independent medical internist, who were not informed about the subjects' behavioral patterns. Results included the following: after two and a half years of the study Type A men between the ages of forty and forty-nine and fifty and fifty-nine had 6.5 and 1.9 times respectively the incidence of CHD as compared with Type B men. (See CORONARY-PRONE BEHAVIOR.)

Later work exploring concomitants of Type A behavior pattern has shown that Type A people are more successful than Type B (e.g. Waldron 1978). There have been mixed results in studies which have looked at the psychological well-being of

the two types. Strube et al. (1985) found that younger Type A people (male and female) reported greater satisfaction with their lives, but that older Type B people's satisfaction was greater.

H. Friedman et al. (1985) suggested that the normal assessment of Types A and B is inadequate, and claimed there are, at least, two distinct categories within each type. The distinction within type is based on self-rated expressive style. Among a Type A group of high-risk middle-aged men some were defined as "charismatic" and others as "hostile". Among, high-risk Type Bs some were defined as "relaxed" and some as "tense" and "inhibited". There were differences in perceived verbal and non-verbal expression among these groups. There was also a (marginally significant) tendency for the "hostile" Type As and the "tense" Type Bs to have more peripheral artery problems than the other two groups. Friedman et al. therefore argued that not all Type A behavior is necessarily a likely cause of coronary heart disease, nor all Type B behavior a likely prophylactic.   CI.C/RI.

Bibliography

Friedman, H.S., Hall, J.A. and Harris, M.J. 1985: Type A behavior, nonverbal expressive style and health. *Journal of personality and social psychology* 48, 1299–1315.

Friedman, M. and Rosenman, R.H. 1974: *Type A behavior and your heart*. Greenwich, Conn.: Fawcett Publications, Inc.

Rosenman, R.H., Friedman, M., and Strauss, R. 1964: A predictive study of CHD. *Journal of the American medical association* 189, 15–22.

—— 1966: CHD in the Western Collaborative Group Study. *Journal of the American medical association* 195, 86–92.

Strube, M.J., Berry, J.M., Goza, B.K. and Fennimore, D. 1985: Type A behavior, age, and psychological well-being. *Journal of personality and social psychology* 49, 203–18.

Waldron, I. 1978: The coronary-prone behavior pattern, blood pressure, employment and socioeconomic status in women. *Journal of psychosomatic research* 22, 79–87.

U

unconscious drive A psychoanalytic concept used to describe a basic urge that is associated with a state of psychic energy and which leads to a specific form of behavior that discharges the energy. The word "drive" is used interchangeably with instinct, both being translations of the German word *Trieb*. There is no agreed classification of drives, and terms overlap. Examples are sex, life, death and aggressive drives. The expression of drives is affected by the DEFENSE MECHANISMS.   RAM

unconscious mind The hypothetical location of those mental processes and properties which cannot be consciously recalled but which nevertheless influence actions and mental life, often (but not necessarily) by disrupting them in puzzling ways, and thought by the ancients, mystics and Jungians to be a means of access to external spiritual or transcendental powers. Many philosophers from Plato onwards have felt compelled to postulate its existence in order to explain certain aspects of memory, selective perception or intuition. Thus in the *Meno* Plato depicts Socrates eliciting "unconscious knowledge" of a geometric theorem from an illiterate boy; and at the beginning of *Republic* IX he in effect attributes to the mind an unconscious layer whose incestuous desires break out in dreams. Although the concept gradually became more familiar to European philosophy after Aquinas, so that it was even "topical" by 1800, it was not investigated empirically by clinicians or experimenters until the last decades of the nineteenth century. As Whyte shows (1960, chs. 6–8), there were several fairly specific statements of the ubiquity, importance and passionate nature of unconscious processes even before 1800 (e.g. Rousseau, Herder), and the current

state of speculation by the mid-nineteenth century was reviewed massively, derivatively and somewhat uncritically by von Hartmann (1869) whose work made a strong impact in France and England as well as his native Germany. But earlier, in 1846, the German physician C.G. Carus (whose works were known to FREUD) had written that 'the key to the understanding of the conscious life lies in the region of the unconscious' (Whyte 1960, p.149). This view was echoed and emphasized by British psychiatrist Henry Maudsley (1867); and his work was reviewed by Freud's philosophy teacher at Vienna University, Franz Brentano, in 1874 just as Freud was beginning his studies, and a few years before GALTON published some experimental studies of memory which required him to think in terms of unconscious mental processes.

Freud initially studied these processes clinically as the determinants of neurotic symptoms in hysteria; in which case they were identified as painful memories and anxiety-laden wishes which had been subjected to repression, to which he gained access through hypnosis, free-association and dream-interpretation. The last of these came to be called the "royal road" to the Unconscious. He soon began to illustrate the general hypothesis, that the pattern of much normal behavior and mental life is also determined unconsciously by memories, associations and wishes that have been repressed, in the investigation of dreams, mishaps and jokes drawn from everyday life (1900, 1901, 1905). Seen in this way the forgotten appointment is not just due to a faded memory-trace etc. but is positively, if indirectly, determined by an unconscious (repressed) wish to avoid it.

Since, however, that wish is unconscious it has been subject to the transformations of "primary process" ideation and to the motivation of the "pleasure-principle", and has achieved only indirect expression. The primary process is non-rational, and does not acknowledge logical contradiction: an idea and its opposite are the same. In this process, an idea may be "displaced", and hence represented in consciousness or action by another which is contingently, concretely (or otherwise non-rationally) connected; or it may become "condensed" with others into a composite symbol. Both transformations are evident in dream imagery, and the former both in the form of irrelevant perceptual similarity and also in the acoustic *Klang* – associations which divert the course of psychotic thinking. When such transformations are deployed consciously, in the context of (and not instead of) a rational train of thought (reality-principle) then that is a source of humor – as when a *Klang* association is perceived as a pun (Freud 1915, ch. 5).

That association between conscious and unconscious processes Freud called "Pre-conscious", for he realized that much of what was unconscious in a descriptive sense had not actually been repressed from consciousness in a dynamic sense, but was "latent" and available to voluntary recall in certain conditions (e.g. one's knowledge of a foreign language). The other main component of the Unconscious is the "mental representations" of the instincts.

Freud was definite that his concept of the Unconscious was a system or structure in the "topography" of the mental apparatus; it is not just the logical class of unconscious processes, or the figure of speech that Janet seemed to want to make it (Freud 1917, ch. 17). This insistence upon the spatial metaphor makes for philosophical embarrassment, especially after the strictures of Ryle (1949), and may be symptomatic of his having the early neurological model of the *Project*... (Freud 1895) at the back of his mind. Problematical also is Freud's insistence that all psychological processes that occur consciously can also occur unconsciously, or *in* the Unconscious. This applies even to those, such as feeling and awareness, of which consciousness seems a necessary

quality; and he explicitly defends the concept of "unconscious emotion", and even "unconscious consciousness of guilt", recognizing the apparent contradiction in the essay on *The unconscious* (1915, ch. 3).

Freud argued that his clinical data (especially) compelled him to such a postulate: it was both "necessary" and "legitimate" (ibid. ch. 1). But it may be objected (i) that such data were contaminated by his own methods and expectations, so that what has to be explained is something less elaborate which can be accommodated more parsimoniously by the conditioning theories of Pavlov or Skinner (see Wolpe and Rachmann 1960; Conway 1978); (ii) that references to unconscious processes are necessarily untestable and therefore scientifically worthless (but see Cheshire 1975, chs. 5 and 6); (iii) that everything Freud needs to say, for the sake of his system, can be construed logically into propositions about learned dispositions, underlying neurological processes or (after Harré 1970) into conceptual models of the unknown mechanisms which generate certain actions and experiences (Cheshire ibid.); (iv) that Freud's hypotheses and concepts can be translated adequately into an "action-language" qualified with similes and adverbs (Schafer 1976; MacIntyre 1958). The analogy of language and translation, with respect to the organization of unconscious processes, was much elaborated by Lacan, and resisted by Wittgenstein.   NMC

Bibliography

Cheshire, N.M. 1975: *The nature of psychodynamic interpretation*. London and New York: Wiley.

Conway, A.V. 1978: Little Hans: misrepresentation of the evidence? *Bulletin of the British psychological society* 31, 285–7.

Ellengerger, H.F. 1970: *The discovery of the unconscious*. New York: Basic Books.

Freud, S. 1895, 1900, 1901, 1905, 1915, 1916–17: Project for a scientific psychology (vol. 1); The interpretation of dreams (vols. 4–5); The psychopathology of everyday life (vol. 6); *Jokes and their relation to the unconscious (vol. 8); The unconscious (vol. 14); Introductory lectures on psychoanalysis (vol. 16): *Standard edition of the* *psychological works of Sigmund Freud*. London: Hogarth Press; New York: Norton.

Harré, R. 1970: *The principles of scientific thinking*. London: Macmillan.

MacIntyre, A.C. 1958: *The unconscious*. London: Routledge and Kegan Paul.

Miles, T.R. 1966: *Eliminating the unconscious*. Oxford: Pergamon.

Ryle, G. 1949: *The concept of mind*. London: Hutchinson; Totowa, N.J.: Barnes and Noble (1975).

Schafer, R. 1976: *A new language for psychoanalysis*. New Haven, CT.: Yale University Press; London: Yale University Press (1981).

Whyte, L.L. 1960: *The unconscious before Freud*. New York: Basic Books; London: Tavistock (1962).

Wolpe, J. and Rachmann, S. 1960: Psychoanalytic evidence. *Journal of nervous and mental diseases* 131, 135–48.

unemployment may be defined as the condition of being without employment whilst at the same time desiring employment.

Such a definition is inevitably vague, and one needs to be aware of the ambiguities which surround it. A person may desire only a particular type of employment, and may actively avoid other kinds. Another may fulfill all the bureaucratic criteria of being unemployed, and may register him- or herself as unemployed, whilst at the same time not desire any form of employment. It is also important to bear in mind the distinction between employment and work. The former is a relationship between two parties which involves the exchange of labor for reward. Work is a purposeful activity which can be performed inside or outside the employment relationship. Academic study, domestic chores and DIY are all examples of work which need not entail employment.

Although concern with the human costs of unemployment can be traced back several centuries, psychological research into the effects of unemployment has its origins in the economic recession of the 1930s. The classic empirical study of that period was that of *Marienthal* (Jahoda, Lazarsfeld and Zeisel 1933). Marienthal was an Austrian village where the major source of employment, a textile factory, closed down in 1929. The researchers lived there while collecting their data, observing and measuring the effects of unemployment on all manner of personal and social life in the village. Their conclusion was that the unemployed experienced a disintegration in their sense of time, a deterioration in their social and familial relations, and that they progressively abandoned budgeting even though this was more important than ever.

Other studies conducted during that era and worthy of mention are *Men without work* (Pilgrim Trust 1938) and *The unemployed man* (Bakke 1933). The former found depression and apathy to be the root of most of the problems connected with unemployment. Bakke's study of unemployed men in Greenwich, London, pointed to loss of confidence and self-respect, discouragement, and bewilderment.

In 1938 Eisenberg and Lazarsfeld published their review of the psychological effects of unemployment. Covering 112 sources, the article represents probably the most extensive summary of psychological research conducted during the 1930s. The effects attributed to unemployment are divided broadly into categories covering personality changes (e.g. increased emotional instability), effects of socio-political attitudes (e.g. political radicalization), attitudes (e.g. increased determination, resignation), and effects on children and youth (e.g. deterioration in school work, increased delinquency).

Although highlighting some important processes, there are limits to the extent to which research findings obtained during the 1930s can inform current concern with the psychological effects of unemployment. Jahoda (1982) draws attention to four cultural differences between the two eras. Unemployment rates are much lower today (although absolute numbers of unemployed people are similar); there is less real poverty today due to increased welfare benefits; the general health of the population is better than it was some fifty years ago; and the level of education is higher now resulting in greater resourcefulness.

Despite these differences one idea common to both periods is that the unemployed person passes through a number of distinct psychological stages during the course of his/her unemployment. Beales and Lambert (1934), on the basis of essays written by unemployed people, concluded that the initial effect of unemployment was one of optimism, followed in time by pessimism, and ending with fatalism. Eisenberg and Lazarsfeld (1938) stated that such a pattern of change is described by all those who have studied the course of unemployment. More recently Hill (1978) has added a period of shock to the beginning of this sequence, producing a four-stage model. Although attractive, stage models of the psychological effects of unemployment are fraught with difficulties. In an excellent review of psychological research into unemployment, both past and present, Fryer and Payne (1986) point out that there is widespread disagreement concerning the number of stages which are thought to occur, ranging from two to seven. Moreover, most of the studies purporting to demonstrate distinct phases use cross-sectional data. Longitudinal data obtained from successive interviews over a period of time would clearly be preferable.

Today the most common approach to identifying the psychological effects of unemployment is to use clinical instruments to measure various aspects of psychological well-being in unemployed people. These are normally self-completion inventories, in which the respondent indicates the frequency of occurrence of certain psychological symptoms. For example, the General Health Questionnaire (GHQ), which has been used in several UK studies of unemployment, contains items covering feelings of worry, strain, depression, sleeplessness, and so on. Other clinical instruments have been used to obtain measures of depression, anxiety, self-esteem, and positive and negative affect.

Results from studies comparing employed and unemployed people on such measures consistently show the unemployed to be suffering poorer psychological health. More sophisticated longitudinal studies (e.g. Banks and Jackson 1982) have been used to disentangle cause from effect in this relationship. By examining the scores of well-being for people as they move in and out of unemployment, it has been possible to provide persuasive evidence that unemployment causes a significant deterioration in psychological health.

An explanation of why these effects occur has been provided by Jahoda (1982). She points out that although the intended, or manifest, consequence of employment is financial reward, it also provides the employee with a number of unintended, or latent, benefits. Five of these latent benefits are mentioned: time-structure, shared experiences and contacts, goals and purposes, personal status and identity, and enforced activity. Jahoda suggests that these features help to promote psychological health. Hence it is the removal of these latent benefits of employment which causes a deterioration in psychological well-being among the unemployed.

A similar analysis has been provided by Warr (1983). However, in addition to referring to the benefits of employment he also lists the negative features of unemployment. These include the reduced decision latitude which unemployment entails, and an increase in psychologically threatening activities (such as claiming benefits or making job applications).

Much of the current psychological research into unemployment is seeking to discover the variables which mediate its harmful effects. Not all people suffer from unemployment to the same extent, and this has prompted questions as to why this might be so. Attention has been directed to demographic differences in the unemployed population, such as differences in age, social class, gender and ethnicity. Psychological responses to unemployment have been found to differ by each of these variables. In addition, greater commitment to obtaining a job, low levels of activity, and financial strain have all been found to be associated with lower psychological well-being during unemployment. PU

Bibliography

Bakke, E.W. 1933: *The unemployed man: a social study*. London: Nisbet.

Banks, M.H. and Jackson, P.R. 1982: Unemployment and risk of minor psychiatric disorder in young people: cross-sectional and longitudinal evidence. *Psychological medicine* 12, 789–98.

Beales, H.L. and Lambert, R.S. 1934: *Memoirs of the unemployed*. Wakefield: E.P. Publishing.

Eisenberg, P. and Lazarsfeld, P.F. 1938: The psychological effects of unemployment. *Psychological bulletin* 35, 358–90.

Fryer, D. and Payne, R. 1986: Being unemployed: a review of the literature on the psychological experience of unemployment. In *Review of industrial and organizational psychology*, eds. C.L. Cooper and I. Robertson. Chichester: Wiley.

Hill, J.M.M. 1978: The psychological impact of unemployment. *New society* 43 (798), 118–20.

Jahoda, M. 1982: *Employment and unemployment*. Cambridge: Cambridge University Press.

—— Lazarsfeld, P.R., and Zeisel, H. 1933 (1972): *Marienthal: the sociography of an unemployed community*. New York: Aldine-Atherton.

Pilgrim Trust 1938: *Men without work*. Cambridge: Cambridge University Press.

Warr, P.B. 1983: Work, jobs and unemployment. *Bulletin of the British psychological society* 36, 305–11.

universals (social) Structures, traits, and properties of persons, or groups of persons, and their behavior. Social universals are supposed to exist, or are empirically demonstrated to hold, independently of historical and cultural conditions. According to Lonner (1980, p.165), the study of psychology is '*de facto* the study of universals', whatever the definition of its scope as to geographic, temporal, or other domains may be. It aims at the exploration of simple universals such as human sexuality, aggression, communication; of functional universals such as, for example, the need for achievement (McClelland 1961). Psychology furthermore analyzes ethologically oriented universals of behavior with a definite link to the phylogeny of *homo sapiens* such as inherited facial expression of anger or of fear (Ekman 1972). Ekman asserts that some facial expressions are universal, i.e. not bound to learning of whatever kind, whereas other authors maintain that nonlinguistic and paralinguistic modes of expression cannot be understood across cultures (Birdwhistell 1970).

With regard to universals in interpersonal structures the results of cross-cultural psychology vary greatly. Some authors distinguish between just two universals, viz. association/dissociation and superordination/subordination (e.g. Brown 1965), whereas others list up to eight (Foa 1961).   AM

Bibliography

Birdwhistell, R.L. 1970: *Kinesics and context*. Philadelphia: University of Pennsylvania Press.

Brislin, R.W. 1983: Cross-cultural research in psychology. *Annual review of psychology* 34, 363–400.

Brown, R. 1965: *Social psychology*. New York: Free Press.

Ekman, P. 1972: Universality and cultural differences in facial expressions of emotion. In *Nebraska symposium on motivation*, ed. J.K. Cole. Lincoln: University of Nebraska Press.

Foa, U.G. 1961: Convergences in the analysis of the structure of interpersonal behavior. *Psychological review* 68, 341–53.

Lonner, W.J. 1980: The search for psychological universals. In *Handbook of cross-cultural psychology*, eds. H.C. Triandis and W.W. Lambert. Boston and London: Allyn and Bacon.

McLelland, D.C. 1961: *The achieving society*. Princeton, N.J.: Van Nostrand.

Van de Vijver, S. and Poortinga, J. 1982: Cross-cultural generalization and universality. *Journal of cross-cultural psychology* 13, 387–408.

V

values Biddle (1979) described "value" as one of 'those wonderful terms in the social sciences that has scores of meanings', but himself defined it as 'a prescriptive statement that is accepted ... as an absolute'. Rokeach (1973) distinguished values from beliefs and attitudes, regarding values as the class of 'enduring beliefs concerning modes of conduct and states of existence that transcend specific objects and situations' (Braithwaite and Law 1985).

Thomas and Znaniecki (1918) took the study of values and attitudes as their principal object since 'there can be ... no change of social reality which is not the common effect of pre-existing social values and individual attitudes'. They defined attitude as 'the individual counterpart of social value'. Thomas was, of course, an early exponent of SYMBOLIC INTERACTIONISM, but sociologists in general (and anthropologists) have tended, as in this quote, to treat values as common to members of a group or a whole culture. Parsons (1951) devised a system for contrasting different societies on the basis of their patterns of values.

Value is a key concept in expectancy-value theories such as Edwards's (1954) subjective expected utility model (cf. EXPECTANCY). A similar model has more recently been propounded by Fishbein and Ajzen (1975 – see ATTITUDES).   RI.

Bibliography

Biddle, B.J. 1979: *Role theory: expectations, identities, and behaviors.* New York and London: Academic Press.

Braithwaite, V.A. and Law, H.G. 1985: Structure of human values: testing the adequacy of the Rokeach value survey. *Journal of personality and social psychology* 49, 250–63.

Edwards, W. 1954: The theory of decision making. *Psychological bulletin* 51, 380–417.

Fishbein, M. and Ajzen, I. 1975: *Belief, attitude, intention and behavior.* Reading, Mass.: Addison-Wesley.

Parsons, T. 1951: *The social system.* Glencoe, Ill.: The Free Press.

Thomas, W.I. and Znaniecki, F. 1918: *The Polish peasant in Europe and America.* 5 vols. Boston: Badger.

Veblen, Thorstein was born in 1857 in rural Wisconsin, USA. The family were Norwegian, and for the first fifteen years of his life young Thorstein lived in the extreme isolation of a Norwegian-speaking family, with little contact with neighbors. He learned English at school, but even at that age his sardonic wit earned him considerable personal unpopularity. After secondary schooling he studied for the Lutheran ministry at Carleton College but took a job teaching mathematics after graduation. After all sorts of vicissisitudes he took a doctorate at Yale in 1884. Unable to find work he returned to a socially lonely but intellectually active life on his father's farm. Marrying in 1888 seems to have propelled him out into the world again, this time to Cornell and finally to Chicago as assistant professor of economics in 1892. He wrote extensively during those years, mainly developing his important distinction between industry and finance. He came to see that capitalism was changing in ways unanticipated by Marx. Financial institutions were overwhelming individual capitalists and gaining control of manufacturing industry from afar, so to speak. Of equal importance the inevitable widening of the gap between the bourgeoisie and the workers of Marx's theory was giving way to a gradual merging, necessitated by the fairly obvious fact that manufacturing industry needed its own workers' purchasing power to survive.

It was during this period that Veblen began to work on the study which stands beside Marx's famous writings as a source of fundamental, and some would say, more subtle ideas. Veblen realized that no theory of industrial society could dispense with a social psychology, a theory of motivation. Amongst his earliest writings are very thorough criticisms of hedonistic theories of human motivation. 'Pleasure, or the desire for pleasure' he said, 'is not itself a primary factor of consciousness . . . pleasure . . . results from the attainment of some already existent end of action; it is not itself an end.' Looking around him this ironic outsider developed a mordant eye equalled only in our time by that of GOFFMAN. It is the conscious striving after prestige that powers the social and industrial "engine". Status and dignity begin as a testimony to economic success and then become that to which economic activity is directed. Veblen saw that there must be two "orders" in society. An ignoble order: 'the hard, continuous, productive labor to furnish the needs of existence'; and that in which honor, prestige and dignity are created, the 'prestigious and predatory life of [the] exploit.' An "exploit" is a practically worthless but honor enhancing success. The practical order is demeaning. New types of persons whom the lowly can honor appear only in the expressive order. Honor attaches to an activity, display, etc. 'just in so far as there is no biological utility in it'. In a brilliant anticipation of Goffman's backstage/frontstage distinction Veblen notes how among the middle classes home life is so arranged as to display only activities proper to the expressive order.

The overwhelming motivation of human life is directed towards attaining a place in the expressive order. The psychological foundation of this striving is to be found in the motive of emulation and the emotion of jealousy. 'The outcome of modern industrial developments,' says Veblen, 'has been to intensify emulation and the jealousy that goes with that emulation . . .'. It is not wealth but the *display* of wealth that is to be emulated. In his great classic *The theory of the leisure class* Veblen draws out the consequences of this social psychological theory in a marvelous parade of detailed illustrative examples. By 1899 the first motor cars were on the streets; they had ceased already to be a means of transport only, and had become objects of display and of course emulation. The theory of fashion is also illuminated by Veblen's observation that the higher social strata continually strive to keep ahead of those below, whose skill in emulation is always threatening to overtake them, by continually elaborating style, until in a final coup the upper levels of society suddenly find that only in the simplest things does aesthetic merit lie. The vulgar are left stranded in their frills and furbelows. There is even a wonderful analysis of the underlying psychology of the breeding of dogs.

Shortly after publishing this master work Veblen moved to Stanford University where for three years he is alleged to have emptied the classrooms of the economics department with his unintelligible lectures and his irony. His private life fared little better, since as one biographer coyly puts it, he was much troubled with "personal affairs", indulgence in which had led to the collapse of his marriage in the Chicago days. From 1911 Veblen taught at Columbia, serving the Wilson administration as an adviser, particularly about the settlement of Europe in 1919. For the next ten years he edited the left-wing periodical *Dial*, but this earned him little but obloquy. He returned to California in 1927 to die in obscurity and poverty at the age of 73.   RHa

Bibliography

Hobson, J.A. 1936: *Veblen*. London: Chapman and Hall.

Veblen, T. 1899 (1970): *The theory of the leisure class*. London: Unwin.

verstehende Psychologie An approach to psychology applying the method of *Verstehen*, i.e. understanding mental processes in others through observation of physical processes and analogy to one's own (directly accessible) mental processes. Though the term was coined by Jaspers,

Dilthey is considered the first to have advocated this "descriptive and analytic" approach which he opposed to a causally explanatory psychology. The latter follows natural sciences in searching for general (causal) laws, neglecting individuality, meaning, sense and value. *Verstehende Psychologie* is idiographic, employing description, empathy, interpretation and sympathetic understanding.

(See also HERMENEUTIC INTERPRETATIVE THEORY; GEISTESWISSENSCHAFTLICHE PSYCHOLOGIE.)

HUKG

Bibliography

Dilthey, W. (1923) 1959: The understanding of other persons and their life-expressions. From Gesammelte Schriften, vol. 1. Leipzig and Berlin: Teubner. In *Theories of history*, ed. P. Gardiner. Glencoe, Ill.: Free Press.

Taylor, C. 1980: Understanding in human science. *Review of metaphysics* 34, 3–23.

W

Weber, Max (1864–1920) A German sociologist, regarded, with DURKHEIM, as one of the two founders of modern sociology (in fact, according to Raymond Aron, 'the sociologist'). His father was a lawyer by training, and involved in Prussian politics. Weber was educated at Heidelberg, Göttingen and Berlin. He studied law, economics, history and philosophy. He completed his academic training in 1891, and became *Privatdozent* in law in Berlin. He moved to Freiburg as professor of political economy (1894), and to Heidelberg in 1896. In 1898 he had a nervous breakdown and, after attempting and failing to resume his teaching, he was given leave without pay. He took up his scholarly activities again in 1903, as co-editor of *Archiv für Sozialwissenschaft und Sozialpolitik*. In 1904 he began publishing his own work. After World War I (in which he was a hospital administrator) he took up a specially created chair in Vienna, and then in 1919 moved to Munich, where he died.

Intellectually, he was influenced by Marx, especially in his early work, and by Nietzsche. He wrote extensively on methodology in social science, on history, and on general sociology and the sociology of religion, and was even involved in an industrial psychology survey which attempted (unsuccessfully) to discover the determinants of workers' productivity. He was particularly interested in the different ways in which people live in different societies as a result of their different values and beliefs. This interest went back to the 1890s when he was studying the conditions of farm laborers east of the Elbe. Weber showed that economic self-interest alone could not explain the exodus to the cities. The farm workers also desired the independence offered by urban life, and preferred that to the security of their traditional role.

In *The Protestant ethic and the spirit of capitalism* (1904/5, 1930) Weber explored the effect of a particular set of religious beliefs on economic and technological development. His starting point was the fact that Protestantism (particularly Calvinist, puritan Protestantism) seems to be correlated with the rise of the phenomenon of capitalism. This must surely be more than a coincidence. Yet it is a paradox if puritanical beliefs have led to economic achievement, since they apparently deny the worth of material, worldly goods. Nevertheless it was Weber's thesis that these religious beliefs played a major role in that development. He pointed out that both puritan religion and capitalist enterprise lead to organization. Puritan creeds stress the value of action in this world. The frugal, active lives of Protestants therefore led to the accumulation of wealth in a continuous way, since they favored reinvestment rather than consumption.

Attributing the rise of capitalism to a particular set of religious beliefs requires one to show that where capitalism was not developed, the necessary *material* conditions for its development were present, but the religious beliefs lacked the features of Protestantism. In later work, Weber did attempt to explain the traits which distinguish one religion from another, and to see what (often unintended) consequences different theological and eschatological beliefs have for social and economic organization. He outlined, for instance, the beliefs inherent in certain oriental systems (Confucianism, Hinduism) which probably tended to retard economic development. He did not, however, hold that there was a unidirectional causal relation between religious belief and social and economic organization, since he believed that groups with particular economic interests are more receptive to some religious ideals than to others. As he said, 'Not ideas, but ideals and material interests, directly govern men's concepts'.

He was a "methodological individualist" believing that the data of sociological analysis are the activities of individual men and women. This meant that he wanted to avoid any tendency to treat collective constructs, such as "society" as "things" which exist separately from individuals (cf. in contrast Durkheim). At the same time, however, he believed that sociology is not reducible to psychology. He therefore attempted to ground his sociological theory in social action (1922, 1978). Collectivities are to be understood in terms of the meaningful behavior of their members. Actions are defined by reference to the agents' motives. Even his typology of powers or "domination" (*Herrschaft*) into traditional, charismatic, and legal/rational depends on the particular motivation to obedience of the governed. For him, in fact, sociology was the science of social action.

He argued that comprehension of natural (non-human) phenomena cannot be immediate. We can establish systems of laws, as in physics, based on the observed relations between the phenomena. In contrast, we can have immediate (*aktuell*) understanding of human behavior. He borrowed this idea from Jaspers, who distinguished between explanation and comprehension in psychopathology. Neurosis is immediately comprehensible, because of the similarity between the phenomena of neurosis and the common phenomena of emotion, mood and behavior. Psychosis, on the other hand, is not comprehensible in this immediate way. This kind of understanding does not require magical intuition or empathy. We understand or make sense of others' actions because they fit recognizable patterns with which we are familiar in our own behavior and the behavior of those around us. This comprehension is not based on the observation of regularities, but on our subjective understanding of matters such as what a rule is and what it is to follow a rule (see Runciman 1972). According to

Weber, these kinds of understanding are the basis of the cultural sciences, history and sociology, which offer understanding without having general historical or sociological laws. Nevertheless they only explain (*erklären*) by outlining the causal conditions of an event. The historian, who deals with unique events, tests the adequacy of a causal explanation by performing "thought experiments" in which he tries to imagine what would have happened if any one of the antecedent conditions had been different.

Weber (1922, 1978) divided social action into four types: (1) *Zweckrational* – rational action in pursuit of a goal; (2) *Wertrational* – rational action with reference to a value; (3) emotional; (4) traditional. The first type involves practical conduct which is performed as a means to an end. The second type, as of someone who sacrifices himself as a martyr or a hero, may have no practical purpose, but still rests on a rational choice to keep faith with an ideal. Emotional action involves impulse, as when one flares up with anger or abandons oneself to grief. Traditional actions are customs and habits which have been inculcated into one, and may be performed without planning or even attention. In general a traditional action is one for which the agent has not considered an alternative.

According to Weber, social action includes all human behavior which 'by virtue of the subjective meaning (*Sinn*) attached to it by the acting individual . . . takes account of the behavior of others and is thereby oriented in its course' (1922, 1978). History and sociology are (or should be) attempts to understand action by reference to the "complex of subjective meaning" (*Sinnzusammenhang*) which appears to the agent himself or the observer to be a ground of the behavior. Weber believed that the social sciences provide causal explanations of the impact of ideas on actions or of the impact of political organization on economic organization. But if action can be understood only in terms of the agent's meanings, causal explanations of action in terms of regular relations among phenomena are obviously at least unsatisfactory. In fact such mediate understanding may actually be impossible without reference to meaning. For our ability to recognize that events of type *a* cause events of type *b* depends upon our ability to categorize events correctly into the two types. If either (or both) of *a* and *b* are types of action or behavior, and we cannot categorize them without knowing the meaning attached to them, it follows that we cannot tell whether a causal relation exists or not. In that case causal explanation of human behavior depends upon the prior understanding in terms of meaning.

This does not, of course, imply that causal explanation is out of place. Action is done for a reason, but that does not exclude the possibility, or indeed the need to explain it by reference to causes. In fact, in his 1904 editorial in the *Archiv* Weber stated that '"purpose" is . . . the cause of an action; and it must be taken into account just as much as any cause'. We can directly perceive the agent's (possible) motives, and this allows us to classify actions. Our perception, however, is fallible. Having intuitively established possible ways in which the action can be understood, we must still look for evidence to see whether we are correct. The social sciences are scientific exactly because they employ empirical methods, and any practitioner's claim can be supported or proved false by others. Evidence may include what the agent says, but is not confined to that. We can also use evidence about what people, like the agent, (in that society) typically do and why, and other knowledge we have about common patterns of behavior and motivation.

This point brings us to another aspect of Weber's analysis which if often mentioned – his use of "ideal types". These are constructs which have the characteristic features of particular kinds of entity or relationship. They do not have the average features or act as summary descriptions. Rather, says Weber, 'An ideal type is formed by the one-sided *accentuation* . . . and by the synthesis of a great many diffuse, discrete, more or less present and occasionally absent concrete individual phenomena, which are arranged . . . into a unified analytical construct'. His three types of domination or power (legal, traditional and charismatic), for instance, are discussed in terms of their ideal-typical features, which bring out the relationship between governments and the motives of those governed. He held, however, that real examples of power contain a mixture of features and do not embody just one type. Furthermore, events in history can be explained by reference to ideal-typical motives of people in particular social roles. It may be impossible to verify whether the individuals actually had the imputed motives. But historical understanding may be provided by reference to them if there is no evidence that they were not held, and if it is likely that people in that position would have entertained such motives. "Ideal types" are remarkably similar conceptually to the "prototypes" which many cognitive psychologists believe underlie our everyday understanding of reality (see SOCIAL COGNITION). They differ from them because the social scientist's ideal types are explicit, and are used as a model with which the empiricial cases are compared. Although categorization in everday life may also proceed by similar comparison, the process is not explicit.

Weber was able to build his analysis of social phenomena from the starting point of social action by stating that social relationships consist in the meaningful behavior of several persons who take account of each other's behavior in their own. Hence political power can be understood in terms of the beliefs, expectations and consequent behavior of those who are governed. A state is therefore an association which successfully claims the monopoly of legitimate use of force within a territory. In other words, a state compels because its citizens recognize its legitimacy.   RL

Bibliography

Weber's complete works have been published in Germany by Mohr (Tübingen). Many are available in translation, either complete or in selections. Of particular importance are: *Economy and society* (*Wirtschaft und Gesellschaft*. Tübingen: Mohr, 1922), rev. edn. G. Roth and C. Wittich. 2 vols. Berkeley: University of California Press, 1978; *The Protestant ethic and the spirit of capitalism* (*Die Protestantische Ethik und der Geist des Kapitalismus*. Archiv für Sozialwissenschaft und Sozialpolitik xx, 1904, and xxi, 1905). Trans. T. Parsons. London and New York: Allen and Unwin, 1930; *The methodology of the social sciences* (3 essays originally published in the *Archiv* and *Logos*), ed. and trans. E. Shils and H.A. Finch, Glencoe, Ill.: Free Press, 1949. There is a selection from *Economy and society* in *From Max Weber*, eds. H.H. Gerth and B. Wright Mills. New York: Oxford University Press, 1946; London: Routledge and Kegan Paul, 1948.

Secondary sources in English

Bendix, R. 1962: *Max Weber: an intellectual portrait*, rev. edn. New York: Doubleday; London: Heinemann.

Freund, J. 1968: *The sociology of Max Weber*. Trans. M. Ilford. London: Allen Lane.

Parsons, T. 1937: *The structure of social action: a study in social theory with special reference to a group of recent European writers*. Glencoe, Ill.: Free Press.

Runciman, W.G. 1972: *A critique of Max Weber's philosophy of social science*. Cambridge: Cambridge University Press.

word association test

A word association test (WAT) is elegantly simple: provide someone with a stimulus word, and ask for the first word that comes to mind. For example, say "table", and the response may well be "chair". Psychologists examine the nature and probabilities of response words, and sometimes how long it takes for a response. Word associations reveal people's verbal habits, the structure of their verbal memory, thought processes, and occasionally even emotional states and personality. They can be used both to understand individual people and to study the structure of language itself.

Response patterns

The father of WAT was the British scientist GALTON, who in the nineteenth century tested one subject, himself. In a less personal WAT in 1901 the German linguist-psychologist team Thumb and Marbe used eight subjects and sixty stimulus words. They found the following response trends, which have also been found in many subsequent WATs.

Words of one type evoked a response of the same type: e.g., "brother" led to "sister"; a noun led to another noun.

More common responses occurred more rapidly than less common ones: e.g. to "table" the most frequent response "chair" might occur within 1.3 sec.; the next most frequent "furniture" within 1.6 sec.; the third "eat" within 2 sec., and so on.

A given stimulus word often elicited an identical response from different subjects. In the first large scale WAT, Kent and Rosanoff (1910) tested 1,000 subjects' responses to 100 stimulus words, establishing a set of norms for future WATs. Between 1910 and 1954 there was an increase in primary (the most frequently given) responses. For example, to "table" the primary response "chair" was given by 26.7% of subjects in 1910; by 33.8% in 1928; and by 84.0% in 1954. Idiosyncratic responses (such as "mensa", which was given to "table" by 1 out of 1,008 subjects) became rarer. These trends may be due to the influence of mass media, to advertising, and to the standardization of school instruction. We are in the "group-think" age.

Between men and women, response times tend to be faster for men (1.3 sec. for educated, 1.8 for uneducated) than for women (1.7 sec. for educated, 2.2 for uneducated) (Jung 1918). Males tend to respond with antonyms and females with synonyms (Goodenough 1946). At every age female subjects may be characterized as stereotyped: compared to males, females give fewer different responses to each stimulus, and are more likely to give one of the four most frequent responses.

Conformity-minded people or people who are exposed to uniform mass media are likely to show more common responses, or less richness. All groups may be moving toward giving more common responses over the years.

Diagnostic use of WAT

WATs can reveal a person's emotional state. The noted Swiss psychoanalyst JUNG (1918) pioneered the use of word association in clinical diagnosis. He used emotionally loaded words to probe into patients' repressed images, wishes, or emotions. Both the time it takes for a person to produce a response word and the type of response word are supposed to reflect the emotional state. For example, a thirty-seven year old female teacher, single, came to him with a severe case of insomnia. She responded with an unusual word "home-sick" to the stimulus "foreign", taking 14.8 sec. (compared to normal people's 2 sec. in responding to neutral words). In a subsequent interview, she revealed her love affair with a foreigner who left her without saying good-bye.

In earlier times, schizophrenics were believed to have unusual and "unlogical" associations, remote associations and clang associations (or rhymes). Modern word association tests show that schizophrenics have intact associative structure, though they tend to have longer response times, fewer common responses, and more repetitions, than do normals (Mefford 1979).

Rapaport and his associates at the Menninger Clinic developed a diagnostic WAT, containing sixty stimulus words, of which twenty are such "traumatic" words as "love, breast, suicide, masturbate, bite", and the rest are such neutral words as "hat, chair, man, city" (Rapaport, Gill and Schafer 1946). Shiomi (1979) in Japan used the words of Rapaport et al. to study the personality of normal people. For male adults response times of extroverts to "traumatic" words were shorter than those of introverts. According to Shiomi, introverts defend themselves against responding to traumatic words whereas extroverts do not.

In a WAT a person is free to respond, free to reveal, unconsciously, aspects of his or her inner life.   IT

Bibliography

Goodenough, F.L. 1946: Semantic choice and personality structure. *Science* 104, 451–6.

Jung, C.G. 1918: *Studies in word-association.* London: Heinemann.

Kent, H.G. and Rosanoff, A.J. 1910: A study of association in insanity. *American journal of insanity* 67, 37–96.

Mefford Jr, R.B. 1979: Word association: capacity of chronic schizophrenics to follow formal semantic, syntactic, and instructional rules. *Psychological reports* 45, 431–42.

Rapaport, D., Gill, M. and Schafer, R. 1946: *Diagnostic psychological testing.* Chicago: Yearbook Publications.

Shiomi, K. 1979: Differences in RTs of extraverts and introverts to Rapaport's word association test. *Psychological reports* 45, 75–80.

work ethic Originally known as the Protestant ethic, this is the view that hard work and career progress are moral virtues in themselves, independent of any practical results. In the early part of this century the German sociologist, WEBER, put forward the idea that the rise of capitalism was helped on by the Protestant Reformation which fostered the notion that hard work was a moral duty and that a person's good works constituted proof that he had been chosen by God for salvation; people therefore worked hard to prove that they had been chosen. The work ethic is a secularization of the Protestant ethic. It is widely held to be declining in Western society as a result of such influences as welfare state policies, increasing wealth, the declining influence of religion, and more relaxed child-rearing practices. Research by Cherrington (1980) supports this claim, especially among younger workers. Cherrington estimated that one-third of the current US workforce believes in the work ethic. Those people who do are slightly more likely to be high producers and to be satisfied with their work than those who do not. Cherrington found work ethic values to be related to child-rearing practices which encouraged firm discipline, personal responsibility and high standards of personal conduct. Jackson et al. (1983) found that among unemployed young people commitment to a work ethic caused higher levels of distress.

EAL

Bibliography

Cherrington, D.J. 1980: *The work ethic.* New York: AMACOM.

Jackson, P.R., Stafford, E.M., Banks, M.H. and Warr, P.B. 1983: Unemployment and psychological distress in young people: the moderating role of employment commitment. *Journal of applied psychology* 68, 525–35.

Weber, M. 1904–05 (1958): *The Protestant ethic and the spirit of capitalism*. Trans. T. Parsons. New York: Scribner.

work stress Many of the current definitions of stress come from homeostatic, energy-exchange models of physical phenomena espoused by earlier scientists such as Royle, Cannon, and others, suggesting that stress results from the interaction of stimuli and an organism. Lazarus (1971) summarizes the definition in human stress terms thus: 'Stress refers to a very broad class of problems differentiated from other problem areas because it deals with *any demands which tax the system*, whether it is a physiological system, a social system, or a psychological system, *and the response of that system.*'

In any form of paid employment there are a large number of potential sources of stress: the characteristics of the job itself, the role of the person in the organization, interpersonal relationships at work, career development pressures, the climate and structure of the organization, and problems associated with the interface between the organization and the outside world.

Factors intrinsic to the job were a first and vital focus of study for early researchers of stress. Stress can be caused by too much or too little work, time pressures and deadlines, having to make too many decisions, fatigue from the physical strains of the work environment (e.g. an assembly line), excessive travel, long hours, having to cope with changes at work, and the expenses (monetary and career) of making mistakes. Karasek (1979) found that reports of stress were a joint function of high job demands and low decision latitude.

Another major source of work stress is associated with a person's role in the organization. A great deal of research in this area has concentrated on ROLE AMBIGUITY AND CONFLICT.

A third major source of stress at work has to do with the nature of relationships with superiors, subordinates, and colleagues. A number of writers (e.g. Argyris 1964; Cooper and Marshall 1978) have suggested that good relationships between

members of a work group are a central factor in individual and organizational health.

Buck (1972) focused on the attitude of workers and managers to their immediate bosses and their relationships with them, using Fleishman's (1969) leadership questionnaire on consideration and initiating structure. As described in Chapter 10, the consideration factor is associated with behavior indicative of friendship, mutual trust, respect and a certain warmth between boss and subordinate. Buck found that those workers who felt that their bosses were low on consideration reported feeling more job pressure. Workers who were under pressure reported that their bosses did not give them criticism in a helpful way, played favorites with subordinates, "pulled rank", and took advantage of them whenever they got a chance. Buck concludes that the 'lack of considerate behaviour of supervisors appears to have contributed significantly to feelings of job pressure'.

Officially one of the most critical functions of a manager is his supervision of other people's work. It has long been accepted that "inability to delegate" can be a problem, but now a new strain is being put on the manager's interpersonal skills: he must learn to work "participatively". In respect of relationships with colleagues more generally stress can be caused not only by interpersonal rivalry and competition but also by a lack of adequate social support in difficult situations (Lazarus 1966). At highly competitive managerial levels, for example, it is likely that problem sharing will be inhibited for fear of appearing weak, and much American literature identifies the isolated life of the top executive as an added source of strain.

Two major clusters of potential stressors have been identified in the area of career development: lack of job security and fear of redundancy, obsolescence or early retirement; and status incongruity (under- or over-promotion) or frustration at having reached a career ceiling.

For many workers, especially managers and professional staff, career progression is of overriding importance: by promotion they earn not only money, but also enhanced status and the new job challenges for which they strive. Typically, in the early years at work this striving and the ability to come to terms quickly with a rapidly changing environment is fostered and suitably rewarded by the company. At middle age a person's career becomes more problematic, and most employees find their progress slowed if not actually stopped. Job opportunities become fewer, those jobs that are available take longer to master, past (mistaken?) decisions cannot be revoked, old knowledge and methods become obsolete, energies may be flagging or demanded for family activities, and there is the press of fresh young recruits to face in competition.

A fifth potential source of work stress is simply "being in the organization", and the threat to an individual's freedom, autonomy and identity that this poses. Criticisms such as little or no participation in the decision-making process, no sense of belonging, lack of effective consultation and communication, restrictions on behavior (e.g. through tight budgets) and office politics are frequent.

The sixth and final source of work stress is more a "catch-all" for all those exchanges between life outside and life inside the organization that might put pressure on an individual: family problems (Pahl and Pahl 1971), life crises (Cooper and Marshall 1978), financial difficulties, conflict of personal beliefs with those of the company, and the conflict of company with family demands.

The individual worker has two stress-related problems with respect to his family and his work. The first is that of managing time and conflicting commitments. Not only does the busy work life leave few resources to cope with other people's needs, but in order to do a job well, the individual usually needs support from others to cope with the details of home management, to relieve stress when possible, and to maintain contact with the world outside work. The second problem, often a result of the first, is the spill-over of crises or stresses from one system to the other.   CLC

Bibliography

Argyris, C. 1964: *Integrating the individual and the organisation*. New York: Wiley.

Buck. V.E. 1972: *Working under pressure*. London: Staples Press; New York: Crane Rusak.

Cooper. C.L. and Marshall, J. 1978: *Understanding executive stress*. London: Macmillan.

Fleishman, E.A. 1969: *Manual for the leadership opinion questionnaire*. Science Research Associates.

French, J., Caplan, R. and van Harrison, R. 1982: *The mechanisms of job stress and strain*. New York: Wiley.

Karasek, R.A. 1979: Job demands, job decision latitude, and mental strain: implications for job redesign. *Administrative science quarterly* 29, 285–307.

Lazarus, R.S. 1966: *Psychological stress and the coping process*. New York: McGraw-Hill.

—— 1971: The concepts of stress and disease. In *Society, stress and disease*, ed. L. Levi. Oxford: Oxford University Press.

Pahl, J.M. and R.E. 1971: *Managers and their wives*. London: Allen Lane.

Wundt, Wilhelm (1832–1920) Philosopher, physiologist, psychologist, at the universities of Heidelberg and (from 1875) Leipzig. In Heidelberg, after his medical training, Wundt moved into research in sensory and neural physiology and then into specifically psychological experimentation. He thereby elaborated his ideas for a new, scientific psychology anchored in physiology which he expounded in *Grundzüge der physiologischen Psychologie* (1st edn. 1873/74). As professor of philosophy in Leipzig he became the celebrated organizer of psychology as an autonomous and scientific discipline: he founded the prototypical psychological institute around a laboratory, wrote influential treatises and textbooks, edited journals and attracted an international group of students (the Wundt-school). They disseminated the institutional structure Wundt had given to the field (including some idiosyncrasies, among them a relative neglect of differential, animal, child and applied psychology). For many years this school was so predominant that most opposing views chose to define themselves in contrast to it.

Yet there is no brief way in which to summarize Wundt's psychology since it was constantly remodeled in the course of his research which spanned simple sensory impressions, reaction time, and highly complex mental processes. Though close to the associationist tradition Wundt criticized it for its disregard of volitional processes and proposed the principle of creative synthesis by which a combination of mental elements acquires new, emergent properties not contained in the elements themselves.

In psychological method Wundt perceived a basic dichotomy. Simpler mental processes are the object of experimental physiological psychology. This is unsuitable for the more complex, which are explored through the study of their trans-individual products (e.g. language, custom, myth, religion), and are the domain of *Völkerpsychologie* (mis-termed "folk psychology"). Important for an understanding of Wundt's methodology is the philosophy of science as put forward in his *Logik*. Wundt embedded his psychology in an elaborate philosophy to which belong the conception of mind as an activity, not a substance; psychological (not meta-physical) voluntarism; the a priori unity of consciousness; and the dominant role assigned to apperception.

Wundt's seldom read and often misunderstood *Völkerpsychologie* is not a social but an anthropological psychology which would elucidate the mental and cultural evolution of man by examining, as Wundt put it, the record *above* the ground, not beneath it. Nor was this ambitious project a late-life substitute for the rigors of science as Boring intimated. As early as Wundt's 1862 Lectures at Heidelberg (*Lectures on human and animal psychology*) his interest in the psychological aspects of culture is noted as is his recognition that these were not to be understood by the limited methods of experimental science.

As Wundt was a voluntarist his anthropology reserves a special place for human character as the engine of progress and creation. (Interestingly, J.S. Mill would use the same word in explaining the difference between his social science and the radical determinist's "Asiatic fatalism".) In light of his unarguable standing in the history of scientific psychology, his somewhat humanistic position on human agency, human character and the sources of human culture provided something of an authorization for "serious" psychologists to retain these subjects among the officially sanctioned ones early in the present century. Additionally, the *Völkerpsychologie* preserved elements of Continental social theory and thus gave these a currency that would otherwise have been rejected in the Anglo-American world of "scientific" psychology. His four-stage theory of cultural evolution – *primitive, totemic, heroic-deistic, humanistic* – is redolent not only of obvious Darwinian accounts but of those dialectical theories so favored by the nineteenth-century German writers Fichte, Hegel and Marx.

This said, it is still the case that Wundt did not play an influential part in the direction taken in this century by the fields of personality and social psychology. His major writings did not focus on "personality" as such – even if character-formation and human will were central to many of his essays – and his treatments of human collectives were, as noted, anthropological and broadly cultural, not "social" in the sense in which the term is now used. In the tradition of Leibniz and Kant, he regarded the domain of consequential human actions (the domain of history, society, art, politics) as arising from human purposes and reasons, themselves not reducible to biological or elemental natural causes. Accordingly, he did not regard such subjects as accessible to purely experimental or (narrowly) scientific modes of inquiry. In light of his position on such matters, it seems that he would have regarded current research in the areas of "personality and social psychology" to be "scientific" only to the extent that the genuinely personal and social dimensions of the phenomena have been systematically excluded! HUKG/DNR

Bibliography

*Bringmann, W.G. and Scheerer, E. eds. 1950: Wundt centennial issue. *Psychological research* 42, 1–189.

*—— and Tweney, R. eds. 1980: *Wundt studies: a centennial collection*. Toronto: Hogrefe.

*Rieber, R.W. ed. 1980: *Wilhelm Wundt and the making of scientific psychology*. New York: Plenum.

Robinson, D.N. 1982: *Toward a science of human nature: essays on the psychologies of Hegel, Mill, Wundt and James*. New York: Columbia University Press.

Wundt, W. 1863–4 (1904): *Lectures on human and animal psychology*. Trans. J.E. Creighton and E.B. Tichener. New York: Macmillan.

—— 1907: *Outlines of psychology*. 3rd edn. Trans. C.H. Judd. Leipzig: Engelmann.

—— 1908–1911: *Grundzüge der physiologischen Psychologie*. 6th edn. 3 vols. Leipzig: Engelmann.

—— 1917–1926: *Völkerpsychologie*, 1st to 4th edns. 10 vols. Leipzig: Kröner.

—— 1919: *System der Philosophie*, 4th edn. 2 vols. Leipzig: Kröner.

Index

The figures in **bold** index the main article on that subject. Columns (designated a & b) are only differentiated where the subject is restricted to one column on any page. For clarity, entries have been only minimally divided into sub-headings: references should be used in conjunction with article headings to obtain the required degree of detail.

77b, 159a, 220a, 350a, 376b, 379b, 383b
cathexis 229a, 254a, 256a
Cattell, R. B. 12a, 17a, **38–9**, 86b, 107, 185b, 242b, 250b, 253a, 255b, 314b, 369b
  16PF test 17a, 38–9, 57a, 107b, 116a, 245b, 249b–50, 364a
Chicago 72a, 143a, 163b–4a, 210, 233a, 352b–5a
childhood 6a, 132a, 229a, 232–3, 247–9a, 255–7, 282b, 297b, 338a, 366b
children
  studies of 10a, 31a, 43b–4a, 57b–8, 74a, 87a, 92b, 96b–7a, 105b–6, 111, 116b, 175a, 200a, 209b–11a, 212b, 247–8, 251b, 256a, 277a, 289b, 305b, 316a, 317a, 319a, 323a, 333b–4a, 365, 373b, 383b, 385b
  training of 1a, 60–1, 151b, 339b, 383b
choice *see* decision
cognition *see* social cognition
cognitive
  balance 26a, **39b–40a**, 41, 65a, 153b
  behavior 2b–3, 32b, 40a, 207
  complexity **40**
  consistency 26a, **40b–2a**, 54a, 153b, 291a, 335b
  development 13a, 98a, 221a, 317b
  dissonance 24b, 41a, 42a, **42–3a**, 53b, 303b, 309b, 320b
  personality theory 16a, 32a, 36a, **43–6a**, 79b, 166a, 175b, 207, 233b, 334
  structure 16a, 40a, 45a, 122b, 226, 332a
  style 40b, 45, **46**, 120b–1a
  units 41a, 45a, 103b, 133a, 162a
cohesiveness **46b**
common-sense views 27b–8a, 29b, 41a, 100, 217a, 316b
communication 23b, 26b, 41b, 43b, **46b–50a**, 133b–4a, 146, 213b, 219b, 240b, 259b, 264a, 266b–7a, 282b, 297b, 302b, 337a, 354, 366b–7a, 375a

failures in 32b, 87a, 113b, 231a, 241b, 267a, 278b, 283a, 385a
and language 20b–1, 48a, 51b, 63b, 84b, 94b, 101a, 118b–19a, 141–2, 146, 154–6, 252a, 264–5a, 297b–8, 312, 330b, 343; *see also* speech
  network **52b–3a**, 65b–6, 82a, 140a, 148b, 192b, 217a, 283a
  non-verbal 15a, 25b, 47b–9, **50a–2b**, 92a, 105b–6a, 111–14a, 135–6, 141–2, 143b, 149b, 172a, 195b, 223b–4, 241b, 251b–2a, 272b, 289, 297b–8, 320b, 330b–1, 335a, 336a, 363, 366b, 375b
  relational theory of 48b–9a, 50b
  see also interaction, relationships
competition **53a**, 56a, 132–4, 150b, 229–31, 270, 316a, 325b, 332a
complex 198b–9a
compulsion 42b, 60a, 61b, 127b, 226, 247a
Comte, Auguste 70, 264
conflict **53**
  approach/avoid **17b–18a**, 135b
  armed 267b–8a
  behavior 56a, 66a, 123, 224b, 327b
  dilemma 56a, 327b
  Freud on 233b, 247b
  intellectual 76a, 224b
  intergroup 66a, 270, 329
  internal 249a, 273, 303b, 333b, 342b
  Lewin on 208a
  occupational 229b–31, 385a
  role 118a, 119a, **292a**, 293a, 351b, 384b–5a
  sex-role 118–9
  social 75b, 224b, 229b–31, 282b, 329, 332a, 352b, 354b
  theory 159a, 170a, 171b, 267b–8a
  unconscious 58b, 170a, 233b
  work on 227b
conformity 5b, 19–20a, 46b, 80a, 146b–7a, 150, 233a, 235a, 238a, 292b, 304a,

310a, 328b–9a, 382b; *see also* Asch, social influence
congruity principle 41, 42b, **54a**
  incongruity 171b–2a
conscience **54a**, 60, 65b, 74a, 352a
collective 16a, 81b
consistency *see* cognitive, self
contagion **54b–5a**, 67a
context 178a, 179b–80a; *see also* environment
contextualism **55a**, 55b
control
  of environment 206a, 211a, 232b, 240, 270b, 334a, 336b, 363a
  locus of 31b, 45b, 180b–1a, **211**, 252b, 364b
  parental 86a, 291a, 352a
  self- 32a, 56b, 57b, 180b–1a, 247a, 248a, 290b, 303b, **304**, 334
  systems 74a, 356a
Cooley, Charles Horton 192b, 297b, 300b, 309b, 321a, 353b
co-operation 25b, 53a, **56**, 58b–9a, 96–7, 132–4, 150b, 229–31, 232b, 233b, 256b, 332a
coronary-prone behavior **56b–7a**, 369b–70
correlations **64a**
  attitude/behavior 23, 302a, 369b
  discovery of 132a
  factor analysis 23, 114b–16, 308b, 346b, 364a
  genetic 138a, 368b
  questionnaires and tests 38b–9a, 94a, 107b, 360b, 362a
  statistical 23, 546, 94a, 346
  trait/personality factors 38b–9a, 54b, 107b, 120b, 177, 183a, 186–7, 242b–5, 253a, 308b, 311b, 341b, 364–6a, 368b
counseling 169, 197a, 285b, 289b–90a, 339a
courtship 281b–3a, 313a; *see also* marital relations
creativity **57a–9b**, 159b, 221b, 232b, 261a, 306b, 366b, 386a
crime 74b, 84a, 108a, 109a, 318b
criminal psychology **59b–61b**,